Automation, Production Systems, and Computer Integrated Manufacturing

MIKELL P. GROOVER

Professor of Industrial Engineering
Lehigh University

PRENTICE-HALL, INC., Englewood Cliffs, New Jersey 07632
201-592-2996

Library of Congress Cataloging-in-Publication Data

GROOVER, MIKELL P., 1939–
  Automation, production systems, and computer
integrated manufacturing.

  Rev. ed. of: Automation, production systems,
and computer-aided manufacturing. c1980.
  Includes bibliographies and index.
    1. Manufacturing processes—Automation.
2. Production control.   3. CAD/CAM systems.
4. Robots, Industrial.   I. Groover, Mikell P.,
1939–   . Automation, production systems, and
computer-aided manufacturing.   II. Title.
TS183.G76 1987   670.42'7   86–25529
ISBN   0–13–054652–6

Editorial/production supervision
  and interior design: **PATRICK WALSH**
Cover design: **WANDA LUBELSKA DESIGN**
Manufacturing buyer: **RHETT CONKLIN**

Printed in the United States of America

10 9 8 7 6 5 4 3 2 1

ISBN 0-13-054652-6 025

Prentice-Hall International (UK) Limited, *London*
Prentice-Hall of Australia Pty. Limited, *Sydney*
Prentice-Hall Canada Inc., *Toronto*
Prentice-Hall Hispanoamericana, S.A., *Mexico*
Prentice-Hall of India Private Limited, *New Delhi*
Prentice-Hall of Japan, Inc., *Tokyo*
Prentice-Hall of Southeast Asia Pte. Ltd., *Singapore*
Editora Prentice-Hall do Brasil, Ltda., *Rio de Janeiro*

To
Bonnie

Contents

Preface   xiii

List of Symbols   xvii

1 Introduction   1

    1.1 Automation Defined, 1
    1.2 Reasons for Automating, 6
    1.3 Arguments for and against Automation, 7
    1.4 Organization of the Book, 9
        References, 10

part I   FUNDAMENTALS OF MANUFACTURING AND AUTOMATION   13

2 Production Operations and Automation Strategies   15

    2.1 Manufacturing Industries, 15
    2.2 Types of Production, 18
    2.3 Functions in Manufacturing, 20

2.4 Organization and Information Processing in Manufacturing, 24
2.5 Plant Layout, 27
2.6 Production Concepts and Mathematical Models, 30
2.7 Automation Strategies, 40
References, 41
Problems, 42
Appendix: Averaging Procedures for Manufacturing Lead Time
Equations, 45

3 Production Economics   47

3.1 Methods of Evaluating Investment Alternatives, 48
3.2 Costs in Manufacturing, 52
3.3 Break-even Analysis, 56
3.4 Unit Cost of Production, 60
3.5 Cost of Manufacturing Lead Time and Work-in-process, 62
3.6 Other Difficult-to-quantify Factors, 66
References, 67
Problems, 67
Appendix: Interest and Interest Tables, 70

part II   HIGH VOLUME PRODUCTION SYSTEMS   81

4 Detroit-Type Automation   83

4.1 Automated Flow Lines, 83
4.2 Methods of Workpart Transport, 87
4.3 Transfer Mechanism, 89
4.4 Buffer Storage, 93
4.5 Control Functions, 95
4.6 Automation for Machining Operations, 97
4.7 Design and Fabrication Considerations, 101
References, 104
Problems, 105

5 Analysis of Automated Flow Lines   106

5.1 General Terminology and Analysis, 107
5.2 Analysis of Transfer Lines Without Storage, 111
5.3 Partial Automation, 114
5.4 Automated Flow Lines with Storage Buffers, 119
5.5 Computer Simulation of Automated Flow Lines, 128
References, 129
Problems, 130

6   Assembly Systems and Line Balancing   137

6.1   The Assembly Process, 137
6.2   Assembly Systems, 139
6.3   Manual Assembly Lines, 139
6.4   The Line Balancing Problem, 143
6.5   Methods of Line Balancing, 149
6.6   Computerized Line Balancing Methods, 156
6.7   Other Ways to Improve the Line Balancing, 159
6.8   Flexible Manual Assembly Lines, 162
        References, 165
        Problems, 166

7   Automated Assembly Systems   170

7.1   Design for Automated Assembly, 171
7.2   Types of Automated Assembly Systems, 173
7.3   Parts Feeding Devices, 175
7.4   Analysis of Multi-station Assembly Machines, 180
7.5   Analysis of a Single station Assembly Machine, 188
        References, 191
        Problems, 191

part III   NUMERICAL CONTROL PRODUCTION SYSTEMS   197

8   Numerical Control   199

8.1   What is Numerical Control?, 199
8.2   Coordinate System and Machine Motions, 201
8.3   Types of NC Systems, 204
8.4   The MCU and Other Components of the NC System, 207
8.5   Machine Tool Applications, 215
8.6   Other Applications, 221
8.7   Economics of NC, 223
        References, 224
        Problems, 225

9   NC Part Programming   229

9.1   Punched Tape and Tape Format, 230
9.2   Methods of NC Part Programming, 237
9.3   Manual Part Programming, 239
9.4   Computer-assisted Part Programming, 242
9.5   The APT Language, 248

9.6   Manual Data Input, 260
9.7   NC Part Programming Using CAD/CAM, 261
9.8   Computer-automated Part Programming, 263
      References, 264
      Problems, 264
      Appendix: APT Word Definitions, 268

10   DNC, CNC, and Adaptive Control   279

10.1   Problems with Conventional NC, 280
10.2   Direct Numerical Control, 281
10.3   Computer Numerical Control, 284
10.4   Adaptive Control Machining, 287
10.5   Current Trends in NC, 294
       References, 295
       Problems, 296

part IV   **INDUSTRIAL ROBOTICS**   **299**

11   Robotics Technology   301

11.1   Robot Anatomy, 302
11.2   Control Systems, 308
11.3   Accuracy and Repeatability, 310
11.4   Other Specifications, 313
11.5   End Effectors, 314
11.6   Sensors in Robotics, 315
       References, 316
       Problems, 317

12   Robot Programming   319

12.1   Types of Programming, 319
12.2   Leadthrough Programming, 320
12.3   Robot Languages, 325
12.4   Simulation and Off-line Programming, 330
12.5   Workcell Control, 332
       References, 335
       Problems, 335

13   Robot Applications   338

13.1   Characteristics of Robot Applications, 338
13.2   Robot Cell Design, 340

13.3   Types of Robot Applications, 342
13.4   Material Handling Applications, 342
13.5   Processing Operations, 346
13.6   Assembly and Inspection, 351
       References, 354
       Problems, 355

part V   MATERIALS HANDLING AND STORAGE   359

   14 Automated Materials Handling   361

       14.1   The Materials Handling Function, 362
       14.2   Types of Material Handling Equipment, 362
       14.3   Analysis for Material Handling Systems, 365
       14.4   Design of the System, 370
       14.5   Conveyor Systems, 373
       14.6   Automated Guided Vehicle Systems, 383
              References, 398
              Problems, 399

   15 Automated Storage Systems   404

       15.1   Storage System Performance, 404
       15.2   Automated Storage/Retrieval Systems, 407
       15.3   Carousel Storage Systems, 417
       15.4   Work-in-process Storage, 422
       15.5   Interfacing Handling and Storage with Manufacturing, 425
              References, 428
              Problems, 429

part VI   GROUP TECHNOLOGY AND FLEXIBLE MANUFACTURING   431
          SYSTEMS

   16 Group Technology   433

       16.1   Part Families, 434
       16.2   Parts Classification and Coding, 437
       16.3   Production Flow Analysis, 445
       16.4   Machine Cell Design, 447
       16.5   Benefits of Group Technology, 454
              References, 456
              Problems, 457

17   Flexible Manufacturing Systems   462

17.1   What Is an FMS?, 463
17.2   FMS Workstations, 466
17.3   Materials Handling and Storage System, 468
17.4   Computer Control System, 472
17.5   Planning the FMS, 476
17.6   Analysis Methods for Flexible Manufacturing Systems, 478
17.7   Applications and Benefits, 479
        References, 481

part VII   **QUALITY CONTROL AND AUTOMATED INSPECTION**   **485**

18   Automated Inspection and Testing   487

18.1   Inspection and Testing, 488
18.2   Statistical Quality Control, 489
18.3   Automated Inspection Principles and Methods, 493
18.4   Sensor Technologies for Automated Inspection, 497
18.5   Coordinate Measuring Machines, 499
18.6   Other Contact Inspection Methods, 504
18.7   Machine Vision, 506
18.8   Other Optical Inspection Methods, 513
18.9   Other Noncontact Inspection Methods, 516
        References, 517
        Problems, 518

part VIII   **CONTROL SYSTEMS**   **521**

19   Linear Feedback Control Systems   523

19.1   Process Model Formulation, 524
19.2   Transfer Functions and Block Diagrams, 533
19.3   Laplace Transforms, 546
19.4   Control Actions, 553
19.5   Linear Systems Analysis, 560
19.6   Root-locus Method, 565
19.7   System Design, 572
        References, 582
        Problems, 582

20   Optimal Control   590

20.1   Structural Model of a Manufacturing Process, 590
20.2   Steady-state Optimal Control, 592

20.3   Adaptive Control, 600
20.4   On-line Search Strategies, 622
        References, 635
        Problems, 636

21   Sequence Control and Programmable Controllers   642

21.1   Logic Control and Sequencing, 643
21.2   Logic Control Elements, 644
21.3   Sequencing Elements, 653
21.4   Ladder Logic Diagrams, 656
21.5   Programmable Logic Controllers, 662
        References, 670
        Problems, 670

22   Computer Process Control   673

22.1   The Computer-process Interface, 674
22.2   Interface Hardware, 679
22.3   Computer Process Monitoring, 690
22.4   Types of Computer Process Control, 691
22.5   Direct Digital Control, 692
22.6   Supervisory Computer Control, 696
22.7   Programming for Computer Process Control, 699
        References, 705
        Problems, 705

part IX   COMPUTER INTEGRATED MANUFACTURING   707

23   Fundamentals of CAD/CAM   709

23.1   Computer-aided Design, 709
23.2   Computer-aided Manufacturing, 718
23.3   Computer Integrated Manufacturing, 720
        References, 723

24   Computerized Manufacturing Planning Systems   724

24.1   Computer-aided Process Planning, 724
24.2   Computer Integrated Production Planning Systems, 729
24.3   Material Requirements Planning, 732
24.4   Capacity Planning, 740
        References, 741
        Problems, 742

25 Shop Floor Control and Automatic Identification Techniques   743

25.1   Shop Floor Control, 743
25.2   Factory Data Collection Systems, 748
25.3   Automatic Identification Systems, 751
25.4   Bar Code Technology, 754
25.5   Automated Data Collection Systems, 760
         References, 762

26 Computer Networks for Manufacturing   764

26.1   Hierarchy of Computers in Manufacturing, 765
26.2   Local Area Networks, 768
26.3   Manufacturing Automation Protocol, 772
         References, 775

27 The Future Automated Factory   776

27.1   Trends in Manufacturing, 776
27.2   The Future Automated Factory, 779
27.3   Human Workers in the Future Automated Factory, 786
27.4   The Social Impact, 787
         References, 789

Answers to Selected Problems   790

Index   799

Preface

This book is intended to provide a comprehensive technical survey of the important topics in production automation and related systems. These topics include flow line production, numerical control, industrial robotics, material handling, group technology, flexible manufacturing systems, automated inspection, process control, and computer integrated manufacturing (CIM). The book is virtually a one-volume encyclopedia on modern manufacturing systems: everything you always wanted to know about production automation but could not find in one book.

The book has been designed primarily as a text for engineering students at the advanced undergraduate or beginning graduate levels. It has the characteristic features of an engineering textbook: diagrams, equations, example problems which illustrate the use of the equations, and end-of-chapter exercises. There is even a *Solutions Manual* available from Prentice-Hall for the end-of-chapter problems. The book should be suitable for such curricula as industrial engineering, mechanical engineering, and manufacturing engineering. Many colleges and universities throughout the United States are introducing new programs in manufacturing systems, and this book should be suitable for certain courses in these programs.

There is probably more material in the book than most instructors would want to cover in a single-semester course. The text is designed to fit a variety of course requirements. Each instructor can select those portions of the book that coincide with the topics he or she wants to include in a particular course. Students will subsequently find the book to be a useful reference for other topics that were not covered during the course.

The book should also be useful for practicing engineers who wish to learn about automation technology in modern manufacturing. Managers and students of business should also find the book useful for its emphasis on economic as well as technical issues related to automation.

The present text is actually a second edition, even though the title has been changed. The previous edition was *Automation, Production Systems, and Computer-Aided Manufacturing*. The last part of the title has been changed to *Computer Integrated Manufacturing* in the current edition to reflect the terminology that enjoys more common use today. Perhaps the change in the title seems subtle; the change in the text is substantial. Major revisions have been made to update the existing material on basic manufacturing concepts and associated mathematical models, production economics, numerical control, flexible manufacturing systems, computer process control, CAD/CAM, and computer-aided process planning. New chapters have been added on industrial robotics, automated assembly, automated material handling and storage, automated inspection (e.g., machine vision, coordinate measuring machines), programmable logic controllers, shop floor control using automatic identification techniques (e.g., bar codes), and computer networking in manufacturing including the Manufacturing Automation Protocol (MAP). There is a final chapter that explores the technology and social impact of the future automated factory. I believe readers will find this new edition to be a significant enhancement of the first work.

ACKNOWLEDGMENTS

I am indebted to many persons and organizations for their help and contributions during the preparation of this book. Acknowledgement is hereby given to the many companies that contributed photos and other materials used in the text. I have attempted to provide the proper credits to these companies in the figure captions. There are individuals who deserve special mention in this section for their help in providing reviews, ideas, and/or suggestions that improved the text. These persons include: Joel Elston, research engineer in our Institute for Robotics at Lehigh; Mark Forrester, brother-in-law and good friend who helped me develop the "pipe-and-ring" model of manufacturing used in the text; Steve Howard, graduate student in our Manufacturing Systems Engineering Program who was very helpful in the chapter on programmable logic controllers; James Lin, one of my doctoral students at Lehigh who stimulated my thinking on material handling systems; Judy Swartley-Loush, another doctoral student who did background research for me in the area of automated storage systems; and John Wiginton, colleague at Lehigh and specialist in information and communications systems. I am also grateful to the Manufacturing Systems Engineering Class of 1986 for permitting me to try out some of the new material on them.

Finally, I would be remiss if I did not thank Matthew Fox, my editor at Prentice-Hall, for his perseverance and patience with me during manuscript preparation.

DEDICATION

The dedication of a book is not something that an author takes lightly. One hopes to reflect great honor and credit on an individual or an organization through the dedication of a major work such as a book. It is as if the author is dedicating a major portion of his life that is represented by the book. In my case there are many who deserve credit for various contributions they have made to my personal and professional development. Presumably, the net result of that development is somehow reflected in the book. However, there is one person who stands far above all others in deserving to be honored here. That person is my wife. I therefore dedicate this book to Bonnie, my loving wife and companion for many years. As I have told her on numerous occasions, she is the best thing that ever happened to me. Considering that I have written several other books before this one, I don't know why I never thought of doing this until now.

MIKELL P. GROOVER

List of Symbols

The following symbols are used to represent the various terms and parameters in equations throughout the book. In some instances, the same symbol is used in different equations; however, these instances occur in different chapters of the book where there is little likelihood of confusion.

A	Equivalent uniform annual cash value
A	Area
a	Parameter used in various equations
a	Rate of change of V in a first order hold digital-to-analog converter
B	Parameter value used in storage buffer computations (Table 5.1 in text)
B_i	Bit status (values $= 0$ or 1) in a binary register
b	Buffer capacity of a storage buffer zone on a production line
b	Parameter used in various equations
C	Circumference of a storage carousel track
C	Constant used in various equations
C	Controller transfer function $C = C(s)$
C_{as}	Cost rate for an automatic workstation on a production line
C_{at}	Cost rate for the mechanized transport system on a production line
C_L	Cost rate of production line, including operators and equipment

C_m	Material costs per unit of production
C_{no}	Nonoperation costs per operation (e.g., handling, storage, etc.)
C_o	Cost rate of operator with appropriate overheads included
C_{pc}	Cost per piece
C_t	Cost of tooling per unit of production
CR	Control resolution for a positioning system
D	Proportion of downtime on a production line
D	Diameter
D_1'	Downtime proportion of stage 1 in a two stage production line
$\mathbf{D}_p$	Direction of the gradient
D_w	Demand rate in number of parts (or products) per week
d	Balance delay (measure of inefficiency) in assembly line balancing
d	Depth of cut in a machining operation
E	Production line efficiency, defined as proportion uptime
E_h	Efficiency of a material handling system
E_k	Production line efficiency for stage k in an automated production line
E_0	Production line efficiency for a line with zero buffer capacity
E_∞	Production line efficiency for a line with infinite buffer capacity
e	Abbreviation for exponent
e	Error signal
e_n	Error signal for time period n
F	Future cash value
F	Frequency of production line stops
F	Force variable
F_c	Cutting force in a machining operation
F_t	Traffic factor in a material handling system
f	Feed rate of the parts feeder at an automatic assembly workstation
f	Feed in a machining operation (in/rev)
f_p	Feed rate of parts on a manual production line
f_p	Frequency of the pulse train (pulse rate) to drive a stepping motor
f_r	Feed rate in a machining operation (in/min)
G	Forward transfer function in a control system $G = G(s)$
$\mathbf{G}_p$	Gradient, a vector quantity used in certain search methods
H	Hours of operation during a work shift
H	Feedback transfer function in a control system $H = H(s)$
H_s	Height of an automated storage/retrieval system
h	Holding cost rate
h	Head or liquid level in a tank
$h(b)$	Ideal proportion of time in a two stage production line when stage 1 is down that stage 2 is operating, within the limits imposed by buffer capacity b
I	Interest payment
I	Electrical current
IC	Initial cost of an investment project
i	Interest rate (per year), also used to indicate rate of return
i	Subscript used to identify the sequence of production operations or workstations in a production line
i	Subscript used to identify data in statistical calculations
j	Subscript used to identify production batches in a factory

j	Subscript used to denote reason for a breakdown in a production line
j	Subscript used to denote work elements in line balancing
K	Parameter value used in storage buffer computations (Table 5.1 in text)
K	Constant used in various equations
K_d	Damping coefficient
K_s	Spring constant
k	Subscript used to identify stages in a production line
L	Parameter value used in storage buffer computations (Table 5.1 in text)
L	Length of a machined workpart in the direction of the feed
L_c	Length of a component in the feed track of an automatic assembly station
L_d	Length or distance of a delivery in a material handling system
L_e	Length or distance of the empty trip associated with a delivery
L_{f1}	Length of the feed track of an automatic assembly station at the low level sensor
L_{f2}	Length of the feed track of an automatic assembly station at the high level sensor
L_r	Length of travel associated with a carousel storage system retrieval
L_s	Length of a workstation on a manual assembly line or production line
L_s	Length of an automated storage/retrieval system
M	Mass
M_p	Magnitude of the gradient
MLT	Manufacturing lead time
MRR	Metal removal rate in a machining operation
$MTBF$	Mean time between failure
$MTTR$	Mean time to repair
m	Probability that a defective component delivered from the parts feeder will jam an automatic assembly station
$NACF$	Net annual cash flow
n	Number of years (or other periods) in engineering economy calculations
n	Payback period, in years, until investment pays for itself
n	Number of workstations on a production line
n	Number of work elements performed on a single station assembly machine
n	Number of bits
n	Exponent in the Taylor tool life equation
n_a	Number of automatic workstations on a production line
n_b	Number of storage bins suspended from a carrier in a storage carousel
n_c	Number of carriers in a material handling system
n_d	Number of openings in an optical encoder disk
n_e	Number of minimum rational work elements in line balancing
n_{f1}	Number of parts in the feed track of an automatic assembly station at the low level sensor
n_{f2}	Number of parts in the feed track of an automatic assembly station at the high level sensor
n_h	Number of horizontal load compartments in an automated storage system
n_m	Number of machines through which part is routed during its production
n_o	Number of manually operated workstations on a production line
n_Q	Number of batches
n_p	Number of individual parts in a carrier or unit load in material handling
n_p	Number of poles in the root locus plot
n_s	Number of step angles in a stepping motor
n_v	Number of vertical load compartments in an automated storage system
n_z	Number of zeros in the root locus plot

P	Present cash value (starting amount of an investment or deposit)
P	Number of pulses received by a stepping motor
P	Numerical value of a pole in the root locus plot
P_{ap}	Proportion of acceptable product (yield) produced on an automated assembly machine
P_{qp}	Proportion of assemblies made that contain one or more defects
PC	Production capacity of a plant, department, or other facility
PW	Present worth of an investment project
p	Probability (or frequency) of workstation failure resulting in downtime
p	Point on a response surface defined by its coordinates x_1, x_2
Q	Quantity of parts in a batch, number of units to be produced per year
Q	Parameter in automated storage/retrieval system calculations
Q_T	Total dose in the ion implantation process
q	Scrap rate or fraction defect rate
R	Resistance to fluid flow
R_c	Ideal or theoretical production rate, based on ideal cycle time
R_f	Rate of flow in a material handling system (e.g., pieces/hour)
R_p	Actual average production rate
r	Ratio of breakdown rates for a two stage production line
r	Correlation coefficient
r_i	Root of the characteristic equation
S	Rotational speed of a motor or spindle
S_w	Number of work shifts per week (or month or other period)
SR	Spatial resolution for a positioning system
s	Storage cost rate
s	Differential operator and Laplace transform variable
s_c	Spacing between carriers along a conveyor
s_e	Standard error of estimate
s_p	Spacing between parts along a conveyor on a manual production line
T	Time parameter in automated storage/retrieval system calculations
T	Tool life of a cutting tool
T_c	Ideal or theoretical cycle time for a production line
T_d	Average downtime per line stop occurrence
T_{dc}	Dual-command transaction time of an automated storage/retrieval system
T_{ej}	Time to perform minimum rational work element j on a production line
T_h	Handling time for part or load (loading and unloading)
T_m	Time to machine a workpart length
T_{no}	Average nonoperation time per part
T_o	Average operation time per part for process or assembly
T_p	Average production time per unit
T_{pd}	Pick-and-deposit time of an automated storage/retrieval system
T_r	Time to complete a retrieval transaction for a carousel storage system
T_s	Sum of element times at a station on a manual production line
T_{sc}	Single-command transaction time of an automated storage/retrieval system
T_{su}	Setup time
T_t	Tolerance time on a manual assembly line or production line
T_{th}	Tool handling time per workpiece
T_v	Total time associated with a delivery cycle in material handling
T_{wc}	Total work content time of the work to be done on a production line

TTW	Total transport work in material handling
TWR	Tool wear rate
t	Time variable
t_h	Time to travel the full horizontal distance of an automated storage/retrieval system
t_v	Time to travel the full vertical distance of an automated storage/retrieval system
U	Utilization (of equipment)
UAC	Uniform annual cost of an investment project
V	Velocity or cutting speed in a machining operation
V	Voltage
V_c	Velocity (ft/min) of a conveyor or cart in a material handling system or along a mechanized production line
V_h	Horizontal travel velocity in an automated storage/retrieval system
V_o	Output voltage of a digital-to-analog converter
V_{ref}	Reference voltage of a digital-to-analog converter
V_v	Vertical travel velocity in an automated storage/retrieval system
W	Number of work centers
W_s	Width of a storage carousel track
WIP	Work-in-process
x	Variable in a differential equation
x_p	Controller output variable and input to the process in a control system
x_{pn}	Value of the process input in a direct digital control system
y	Variable in a differential equation
Y	Desired steady state value of y
Z	Numerical value of a zero in the root locus plot
z	Objective function or index of performance
α	Step angle in a stepping motor, angle between openings in an encoder disk
α	Asymptote angles in the root locus plot
β	Angle corresponding to the damping ratio in the root locus plot
ζ	Damping ratio
θ	Proportion of components that pass through the selector-orientor device for delivery into the feed track at an automatic assembly workstation
θ_p	Departure angle in the root locus plot
θ_z	Arrival angle in the root locus plot
σ	Real part of a complex number
σ_b	Breakaway point in the root locus plot
σ_c	Center of asymptotes in the root locus plot
τ	Time constant
τ	Time interval between sampling instants
ω	Imaginary part of a complex number
ω_d	Damped natural frequency
ω_n	Natural frequency

chapter **1**

Introduction

This is a book about production automation. New terms have been developed to describe various aspects of this technology. Many of these terms, such as *robotics*, *CAD/CAM* (computer-aided design/computer-aided manufacturing), *flexible manufacturing systems*, and *machine vision*, were unknown 30 years ago. Old words, such as *mechanization*, have virtually disappeared from the technical vocabulary. Automation is a dynamic technology that represents a continuous evolutionary process that began many decades ago. Some might even argue that the process began with the industrial revolution (circa 1770), when machines began to take over the work previously performed by manual labor. Automation is a process of technological development that will proceed into the foreseeable future.

In this first chapter, we define automation, describe the various types of automation, provide reasons why companies install automated systems, and present the social arguments for and against this technology.

1.1 AUTOMATION DEFINED

Automation is a technology concerned with the application of mechanical, electronic, and computer-based systems to operate and control production. This technology includes:

- Automatic machine tools to process parts
- Automatic assembly machines
- Industrial robots
- Automatic material handling and storage systems
- Automatic inspection systems for quality control
- Feedback control and computer process control
- Computer systems for planning, data collection, and decision making to support manufacturing activities

The scope of this text will be limited primarily to automated systems used in discrete-product manufacturing. Examples of industries using these types of systems include: metalworking, electronics, automotive, appliances, aircraft, and many others.

Types of automation

For our purposes in this book, automated production systems can best be classified into three basic types:

1. Fixed automation   = mass produ. lines
2. Programmable automation
3. Flexible automation

Fixed automation is a system in which the sequence of processing (or assembly) operations is fixed by the equipment configuration. The operations in the sequence are usually simple. It is the integration and coordination of many such operations into one piece of equipment that makes the system complex. The typical features of fixed automation are:

- High initial investment for custom-engineered equipment
- High production rates
- Relatively inflexible in accommodating product changes

The economic justification for fixed automation is found in products with very high demand rates and volumes. The high initial cost of the equipment can be spread over a very large number of units, thus making the unit cost attractive compared to alternative methods of production. Examples of fixed automation include mechanized assembly lines (starting around 1913—the product moved along mechanized conveyors, but the workstations along the line were manually operated) and machining transfer lines (beginning around 1924).

In *programmable automation*, the production equipment is designed with the capability to change the sequence of operations to accommodate different product configurations. The operation sequence is controlled by a program, which is a set of instructions

coded so that the system can read and interpret them. New programs can be prepared
and entered into the equipment to produce new products. Some of the features that
characterize programmable automation include:

- High investment in general-purpose equipment
- Low production rates relative to fixed automation
- Flexibility to deal with changes in product configuration
- Most suitable for batch production

Automated production systems that are programmable are used in low and medium-
volume production. The parts or products are typically made in batches. To produce each
new batch of a different product, the system must be reprogrammed with the set of
machine instructions that correspond to the new product. The physical setup of the machine
must also be changed over: Tools must be loaded, fixtures must be attached to the machine
table, and the required machine settings must be entered. This changeover procedure
takes time. Consequently, the typical cycle for a given product includes a period during
which the setup and reprogramming takes place, followed by a period in which the batch
is produced. Examples of programmable automation include numerically controlled machine tools (first prototype demonstrated in 1952) and industrial robots (initial applications
around 1961), although the technology has its roots in the Jacquard loom (1801).

Flexible automation is an extension of programmable automation. The concept of
flexible automation has developed only over the last 15 or 20 years, and the principles
are still evolving. A flexible automated system is one that is capable of producing a
variety of products (or parts) with virtually no time lost for changeovers from one product
to the next. There is no production time lost while reprogramming the system and altering
the physical setup (tooling, fixtures, machine settings). Consequently, the system can
produce various combinations and schedules of products, instead of requiring that they
be made in separate batches. The features of flexible automation can be summarized as
follows:

- High investment for a custom-engineered system
- Continuous production of variable mixtures of products
- Medium production rates
- Flexibility to deal with product design variations

The essential features that distinguish flexible automation from programmable automation are (1) the capacity to change part programs with no lost production time, and
(2) the capability to change over the physical setup, again with no lost production time.
These features allow the automated production system to continue production without the
downtime between batches that is characteristic of programmable automation. Changing
the part programs is generally accomplished by preparing the programs off-line on a
computer system and electronically transmitting the programs to the automated production
system. Therefore, the time required to do the programming for the next job does not

interrupt production on the current job. Advances in computer systems technology are largely responsible for this progamming capability in flexible automation. Changing the physical setup between parts is accomplished by making the changeover off-line and then moving it into place simultaneously as the next part comes into position for processing. The use of pallet fixtures that hold the parts and transfer into position at the workplace is one way of implementing this approach. For these approaches to be successful, the variety of parts that can be made on a flexible automated production system is usually more limited than a system controlled by programmable automation. Examples of flexible automation are the flexible manufacturing systems for performing machining operations that date back to the late 1960s.

The relative positions of the three types of automation for different production volumes and product varieties are depicted in Figure 1.1.

Computer integrated manufacturing

The computer has had and continues to have a dramatic impact on the development of production automation technologies. Nearly all modern production systems are implemented today using computer systems. The term *computer integrated manufacturing* (CIM) has been coined to denote the pervasive use of computers to design the products, plan the production, control the operations, and perform the various business related

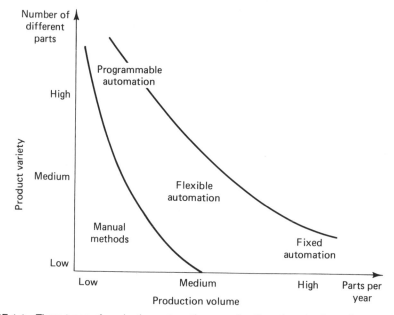

FIGURE 1.1   Three types of production automation as a function of production volume and product variety.

functions needed in a manufacturing firm. *CAD/CAM* (computer-aided design and computer-aided manufacturing) is another term that is used almost synonymously with CIM.

Let us attempt to define the relationship between automation and CIM by developing a conceptual model of manufacturing. In a manufacturing firm, the physical activities related to production that take place in the factory can be distinguished from the information-processing activities, such as product design and production planning, that usually occur in an office environment. The physical activities include all of the manufacturing processing, assembly, material handling, and inspections that are performed on the product. These operations come in direct contact with the product during manufacture. They touch the product. The relationship between the physical activities and the information-processing activities in our model is depicted in Figure 1.2. Raw materials flow in one end of the factory and finished products flow out the other end. The physical activities (processing, handling, etc.) take place inside the factory. The information-processing functions form a ring that surrounds the factory, providing the data and knowledge required to produce the product successfully. These information-processing functions include (1) certain business activities (e.g., marketing and sales, order entry, customer billing, etc.), (2) product design, (3) manufacturing planning, and (4) manufacturing control. These four functions form a cycle of events that must accompany the physical production activities but which do not directly touch the product.

Now consider the difference between automation and CIM. Automation is concerned with the physical activities in manufacturing. Automated production systems are designed to accomplish the processing, assembly, material handling, and inspecting activities with little or no human participation. By comparison, computer integrated manufacturing is

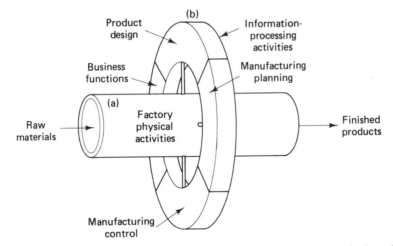

FIGURE 1.2 Model of manufacturing, showing (a) the factory as a processing pipeline where the physical manufacturing activities are performed, and (b) the information-processing activities that support manufacturing as a ring that surrounds the factory.

concerned more with the information-processing functions that are required to support the production operations. CIM involves the use of computer systems to perform the four types of information-processing functions. Just as automation deals with the physical activities, CIM deals with automating the information-processing activities in manufacturing. The growing applications of computer systems in manufacturing are leading us toward the computer-automated factory of the future.

We will return to our model of manufacturing in Chapter 2 and to the topics of CIM, CAD/CAM, and the future automated factory in the final chapters. For now let us consider some of the more general issues related to automation and computer-integrated manufacturing.

1.2 REASONS FOR AUTOMATING

Companies undertake projects in automation and CIM for a variety of good reasons. Some of the important reasons for automating include the following:

1. *Increased productivity.* Automation of manufacturing operations holds the promise of increasing the productivity of labor. This means greater output per hour of labor input. Higher production rates (output per hour) are achieved with automation than with the corresponding manual operations.

2. *High cost of labor.* The trend in the industrialized societies of the world has been toward ever-increasing labor costs. As a result, higher investment in automated equipment has become economically justifiable to replace manual operations. The high cost of labor is forcing business leaders to substitute machines for human labor. Because machines can produce at higher rates of output, the use of automation results in a lower cost per unit of product.

3. *Labor shortages.* In many advanced nations there has been a general shortage of labor. West Germany, for example, has been forced to import labor to augment its own labor supply. Labor shortages also stimulate the development of automation as a substitute for labor.

4. *Trend of labor toward the service sector.* This trend has been especially prevalent in the United States. At this writing (1986), the proportion of the work force employed in manufacturing stands at about 20%. In 1947, this percentage was 30%. By the year 2000, some estimates put the figure as low as 2% [7].[1] Certainly, automation of production jobs has caused some of this shift. However, there are also social and institutional forces that are responsible for the trend. The growth of government employment at the federal, state, and local levels has consumed a certain share of the labor market which might otherwise have gone into manufacturing. Also, there has been a tendency for people to view factory work as tedious, demeaning, and dirty. This view

---

[1]Numbers in brackets refer to the References at the end of the chapter.

has caused them to seek employment in the service sector of the economy (government, insurance, personal services, legal, sales, etc.).

5. *Safety.* By automating the operation and transferring the operator from an active participation to a supervisory role, work is made safer. The safety and physical well-being of the worker has become a national objective with the enactment of the Occupational Safety and Health Act of 1970 (OSHA). It has also provided an impetus for automation.

6. *High cost of raw materials.* The high cost of raw materials in manufacturing results in the need for greater efficiency in using these materials. The reduction of scrap is one of the benefits of automation.

7. *Improved product quality.* Automated operations not only produce parts at faster rates than do their manual counterparts, but they produce parts with greater consistency and conformity to quality specifications.

8. *Reduced manufacturing lead time.* For reasons that we shall examine in subsequent chapters, automation allows the manufacturer to reduce the time between customer order and product delivery. This gives the manufacturer a competitive advantage in promoting good customer service.

9. *Reduction of in-process inventory.* Holding large inventories of work-in-process represents a significant cost to the manufacturer because it ties up capital. In-process inventory is of no value. It serves none of the purposes of raw materials stock or finished product inventory. Accordingly, it is to the manufacturer's advantage to reduce work-in-progress to a minimum. Automation tends to accomplish this goal by reducing the time a workpart spends in the factory.

10. *High cost of not automating.* A significant competitive advantage is gained by automating a manufacturing plant. The advantage cannot easily be demonstrated on a company's project authorization form. The benefits of automation often show up in intangible and unexpected ways, such as improved quality, higher sales, better labor relations, and better company image. Companies that do not automate are likely to find themselves at a competitive disadvantage with their customers, their employees, and the general public.

All of these factors act together to make production automation a feasible and attractive alternative to manual methods of manufacture.

1.3 ARGUMENTS FOR AND AGAINST AUTOMATION

Since the time when production automation became a national issue in the late 1950s and early 1960s, labor leaders and government officials have debated the pros and cons of automation technology. Even business leaders, who generally see themselves as advocates of technological progress, have on occasion questioned whether automation was really worth its high investment cost. There have been arguments to limit the rate at which new production technology should be introduced into industry. By contrast, there have been proposals that government (federal and state) should not only encourage the introduction of new automation, but should actually finance a portion of its cost. (The Japanese government does it.) In this section we discuss some of these arguments for and against automation.

Arguments against automation

First, the arguments against automation include the following:

1.   Automation will result in the subjugation of the human being by a machine. This is really an argument over whether workers' jobs will be downgraded or upgraded by automation. On the one hand, automation tends to transfer the skill required to perform work from human operators to machines. In so doing, it reduces the need for skilled labor. The manual work left by automation requires lower skill levels and tends to involve rather menial tasks (e.g., loading and unloading workparts, changing tools, removing chips, etc.). In this sense, automation tends to downgrade factory work. On the other hand, the routine monotonous tasks are the easiest to automate, and are therefore the first jobs to be automated. Fewer workers are thus needed in these jobs. Tasks requiring judgment and skill are more difficult to automate. The net result is that the overall level of manufacturing labor will be upgraded, not downgraded.

2.   There will be a reduction in the labor force, with resulting unemployment. It is logical to argue that the immediate effect of automation will be to reduce the need for human labor, thus displacing workers. Because automation will increase productivity by a substantial margin, the creation of new jobs will not occur fast enough to take up the slack of displaced workers. As a consequence, unemployment rates will accelerate.

3.   Automation will reduce purchasing power. This follows from argument 2. As machines replace workers and these workers join the unemployment ranks, they will not receive the wages necessary to buy the products brought by automation. Markets will become saturated with products that people cannot afford to purchase. Inventories will grow. Production will stop. Unemployment will reach epidemic proportions. And the result will be a massive economic depression.

Arguments in favor of automation

Some of the arguments against automation are perhaps overstated. The same can be said of some of the declarations that advocate the new manufacturing technologies. The following is a sampling of the arguments for automation:

1.   Automation is the key to the shorter workweek. There has been and is a trend toward fewer working hours and more leisure time. (College engineering professors seem excluded from this trend). Around the turn of the century, the average workweek was about 70 hours per week. The standard is currently 40 hours (although many in the labor force work overtime). The argument holds that automation will allow the average number

of working hours per week to continue to decline, thereby allowing greater leisure hours and a higher quality of life.

2.   Automation brings safer working conditions for the worker. Since there is less direct physical participation by the worker in the production process, there is less chance of personal injury to the worker.

3.   Automated production results in lower prices and better products. It has been estimated that the cost to machine one unit of product by conventional general-purpose machine tools requiring human operators may be 100 times the cost of manufacturing the same unit using automated mass-production techniques. Examples abound. The machining of an automobile engine block by transfer line techniques (discussed in Chapter 4 and 5) may cost $25 to $35. If conventional techniques were used on reduced quantities (and the quantities would indeed be much lower if conventional methods were used), the cost would increase to around $3000. The electronics industry offers many examples of improvements in manufacturing technology that have significantly reduced costs while increasing product value (e.g., color TV sets, stereo equipment, hand-held calculators, and computers).

4.   The growth of the automation industry will itself provide employment opportunities. This has been especially true in the computer industry. As the companies in this industry have grown (IBM, Burroughs, Digital Equipment Corp., Honeywell, etc.), new jobs have been created. These new jobs include not only workers directly employed by these companies, but also computer programmers, systems engineers, and others needed to use and operate the computers.

5.   Automation is the only means of increasing our standard of living. Only through productivity increases brought about by new automated methods of production will we be able to advance our standard of living. Granting wage increases without a commensurate increase in productivity will result in inflation. In effect, this will reduce our standard of living. To afford a better society, we must increase productivity faster than we increase wages and salaries. Therefore, as this argument proposes, automation is a requirement to achieve the desired increase in productivity.

No comment is offered on the relative merits of these arguments for and against automation. This book is concerned principally with the technical and engineering aspects of automated production systems. Included within the engineering analysis is, of course, consideration of the economic factors that determine the feasibility of an automation project.

1.4   ORGANIZATION OF THE BOOK

The following 26 chapters of this book are organized into nine parts. This introductory chapter has attempted to set the stage and whet the reader's appetite for the technical chapters that follow on automation, production systems, and computer integrated manufacturing.

Part I contains two chapters, the first of which covers some of the fundamental concepts and principles of manufacturing and automation. The second chapter in Part I discusses production economics, an essential subject for justifying an automation project.

Part II is concerned with high-volume production of discrete products. The type of automation used here is sometimes called "Detroit automation" because of its extensive applications in the automobile industry. The four chapters in Part II discuss the production lines, both automated and manually operated, that perform processing and assembly operations. The automated production lines are examples of fixed automation.

Part III covers numerical control, an example of programmable automation. Numerical control is used for batch production of parts and products. The program is formed out of numbers, hence the name *numerical control*. An extension of numerical control technology is industrial robotics.

Part IV provides three chapters on industrial robotics: its technology, programming, and applications.

Part V deals with material handling, one of the physical activities in the factory that "touch" the product. We concentrate, of course, on automated systems. The two chapters in Part V discuss automated material handling systems and automated storage systems.

Part VI is concerned with group technology and flexible manufacturing systems. A flexible manufacturing system (FMS) is a representative application of flexible automation. Group technology is considered a necessary principle to achieving a successful FMS.

Part VII contains only one chapter—on quality control and automated inspection. Please do not interpret the one chapter as meaning that quality control (QC) is not important. The chapter is substantial, both in length and importance. We learn that automated inspection methods do not always have to "touch" the product.

Part VIII covers automatic control systems. We survey the traditional linear feedback control theory and then proceed to consider how computer systems are used to achieve control over manufacturing operations in a modern factory.

Finally, Part IX presents an introduction to computer integrated manufacturing. The five chapters describe the elements of CIM: computer-aided design, computer-aided manufacturing, manufacturing planning, manufacturing control, and the glue that holds these computer systems together—computer networks. We conclude the book with a description of what the future automated factory will be like, and the social impact that it will have.

REFERENCES

[1] BUCKINGHAM, W., *Automation,* Harper & Row, Publishers, Inc., New York, 1961.

[2] DRUCKER, P. F., "Automation Payoffs Are Real," *The Wall Street Journal,* September 20, 1985.

[3] GROOVER, M. P, and J. C. WIGINTON, "CIM and the Flexible Automated Factory of the Future," *Industrial Engineering,* January 1986, pp. 74–85.

[4]   GROOVER, M. P., M. WEISS, R. N. NAGEL, and N. G. ODREY, *Industrial Robotics: Technology, Programming, and Applications,* McGraw-Hill Book Company, New York, 1986, Chapter 1.

[5]   HARRINGTON, J., *Computer Integrated Manufacturing,* Industrial Press, Inc., New York, 1973.

[6]   LUKE, H. D. *Automation for Productivity,* John Wiley & Sons, Inc., New York, 1972.

[7]   MERCHANT, M. E., "The Inexorable Push for Automated Production," *Production Engineering,* January 1977, pp. 44–49.

[8]   SILBERMAN, C. E., and the Editors of *Fortune, The Myths of Automation,* Harper & Row, Publishers, Inc., New York, 1966.

[9]   TERBORGH, G., *The Automation Hysteria,* W. W. Norton & Company, Inc., New York, 1966.

part **I**

Fundamentals
of Manufacturing
and Automation

In Chapter 1 we defined automation and discussed its social and economic basis. Before proceeding to examine various examples of automated production systems that are used in industry, there are certain general concepts and principles related to manufacturing that should be understood. It is our objective in this first part of the book to present these concepts and principles of manufacturing. Part I consists of two chapters: Chapter 2 on production operations and automation strategies, and Chapter 3 on production economics.

In Chapter 2 we define production and survey the variety of industries that are engaged in production activities. The different categories of production systems, manufacturing operations, plant layouts, and organizational structures are also discussed. We present a set of mathematical models to describe how production is accomplished and how the performance of a production system is measured. Manufacturing lead time, production rate, plant capacity, work-in-process, and utilization are among the basic concepts that are given quantitative meanings in this section. These performance measures will be referred to throughout the book. The chapter concludes by presenting a list of 10 automation strategies: a checklist of approaches for automating production operations.

Chapter 3 is concerned with production economics. It is important for technical specialists in automation to understand the economic criteria that determine whether a given production system will be successful. The chapter begins with an introductory treatment of engineering economy, emphasizing the methods for evaluating investment proposals that are used by companies. The types of costs encountered in production are discussed, including overhead costs. A rational method for costing an automated production workcell is developed which distinguishes the cost of labor from the cost of equipment. Other topics in Chapter 3 include breakeven analysis, analysis of unit costs of production, and evaluation of the cost of work-in process. An appendix to this chapter presents a tabulation of the interest factors used in engineering economy calculations.

It is important for the reader to possess the background contained in these two chapters in order to appreciate the opportunities and limitations of the various automated systems discussed in the remaining chapters.

chapter 2

Production Operations and Automation Strategies

Production is a transformation process that converts raw materials into finished products that have value in the marketplace. The products are made by a combination of manual labor, machinery, tools, and energy. The transformation process usually involves a sequence of steps, each step bringing the materials closer to the desired final state. The individual steps are referred to as production operations.

In this chapter we define some fundamental concepts about production and automation. We begin by examining the industries that are engaged in manufacturing. This leads into the types of production and the various functions that are associated with it. Many of the functions can be described by mathematical models, and several equations are derived to define concepts such as production rate and plant capacity. The chapter concludes by developing a list of 10 automation strategies. These strategies form the basis for the specific topics covered in this book.

2.1 MANUFACTURING INDUSTRIES

There is a wide variety of basic industries, including not only manufacturing but all others as well. By examining the publicly held corporations whose shares are traded on the major stock exchanges, it is possible to compile a list of industry types. Such a list is presented in Table 2.1. This list includes all types of industrial corporations, banks,

TABLE 2.1   Basic Industries: General

Advertising
Aerospace
Automotive (cars, trucks, buses)
Beverages
Building materials
Cement
Chemicals
Clothing (garments, shoes)
Construction
Drugs, soaps, cosmetics
Equipment and machinery
Financial (banks, investment companies, loans)
Foods (canned, dairy, meats, etc.)
Hospital supplies
Hotel/motel
Insurance
Metals (steel, aluminum, etc.)
Natural resources (oil, coal, forest, etc.)
Paper
Publishing
Radio, TV, motion pictures
Restaurant
Retail (food, department store, etc.)
Shipbuilding
Textiles
Tire and rubber
Tobacco
Transportation (railroad, airlines, trucking, etc.)
Utilities (electric power, natural gas, telephone)

utilities, and so on. Our interest in this book is on industrial firms that are engaged in production.

Table 2.2 is a list of basic industries that produce goods, together with examples of companies that are members of these industries. The companies represented in this table can be divided into two types, depending on the nature of their production operations. The two types are the manufacturing industries and the process industries. *Manufacturing companies* are typically identified with discrete-item production: cars, computers, machine tools, and the components that go into these products. The *process industries* are represented by chemicals and plastics, petroleum products, food processing, soaps, steel, and cement. Our focus in this book is on manufacturing.

There are other ways to classify companies. One alternative is to place a company into one of three categories:

1. Basic producer
2. Converter
3. Fabricator

TABLE 2.2 Basic Industries: Manufacturing and Process Industries

Basic industry	Representative company
Aerospace	Boeing Co.
Automotive	General Motors
Beverages	Coca-Cola
Building materials	U.S. Gypsum
Cement	Lone Star Industries
Chemicals	E.I. du Pont
Clothing	Hanes Corp.
Drugs, soaps, cosmetics	Proctor & Gamble
Equipment and machinery	
Agricultural	Deere
Construction	Caterpillar Tractor
Electrical	General Electric
Electronics	Hewlett-Packard
Household appliances	Maytag
Industrial	Ingersoll-Rand
Machine tools	Cincinnati Milacron
Office equipment, computers	IBM
Railroad equipment	Pullman
Steam generating	Combustion Engineering
Foods	
Canned foods	Green Giant
Dairy products	Borden
Meats	Oscar Mayer
Packaged foods	General Mills
Hospital supplies	American Hospital Supply
Metals	
Aluminum	Alcoa
Copper	Kennecott
Steel	U.S. Steel
Natural resources	
Coal	Pittston
Forest	Georgia-Pacific
Oil	Exxon
Paper	Kimberly Clark
Textiles	Burlington Industries
Tire and rubber	Goodyear

The three types form a connecting chain in the transformation of natural resources and basic raw materials into goods for the consuming public. The *basic producers* take the natural resources and transform these into the raw materials used by other industrial manufacturing firms. For example, steel producers transform iron ore into steel ingots. The *converter* represents the intermediate link in the chain. The converter takes the output of the basic producer and transforms these raw materials into various industrial products and some consumer items. For example, the steel ingot is converted into bar stock or sheet metal. Chemical firms transform petroleum products into plastics for molding. Paper mills convert wood pulp into paper. A distinguishing characteristic of the converter is that its products are uncomplicated in physical form. The products are not assembled items. The production processes used to make the products may be complex but the products themselves are not.

The third category of manufacturing firms is the *fabricator*. These firms fabricate and assemble final products. The bar stock and sheet metal are transformed into machined engine components and automobile body panels. The plastics are molded into various shapes. Then these parts are assembled into final products, such as trucks, automobiles, appliances, garments, and machine tools. Fabricators include both the firms that produce the components and those which assemble the components into consumer goods.

There are several complicating factors in this classification. Some firms possess a high degree of *vertical integration,* which means that their operations include all three categories. The major oil firms are examples of vertical integration. They convert natural resources into finished petroleum products and then market these products directly to the consumer. Another complicating factor is that some companies—the conglomerates—are in so many different types of business that it is difficult to classify them. Some of their operations are in the basic producer category; others are converters; and still other lines of business fall into the fabricator category.

2.2 TYPES OF PRODUCTION

Another way of classifying production activity is according to the quantity of product made. In this classification, there are three types of production:

1. Job shop production
2. Batch production
3. Mass production

This classification is normally associated with discrete-product manufacture, but it can also serve for plants used in the process industries. For example, some chemicals are produced in batches (batch production), whereas others are produced by continuous-flow processes (mass production). The three types of production are related to production volume as shown in Figure 2.1.

JOB SHOPS. The distinguishing feature of job shop production is low volume. The manufacturing lot sizes are small, often one of a kind. Job shop production is commonly used to meet specific customer orders, and there is a great variety in the type of work the plant must do. Therefore, the production equipment must be flexible and general-purpose to allow for this variety of work. Also, the skill level of job shop workers must be relatively high so that they can perform a range of different work assignments. Examples of products manufactured in a job shop include space vehicles, aircraft, machine tools, special tools and equipment, and prototypes of future products.

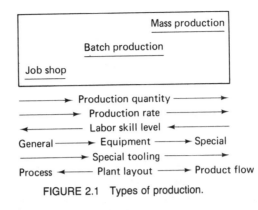

FIGURE 2.1   Types of production.

Construction work and shipbuilding are not normally identified with the job shop category, even though the quantities are in the appropriate range. Although these two activities involve the transformation of raw materials into finished products, the work is not performed in a factory.

BATCH PRODUCTION.   This category involves the manufacture of medium-sized lots of the same item or product. The lots may be produced only once, or they may be produced at regular intervals. The purpose of batch production is often to satisfy continuous customer demand for an item. However, the plant is capable of a production rate that exceeds the demand rate. Therefore, the shop produces to build up an inventory of the item. Then it changes over to other orders. When the stock of the first item becomes depleted, production is repeated to build up the inventory again.

The manufacturing equipment used in batch production is general-purpose but designed for higher rates of production. For example, turret lathes capable of holding several cutting tools are used rather than engine lathes. The machine tools used in batch manufacture are often combined with specially designed jigs and fixtures which increase the output rate. Examples of items made in batch-type shops include industrial equipment, furniture, textbooks, and component parts for many assembled consumer products (household appliances, lawn mowers, etc.). Batch production plants include machine shops, casting foundries, plastic molding factories, and pressworking shops. Some types of chemical plants are also in this general category.

It has been estimated that perhaps as much as 75% of all parts manufacturing is in lot sizes of 50 pieces or less. Hence, batch production and job shop production constitute an important portion of total manufacturing activity.

MASS PRODUCTION.   This is the continuous specialized manufacture of identical products. Mass production is characterized by very high production rates, equipment that is completely dedicated to the manufacture of a particular product, and very high demand rates for the product. Not only is the equipment dedicated to one product, but the entire plant is often designed for the exclusive purpose of producing the particular product. The equipment is special-purpose rather than general-purpose. The investment in machines and specialized tooling is high. In a sense, the production skill has been transferred from the operator to the machine. Consequently, the skill level of labor in a mass production plant tends to be lower than in a batch plant or job shop.

Two categories of mass production can be distinguished:

1. Quantity production
2. Flow production

Quantity production involves the mass production of single parts on fairly standard machine tools such as punch presses, injection molding machines, and automatic screw machines. These standard machines have been adapted to the production of the particular part by means of special tools—die sets, molds, and form cutting tools, respectively—designed for the part in question. The production equipment is devoted full time to satisfy a very large demand rate for the item. In mass production, the demand rate and the production rate are approximately equal. Examples of items in quantity production include components for assembled products that have high demand rates (automobiles, some household appliances, light bulbs, etc.), hardware items (such as screws, nuts, and nails), and many plastic molded products.

Flow production is the other category of mass production. The term suggests the physical flow of the product in oil refineries, continuous chemical process plants, and food processing. While these are examples of flow production, the term also applies to the manufacture of either complex single parts (such as automotive engine blocks) or assembled products. In these cases, the items are made to "flow" through a sequence of operations by material handling devices (conveyors, moving belts, transfer devices, etc.). Examples of flow production include automated transfer machines for the production of complex discrete parts, and manual assembly lines for the assembly of complex products.

Figure 2.1 summarizes some of the important characteristics of these different types of production plants. It will be noted that the production ranges of the three major categories overlap to some degree. The reason is simply that it is difficult to draw a clear dividing line between the different types.

2.3 FUNCTIONS IN MANUFACTURING

For any of the three types of production, there are certain basic functions that must be carried out to convert raw materials into finished product. For a firm engaged in making discrete products, the functions are:

1. Processing
2. Assembly
3. Material handling and storage
4. Inspection and test
5. Control

The first four of these functions are the physical activities mentioned in Chapter 1 that "touch" the product as it is being made. Processing and assembly are operations that add value to the product. The third and fourth functions must be performed in a manufacturing plant, but they do not add value to the product. As shown in Figure 2.2, derived from Figure 1.2, these four functions occur inside the factory directly on the product. The fifth function, control, is required to coordinate and regulate the physical activities. The following subsections describe the five functions.

Processing operations

Processing operations transform the product from one state of completion into a more advanced state of completion. No materials or components are assembled or added to accomplish the transformation. Instead, energy (i.e., mechanical, heat, electrical, chemical, etc.) is added to change the shape of the part, remove material from it, alter its physical properties, or accomplish other forms of work to change it. Processing operations can be classified into one of the following four categories:

1. Basic processes
2. Secondary processes
3. Operations to enhance physical properties
4. Finishing operations

Basic processes are those which give the work material its initial form. Metal casting and plastic molding are examples. In both cases, the raw materials are converted into the basic geometry of the desired product. It is common for additional processing to be required to achieve the final shape and size of the workpart.

Secondary processes follow the basic process and are performed to give the workpart its final desired geometry. Examples in this category include machining (turning, drilling, milling, etc.) and pressworking operations (blanking, forming, drawing, etc.).

Operations to enhance physical properties do not perceptibly change the physical geometry of the workpart. Instead, the physical properties of the material are improved

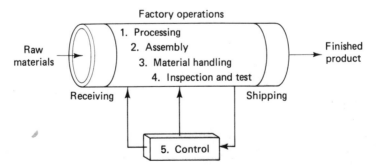

FIGURE 2.2 Model of the factory showing five functions of manufacturing.

in some way. Heat-treating operations to strengthen metal parts and preshrinking used in the garment industry are examples in this category.

Finishing operations are the final processes performed on the workpart. Their purpose is, for example, to improve the appearance, or to provide a protective coating on the part. Examples in this fourth category include polishing, painting, and chrome plating.

Figure 2.3 presents an input/output model of a typical processing operation in manufacturing. Most manufacturing processes require five inputs:

1. Raw materials
2. Equipment (machine tools)
3. Tooling and fixtures
4. Energy (electrical energy)
5. Labor

The manufacturing process adds value to the raw materials (or work-in-progress) by transforming them into a more desirable state. The process is usually carried out on production equipment that reflects a capital investment by the firm. The equipment is adapted to the particular workpart by the use of tools, fixtures, molds, die sets, and so on. This tooling must often be designed specifically for the given workpart. Electrical energy is required to operate the production equipment. Finally, labor is required to operate the equipment, load the raw workpart, unload the piece when the process is completed, check for malfunctions of the machine, and so on.

The manufacturing process produces two outputs:

1. The completed workpiece
2. Scrap and waste

The term *completed workpiece* refers to the desired output of the particular manufacturing process. Since the workpart must be routed through several operations, only the last operation yields the finished part. The other operations produce work-in-progress for succeeding processes. As a by-product of all manufacturing processes, some scrap material and waste results. The scrap is in the form of metal chips (machining operations),

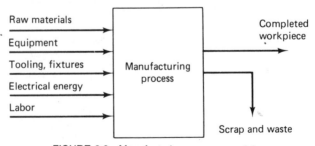

FIGURE 2.3 Manufacturing process model.

skeleton (sheet metal pressworking operations), sprue and runner (plastic molding), and so on. The waste is represented by tools consumed in the operation, the mechanical inefficiency of the machine tool, and heat losses.

Assembly operations

Assembly and joining processes constitute the second major type of manufacturing operation. In assembly, the distinguishing feature is that two or more separate components are joined together. Included in this category are mechanical fastening operations, which make use of screws, nuts, rivets, and so on, and joining processes, such as welding, brazing, and soldering. In the fabrication of a product, the assembly operations follow the processing operations.

Material handling and storage

A means of moving and storing materials between the processing and assembly operations must be provided. In most manufacturing plants, materials spend more time being moved and stored than being processed. In some cases, the majority of the labor cost in the factory is consumed in handling, moving, and storing materials. It is important that this function be carried out as efficiently as possible. In Chapters 14 and 15 we consider the materials handling and storage function and the methods by which it can be automated.

Inspection and testing

Inspection and testing are generally considered part of quality control. The purpose of inspection is to determine whether the manufactured product meets the established design standards and specifications. For example, inspection examines whether the actual dimensions of a mechanical part are within the tolerances indicated on the engineering drawing for the part.

Testing is generally concerned with the functional specifications of the final product rather than the individual parts that go into the product. For example, final testing of the product ensures that it functions and operates in the manner specified by the product designer.

In Chapter 18 we examine the inspection and testing function, with particular attention to methods used for automating it.

Control

The control function in manufacturing includes both the regulation of individual processing and assembly operations, and the management of plant-level activities. Control at the process level involves the achievement of certain performance objectives by proper manipulation of the inputs to the process. We devote a major part of our book to the subject of process control.

Control at the plant level includes effective use of labor, maintenance of the equipment, moving materials in the factory, shipping products of good quality on schedule, and keeping plant operating costs at the minimum level possible. The manufacturing control function at the plant level represents the major point of intersection between the physical operations in the factory and the information-processing activities that occur in production. Let us examine the complete cycle of information processing that takes place in a manufacturing firm.

2.4 ORGANIZATION AND INFORMATION PROCESSING IN MANUFACTURING

Manufacturing firms must organize themselves to accomplish the five functions described above. In the present section we consider the organizational functions within a manufacturing firm. Many companies make hundreds of different products, each product consisting of individual components perhaps numbering in the thousands. The task of coordinating all of the individual activities required to make the parts, assemble them, and deliver the product to the customer is complex indeed. It is a problem in information processing. We therefore resort to the manufacturing model presented in Chapter 1 (Figure

FIGURE 2.4   Information-processing cycle in a typical manufacturing firm.

1.2) and expand our discussion of the information-processing activities that take place. Figure 2.4 illustrates the cycle of information-processing activities that typically occur in a manufacturing firm which produces discrete parts and assembles them into final products for sale to its customers. The factory operations described in the preceding section are pictured in the center of the figure. The information-processing cycle, represented by the outer ring, can be described as consisting of four functions:

1. Business functions
2. Product design
3. Manufacturing planning
4. Manufacturing control

Business functions

The *business functions* are the principal means of communicating with the customer. They are therefore the beginning and the end of the information-processing cycle. Included within this category are sales and marketing, sales forecasting, order entry, cost accounting, customer billing, and others.

An order to produce a product will typically originate from the sales and marketing department of the firm. The production order will be one of the following forms: (1) an order to manufacture an item to the customer's specifications, (2) a customer order to buy one or more of the manufacturer's proprietary products, or (3) an order based on a forecast of future demand for a proprietary product.

Product design

If the product is to be manufactured to customer specifications, the design will have been provided by the customer. The manufacturer's product design department will not be involved.

If the product is proprietary, the manufacturing firm is responsible for its development and design. The cycle of events that initiates a new product design often originates in the sales and marketing department. Figure 2.4 indicates the information flow in this way. The departments of the firm that are organized to perform the product design function might include: research and development, design engineering, drafting, and perhaps a prototype shop.

The product design is documented by means of component drawings, specifications, and a bill of materials that defines how many of each component go into the product. A prototype is often built for testing and demonstration purposes. The manufacturing engineering department is sometimes consulted to lend advice on matters of produceability. A typical question might be: What changes in design could be made to reduce production costs without sacrificing function? Cost estimates are prepared to establish an anticipated price for the product.

Upon completion of the design and fabrication of the prototype, the top company management is invited in for a "show-and-tell" presentation. The design engineer in charge gives a presentation and demonstration of the product so that management can decide whether to manufacture the item. This decision is often a two-step procedure. The first is a decision by engineering management that the design is approved. Many companies call this an "engineering release." The second step is a decision by corporate management as to the general suitability of the product. This second decision represents an authorization to produce the item.

Manufacturing planning

The information and documentation that constitute the design of the product flow into the *manufacturing planning* function. The departments in the organization that perform manufacturing planning include manufacturing engineering, industrial engineering, and production planning and control. (The production planning and control department is usually involved with both manufacturing planning and manufacturing control.)

As shown in Figure 2.4, the information-processing activities in manufacturing planning include process planning, master scheduling, requirements planning, and capacity planning. *Process planning* consists of determining the sequence of the individual processing and assembly operations needed to produce the part. The document used to specify the process sequence is called a *route sheet*. The route sheet lists the production operations and associated machine tools for each component (and subassembly) of the product. The manufacturing engineering and industrial engineering departments are responsible for planning the processes and related manufacturing details.

The authorization to produce the product must be translated into the master schedule or master production schedule. The *master schedule* is a listing of the products to be made, when they are to be delivered, and in what quantities. Units of months are generally used to specify the deliveries on the master schedule. Based on this schedule, the individual components and subassemblies that make up each product must be planned. Raw materials must be requisitioned, purchased parts must be ordered from suppliers, and all of these items must be planned so that they are available when needed. This whole task is called *requirements planning* or *material requirements planning*. In addition, the master schedule must not list more quantities of products than the factory is capable of producing with its given number of machines and workers each month. The production quantity that the factory is capable of producing is referred to as the plant capacity. We will define and discuss this term later in the chapter. *Capacity planning* is concerned with planning the manpower and machine resources of the firm.

Manufacturing control

Manufacturing control is concerned with managing and controlling the physical operations in the factory to implement the manufacturing plans. The flow of information is from planning to control, as indicated in Figure 2.4. Information also flows back and forth between manufacturing control and the factory operations, as indicated in Figure 2.2.

Included with the control function are shop floor control, inventory control, quality control, and various other control activities. Process control is also included if the plant uses automatic process control in its operations.

Shop floor control is concerned with the problem of monitoring the progress of the product as it is being processed, assembled, moved, and inspected in the factory. The sections of a traditional production planning and control department that are involved in shop floor control include scheduling, dispatching, and expediting. Production scheduling is concerned with assigning start dates and due dates to the various parts (and products) that are to be made in the factory. This requires that the parts be scheduled one by one through the various production machines listed on the route sheet for each part. Based on the production schedule, *dispatching* involves issuing the individual work orders to the machine operators to accomplish the processing of the parts. The dispatching function is performed in some plants by the shop foremen, in other plants by a person called the dispatcher. Even with the best plans and schedules, things sometimes go wrong (e.g., machine breakdowns, improper tooling, parts delayed at the vendor). The *expediter* compares the actual progress of a production order against the schedule. For orders that fall behind, the expediter attempts to take the necessary corrective action to complete the order on time.

Inventory control overlaps with shop floor control to some extent. *Inventory control* attempts to strike a proper balance between the danger of too little inventory (with possible stock-outs of materials) and the expense of having too much inventory. Shop floor control is also concerned with inventory in the sense that the materials being processed in the factory represent inventory (called work-in-process).

The mission of *quality control* is to assure that the quality of the product and its components meet the standards specified by the product designer. To accomplish its mission, quality control depends on the inspection activities performed in the factory at various times throughout the manufacture of the product. Also, raw materials and components from outside sources must be inspected when they are received. Final inspection and testing of the finished product is performed to ensure functional quality and appearance.

2.5 PLANT LAYOUT

In addition to the organizational structure, a firm engaged in manufacturing must also be concerned with its physical facilities. The term *plant layout* refers to the arrangement of these physical facilities in a production plant. A layout suited to flow-type mass production is not appropriate for job shop production, and vice versa. There are three principal types of plant layout associated with traditional production shops:

1. Fixed-position layout
2. Process layout
3. Product-flow layout

We will see that there is a considerable correlation between the type of plant layout and the types of production previously classified according to quantity.

FIXED-POSITION LAYOUT. In this type of layout, the term "fixed-position" refers to the product. Because of its size and weight, the product remains in one location and the equipment used in its fabrication is brought to it. Large aircraft assembly and ship-building are examples of operations in which fixed-position layout is utilized. Fixed-position layout is illustrated in Figure 2.5(a).

Another arrangement of facilities, similar to the fixed-position type, is *project layout*. This is used for construction jobs such as buildings, bridges, and dams. As with fixed-position layout, the product is large and the construction equipment and workers must be moved to the product. Unlike the fixed-position arrangement, when the job is completed, the equipment is removed from the construction site. In fixed-position layout, the product is eventually moved out of the plant and the plant remains for the next job. This type of arrangement is often associated with job shops in which complex products are fabricated in very low quantities.

PROCESS LAYOUT. In a process layout, the production machines are arranged into groups according to general type of manufacturing process. The lathes are in one department, drill presses are in another, plastic molding in still another department, and so on. The advantage of this type of layout is its flexibility. Different parts, each requiring its own unique sequence of operations, can be routed through the respective departments in the proper order. Forklift trucks and hand carts are used to move materials from one work center to the next.

Process layout is typical in job shops and batch production. It is also used in quantity-type mass production. The process layout is illustrated in Figure 2.5(b).

PRODUCT-FLOW LAYOUT. If a plant specializes in the production of one product or one class of product in large volumes, the plant facilities should be arranged to produce the product as efficiently as possible. For complex assembled products, or items requiring a long sequence of operations, this efficiency is usually best achieved with product-flow layout. With this type of layout, the processing and assembly facilities are placed along the line of flow of the product. The work-in-progress is moved by conveyor or similar means from one workstation to the next. The product is progressively fabricated as it flows through the sequence of workstations. As the name implies, this type of layout is appropriate for flow-type mass production. The arrangement of facilities within the plant is relatively inflexible and is warranted only when the production quantities are large enough to justify the investment. Figure 2.5(c) illustrates a product-flow layout.

These three layouts (fixed-position, process, and product-flow) are the conventional types found in manufacturing plants today. As we shall see in Chapter 16, a fourth type, called group technology layout, represents an attempt to combine the efficiency of flow layout with the flexibility of process layout.

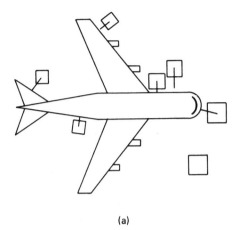

(a)

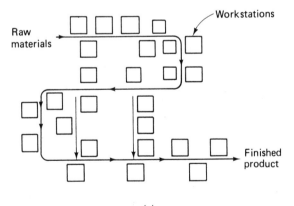

(b)

(c)

FIGURE 2.5   Types of plant layout: (a) fixed-position layout; (b) process layout; (c) product-flow layout.

2.6 PRODUCTION CONCEPTS AND MATHEMATICAL MODELS

A number of production concepts are quantitative, or require a quantitative approach to measure them. In this section we define some of these concepts. In subsequent chapters we refer back to these production concepts as we discuss specific topics in automation.

Manufacturing lead time

Our description of production is that it consists of a series of individual steps: processing and assembly operations. Between the operations are material handling, storage, inspections, and other nonproductive activities. Let us therefore divide the activities in production into two main categories, operations and nonoperation elements. An operation on a product (or workpart) takes place when it is at the production machine. The nonoperation elements are the handling, storage, inspections, and other sources of delay. Let us use T_o to denote the time per operation at a given machine or workstation, and T_{no} to represent the nonoperation time associated with the same machine. Further, let us suppose that there are n_m separate machines or operations through which the product must be routed in order to be completely processed. If we assume a batch production situation, there are Q units of the product in the batch. A setup procedure is generally required to prepare each production machine for the particular product. The setup typically includes arranging the workplace and installing the tooling and fixturing required for the product. Let this setup time be denoted as T_{su}.

Given these terms, we can define an important production concept, manufacturing lead time. The *manufacturing lead time* (MLT) is the total time required to process a given product (or workpart) through the plant. We can express it as follows:

$$\text{MLT} = \sum_{i=1}^{n_m} (T_{sui} + QT_{oi} + T_{noi}) \tag{2.1}$$

where i indicates the operation sequence in the processing; $i = 1, 2, \ldots, n_m$. The MLT equation does not include the time the raw workpart spends in storage before its turn in the production schedule begins.

For our purposes in the following definitions, let us assume that all operation times, setup times, and nonoperation times are equal, respectively. We can therefore transform the summation process in Eq. (2.1) to the following multiplication process:

$$\text{MLT} = n_m (T_{su} + QT_o + T_{no}) \tag{2.2}$$

In addition to parameters T_{su}, T_o, and T_{no} being equal for all n_m machines in Eq. (2.2), we have also generalized by suggesting that Q and n_m are the same for all products. In an actual batch production factory, which this equation is intended to represent, these terms vary by product. These discrepancies can be accounted for by using the proper weighted-average values of the various terms. The averaging procedure is explained in the Appendix at the end of this chapter.

Equation (2.2) can be adapted for job shop production and mass-production situations by adjusting the parameter values. For a job shop in which the batch size is 1, Eq. (2.2) can be used by setting the value of $Q = 1$. That is,

$$\text{MLT} = n_m (T_{su} + T_o + T_{no}) \qquad (2.3)$$

For mass production, the Q term in Eq. (2.2) is very large and dominates the other terms. In the case of quantity-type mass production in which a large number of units are made on a single machine, the MLT simply becomes the operation time for the machine after the setup has been completed and production begins.

For flow-type mass production, the entire production line is set up in advance. Also, the nonoperation time between processing steps consists simply of the time to transfer the product (or part) from one machine or workstation to the next. If the workstations are integrated so that parts are being processed simultaneously at each station, the station with the longest operation time will determine the MLT value. Hence,

$$\text{MLT} = n_m (\text{transfer time} + \text{longest } T_o) \qquad (2.4)$$

In this case, n_m represents the number of separate workstations on the production line. (In Chapter 4 we shall refer to the transfer time plus the longest operation time in Eq. (2.4) as the ideal cycle time for an automated production line.) One might argue that the manufacturing lead time for the first product coming off the line should include the time required to set up the production line.

The values of setup time, operation time, and nonoperation time are different for the different production situations. Setting up a flow line for high production requires much more time than setting up a general-purpose machine in a job shop. However, the concept of how time is spent in the factory for the various situations is valid.

EXAMPLE 2.1

A certain part is produced in a batch size of 50 units and requires a sequence of eight operations in the plant. The average setup time is 3 h, and the average operation time per machine is 6 min. The average nonoperation time due to handling, delays, inspections, and so on, is 7 h. Compute how many days it will take to produce a batch, assuming that the plant operates on a 7-h shift per day.

Solution:

The manufacturing lead time is computed from Eq. (2.2):

$$\text{MLT} = 8(3 + 50 \times 0.1 + 7) = 120 \text{ h}$$

At 7 h per day, this amounts to $120/7 = 17.14$ days.

Production rate

The production rate for an individual manufacturing process or assembly operation is usually expressed as an hourly rate (e.g., units of product per hour). The rate will be symbolized as R_p. Again we will begin with the batch production case and then generalize to the job shop and mass-production cases.

Consider the terms in Eq. (2.2) representing setup time and operation time at any given machine. These terms give the total batch time for the machine:

$$\frac{\text{batch time}}{\text{machine}} = T_{su} + QT_o \qquad - \quad excl. \; non-oper. \; time$$

If the value of Q represents the desired quantity to be produced, and there is a significant scrap rate, denoted by q, the quantity started through the process must be $Q/(1 - q)$ and the batch time therefore becomes

*ie., q denotes
the fraction of
units defective*

$$\frac{\text{batch time}}{\text{machine}} = T_{su} + \frac{QT_o}{(1 - q)}$$

Dividing the batch time by the quantity in the batch yields the average production time per unit of product for the given machine:

$$T_p = \frac{\text{batch time/machine}}{Q} \qquad (2.5)$$

The average production rate for the machine is simply the reciprocal of the production time:

$$R_p = \frac{1}{T_p} \qquad (2.6)$$

For job shop production, if the quantity $Q = 1$, the production time per unit is

$$T_p = T_{su} + T_o \qquad (2.7)$$

For quantity-type mass production, the production rate equals the cycle rate of the machine (reciprocal of operation time) after production has started and the effects of setup are neglected.

For flow-type mass production, the production time approximates to the cycle time of the production line (transfer time + longest operation time), again neglecting setup time. The problem in production flow lines is the interdependence among workstations on the line. If one workstation breaks down, the entire line must often be stopped. We examine methods of analyzing this breakdown issue in Chapter 5 for automated processing lines and in Chapter 7 for automated assembly lines.

Components of the operation time

Next we consider the components of the operation time T_o. The operation time is the time an individual workpart spends on a machine, but not all of this time is productive. Let us try to relate the operation time to a specific process. To illustrate, we use a machining operation, as machining is common in discrete-parts manufacturing. Operation *(or, m/c processing)* time for a machining operation is composed of three elements: the actual machining time T_m, the workpiece handling time T_h, and any tool handling time per workpiece T_{th}. Hence,

— here T_o includes direct handling w.r.t. the m/c

$$T_o = T_m + T_h + T_{th} \tag{2.8}$$

The tool handling time represents all the time spent in changing tools when they wear out, changing from one tool to the next for successive operations performed on a turret lathe, changing between the drill bit and tap in a drill-and-tap sequence performed at one drill press, and so on. T_{th} is the average time per workpiece for any and all of these tool handling activities.

Each of the terms T_m, T_h, and T_{th} has its counterpart in many other types of discrete-item production operations. There is a portion of the operation cycle, when the material is actually being worked (T_m), and there is a portion of the cycle when either the workpart is being handled (T_h) or the tooling is being adjusted or changed (T_{th}). We can therefore generalize on Eq. (2.8) to cover many other manufacturing processes in addition to machining.

Capacity

The term *capacity,* or *plant capacity,* is used to define the maximum rate of output that a plant (or other production facility) is able to produce under a given set of assumed operating conditions. It is closely related to production rate. The assumed operating conditions refer to the number of shifts per day (one, two, or three), number of days in the week (or month) that the plant operates, employment levels, whether or not overtime is included, and so on. For continuous chemical production, the plant may be operated 24 h per day, 7 days per week. For an automobile assembly plant, capacity is typically defined as one shift, but with an allowance for overtime.

Capacity for a production plant is usually measured in terms of the types of output produced by the plant (e.g., tons of steel for a steel mill, number of cars for an automobile assembly plant, and barrels of oil for a refinery). When the output units are nonhomogeneous, input units may be more appropriate. A job shop, for example, might use available labor hours or available machine hours as its measures of capacity.

Quantitative measures of plant capacity can be developed based on the production models derived earlier. Let PC be the production capacity (plant capacity) of a given work center or group of work centers under consideration. Capacity will be measured as the number of good units produced per week. Let W represent the number of work centers under consideration. A work center is a production system in the plant typically consisting of one worker and one machine. It might also be one automated machine with no worker, or several workers acting together on a production line. It is capable of producing at a rate R_p units per hour. Each work center operates for H hours per shift. H is an average that excludes time for machine breakdowns and repairs, maintenance, operator delays, and so on. Provision for setup time is included in R_p, according to Eq. (2.5). Let S_w denote the number of shifts per week (or other suitable time period for the plant).

These parameters can be used to calculate the production capacity for the group of work centers as follows:

— simplified eqn.

$$PC = WS_wHR_p \qquad (2.9)$$

As in the previous equations, our assumption is that the units processed through the group of work centers are homogeneous, and therefore the value of R_p is the same for all units produced.

EXAMPLE 2.2

The turret lathe section has six machines, all devoted to production of the same part. The section operates 10 shifts per week. The number of hours per shift averages 6.4 because of operator delays and machine breakdowns. The average production rate is 17 units/h. Determine the production capacity of the turret lathe section.

Solution:

From Eq. (2.9),

$$PC = 6(10)(6.4)(17) = 6528 \text{ units/week}$$

If we include the possibility that in a batch production plant, each product is routed through n_m machines, the plant capacity equation must be amended as follows:

for each m/c
(on the avg)

$$PC = \frac{WS_wHR_p}{n_m} \qquad (2.10)$$

Another way of using the production capacity equation is for determining how resources might be allocated to meet a certain weekly demand rate requirement. Let D_w be the demand rate for the week in terms of number of units required. Replacing PC by D_w in Eq. (2.10) and rearranging, we get

 # m/c hrs. reqd. per wk.

$$WS_wH = \frac{D_wn_m}{R_p} \qquad (2.11)$$

 # m/c hrs. reqd. per wk. to meet dem.

Given a certain hourly production rate for the manufacturing process, Eq. (2.11) indicates three possible ways of adjusting the capacity up or down to meet changing weekly demand requirements:

1. Change the number of work centers, W, in the shop. This might be done by using equipment that was formerly not in use and by hiring new workers. Over the long term, new machines might be acquired.

2. Change the number of shifts per week, S_w. For example, Saturday shifts might be authorized.

3. Change the number of hours worked per shift, H. For example, overtime might be authorized.

In cases where production rates differ, the capacity equations can be revised, summing the requirements for the different products. Equation (2.10) would be rewritten as follows:

$$WS_wH = \Sigma \frac{D_w n_m}{R_p} \qquad (2.12)$$

The following example illustrates the use of this equation.

EXAMPLE 2.3

Three products are to be processed through a certain type of work center. Pertinent data are given in the following table.

Product	Weekly demand	Production rate (units/h)
1	600	10
2	1000	20
3	2200	40

Determine the number of work centers required to satisfy this demand, given that the plant works 10 shifts per week and there are 6.5 h available for production on each work center for each shift. The value of $n_m = 1$.

Solution:

$$\text{Product 1: } D_w/R_p = 600/10 = 60 \text{ h}$$

$$\text{Product 2: } D_w/R_p = 1000/20 = 50 \text{ h}$$

$$\text{Product 3: } D_w/R_p = 2200/40 = 55 \text{ h}$$

$$\text{Total production hours required} = \overline{165 \text{ h}}$$

Since each work center can operate (10 shifts/week)(6.5 h) or 65 h/week, the total number of work centers is

$$W = \frac{165}{65} = 2.54 \text{ work centers}$$

This number would be rounded up to 3.

These capacity models assume that there are no bottleneck operations that prohibit smooth flow of product through the plant. In most batch production machine shops where each product has a different operation sequence, the work distribution among the productive resources is not perfectly balanced. Consequently, there are some operations that are fully utilized, while other operations stand idle waiting for work. In Problem 2.9 we see the effect of a bottleneck situation.

Utilization and availability

Utilization refers to the amount of output of a production facility relative to its capacity. Letting U represent utilization, we have

$$U = \frac{\text{output}}{\text{capacity}} \tag{2.13}$$

The term can be applied to an entire plant, a single machine in the plant, or any other productive resource (e.g., labor). For convenience, it is often defined as the proportion of time that the facility is operating relative to the time available under the definition of capacity. Utilization is usually expressed as a percentage.

EXAMPLE 2.4

A production machine is operated 65 h/week at full capacity. Its production rate is 20 units/h. During a certain week, the machine produced 1000 good parts and was idle the remaining time.

    (a) Determine the production capacity of the machine.
    (b) What was the utilization of the machine during the week under consideration?

Solution:

(a) The capacity of the machine can be determined using the assumed 65-h week as follows:

$$PC = 65(20) = 1300 \text{ units/week}$$

(b) The utilization can be determined as the ratio of the number of parts made during productive use of the machine relative to its capacity.

$$U = \frac{1000}{1300} = 0.7692 = 76.92\%$$

The alternative way of assessing utilization is by the time during the week that the machine was actually used. To produce 1000 units, the machine was operated

$$H = \frac{1000}{20} = 50 \text{ h}$$

The utilization is defined relative to the 65 h available.

$$U = \frac{50}{65} = 76.92\%$$

The term *availability* is sometimes used as a measure of reliability for equipment. It is especially germane for automated production equipment. Availability is defined using two other reliability terms, the *mean time between failures* (MTBF) and the *mean time to repair* (MTTR). The MTBF indicates the average length of time between breakdowns of the piece of equipment. The MTTR indicates the average time required to service the equipment and place it back into operation when a breakdown does occur:

$$\text{availability} = \frac{\text{MTBF} - \text{MTTR}}{\text{MTBF}} \qquad (2.14)$$

Availability is typically expressed as a percentage.

Work-in-process

Work-in-process (WIP) is the amount of product currently located in the factory that is either being processed or is between processing operations. WIP is inventory that is in the state of being transformed from raw material to finished product. A rough measure of work-in-process can be obtained from the following, using symbols defined previously:

$$\text{WIP} = \frac{PC \, U}{S_w \, H} \, (\text{MLT}) \qquad (2.15)$$

where WIP represents the number of units in-process. The equation states that the level of WIP will equal the rate at which parts flow through the factory (recall the pipeline model of the factory in Figure 2.2) multiplied by the length of time the parts spend in the factory. The units for $PC \times U/S_w H$ (e.g., parts per week) must be consistent with the units for MLT (e.g., weeks).

Work-in-process represents an investment by the firm, but one that cannot be turned into profit until the processing is completed. Many manufacturing companies sustain major costs because work remains in-process in the factory too long. In Chapter 3 we examine how these costs can be assessed.

Eugene Merchant, an advocate and spokesman for the manufacturing industry for many years, has observed [1] that materials in a typical metal machining batch factory spend more time waiting or being moved than in processing. His observation is illustrated in Figure 2.6. About 95% of the time of a workpart is spent either moving or waiting; only 5% of its time is spent on the machine tool. Of this 5%, less than 30% of the time at the machine (1.5% of the total time of the part) is time during which actual cutting is taking place. The remaining 70% (3.5% of the total) is required for loading and unloading,

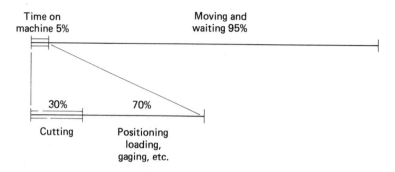

FIGURE 2.6   How time is spent by a typical part in a batch production machine shop.

positioning, gaging, and other causes of nonprocessing time. These time proportions are evidence of the inefficiencies with which work-in-process is managed in the factory.

Two measures that can be used to assess the magnitude of the work-in-process problem in a given factory are the WIP ratio and the TIP ratio [2]. The *WIP ratio* provides an indication of the amount of inventory-in-process relative to the work actually being processed. It is the total quantity of a given part (or assembly) in the plant or section of the plant divided by the quantity of the same part that is being processed (or assembled). The WIP ratio can be obtained by dividing the WIP level determined from Eq. (2.15) by the number of machines currently engaged in processing parts. Using parameters previously defined, the divisor is calculated as

$$\text{Number of machines processing} = WU \frac{QT_o}{T_{su} + QT_o}$$

where W = number of available work centers in the plant

U = plant utilization

Q = average batch quantity

T_o, T_{su} = operation time and setup time

The WIP ratio is therefore determined as

$$\text{WIP ratio} = \frac{\text{WIP}}{\text{Number of machines processing}} \tag{2.16}$$

The ideal WIP ratio is 1 : 1, which implies that all parts in the plant are being processed. In a high-volume flow line operation, we would expect the WIP ratio to be relatively close to 1 : 1 if we ignore the raw product that is waiting to be launched onto the line and the finished product that has been completed. In a batch production shop, the WIP ratio is significantly higher, perhaps 50 : 1 or higher, depending on the average batch size, nonproductive time, and other factors in the plant.

The *TIP ratio* measures the time that the product spends in the plant relative to its actual processing time. It is computed as the total manufacturing lead time for a part divided by the sum of the individual operation times for the part. Referring to the parameters defined for our earlier equations, we obtain

$$\text{TIP ratio} = \frac{\text{MLT}}{n_m T_o} \tag{2.17}$$

Again, the ideal TIP ratio is 1 : 1, and again it is very difficult to achieve such a low ratio in practice. In the Merchant observation of Figure 2.6, the TIP ratio = 20 : 1.

It should be noted that the WIP and TIP ratios reduce to the same value in our simplified model of manufacturing presented in this section. This can be demonstrated mathematically. In an actual factory situation, the WIP and TIP ratios would not necessarily be equal, owing to the complexities and realities encountered in the real world. For example, assembled products create complications in evaluating the ratio values because of the combination of parts into one assembly.

Some comments on the production concepts

All of the preceding concepts are important in production and are relevant in our discussion of automation.

Manufacturing lead time determines to a large extent how long it will take to deliver a product to the customer. In the competitive environment of modern business, the ability of a manufacturing firm to deliver the product to the customer in the shortest possible time often wins the order. Flexible automated manufacturing systems are being designed today to make parts of different designs in the minimum possible MLT.

High production rate and high productivity are both important objectives in automation. These objectives are accomplished by reducing handling time (T_h), processing time (T_m), tool-changing time (T_{th}), and setup time (T_{su}). Another objective of automation is to increase plant production capacity, or to make changes in capacity without the need for drastic adjustments in employment levels.

Availability and utilization are both useful measures of performance in a manufacturing plant. Availability gives an indication of how well the maintenance personnel are servicing and maintaining the equipment in the plant. If this measure is close to 100%, it means that the equipment is reliable and the maintenance personnel are doing a good job. When a piece of equipment is brand new (and experiencing debugging problems), and later when it begins to age, its availability tends to be lower. Maintenance is especially important for automated equipment, because the success of the production operation depends on the reliability and availability of the machine.

Utilization provides a measure of how well production resources are being used, given that they are available. If the utilization is low, the facility is not being operated nearly to its capacity. This usually has a financial penalty because the firm has paid for a production resource it is not utilizing fully. When the utilization is very high (near 100%), it may mean that the company should expand to increase its capacity.

Finally, work-in-process is an important issue in manufacturing. Many firms are attempting to reduce the high cost of WIP, and one of the approaches that is being used is to automate their operations.

2.7 AUTOMATION STRATEGIES

There are certain fundamental strategies that can be employed to improve productivity in manufacturing operations. Since these strategies are often implemented by means of automation technology, we refer to them as *automation strategies*. Table 2.3 presents a summary list of the 10 strategies. The table also indicates the probable effects of each strategy on the parameters in the various equations of Section 2.6. Each strategy is discussed in the following list.

    1. *Specialization of operations.* The first strategy involves the use special-purpose equipment designed to perform one operation with the greatest possible efficiency. This is analogous to the concept of labor specialization, which has been employed to improve labor productivity.

    2. *Combined operations.* Production occurs as a sequence of operations. Complex parts may require dozens, or even hundreds, of processing steps. The strategy of combined operations involves reducing the number of distinct production machines or workstations through which the part must be routed. This is accomplished by performing more than one operation at a given machine, thereby reducing the number of separate machines needed. Since each machine typically involves a setup, setup time can usually be saved as a consequence of this strategy. Material handling effort and nonoperation time are also reduced.

    3. *Simultaneous operations.* A logical extension of the combined operations

TABLE 2.3 Ten Automation Strategies

Strategy	*Effect*[a]
1. Specialization of operations	Reduce T_o
2. Combined operations	Reduce n_m, T_h, T_{no}
3. Simultaneous operations	Reduce n_m, T_o, T_h, T_{no}
4. Integration of operations	Reduce n_m, T_h, T_{no}
5. Increase flexibility	Reduce T_{su}, MLT, WIP; increase U
6. Improved material handling and storage	Reduce T_{no}, MLT, WIP
7. On-line inspection	Reduce T_{no}, q
8. Process control and optimization	Reduce T_o, q
9. Plant operations control	Reduce T_{no}, MLT; increase U
10. Computer-integrated manufacturing	Reduce MLT, design time, production planning time; increase U

[a]T_o, operation time (process or assembly); T_{no}, nonoperation time; T_h, work handling time; n_m, number of machines through which part must be routed; MLT, manufacturing lead time; WIP, work-in-process; q, scrap rate or fraction defect rate; U, utilization.

strategy is to perform at the same time the operations that are combined at one workstation. In effect, two or more processing (or assembly) operations are being performed simultaneously on the same workpart, thus reducing total processing time.

4. *Integration of operations.* Another strategy is to link several workstations into a single integrated mechanism using automated work handling devices to transfer parts between stations. In effect, this reduces the number of separate machines through which the product must be scheduled. With more than one workstation, several parts can be processed simultaneously, thereby increasing the overall output of the system.

5. *Increased flexibility.* This strategy attempts to achieve maximum utilization of equipment for job shop and medium-volume situations by using the same equipment for a variety of products. It involves the use of the flexible automation concepts explained in Chapter 1. Prime objectives are to reduce setup time and programming time for the production machine. This normally translates into lower manufacturing lead time and lower work-in-process.

6. *Improved material handling and storage.* A great opportunity for reducing nonproductive time exists in the use of automated material handling and storage systems. Typical benefits included reduced work-in-process and shorter manufacturing lead times.

7. *On-line inspection.* Inspection for quality of work is traditionally performed after the process. This means that any poor-quality product has already been produced by the time it is inspected. Incorporating inspection into the manufacturing process permits corrections to the process as product is being made. This reduces scrap and brings the overall quality of product closer to the nominal specifications intended by the designer.

8. *Process control and optimization.* This includes a wide range of control schemes intended to operate the individual processes and associated equipment more efficiently. By this strategy, the individual process times can be reduced and product quality improved.

9. *Plant operations control.* Whereas the previous strategy was concerned with the control of the individual manufacturing process, this strategy is concerned with control at the plant level. It attempts to manage and coordinate the aggregate operations in the plant more efficiently. Its implementation usually involves a high level of computer networking within the factory.

10. *Computer integrated manufacturing (CIM).* Taking the previous strategy one step further, we have the integration of factory operations with engineering design and many of the other business functions of the firm. CIM involves extensive use of computer applications, computer data bases, and computer networking in the company.

REFERENCES

[1] MERCHANT, M. E., "The Inexorable Push for Automated Production," *Production Engineering,* January 1977, pp. 45–46.

[2] SNIDERMAN, A., Burroughs Corporation, personal communications, October 1985 and February 1986.

PROBLEMS

2.1 A certain part is routed through six machines in a batch production plant. The setup and operation times for each machine are given in the following table:

Machine	Setup time (h)	Operation time (min)
1	4	5.0
2	2	3.5
3	8	10.0
4	3	1.9
5	3	4.1
6	4	2.5

The batch size is 100 and the average nonoperation time per machine is 12 h.
(a) Determine the manufacturing lead time.
(b) Determine the production rate for operation 3.

2.2. Suppose that the part in Problem 2.1 is made in very large quantities on a flow production line in which an automated work handling system is used to transfer parts between the machines. The transfer time between stations is 15 s. The total time required to set up the entire line is 150 h. Assume that the operation times at the individual machines remain the same.
(a) Determine the manufacturing lead time for a part coming off the line.
(b) Determine the production rate for operation 3.
(c) What is the theoretical production rate for the entire production line?

2.3. The average part produced in a certain batch manufacturing plant must be processed through an average of six machines. There are 20 new batches of parts launched each week. Other pertinent data are as follows:

$$\text{average operation time} = 6 \text{ min}$$

$$\text{average setup time} = 5 \text{ h}$$

$$\text{average batch size} = 25 \text{ parts}$$

$$\text{average nonoperation time per batch} = 10 \text{ h}$$

There are 18 machines in the plant. The plant operates an average of 70 production hours per week. Scrap rate is negligible.
(a) Determine the manufacturing lead time for an average part.
(b) Determine the plant capacity.
(c) Determine the plant utilization.
(d) How would you expect the nonoperation time to be affected by the plant utilization?

2.4. Based on the data provided in Problem 2.3 and your answers to that problem, determine (a) the average level of work-in-process (number of parts-in-process) in the plant, (b) the WIP ratio, and (c) the TIP ratio.

2.5. An average of 20 new orders are started through a certain factory each month. On average, an order consists of 50 parts to be processed through 10 machines in the factory. The operation time per machine for each part = 15 min. The nonoperation time per order at each machine averages 8 hours, and the required setup time per order = 4 h. There are 25 machines in the factory, 80% of which are operational at any time (the other 20% are in repair or maintenance). The plant operates 160h/month. However, the plant manager complains that a total of 100 overtime machine hours must be authorized each month in order to keep up with the production schedule.

(a) What is the manufacturing lead time for an average order?

(b) What is the plant capacity (on a monthly basis), and why must the overtime be authorized?

(c) What is the utilization of the plant according to the definition given in the text?

(d) Determine the average level of work-in-process (number of parts-in-process) in the plant.

(e) Determine the WIP ratio and the TIP ratio.

2.6. Four products are to be manufactured in department A, and it is desired to determine how to allocate the resources in that department to meet the required demand for these products for a certain week. The demand and other data for the products are given as follows:

Product	Weekly demand	Setup time (h)	Operation time (min)	Scrap rate
1	750	6	4.0	0.02
2	900	5	3.0	0.04
3	400	7	2.0	0.05
4	400	6	3.0	0.03

The plant normally operates one shift (6.75 h per shift) 6 days per week, and there are currently three available work centers in the department.

(a) Propose a way of scheduling the machines to meet the weekly demand.

(b) Propose a way of scheduling to meet the weekly demand if there were four machines instead of three.

(c)Discuss the issues and problems encountered in developing your machine schedule in parts (a) and (b).

2.7. The mean time between failures for a certain production machine is 250 h, and the mean time to repair is 6 h. Determine the availability of the machine.

2.8. The mean time between failures and mean time to repair in a certain department of the factory are 400 h and 8 h, respectively. The department operates 25 machines during one 8-h shift per day, 5 days per week, 52 weeks per year. Each time a machine breaks down, it costs the company $200 per hour (per machine) in lost revenue. A proposal has been submitted to install a preventive maintenance program in this department. In this program, preventive maintenance would be performed on the machines during the evening so that there will be no interruptions to production during the regular shift. The effect of this program is expected to be that the average MTBF will double, and half of the emergency repair time normally accomplished during the day shift will be performed during the evening shift. The cost of the maintenance crew will be $1500 per week. However, a reduction of maintenance personnel on the day shift will result in a savings during the regular shift of $700 per week.

(a) Compute the availability of machines in the department both before and after the preventive maintenance program is installed.

(b) Determine how many total hours per year the 25 machines in the department are under repair both before and after the preventive maintenance program is installed. In this part and in part (c), ignore the effects of queueing of the machines that might have to wait for a maintenance crew.

(c) Will the preventive maintenance program pay for itself in terms of savings in the cost of lost revenues?

2.9. There are nine machines in the automatic lathe section of a certain machine shop. The setup time on an automatic lathe averages 6 h. The average batch size for parts processed through the section is 90. The average operation time is 8.0 min. Under shop rules, an operator is permitted to be assigned to run up to three machines. Accordingly, there are three operators in the section for the nine lathes. In addition to the lathe operators, there are two setup workers who perform machine setups exclusively. These setup workers are kept busy for the full shift. The section runs one 8-hr shift per day, 6 days per week. However, an average of 15% of the production time is lost due to machine breakdowns. Scrap losses are negligible. The production control manager claims that the capacity of the section should be 1836 pieces per week. However, the actual output averages only 1440 units per week. What is the problem? Recommend a solution.

2.10. A certain job shop specializes in one-of-a-kind orders dealing with parts of medium-to-high complexity. A typical part is processed through 10 machines in batch sizes of 1. The shop contains eight conventional machine tools and operates 35 h per week of production time. Pertinent data on the part are given below:

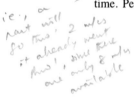

average machining time per machine = 0.5 h

average work handling time per machine = 0.3 h

average tool change time per machine = 0.2 h

average setup time per machine = 6 h

average nonoperation time per machine = 12 h

A new programmable machine has been purchased by the shop which is capable of performing all 10 operations in a single setup. The programming of the machine for this part will require 20 h; however, the programming can be done off-line, without tieing up the machine. The setup time will be 10 h. The total machining time will be reduced to 80% of its previous value due to advanced tool control algorithms; the work handling time will be the same as for one machine; and the total tool change time will be reduced by 50% because it will be accomplished automatically under program control. For the one machine, nonoperation time is expected to be 12 h.

(a) Determine the manufacturing lead time for the traditional method and for the new method.

(b) Compute the plant capacity for the following alternatives: (i) a job shop containing the eight traditional machines, and (ii) a job shop containing two of the new programmable machines. Assume that the typical jobs are represented by the data given above.

(c) Determine the average level of work-in-process for the two alternatives in part (b) if the alternative shops operate at capacity.

(d) Identify which of the 10 automation strategies are represented (or probably represented) by the new machine.

APPENDIX: AVERAGING PROCEDURES FOR MANUFACTURING LEAD TIME EQUATIONS

As indicated in our presentation of the manufacturing lead time equations in Section 2.6, Eq. (2.2) can be used for actual factory data, with its inherent variations in parameter values, if an appropriate averaging procedure is used. This appendix explains the averaging procedure.

Straight arithmetic averages are used to compute values for Q and n_m. Weighted-average values for T_{su}, T_o, and T_{no} are computed as follows.

First, let n_Q equal the number of batches of various parts to be considered. This number might represent the batches processed through the shop during a certain time period (e.g., month or year), or it might be a sample of batches to be used in the analysis. Given n_Q, the average batch quantity Q is calculated by

$$Q = \frac{\sum_{j=1}^{n_Q} Q_j}{n_Q} \tag{A2.1}$$

where Q_j represents the batch quantity of batch j among n_Q batches. The value of n_m for use in Eq. (2.2) is also an arithmetic average:

$$n_m = \frac{\sum_{j=1}^{n_Q} n_{mj}}{n_Q} \tag{A2.2}$$

where n_{mj} represents the number of operations (or machines) in the process routing for batch j. The setup time is given by

$$T_{su} = \frac{\sum_{j=1}^{n_Q} n_{mj} \, \bar{T}_{suj}}{\sum_{j=1}^{n_Q} n_{mj}} \tag{A2.3}$$

where $\bar{T}_{suj}$ represents the average setup time for batch j. The nonoperation time is calculated similarly:

$$T_{no} = \frac{\sum_{j=1}^{n_Q} n_{mj} \, \bar{T}_{noj}}{\sum_{j=1}^{n_Q} n_{mj}} \tag{A2.4}$$

where $\bar{T}_{noj}$ represents the average nonoperation time for batch j. Finally, the average operation time for use in Eq. (2.2) must be computed as the following weighted average:

$$T_o = \frac{\displaystyle\sum_{j=1}^{n_Q} n_{mj} \, Q_j \, \bar{T}_{oj}}{n_m Q n_Q} \qquad (A2.5)$$

where $\bar{T}_{oj}$ represents the average operation time per operation for batch j, and n_m and Q are the average values calculated by Eqs. (A2.1) and (A2.2).

chapter **3**

Production Economics

In Chapter 1 a list of reasons for considering automation was presented. In the final analysis, a proposed automation project should be evaluated against the same economic criteria as those used to assess any other investment opportunity: Will the investment pay for itself and contribute to the profits of the firm?

In the present chapter we consider production economics, a subject closely related to (and based on) engineering economy. For the reader unfamiliar with engineering economy, we have included some of the introductory principles in the Appendix to this chapter. The Appendix also includes interest tables that will be of use in solving the problems at the end of the chapter.

Production economics is concerned with issues and problems in engineering economy and investment analysis that are specifically relevant to the production function. The subject includes methods of evaluating investment proposals for manufacturing, production costs, and break-even analysis. These topics are generally covered in texts on engineering economy [1,4].

Production economics also includes certain issues that are not covered in the usual textbooks. These issues are often overlooked in most corporate investment analyses. As a consequence of the omission, many projects in automation are not approved because they fail to meet the company's investment objectives. A good example of these omitted issues is work-in-process. A reduction in WIP achieved by automating a certain series of production operations will have a beneficial effect on the firm's annual cash flow. In this chapter an attempt is made to address these types of issues so that the full opportunities offered by automation can be considered. We begin with the more traditional topics.

3.1 METHODS OF EVALUATING INVESTMENT ALTERNATIVES

There are several methods of evaluating and comparing investment proposals, including the following:

1. Payback period method
2. Present worth (PW) method
3. Uniform annual cost (UAC) method
4. Rate-of-return method

In the discussion of these methods in this section, we adopt the convention that positive cash flows represent money coming in (revenues and/or profits) and negative cash flows represent money expended (costs).

Payback method

The *payback method* uses the simple concept that the net revenues derived from an investment should pay back the investment in a certain period of time (the payback period). Let us refer to the net revenue in a given year as the net annual cash flow (NACF). If the revenues exceed costs for the year, the NACF is positive. If costs exceed revenues, the NACF is negative.

Assuming for the moment that the net annual cash flows are positive and equal from one year to the next, the payback period can be defined as follows:

$$n = \frac{\text{IC}}{\text{NACF}} \tag{3.1}$$

where IC is the initial cost of the investment project, and n is the payback period (expressed in years).

EXAMPLE 3.1

A new production machine costs $85,000 installed and is expected to generate revenues of $55,000 per year for 7 years. It will cost $30,000 per year to operate the machine. At the end of 7 years, the machine will be scrapped at zero salvage value. Determine the payback period for this investment.

Solution:

The NACF = 55,000 − 30,000 = $25,000 per year for 7 years. The IC = $85,000, so the payback period is

$$n = \frac{85,000}{25,000} = 3.4 \text{ years}$$

The production machine will pay for itself through the net revenues generated in 3.4 years.

    In most real-life situations, the net annual cash flows will not be equal year after year. The concept of payback period is nevertheless applicable. Instead of using Eq. (3.1), a summation procedure is used to determine how many years are required for the initial cost to be recovered by the accumulated net annual cash flows. The procedure is best summarized by the following:

$$0 = -(\text{IC}) + \sum_{j=1}^{n} (\text{NACF}_j) \tag{3.2}$$

zero

where NACF_j represents the net annual cash flow for year j. The value of n is determined so that the sum of the NACF values equals the IC value.

Present worth method

The *PW method* uses the equivalent present value of all current and future cash flows to evaluate the investment proposal. The future cash flows are converted into their present worths by using the appropriate interest factors. Accordingly, some interest rate must be used in the factors. This interest rate is decided in advance and represents the rate-of-return criterion that the company is using to evaluate its investment opportunities. If the aggregate present worth of the project is positive, the return from the project exceeds the rate-of-return criterion. If the present worth of the project is negative, the project does not meet the rate-of-return criterion.

EXAMPLE 3.2

The data from Example 3.1 will be used here. Assume that the company considering the investment uses a rate-of-return criterion of 20%. Determine the equivalent present worth of the proposal.

Solution:

Using the interest factors from the tables in the Appendix, all cash flows are converted to their present values. The IC is already a present value.

PW = −85,000 + 55,000(*P*/*A*, 20%, 7) − 30,000(*P*/*A*, 20%, 7)

    = −85,000 + 25,000(3.6046)

    = +$5,115

Since the present worth is positive, we conclude that the return from the investment exceeds the rate-of-return criterion of 20%, and the project is therefore meritorious.

Uniform annual cost method

The *UAC method* converts all current and future cash flows to their equivalent uniform annual costs using the given rate of return. As with the present worth method, a positive aggregate uniform annual cost means that the project exceeds the criterion.

EXAMPLE 3.3

Again, the data from Example 3.1 will be used. The problem is to determine the equivalent uniform annual cost for the project.

Solution:

Using the interest factors from the tables in the Appendix, all cash flows not already expressed as UAC values are converted to their uniform annual cost equivalents.

$$UAC = -85,000(A/P, 20\%, 7) + 55,000 - 30,000$$
$$= -85,000(0.2774) + 25,000$$
$$= +\$1421$$

Since the UAC value is positive, the actual rate of return is greater than 20%, just as we found using the present worth method.

Rate-of-return method

The *rate-of-return method,* also called the *return-on-investment* (ROI) *method,* goes slightly beyond the PW and UAC methods by actually calculating the rate of return that is provided by the investment. If the calculated rate is greater than the criterion rate of return, the investment is acceptable.

To determine the return on investment, an equation must be set up with the rate of return as the unknown. Either the PW method or the UAC method can be used to establish the equation. Then the value of the interest rate i that drives the aggregate PW or UAC to zero is determined.

EXAMPLE 3.4

The data from Example 3.1 will be used to demonstrate computation of the rate of return.

Solution:

A uniform annual cost equation will be set up to illustrate determination of the rate of return.

$$UAC = -85,000(A/P, i, 7) + 55,000 - 30,000$$

Putting LHS = 0 =>

$$(A/P, i, 7) = \frac{25,000}{85,000} = 0.2941$$

Scanning the A/P values in the interest tables at $n = 7$ years for different values of i, we find that $(A/P, 20\%, 7) = 0.2774$ and $(A/P, 25\%, 7) = 0.3163$. By interpolation, a value of $i = 22.15\%$ corresponding to our $(A/P, i, 7) = 0.2941$ is computed.

Comparison of investment alternatives

Any of the four methods can be used to compare investment alternatives. Each method has its relative advantages and disadvantages. The payback method is easy to comprehend but does not incorporate the concept of time value of money into its evaluation. Despite this deficiency, this is a common method used in industry and provides a quick performance measure for the investment proposal. The present worth method is also easy to understand, and it does include interest rates in the evaluation. The UAC method is convenient to use when the service lives of the alternatives are different. Awkward adjustments must be made in the PW method when comparing alternatives with different service lives. The advantage of the rate-of-return method, as we saw in Example 3.4, is that it provides a value for the expected return on the investment. Its disadvantage is that a trial-and-error approach is usually required for problems containing more than one interest factor.

One of the most practical uses of the methods described above is to compare investment alternatives. The following example illustrates how the uniform annual cost method can be used to compare two production methods.

EXAMPLE 3.5

Two production methods, one manual and the other automated, are to be compared using the UAC method. The data for the manual method are the same data we have used in Examples 3.1 through 3.4. For the automated method, IC = \$150,000, the annual operating cost = \$5000, and the service life is expected to be 5 years. In addition, the equipment associated with this alternative will have a salvage value = \$15,000 at the end of the 5 years. Revenues from either alternative will be \$55,000 per year. A 20% rate of return is to be used as the criterion.

Solution:

The equivalent UAC for the manual method has already been calculated. From Example 3.3,

$$\text{manual UAC} = +\$1421$$

For the automated method,

$$\text{UAC} = -150,000(A/P, 20\%, 5) + 55,000 - 5000 + 15,000(A/F, 20\%, 5)$$

$$= -150,000(0.3344) + 50,000 + 15,000(0.1344)$$

$$\text{automated UAC} = +\$1856$$

The automated method has the higher positive net uniform annual cash value. Assuming that money is available to make the larger investment, it would be selected.

The situation depicted in this example is typical of automation projects: A larger initial investment must be made for the sake of lower annual operating costs. Less labor is required to run the automated process.

In many of the problems in this book, we will make use of annual costs or costs per other time period (e.g., cost per hour) which can be determined from the annual cost. The annual cost given will often be a calculated equivalent UAC. Let us consider next the types of costs in manufacturing and how these costs can be reduced to their equivalent annual or hourly rates.

3.2 COSTS IN MANUFACTURING

Fixed and variable costs

Manufacturing costs can be divided into two major categories, fixed costs and variable costs. The difference between the two is based on whether the expense varies in relation to the level of output.

A *fixed cost* is one that is constant for any level of production output. Examples of fixed costs include cost of the factory building, insurance, property taxes, and the cost of production equipment. All of these fixed costs can be expressed as annual costs. Those items that are capital investments (e.g., factory building and production equipment) can be converted to their equivalent uniform annual costs by the methods of the preceding section.

A *variable cost* is one that increases as the level of production increases. Direct labor costs (plus fringe benefits), raw materials, and electrical power to operate the production machines are examples of variable costs. The ideal concept of variable cost is that it is directly proportional to output level. When fixed and variable costs are combined, we get the total cost of manufacturing as a function of output. A general plot of the relationship is shown in Figure 3.1.

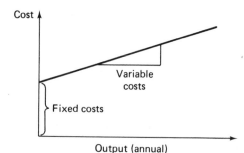

FIGURE 3.1   Plot of fixed and variable costs as a function of production output.

Overhead costs

Classification of costs as either fixed or variable is not always convenient for accountants and finance people. Fixed costs and variable costs are valid concepts, but the financial specialists of a manufacturing firm usually prefer to think in terms of direct labor cost, material cost, and overhead costs. The *direct labor cost* is the sum of the wages paid to the people who operate the production machines and perform the processing and assembly operations. The *material cost* is the cost of all the raw materials that are used to produce the finished product of the firm. In terms of fixed and variable costs, direct labor and material costs must be considered as variable.

Overhead costs are all the other costs associated with running a manufacturing firm. Overhead can be divided into two categories: factory overhead (sometimes called factory expense) and corporate overhead. *Factory overhead* includes the costs of operating the factory other than direct labor and materials. The types of expenses included in this category are listed in Table 3.1. It can be seen that some of these costs are variable whereas others are fixed. The *corporate overhead cost* is the cost of running the company other than its manufacturing activities. A list of many of the expenses included under corporate overhead is presented in Table 3.2. Many manufacturing firms operate more than one plant, and this is one of the reasons for dividing overhead into factory and corporate categories.

FACTORY OVERHEAD.   The overhead costs of a firm can amount to several times the cost of direct labor. The overhead can be allocated according to a number of different bases, including direct labor cost, direct labor hours, space, material cost, and so on. We will use direct labor cost to illustrate how factory overhead rates are determined. Suppose that the total cost of operating a plant amounts to $900,000 per year. Of this total, $400,000 is direct labor cost. This means that $500,000 is indirect or overhead expense: plant supervision, line foremen, annual cost of equipment, energy, maintenance personnel, and so on. The factor overhead rate for this plant would be figured as

$$\text{factory overhead rate} = \frac{\$500,000}{\$400,000} = 1.25$$

TABLE 3.1   Typical Factory Overhead Expenses

Plant supervision	Applicable taxes
Line foremen	Insurance
Maintenance crew	Heat
Custodial services	Light
Security personnel	Power for machines
Tool crib attendant	Factory cost
Materials handling crew	Equipment cost
Shipping and receiving	Fringe benefits

TABLE 3.2   Typical Corporate Overhead Expenses

Corporate executives	Applicable taxes
Sales personnel	Cost of office space
Accounting department	Security personnel
Finance department	Heat
Legal counsel	Light
Research and development	Air conditioning
Design and engineering	Insurance
Other support personnel	Fringe benefits

Overhead rates are often expressed as percentages, so this equals 125%. This rate could be applied to a particular production job, as illustrated in Example 3.6.

CORPORATE OVERHEAD. The corporate overhead rate can be determined in a manner similar to that used for factory overhead. We will use an oversimplified example to illustrate. Suppose that the firm operates two plants with direct labor and factory overhead expenses as follows:

	Plant 1	*Plant 2*	*Total*
Direct labor	$400,000	$200,000	$600,000
Factory expense	$500,000	$300,000	$800,000
Total cost	$900,000	$500,000	$1,400,000

In addition, the cost of management, sales staff, engineering, accounting, and so on, amounts to $960,000. The corporate overhead rate would be based on the total direct labor of the two plants:

$$\text{corporate overhead rate} = \frac{\$960,000}{\$600,000} (100\%) = 160\%$$

Overhead rates, both factory and corporate, are simply a means for allocating expenses that are not directly associated with production. The principal concern in this book will be with determining the appropriate allocation of factory expenses, not corporate overhead.

EXAMPLE 3.6

A batch of 50 parts is to be processed through the factory for a particular customer. Raw materials and tooling are supplied by the customer. The total time for processing the parts (including setup and other direct labor) is 100 h. Direct labor cost is $9.00 per hour. The factory overhead rate is 125% and the corporate overhead rate is 160%. Compute the cost of the job.

Solution:

(1) The direct labor cost for the job is

$$(100 \text{ h})(\$9.00/\text{h}) = \$900$$

(2) The allocated factory overhead charge, at 125% of direct labor, would be

$$(\$900)(1.25) = \$1125$$

(3) The allocated corporate overhead charge, at 160% of direct labor, would be

$$(\$900)(1.60) = \$1440$$

Interpretation: (1) The direct labor cost of the job, representing actual cash spent on the customer's order, is $900.

(2) The total factory cost of the job, including allocated factory overhead, is $900 + $1125 = $2025. To evaluate alternative production methods, at least some of the factory overhead expenses should be included in the cost comparison.

(3) The total cost of the job, including corporate overhead, is $2025 + $1440 = $3465. To price the job for the customer, and to earn a profit over the long run on jobs like this, the price would have to be greater than $3465. For example, if the company uses a 10% markup, the price quoted to the customer would be (1.10)($3465) = $3811.50.

Cost of equipment usage

The trouble with overhead rates as we have developed them is that they are based on direct labor cost alone. A machine operator who runs an old, small engine lathe will be costed at the same overhead rate as the operator who runs a modern NC machining center representing a $250,000 investment. Obviously, the time on the automated machine should be valued at a higher rate. If differences between rates of different production machines are not recognized, manufacturing costs will not be accurately measured by the overhead rate structure.

To overcome this difficulty, it is appropriate to divide production costs (excluding raw materials) into two components: direct labor and machine cost. Associated with each will be the applicable factory overhead. These cost components will apply not to the aggregate factory operations but to individual production work centers. A work center would typically be one worker–machine system or a small group of machines plus the labor to operate them.

The direct labor cost consists of the wages paid to operate the work center. The applicable factory overhead allocated to direct labor might include fringe benefits and line supervision. These are factory expense items which are appropriately charged as direct labor overhead.

The machine cost is the capital cost of the machine apportioned over the life of the asset at the appropriate rate of return used by the firm. This provides an annual cost that may be expressed as an hourly rate (or any other time unit) by dividing the annual cost by the number of hours of use per year. The machine overhead rate is based on those factory expenses which are directly applicable to the machine. These would include power for the machine, floor space, maintenance and repair expenses, and so on. In separating the applicable factory overhead items of Table 3.1 between direct labor and machine, some arbitrary judgment must be used.

EXAMPLE 3.7

The determination of an hourly rate for a given work center can best be illustrated by means of an example. Given the following:

direct labor rate = $7.00/h

applicable labor factory overhead rate = 60%

capital investment in machine = $100,000

service life = 8 years

salvage value = zero

applicable machine factory overhead rate = 50%

rate of return used 10%

The machine is operated one 8-h shift per day, 250 days per year. Determine the appropriate hourly cost for this worker–machine system.

Solution:

The labor cost per hour is $7.00(1 + 60%) = $11.20/h. The machine cost must first be annualized:

$$UAC = 100,000(A/P, \ 10\%,8)$$
$$= 100,000(0.18744) = \$18,744/yr$$

— w/o considering depreciation methods

The number of hours per year is 8 × 250 = 2000 hr/yr. Dividing the $18,744 by 2000 gives $9.37/h. Applying the 50% overhead rate, the machine cost per hour is $9.37(1 + 50%) = $14.06/h. So the

$$total \ work \ center \ rate = \$11.20 + \$14.06$$
$$= \$25.26/h$$

In subsequent chapters there will be problems in which an hourly rate must be applied to a particular automated production system. Example 3.7 illustrates the general method by which this hourly rate is determined.

3.3 BREAK-EVEN ANALYSIS

Break-even analysis is a method of assessing the effect of changes in production output on costs, revenues, and profits. It is most commonly conceptualized in the form of a break-even chart. To construct the break-even chart, the manufacturing costs are divided into fixed costs and variable costs. The sum of these costs is plotted as a function of production output. To plot the total cost, the variable cost per unit change in output must be determined. Revenues can also be plotted on a break-even chart as a function of production output.

Break-even analysis can be used for either of two main purposes:

1. *Profit analysis*. In this case the break-even chart shows the effect of changes in output on costs and revenues. This gives a picture of how profits (or losses) will vary for different output levels. The break-even point is the output level at which total costs

equal revenues and the profit is zero. An example of a break-even chart used for profit analysis is shown in Figure 3.2.

 2. *Production method cost comparison.* In this case the break-even chart shows the effect of changes in output level on the costs of two (or more) different methods of production. The break-even point for this chart is the output level at which the costs for the two production methods are equal. (When more than two production methods are plotted on the same chart, there will be a break-even point for each pair of production methods.) Figure 3.3 shows a break-even chart used for production method cost comparison.

 We will illustrate the two types of break-even analysis by means of two examples.

EXAMPLE 3.8

This example illustrates the use of a break-even chart for profit analysis. A manually operated production machine costs $66,063. It will have a service life of 7 years with an anticipated salvage value of $5000 at the end of its life. The machine will be used to produce one type of part at a rate of 20 units/h. The annual cost to maintain the machine is $2000. A machine overhead rate of 15% is applicable to capital cost and maintenance. Labor to run the machine costs $10.00/h and the applicable overhead rate is 30%. Determine the profit break-even point if the value added is $1.00/unit and the rate-of-return criterion is 20%.

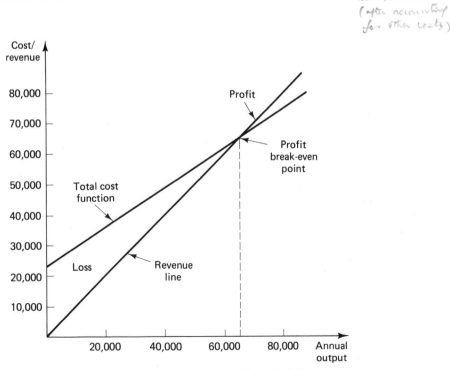

FIGURE 3.2   Profit break-even chart (see Example 3.8).

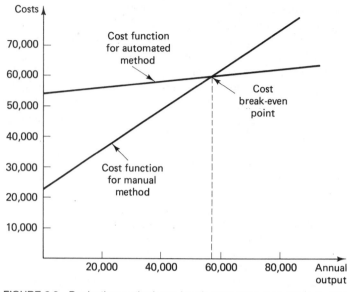

FIGURE 3.3   Production method cost break-even chart (see Example 3.9).

Solution:

Let Q be the annual level. Variable cost is labor cost, including applicable overhead, divided by production rate.

$$\frac{\$10.00/\text{h}(1 + 30\%)}{20 \text{ pieces/h}} = \$0.65/\text{unit}$$

The variable cost as a function of Q is $0.65Q$.

The annual fixed cost is figured on the machine investment plus the maintenance. First, ignoring overhead, we have

$$\text{UAC} = 66{,}063(A/P, 20\%, 7) + 2000 - 5000(A/F, 20\%, 7)$$

$$= \$19{,}939$$

Adding the 15% overhead, the fixed cost $= \$22{,}930$.

The sum of the fixed and variable costs provides the total cost equation as a function of Q:

$$\text{total cost} = \$22{,}930 + 0.65Q$$

Revenues as a function of Q are the product of value added per unit multiplied by Q. Revenues $= \$1.00Q$. This is plotted in Figure 3.2. The break-even point occurs where the revenue line intersects the total cost line. To calculate the break-even point, the following equation can be set up:

$$\text{profit} = 1.00Q - 22{,}930 - 0.65Q = 0$$

$$1.00Q = 22,930 + 0.65Q$$

$$0.35Q = 22,930$$

$$Q = 65,514 \text{ units/yr}$$

At a production rate of 20 units/h this would require $65,514/20 = 3276$ h/yr.

may require addl. shifts (w/ often addl. costs·)

EXAMPLE 3.9

This example illustrates the cost break-even analysis. Suppose that an alternative to the manually operated production machine of Example 3.8 is available. The alternative is an automated machine, costing $125,000, but capable of a production rate of 50 units/h. Its service life is 5 years with no salvage value at the end of that time. Annual maintenance will cost $5000. One-third of one operator costing $12.00/h will be required to run the machine. The overhead rates and rate of return used in Example 3.8 are applicable. Determine the break-even point for the automated and manual methods of production.

Solution:

Variable cost for the automated machine is

$$\frac{(\$12.00/\text{h})(1/3)(1 + 30\%)}{50 \text{ pieces/h}} = \$0.104/\text{unit}$$

Fixed cost is the capital cost plus maintenance, with machine overhead added.

$$[125,000(A/P, 20\%, 5) + 5000](1 + 15\%) = \$53,820$$

Total cost is variable cost plus fixed cost:

$$\text{total cost} = 53,820 + 0.104Q$$

The total cost functions for the two production methods are plotted in Figure 3.3. The break-even point is represented by the intersection point for the two methods. Setting the two total cost equations equal yields

$$53,820 + 0.104Q = 22,930 + 0.65Q$$

$$53,820 - 22,930 = 0.65Q - 0.104Q$$

$$30,890 = 0.546Q$$

$$Q = 56,575 \text{ units/yr}$$

For the manual method, this corresponds to 2829 h of production per year, and for the automated method this quantity would require 1131.5 h of operation per year.

Just to complete the example, let us compute the profit break-even point for the automated method given that the value added per unit is $1.00.

$$\text{profit} = 1.00Q - 53,820 - 0.104Q = 0$$

$$1.00Q = 53,820 + 0.104Q$$

$$0.896Q = 53,820$$

$$Q = 60,067 \text{ units/yr}$$

This would require 1201.3 h of operation per year.

3.4 UNIT COST OF PRODUCTION

In Examples 3.8 and 3.9, one of the complications in the problems was the difference in production rates for the two alternatives. The automated method outproduced the manual method, which is often the case in comparing automation against manual production. To help decide between the alternatives, it is often useful to determine the unit cost of production for the two (or more) methods under consideration.

The unit cost for a certain operation is the total cost of production divided by the number of units produced. The total cost of production includes both fixed and variable costs. Accordingly, because of the fixed portion of the cost of production, the unit cost will vary as a function of annual output Q. As the annual output increases, the unit cost decreases. Using the manual production method from Example 3.8 to illustrate, dividing the total cost equation by the quantity Q, we get the unit cost equation, which we will symbolize by C_{pc} (cost per piece):

$$C_{pc} = \frac{22,930 + 0.65Q}{Q} = 0.65 + \frac{22,930}{Q}$$

Similarly, the unit production cost for the automated method of Example 3.9 is given by

$$C_{pc} = 0.104 + \frac{53,820}{Q}$$

The two relationships are plotted as a function of Q in Figure 3.4. Note that the unit costs are equal at the previously determined break-even point of Example 3.9 (56,575 units per year).

In subsequent chapters we will sometimes use the unit cost as a measure of performance for a production system. The reader should recall that these unit costs are calculated under assumed conditions of annual cost and production rate. As indicated in Figure 3.4, the actual cost per unit of production is strongly dependent on the level of annual output.

One other observation about Examples 3.8 and 3.9 is that the total cost equations for the two alternatives ignore certain practical realities that might influence how the production methods are implemented. For both methods, the number of hours of operation were calculated at the various break-even points. In the case of the manual method, the number of annual hours of operation at the profit break-even point = 3276 h. This is

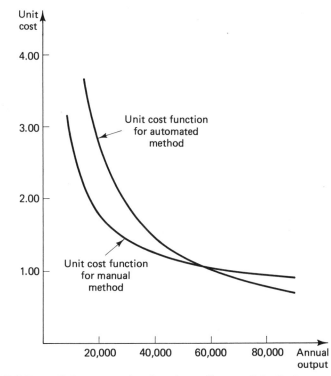

FIGURE 3.4   Unit cost as a function of annual output Q for the two production methods of Examples 3.8 and 3.9.

greater than the number of hours normally worked by one person per year (40/week $\times$ 50 weeks/yr = 2000 h/yr). Will the extra hours be achieved by using two machines, or by using two shifts on one machine, or by working overtime by one production worker? In each instance, there are additional costs which are not included in the total cost equation. If two machines are used, the capital cost (fixed cost) is doubled. If two shifts are used, the worker on the second shift will probably be paid at a higher rate, and there will be other additional costs if the plant does not normally operate a second shift. If overtime is used to achieve the 3276 annual hours of operation, the cost will increase, as the overtime rate is higher (typically time-and-a-half) than the regular shift rate. Problem 3.12 requires the reader to determine the total cost equation and unit cost equation for the three alternatives described here.

In the case of the automated production machine, the number of hours of annual operation to reach the profit break-even point is 1201.3 h, well under 2000 h/yr. If the company operates the machine at that point or only slightly above, it will be running below capacity and the utilization will be low. In this case, the company might want to consider ways of increasing demand for the product in order to raise the machine utilization.

These complicating factors must be considered when alternative production methods are compared in a real-life industrial setting.

3.5 COST OF MANUFACTURING LEAD TIME AND WORK-IN-PROCESS

One of the considerations that is often overlooked in an automation proposal is the effect that the automated method will have on manufacturing lead time and in-process inventory. Automation will often result in dramatic reductions in both of these factors by comparison to previous conventional manufacturing methods. In this section we present a method for evaluating the cost of these factors, based on concepts suggested by Meyer [3].

Our definition in Chapter 2 indicated that production typically consists of a series of separate manufacturing steps or operations. An operation time is required for each step, and that time has an associated cost. There is also a time between each operation, at least for most manufacturing situations, which we have referred to as the nonoperation time. The nonoperation time includes material handling, inspection, and storage. There is also a cost associated with the nonoperation time. These times and costs for a given part can be illustrated graphically as shown in Figure 3.5. At time $t = 0$, the cost of the part is simply its material cost C_m. The cost of each processing step on the part will be the production time multiplied by the rate for the machine and labor. The production time T_p is determined from Eq. (2.5) and accounts for both setup time and operation

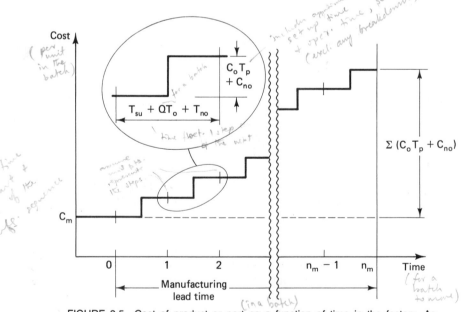

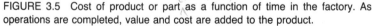

FIGURE 3.5   Cost of product or part as a function of time in the factory. As operations are completed, value and cost are added to the product.

time. We will symbolize the rate as C_o. The determination of this rate was illustrated in Example 3.7. The nonoperation costs (e.g., inspection, material handling, etc.) that are related to the processing step will be symbolized by the term C_{no}. Accordingly, the cost associated with each processing step in the manufacturing sequence will be

$$C_o T_p + C_{no}$$

The cost for each step is shown in Figure 3.5 as a vertical line, suggesting no time lapse. This is a simplification in the graph, since the time between operations spent waiting and in storage is generally much greater than the time for processing, handling, and inspection.

The total cost that has been invested in the part at the end of all operations is the sum of the material cost and the accumulated processing, inspection, and handling costs. Symbolizing this part cost as C_{pc}, we can utilize the following equation to evaluate it:

$$C_{pc} = C_m + \sum_i (C_o T_{pi} + C_{noi})$$

where i is used to indicate the sequence of operations. If we assume that T_p and C_{no} are equal for all n_m operations, then

$$C_{pc} = C_m + n_m (C_o T_p + C_{no}) \tag{3.3}$$

The part cost function shown in Figure 3.5 and represented by Eq. (3.3) can be approximated by a straight line as shown in Figure 3.6. The line starts at time $t = 0$ with a value $= C_m$ and slopes upward to the right so that its final value is the same as

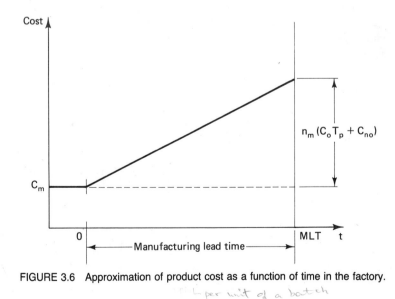

FIGURE 3.6 Approximation of product cost as a function of time in the factory.

the final part cost in Figure 3.5. The approximation becomes more accurate as the number of processing steps increases. The equation for this line is

$$C_m + \frac{n_m(C_oT_p + C_{no})}{\text{MLT}} t$$

where MLT is the manufacturing lead time for the part and t is the time in Figure 3.6.

In addition to the costs shown in Figure 3.5 (and approximated in Figure 3.6), there are two other sources of costs that should be accounted for. These are the cost of investing in work-in-process and the cost of storing the work-in-process. Both are related to the time that the parts spend in the factory. The investment cost results because the company must pay its operating costs before receiving payment from the customer for the parts. This investment cost is the accumulated cost of the part, depicted as a function of time in Figure 3.5, multiplied by the rate of return or interest rate, i, used by the company.

The storage cost results because work-in-process takes up space in the factory. In some plants, WIP is placed in a special storage facility (e.g., an automated storage system) between processing steps. In either case, there is a cost of storing the WIP. The magnitude of the cost is generally related to the size of the part and how much space it occupies. As an approximation, it can be related to the value or cost of the item stored. For our purposes, this is the most convenient method of valuating the storage cost of the part. By this method, the storage cost is equal to the accumulated cost of the part multiplied by the storage rate, s. The term s is the storage cost as a percentage of the value of the item in inventory.

Combining the interest rate and the storage rate into one factor, we have $h = i + s$. The term h is called the holding cost rate. Like i and s, it is a percentage that is multiplied by the accumulated cost of the part to evaluate the holding cost of investing in and storing work-in-process. Applying the holding cost rate to the accumulated part cost defined by Eq. (3.3) but substituting straight-line approximation in place of the stepwise cost accumulation in Figure 3.5, we have an equation for total cost per part which includes the WIP investment and storage components:

$$TC_{pc} = C_m + n_m (C_oT_p + C_{no}) + \int_o^{\text{MLT}} \left[C_m + \frac{n_m(C_oT_p + C_{no}) t}{\text{MLT}} \right] h \, dt$$

This can be reduced to simpler form.

$$\text{Let } C_1 = n_m (C_oT_p + C_{no})$$

Then

$$TC_{pc} = C_m + C_1 + \int_o^{\text{MLT}} \left(C_m + \frac{C_1 t}{\text{MLT}} \right) h \, dt \qquad (3.4)$$

which reduces to

$$TC_{pc} = C_m + C_1 + \left(C_m + \frac{C_1}{2}\right) h(\text{MLT}) \qquad (3.5)$$

The holding cost is the last term on the right-hand side.

$$\frac{\text{holding cost}}{\text{piece}} = \left(C_m + \frac{C_1}{2}\right) h(\text{MLT}) \qquad (3.6)$$

shorter MLT will reduce holding cost

Figure 3.7 shows the effect of adding the holding cost to the material, operation, and nonoperation costs of a part or product during production in the plant.

EXAMPLE 3.10

The cost of the raw material for a certain part is $100. The part is processed through 20 processing steps in the plant and the manufacturing lead time is 15 weeks. The production time per processing step is 0.8 h and the machine and labor rate is $25.00/h. Inspection, material handling, and related costs average $10 per processing step by the time the part is finished. The interest rate i used by the company is 20% and the storage rate $s = 13\%$. Determine the cost per part and the holding cost.

incl. set up, per pc.

have all values due for 1 part (unit)

Solution:

The material cost, operation costs, and nonoperation costs are, by Eq. (3.3),

$$C_{pc} = \$100 + 20(\$25.00/\text{h} \times 0.8\ \text{h} + \$10) = \$700/\text{piece}$$

To compute the holding cost, first calculate C_1:

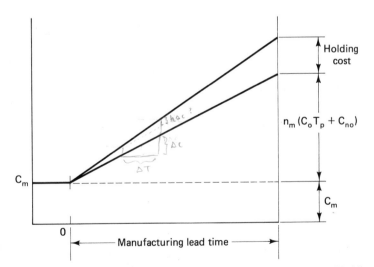

FIGURE 3.7 Approximation of product cost showing additional cost of holding work-in-process during the manufacturing lead time.

$$C_1 = 20(\$25.00/h \times 0.8\ h + \$10) = \$600/piece$$

Next, determine the holding cost rate $h = 20\% + 13\% = 33\%$. Expressing this as a weekly rate $h = (33\%)/(52\ weeks) = 0.6346\%/week = 0.006346/week$. According to Eq. (3.6),

$$holding\ cost = \left(100 + \frac{600}{2}\right)(0.006346)(15\ weeks)$$

$$= \$38.08/piece$$

$$TC_{pc} = 700.00 + 38.08 = \$738.08/piece$$

The \$38.08 represents over 5% of the cost of the part, yet the holding cost is usually not included directly in the company's evaluation of part cost. Rather, it is considered to be overhead. Suppose that this is a typical part for the company, and 5000 similar parts are processed through the plant each year; then the annual inventory cost for WIP = 5000 × \$38.08 = \$190,400. If the manufacturing lead time could be reduced to half its current value, this would translate into a 50% savings in WIP holding cost.

3.6 OTHER DIFFICULT-TO-QUANTIFY FACTORS

There are a number of cost components that are more difficult to quantify than the material, labor, machine, and holding costs discussed in the preceding sections. These costs include:

- *Floor space.* A difference in production method can have an effect on the amount of floor space consumed at the workcell. Automated methods generally require less floor space than is required using manual methods. If the accumulated floor space savings of many automated workcells means that new plant construction can be avoided, the financial benefit to the company is substantial. This cost difference can be evaluated by assessing the cost per square foot of building space and multiplying by the floor space occupied by the alternative production methods.
- *Product quality.* Automated production methods often lead to less scrap and rework by performing the manufacturing process with greater consistency than human workers are capable of. One of the automation strategies discussed in Chapter 2 involved the use of automated inspection to achieve closer agreement between manufactured product and design specifications. The amount of the savings is difficult to estimate. If a current manual method produces a high rate of scrap, the potential exists for significant improvements in quality through automation. It should be possible to include the effect of scrap into the analysis as we did in our production rate formulas in Chapter 2.
- *Customer delivery.* Different production methods provide different manufacturing lead times, which directly influences customer delivery. Customers who appreciate faster deliveries tend to order more from vendors who can respond quickly. Assessing the value of manufacturing lead times in terms of customer satisfaction and the resulting increases in volume of business is difficult.

• *Safety.* One of the reasons for automating given in Chapter 1 was safety. Removing the worker from a hazardous environment improves safety conditions. What is the financial worth of that benefit?

• *Improved scheduling.* If the number of separate steps required to process the product can be reduced through the use of automated production systems, this should lead to better scheduling in the shop. Fewer separate machines need to be included in the schedule, and cycle times are more consistent. There is a value to the company of this improved scheduling, but it is nearly impossible to evaluate with confidence.

• *Corporate image.* Finally, a company that is employing innovative new manufacturing methods and technologies generally has a better corporate image. This will often make work easier for the company sales staff.

REFERENCES

[1] BLANK, L. T. and A. J. TARQUIN, *Engineering Economy,* 2nd ed., McGraw-Hill Book Company, New York, 1983.

[2] GROOVER, M. P., M. WEISS, R. N. NAGEL, and N. G. ODREY, *Industrial Robotics: Technology, Programming, and Applications,* McGraw-Hill Book Company, New York, 1986, Chapter 12.

[3] MEYER, R. J., "A Cookbook Approach to Robotics and Automation Justification," *Technical Paper MS82-192,* Society of Manufacturing Engineers, Dearborn, Mich., 1982.

[4] THUESEN, G. J., and W. FABRYCKY, *Engineering Economy,* 6th ed., Prentice-Hall, Inc., Englewood Cliffs, N.J., 1984.

PROBLEMS

3.1. Two alternative production methods have been proposed: one a manual method, the other an automatic machine. Data are given in the following table.

	Manual	*Automatic*
First cost	$15,000	$95,000
Annual operating cost	$30,000	$10,000
Salvage value	0	$15,000
Service life (years)	10	7

Use a rate of return of 10% to select the more economical alternative if the two alternatives are equivalent in terms of capability.

3.2. Solve Problem 3.1 using a rate of return of 20%. Why is the selection of method different from that of Problem 3.1?

3.3. A proposed automatic machine is to be used exclusively to produce one type of workpart. The machine has a first cost of $50,000 and its expected service life is 3 years with a salvage value of $20,000 at the end of the 3 years. The machine will be operated 4000 h/yr (two shifts) at $8.00/h (labor, power, maintenance, etc.). Its production rate is 10 units/h. Excluding raw material costs, compute the production cost per unit using a rate of return of 25%.

3.4. The following data apply to the operation of a particular automated manufacturing system:

$$\text{direct labor rate} = \$10.00/h$$

$$\text{number of operators required} = 1$$

$$\text{applicable labor factory overhead rate} = 50\%$$

$$\text{capital investment in system} = \$300,000$$

$$\text{service life} = 10 \text{ years}$$

$$\text{salvage value} = \$30,000$$

$$\text{applicable machine factory overhead rate} = 30\%$$

The system is operated one shift (2000 h/yr). Use a rate of return of 25% to determine the appropriate hourly rate for this worker–machine system.

3.5. Solve Problem 3.4 except using three-shift operation (6000h/yr). Note the effect of increased machine utilization on the hourly rate for the system as compared to the results of Problem 3.4.

3.6. A piece of automated production equipment has a first cost of $100,000. The service life is 6 years, the anticipated salvage value is $10,000, and the annual maintenance costs are $3000. The equipment will produce at the rate of 10 units/h, each unit worth $2.00 in added revenue. (gross) One operator is required full time to tend the machine at a rate of $10.00/h. Assume that no overhead rates are applicable. Raw material costs equal $0.20/unit. Use a rate of return of 20%.
(a) Compute the profit break-even point.
(b) How many hours of operation are required to produce the number of units indicated by the break-even point?
(c) How much profit (or loss) will be made if 50,000 units/yr are produced?

3.7. In Problem 3.6, recompute the break-even point if the applicable overhead rates are 20% for the machine and 40% for labor.

3.8. The break-even point is to be determined for two methods of production, a manual method and an automated method. The manual method requires two operators at $9.00/h each. Together, they produce at a rate of 36 units/h. The automated method has an initial cost of $125,000, a 4-year service life, no salvage value, and annual maintenance costs of $3000. No labor (except for maintenance) is required to operate the machine, but the machine consumes energy at the rate of 50 kW when running. Cost of electricity is $0.05/kWh. If the production rate for this automated machine is 100 units/h, determine the break-even point for the two methods if a 25% rate of return is required.

3.9. Determine the unit cost equation as a function of quantity Q for the data given in Problem 3.6.

3.10. Determine the unit cost equation as a function of quantity Q for the data given in Problem 3.7.

3.11. Determine the unit cost equation as a function of quantity Q for the two production methods in Problem 3.8.

3.12. For the manual method of Example 3.8, three possible ways of implementing the method were discussed in Section 3.4. The three ways were:
(a) Use two machines to achieve the total hours required.
(b) Use a two-shift operation to achieve the total hours.
(c) Use overtime at time-and-a-half to achieve the total hours.
For each of the three ways, determine the total cost equation and the unit cost equation, indicating the values of Q where the equation changes form. Plot each case. The following ground rules apply: (1) 2000 h of operation per year on regular shift; (2) costs as given in Example 3.8; (3) second shift differential = $0.20/h (the labor rate increment of 25 cents/h applies to the labor rate only, not to overheads); (4) labor rate for overtime is $15.00/h, but overhead costs remain constant.

3.13. A proposal has been submitted to construct a new warehouse with 16,000 ft² of storage floor space. Assume that 80% of the floor space in the warehouse is available for storage purposes. The building will cost $500,000 to build and is expected to have a 20-year life with a salvage value at that time of $100,000. Annual maintenance and operating costs will be $120,000. The rate of return used by the firm in this problem is 25%. This rate applies to investments in building or in inventory.
(a) For a given item that costs $125.00 to purchase and requires 5 ft² of floor space, how much will it cost the company to store the item in the warehouse for 3 months? Your answer must consider both storage costs and inventory investment costs.
(b) If the item indicated in part (a) is typical in size and cost of the company's inventory stored in the warehouse, determine a value for h, the holding cost rate.
(c) Determine an estimate of the total cost of inventory in the warehouse on an annual basis, assuming that the warehouse is filled to its 80% of floor space throughout the year.

3.14. For the data given in Problem 3.13, solve the problem given that a shelving structure is included in the warehouse cost that permits the parts to be stacked vertically six high.

3.15. A workpart costing $80 is processed through the factory. The manufacturing lead time for the part is 12 weeks, and the total time spent in processing during the lead time is 30 h for all operations at a rate of $35/h. Nonoperation costs total $70 during the lead time. The holding cost rate used by the company for work-in-process is 26%. The plant operates 40h/week, 52 weeks per year. If this part is typical of the 200 parts per week processed through the factory:
(a) Determine the holding cost per part during the manufacturing lead time.
(b) Determine the total annual holding costs to the factory.
(c) If the manufacturing lead time were to be reduced from 12 weeks to 8 weeks, how much would the total holding costs be reduced on an annual basis?

3.16. A batch of large castings is processed through a machine shop. The batch size is 20. Each raw casting costs $175. There are 22 machining operations performed on each casting at an average operation time of 0.5 h per operation. Setup time per operation averages 5 h. The cost rate for the machine and labor is $40/h. Nonoperation costs (inspection, handling between operations, etc.) average $5 per operation per part. The corresponding nonoperation time between each operation averages 2 working days. The shop works five 8-h days per week, 52 weeks per year. The interest rate used by the company is 25% for investing in WIP inventory, and the storage cost rate is 14% of the value of the item held. Both of these rates are annual rates. Determine the following:

(a) Manufacturing lead time for the batch of castings.
(b) Total cost to the shop of each casting when it is completed, including the holding cost.
(c) Total holding cost of the batch for the time it spends in the machine shop as work-in-process.

APPENDIX: INTEREST AND INTEREST TABLES

Basic concepts

Money is considered to possess a *time value* because when money is borrowed for a period of time, it is expected that the amount paid back will be greater than that which was borrowed. The difference is referred to as *interest*. The amount of interest is determined by three factors: the length of time the money was borrowed, the interest rate, and whether simple interest or compound interest was used to compute the amount. To explain these factors, let us concern ourselves with the difference between simple and compound interest.

SIMPLE INTEREST.   The interest rate is generally expressed in terms of an annual rate. To compute the interest for a certain amount of money borrowed for exactly 1 year, the amount is multipled by the interest rate. We can reduce this to the following formula:

$$I = Pi$$

$$\text{where } i = \text{annual interest rate}$$

$$P = \text{principal (the starting amount)}$$

$$I = \text{interest}$$

With simple interest, when an amount of money is borrowed for a period greater than 1 year, the interest charge is determined by multiplying the yearly interest charge by the number of years:

$$I = Pni$$

where n represents the number of years. The amount of money paid back at the end of n years can be determined from the formula

$$F = P + I = P(1 + ni) \tag{A3.1}$$

where F represents the future amount to be paid, in this case under simple interest.

COMPOUND INTEREST.   With simple interest, the amount I is directly proportional to the length of time n. If interest is compounded during the length of time, the final amount F (principal plus interest) grows at a faster rate. To illustrate compound interest, consider the manner in which a savings account might grow if the interest were compounded annually. Using an initial deposit of $1000 and an interest rate of 5%, the savings account at the end of the first year would be worth

$$F_1 = \$1000(1 + 0.05) = \$1050$$

This amount is used to compute the interest for the second year. Thus, the savings would have grown by the end of the second year to

$$F_2 = \$1050(1 + 0.05) = \$1102.50$$

The general equation for calculating the future equivalent of some present value P can be determined by the equation

$$F = P(1 + i)^n \tag{A3.2}$$

In engineering economy calculations, compound interest is almost always used, because it reflects more accurately the time value of money.

Interest factors

Equation (A3.2) represents one of six common interest-rate problems: the problem of computing the future worth of some present value, given the rate of return i and the number of years n. There are a total of six of these problems. They occur frequently enough that an interest factor has been defined to cover each problem. In the paragraphs below the six interest factors are described.

1. *Single-payment compound amount factor (SPCAF)*. This is the case we have previously considered: finding the future value F of a present sum P. As the reader can deduce from Eq. (A3.2), the formula used to calculate the single-payment compound amount factor is

$$SPCAF = (1 + i)^n \tag{A3.3}$$

We shall adopt the following notation for the SPCAF, which will be easier to remember and use than the name of the factor:

$$SPCAF = (F/P, i\%, n) \tag{A3.4}$$

The terms in parentheses can be read: Find F, given P, i, and n. This general form will be used for the interest factors that follow.

2. *Single-payment present worth factor (SPPWF)*. This is the inverse of the previous interest problem. The SPPWF is used to compute the present worth of some future value.

$$\text{SPPWF} = (P/F, \, i\%, \, n) = \frac{1}{(1 + i)^n} \tag{A3.5}$$

3. *Capital recovery factor (CRF).* Instead of paying off a borrowed sum with a single future payment, another common method is to make uniform annual payments at the end of each of n years. The amount of each payment is figured to yield the required interest rate i. The capital recovery factor is designed specifically for this case.

$$\text{CRF} = (A/P, \, i\%, \, n) = \frac{i(1 + i)^n}{(1 + i)^n - 1} \tag{A3.6}$$

where A represents the amount of the annual payment.

4. *Uniform series present worth factor (USPWF).* This solves the preceding problem in reverse: finding the present value of a series of n future end-of-year equal payments.

$$\text{USPWF} = (P/A, \, i\%, \, n) = \frac{(1 + i)^n - 1}{i(1 + i)^n} \tag{A3.7}$$

5. *Sinking fund factor (SFF).* "Sinking fund" refers to the situation in which we want to put aside a certain sum of money at the end of each year so that after n years, the accumulated fund, with interest compounded, will be worth F. The sinking fund factor allows us to determine the amount A to be put aside each year.

$$\text{SFF} = (A/F, \, i\%, \, n) = \frac{i}{(1 + i)^n - 1} \tag{A3.8}$$

6. *Uniform series compound amount factor (USCAF).* The reverse of the preceding problem arises when it is desired to know how much money has accumulated after n years of uniform annual payments at interest rate i.

$$\text{USCAF} = (F/A, \, i\%, \, n) = \frac{(1 + i)^n - 1}{i} \tag{A3.9}$$

TABLES OF INTEREST FACTORS. Instead of calculating the value of the interest factor needed in a given problem, values are tabulated for a wide variety of interest rates and years. In this appendix, the interest factors are given for interest rates equal to 10%, 12%, 15%, 20%, 25%, 30%, 40%, and 50%. Although this list is not nearly complete, these values cover the range of annual rates of return that seem to prevail during the period in which this book is being written.

TABLE A3.1   10% Interest Factors for Annual Compounding*

n	Single Payment — Compound-amount factor — To find F Given P — $F/P, i, n$	Single Payment — Present-worth factor — To find P Given F — $P/F, i, n$	Equal Payment Series — Compound-amount factor — To find F Given A — $F/A, i, n$	Equal Payment Series — Sinking-fund factor — To find A Given F — $A/F, i, n$	Equal Payment Series — Present-worth factor — To find P Given A — $P/A, i, n$	Equal Payment Series — Capital-recovery factor — To find A Given P — $A/P, i, n$	Uniform gradient-series factor — To find A Given G — $A/G, i, n$
1	1.100	0.9091	1.000	1.0000	0.9091	1.1000	0.0000
2	1.210	0.8265	2.100	0.4762	1.7355	0.5762	0.4762
3	1.331	0.7513	3.310	0.3021	2.4869	0.4021	0.9366
4	1.464	0.6830	4.641	0.2155	3.1699	0.3155	1.3812
5	1.611	0.6209	6.105	0.1638	3.7908	0.2638	1.8101
6	1.772	0.5645	7.716	0.1296	4.3553	0.2296	2.2236
7	1.949	0.5132	9.487	0.1054	4.8684	0.2054	2.6216
8	2.144	0.4665	11.436	0.0875	5.3349	0.1875	3.0045
9	2.358	0.4241	13.579	0.0737	5.7590	0.1737	3.3724
10	2.594	0.3856	15.937	0.0628	6.1446	0.1628	3.7255
11	2.853	0.3505	18.531	0.0540	6.4951	0.1540	4.0641
12	3.138	0.3186	21.384	0.0468	6.8137	0.1468	4.3884
13	3.452	0.2897	24.523	0.0408	7.1034	0.1408	4.6988
14	3.798	0.2633	27.975	0.0358	7.3667	0.1358	4.9955
15	4.177	0.2394	31.772	0.0315	7.6061	0.1315	5.2789
16	4.595	0.2176	35.950	0.0278	7.8237	0.1278	5.5493
17	5.054	0.1979	40.545	0.0247	8.0216	0.1247	5.8071
18	5.560	0.1799	45.599	0.0219	8.2014	0.1219	6.0526
19	6.116	0.1635	51.159	0.0196	8.3649	0.1196	6.2861
20	6.728	0.1487	57.275	0.0175	8.5136	0.1175	6.5081
21	7.400	0.1351	64.003	0.0156	8.6487	0.1156	6.7189
22	8.140	0.1229	71.403	0.0140	8.7716	0.1140	6.9189
23	8.954	0.1117	79.543	0.0126	8.8832	0.1126	7.1085
24	9.850	0.1015	88.497	0.0113	8.9848	0.1113	7.2881
25	10.835	0.0923	98.347	0.0102	9.0771	0.1102	7.4580
26	11.918	0.0839	109.182	0.0092	9.1610	0.1092	7.6187
27	13.110	0.0763	121.100	0.0083	9.2372	0.1083	7.7704
28	14.421	0.0694	134.210	0.0075	9.3066	0.1075	7.9137
29	15.863	0.0630	148.631	0.0067	9.3696	0.1067	8.0489
30	17.449	0.0573	164.494	0.0061	9.4269	0.1061	8.1762
31	19.194	0.0521	181.943	0.0055	9.4790	0.1055	8.2962
32	21.114	0.0474	201.138	0.0050	9.5264	0.1050	8.4091
33	23.225	0.0431	222.252	0.0045	9.5694	0.1045	8.5152
34	25.548	0.0392	245.477	0.0041	9.6086	0.1041	8.6149
35	28.102	0.0356	271.024	0.0037	9.6442	0.1037	8.7086
40	45.259	0.0221	442.593	0.0023	9.7791	0:1023	9.0962
45	72.890	0.0137	718.905	0.0014	9.8628	0.1014	9.3741
50	117.391	0.0085	1163.909	0.0009	9.9148	0.1009	9.5704
55	189.059	0.0053	1880.591	0.0005	9.9471	0.1005	9.7075
60	304.482	0.0033	3034.816	0.0003	9.9672	0.1003	9.8023
65	490.371	0.0020	4893.707	0.0002	9.9796	0.1002	9.8672
70	789.747	0.0013	7887.470	0.0001	9.9873	0.1001	9.9113
75	1271.895	0.0008	12708.954	0.0001	9.9921	0.1001	9.9410
80	2048.400	0.0005	20474.002	0.0001	9.9951	0.1001	9.9609
85	3298.969	0.0003	32979.690	0.0000	9.9970	0.1000	9.9742
90	5313.023	0.0002	53120.226	0.0000	9.9981	0.1000	9.9831
95	8556.676	0.0001	85556.760	0.0000	9.9988	0.1000	9.9889
100	13780.612	0.0001	137796.123	0.0000	9.9993	0.1000	9.9928

*Tables are reprinted by permission from G. J. Thuesen and W. Fabrycky, *Engineering Economy*, 6th ed. (Englewood Cliffs, NJ: Prentice-Hall Inc., 1984), pp. 574–588.

TABLE A3.2   12% Interest Factors for Annual Compounding

	Single Payment		Equal Payment Series				Uniform gradient-series factor
	Compound-amount factor	Present-worth factor	Compound-amount factor	Sinking-fund factor	Present-worth factor	Capital-recovery factor	
n	To find F Given P $F/P, i, n$	To find P Given F $P/F, i, n$	To find F Given A $F/A, i, n$	To find A Given F $A/F, i, n$	To find P Given A $P/A, i, n$	To find A Given P $A/P, i, n$	To find A Given G $A/G, i, n$
1	1.120	0.8929	1.000	1.0000	0.8929	1.1200	0.0000
2	1.254	0.7972	2.120	0.4717	1.6901	0.5917	0.4717
3	1.405	0.7118	3.374	0.2964	2.4018	0.4164	0.9246
4	1.574	0.6355	4.779	0.2092	3.0374	0.3292	1.3589
5	1.762	0.5674	6.353	0.1574	3.6048	0.2774	1.7746
6	1.974	0.5066	8.115	0.1232	4.1114	0.2432	2.1721
7	2.211	0.4524	10.089	0.0991	4.5638	0.2191	2.5515
8	2.476	0.4039	12.300	0.0813	4.9676	0.2013	2.9132
9	2.773	0.3606	14.776	0.0677	5.3283	0.1877	3.2574
10	3.106	0.3220	17.549	0.0570	5.6502	0.1770	3.5847
11	3.479	0.2875	20.655	0.0484	5.9377	0.1684	3.8953
12	3.896	0.2567	24.133	0.0414	6.1944	0.1614	4.1897
13	4.364	0.2292	28.029	0.0357	6.4236	0.1557	4.4683
14	4.887	0.2046	32.393	0.0309	6.6282	0.1509	4.7317
15	5.474	0.1827	37.280	0.0268	6.8109	0.1468	4.9803
16	6.130	0.1631	42.753	0.0234	6.9740	0.1434	5.2147
17	6.866	0.1457	48.884	0.0205	7.1196	0.1405	5.4353
18	7.690	0.1300	55.750	0.0179	7.2497	0.1379	5.6427
19	8.613	0.1161	63.440	0.0158	7.3658	0.1358	5.8375
20	9.646	0.1037	72.052	0.0139	7.4695	0.1339	6.0202
21	10.804	0.0926	81.699	0.0123	7.5620	0.1323	6.1913
22	12.100	0.0827	92.503	0.0108	7.6447	0.1308	6.3514
23	13.552	0.0738	104.603	0.0096	7.7184	0.1296	6.5010
24	15.179	0.0659	118.155	0.0085	7.7843	0.1285	6.6407
25	17.000	0.0588	133.334	0.0075	7.8431	0.1275	6.7708
26	19.040	0.0525	150.334	0.0067	7.8957	0.1267	6.8921
27	21.325	0.0469	169.374	0.0059	7.9426	0.1259	7.0049
28	23.884	0.0419	190.699	0.0053	7.9844	0.1253	7.1098
29	26.750	0.0374	214.583	0.0047	8.0218	0.1247	7.2071
30	29.960	0.0334	241.333	0.0042	8.0552	0.1242	7.2974
31	33.555	0.0298	271.293	0.0037	8.0850	0 1237	7.3811
32	37.582	0.0266	304.848	0.0033	8.1116	0.1233	7.4586
33	42.092	0.0238	342.429	0.0029	8.1354	0.1229	7.5303
34	47.143	0.0212	384.521	0.0026	8.1566	0.1226	7.5965
35	52.800	0.0189	431.664	0.0023	8.1755	0.1223	7.6577
40	93.051	0.0108	767.091	0.0013	8.2438	0.1213	7.8988
45	163.988	0.0061	1358.230	0.0007	8.2825	0.1207	8.0572
50	289.002	0.0035	2400.018	0.0004	8.3045	0.1204	8.1597

TABLE A3.3 15% Interest Factors for Annual Compounding

n	Single Payment		Equal Payment Series				Uniform gradient-series factor
	Compound-amount factor	Present-worth factor	Compound-amount factor	Sinking-fund factor	Present-worth factor	Capital-recovery factor	
	To find F Given P $F/P, i, n$	To find P Given F $P/F, i, n$	To find F Given A $F/A, i, n$	To find A Given F $A/F, i, n$	To find P Given A $P/A, i, n$	To find A Given P $A/P, i, n$	To find A Given G $A/G, i, n$
1	1.150	0.8696	1.000	1.0000	0.8696	1.1500	0.0000
2	1.323	0.7562	2.150	0.4651	1.6257	0.6151	0.4651
3	1.521	0.6575	3.473	0.2880	2.2832	0.4380	0.9071
4	1.749	0.5718	4.993	0.2003	2.8550	0.3503	1.3263
5	2.011	0.4972	6.742	0.1483	3.3522	0.2983	1.7228
6	2.313	0.4323	8.754	0.1142	3.7845	0.2642	2.0972
7	2.660	0.3759	11.067	0.0904	4.1604	0.2404	2.4499
8	3.059	0.3269	13.727	0.0729	4.4873	0.2229	2.7813
9	3.518	0.2843	16.786	0.0596	4.7716	0.2096	3.0922
10	4.046	0.2472	20.304	0.0493	5.0188	0.1993	3.3832
11	4.652	0.2150	24.349	0.0411	5.2337	0.1911	3.6550
12	5.350	0.1869	29.002	0.0345	5.4206	0.1845	3.9082
13	6.153	0.1625	34.352	0.0291	5.5832	0.1791	4.1438
14	7.076	0.1413	40.505	0.0247	5.7245	0.1747	4.3624
15	8.137	0.1229	47.580	0.0210	5.8474	0.1710	4.5650
16	9.358	0.1069	55.717	0.0180	5.9542	0.1680	4.7523
17	10.761	0.0929	65.075	0.0154	6.0472	0.1654	4.9251
18	12.375	0.0808	75.836	0.0132	6.1280	0.1632	5.0843
19	14.232	0.0703	88.212	0.0113	6.1982	0.1613	5.2307
20	16.367	0.0611	102.444	0.0098	6.2593	0.1598	5.3651
21	18.822	0.0531	118.810	0.0084	6.3125	0.1584	5.4883
22	21.645	0.0462	137.632	0.0073	6.3587	0.1573	5.6010
23	24.891	0.0402	159.276	0.0063	6.3988	0.1563	5.7040
24	28.625	0.0349	184.168	0.0054	6.4338	0.1554	5.7979
25	32.919	0.0304	212.793	0.0047	6.4642	0.1547	5.8834
26	37.857	0.0264	245.712	0.0041	6.4906	0.1541	5.9612
27	43.535	0.0230	283.569	0.0035	6.5135	0.1535	6.0319
28	50.066	0.0200	327.104	0.0031	6.5335	0.1531	6.0960
29	57.575	0.0174	377.170	0.0027	6.5509	0.1527	6.1541
30	66.212	0.0151	434.745	0.0023	6.5660	0.1523	6.2066
31	76.144	0.0131	500.957	0.0020	6.5791	0.1520	6.2541
32	87.565	0.0114	577.100	0.0017	6.5905	0.1517	6.2970
33	100.700	0.0099	664.666	0.0015	6.6005	0.1515	6.3357
34	115.805	0.0086	765.365	0.0013	6.6091	0.1513	6.3705
35	133.176	0.0075	881.170	0.0011	6.6166	0.1511	6.4019
40	267.864	0.0037	1779.090	0.0006	6.6418	0.1506	6.5168
45	538.769	0.0019	3585.128	0.0003	6.6543	0.1503	6.5830
50	1083.657	0.0009	7217.716	0.0002	6.6605	0.1501	6.6205

TABLE A3.4 20% Interest Factors for Annual Compounding

	Single Payment		Equal Payment Series				Uniform gradient-series factor
	Compound-amount factor	Present-worth factor	Compound-amount factor	Sinking-fund factor	Present-worth factor	Capital-recovery factor	
n	To find *F* Given *P* $F/P, i, n$	To find *P* Given *F* $P/F, i, n$	To find *F* Given *A* $F/A, i, n$	To find *A* Given *F* $A/F, i, n$	To find *P* Given *A* $P/A, i, n$	To find *A* Given *P* $A/P, i, n$	To find *A* Given *G* $A/G, i, n$
1	1.200	0.8333	1.000	1.0000	0.8333	1.2000	0.0000
2	1.440	0.6945	2.200	0.4546	1.5278	0.6546	0.4546
3	1.728	0.5787	3.640	0.2747	2.1065	0.4747	0.8791
4	2.074	0.4823	5.368	0.1863	2.5887	0.3863	1.2742
5	2.488	0.4019	7.442	0.1344	2.9906	0.3344	1.6405
6	2.986	0.3349	9.930	0.1007	3.3255	0.3007	1.9788
7	3.583	0.2791	12.916	0.0774	3.6046	0.2774	2.2902
8	4.300	0.2326	16.499	0.0606	3.8372	0.2606	2.5756
9	5.160	0.1938	20.799	0.0481	4.0310	0.2481	2.8364
10	6.192	0.1615	25.959	0.0385	4.1925	0.2385	3.0739
11	7.430	0.1346	32.150	0.0311	4.3271	0.2311	3.2893
12	8.916	0.1122	39.581	0.0253	4.4392	0.2253	3.4841
13	10.699	0.0935	48.497	0.0206	4.5327	0.2206	3.6597
14	12.839	0.0779	59.196	0.0169	4.6106	0.2169	3.8175
15	15.407	0.0649	72.035	0.0139	4.6755	0.2139	3.9589
16	18.488	0.0541	87.442	0.0114	4.7296	0.2114	4.0851
17	22.186	0.0451	105.931	0.0095	4.7746	0.2095	4.1976
18	26.623	0.0376	128.117	0.0078	4.8122	0.2078	4.2975
19	31.948	0.0313	154.740	0.0065	4.8435	0.2065	4.3861
20	38.338	0.0261	186.688	0.0054	4.8696	0.2054	4.4644
21	46.005	0.0217	225.026	0.0045	4.8913	0.2045	4.5334
22	55.206	0.0181	271.031	0.0037	4.9094	0.2037	4.5942
23	66.247	0.0151	326.237	0.0031	4.9245	0.2031	4.6475
24	79.497	0.0126	392.484	0.0026	4.9371	0.2026	4.6943
25	95.396	0.0105	471.981	0.0021	4.9476	0.2021	4.7352
26	114.475	0.0087	567.377	0.0018	4.9563	0.2018	4.7709
27	137.371	0.0073	681.853	0.0015	4.9636	0.2015	4.8020
28	164.845	0.0061	819.223	0.0012	4.9697	0.2012	4.8291
29	197.814	0.0051	984.068	0.0010	4.9747	0.2010	4.8527
30	237.376	0.0042	1181.882	0.0009	4.9789	0.2009	4.8731
31	284.852	0.0035	1419.258	0.0007	4.9825	0.2007	4.8908
32	341.822	0.0029	1704.109	0.0006	4.9854	0.2006	4.9061
33	410.186	0.0024	2045.931	0.0005	4.9878	0.2005	4.9194
34	492.224	0.0020	2456.118	0.0004	4.9899	0.2004	4.9308
35	590.668	0.0017	2948.341	0.0003	4.9915	0.2003	4.9407
40	1469.772	0.0007	7343.858	0.0002	4.9966	0.2001	4.9728
45	3657.262	0.0003	18281.310	0.0001	4.9986	0.2001	4.9877
50	9100.438	0.0001	45497.191	0.0000	4.9995	0.2000	4.9945

TABLE A3.5   25% Interest Factors for Annual Compounding

n	Single Payment		Equal Payment Series				Uniform gradient-series factor
	Compound-amount factor	Present-worth factor	Compound-amount factor	Sinking-fund factor	Present-worth factor	Capital-recovery factor	
	To find F Given P $F/P, i, n$	To find P Given F $P/F, i, n$	To find F Given A $F/A, i, n$	To find A Given F $A/F, i, n$	To find P Given A $P/A, i, n$	To find A Given P $A/P, i, n$	To find A Given G $A/G, i, n$
1	1.250	0.8000	1.000	1.0000	0.8000	1.2500	0.0000
2	1.563	0.6400	2.250	0.4445	1.4400	0.6945	0.4445
3	1.953	0.5120	3.813	0.2623	1.9520	0.5123	0.8525
4	2.441	0.4096	5.766	0.1735	2.3616	0.4235	1.2249
5	3.052	0.3277	8.207	0.1219	2.6893	0.3719	1.5631
6	3.815	0.2622	11.259	0.0888	2.9514	0.3388	1.8683
7	4.768	0.2097	15.073	0.0664	3.1611	0.3164	2.1424
8	5.960	0.1678	19.842	0.0504	3.3289	0.3004	2.3873
9	7.451	0.1342	25.802	0.0388	3.4631	0.2888	2.6048
10	9.313	0.1074	33.253	0.0301	3.5705	0.2801	2.7971
11	11.642	0.0859	42.566	0.0235	3.6564	0.2735	2.9663
12	14.552	0.0687	54.208	0.0185	3.7251	0.2685	3.1145
13	18.190	0.0550	68.760	0.0146	3.7801	0.2646	3.2438
14	22.737	0.0440	86.949	0.0115	3.8241	0.2615	3.3560
15	28.422	0.0352	109.687	0.0091	3.8593	0.2591	3.4530
16	35.527	0.0282	138.109	0.0073	3.8874	0.2573	3.5366
17	44.409	0.0225	173.636	0.0058	3.9099	0.2558	3.6084
18	55.511	0.0180	218.045	0.0046	3.9280	0.2546	3.6698
19	69.389	0.0144	273.556	0.0037	3.9424	0.2537	3.7222
20	86.736	0.0115	342.945	0.0029	3.9539	0.2529	3.7667
21	108.420	0.0092	429.681	0.0023	3.9631	0.2523	3.8045
22	135.525	0.0074	538.101	0.0019	3.9705	0.2519	3.8365
23	169.407	0.0059	673.626	0.0015	3.9764	0.2515	3.8634
24	211.758	0.0047	843.033	0.0012	3.9811	0.2512	3.8861
25	264.698	0.0038	1054.791	0.0010	3.9849	0.2510	3.9052
26	330.872	0.0030	1319.489	0.0008	3.9879	0.2508	3.9212
27	413.590	0.0024	1650.361	0.0006	3.9903	0.2506	3.9346
28	516.988	0.0019	2063.952	0.0005	3.9923	0.2505	3.9457
29	646.235	0.0016	2580.939	0.0004	3.9938	0.2504	3.9551
30	807.794	0.0012	3227.174	0.0003	3.9951	0.2503	3.9628
31	1009.742	0.0010	4034.968	0.0003	3.9960	0.2503	3.9693
32	1262.177	0.0008	5044.710	0.0002	3.9968	0.2502	3.9746
33	1577.722	0.0006	6306.887	0.0002	3.9975	0.2502	3.9791
34	1972.152	0.0005	7884.609	0.0001	3.9980	0.2501	3.9828
35	2465.190	0.0004	9856.761	0.0001	3.9984	0.2501	3.9858

TABLE A3.6   30% Interest Factors for Annual Compounding

	Single Payment		Equal Payment Series				Uniform gradient-series factor
	Compound-amount factor	Present-worth factor	Compound-amount factor	Sinking-fund factor	Present-worth factor	Capital-recovery factor	
n	To find F Given P $F/P, i, n$	To find P Given F $P/F, i, n$	To find F Given A $F/A, i, n$	To find A Given F $A/F, i, n$	To find P Given A $P/A, i, n$	To find A Given P $A/P, i, n$	To find A Given G $A/G, i, n$
1	1.300	0.7692	1.000	1.0000	0.7692	1.3000	0.0000
2	1.690	0.5917	2.300	0.4348	1.3610	0.7348	0.4348
3	2.197	0.4552	3.990	0.2506	1.8161	0.5506	0.8271
4	2.856	0.3501	6.187	0.1616	2.1663	0.4616	1.1783
5	3.713	0.2693	9.043	0.1106	2.4356	0.4106	1.4903
6	4.827	0.2072	12.756	0.0784	2.6428	0.3784	1.7655
7	6.275	0.1594	17.583	0.0569	2.8021	0.3569	2.0063
8	8.157	0.1226	23.858	0.0419	2.9247	0.3419	2.2156
9	10.605	0.0943	32.015	0.0312	3.0190	0.3312	2.3963
10	13.786	0.0725	42.620	0.0235	3.0915	0.3235	2.5512
11	17.922	0.0558	56.405	0.0177	3.1473	0.3177	2.6833
12	23.298	0.0429	74.327	0.0135	3.1903	0.3135	2.7952
13	30.288	0.0330	97.625	0.0103	3.2233	0.3103	2.8895
14	39.374	0.0254	127.913	0.0078	3.2487	0.3078	2.9685
15	51.186	0.0195	167.286	0.0060	3.2682	0.3060	3.0345
16	66.542	0.0150	218.472	0.0046	3.2832	0.3046	3.0892
17	86.504	0.0116	285.014	0.0035	3.2948	0.3035	3.1345
18	112.455	0.0089	371.518	0.0027	3.3037	0.3027	3.1718
19	146.192	0.0069	483.973	0.0021	3.3105	0.3021	3.2025
20	190.050	0.0053	630.165	0.0016	3.3158	0.3016	3.2276
21	247.065	0.0041	820.215	0.0012	3.3199	0.3012	3.2480
22	321.184	0.0031	1067.280	0.0009	3.3230	0.3009	3.2646
23	417.539	0.0024	1388.464	0.0007	3 3254	0.3007	3.2781
24	542.801	0.0019	1806.003	0.0006	3.3272	0.3006	3.2890
25	705.641	0.0014	2348.803	0.0004	3.3286	0.3004	3.2979
26	917.333	0.0011	3054.444	0.0003	3.3297	0.3003	3.3050
27	1192.533	0.0008	3971.778	0.0003	3.3305	0.3003	3.3107
28	1550.293	0.0007	5164.311	0.0002	3.3312	0.3002	3.3153
29	2015.381	0.0005	6714.604	0.0002	3.3317	0.3002	3.3189
30	2619.996	0.0004	8729.985	0.0001	3.3321	0.3001	3.3219
31	3405.994	0.0003	11349.981	0.0001	3.3324	0.3001	3.3242
32	4427.793	0.0002	14755.975	0.0001	3.3326	0.3001	3.3261
33	5756.130	0.0002	19183.768	0.0001	3.3328	0.3001	3.3276
34	7482.970	0.0001	24939.899	0.0001	3.3329	0.3001	3.3288
35	9727.860	0.0001	32422.868	0.0000	3.3330	0.3000	3.3297

TABLE A3.7   40% Interest Factors for Annual Compounding

	Single Payment		Equal Payment Series				Uniform gradient-series factor
	Compound-amount factor	Present-worth factor	Compound-amount factor	Sinking-fund factor	Present-worth factor	Capital-recovery factor	
n	To find F Given P $F/P, i, n$	To find P Given F $P/F, i, n$	To find F Given A $F/A, i, n$	To find A Given F $A/F, i, n$	To find P Given A $P/A, i, n$	To find A Given P $A/P, i, n$	To find A Given G $A/G, i, n$
1	1.400	0.7143	1.000	1.0001	0.7143	1.4001	0.0000
2	1.960	0.5103	2.400	0.4167	1.2245	0.8167	0.4167
3	2.744	0.3645	4.360	0.2294	1.5890	0.6294	0.7799
4	3.842	0.2604	7.104	0.1408	1.8493	0.5408	1.0924
5	5.378	0.1860	10.946	0.0914	2.0352	0.4914	1.3580
6	7.530	0.1329	16.324	0.0613	2.1680	0.4613	1.5811
7	10.541	0.0949	23.853	0.0420	2.2629	0.4420	1.7664
8	14.758	0.0678	34.395	0.0291	2.3306	0.4291	1.9186
9	20.661	0.0485	49.153	0.0204	2.3790	0.4204	2.0423
10	28.925	0.0346	69.814	0.0144	2.4136	0.4144	2.1420
11	40.496	0.0247	98.739	0.0102	2.4383	0.4102	2.2215
12	56.694	0.0177	139.234	0.0072	2.4560	0.4072	2.2846
13	79.371	0.0126	195.928	0.0052	2.4686	0.4052	2.3342
14	111.120	0.0090	275.299	0.0037	2.4775	0.4037	2.3729
15	155.568	0.0065	386.419	0.0026	2.4840	0.4026	2.4030
16	217.794	0.0046	541.986	0.0019	2.4886	0.4019	2.4262
17	304.912	0.0033	759.780	0.0014	2.4918	0.4014	2.4441
18	426.877	0.0024	1064.691	0.0010	2.4942	0.4010	2.4578
19	597.627	0.0017	1491.567	0.0007	2.4959	0.4007	2.4682
20	836.678	0.0012	2089.195	0.0005	2.4971	0.4005	2.4761
21	1171.348	0.0009	2925.871	0.0004	2.4979	0.4004	2.4821
22	1639.887	0.0007	4097.218	0.0003	2.4985	0.4003	2.4866
23	2295.842	0.0005	5737.105	0.0002	2.4990	0.4002	2.4900
24	3214.178	0.0004	8032.945	0.0002	2.4993	0.4002	2.4926
25	4499.847	0.0003	11247.110	0.0001	2.4995	0.4001	2.4945
26	6299.785	0.0002	15746.960	0.0001	2.4997	0.4001	2.4959
27	8819.695	0.0002	22046.730	0.0001	2.4998	0.4001	2.4970
28	12347.570	0.0001	30866.430	0.0001	2.4998	0.4001	2.4978
29	17286.590	0.0001	43213.990	0.0001	2.4999	0.4001	2.4984
30	24201.230	0.0001	60500.580	0.0001	2.4999	0.4001	2.4988

TABLE A3.8 50% Interest Factors for Annual Compounding

	Single Payment		Equal Payment Series				Uniform gradient-series factor
	Compound-amount factor	Present-worth factor	Compound-amount factor	Sinking-fund factor	Present-worth factor	Capital-recovery factor	
n	To find *F* Given *P* *F/P, i, n*	To find *P* Given *F* *P/F, i, n*	To find *F* Given *A* *F/A, i, n*	To find *A* Given *F* *A/F, i, n*	To find *P* Given *A* *P/A, i, n*	To find *A* Given *P* *A/P, i, n*	To find *A* Given *G* *A/G, i, n*
1	1.500	0.6667	1.000	1.0000	0.6667	1.5000	0.0001
2	2.250	0.4445	2.500	0.4000	1.1112	0.9001	0.4001
3	3.375	0.2963	4.750	0.2106	1.4075	0.7106	0.7369
4	5.063	0.1976	8.125	0.1231	1.6050	0.6231	1.0154
5	7.594	0.1317	13.188	0.0759	1.7367	0.5759	1.2418
6	11.391	0.0878	20.781	0.0482	1.8245	0.5482	1.4226
7	17.086	0.0586	32.172	0.0311	1.8830	0.5311	1.5649
8	25.629	0.0391	49.258	0.0204	1.9220	0.5204	1.6752
9	38.443	0.0261	74.887	0.0134	1.9480	0.5134	1.7597
10	57.665	0.0174	113.330	0.0089	1.9654	0.5089	1.8236
11	86.498	0.0116	170.995	0.0059	1.9769	0.5059	1.8714
12	129.746	0.0078	257.493	0.0039	1.9846	0.5039	1.9068
13	194.620	0.0052	387.239	0.0026	1.9898	0.5026	1.9329
14	291.929	0.0035	581.858	0.0018	1.9932	0.5018	1.9519
15	437.894	0.0023	873.788	0.0012	1.9955	0.5012	1.9657
16	656.841	0.0016	1311.681	0.0008	1.9970	0.5008	1.9757
17	985.261	0.0011	1968.522	0.0006	1.9980	0.5006	1.9828
18	1477.891	0.0007	2953.783	0.0004	1.9987	0.5004	1.9879
19	2216.837	0.0005	4431.671	0.0003	1.9991	0.5003	1.9915
20	3325.256	0.0004	6648.511	0.0002	1.9994	0.5002	1.9940
21	4987.882	0.0003	9973.765	0.0002	1.9996	0.5002	1.9958
22	7481.824	0.0002	14961.640	0.0001	1.9998	0.5001	1.9971
23	11222.730	0.0001	22443.470	0.0001	1.9999	0.5001	1.9980
24	16834.100	0.0001	33666.210	0.0001	1.9999	0.5001	1.9986
25	25251.160	0.0001	50500.330	0.0001	2.0000	0.5001	1.9991

COMMENTS ON THE USE OF THE INTEREST FACTORS. In using the interest factors, we must be clear as to when the various cash flow transactions represented by *P*, *F*, and *A* occur during the year. The present worth transaction, *P*, occurs at the beginning of the year. *F* and *A* transactions are assumed to be end-of-year cash flows.

Our definitions of the six interest factors were based on 1-year intervals or periods. Actually, interest can be compounded more frequently than annually. Savings accounts are often compounded quarterly. The foregoing interest factors can be adapted to periods other than annual periods. However, for our purposes it will be sufficient and convenient to maintain the annual compounding convention.

part II

High-Volume Production Systems

The traditional symbol of automation is the mechanized flow line. Chronologically, this was the first example of automated production to appear. Its origins can be traced largely to the work of Henry Ford in the manufacture of automobiles. To be sure, Mr. Ford did not invent the automated flow line or its predecessor, the moving assembly line. However, in his efforts to improve the methods of automobile manufacture, he achieved such significant advances in assembly-line mass-production techniques that the feasibility and potential of these methods were demonstrated. In turn, this led to the development of the fully automated transfer line. Because of the contributions of Henry Ford and others in the automotive industry, this type of mechanized production is often referred to as Detroit automation.

This part of the book is concerned with the mass production of discrete products using mechanized and automated flow lines. Chapters 4 and 5 deal with flow lines that perform processing operations on discrete parts. In Chapter 4 we describe the transfer line and similar systems that perform a sequence of operations simultaneously on a number of parts. We examine the various configurations of these transfer systems, their features, and how they work. Chapter 5 is concerned with the quantitative analysis of transfer systems. Certain measures of line performance are defined, and equations are derived for computing these measures of performance.

In Chapters 6 and 7 we consider assembly operations. Assembly is a subject of considerable interest in manufacturing today because of the high cost of labor required to accomplish it. In some industries, assembly operations constitute 30% or more of the total labor cost. There is substantial motivation to perform these operations as efficiently as possible.

Some basic definitions and concepts about the assembly process and the systems used for assembly are presented in Chapter 6. Assembly operations are often carried out on production lines which are very similar to the mechanized flow lines discussed in Chapters 4 and 5. Assembly production lines can be either manually operated or automated. In manual assembly lines, human beings perform the various assembly operations required to put the product or subassembly together. One of the important problems in these manual lines is called line balancing. Chapter 6 includes a discussion of the methods used to solve the line balancing problem.

In Chapter 7 we describe automated assembly systems. Many of the concepts developed in Chapters 4 and 5 for automated processing lines can be applied to automated assembly systems. Equations are derived to compute the performance and operating characteristics of these assembly systems.

chapter 4

Detroit-Type Automation

In this chapter we consider the automated equipment used in the processing of discrete parts in large volumes. The equipment is often in the configuration of mechanically integrated flow lines, consisting of a number of workstations that perform the processing operations on the line. These flow lines are called transfer machines or transfer lines. The methods used to transport parts between stations are examined in this chapter as well as the other features that characterize these production systems. We emphasize machining operations as the typical process carried out on these systems, although the automated flow line concept is used in a variety of industries and processes.

4.1 AUTOMATED FLOW LINES

An automated flow line consists of several machines or workstations which are linked together by work handling devices that transfer parts between the stations. The transfer of workparts occurs automatically and the workstations carry out their specialized functions automatically. The flow line can be symbolized as shown in Figure 4.1 using the symbols presented in Table 4.1. A raw workpart enters one end of the line and the processing steps are performed sequentially as the part moves from one station to the

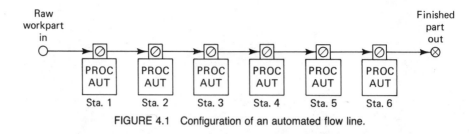

FIGURE 4.1   Configuration of an automated flow line.

next. It is possible to incorporate buffer storage zones into the flow line, either at a single location or between every workstation. It is also possible to include inspection stations in the line to automatically perform intermediate checks on the quality of the workparts. Manual stations might also be located along the flow line to perform certain operations

TABLE 4.1   Symbols used in the Production Systems Diagrams

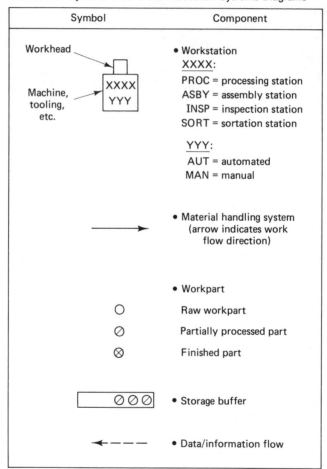

which are difficult or uneconomical to automate. These various features of mechanized flow lines will be discussed in subsequent sections.

Automated flow lines are generally the most appropriate means of production in cases of relatively stable product life; high product demand, which requires high rates of production; and where the alternative method of manufacture would involve a large labor content. The objectives of the use of flow line automation are, therefore:

To reduce labor costs

To increase production rates

To reduce work-in-process

To minimize distances moved between operations

To achieve specialization of operations

To achieve integration of operations

Although Figure 4.1 shows the flow pattern of operations in a straight line, there are actually two general forms that the work flow can take. These two configurations are in-line and rotary.

In-line type

The *in-line* configuration consists of a sequence of workstations in a more-or-less straight-line arrangement. The flow of work can take a few 90° turns, either for workpiece reorientation, factory layout limitations, or other reasons, and still qualify as a straight-line configuration. A common pattern of work flow, for example, is a rectangular shape, which would allow the same operator to load the starting workpieces and unload the finished workpieces. An example of an in-line transfer machine used for metal-cutting operations is illustrated in Figure 4.2.

Rotary type

In the *rotary* configuration, the workparts are indexed around a circular table or dial. The workstations are stationary and usually located around the outside periphery of the dial. The parts ride on the rotating table and are registered or positioned, in turn, at each station for its processing or assembly operation. This type of equipment is often referred to as an *indexing machine* or *dial index machine* and the configuration is shown in Figure 4.3.

Selection

The choice between the two types depends on the application. The rotary type is commonly limited to smaller workpieces and to fewer stations. There is generally not as much flexibility in the design of the rotary configuration. For example, the dial-type design does not lend itself to providing for buffer storage capacity. On the other hand, the rotary

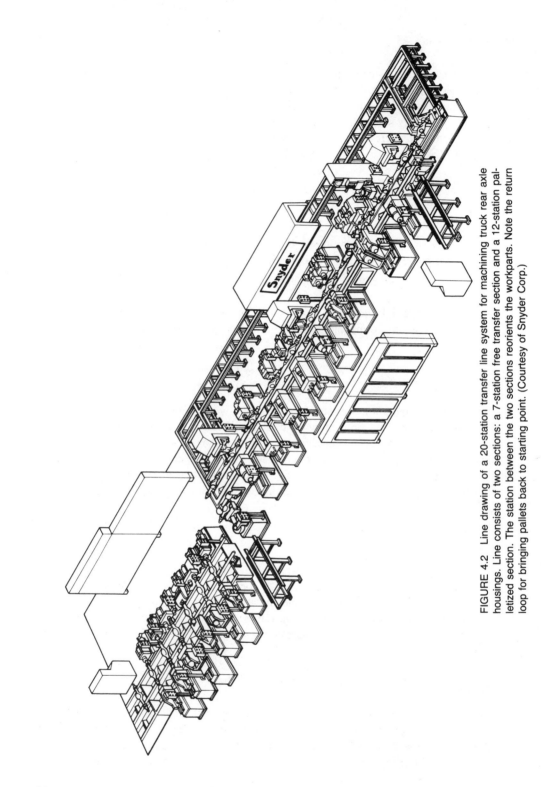

FIGURE 4.2 Line drawing of a 20-station transfer line system for machining truck rear axle housings. Line consists of two sections: a 7-station free transfer section and a 12-station palletized section. The station between the two sections reorients the workparts. Note the return loop for bringing pallets back to starting point. (Courtesy of Snyder Corp.)

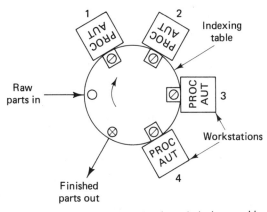

FIGURE 4.3   Configuration of a rotary indexing machine.

configuration usually involves a lower-cost piece of equipment and typically requires less factory floor space.

The in-line design is preferable for larger workpieces and can accommodate a larger number of workstations. The number of stations on the dial index machine is more limited due to the size of the dial. In-line machines can be fabricated with a built-in storage capability to smooth out the effect of work stoppages at individual stations and other irregularities.

4.2   METHODS OF WORKPART TRANSPORT

The transfer mechanism of the automated flow line must not only move the partially completed workparts or assemblies between adjacent stations, it must also orient and locate the parts in the correct position for processing at each station. The general methods of transporting workpieces on flow lines can be classified into the following three categories:

1.   Continuous transfer
2.   Intermittent or synchronous transfer
3.   Asynchronous or power-and-free transfer

These three categories are distinguished by the type of motion that is imparted to the workpiece by the transfer mechanism. The most appropriate type of transport system for a given application depends on such factors as:

The types of operation to be performed
The number of stations on the line
The weight and size of the workparts

Whether manual stations are included on the line

Production rate requirements

Balancing the various process times on the line

Before discussing the three types of work transport system, we should try to clarify a possible source of confusion. These transfer systems are used for both processing and assembly operations. In the case of automatic assembly machines, we are referring to the mechanisms that transport the partially completed assemblies between stations, not the feed mechanisms that present new components to the assemblies at a particular station. The devices that feed and orient the components are normally an integral part of the workstation. We take a closer look at these devices in Chapter 7 when we discuss automatic assembly in more detail.

Continuous transfer

With the continuous method of transfer, the workparts are moved continuously at constant speed. This requires the workheads to move during processing in order to maintain continuous registration with the workpart. For some types of operations, this movement of the workheads during processing is not feasible. It would be difficult, for example, to use this type of system on a machining transfer line because of inertia problems due to the size and weight of the workheads. In other cases, continuous transfer would be very practical. Examples of its use are in beverage bottling operations, packaging, manual assembly operations where the human operator can move with the moving flow line, and relatively simple automatic assembly tasks. In some bottling operations, for instance, the bottles are transported around a continuously rotating drum. Beverage is discharged into the moving bottles by spouts located at the drum's periphery. The advantage of this application is that the liquid beverage is kept moving at a steady speed and hence there are no inertia problems.

Continuous transfer systems are relatively easy to design and fabricate and can achieve a high rate of production.

Intermittent transfer

As the name suggests, in this method the workpieces are transported with an intermittent or discontinuous motion. The workstations are fixed in position and the parts are moved between stations and then registered at the proper locations for processing. All workparts are transported at the same time and, for this reason, the term "synchronous transfer system" is also used to describe this method of workpart transport. Examples of applications of the intermittent transfer of workparts can be found in machining operations, pressworking operations or progressive dies, and mechanized assembly. Most of the transfer mechanisms reviewed in Section 4.3 provide the intermittent or synchronous type of workpart transport.

Asynchronous transfer

This system of transfer, also referred to as a "power-and-free system," allows each workpart to move to the next station when processing at the current station has been completed. Each part moves independently of other parts. Hence, some parts are being processed on the line at the same time that others are being transported between stations.

Asynchronous transfer systems offer the opportunity for greater flexibility than do the other two systems, and this flexibility can be a great advantage in certain circumstances. In-process storage of workparts can be incorporated into the asynchronous systems with relative ease. Power-and-free systems can also compensate for line balancing problems where there are significant differences in process times between stations. Parallel stations or several series stations can be used for the longer operations, and single stations can be used for the shorter operations. Therefore, the average production rates can be approximately equalized. Asynchronous lines are often used where there are one or more manually operated stations and cycle-time variations would be a problem on either the continuous or synchronous transport systems. Larger workparts can be handled on the asynchronous systems. A disadvantage of the power-and-free systems is that the cycle rates are generally slower than for the other types.

Pallet fixtures

The transfer system is sometimes designed to accommodate some sort of pallet fixture. Workparts are attached to the pallet fixtures and the pallets are transferred between stations, carrying the part through its sequence of operations. The pallet fixture is designed so that it can be conveniently moved, located, and clamped in position at successive stations. Since the part is accurately located in the fixture, it is therefore correctly positioned for each operation. In addition to the obvious advantage of convenient transfer and location of workparts, another advantage of pallet fixtures is that they can be designed to be used for a variety of similar parts.

The other method of workpart location and fixturing does not use pallets. With this method, the workparts themselves are indexed from station to station. When a part arrives at a station, it is automatically clamped in position for the operation.

The obvious benefit of this transfer method is that it avoids the cost of pallet fixtures.

4.3 TRANSFER MECHANISMS

There are various types of transfer mechanisms used to move parts between stations. These mechanisms can be grouped into two types: those used to provide linear travel for in-line machines, and those used to provide rotary motion for dial indexing machines.

Linear transfer mechanisms

We will explain the operation of three of the typical mechanisms: the walking beam transfer bar system, the powered roller conveyor system, and the chain-drive conveyor system. This is not a complete listing of all types, but it is a representative sample.

WALKING BEAM SYSTEMS.   With the walking beam transfer mechanism, the work-parts are lifted up from their workstation locations by a transfer bar and moved one position ahead, to the next station. The transfer bar then lowers the parts into nests which position them more accurately for processing. This type of transfer device is illustrated in Figure 4.4.

POWERED ROLLER CONVEYOR SYSTEM.   This type of system is used in general stock handling systems as well as in automated flow lines. The conveyor can be used to move parts or pallets possessing flat riding surfaces. The rollers can be powered by either

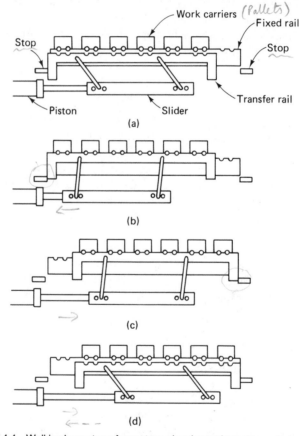

FIGURE 4.4   Walking beam transfer system, showing various stages during transfer cycle. (Reprinted from Boothroyd and Redford [1].)

of two mechanisms. The first is a belt drive, in which a flat moving belt beneath the rollers provides the rotation of the rollers by friction. A chain drive is the second common mechanism used to power the rollers. Powered roller conveyors are versatile transfer systems because they can be used to divert work pallets into workstations or alternate tracks. We discuss roller conveyor systems in Chapter 14.

CHAIN-DRIVE CONVEYOR SYSTEM. Figure 4.5 illustrates this type of transfer system. Either a chain or a flexible steel belt is used to transport the work carriers. The chain is driven by pulleys in either an "over-and-under" configuration, in which the pulleys turn about a horizontal axis, or an "around-the-corner" configuration, in which the pulleys rotate about a vertical axis.

This general type of transfer system can be used for continuous, intermittent, or nonsynchronous movement of workparts. In the nonsynchronous motion, the workparts are pulled by friction or ride on an oil film along a track with the chain or belt providing the movement. It is necessary to provide some sort of final location for the workparts when they arrive at their respective stations.

Rotary transfer mechanisms

There are several methods used to index a circular table or dial at various equal angular positions corresponding to workstation locations. Those described below are meant to be a representative rather than a complete listing.

RACK AND PINION. This mechanism is simple but is not considered especially suited to the high-speed operation often associated with indexing machines. The device is pictured in Figure 4.6 and uses a piston to drive the rack, which causes the pinion gear and attached indexing table to rotate. A clutch or other device is used to provide rotation in the desired direction.

RATCHET AND PAWL. This drive mechanism is shown in Figure 4.7. Its operation is simple but somewhat unreliable, owing to wear and sticking of several of the components.

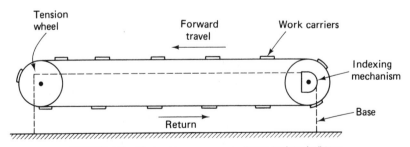

FIGURE 4.5 Chain-driven conveyor, "over-and-under" type.

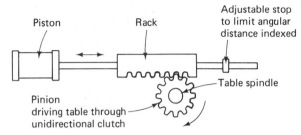

FIGURE 4.6   Rack-and-pinion mechanism for rotary indexing table. (Reprinted from Boothroyd and Redford [1].)

GENEVA MECHANISM.   The two previous mechanisms convert a linear motion into a rotational motion. The Geneva mechanism uses a continuously rotating driver to index the table, as pictured in Figure 4.8. If the driven member has six slots for a six-station dial indexing machine, each turn of the driver will cause the table to advance one-sixth of a turn. The driver only causes movement of the table through a portion of its rotation. For a six-slotted driven member, 120° of a complete rotation of the driver is used to index the table. The other 240° is dwell. For a four-slotted driven member, the ratio would be 90° for index and 270° for dwell. The usual number of indexings per revolution of the table is four, five, six, and eight.

EXAMPLE 4.1

Let us examine the operation of a six-slotted Geneva mechanism. Suppose that the driver rotates at 6 rpm. Determine the cycle time of the indexing machine, the process time, and the time spent each cycle in indexing the table to the next work position.

Solution:

As indicated above, for a six-slotted Geneva mechanism, the driver spends 120° of its rotation to index the table, and the remaining 240° of rotation correspond to dwell of the table. At 6 rev/min,

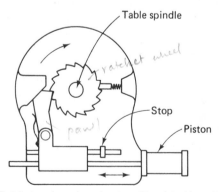

FIGURE 4.7   Ratchet-and-pawl mechanism. (Reprinted from Boothroyd and Redford [1].)

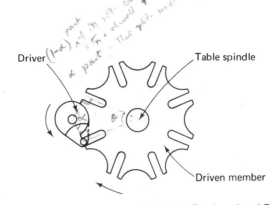

Driver

Table spindle

Driven member

FIGURE 4.8   Geneva mechanism. (Reprinted from Boothroyd and Redford [1].)

the cycle time of the indexing machine is 10 s. The portion of this cycle time devoted to processing (dwell of the indexing table) is 240/360 = 0.667. This corresponds to 6.67 s. The indexing time is 120/360 = 0.333 × 10 s = 3.33 s.

CAM MECHANISMS.   Various forms of cam mechanism, an example of which is illustrated in Figure 4.9, provide probably the most accurate and reliable method of indexing the dial. They are in widespread use in industry despite the fact that the cost is relatively high compared to alternative mechanisms. The cam can be designed to give a variety of velocity and dwell characteristics.

4.4 BUFFER STORAGE

Automated flow lines are often equipped with additional features beyond the basic transfer mechanisms and workstations. For example, the idea of using a buffer storage capacity between stations was introduced in Section 4.1. It is not uncommon for production flow lines to include storage zones for collecting banks of workparts along the line. One example of the use of storage zones would be two intermittent transfer systems, each

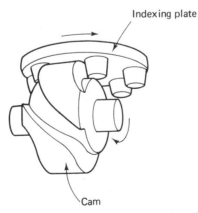

Indexing plate

Cam

FIGURE 4.9   Cam mechanism. (Reprinted from Boothroyd and Redford [1].)

without any storage capacity, linked together with a workpart inventory area. It is possible to connect three, four, or even more lines in this manner. Another example of workpart storage on flow lines is the asynchronous transfer line. With this system, it is possible to provide a bank of workparts for every station on the line.

There are two principal reasons for the use of buffer storage zones. The first is to reduce the effect of individual station breakdowns on the line operation. The continuous or intermittent transfer system acts as a single integrated machine. When breakdowns occur at the individual stations or when preventive maintenance is applied to the machine, production must be halted. In many cases, the proportion of time the line spends out of operation can be significant, perhaps reaching 50% or more. Some of the common reasons for line stoppages are:

Tool failures or tool adjustments at individual processing stations

Scheduled tool changes

Defective workparts or components at assembly stations, which require that the feed mechanism be cleared

Feed hopper needs to be replenished at an assembly station

Limit switch or other electrical malfunction

Mechanical failure of transfer system or workstation

When a breakdown occurs on an automated flow line, the purpose of the buffer storage zone is to allow a portion of the line to continue operating while the remaining portion is stopped and under repair. For example, assume that a 20-station line is divided into two sections and connected by a parts storage zone which automatically collects parts from the first section and feeds them to the second section. If a station jam were to cause the first section of the line to stop, the second section could continue to operate as long as the supply of parts in the buffer zone lasts. Similarly, if the second section were to shut down, the first section could continue to operate as long as there is room in the buffer zone to store parts. Hopefully, the average production rate on the first section would be about equal to that of the second section. By dividing the line and using the storage area, the average production rate would be improved over the original 20-station flow line. A quantitative analysis of the effect of adding buffer inventory zones will be presented in Chapter 5. Figure 4.10 illustrates the case of two processing lines separated by a storage buffer.

The second reason for using storage on flow lines is to smooth out the effects of

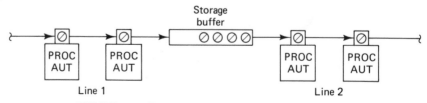

FIGURE 4.10   Two flow lines separated by storage buffer.

variations in cycle times. These variations occur either between stations or, in the case of flow lines with one or more manual stations, they can occur from cycle to cycle at the same station. To illustrate the second case, suppose that we are considering an assembly line on which all the stations are mechanized except one. The manual station requires the operator to perform an alignment of two components and the time required tends to vary from cycle to cycle. For the transfer system in this line, we must choose between a synchronous system with no parts storage capacity and an asynchronous system which allows a "float" of parts ahead of each station. To illustrate this difference in operation, let us consider the following example.

EXAMPLE 4.2

Assume that we have collected data on the operation and found the following distribution of operation times for a total of 100 cycles: 7 s: two occurrences, or 2%; 8 s: 10%; 9 s: 18%; 10 s: 38%; 11 s: 20% and 12 s: 12%. This gives an average of 10 s. If this manual operation were used on the synchronous machine, the line would have to be set up with cycle time of 12 s to allow the operator time to finish all assemblies. This would give a production rate of 300 units/h from the line. If the cycle time were adjusted to 11 s, the cycle rate would increase to 327 per hour, but the operator would be unable to complete 12% of the assemblies. Thus, the actual production rate of completed assemblies would be only 288 units/h. If the cycle time were decreased to 10 s, the cycle rate would increase to 360 per hour. However, the operator would be unable to complete the assemblies requiring 11 s and 12 s. The actual production rate would suffer a decrease to 245 units/h.

With the asynchronous transfer system, the line could be arranged to collect a bank of workparts immediately before and after the manual station. Thus, the operator would be allowed a range of times to complete the alignment process. As long as the operator's average time were compatible with the cycle time of the transfer system, the flow line would run smoothly. The line cycle time could be set at 10 s and the production rate would be 360 good assemblies per hour.

The disadvantages of buffer storage on flow lines are increased factory floor space, higher in-process inventory, more material handling equipment, and greater complexity of the overall flow line system. The benefits of buffer storage are often great enough to more than compensate for these disadvantages.

4.5 CONTROL FUNCTIONS

Controlling an automated flow line is a complex problem, owing to the sheer number of sequential steps that must be carried out. There are three main functions that are utilized to control the operation of an automatic transfer system. The first of these is an operational requirement, the second is a safety requirement, and the third is dedicated to improving quality.

1. *Sequence control.* The purpose of this function is to coordinate the sequence of actions of the transfer system and its workstations. The various activities of the automated flow line must be carried out with split-second timing and accuracy. On a metal machining transfer line, for example, the workparts must be transported, located, and clamped in place before the workheads can begin to feed. Sequence control is basic to the operation of the flow line.

2. *Safety monitoring.* This function ensures that the transfer system does not operate in an unsafe or hazardous condition. Sensing devices may be added to make certain that the cutting tool status is satisfactory to continue to process the workpart in the case of a machining-type transfer line. Other checks might include monitoring certain critical steps in the sequence control function to make sure that these steps have all been performed and in the correct order. Hydraulic or air pressures might also be checked if these are crucial to the operation of automated flow lines.

3. *Quality monitoring.* The third control function is to monitor certain quality attributes of the workpart. Its purpose is to identify and possibly reject defective workparts and assemblies. The inspection devices required to perform quality monitoring are sometimes incorporated into existing processing stations. In other cases, separate stations are included in the line for the sole purpose of inspecting the workpart.

It is possible to extend the notion of quality monitoring and to incorporate a control loop into the flow line as illustrated in Figure 4.11. An inspection station would be used to monitor certain quality characteristics of the part and to feed back information to the preceding workstations so that adjustments in the process could be made.

The traditional means of controlling the sequence of steps on the transfer system has been to use electromechanical relays. Relays are employed to maintain the proper order of activating the workheads, transfer mechanism, and other peripheral devices on the line. However, owing to their comparatively large size and relative unreliability, relays have lost ground to other control devices, such as programmable controllers and computers. These more modern components offer opportunities for a higher level of control over the flow line, particularly in the areas of safety monitoring and quality monitoring.

Conventional thinking on the control of the line has been to stop operation when a malfunction occurred. While there are certain malfunctions representing unsafe conditions that demand shutdown of the line, there are other situations where stoppage of the line is not required and perhaps not even desirable. For example, take the case of a feed mechanism on an automatic assembly machine that fails to feed its component. Assuming that the failures are random and infrequent, it may be better to continue to operate the machine and lock out the affected assembly from further operations. If the

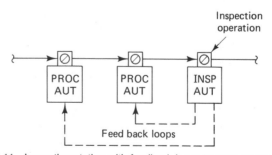

FIGURE 4.11   Inspection station with feedback loops to upstream workstations.

assembly machine were stopped, production would be lost at all other stations while the machine is down. Deciding whether it is better to stay in operation or stop the line must be based on the probabilities and economics of the particular case. The point is that there are alternative control strategies to choose between, instantaneous control and memory control.

     1. *Instantaneous control.* This mode of control stops the operation of the flow line immediately when a malfunction is detected. It is relatively simple, inexpensive, and trouble-free. Diagnostic features are often added to the system to aid in identifying the location and cause of the trouble to the operator so that repairs can be quickly made. However, stopping the machine results in loss of production from the entire line, and this is the system's biggest drawback.

     2. *Memory control.* In contrast to instantaneous control, the memory system is designed to keep the machine operating. It works to control quality and/or protect the machine by preventing subsequent stations from processing the particular workpart and by segregating the part as defective at the end of the line. The premise upon which memory-type control is based is that the failures which occur at the stations will be random and infrequent. If, however, the station failures result from cause (a workhead that has gone out of alignment, for example) and tend to repeat, the memory system will not improve production but, rather, degrade it. The flow line will continue to operate, with the consequence that bad parts will continue to be produced. For this reason, a counter is sometimes used so that if a failure occurs at the same station for two or three consecutive cycles, the memory logic will cause the machine to stop for repairs.

4.6 AUTOMATION FOR MACHINING OPERATIONS

Transfer systems have been designed to perform a great variety of different metal-cutting processes. In fact, it is difficult to think of machining operations that must be excluded from the list. Typical applications include operations such as milling, boring, drilling, reaming, and tapping. However, it is also feasible to carry out operations such as turning and grinding on transfer-type systems.

     There are various types of mechanized and automated machines that perform a sequence of operations simultaneously on different workparts. These include dial indexing machines, trunnion machines, and transfer lines. To consider these machines in approximately the order of increasing complexity, we begin with one that really does not belong in the list at all, the single-station machine.

Single-station machine

These mechanized production machines perform several operations on a single workpart which is fixtured in one position throughout the cycle. The operations are performed on several different surfaces by workheads located around the piece. The available space surrounding a stationary workpiece limits the number of machining heads that can be used. This limit on the number of operations is the principal disadvantage of the single-station machine. Production rates are usually low to medium.

Rotary indexing machine

To achieve higher rates of production, the rotary indexing machine performs a sequence of machining operations on several workparts simultaneously. Parts are fixtured on a horizontal circular table or dial, and indexed between successive stations. An example of a dial indexing machine is shown in Figure 4.12.

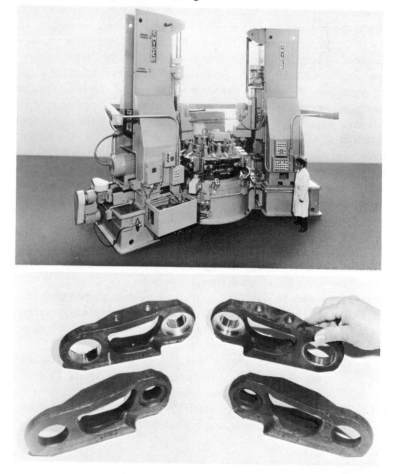

FIGURE 4.12 (Top view) Five-station dial index machine showing vertical and horizontal machining stations around periphery of rotary table. (Bottom view) Rough forgings and finished parts processed on the dial index machine. (Courtesy of Snyder Corp.)

Trunnion machine

This machine, shown in Figure 4.13, uses a vertical drum mounted on a horizontal axis, so it is a variation of the dial indexing machine. The vertical drum is called a trunnion. Mounted on it are several fixtures which hold the workparts during processing.

Trunnion machines are most suitable for small workpieces. The configuration of the machine, with a vertical rather than a horizontal indexing dial, provides the opportunity to perform operations on opposite sides of the workpart. Additional stations can be located on the outside periphery of the trunnion if this is required. The trunnion-type machine is appropriate for workparts in the medium production range.

Center column machine

Another version of the dial indexing arrangement is the center column type, pictured in Figure 4.14. In addition to the radial machining heads located around the periphery of the horizontal table, vertical units are mounted on the center column of the machine. This increases the number of machining operations that can be performed as compared

FIGURE 4.13   Six-station trunnion machine. (Courtesy of Snyder Corp.)

FIGURE 4.14   Ten-station center column machine that can be tooled for 34 different pump housing components. (Courtesy of Snyder Corp.)

to the regular dial indexing type. The center column machine is considered to be a high-production machine which makes efficient use of floor space.

Transfer machine

The most highly automated and versatile of the machines is the transfer line, illustrated in Figures 4.2 and 4.15. The workstations are arranged in a straight-line flow pattern and parts are transferred automatically from station to station. The transfer system can be synchronous or asynchronous, workparts can be transported with or without pallet fixtures, buffer storage can be incorporated into the line operation if desired, and a variety of different monitoring and control features can be used to manage the line. Hence, the transfer machine offers the greatest flexibility of any of the machines discussed. The

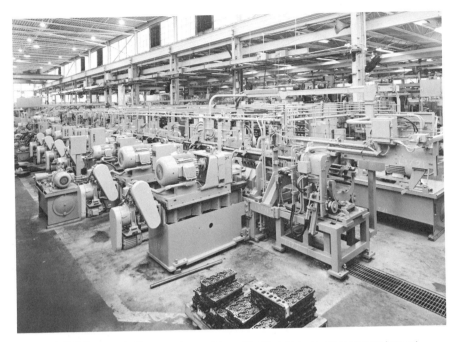

FIGURE 4.15   In-line transfer machine with 33 stations to process cast-iron cylinder heads in foreground. (Courtesy of F. Jos. Lamb Co.)

transfer line can accommodate larger workpieces than the rotary-type indexing systems. Also, the number of stations, and therefore the number of operations, which can be included on the line is greater than for the circular arrangement. The transfer line has traditionally been used for machining a single product in high quantities over long production runs. More recently, transfer machines have been designed for ease of changeover to allow several different but similar workparts to be produced on the same line. These attempts to introduce flexibility into transfer line design add to the appeal of these high-production systems.

4.7   DESIGN AND FABRICATION CONSIDERATIONS

When a manufacturing firm decides that some form of automated flow line represents the best method of producing a particular workpart or assembly, there are then a series of specifications that must be decided. In designing and building an automated flow line, some of the details to consider are the following:

Whether the flow line is to be engineered in-house or by a machine tool builder

Size, weight, geometry, and material if a processed workpart

Size, weights, and number of components if an assembly

Tolerance requirements

Type and sequence of operations

Production-rate requirements

Type of transfer system

Methods of fixturing and locating workparts

Methods of orienting and feeding components in the case of assemblies

Reliability of individual stations and transfer mechanisms, as well as overall reliability of the line

Buffer storage capability

Ease of maintenance

Control features desired

Floor space available

Flexibility of line in terms of possible future changes in product design

Flexibility of line to accommodate more than a single workpart

Initial cost of the line

Operational and tooling cost for the line

In developing the concept for a mechanized flow line, there are two general approaches that can be considered. The first is to use standard machine tools and other pieces of processing equipment at the workstations and to connect them with standard or special material handling equipment. The material handling hardware serves as the transfer system and moves, feeds, and ejects the work between the standard machines. The line of machines is sometimes referred to as a *link line*. The individual machines must either be capable of operating on an automatic cycle or they must be manually operated. There may also be fixturing and location problems at the stations which are difficult to solve without some form of human assistance during the cycle. A firm will often prefer the link line because it can be made up from machine tools that are already in the plant, these machine tools can be reused when the production run is finished, and there is less debugging and maintenance. These flow lines can also be engineered by personnel within the firm, perhaps with the aid of material handling experts. The limitation of these flow lines is that they favor simpler workpiece shapes and smaller sizes since the work handling equipment is less sophisticated and more general-purpose. Greater future use of industrial robots as material handling devices will increase the attractiveness of the link line. This type of flow line is used in such processes as plating and finishing operations, press-working, rolling mill operations, gear manufacturing, and a variety of machining operations.

The alternative approach to developing an automated line is to turn the problem over to a machine tool builder specializing in the fabrication of transfer lines, assembly machines, or other flow line equipment. Using the customer's blueprints and specifications, the builder will submit a proposal for the line. Typically, several machine tool

FIGURE 4.16　Standard rotary table component used on dial indexing machines. (Courtesy of Ferguson Machine Co.)

FIGURE 4.17　Standard power feed unit used on machining transfer lines. (Courtesy of Ferguson Machine Co.)

builders will be asked to make proposals. Each proposed design will be based on the machine components comprising the builder's product line as well as the ingenuity and experience of the engineer preparing the proposal.

Once a particular proposal is accepted, the machine tool builder will proceed with the final detailed design. The resulting machine will utilize a "building-block" principle. That is, the specialized flow line, designed to produce the customer's particular product, will be constructed out of standard components. These standard components consist of the base or transfer system, and workheads for performing the various processing or assembly operations. These standard components will be fabricated into the special configuration required for the customer's product. Several examples of these standard transfer line components are pictured in Figures 4.16 and 4.17. For metal-cutting transfer lines, the workheads consist of the feed mechanism, spindle, and power source. The workheads must then be fitted with special tools to carry out the particular process. These workheads do not have a frame or worktable. Instead, they are attached to the transfer system frame, which has been specially adapted for the workpart. When a flow line has been fabricated using this building-block principle, it is sometimes referred to as a *unitized flow line*. The standard machine tool components all go together and act as a single mechanical unit.

Higher production rates are generally possible with unitized construction compared to link lines. Also, less floor space is required because the unitized lines are typically much more compact. The higher cost of unitized equipment makes it suitable only for long production runs and on products not subject to frequent design changes. Equipment obsolescence becomes a danger if these two requirements are not met. Applications of this type of flow line construction are found in transfer lines for machining automotive engine parts and in assembly machines for pens, small hardware items, electrical assemblies, and so on. Figures 4.2, 4.12, 4.13, 4.14, and 4.15 illustrate this type of flow line construction.

REFERENCES

[1] BOOTHROYD, G., and A. H. REDFORD, *Mechanized Assembly,* McGraw-Hill Publishing Co., London, 1968.

[2] DROZDA, T. J., and C. WICK, Editors, *Tool and Manufacturing Engineers Handbook,* 4th ed., Volume I, Society of Manufacturing Engineers, Dearborn, Mich. 1983, Chapter 15.

[3] EARY, D., and G. E. JOHNSON, *Process Engineering for Manufacturing,* Prentice-Hall, Inc., Englewood Cliffs, N.J., 1962, Chapter 13.

[4] LAWSON, E. A., F. E. BLOCK, F. J. LONG, and D. C. COONFER, "Transfer Machines Today," *Automation,* June 1971.

[5] RILEY, F. J., "Selecting Controls for Automatic Assembly," *Manufacturing Engineering and Management,* Part I, October 1974; Part II, November 1974.

PROBLEMS

4.1. For the eight-slotted driven member of the Geneva mechanism in Figure 4.8, determine the proportion of each complete revolution of the driver that motion is being imparted to the driven member. Express this in degrees. How many degrees of rotation represent dwell?

4.2. A Geneva mechanism with a six-slotted driven member is used in a dial-type assembly machine. The longest assembly operation takes exactly 1 s to complete, so the driven member must be in a stopped (dwell) position for this length of time.
(a) At what rotational speed must the driver be turned to accomplish this 1-s dwell?
(b) How much time will be required to index the dial to the next position?
(c) Determine the ideal production rate of the assembly machine if each index of the dial produces a completed workpart.

4.3. A certain transfer line performs a sequence of machining and assembly operations. One of the assembly operations near the end of the line is performed manually. The distribution of operation times for the manual station is given in the following table.

Operation time(s)	Frequency of occurrence (%)
15	2.7
16	6.1
17	12.1
18	25.9
19	32.1
20	10.9
21	6.9
22	3.3
	100.0

The slowest automatic station has a cycle time of 18 s.
(a) If the line uses a synchronous (intermittent) transfer system, determine the cycle rate and actual production rate per hour if the transfer system were set to index parts at each of the following intervals: once every 22 s, 21 s, 20 s, 19 s, 18 s. Time taken to move parts is negligible.
(b) If an asynchronous parts transfer system were used on this line to accumulate a float of parts before the manual station, at what cycle rate should the system be operated? Determine the corresponding production rate.

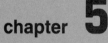

chapter **5**

Analysis
of Automated Flow Lines

In analyzing the performance of automated flow lines, two general problem areas must be distinguished. The first is related to the production processes used on the line. For example, consider a transfer line that performs a series of machining operations. There is an extensive body of knowledge related to the theory and practice of metal machining. This technology includes the proper specification and use of cutting tools, the metallurgy and machinability of the work material, chip control, machining economics, machine tool vibrations, and a host of other topics. Many of the problems encountered in the operation of a metal-cutting transfer line are directly related to and can be solved by the application of good machining principles. The same is true for other production processes. In each area of production, a technology has developed after many years of research and practical experience in the area. By making the best use of the given process technology, each individual workstation on the line can be made to operate at or near its maximum productive capability. However, even if it were possible to operate each station in an optimal way, this does not guarantee that the overall flow line will be optimized.

It is with this viewpoint of the overall flow line operation that we identify the second general problem area of flow line performance. This second area is concerned with the systems aspects of designing and running the line. Normally associated with the operation of an automated flow line is the problem of reliability. Since the line often operates as a single mechanism, failure of one component of the mechanism will often result in stoppage of the entire line. There are approaches to this problem that transcend the manufacturing processes at individual stations. What is the effect of the number of workstations on the performance of the line? How much improvement can be obtained by using one or more buffer storage zones? What is the effect of component quality on the operation of an automated assembly machine? How will the use of manual workstations affect the line? These are questions that can be analyzed using a systems approach.

In addition to the reliability problem, another systems design problem is one of properly balancing the line. In line balancing, the objective is to spread the total work load as evenly as possible among the stations in the line. The problem is normally associated with the design of manual assembly lines. It is also a consideration in automated flow lines, but the reliability problem usually predominates. We will consider line balancing in Chapter 6. The reliability of the line will be the principal concern of the present chapter.

5.1 GENERAL TERMINOLOGY AND ANALYSIS

Flow line performance can be analyzed by means of three basic measures: average production rate, proportion of time the line is operating (line efficiency), and cost per item produced on the line. We will concern ourselves initially with flow lines that possess no internal buffer storage capacity.

To begin the analysis, we must assume certain basic characteristics about the operation of the line. A synchronous transfer system is assumed. Parts are introduced into the first workstation and are processed and transported at regular intervals to succeeding stations. This interval defines the ideal or theoretical cycle time T_c of the flow line. T_c is equal to the time required for parts to transfer plus the processing time at the longest workstation. The processing times at different stations will not be the same. Long holes take more time to drill than short holes. A milling operation may take longer than a tapping operation. The stations which require less time than the longest station will have a certain amount of idle time. The components of T_c are illustrated graphically in Figure 5.1.

Because of breakdowns of the line, the actual average production time T_p will be longer than the ideal cycle time. When a breakdown occurs at any one station, we assume

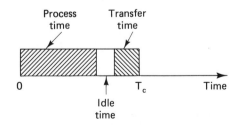

FIGURE 5.1   Components of cycle time at a typical workstation on a transfer line.

that the entire line is shut down. Let T_d represent the average downtime to diagnose the problem and make repairs when a breakdown occurs. Since there may be more than one reason why a line is down, it is sometimes convenient to distinguish between the different reasons by subscripting the term as T_{dj}. The subscript j is used to identify the reason for the breakdown (e.g., tool failure, part jam, feed mechanism, etc.). The frequency with which line stops per cycle occur for reason j is denoted by F_j. Multiplying the frequency F_j by the average downtime per stop T_{dj} gives the mean time per cycle the machine will be down for reason j. If there is only one reason why the transfer machine may be down, the average production time T_p is given by

$$T_p = T_c + FT_d \qquad (5.1)$$

The effect of this apportioned downtime on the cycle time is illustrated in Figure 5.2.

If there are several reasons why the line is down and we wish to distinguish among them, the average production time becomes

$$T_p = T_c + \sum_j F_j T_{dj} \qquad (5.2)$$

It is possible that there are interactions between some of the causes of line stops. For example, if we were to introduce a scheduled maintenance or tool change program, this would presume to favorably influence the frequency of unplanned station breakdowns.

One of the important measures of performance for a transfer line is the average production rate R_p. We must differentiate between this production rate, which represents the actual output of the machine, and the theoretical production rate. The actual average production rate is based on the average production time T_p:

incl. defective parts (in this context)

$$R_p = \frac{1}{T_p} \qquad (5.3)$$

If the flow line produces less than a 100% yield, this production rate must be adjusted for the yield. For example, if 2% of the workparts are scrapped during processing, the production rate would be 98% of that calculated by Eq. (5.3). The theoretical production rate of the flow line, rarely achieved in practice, is computed as

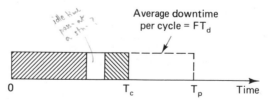

FIGURE 5.2   Apportioned downtime added to cycle time to obtain average production time.

$$R_c = \frac{1}{T_c} \tag{5.4}$$

The machine tool builder will use this value in describing the flow line, and will speak of it as the production rate at 100% efficiency. Unfortunately, the machine will not operate at 100% efficiency.

The line efficiency E is simply the proportion of time the line is up and operating. We can compute it as follows:

uptime ~ proportion
$$E = \frac{T_c}{T_p} = \frac{T_c}{T_c + FT_d} \tag{5.5}$$

An alternative measure of performance is the proportion of downtime D on the line:

$$D = \frac{FT_d}{T_p} = \frac{FT_d}{T_c + FT_d} \tag{5.6}$$

Certainly, the downtime proportion and the uptime proportion must add to 1:

$$E + D = 1 \tag{5.7}$$

The third measure of flow line performance is the cost per item produced. Let C_m equal the cost of raw materials per product, where the product refers to the unit of output from the line. Let C_L represent the cost per minute to operate the line. This would include labor, overhead, maintenance, and the allocation of the capital cost of the equipment over its expected service life. The last item, capital cost, will likely be the largest portion of C_L. The cost of any disposable tooling should be computed on a per workpiece basis and is symbolized by C_t. Using these components, the general formula for calculating the cost per workpiece C_{pc} is
w/o MLT/WIP

$$C_{pc} = C_m + C_L T_p + C_t \tag{5.8}$$

This equation does not account for such things as yield or scrap rates, inspection cost associated with identifying defective items produced, or repair cost associated with fixing the defective items. However, these factors can be incorporated into Eq. (5.8) in a fairly straightforward manner.

We will let n represent the number of workstations on the flow line and Q will designate the quantity of workparts produced off the line. Q may represent a batch size or it may mean the number of parts produced over a certain time period. We will use it in whatever way we find convenient. However, one note of caution is this: Q may include a certain number of defects if the flow line has a habit of not producing 100% good product.

Let us consider an example to illustrate the terminology of flow line performance.

EXAMPLE 5.1

Suppose that a 10-station transfer machine is under consideration to produce a component used in a pump. The item is currently produced by more conventional means, but demand for the item cannot be met. The manufacturing engineering department has estimated that the ideal cycle time will be $T_c = 1.0$ min. From similar transfer lines, it is estimated that breakdowns of all types will occur with a frequency, $F = 0.10$ breakdown/cycle, and that the average downtime per line stop will be 6.0 min. The scrap rate for the current conventional processing method is 5% and this is considered a good estimate for the transfer line. The starting casting for the component costs $1.50 each and it will cost $60.00/h or $1.00/min to operate the transfer line. Cutting tools are estimated to cost $0.15/workpart.   ↳ assume incl oH ?

Using the foregoing data, it is desired to compute the following measures of line performance:

(a) Production rate.

(b) Number of hours required to meet a demand of 1500 units/week.

(c) Line efficiency.

(d) Cost per unit produced.

Solution:

(a) The average production time per piece can be calculated from Eq. (5.1).

$$T_p = 1.0 + 0.10(6.0) = 1.6 \text{ min}$$

The average production rate for the line would be determined by Eq. (5.3).

$$R_p = \frac{1}{1.6} = 0.625 \text{ piece/min or } 37.5 \text{ pieces/h}$$

However, correcting for the scrap rate of 5%, the actual production rate of good products is

$$R_p' = 0.95(37.5) = 35.625 \text{ pieces/h}$$

(b) To compute the number of hours required to produce 1500 units/week (we assume that this means 1500 good units plus scrap rather than 1500 with 5% scrap included), we divide the production rate of 35.625 units/h into the 1500-unit requirement:

$$\text{hours} = \frac{1500}{35.625} = 42.1 \text{ h}$$

(c) The line efficiency is found by taking the ratio of the ideal cycle time to the average production time, according to Eq. (5.5).

$$E = \frac{1.0}{1.6} = 0.625$$

The proportion downtime is determined by Eq. (5.6).

$$D = \frac{0.10(6)}{1.6} = 0.375$$

(d) The cost per product can be computed from Eq. (5.8) except that we must account for the scrap rate. This is accomplished by dividing the cost determined by Eq. (5.8) by the yield of good parts. In our example the yield is 0.95.

$$C_{pc} = \frac{1}{0.95}(1.50 + 1.00 \times 1.60 + 0.15)$$

$$= \$3.42/\text{good unit}$$

The \$3.42 represents the average cost per acceptable product under the assumption that we are discarding the 5% bad units at no salvage value and no disposal cost. Suppose that we could repair these units at a cost of \$5.00/unit. Would it be economical to do so? To compute the cost per piece, the repair cost would have to be added to the other components of Eq. (5.8). Also, since repair of the defects means that our yield will be 100%, the 0.95 used above to obtain a cost of \$3.42 can be ignored.

$$C_{pc} = 1.50 + 1.00 \times 1.60 + 0.15 + 0.05(5.00)$$

$$= \$3.50/\text{unit}$$

The lower cost per unit is associated with the policy of scrapping the 5% defects rather than repairing them. Unless the extra units are needed to meet demand, the scrap policy seems preferable.

5.2 ANALYSIS OF TRANSFER LINES WITHOUT STORAGE

In this section we consider the analysis of continuous and intermittent transfer machines without internal storage capacity. We will supplement the results of Section 5.1 by considering what happens at a workstation when it breaks down. There are two possibilities and we refer to their analyses as the upper-bound approach and the lower-bound approach. In practical terms, the difference between the two approaches is simply this: With the *upper-bound approach*, we assume that the workpart is not removed from the station when a breakdown occurs at that station. With the *lower-bound approach*, the workpart is taken out of the station when the station breaks down. The circumstances under which each approach is appropriate are discussed in the following subsections.

Upper-bound approach

The upper-bound approach provides an estimate of the upper limit on the frequency of line stops per cycle. We assume here that a breakdown at a station does not cause the part to be removed from that station. In this case it is possible, perhaps likely, that there will be more than one line stop associated with a particular workpart. An example of this

Here a cycle corresponds to an indexing of the transfer line when a new part is put on the system & a finished part comes off the 'sys

situation is that of a hydraulic failure at a workstation which prevents the feed mechanism from working. Another possibility is that the cutting tool has nearly worn out and needs to be changed. Or, the workpart is close to being out of tolerance and a tool adjustment is required to correct the condition. With each of these examples, there is no reason for the part to be removed from the transfer machine. *ie., have a breakdown associated*

Let p_i represent the probability that a part will jam at a particular station i, where $i = 1, 2, \ldots, n$. Since the parts are not removed when a station jam occurs, it is possible (although not probable) that the part will jam at every station. The expected number of line stops per part passing through the line can be obtained merely by summing up the probabilities p_i over the n stations. Since each of the n stations is processing a part each cycle, this expected number of line stops per part passing through the line is equal to the frequency of line stops per cycle. Thus,

ie., over if a batch of
given N parts
p_i will jam at stn. i
chr. 2
(= if N_i) p_i^N etc.

$$F = \sum_{i=1}^{n} p_i \tag{5.9}$$

If the probabilities p_i are all equal, $p_1 = p_2 = \cdots = p_n = p$, then

$$F = np \tag{5.10}$$

(this is the max. value for F, since we consider the breakdowns at stns. to happen independently & there is no part removal here. hence F is not same as)

EXAMPLE 5.2

In a 10-station transfer line, the probability that a station breakdown will occur for a given workpart is equal to 0.01. This probability is the same for all 10 stations. Determine the frequency of line stops per cycle on this flow line using the upper-bound approach.

Solution:

The value of F can be calculated from Eq. (5.10).

$$F = 10(0.01) = 0.10$$

This is the value of F used in Example 5.1.

(here there's no scrap) since problem is corrected

Lower-bound approach

The lower-bound approach gives an estimate of the lower limit on the expected number of line stops per cycle. In this approach we assume that the station breakdown results in the destruction or damage of the workpiece. For example, a drill or tap breaks off in the part during processing. The broken tool must be replaced at the workstation and the workpart must be removed from the line for subsequent rework or scrap. Accordingly, the part cannot proceed to the next stations for further processing.

Again, let p_i be the probability that a part will jam at a particular station i. Then, considering a given workpart as it proceeds through the line, p_1 is the probability that

i.e., the # parts actually passing thru' the entire line, from a given batch (say 100), will be less than the batch qty. started with (ie. & .:. less prob. of breakdowns (esp. at later stns.)). F is mainly a measure of line ineff. due to breakdowns ...

the part will jam at station 1, and $(1 - p_1)$ is the probability that the part will not jam at station 1 and thus be available for subsequent processing. The quantity $p_2(1 - p_1)$ is the probability that this given part will jam at station 2. Generalizing, the quantity

$$p_i(1 - p_{i-1})(1 - p_{i-2}) \cdots (1 - p_2)(1 - p_1) \qquad i = 1, 2, \ldots, n$$

is the probability that the given part will jam at any station i. Summing all these probabilities from $i = 1$ through n would give the probability or what has previously been called the frequency of line stops per cycle. There is an easier way to determine this frequency.

The probability that a given part will pass through all n stations without a line stop associated with its processing is given by

$$\prod_{i=1}^{n} (1 - p_i)$$

Therefore, the frequency of line stops per cycle is provided by

$$F = 1 - \prod_{i=1}^{n} (1 - p_i) \qquad (5.11)$$

If the probabilities p_i that a part will jam at a particular station are all equal, $p_1 = p_2 = \cdots = p_n = p$, then

$$F = 1 - (1 - p)^n \qquad (5.12)$$

We might be tempted to view this frequency, F, as the probability of a line stop per cycle, except that it is possible, in the upper-bound approach, for the frequency of line stops per cycle to exceed unity. A probability greater than 1 cannot be interpreted.

With the lower-bound approach, the number of workparts coming off the line will be less than the number starting. If the parts are removed from the line when a breakdown occurs, they are not available to be counted as part of the output of the line. Therefore, the production-rate formula given by Eq. (5.3) must be amended to reflect this reduction in output. Using the lower-bound approach, the production-rate formula becomes

$$R_p = \frac{1 - F}{T_p}$$

where F not only stands for the frequency of line stops but also the frequency of parts removal. If no rework is performed, F is the scrap rate. Therefore, the term $(1 - F)$ represents the yield of the transfer machine. T_p is interpreted to mean the average cycle time of the machine.

EXAMPLE 5.3

Compute the value of F using the lower-bound approach for the data of Example 5.2. Also compute the production rate.

Solution:

From Eq. (5.12) the value of F is

$$F = 1 - (1 - 0.01)^{10} = 0.0956 \quad = \text{scrap rate, here}$$

Although the value of F is smaller as calculated by the lower-bound approach, the difference is small. This difference grows as the value of p and the number of workstations increase.

To compute the production rate, we must adjust Eq. (5.3), as indicated in the previous discussion, by the value of F. Production time T_p was calculated in Example 5.1 as 1.6 min. Therefore, the production rate

$$R_p = \frac{1 - 0.0956}{1.6} = 0.565 \text{ piece/min or 33.9 pieces/h}$$

This is somewhat below the 35.6 pieces/h obtained in Example 5.1, where the scrap rate was 0.05 rather than the 0.0956 computed here. We can reason that the 5% scrap rate probably represents a mixture of the two cases assumed by the upper- and lower-bound approaches. When breakdowns occur, the workparts are sometimes removed from the line and other times they are not. The upper- and lower-bound approaches, as their names imply, provide upper and lower limits on the frequency of downtime occurrences. However, these two approaches also generate upper and lower limits on the production rate, assuming that station breakdowns are the sole cause of scrap. Of course, the 5% scrap figure may also include other conditions, such as poor quality of the workparts.

Some comments and observations

Determining whether the upper- or the lower-bound approach is more appropriate for a particular transfer line requires knowledge about the operation of the line. The operator may be required to use judgment in each breakdown to determine whether the workpart should be removed. If parts are sometimes removed and sometimes not, the actual frequency of breakdowns will fall somewhere between the upper and lower bounds. Of the two approaches, the upper-bound approach is preferred, certainly for convenience of calculation and probably for accuracy also.

There are other reasons why line stops occur which are not directly related to workstations (e.g., transfer mechanism failure, schedule tool changes for all stations, preventive maintenance, product changeover, etc.). These other factors must be taken into consideration when determining line performance.

The biggest difficulty in using Eqs. (5.9) through (5.12) lies in determining the values of p_i for the various stations. Perhaps the best approach is to base the values of p_i on previous historical data and experience with similar workstations.

There are a number of general truths about the operation of transfer lines which are revealed by the equations of Sections 5.1 and 5.2. First, the line efficiency decreases

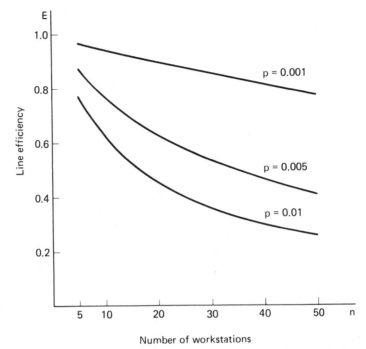

FIGURE 5.3   Relationship between line efficiency (E) and number of workstations (n) for various workstation breakdown rates (p).

substantially as the number of stations increases. It is not uncommon for large transfer lines consisting of up to 100 stations to be down more than 50% of the time. It is doubtful that such lines achieve the return on investment which their owners anticipated from them. The influence of the number of stations on line efficiency is dramatically displayed in Figure 5.3 for several assumed values of station breakdown probabilities.

This figure was calculated using the upper-bound approach. In comparing the upper- and lower-bound approaches, we find that the upper-bound calculations lead to a lower value of line efficiency but a higher value for the production rate. The reason for this apparent anomaly is this: Using the lower-bound approach with its assumption of parts removal, the removed parts are not available at subsequent workstations to cause line stoppages. Hence, the proportion of uptime on the line is greater. However, if the parts are removed from the line, the production rate of the line is reduced.

5.3   PARTIAL AUTOMATION

There are many examples of flow lines in industry that contain both automated and manually operated workstations. These cases of partially automated production lines occur for two main reasons. First, mechanization of a manually operated flow line is often introduced gradually. Automation of the simpler manual operations is carried out initially, and the transition toward a fully automated line is accomplished progressively. A long period of time may elapse before the transformation has been completed. Meanwhile, the line operates as a partially automated system. The second reason for partial automation is based strictly on economics. Some manual operations are difficult to automate and it may be uneconomical to do so. Therefore, when the sequence of workstations is planned for the flow line, certain stations are designed to be manually operated while the rest are designed to be automatic. Examples of operations that are often difficult to automate are processes requiring alignment or special human skills to carry out. Many assembly operations fall into this category. Also, inspection operations often create problems when automation is being considered to substitute for a human operator. Defects in a workpart that can be easily perceived by a human inspector are sometimes extremely difficult to identify by an automatic inspection device. Another problem is that the automatic device can only check the defects for which it was designed, whereas a human operator is capable of sensing a variety of unforeseen imperfections in the part.

To analyze the performance of a partially automated flow line, we will build on the developments of the previous sections. Our analysis will be confined to the operation of a system without buffer storage. Later in this section we will speculate on the improvements that would result if in-process inventory banks were used for the manual workstations. The ideal cycle time T_c will be determined by the slowest station in the line, which generally will be one of the manual stations. We assume that breakdowns occur only at the automatic stations and that the reasons for breakdowns are as varied as they are for a completely automated system (e.g., tool failures, defective components, electrical and mechanical malfunctions, etc.). Breakdowns do not occur at the manual stations because the human operators are flexible enough, we assume, to adapt to the kinds of variations and disruptions that cause an automatic workhead to stop. This, of course, is not always true, but our analysis will be based on this assumption. Let p equal the probability of a station breakdown for an automatic workhead. The values of p may be different for different stations, but we will leave to the reader the task of generalizing on our particular case of equal p for all stations.

Since n is the total number of workstations on the line, let n_a equal the number of automatic stations and n_o equal the number of manual operator stations. The sum of n_a and n_o must be n. In our previous discussion of costs in Section 5.1, C_L was used to represent the cost to operate the line, including labor, capital, and overhead. For a partially automated system, we must separate this term into several components. Let C_o equal the operator cost per manual station. This is a labor cost in \$/minute which applies to each manually operated workstation. The cost per automatic workstation in \$/minute will be denoted by C_{as}. This cost will often vary for different stations, depending on the level of sophistication of the mechanism. We can allow for these differences in C_{as} with little difficulty, as will be shown in a subsequent example. The last cost component of C_L is the cost per minute of the automatic transfer mechanism which will be used for all stations, manual and automatic, to transport the workparts. Let this cost be symbolized by C_{at}. It is not a cost per station, but rather a cost that includes all n stations. Combining these costs, the total line cost C_L is given by *(handwritten margin notes at top)* line cost rate ($/time) # man. stns # auto. stns. cost rate for transfer — medi. are a while

$$C_L = n_o C_o + n_a C_{as} + C_{at} \tag{5.13}$$

To figure the average production time, the ideal cycle time is added to the average downtime per cycle as follows:

$$T_p = T_c + F T_d$$

(handwritten: based on upper bound --)

$$= T_c + n_a p T_d \tag{5.14}$$

By using n_a (the number of automatic workstations), we are consistent with our assumption that breakdowns do not occur at manual stations. Equation (5.14) is based on the upper-bound approach of Section 5.2.

By substituting Eqs. (5.13) and (5.14) into Eq. (5.8), we obtain the cost per unit produced:

$$C_{pc} = C_m + (n_o C_o + n_a C_{as} + C_{at})(T_c + n_a p T_d) + C_t \tag{5.15}$$

(handwritten: C_L under first group, T_p under second group)

EXAMPLE 5.4

A proposal has been made to replace one of the current manual stations with an automatic workhead on a 10-station transfer line. The current system has six automatic workheads and four manual stations. The current cycle time is 30 s. The bottleneck station is the manual station that is the candidate for replacement. The proposed automatic station would allow the cycle time to be reduced to 24 s. The new station is costed at $0.25/min. Other cost data for the existing line:

$$C_o = \$0.15/\text{min}$$

$$C_{as} = \$0.10/\text{min}$$

$$C_{at} = \$0.10/\text{min}$$

Breakdowns occur at each of the six automatic workstations with a probability $p = 0.01$. The average downtime per breakdown is 3 min. It is estimated that the value of p for the new automatic station would be $p = 0.02$. The average downtime for the line would be unaffected. Material for the product costs $0.50/unit. Tooling costs can be neglected ($C_t = 0$). It is desired to compare the challenger (the new automated station) with the defender (the current manual station) on the basis of cost per unit.

Solution:

For the current line, the production time is

$$T_p = 0.5 + 6(0.01)(3) = 0.68 \text{ min/unit}$$

$$C_L = 4(0.15) + 6(0.10) + 0.10 = \$1.30/\text{min}$$

$$C_{pc} = 0.50 + 1.30(0.68) = \$1.384/\text{unit}$$

For the transfer line with the new workhead replacing the current manual station, similar computations are as follows:

$$T_p = 0.4 + (6 \times 0.01 + 0.02)(3) = 0.64 \text{ min/unit}$$

$$C_L = 3(0.15) + 6(0.10) + 0.25 + 0.10 = \$1.40/\text{min}$$

$$C_{pc} = 0.50 + 1.40(0.64) = \$1.396/\text{unit}$$

The conclusion is that the improved performance of the automatic workhead does not justify its greater cost. It should be noted that the reduced reliability of the automatic workheads figures prominently in the cost calculations. If the value of p for the new automatic workhead had been equal to 0.01 instead of 0.02, the conclusion would have been reversed.

Buffer storage

The preceding analysis assumes no buffer storage between stations on the line. Therefore, when the automated portion of the line breaks down, the manual stations must also stop working for lack of workparts. It would be beneficial to the line operation to build up an inventory of parts before and after each manual station. In this manner, these stations, which usually operate at a slower pace than the automatics, could continue to produce while the automated portion of the line is down. This would tend to help solve the line balancing problem that often occurs on partially automated machines. To illustrate, consider the previous example of the current transfer system whose ideal cycle time is 0.50 min. Under the current method of operation, both manual and automatic stations are out of operation when a breakdown occurs. The 0.50-min cycle time is caused by one of the manual stations. Suppose that the ideal cycle time on the automatic portion of the line could be set at 0.32 min. The resulting average production time on the automatic stations would then be

$$T_p = 0.32 + 6(0.01)(3) = 0.50 \text{ min}$$

If a bank of workparts could be provided for the human operators to work on during the downtime occurrences, the average production time of the entire assembly system would be 0.50 min rather than 0.68 min as computed in Example 5.4. The resulting cost per assembly, ignoring any added cost as a result of the buffer storage capacity, would be

$$C_{pc} = 0.50 + 1.30(0.50) = \$1.15/\text{unit}$$

which is a substantial reduction from the \$1.384/unit previously calculated for the current line.

We treat the topic of buffer storage in more detail in the next section.

5.4 AUTOMATED FLOW LINES
WITH STORAGE BUFFERS

One of the methods by which flow lines can be made to operate more efficiently is to add one or more parts storage buffers between workstations along the line. The buffer zones divide the line into stages. If one storage buffer is used, the line is divided into two stages. If two storage buffers are used at two different locations along the line, a three-stage line results. The upper limit on the number of storage zones is to have in-process inventory capacity between every workstation. The number of stages will then be equal to the number of stations. For an n-stage line, there will be $n - 1$ storage buffers. This, of course, does not include the inventory of raw workparts which are available for feeding onto the front of the flow line. Nor does it include the inventory of finished parts that accumulate at the end of the line.

In a flow line without internal workpart storage, the workstations are interdependent. When one stations breaks down, all the other stations will be affected, either immediately or by the end of a few cycles of operation. The other workstations will be forced to stop production for one of two reasons:

1. *Starving of stations.* If a workstation cannot continue to operate because it has no parts to work on, the station is said to be *starved* of parts. When a breakdown occurs at a given station in the line, the stations following the broken-down station will become starved.

2. *Blocking of stations.* This occurs when a station is prevented from passing its workpart along to the following station. When a station breakdown occurs, the preceding or upstream stations are said to be *blocked,* because they are unable to transfer workparts to the station that is down.

The terms "starving" and "blocking" are often used in reference to manual flow lines. However, they are useful for explaining how buffer storage zones can be used to improve the efficiency of automated flow lines. When an automated flow line is divided into stages by storage buffers, the overall efficiency and production rate of the line are improved. When one of the stages in the line breaks down, the storage buffers prevent the other stages from being immediately affected. Consider a two-stage transfer line with one storage buffer between the stages. If the first stage breaks down, the inventory of workparts that has accumulated in the storage buffer will allow the second stage to continue operating until the inventory has been exhausted. Similarly, if the second stage breaks down, the storage zone will accept the output of the first stage. The first stage can continue to operate until the capacity of the storage buffer is reached.

The purpose served by the storage buffer can be extended to flow lines with more than two stages. The presence of these in-process inventories allows each stage to operate somewhat independently. It is clear that the extent of this independence between one stage and the next depends on the storage capacity of the buffer zone separating the stages.

Limits of storage buffer effectiveness

The two extreme cases of storage buffer effectiveness can be identified as:

1. No buffer storage capacity at all
2. Storage buffers with infinite capacity

NO BUFFER STORAGE CAPACITY.   In this case, the flow line acts as one machine. When a station breakdown occurs, the entire line is forced down. The efficiency of the line was previously given by Eq. (5.5). We will rewrite this equation as

$$E_0 = \frac{T_c}{T_c + FT_d} \tag{5.16}$$

The subscript 0 identifies this as the efficiency of the line with no buffer storage capacity. It represents a starting point from which the line efficiency can be improved by adding provision for in-process storage.

INFINITE-CAPACITY STORAGE BUFFERS.   The opposite extreme is the case where buffer zones of infinite capacity are installed between each stage. If we assume that each of these buffer zones is half full (in other words, each buffer zone has an infinite supply of parts as well as the capacity to accept an infinite number of additional parts), then each stage is independent of the rest. Infinite storage buffers means that no stage will ever be blocked or starved because of the breakdown of some other stage.

Of course, a flow line with infinite-capacity buffers cannot be realized in practice. However, if such a line could be approximated in real life, the overall line efficiency would be determined by the bottleneck stage. We would have to limit the production on the other stages to be consistent with that of the bottleneck stage. Otherwise, the in-process inventory upstream from the bottleneck would grow indefinitely, eventually reaching some practical maximum, and the in-process inventory in the downstream buffers would decline to zero. As a practical matter, therefore, the upper limit on the efficiency of any such a line is defined by the efficiency of the bottleneck stage. If we assume the cycle time T_c to be the same for all stages, the efficiency of any stage is given by

$$E_k = \frac{T_c}{T_c + F_k T_{dk}} \tag{5.17}$$

where the subscript k is used to identify the stage.

The overall line efficiency would be given by

$$E_\infty = \min_k E_k \tag{5.18}$$

where the subscript ∞ is used to indicate the infinite storage buffers between stages.

BUFFER STOCK EFFECTIVENESS IN PRACTICE. By providing one or more buffer zones on a flow line, we expect to improve the line efficiency above E_0 but we cannot expect to achieve E_∞, simply because buffer zones of infinite capacity are not possible. Hence, the actual value of E will lie somewhere between these extremes:

$$E_0 < E < E_\infty \tag{5.19}$$

Before embarking on the problem of evaluating E for realistic levels of buffer capacity, it seems appropriate to comment on the practical implications of Eqs. (5.16) through (5.19):

    1. Equation (5.19) indicates that if E_0 and E_∞ are nearly equal in value, relatively little advantage will be gained from the addition of storage buffers to the line. If E_∞ is significantly larger than E_0, storage buffers can provide a pronounced improvement in the line's efficiency.

    2. The workstations along the line should be divided into stages so as to make the efficiencies of all stages as equal as possible. In this way the maximum difference between E_0 and E_∞ will be achieved, and no single stage will stand out as a significant bottleneck.

    3. The efficiency of an automated flow line with buffer storage can be maximized under the following conditions:

        a. By setting the number of stages equal to the number of workstations. That is, all adjacent stations will be separated by storage buffers.

        b. By providing that all workstations have an equal probability of breakdown.

        c. By designing the storage buffers to be of large capacity. The actual capacity would be determined by the average downtime. If the average downtime (in particular, the ratio T_d/T_c) is large, more buffer capacity must be provided to ensure adequate insulation between workstations.

    4. Although it is not obvious from Eqs. (5.16) through (5.19), the "law of diminishing returns" operates as the number of stages increases. The biggest improvement in line efficiency comes from adding the first storage buffer to the line. As more storage buffers are added, the efficiency improves, but at an ever-slower rate. This will be demonstrated in Example 5.6 later in this section.

Analysis of a two-stage line

Much of the preceding discussion is based on the work of Buzacott [2], who has pioneered the analytical research on flow lines with buffer stocks. Several of his publications on the subject are listed in the references at the end of this chapter [2,4,5,6,7]. Other researchers have also studied the problem of flow lines with storage buffers, especially the two-stage line, and the interested reader is referred to their work [12,15,16].

    Our presentation of the two-stage flow line problem will closely follow Buzacott's analysis developed in reference [2]. The two-stage line is separated by a storage buffer of capacity b. The capacity is expressed in terms of the number of workparts the storage zone can hold. Let F_1 and F_2 represent, respectively, the breakdown rates of stages 1 and 2. We will use the term r to define the ratio of breakdown rates as follows:

$$r = \frac{F_2}{F_1} \qquad (5.20)$$

The ideal cycle time, T_c, is the same for both stages. We assume that the downtime distributions of all stations within a stage are the same, and that the average downtimes of stages 1 and 2 are T_{d1} and T_{d2}.

Over the long run, both stages must have equal efficiencies. For example, if the efficiency of stage 1 would tend to be greater than the stage 2 efficiency, the inventory in the storage buffer would tend to build up until its capacity b is reached. Thereafter, stage 1 would eventually be blocked when it tried to outproduce stage 2. Similarly, if the efficiency of stage 2 is greater, the buffer inventory would become depleted, thus starving stage 2. Accordingly, the efficiencies of the two stages would tend to equalize over time.

The overall line efficiency for the two stages can be expressed as

$$E = E_0 + D_1'h(b) \qquad (5.21)$$

where E_0 is the line efficiency without buffer storage. The value of E_0 was given by Eq. (5.16), but we will write it below to explicitly define the two-stage system efficiency when $b = 0$:

$$E_0 = \frac{T_c}{T_c + F_1 T_{d1} + F_2 T_{d2}} \qquad (5.22)$$

The term $D_1'h(b)$ appearing in Eq. (5.21) represents the improvement in efficiency that results from adding buffer capacity ($b > 0$).

D_1' is the proportion of total time that stage 1 is down. However, Buzacott defines D_1' as

$$D_1' = \frac{F_1 T_{d1}}{T_c + F_1 T_{d1} + F_2 T_{d2}} \qquad (5.23)$$

Note that the form of this equation is different from the case given by Eq. (5.6) when we were considering the flow line to be an integral mechanism, uncomplicated by the presence of buffer stocks.

The term $h(b)$ is the ideal proportion of the downtime D_1' (when stage 1 is down) that stage 2 could be up and operating within the limits of buffer capacity b. Buzacott [2] presents equations for evaluating $h(b)$ using a Markov chain analysis. The equations cover several different downtime distributions and are based on the assumption that the probability of both stages being down at the same time is negligible. Four of these equations are presented in Table 5.1.

In sample calculations, the author has found that Eq. (5.21) tends to overestimate line efficiency. This is because of the assumption implicit in the computation of $h(b)$ that both stages will not be broken down at the same time. Another way of stating this assumption is this: During the downtime of stage 1, stage 2 is assumed to always be operating. However, it is more realistic to believe that during the downtime of stage 1, stage 2 will be down a certain portion of the time, this downtime determined by the efficiency of stage 2. Hence, it seems more accurate to express the overall line efficiency of a two-stage line as follows, rather than by Eq. (5.21):

$$E = E_0 + D_1' h(b) E_2 \tag{5.29}$$

where E_2 represents the efficiency of stage 2 by Eq. (5.17).

In work subsequent to the research documented in reference [2], Buzacott develops a more exact solution to the two-stage problem than that provided by Eq. (5.21). This is reported in reference 5 and seems to agree closely with the results given by Eq. (5.29).

EXAMPLE 5.5

This example will illustrate the use of Eq. (5.29) and Table 5.1 to calculate line efficiency for a transfer line with one storage buffer. The line has 10 workstations, each with a probability of breakdown of 0.02. The cycle time of the line is 1 min, and each time a breakdown occurs, it takes exactly 5 min to make repairs. The line is to be divided into two stages by a storage bank so that each stage will consist of five stations. We want to compute the efficiency of the two-stage line for various buffer capacities.

Solution:

First, let us compute the efficiency of the line with no buffer capacity.

$$F = np = 10(0.02) = 0.2$$

By Eq. (5.16),

$$E_0 = \frac{1.0}{1.0 + 0.2(5)} = 0.50$$

Next, dividing the line into two equal stages by a buffer zone of infinite capacity, each stage would have an efficiency given by Eq. (5.17).

$$F_1 = F_2 = 5(0.02) = 0.1$$

$$E_1 = E_2 = \frac{1.0}{1.0 + 0.1(5)} = 0.6667$$

By Eq. (5.18), $E_\infty = 0.6667$ represents the maximum possible efficiency that could be achieved by using a storage buffer of infinite capacity.

TABLE 5.1 Formulas for Computing $h(b)$ for a Two-Stage Flow Line under Several Downtime Situations

The following definitions and assumptions apply to Eqs. (5.25) through (5.28) used to compute $h(b)$: Assume that the two stages have equal repair times and equal cycle times. That is,

$$T_{d_1} = T_{d_2} = T_d$$

and

$$T_{c_1} = T_{c_2} = T_c$$

Let

$$b = B\frac{T_d}{T_c} + L \tag{5.24}$$

where B is the largest integer satisfying the relation

$$b\frac{T_c}{T_d} \geq B$$

and L represents the leftover units, the number by which b exceeds BT_d/T_c. Finally, let $r = F_2/F_1$, as given by Eq. (5.20).

With these definitions and assumptions, we can express the relationships for two theoretical downtime distributions as developed by Buzacott [2]:

1. *Constant repair distribution.* Each downtime occurrence is assumed to require a constant repair time T_d.

$$r \neq 1: h(b) = r\frac{1 - r^B}{1 - r^{B+1}} + L\frac{T_c}{T_d}\frac{r^{B+1}(1 - r)^2}{(1 - r^{B+1})(1 - r^{B+2})} \tag{5.25}$$

$$r = 1: h(b) = \frac{B}{B + 1} + L\frac{T_c}{T_d}\frac{1}{(B + 1)(B + 2)} \tag{5.26}$$

2. *Geometric repair distribution.* This downtime distribution assumes that the probability that repairs are completed during any cycle is independent of the time since repairs began. Define the parameter K:

$$K = \frac{1 + r - T_c/T_d}{1 + r - rT_c/T_d}$$

Then for the two cases

$$r \neq 1: h(b) = \frac{r(1 - K^b)}{1 - rK^b} \tag{5.27}$$

$$r = 1: h(b) = \frac{bT_c/T_d}{2 + (b - 1)T_c/T_d} \tag{5.28}$$

Now, we will see how Eq. (5.29) and the formulas in Table 5.1 are used. Let us investigate the following buffer capacities: $b = 1, 10, 100,$ and ∞.

When $b = 1$, according to Eq. (5.24) in Table 5.1, the buffer capacity is converted to $B = 0$, and $L = 1$. We are dealing with a constant repair-time distribution and the breakdown rates are the same for both stages, so $r = 1$. We will therefore use Eq. (5.26) to compute the value of $h(1)$:

$$h(1) = 0 + \frac{1(1.0)}{5.0} \frac{1}{(0 + 1)(0 + 2)} = 0.10$$

Using Eq. (5.23) to get the proportion of total time that stage 1 is down,

$$D'_1 = \frac{0.1(5.0)}{1.0 + 0.2(5.0)} = 0.25$$

Now the line efficiency can be computed from Eq. (5.29):

$$E = 0.50 + 0.25(0.10)(0.6667) = 0.5167$$

Only a very modest improvement results from the use of a storage buffer with capacity of one workpart.

When $b = 10$, $B = 2$ and $L = 0$. The value of $h(10)$ is again computed from Eq. (5.26):

$$h(10) = \frac{2}{2 + 1} + 0 = 0.6667$$

The resulting line efficiency is

$$E = 0.50 + 0.25(0.6667)(0.6667) = 0.6111$$

We see a 22% increase in line efficiency over E_0 from using a buffer capacity of 10 work units.

When $b = 100$, $B = 20$, $L = 0$, and

$$h(100) = \frac{20}{21} + 0 = 0.952$$

Therefore,

$$E = 0.50 + 0.25(0.952)(0.6667) = 0.6587$$

A 32% increase in line efficiency results when the buffer capacity equals 100. Comparing this to the case when $b = 10$, we can see the law of diminishing returns operating.

When the storage capacity is infinite ($b = \infty$),

$$h(\infty) = 1.0$$

and

$$E = 0.50 + 0.25(1.0)(0.6667) = 0.6667$$

according to Eq. (5.29), which equals the result given by Eq. (5.18).

It is of instructional value to compare this result for $b = \infty$ given by Eq. (5.29), with the result given by Eq. (5.21), which neglects the possibility of overlapping stage downtime occurrences. According to Eq. (5.21), the line efficiency would be calculated as

$$E = 0.50 + 0.25(1.0) = 0.75$$

which, of course, exceeds the maximum possible value given by Eq. (5.18). The corrected formula, Eq. (5.29), provides better calculated results, since it accounts for the occurrence of overlapping breakdowns for the two stages.

Flow lines with more than two stages

We will not consider exact formulas for computing efficiencies for flow lines consisting of more than two stages. It is left to the interested reader to consult some of the references, in particular [1], [2], and [5]. However, the previous discussion in this section should provide a general guide for deciding on the configuration of multistage lines. Let us consider some of these decisions in the context of an example.

EXAMPLE 5.6

Suppose that the flow line under consideration here has 16 stations with cycle time of 15 s (assume that all stations have roughly equal process times). When station breakdowns occur, the average downtime is 2 min. The breakdown frequencies for each station are presented in the following table.

Station	p_i	Station	p_i
1	0.01	9	0.03
2	0.02	10	0.01
3	0.01	11	0.02
4	0.03	12	0.02
5	0.02	13	0.02
6	0.04	14	0.01
7	0.01	15	0.03
8	0.01	16	0.01

We want to consider the relative performances when the line is separated into two, three, or four stages.

Solution:

First, the performance of the line can be determined for the single-stage case (no storage buffer). From the table, the frequency of downtime occurrences is given by Eq. (5.9):

$$F = \sum_{i=1}^{16} p_i = 0.30$$

The line efficiency is, by Eq. (5.16),

$$E_0 = \frac{0.25}{0.25 + 0.30(2)} = 0.2941$$

To divide the line into stages, we must first decide the optimum locations for the storage buffers. The stations should be grouped into stages so as to make the efficiencies of the stages as close as possible. Then, to assess relative performances for the two-, three-, and four-stage lines, we will base the comparison on the use of storage buffers with infinite capacity.

For the two-stage line, the breakdown frequency of $F = 0.30$ should be shared evenly between the two stages. From the foregoing table of p_i values it can be determined that the storage buffer should be located between stations 8 and 9. This will yield equal F values for the two stages.

$$F_1 = \sum_{i=1}^{8} p_i = 0.15$$

$$F_2 = \sum_{i=9}^{16} p_i = 0.15$$

The resulting stage efficiencies are

$$E_1 = E_2 = \frac{0.25}{0.25 + 0.15(2)} = 0.4545$$

From Eq. (5.18), $E_\infty = 0.4545$.

Similarly, for the three-stage configuration, the frequency of breakdowns should be divided as equally as possible among the three stages. Accordingly, the line should be divided as follows:

Stage	Stations	F_k	E_k
1	1–5	0.09	0.5814
2	6–10	0.10	0.5556
3	11–16	0.11	0.5319

The third stage, with the lowest efficiency, determines the overall three-stage line efficiency: $E_\infty = 0.5319$.

Finally, for four stages the division would be the following:

Stage	Stations	F_k	E_k
1	1–4	0.07	0.6410
2	5–8	0.08	0.6098
3	9–12	0.08	0.6098
4	13–16	0.07	0.6410

The resulting line efficiency for the four-stage configuration would be $E_\infty = 0.6098$.

The example shows the proper approach for dividing the line into stages. It also shows how the line efficiency continues to increase as the number of storage banks is increased. However, it can be seen that the rate of improvement in efficiency drops off as more stage buffers are added. In the foregoing calculations we assumed an infinite buffer capacity. For realistic capacities, the efficiency would be less as was illustrated in Example 5.5.

The maximum possible efficiency would be achieved by using an infinite storage bank between every workstation. Station 6 would be the bottleneck stage. We leave it for the reader to figure out the line efficiency for the 16-stage case.

5.5 COMPUTER SIMULATION OF AUTOMATED FLOW LINES

A number of studies have been concerned with simulating the operation of flow lines, both automated and nonautomated. Some of these studies have been performed by large industrial concerns and the models developed as well as the results obtained are often considered proprietary. References [8], [10], [11], [13], and [14] are a sampling of the reports of these studies.

Production magazine [8] reports some of the results provided by a computer simulation model developed by Ingersoll Manufacturing consultants. However, very little information is given about the details of the model itself. Phillips and Slovick [13] report on an analysis of an actual continuous production line at one of the Western Electric plants. The line is manually operated with seven workstations. A GERTS-type simulation language was used to develop the model of the line. Although the study was limited in scope to the particular assembly and test line, the investigators found the GERTS simulation approach to be quite valuable for production control purposes. Phillips and Pritsker [14] explore the possibilities of using GERTS on a number of production system situations.

One of the more comprehensive automated flow line simulation studies reported in the literature was performed by Hanifin [10,11]. Hanifin used as the object of his investigation several actual transfer lines at the Kokomo Works of Chrysler Corporation. His computer model, using GPSS as the simulation language, was based on the operation of these machining flow lines. The model was developed to deal with several specific problem areas at Chrysler. Yet the results of his study can be generalized to some extent. His investigation considered the effect of adding up to three storage buffer areas of three specific locations along the line. He also investigated the effect of different average tool change times.

Simulation has become a much more familiar tool for the analyst to use to study transfer lines and other production systems. Simulation software packages have become available that are much easier to use, yet provide more capabilities to investigate system performance. These languages include SLAM II (Pritsker & Associates, Inc., West Lafayette, Indiana), SIMAN (Systems Modeling Corporation, State College, Pennsylvania), SEE WHY (Istel Inc., Burlington, Massachusetts), and several improved versions of GPSS. Animated graphics capabilities are becoming more common on simulation languages such as these, permitting the user to visualize more clearly the operation of the flow line (or other system). Although the equations presented in this chapter are useful as long as the assumptions underlying them are valid, there are many flow line systems whose complexities are beyond the assumed conditions of these models. Asynchronous transfer lines are good examples of production systems in this category. Robot cells, flexible manufacturing systems, automated material handling systems, and other systems that we cover later in this book are also sometimes too complex to submit to analytic mathematical models. Computer simulation, especially with animated graphics, can be used to assess the performance of these complex production systems and to identify their design flaws and operating problems.

REFERENCES

[1] BOOTHROYD, G., and A. H. REDFORD, *Mechanized Assembly,* McGraw-Hill Publishing Co., London, 1968, Chapters 7 and 8.

[2] BUZACOTT, J. A., "Automatic Transfer Lines with Buffer Stocks," *International Journal of Production Research,* Vol. 5, No. 3, 1967, pp. 183–200.

[3] BUZACOTT, J. A., "Prediction of the Efficiency of Production Systems without Internal Storage," *International Journal of Production Research,* Vol. 6, No. 3, 1968, pp. 173–188.

[4] BUZACOTT, J. A., "Methods of Reliability Analysis of Production Systems Subject to Breakdowns," in *Operations Research and Reliability,* (D. Grouchko, Editor), Gordon and Breach, Science Publishers, Inc., New York, 1971, pp. 211–232.

[5] BUZACOTT, J. A., "The Role of Inventory Banks in Flow-Line Production Systems," *International Journal of Production Research,* Vol. 9, No. 4, 1971, pp. 425–436.

[6] BUZACOTT, J. A., and L. E. HANIFIN, "Models of Automatic Transfer Lines with Inventory Banks—A Review and Comparison," *AIIE Transactions,* Vol. 10, No. 2, 1978, pp. 197–207.

[7] BUZACOTT, J. A., and L. E. HANIFIN, "Transfer Line Design and Analysis—An Overview," *Proceedings,* 1978 Fall Industrial Engineering Conference of AIIE, December 1978.

[8] "Computer Techniques Isolate Production Snags," *Production,* February 1977.

[9] GROOVER, M. P., "Analyzing Automatic Transfer Machines," *Industrial Engineering,* Vol. 7, No. 11, 1975, pp. 26–31.

[10] HANIFIN, L. E., "Increased Transfer Line Productivity Utilizing Systems Simulation," D. Eng. dissertation, University of Detroit, 1975.

[11] HANIFIN, L. E., S. G. LIBERTY, and K. TARAMAN, "Improved Transfer Line Efficiency Utilizing Systems Simulation," *Technical Paper MR* 75—169, Society of Manufacturing Engineers, Dearborn, Mich., 1975.

[12] OKAMURA, K., and H. YAMASHINA, "Analysis of the Effect of Buffer Storage Capacity in Transfer Line Systems," *AIIE Transactions,* Vol. 9, No. 2, 1977, pp. 127–135.

[13] PHILLIPS, D. T., and R. F. SLOVICK, "A GERTS III Q Application to a Production Line," *Proceedings,* 1974 Spring Annual Conference of AIIE, May, 1974.

[14] PHILLIPS, D. T., and A. A. B., PRITSKER, "GERT Network Analysis of Complex Production Systems," *International Journal of Production Research,* Vol. 13, No. 3, 1975, pp. 223–237.

[15]   RAO, N. P., "Two-Stage Production Systems with Intermediate Storage," *AIIE Transactions,* Vol. 7, No. 4, 1975, pp. 414–421.

[16]   SHESKIN, T. J., "Allocation of Interstage Storage along an Automatic Production Line," *AIIE Transactions,* Vol. 8, No. 1, 1976, pp. 146–152.

PROBLEMS

5.1.   An eight-station rotary indexing machine operates with an ideal cycle time of 20 s. The frequency of line stop occurrences is 0.06 stop/cycle on the average. When a stop occurs, it takes an average of 3 min to make repairs. Determine the following:
   (a) Average production time T_p.
   (b) Average production rate R_p.
   (c) Line efficiency E.
   (d) Proportion of downtime D.

5.2.   Assume that the frequency of line stop occurrences in Problem 5.1 is due to random mechanical and electrical failures on the line. Suppose, in addition to the foregoing reasons for line stops, that the workstation tools must be reset and/or changed at regular intervals. It takes an average of 4 min to inspect and adjust or change the tools at all eight stations. This procedure is performed every 200 cycles. Recompute T_p,R_p,E, and D with these additional data for the indexing machine.

5.3.   Component costs associated with the operation of the indexing machine of Problem 5.2 are as follows:

$$\text{cost of raw workpart} = \$0.35/\text{workpiece}$$

$$\text{cost to operate the line} = \$0.50/\text{min}$$

$$\text{cost of disposable tooling} = \$0.02/\text{workpiece}$$

Compute the average cost per workpiece produced off the rotary indexing machine.

5.4.   In the operation of a certain 15-station transfer line, the ideal cycle time is 0.58 min. Breakdowns occur at a rate of once every 10 cycles, and the average downtime per breakdown ranges between 2 and 9 min, with an average of 4.2 min. The plant in which the transfer line is located works an 8-h day, 5 days per week. How many parts will the line be capable of producing during an average week?

5.5.   The following data apply to a 12-station in-line transfer machine:

$$p = 0.01 \text{ (all stations have an equal probability of failure)}$$

$$T_c = 0.3 \text{ min}$$

$$T_d = 3.0 \text{ min}$$

Using the upper-bound approach, compute the following for the transfer machine:
   (a) F, the frequency of line stops.
   (b) R_p, the average production rate.
   (c) E, the line efficiency.

5.6. Solve Problem 5.5 using the lower-bound approach. What proportion of workparts are removed from the transfer line?

5.7. A circular indexing machine performs 10 assembly operations at 10 separate stations. The total cycle time, including transfer time between stations, is 10 s. Stations break down with a probability $p = 0.007$, which can be considered equal for all 10 stations. When these work stoppages occur, it takes an average of 2 min to correct the fault. Parts are not normally removed from the machine when these stops occur. Compute the proportion of downtime, the efficiency, and the production rate of this circular indexing machine.

5.8. A transfer machine has six stations as follows:

Station	Operation	p_i	Process time (min)
1	Load part	0	0.78
2	Drill three holes	0.02	1.25
3	Ream two holes	0.01	0.90
4	Tap two holes	0.04	1.42
5	Mill flats	0.01	1.42
6	Unload part	0	0.45

The time to transfer between stations $= 0.28$ min. If the part stops due to a jam in the line, it is removed as defective. It takes an average of 8 min to determine the fault and correct the problem and remove the part. Also, there is a scheduled tool change every 40 parts which takes 6 min to complete. There are 20,000 parts to be started onto the transfer machine.
(a) How many defective parts will be removed from the line?
(b) How many total hours will be consumed in the manufacturing process? — for the starting batch qty of 2000
(c) Find the proportion of downtime.
(d) Find the rate of production of acceptable parts.

5.9. In Problem 5.8, the cost of operating the transfer machine is $60/h, as estimated by the accounting department of the company. It is proposed that a computer and sensors be installed to aid in diagnosing breakdowns when they occur. The anticipated savings are 2 min off the 8 min to identify and correct the fault when it occurs. The computer will have no effect on tool changes. The estimated cost of installing the monitoring system is $11,000. How many units must the system produce in order to pay for the computer?

5.10. A 23-station transfer line has been logged for 5 days (a total of 2400 min). During this time, there were a total of 158 downtime occurrences on the line. The accompanying table identifies the type of downtime occurrence, how many occurrences, and how much total time for the type of occurrence.

Type of occurrence	Number of occurrences	Total minutes lost
Associated with stations	132	793
Tool-related causes at stations	104	520
Mechanical failures at stations	21	189
Other miscellaneous station failures	7	84
Associated with transfer mechanism	26	78

The transfer line performs a sequence of machining operations, the longest of which takes 0.42 min. The transfer mechanism takes 0.08 min to index a part from one station to the next position. Assuming no parts removal when the line jams, determine the following characteristics for this line for the 5-day period:
(a) How many parts are produced.
(b) Downtime proportion.
(c) Production rate and production time.
(d) Frequency rate p associated with the transfer mechanism breakdowns.

5.11. An eight-station transfer line has the following operations at each station; also given are the processing time and the frequency of line stops for each station. During the observation period there were 2000 parts completed.

Station	Process	Process time (min)	Breakdowns
1	Load part	0.40	0
2	Mill top	0.85	22
3	Mill sides	1.10	31
4	Drill two holes	0.60	47
5	Ream two holes	0.40	8
6	Drill six holes	0.90	58
7	Tap six holes	0.75	84
8	Unload part	0.50	0

Also influencing the cycle time is the operation of the transfer mechanism, which takes 0.15 min each cycle. When breakdowns occur it takes an average of 7.00 min to make repairs and get the line operating again. Assume that the upper-bound approach is operative in your analysis for the following:
(a) Determine the average production time per piece and the hourly production rate for this transfer line.
(b) What is the uptime efficiency of the line and the proportion downtime?
(c) How many hours were required to produce the 2000 parts?

5.12. In Problem 5.11, if the lower-bound approach were used instead of the upper-bound approach, and if the frequency of breakdowns in the lower-bound approach $F = 0.10$, determine the following (assuming that the process times, transfer time, and average downtime per occurrence are the same in Problem 5.11):
(a) How many raw workparts would have started on the line in order to complete the 2000 parts?
(b) How many parts would have been removed from the line as damaged due to breakdowns if 2000 parts were completed?
(c) How many hours would have been required to produce the 2000 completed parts?

5.13. The APSCIM Machine & Foundry operates an automated transfer line with 12 stations. The line is considered to have an efficiency that is unacceptably low. Figure P5.13 is a report of a study on the current line operations. APSCIM would like to improve the efficiency by making the following changes in the line:

First, change over from the current electromechanical relay–type controls to a programmable controller. In addition to controlling the line in the same way as before, the new controller would reduce the average downtime by diagnosing the malfunction, thus allowing repairs to be made more quickly. It is expected that the average downtime per occurrence will be reduced by 25% using this diagnostic system.

APSCIM Machine & Foundry, Inc.
Technology Laboratory Report

Report No. 572

Prepared by: John B. Olderfella

This will document our two-week study of the APSCIM transfer line. The transfer line was observed for a total of 80 hours (one shift per day). During this period, the line was down for a total of 42 hours, and a total of 1689 parts were machined. The following table lists the operation, the process time (in minutes), and the number of downtime occurrences for each station:

Station	Operation	Process time (min)	Number of downtimes
1	Load (manual)	0.50	0
2	Rough mill top	1.10	15
3	Finish mill top	1.25	18
4	Rough mill sides	0.65	23
5	Finish mill sides	1.05	31
6	Mill surfaces for drill	0.80	9
7	Drill two holes	0.75	27
8	Tap two holes	0.40	47
9	Drill three holes	0.85	30
10	Ream three holes	0.70	21
11	Tap three holes	0.45	25
12	Unload and inspect	0.90	0
		9.40	246

The transfer time required to move parts from one station to the next is 6 seconds.

FIGURE P5.13

Second, divide the current line consisting of 12 stations into two stages, each consisting of six stations. An in-process storage buffer would be used between the stages so that each stage could operate as an independent transfer line. This is expected to improve the overall production rate and line efficiency.

Determine the following:

(a) The parameters of the line performance as it currently operates (without the improvements). These should include the ideal cycle time, the frequency of line stops, the line efficiency, and the average hourly production rate.

(b) The effect of the two changes in the line operation described above. Determine the effect of both of the changes together rather than each change separately. Your analysis should result in an assessment of the line performance for each stage (ideal cycle time, the frequency of line stops, the line efficiency, and the average hourly production rate). Also, determine the overall performance of the two-stage system. In your analysis, assume the upper-bound approach. Make any other additional assumptions necessary to solve the problem.

5.14. A 14-station transfer line has been logged for a total of 2400 min. The following table identifies the type of downtime occurrence, how many occurrences, and how much time was lost for each type.

Type of occurrence	Number	Time lost (mins)
Tool changes and failures	70	400
Station failures: mechanical and electrical	45	300
Transfer system failures	25	150

The ideal cycle time for the line is 0.50 min, including transfer time between stations. Half of the downtime occurrences for "tool changes and failures" (35 occurrences and 200 min) involve cases where the part was damaged and has to be removed from the line. The other downtime occurrences follow the assumptions of the upper-bound approach. Determine the following characteristics of the line operation.

(a) How many acceptable parts were produced during the 2400-min period?
(b) What were the line efficiency and downtime proportion?
(c) What was the average actual production rate of acceptable parts in parts per hour?
(d) Determine the frequency p associated with the transfer system failures?

5.15. A partially automated flow line has a mixture of mechanized and manual workstations. There are a total of six stations and the overall theoretical cycle time is 1.0 min. This includes a transfer time of 6 s. The six stations possess characteristics as follows:

Station	Type	Process time (s)	p_i
1	Manual	30	0
2	Automatic	15	0.01
3	Automatic	20	0.02
4	Automatic	25	0.01
5	Manual	54	0
6	Manual	30	0

Cost of the transfer mechanism is $0.10/min to operate. Cost to run each of the automatic workheads is figured at $0.12/min for each of the three automatic stations. Labor cost to operate each of the manual stations is $0.15/min for each of stations 1, 5, and 6. It has been proposed to substitute an automatic workhead for the current manual station 5. The cost of this workhead will be 0.25/min and its breakdown rate p will be 0.02, but its process time will be only 30 s compared to 54 s for the current line. The average downtime per breakdown of the current and proposed configuration is 3.0 min. Should the proposal be accepted?

5.16. A manual flow line has six stations. The time required to process the part at each station is 1.0 min. The parts are transferred by hand from one station to the next, and an additional 12 s is lost each cycle due to lack of operator discipline. Hence, the current cycle time on the line is 1.2 min. The following two proposals have been made: First, install a mechanized transfer system to pace the line. Second, automate one or more of the workstations on the line, resulting in a partially or fully automated line. This requires installation of the mechanized transfer system in the first proposal. The transfer system alone will bring discipline to the line and cause the cycle time to be reduced to 1.0 min. All six stations are candidates for automation; however, there are differences in the reliability with which the automated stations would operate. This is manifested in the value of p, the probability of a station failure. These probability values are given in the following table.

Station	Probability p	Station	Probability p
1	0.01	4	0.04
2	0.02	5	0.05
3	0.03	6	0.06

The average downtime = 3 min when any of these automated stations break down. The ideal cycle time for each automated station is 20 s. The cost of the automated transfer mechanism (which serves all six stations) = $0.10/min. The cost per operator on the line = $0.20/min; and the cost per automated workstation = $0.25/min. Determine if either or both of the proposals should be accepted. If the second proposal is accepted, how many stations should be automated? Use cost per piece as the criterion for your determinations.

5.17. A 16-station automatic transfer line has the following operating characteristics:

$$T_c = 0.75 \text{ min}$$

$$T_d = 3.0 \text{ min}$$

$$p = 0.01 \text{ for all workstations}$$

A proposal has been submitted to place a storage buffer between stations 8 and 9 to improve the overall efficiency of the transfer line. What is the current line efficiency (use the upper-bound approach), and what is the maximum possible efficiency that would result from use of a storage buffer?

5.18. If the capacity of the storage buffer in Problem 5.17 is to be 10 workparts, calculate the line efficiency and the average production rate of the two-stage transfer line. Assume that downtime ($T_d = 3.0$ min) is a constant.

5.19. Solve Problem 5.18 assuming that downtime is geometrically distributed.

5.20. In the transfer line of Problem 5.19, suppose that it is more technically feasible to place the storage buffer between stations 6 and 7. Using a storage buffer capacity of 10 workparts, calculate the line efficiency and the average production rate. Assume that downtime is constant.

5.21. Solve Problem 5.20 but assume that downtime is geometrically distributed.

5.22. A synchronous transfer line has 20 stations and operates with an ideal cycle time of 0.5 min. All stations have an equal probability of breakdown, $p = 0.01$. When breakdowns occur, the average downtime is 5.0 min and the upper-bound approach applies. A proposal has been made to divide the line into two independent stages, each stage having 10 stations, with a buffer storage zone between the stations. The proposal indicates that each stage could operate independently to increase production rate of the overall line. It has been decided that the storage capacity will be 25 units. The cost to operate each station is $4.80/h per station. Installation of the buffer storage zone would increase the line operating cost by $12.00/h. Ignore material and tooling costs in this problem.

(a) Determine the average production rate per hour and the cost per unit of production for the current 20-station line.

(b) Calculate the average production rate per hour and the cost per unit for the proposed two-stage system.

5.23. A certain 16-station transfer line can be conveniently divided into a two-stage line with a buffer storage zone between the eighth and ninth workstations. The probability of a failure at any station is $p = 0.01$. The ideal cycle time is 1.0 min and the downtime on the line is 10.0 min every time a linestop occurs. The downtime should be considered to be constant, and the upper-bound approach should be assumed. The cost of installing the buffer storage zone is a function of its capacity. The cost $= $0.6b/h = $0.01b/min$, where $b =$ the buffer capacity. However, the storage buffer can only be built to hold increments of 10 (i.e., capacity $= 10$ or 20 or 30, etc.). The cost to operate the line is $120 per hour. Material costs and tooling costs should be ignored. Based on cost per unit of product, determine the capacity of the buffer zone that will minimize the product cost.

5.24. The operation of a certain 20-station line is very poor and the management is looking to improve the line's performance. The ideal cycle time is 48 s, and the uptime efficiency is only 40%. The average downtime per occurrence is 3.0 min. Assume that the frequency of breakdowns is equal for all stations and that the repair time distribution is constant. One of the alternatives under consideration is to divide the line into two equal stages by means of a storage buffer. Each stage would have 10 workstations. The company can install a buffer with a 15-unit capacity in the line for $14,000. The present unit cost of production is $4.00 per unit produced (this ignores material and tooling costs). How many units will have to be produced in order for the $14,000 investment in the storage buffer to pay for itself?

chapter **6**

Assembly Systems and Line Balancing

Most discrete products are assembled from components. In this chapter we discuss some of the important aspects of assembly technology, giving most attention to the production systems used to accomplish the assembly process. The first section provides an introduction to assembly process technology, and the second section discusses the various assembly methods and systems used in industry. One of these methods is the manual assembly line, and balancing the work load among the operators along the line is a principal problem in the design and operation of manual assembly lines. We devote Sections 6.3 through 6.7 to a discussion of manual assembly lines and line balancing. In Section 6.8 we discuss a relatively new concept in manual assembly-line design, involving the use of flexible assembly systems.

Another important method of performing assembly operations involves the use of automation. Mechanized and automated assembly systems are discussed in Chapter 7.

6.1 THE ASSEMBLY PROCESS

As defined in Chapter 2, assembly involves the joining together of two or more separate parts to form a new entity. The new entity is called a subassembly, or an assembly, or some similar name. The processes used to accomplish the assembly of the components can be divided into three major categories:

1. Mechanical fastening
2. Joining methods
3. Adhesive bonding

Mechanical fastening consists of a wide variety of techniques that employ a mechanical action to hold the components together. These techniques include:

*   *Threaded fasteners.*   These are screws, nuts, bolts, and so on. The use of threaded fasteners is very common in industry and has the advantage of allowing the assembly to be taken apart (for repair, maintenance, adjustment, etc.) if necessary. Threaded fasteners are readily used by human assembly workers, but are more difficult for robots and automated systems.
*   *Rivets, crimping, and other methods.*   The fastener or one of the components to be assembled is mechanically deformed to retain the mating part(s).
*   *Press fits.*   In this assembly method, there is an interference fit between the two parts that are to be mated. For example, a shaft is fitted into a hole in which the shaft diameter is slightly larger than the hole diameter. To mate the two parts, the shaft must be pressed into the hole under high pressure. Once fitted, the parts are not easily separated.
*   *Snap fits.*   This method involves a temporary interference of the two parts to be mated which occurs only during assembly. One or both of the parts elastically deform when pressed together to overcome the interference and permit them to snap into place. Once together, the snap fit prevents separation of the two parts. Retainers, C-rings, and snap rings are examples of available commercial hardware in this category. Mating parts can sometimes be designed for assembly by snap fitting without the need for these hardware fasteners.
*   *Sewing and stitching.*   These are used to assemble soft, thin materials such as fabrics, cloth, leather, and thin flexible plastics.

The term *joining method* generally refers to the processes of welding, brazing, and soldering. In these processes, molten metal is used to fuse the two or more components together. The process of welding includes a variety of joining techniques whose common feature is that fusing and melting occur in the metal parts being joined. In some welding operations, filler metal is added to promote the joining action between the parent metals. Some of the welding processes used in industry for assembly include resistance welding, arc welding, friction welding, laser beam welding, and electron beam welding.

Brazing and soldering are joining processes that make use of a filler metal which becomes molten for the joining process, but the metal components themselves do not melt. The distinction between brazing and soldering is usually defined by the melting point of the filler metal used in the processes. In brazing, the melting point of the filler is above 450°C, and in soldering the filler melting point is below 450°C. Because there is no fusing of the parent metals in brazing and soldering, these processes do not create as strong an assembly connection as in welding.

Adhesive bonding involves the use of an adhesive material to join components together. The use of adhesives is growing rapidly today as an assembly technology in industry, and new adhesives are being developed to satisfy new applications. Adhesives can be classified into two types: thermoplastic and thermosetting. Thermoplastic adhesives are easy to apply but cannot withstand high-temperature applications. The use of thermosetting adhesives (e.g., epoxies) involves a chemical reaction that is brought on by a chemical hardener and/or heat. This assembly process is therefore more complicated than with thermoplastic adhesives, but the resulting bonds are generally stronger and capable of withstanding higher temperatures in service.

6.2 ASSEMBLY SYSTEMS

There are various methods used in industry to accomplish the assembly processes described above. The methods can be classified as follows:

1. Manual single-stations assembly
2. Manual assembly line
3. Automated assembly system

The *manual single-station assembly* method consists of a single workplace in which the assembly work is accomplished on the product or some major subassembly of the product. This method is generally used on a product that is complex and produced in small quantities, sometimes one of a kind. The workplace may utilize one or more workers, depending on the size of the product and the required production rate. Custom-engineered products such as machine tools, industrial equipment, aircraft, ships, and prototype models of large, complex consumer products (e.g., appliances, cars) make use of a single manual station to perform the assembly work on the product.

Manual assembly lines consist of multiple workstations in which the assembly work is accomplished as the product (or subassembly) is passed from station to station along the line. At each workstation one or more human workers perform a portion of the total assembly work on the product, by adding one or more components to the existing subassembly. When the product comes off the final station, the work has been completed.

Automated assembly systems make use of automated methods at the workstations rather than human beings. As indicated in the chapter introduction, we defer discussion of automated assembly systems until Chapter 7.

6.3 MANUAL ASSEMBLY LINES

Manual assembly lines, or, more generally, manual flow lines, are used in high-production situations where the work to be performed can be divided into small tasks (called *work elements*) and the tasks assigned to the workstations on the line. One of the key advantages of using manual assembly lines is specialization of labor. By giving each worker a limited set of tasks to do repeatedly, the worker becomes a specialist in those tasks and is able to perform them more quickly and more consistently. A typical assembly line is pictured in Figure 6.1. The general configuration of a manual assembly line is illustrated in Figure 6.2.

Transfer of work between workstations

There are two basic ways in which the work (the subassembly that is being built up) is moved on the line between operator workstations:

  1. *Nonmechanical lines.* In this arrangement, no belt or conveyor is used to move the parts between operator workstations. Instead, the parts are passed from station to station by hand. Several problems result from this mode of operation:
   • Starving at stations, where the operator has completed his or her work but must wait for parts from the preceding station.
   • Blocking of stations, where the operator has completed his or her work but must wait for the next operator to finish the task before passing along the part.

FIGURE 6.1   Manual assembly line in which the work proceeds around a long loop, sometimes called a carousel. (Courtesy of Jervis B. Webb Co.)

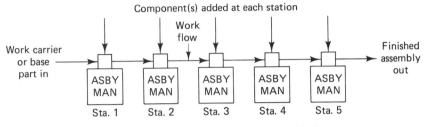

FIGURE 6.2   Diagram of a manual assembly line.

As a result of these problems, the flow of work on a nonmechanical line is usually uneven. The cycle times vary, and this contributes to the overall irregularity. Buffer stocks of parts between workstations are often used to smooth out the production flow.

2.   *Moving conveyor lines.*   These flow lines use a moving conveyor (e.g., a moving belt, conveyor, chain-in-the-floor, etc.) to move the subassemblies between workstations. The transport system can be continuous, intermittent (synchronous), or asynchronous. Continuous transfer is most common in manual assembly lines, although asynchronous transfer is becoming more popular. With the continuously moving conveyor, the following problems can arise:

  • Starving can occur as with nonmechanical lines.
  • Incomplete items are sometimes produced when the operator is unable to finish the current part and the next part travels right by on the conveyor. Blocking does not occur.

Again, buffer stocks are sometimes used to overcome these problems. Also, station overlaps can sometimes be allowed, where the worker is permitted to travel beyond the normal boundaries of the station in order to complete work.

In the moving belt line, it is possible to achieve a higher level of control over the production rate of the line. This is accomplished by means of the feed rate, which refers to the reciprocal of the time interval between workparts on the moving belt. Let f_p denote this feed rate. It is measured in workpieces per time and depends on two factors: the speed with which the conveyor moves, and the spacing of workparts along the belt. Let V_c equal the conveyor speed (feet per minute or meters per second) and s_p equal the spacing between parts on the moving conveyor (feet or meters per workpiece). Then the feed rate is determined by

$$f_p = \frac{V_c}{s_p} \qquad \Rightarrow \text{gives nominal cycle time} \qquad (6.1)$$

To control the feed rate of the line, raw workparts are launched onto the line at regular intervals. As the parts flow along the line, the operator has a certain time period during which he or she must begin work on each piece. Otherwise, the part will flow past the station. This time period is called the tolerance time T_t. It is determined by the conveyor speed and the length of the workstation. This length we will symbolize by L_s, and it is determined largely by the operator's reach at the workstation. The tolerance time is therefore defined by

$$T_t = \frac{L_s}{V_c} \tag{6.2}$$

For example, suppose that the desired production rate on a manual flow line with moving conveyor were 60 units/h. This would necessitate a feed rate of 1 part/min. This could be achieved by a conveyor speed of 0.6 m/min and a part spacing of 0.5 m. (Other combinations of V_c and s_p would also provide the same feed rate.) If the length of each workstation were 1.5 m, the tolerance time available to the operators for each workpiece would be 3 min. It is generally desirable to make the tolerance time large to compensate for worker process time variability.

Model variations

In both nonmechanical lines and moving conveyor lines it is highly desirable to assign work to the stations so as to equalize the process or assembly times at the workstations. The problem is sometimes complicated by the fact that the same production line may be called upon to process more than one type of product. This complication gives rise to the identification of three flow line cases (and therefore three different types of line balancing problems).

The three production situations on flow lines are defined according to the product or products to be made on the line. Will the flow line be used exclusively to produce one particular model? Or, will it be used to produce several different models, and if so, how will they be scheduled on the line? There are three cases that can be defined in response to these questions:

1. *Single-model line.* This is a specialized line dedicated to the production of a single model or product. The demand rate for the product is great enough that the line is devoted 100% of the time to the production of that product.

2. *Batch-model line.* This line is used for the production of two or more models. Each model is produced in batches on the line. The models or products are usually similar in the sense of requiring a similar sequence of processing or assembly operations. It is for this reason that the same line can be used to produce the various models.

3. *Mixed-model lines.* This line is also used for the production of two or more models, but the various models are intermixed on the line so that several different models are being produced simultaneously rather than in batches. Automobile and truck assembly lines are examples of this case.

To gain a better perspective of the three cases, the reader might consider the following. In the case of the batch-model line, if the batch sizes are very large, the batch-model line approaches the case of the single-model line. If the batch sizes become very small (approaching a batch size of 1), the batch-model line approximates to the case of the mixed-model line.

In principle, the three cases can be applied in both manual flow lines and automated flow lines. However, in practice, the flexibility of human operators makes the latter two cases more feasible on the manual assembly line. It is anticipated that future automated lines will incorporate quick changeover and programming capabilities within their designs to permit the batch-model, and eventually the mixed-model, concepts to become practicable.

Achieving a balanced allocation of workload among the stations of the line is a problem in all three cases. The problem is least formidable for the single-model case. For the batch-model line, the balancing problem becomes more difficult; and for the mixed-model case, the problem of line balancing becomes quite complicated.

In this chapter we consider only the single-model line balancing problem, although the same concepts and similar terminology and methodology apply for the batch- and mixed-model cases.

6.4   THE LINE BALANCING PROBLEM

In flow line production there are many separate and distinct processing and assembly operations to be performed on the product. Invariably, the sequence of processing or assembly steps is restricted, at least to some extent, in terms of the order in which the operations can be carried out. For example, a threaded hole must be drilled before it can be tapped. In mechanical fastening, the washer must be placed over the bolt before the nut can be turned and tightened. These restrictions are called *precedence constraints* in the language of line balancing. It is generally the case that the product must be manufactured at some specified production rate in order to satisfy demand for the product. Whether we are concerned with performing these processes and assembly operations on automatic machines or manual flow lines, it is desirable to design the line so as to satisfy all of the foregoing specifications as efficiently as possible.

The line balancing problem is to arrange the individual processing and assembly tasks at the workstations so that the total time required at each workstation is approximately the same. If the work elements can be grouped so that all the station times are exactly equal, we have perfect balance on the line and we can expect the production to flow smoothly. In most practical situations it is very difficult to achieve perfect balance. When the workstation times are unequal, the slowest station determines the overall production rate of the line.

In order to discuss the terminology and relationships in line balancing, we shall refer to the following example. Later, when discussing the various solution techniques, we shall apply the techniques to this problem.

EXAMPLE 6.1

A new small electrical appliance is to be assembled on a production flow line. The total job of assembling the product has been divided into minimum rational work elements. The industrial engineering department has developed time standards based on previous similar jobs. This information is given in Table 6.1. In the right-hand column are the immediate predecessors for each element as determined by precedence requirements. Production demand will be 120,000 units/yr. At 50 weeks/yr and 40 h/week, this reduces to an output from the line of 60 units/h or 1 unit/min.

Terminology

Let us define the following terms in line balancing. Some of the terms should be familiar to the reader from Chapters 4 and 5, but we want to give very specific meanings to these terms for our purposes in this chapter.

MINIMUM RATIONAL WORK ELEMENT. In order to spread the job to be done on the line among its stations, the job must be divided into its component tasks. The minimum rational work elements are the smallest practical indivisible tasks into which the job can be divided. These work elements cannot be subdivided further. For example, the drilling of a hole would normally be considered as a minimum rational work element. In manual assembly, when two components are fastened together with a screw and nut, it would be reasonable for these activities to be taken together. Hence, this assembly task would constitute a minimum rational work element. We can symbolize the time required to carry out this minimum rational work element as T_{ej}, where j is used to identify the element out of the n_e elements that make up the total work or job. For instance, the element time, T_{ej}, for element 1 in Example 6.1 is 0.2 min.

The time T_{ej} of a work element is considered a constant rather than a variable. An automatic workhead most closely fits this assumption, although the processing time could

TABLE 6.1 Work Elements

No.	Element description	T_{ej}	Must be preceded by:
1	Place frame on workholder and clamp	0.2	—
2	Assemble plug, grommet to power cord	0.4	—
3	Assemble brackets to frame	0.7	1
4	Wire power cord to motor	0.1	1, 2
5	Wire power cord to switch	0.3	2
6	Assemble mechanism plate to bracket	0.11	3
7	Assemble blade to bracket	0.32	3
8	Assemble motor to brackets	0.6	3, 4
9	Align blade and attach to motor	0.27	6, 7, 8
10	Assemble switch to motor bracket	0.38	5, 8
11	Attach cover, inspect, and test	0.5	9, 10
12	Place in tote pan for packing	0.12	11

probably be altered by making adjustments in the station. In a manual operation, the time required to perform a work element will, in fact, vary from cycle to cycle.

Another assumption implicit in the use of T_e values is that they are additive. The time to perform two work elements is the sum of the times of the individual elements. In practice, this might not be true. It might be that some economy of motion could be achieved by combining two work elements at one station, thus violating the additivity assumption.

TOTAL WORK CONTENT.   This is the aggregate of all the work elements to be done on the line. Let T_{wc} be the time required for the total work content. Hence,

$$T_{wc} = \sum_{j=1}^{n_e} T_{ej} \qquad (6.3)$$

For the example, $T_{wc} = 4.00$ min.

WORKSTATION PROCESS TIME.   A workstation is a location along the flow line where work is performed, either manually or by some automatic device. The work performed at the station consists of one or more of the individual work elements and the time required is the sum of the times of the work elements done at the station. We use T_{si} to indicate the process time at station i of an n-station line. It should be clear that the sum of the station process times should equal the sum of the work element times.

$$\sum_{i=1}^{n} T_{si} = \sum_{j=1}^{n_e} T_{ej} \qquad (6.4)$$

(excl. idle time)

CYCLE TIME.   This is the ideal or theoretical cycle time of the flow line, which is the time interval between parts coming off the line. The design value of T_c would be specified according to the required production rate to be achieved by the flow line. Allowing for downtime on the line, the value of T_c must meet the following requirement:

any desired cycle time $\quad T_c \le \dfrac{E}{R_p} \quad$ *or* $\; T_c R_p = \dfrac{T_c}{T_p} \le E \quad$ (6.5) *under given R_p* ✳

where E is the line efficiency as defined in Chapter 5, and R_p the required production rate. As we observed in Chapter 5, the line efficiency of an automated line will be somewhat less than 100%. For a manual line, where mechanical malfunctions are less likely, the efficiency will be closer to 100%.

In Example 6.1, the required production rate is 60 units/h or 1 unit/min. At a line efficiency of 100%, the value of T_c would be 1.0 min. At efficiencies less than 100%, the ideal cycle time must be reduced (or what is the same thing, the ideal production rate R_c must be increased) to compensate for the downtime.

✳ *since prod'n. rate* $R_p = \frac{1}{T_p}$ *cannot be lower than a given (reqd.) value,*

& since $T_p = T_c + F T_d$ *where FT_d is a const.*

eg. if $R_p = 1/min \Rightarrow T_p = 1min$, *w/ $FT_d = .2 min$ (i.e. $T_c \le .8 min$)*

then $\frac{T_c}{T_p} = \frac{.8}{1} = .8$ *under* $\frac{}{given} R_p$ — *we can change T_c to a smaller value,*

say $T_c = .6 \Rightarrow \frac{T_c}{T_p} = E = .75 (\le E)$, *but not the other way*

The minimum possible value of T_c is established by the bottleneck station, the one with the largest value of T_s. That is,

$$T_c \geq \max T_{si} \tag{6.6}$$

If $T_c = \max T_{si}$, there will be idle time at all stations whose T_s values are less than T_c. Finally, since the station times are comprised of element times,

$$T_c \geq T_{ej} \quad \text{(for all } j = 1, 2, \ldots, n_e) \tag{6.7}$$

This equation states the obvious: that the cycle time must be greater than or equal to any of the element times.

In Chapter 5 we defined the ideal cycle time to include the transfer time. In Eqs. (6.5) through (6.7), and in the remainder of this chapter, we assume that the transfer time is negligible. If this is not true, a correction must be made in the value of T_c used in Eqs. (6.6) and (6.7) to allow for parts transfer time.

PRECEDENCE CONSTRAINTS.   These are also referred to as "technological sequencing requirements." The order in which the work elements can be accomplished is limited, at least to some extent. In Example 6.1, the switch must be mounted onto the motor bracket before the cover of the appliance can be attached. The right-hand column in Table 6.1 gives a complete listing of the precedence constraints for assembling the hypothetical electrical appliance. In nearly every processing or assembly job, there are precedence requirements that restrict the sequence in which the job can be accomplished.

In addition to the precedence constraints described above, there may be other types of constraints on the line balancing solution. These concern the restrictions on the arrangement of the stations rather than the sequence of work elements. The first is called a *zoning constraint*. A zoning constraint may be either a positive constraint or a negative constraint. A *positive* zoning constraint means that certain work elements should be placed near each other, preferably at the same workstation. For example, all the spray-painting elements should be performed together since a special semienclosed workstation has to be utilized. A *negative* zoning constraint indicates that work elements might interfere with one another and should therefore not be located in close proximity. As an illustration, a work element requiring fine adjustments or delicate coordination should not be located near a station characterized by loud noises and heavy vibrations.

Another constraint on the arrangement of workstations is called a *position constraint*. This would be encountered in the assembly of large products such as automobiles or major appliances. The product is too large for one worker to perform work on both sides. Therefore, for the sake of facilitating the work, operators are located on both sides of the flow line. This type of situation is referred to as a position constraint.

In the example there are no zoning constraints or position constraints given. The line balancing methods presented in Section 6.5 are not equipped to deal with these constraints conveniently. However, in real-life situations, they may constitute a significant consideration in the design of the flow line.

PRECEDENCE DIAGRAM. This is a graphical representation of the sequence of work elements as defined by the precedence constraints. It is customary to use nodes to symbolize the work elements, with arrows connecting the nodes to indicate the order in which the elements must be performed. Elements that must be done first appear as nodes at the left of the diagram. Then the sequence of processing and/or assembly progresses to the right. The precedence diagram for Example 6.1 is illustrated in Figure 6.3. The element times are recorded above each node for convenience.

BALANCE DELAY. Sometimes also called balancing loss, this is a measure of the line inefficiency which results from idle time due to imperfect allocation of work among stations. It is symbolized as d and can be computed for the flow line as follows:

$$d = \frac{nT_c - T_{wc}}{nT_c} \tag{6.8}$$

The balance delay is often expressed as a percent rather than as a decimal fraction in Eq. (6.8).

The balance delay should not be confused with the proportion downtime, D, of an automated flow line, as defined by Eq. (5.6). D is a measure of the inefficiency that results from line stops. The balance delay measures the inefficiency from imperfect line balancing.

Considering the data given in Example 6.1, the total work content $T_{wc} = 4.00$ min.

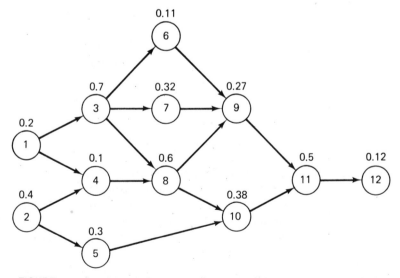

FIGURE 6.3 Precedence diagram for Example 6.1. Nodes represent work elements. The element times are shown above each node. Arrows indicate the sequence in which the work elements must be done.

We shall assume that $T_c = 1.0$ min. If it were possible to achieve perfect balance with $n = 4$ workstations, the balance delay would be, according to Eq. (6.8),

$$d = \frac{4(1.0) - 4.0}{4(1.0)} = 0$$

If the line could only be balanced with $n = 5$ stations for the 1.0-min cycle, the balance delay would be

$$d = \frac{5(1.0) - 4.0}{5(1.0)} = 0.20 \text{ or } 20\%$$

Both of these solutions provide the same theoretical production rate. However, the second solution is less efficient because an additional workstation, and therefore an additional assembly operator, is required. One possible way to improve the efficiency of the five-station line is to decrease the cycle time T_c. To illustrate, suppose that the line could be balanced at a cycle time of $T_c = 0.80$ min. The corresponding measure of inefficiency would be

$$d = \frac{5(0.80) - 4.0}{5(0.80)} = 0$$

This solution (if it were possible) would yield a perfect balance. Although five workstations are required, the theoretical production rate would be $R_c = 1.25$ units/min, an increase over the production rate capability of the four-station line. The reader can readily perceive that there are many combinations of n and T_c that will produce a theoretically perfect balance. Each combination will give a different production rate. In general, the balance delay d will be zero for any values n and T_c that satisfy the relationship

$$nT_c = T_{wc} \tag{6.9}$$

Unfortunately, because of precedence constraints and because the particular values of T_{ej} usually do not permit it, perfect balance might not be achievable for every nT_c combination that equals the total work content time. In other words, the satisfaction of Eq. (6.9) is a necessary condition for perfect balance, but not a sufficient condition.

As indicated by Eq. (6.5), the desired maximum value of T_c is specified by the production rate required of the flow line. Therefore, Eq. (6.9) can be cast in a different form to determine the theoretical minimum number of workstations required to optimize the balance delay for a specified T_c. Since n must be an integer, we can state:

$$\text{minimum } n \text{ is the smallest integer} \geq \frac{T_{wc}}{T_c} \tag{6.10}$$

Applying this rule to our example, with $T_{wc} = 4.0$ min and $T_c = 1.0$ min, the minimum $n = 4$ stations.

In the next section we examine methods that attempt (but do not guarantee) to provide line balancing solutions with minimum balance delay for a given T_c.

6.5 METHODS OF LINE BALANCING

In this section we consider several methods for solving the line balancing problem by hand, using Example 6.1 for purposes of illustration. These methods are heuristic approaches, meaning that they are based on logic and common sense rather than on mathematical proof. None of the methods guarantees an optimal solution, but they are likely to result in good solutions which approach the true optimum. The manual methods to be presented are:

1. Largest-candidate rule
2. Kilbridge and Wester's method
3. Ranked positional weights method

In Section 6.6 we consider some computer procedures for solving the line balancing problem.

Largest-candidate rule

This is the easiest method to understand. The work elements are selected for assignment to stations simply on the basis of the size of their T_e values. The steps used in solving the line balancing problem are listed below, followed by Example 6.2, which is the application of these steps to Example 6.1.

PROCEDURE

Step 1. List all elements in descending order of T_e value, largest T_e at the top of the list.

Step 2. To assign elements to the first workstation, start at the top of the list and work down, selecting the first feasible element for placement at the station. A feasible element is one that satisfies the precedence requirements and does not cause the sum of the T_e values at the station to exceed the cycle time T_c.

Step 3. Continue the process of assigning work elements to the station as in step 2 until no further elements can be added without exceeding T_c.

Step 4. Repeat steps 2 and 3 for the other stations in the line until all the elements have been assigned.

TABLE 6.2   Work Elements Arranged According to T_e
Value for the Largest-Candidate Rule

Work element	T_e	Immediate predecessors
3	0.7	1
8	0.6	3, 4
11	0.5	9, 10
2	0.4	—
10	0.38	5,8
7	0.32	3
5	0.3	2
9	0.27	6, 7, 8
1	0.2	—
12	0.12	11
6	0.11	3
4	0.1	1,2

One comment should be made which applies not only to the largest-candidate rule but to the other methods as well. Starting with a given T_c value, it is not usually clear how many stations will be required on the flow line. Of course, the most desirable number of stations is that which satisfies Eq. (6.10). However, the practical realities of the line balancing problem may not permit the realization of this number.

EXAMPLE 6.2

The work elements of Example 6.1 are listed in Table 6.2 in the manner prescribed by step 1. Also listed are the immediate predecessors for each element. This is of value in determining feasibility of elements that are candidates for assignment to a given station.

TABLE 6.3   Work Elements Assigned to Stations According
to the Largest-Candidate Rule

Station	Element	T_e	ΣT_e at station
1	2	0.4	
	5	0.3	
	1	0.2	
	4	0.1	1.00
2	3	0.7	
	6	0.11	0.81
3	8	0.6	
	10	0.38	0.98
4	7	0.32	
	9	0.27	0.59
5	11	0.5	
	12	0.11	0.62

Following step 2, we start at the top of the list and search for feasible work elements. Element 3 is not feasible because its immediate predecessor is element 1, which has not yet been assigned. The first feasible element encountered is element 2. It is therefore assigned to station 1. We then start the search over again from the top of the list. Steps 2 and 3 result in the assignment of elements 2, 5, 1, and 4 to station 1. The total of their element times is 1.00 min. Hence, $T_{s1} = 1.0$, which equals T_c, and station 1 is filled. Continuing the procedure for the remaining stations results in the allocation shown in Table 6.3. There are five stations, and the balance delay for this assignment is

$$d = \frac{5(1.0) - 4.0}{5(1.0)} = 0.20 = 20\%$$

The solution is illustrated in Figure 6.4. The largest-candidate rule provides an approach that is appropriate for only simpler line balancing problems. More sophisticated techniques are required for more complex problems.

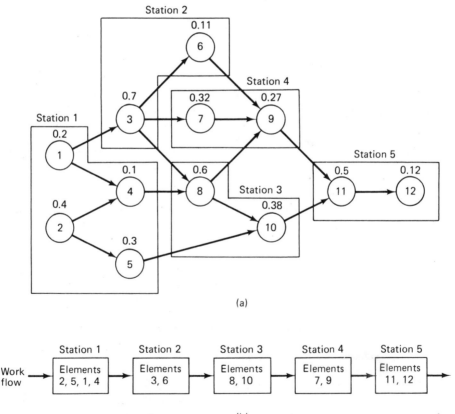

(a)

(b)

FIGURE 6.4   Solution for Example 6.2, illustrating assignment of work elements using largest candidate rule.

Kilbridge and Wester's method

This technique has received a good deal of attention in the literature since its introduction in 1961 [7]. The technique has been applied to several rather complicated line balancing problems with apparently good success [11]. It is a heuristic procedure which selects work elements for assignment to stations according to their position in the precedence diagram. The elements at the front of the diagram are selected first for entry into the solution. This overcomes one of the difficulties with the largest candidate rule, with which elements at the end of the precedence diagram might be the first candidates to be considered, simply because their T_e values are large.

We demonstrate Kilbridge and Wester's method on our sample problem. However, our problem is elementary enough that many of the difficulties which the procedure is designed to solve are missing. The interested reader is invited to consult the references, especially [2], [7], or [11], which apply the Kilbridge and Wester procedure to several more realistic problems.

PROCEDURE AND EXAMPLE 6.3

It will be convenient to discuss the method with reference to our sample problem.

Step 1. Construct the precedence diagram so that nodes representing work elements of identical precedence are arranged vertically in columns. This is illustrated in Figure 6.5. Elements 1 and 2 appear in column I, elements 3, 4, and 5 are in column II, and so on. Note that element 5 could be located in either column II or III without disrupting precedence constraints.

Step 2. List the elements in order of their columns, column I at the top of the list. If an element can be located in more than one column, list all the columns by the element to show the transferability of the element. This step is presented for the problem in Table 6.4. The table also shows the T_e value for each element and the sum of the T_e values for each column.

Step 3. To assign elements to workstations, start with the column I elements. Continue the assignment procedure in order of column number until the cycle time is reached. T_c in our sample problem is 1.0 min. The sum of the T_e values for the columns is helpful because we can see how much of the cycle time is contained in each column. The total time of the elements in column I is 0.6 min, so all of the first-column elements can be entered at station 1. We immediately see that the column II elements cannot all fit at station 1. To select which elements from column II to assign, we must choose those which can still be entered without exceeding T_c. Immediately, element 3 is discarded from consideration since $T_{e3} = 0.7$ min. When added to the column I elements, T_s would exceed 1.0 min. Accordingly, elements 4 and 5 are added to station 1 to make the total process time at that station equal to T_c. Unlike the largest-candidate rule, we need not concern ourselves with precedence requirements, since this is automatically taken care of by ordering the elements according to columns.

To begin on the second station, element 3 from column II would be entered first. The column III elements would be considered next. Element 6 is the only one that can be entered.

The assignment process continues in this fashion until all elements have been allocated. Table 6.5 shows the line balancing solution yielded by the Kilbridge and Wester method. Since five stations are required, the balance delay is again equal to 20%, the same as that provided by the largest-candidate rule. However, note that the work elements which make up the five stations

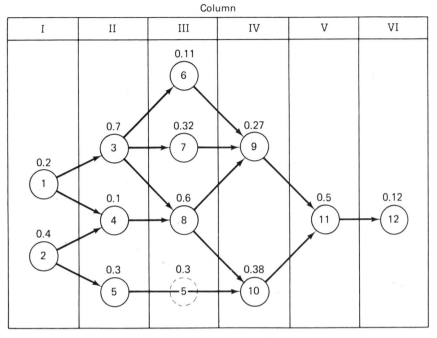

FIGURE 6.5   Work elements in Example 6.3 arranged into columns for the Kilbridge and Wester method.

TABLE 6.4   Work Elements Arranged According to Columns
from Figure 6.3 in the Kilbridge and Wester Method

Work element	Column	T_e	Sum of column $T_e s$
1	I	0.2	
2	I	0.4	0.6
3	II	0.7	
4	II	0.1	
5	II,III	0.3	1.1
6	III	0.11	
7	III	0.32	
8	III	0.6	1.03
9	IV	0.27	
10	IV	0.38	0.65
11	V	0.5	0.5
12	VI	0.12	0.12

TABLE 6.5   Work Elements Assigned to Stations
According to Kilbridge and Wester's Method

Station	Element	T_e	ΣT_e at station
1	1	0.2	
	2	0.4	
	4	0.1	
	5	0.3	1.00
2	3	0.7	
	6	0.11	0.81
3	7	0.32	
	8	0.6	0.92
4	9	0.27	
	10	0.38	0.65
5	11	0.5	
	12	0.12	0.62

are not the same as those in Table 6.3. Also, for stations that do have the same elements, the sequence in which the elements are assigned is not necessarily identical. Station 1 illustrates this difference.

In general, the Kilbridge and Wester method will provide a superior line balancing solution when compared with the largest-candidate rule. However, this is not always true, as demonstrated by our sample problem.

Ranked positional weights method

The ranked positional weights procedure was introduced by Helgeson and Birnie in 1961 [6]. In a sense, it combines the strategies of the largest-candidate rule and Kilbridge and Wester's method. A ranked positional weight value (call it the RPW for short) is computed for each element. The RPW takes account of both the T_e value of the element and its position in the precedence diagram. Then, the elements are assigned to work stations in the general order of their RPW values.

PROCEDURE

Step 1.   Calculate the RPW for each element by summing the element's T_e together with the T_e values for all the elements that follow it in the arrow chain of the precedence diagram.

Step 2.   List the elements in the order of their RPW, largest RPW at the top of the list. For convenience, include the T_e value and immediate predecessors for each element.

Step 3.   Assign elements to stations according to RPW, avoiding precedence constraint and time-cycle violations.

EXAMPLE 6.4

Applying the RPW method to our example problem, we first compute a ranked positional weight value for each element. For element 1, the elements that follow it in the arrow chain (see Figure 6.3) are 3, 4, 6, 7, 8, 9, 10, 11, and 12. The RPW for element 1 would be the sum of the T_e's for all these elements, plus T_e for element 1. This RPW value is 3.30. The reader can see that the trend will be toward lower values of RPW as we get closer to the end of the precedence diagram.

Table 6.6 lists the work elements according to RPW. We begin the assignment process by considering elements at the top of the list and working downward. Each time an element is entered into solution, we go back to the top of the list. The reader should follow through the solution in Table 6.7 to verify the order in which the work elements are assigned.

In the RPW line balance, the number of stations required is five, as before, but the maximum station process time is 0.92 min at number 3. Accordingly, the line could be operated at a cycle time of $T_e = 0.92$ rather than 1.0 min. This would, of course, be beneficial, since the production rate would be increased to $R_c = 1.075$ units/min. The corresponding balance delay is

$$d = \frac{5(0.92) - 4.0}{5(0.92)} = 0.13 = 13\%$$

The RPW solution represents a more efficient assignment of work elements to stations than either of the two preceding solutions. However, it should be noted that we have accepted a cycle time different from that which was originally specified for the problem. If the problem were reworked with $T_c = 0.92$ min using the largest-candidate rule or Kilbridge and Wester's method, it might be possible to duplicate the efficiency provided by the RPW method.

For large balancing problems, involving perhaps several hundred work elements, these manual methods of solution become awkward. A number of computer programs have been developed to deal with these larger assembly line cases. In the following section we survey some of these computerized approaches.

TABLE 6.6   Work Elements Arranged in Order of RPW Value in the Ranked Positional Weights Method

Element	RPW	T_e	Immediate predecessors
1	3.30	0.2	—
3	3.00	0.7	1
2	2.67	0.4	—
4	1.97	0.1	1,2
8	1.87	0.6	3,4
5	1.30	0.3	2
7	1.21	0.32	3
6	1.00	0.11	3
10	1.00	0.38	5,8
9	0.89	0.27	6,7,8
11	0.62	0.5	9,10
12	0.12	0.12	11

TABLE 6.7   Work Elements Assigned to Stations According to the Ranked Positional Weights Method

Station	Element	T_e	ΣT_e at station
1	1	0.2	
	3	0.7	0.9
2	2	0.4	
	4	0.1	
	5	0.3	
	6	0.11	0.91
3	8	0.6	
	7	0.32	0.92
4	10	0.38	
	9	0.27	0.65
5	11	0.5	
	12	0.12	0.62

6.6   COMPUTERIZED LINE BALANCING METHODS

The three methods described in the preceding section are generally carried out manually. This does not preclude their implementation on the digital computer. In fact, computer programs have been developed based on several of the heuristic approaches. However, the use of the computer allows a more complete enumeration of the possible solutions to a line balancing problem than is practical with a manual solution method. Accordingly, the computer line balancing algorithms are normally structured to explore a wide range of alternative allocations of elements to workstations. In this section, we discuss some of the techniques for solving large-scale line balancing problems based on the use of the computer. The first of these, COMSOAL, is the only one for which we will detail the procedure.

Comsoal

This acronym stands for Computer Method of Sequencing Operations for Assembly Lines. It is a method developed at Chrysler Corporation and reported by Arcus in 1966 [1]. Although it was not the first computerized line balancing program to be developed, it seems to have attracted considerably more attention than those which preceded it. The procedure is to iterate through a sequence of alternative solutions and keep the best one. Let us outline the basic algorithm of COMSOAL and proceed to discuss it with regard to our sample problem.

PROCEDURE AND EXAMPLE 6.5

Step 1.   Construct list A, showing all work elements in one column and the total number of elements that immediately precede each element in an adjacent column. This is illustrated in Table 6.8. Note that these types of data would be quite easy to compile and manipulate by the computer.

TABLE 6.8   List A in COMSOAL at the
Beginning of the Sample Problem

Element	Number of immediate predecessors
1	0
2	0
3	1
4	2
5	1
6	1
7	1
8	2
9	3
10	2
11	2
12	1

Step 2.   Construct list B (Table 6.9), showing all elements from list A that have no immediate predecessors.

Step 3.   Select at random one of the elements from list B. The computer would be programmed to perform this random selection process. The only constraint is that the element selected must not cause the cycle time T_c to be exceeded.

Step 4.   Eliminate the element selected in step 3 from lists A and B and update both lists, if necessary. Updating may be needed because the selected element was probably an immediate predecessor for some other elements(s). Hence, there may be changes in the number of immediate predecessors for certain elements in list A; and there may now be some new elements having no immediate predecessors that should be added to list B. To illustrate, suppose in step 3 that element 1 is chosen at random for entry into the first workstation. This would mean that element 3 no longer has any immediate predecessors. Tables 6.10 and 6.11 show the updated lists A and B, respectively.

Step 5.   Again select one of the elements from list B which is feasible for cycle time.

Step 6.   Repeat steps 4 and 5 until all elements have been allocated to stations within the T_c constraint. One possible solution to the problem is shown in Table 6.12. The balance delay is again $d = 20\%$, the same efficiency as obtained with the largest candidate rule and the Kilbridge and Wester method.

Step 7.   Retain the current solution and repeat steps 1 through 6 to attempt to determine an improved solution. If an improved solution is obtained, it should be retained.

TABLE 6.9   List B in COMSOAL at the
Beginning of the Sample Problem

Elements with no immediate predecessors
1
2

TABLE 6.10   List A in COMSOAL after Step 3

Element	Number of immediate predecessors
2	0
3	0
4	1
5	1
6	1
7	1
8	2
9	3
10	2
11	2
12	1

The steps involved in the COMSOAL algorithm represent an uncomplicated data manipulation procedure. It is therefore ideally suited to computer programming. Although there is much iteration in the algorithm, this is of minor consequence because of the speed with which the computer is capable of performing the iterations.

CALB

During the 1970s, the Advanced Manufacturing Methods Program (AMM) of the IIT Research Institute was the nucleus for research in line balancing methodology [8]. In 1968, this group introduced a computer package called CALB (for Computer Assembly Line Balancing or Computer-Aided Line Balancing), which has more or less become the industry standard. Its applications have included a variety of assembled products, including automobiles and trucks, electronic equipment, appliances, military hardware, and others.

CALB can be used for both single-model and mixed-model lines. For the single-model case, the data required to use the program include the identification of each work element T_e for each element, the predecessors, and other constraints that may apply to the line. Also needed to balance the line is information on minimum and maximum allowable time per workstation (in other words, cycle time data). The CALB program starts by sorting the elements according to their T_e and precedence requirements. Based on this sort, elements are assigned to stations so as to satisfy the minimum and maximum allowable station times. Line balancing solutions with less than 2% idle time have been described as common[11].

To use CALB on mixed-model lines, additional data are required such as the

TABLE 6.11   List B in COMSOAL after Step 3

Elements with no immediate predecessors
2
3

TABLE 6.12 One Possible Solution with COMSOAL

Station	Element	T_e	Site at station
1	1	0.2	
	2	0.4	
	5	0.3	
	4	0.1	1.0
2	3	0.7	
	6	0.11	0.81
3	8	0.6	
	10	0.38	0.98
4	7	0.32	
	9	0.27	0.59
5	11	0.5	
	12	0.12	0.62

production requirements per shift for each model to be run on the line, and a definition of relative elements usage per model. The solutions obtained by CALB are described as being nearly optimum.

ALPACA

This computer system was developed by one of the major users of assembly flow lines, General Motors [12]. The acronym represents "Assembly Line Planning and Control Activity." It was first implemented in 1967, but improvements in computer hardware since that time have reduced the cost of using the package to 10% of the original usage cost. ALPACA is described as an interactive line balancing system in which the user can transfer work from one station to another along the flow line and immediately assess the relative efficiency of the change. One of the complex problems facing the automotive industry is the proliferation of car models and options. ALPACA was designed to cope with the complications on the assembly line that arise from this problem. The system user can quickly determine what changes in work element assignments should be made to maintain a reasonable line balance for the ever-changing product flow.

6.7 OTHER WAYS TO IMPROVE THE LINE BALANCE

The line balancing techniques described in Sections 6.5 and 6.6 represent strict and precise procedures for allocating work elements to stations according to a specified cycle time. For most flow line situations, these techniques result in allocations that possess a high degree of balance efficiency. However, the designer of a flow line, either manual or automatic, should not overlook other possible ways for improving the operation of the line. In this section, let us examine some of these possibilities.

Dividing work elements

In Section 6.4, a minimum rational work element was defined as the smallest practical indivisible task, which cannot be subdivided further. In some instances, it may be perfectly reasonable to define certain tasks as minimum rational work elements even though it would be technically possible to further subdivide these elements. For example, it is reasonable to identify the drilling of a hole as a work element, and therefore to perform this work element all at one station. However, if the drilling of a deep hole at one station were to cause a bottleneck situation, it could be argued that the drilling operation should be separated into two steps. The advantage of this would be not only to eliminate the bottleneck but also to increase the tool lives of the drill bits.

This type of situation is more prevalent on mechanized processing lines, where operations such as the drilling process described above are performed. In the initial definition of work elements to be done on the line, it may not seem to be as technologically feasible to subdivide such process operations as it is in the case of assembly operations.

Changing workhead speeds at automatic stations

This again refers to automated (or semiautomated) lines such as machining transfer lines. It may be possible to effect a reduction in the process time of a bottleneck station by increasing its speed or feed rate. There will normally be a penalty associated with such changes in the form of a shorter tool life. This will result in more frequent line stops for tool replacement.

There is an opposite side to the coin. At a station where there is idle time, the workhead feed and speed should probably be reduced to prolong the tool life. This would tend to reduce the frequency of downtime occurrences on the line.

Through a process of increasing the speed/feed combinations at the stations with long process times, and reducing the speed/feed combinations at stations with idle time, it should be possible to improve the balance on the flow line.

Methods analysis

The customary use of the term *methods analysis* implies the study of human work activity for possible improvements. Such an analysis seems an obvious requirement for a manual flow line job, since the work elements need to be defined for the job before any line balancing can be performed. In addition, methods analysis can also be used to increase the rate of production at those stations that turn out to be the bottlenecks. The methods analysis may result in better workplace layout, redesigned tooling and fixturing, or improved hand and body motions. All of these improvements are likely to yield a superior balance of work on the manual flow line.

Analysis of the operations on automated lines may also lead to improvements in work flow and balance. However, attempts to optimize the line balance on automated process lines are usually emphasized during the planning and design stages, since alterations of the finished line are difficult because of the fixed nature of the equipment.

Preassembly of components

To reduce the total amount of work done on the regular assembly line, certain subassemblies can be prepared off-line, either by another assembly cell in the plant, or by purchasing them from an outside vendor that specializes in the type of processes required. Although it may seem like simply a means of moving the work from one location to another, there are several good reasons for organizing the assembly operations in this manner. They include: (1) the required process may be difficult to implement on the regular assembly line; (2) variations in process times (e.g., for adjustments or fitting) for the required assembly operations may result in a longer overall cycle time if done on the regular line; and (3) an assembly cell set up in the plant or a vendor with certain special capabilities to perform the work may be able to achieve higher quality.

Inventory buffers between stations

The justification for using storage buffers on automated flow lines was discussed in Section 5.4. On manual flow lines, storage buffers can also be of benefit. Their principal use is to smooth the flow of work, which might otherwise be disrupted by worker process time variability. Although the line balancing techniques assume that process times are constant, any human activity (and most other physical processes, for that matter) is characterized by random variations. These variations are manifested in process time differences from cycle to cycle. The buffer stocks between workstations help to level these differences.

Parallel stations *(or m/us)*

One of the restrictions implicit in the previous heuristic methods is that the stations must be arranged sequentially. If this restriction can be disregarded, it allows the use of parallel stations where bottlenecks previously existed. To illustrate, suppose that a five-station line had station process times of 1 min at all but the fifth workstation. At this station the process time was 2 min. With the stations arranged in series, the output rate would be limited by the 2-min process time of the fifth station to $R_c = 30$ units/h. However, if two stations were arranged in parallel at the fifth station position, the output could be increased to $R_c = 60$ units/h. Each of the parallel stations would have a production rate of 0.5 unit/min, but since there are two of them, their effective output would be 1 unit/min. Most problems are not as easy at this.

EXAMPLE 6.6

Consider the sample problem (Example 6.1) we have been using to illustrate the various line balancing techniques. The total work content time is $T_{wc} = 4.0$ min. Therefore, with a cycle time of $T_c = 1.0$ min, the theoretical minimum number of workstations needed should be four. However, none of the methods discussed in Sections 6.5 or 6.6 was able to achieve a solution with less than five stations.

By utilizing a configuration with parallel stations, it is possible to achieve a perfectly balanced solution with four stations. The allocation of elements is listed in Table 6.13. Stations 1 and 2

TABLE 6.13   Solution of Sample Problem Using Parallel Stations (Example 6.6)

Station	Elements	T_e	ΣT_e at stations
1 and 2 in parallel	1	0.2	
	2	0.4	
	3	0.7	
	4	0.1	
	8	0.6	2.0
3	5	0.3	
	6	0.11	
	7	0.32	
	9	0.27	1.0
4	10	0.38	
	11	0.5	
	12	0.12	1.0

both have the same work elements: 1, 2, 3, 4, and 8, whose total process time is 2.0 min. Since there are two stations, however, the effective output rate of the parallel arrangement is 1 unit/min. Stations 3 and 4 each have process times of 1 min, so the desired line cycle time of $T_c = 1.0$ min is achieved. The solution is illustrated in Figure 6.6.

There is no formalized procedure for developing a solution that utilizes parallel stations such as the above. Rather, a certain ingenuity and flexibility of mind are required in order for the analyst to perceive that the traditional approaches can be improved upon.

The use of parallel stations in a manual flow line is easily accomplished because of the inherent flexibility of the human operator. In an automated line it is necessary to incorporate a switching device in the workpart transfer mechanism which will alternate work units between the two parallel stations.

6.8   FLEXIBLE MANUAL ASSEMBLY LINES

The well-defined pace of a manual assembly line has merit from the point of view of maximizing production rate. However, the workers on the assembly line often feel as if they are being driven too hard. Frequent complaints by the workers, poor-quality workmanship, sabotage of the line equipment, and other problems have occurred on high-production flow lines. To relieve some of these conditions, a new concept in assembly lines has developed in which the pace of the work is controlled largely by the workers at the individual stations rather than by a powered conveyor moving at a fixed speed.

The new concept was pioneered by Volvo in Sweden. It relies on the use of independently operated work carriers that hold major components and/or subassemblies

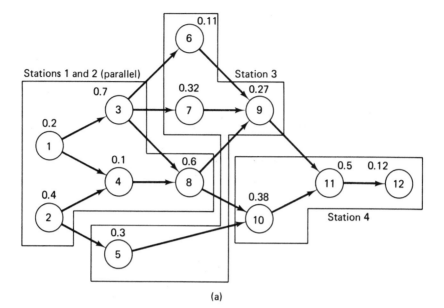

(a)

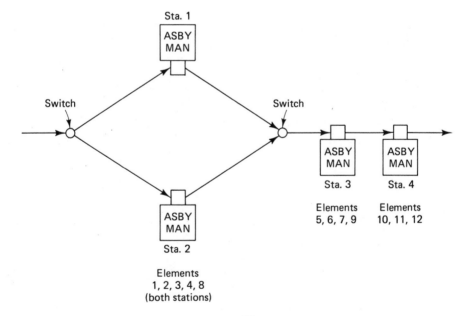

(b)

FIGURE 6.6 Solution for Example 6.6 using parallel workstation configuration: (a) precedence diagram; (b) diagram of workstation layout showing element assignment.

Is be a
buffer
line
(paver + fee
nry.)

of the automobile and deliver them to the manual assembly workstations along the line. The work carriers in the system are called automated guided vehicles (AGVs), and they are designed to follow guidepaths in the factory which are routed to the various stations. The guided vehicles are illustrated in Figure 6.7 operating in an American automobile assembly plant. We describe the technology of automated guided vehicle systems in more detail in Chapter 14, but for now, let us examine the characteristics of assembly systems that use AGVs as the workpart transport system.

The independently operating work carriers allow the assembly system to be configured with parallel paths, queues of parts between stations, and other features not typically found on a conventional in-line assembly system. In addition, these manual assembly lines can be designed to be highly flexible, capable of dealing with variations in product and corresponding variations in assembly cycle times at the different workstations. We have previously referred to this type of assembly system as a mixed-model line.

The type of flexible assembly system described here is generally used when there are many different models to be produced, and the variations in the models result in significant differences in the work content times involved. The work cycle time at any given station might range between 4 and 10 min, depending on model type. Production throughput is determined by the number of similar stations in parallel. A provisioning station is often used before the bank of parallel assembly stations to load the work carrier

FIGURE 6.7   Automated guided vehicles used to carry engines in an automobile assembly plant. Note platforms at side of guided vehicles for assembly workers to ride on. (Courtesy of Eaton-Kenway.)

with the components that will be needed. This permits flexibility in the routing of the carriers to the different stations. Hardware items common to all models are usually stocked at the workstations. The typical operation of the system allows for time variations at a given station resulting from worker skill and effort and from model differences. Instead of the subassembly moving forward at a fixed rate as in a conventional flow line, the worker takes the time needed to accomplish the work elements required for the particular model currently being processed. When the work is completed, the work carrier is released by the worker to proceed toward the next assembly operation.

Benefits of this flexible assembly system compared to the conventional assembly line include greater worker satisfaction, better-quality product, increased capability to accommodate model variations, and greater ability to cope with problems that require more time rather than stopping the entire production line.

REFERENCES

[1] ARCUS, A. L., "COMSOAL—A Computer Method of Sequencing Operations for Assembly Lines," *International Journal of Production Research,* Vol. 4, No. 4, 1966, pp. 259–277.

[2] BUFFA, E. S., and W. H., TAUBERT, *Production-Inventory Systems: Planning and Control,* Richard D. Irwin, Inc., Homewood, Ill., 1972, Chapters 8, 9.

[3] BUXLEY, G. M., H. D. SLACK, and R., WILD, "Production Flow Line System Design—A Review" *AIIE Transactions,* Vol. 5, No. 1, 1973, pp. 37–48.

[4] DAR-EL, E. M., "Solving Large Single-Model Assembly Line Balancing Problems—A Comparative Study," *AIIE Transactions,* Vol. 7., No. 3, 1975, pp. 302–310.

[5] GROOVER, M. P., M. WEISS, R. N. NAGEL, and N. G. ODREY, *Industrial Robotics: Technology, Programming, and Applications,* McGraw-Hill Book Company, New York, 1986, Chapter 15.

[6] HELGESON, W. B., and D. P. BIRNIE, "Assembly Line Balancing Using Ranked Positional Weight Technique," *Journal of Industrial Engineering,* Vol. 12, No. 6, 1961, pp. 394–398.

[7] KILBRIDGE, M. D., and L. WESTER, "A Heuristic Method of Assembly Line Balancing," *Journal of Industrial Engineering,* Vol. 12, No. 4, 1961, pp. 292–298.

[8] MAGAD, E. L., "Cooperative Manufacturing Research," *Industrial Engineering,* Vol. 4, No. 1, 1972, pp. 36–40.

[9] MASTOR, A. A., "An Experimental Investigation and Comparative Evaluation of Production Line Balancing Techniques," Unpublished Ph.D. dissertation, UCLA, Los Angeles, 1966.

[10] MASTOR, A. A., "An Experimental Investigation and Comparative Evaluation of Production Line Balancing Techniques," *Management Science,* Vol. 16, No. 11, 1970, pp., 728–746.

[11] PRENTING, T. O., and N. T. THOMOPOULOS, *Humanism and Technology in Assembly Line Systems,* Spartan Books, Hayden Book Co., Hasbrouk Heights, N. J., 1974.

[12] SHARP, W. I., JR., "Assembly Line Balancing Techniques," *Technical Paper MS77-313,* Society of Manufacturing Engineers, Dearborn, Mich., 1977.

[13] WILD, RAY, *Mass-Production Management,* John Wiley & Sons Ltd., London, 1972.

PROBLEMS

6.1. A manual production flow line is arranged with six stations and a conveyor system is used to move parts along the line. The belt speed is 4 ft/min and the spacing of raw workparts along the line is one every 3 ft. The total line length is 30 ft, hence each station length equals 5 ft. Determine the following:
(a) Feed rate f_p.
(b) Tolerance time T_t.
(c) Theoretical cycle time T_c.

6.2. Given the physical flow line configuration of Problem 6.1, is it likely that the line could be utilized to produce a job whose total work content time = 5.0 min? What about a total work content time of 4.0 min? 3.0 min?

6.3. A manual assembly line is to be designed with a production rate of 100 completed assemblies per hour. The line will have eight stations and the length of each station is 1.0 m. The minimum allowable tolerance time is to be 2.0 min. If the line is figured to have an uptime efficiency of 97% (estimated from previous similar lines), determine the following parameters for the line:
(a) Ideal cycle time T_c.
(b) Conveyor speed V_c.
(c) Feed rate f_p.
(d) Part spacing s_p along the belt.

6.4. The total work content time of a certain assembly job is 7.8 min. The estimated downtime of the line is $D = 5\%$, and the required production rate is $R_p = 80$ units/h.
(a) Determine the theoretical minimum number of workstations required to optimize the balance delay.
(b) For the number of stations determined in part (a), compute the balance delay d.
(c) What feed rate should be specified if a moving belt line is to be used?

6.5. A moving belt assembly line is to be designed for an assembly job that has a total work content of 21 min. From consideration of human factors the length of each station will be 6.0 ft. The belt speed is variable and can be set between 1.1 and 2.0 ft/min. The required production rate for the line must be 30,000 units/yr (assume 2000 h of operation per year). From past experience on similar lines, the uptime proportion of this assembly line (line efficiency), E is expected to be 95%. Production management demands that the line be designed so that the balance delay d is between 0.06 and 0.10, and the line must be designed for a balance delay within this range.
(a) Determine the number of stations that should be designed on the assembly line.
(b) With good design practice in mind, determine the belt speed, spacing between parts on the line, and the tolerance time to be used.

6.6. The following list defines the precedence relationships and element times for a new model toy:

Element	$T_e(min)$	Immediate predecessors
1	0.5	—
2	0.3	1
3	0.8	1
4	0.2	2

(continued)

(*continued*)

Element	$T_e(min)$	Immediate predecessors
5	0.1	2
6	0.6	3
7	0.4	4,5
8	0.5	3,5
9	0.3	7,8
10	0.6	6,9

(a) Construct the precedence diagram for this job.

(b) If the ideal cycle time is to be 1.0 min, what is the theoretical minimum number of stations required to minimize the balance delay?

(c) Compute the balance delay for the answer found in part (b).

6.7. Determine the assignment of work elements to stations using the largest-candidate rule for Problem 6.6.

(a) How many stations are required?

(b) Compute the balance delay.

6.8. Solve Problem 6.6 using the Kilbridge and Wester method.

6.9. Solve Problem 6.6 using the ranked positional weights method.

6.10. Solve for one iteration of Problem 6.6 using COMSOAL.

6.11. A proposal has been submitted to replace a group of assembly workers, each working individually, with an assembly line. The following table gives the individual work elements.

Element	$T_e(min)$	Immediate predecessors
1	1.0	—
2	0.5	—
3	0.8	1,2
4	0.3	2
5	1.2	3
6	0.2	3,4
7	0.5	4
8	1.5	5,6,7

The demand rate for this job is 1600 units/week (assume 40 h/week) and the current number of operators required to meet this demand is eight using the individual manual workers.

(a) Construct the precedence diagram from the data provided on work elements.

(b) Use the largest-candidate rule to assign work elements to stations. What is the balance delay for the solution?

(c) The initial cost to install the assembly line is $20,000. If the hourly rate for workers is $5.00/h, will the assembly line be justified using a 3-year service life? Assume 50 weeks/yr. Use a rate of return $= 10\%$.

6.12. Solve Problem 6.11(b) using the Kilbridge and Wester method.

6.13. Solve Problem 6.12(b) using the ranked positional weights method.

6.14. A manual assembly line operates with a mechanized conveyor. The conveyor moves at a speed of 5 ft/min, and the spacing between base parts launched onto the line is 4 ft. It has been determined that the line operates best when each station is separated from the adjacent stations by 6 ft. There are 14 work elements which must be accomplished to complete the assembly, and the element times and precedence requirements are defined in the following table:

Element	Time (min)	Preceded by:
1	0.2	—
2	0.5	—
3	0.2	1
4	0.6	1
5	0.1	2
6	0.2	3,4
7	0.3	4
8	0.2	5
9	0.4	5
10	0.3	6,7
11	0.1	9
12	0.2	8,10
13	0.1	11
14	0.3	12,13
	3.7 = total work content time (T_{wc})	

(a) Determine the feed rate on the assembly line and the corresponding cycle time.
(b) Determine the tolerance time for each operator on the line.
(c) What is the ideal minimum number of workstations that will allow completion of the assembly on the line?
(d) Draw the precedence diagram for the table of work elements.
(e) Determine an efficient allocation of work elements to stations that can be used for the assembly line. Use one of the line balancing methods discussed in the chapter text. For your line balancing solution, determine the balance delay.

6.15. A manual assembly line is to be designed to make a small consumer product. The work elements, their times, and the precedence constraints are as follows:

Element	Time (min)	Preceded by:	Element	Time (min)	Preceded by:
1	0.4	—	6	0.2	3
2	0.7	1	7	0.3	4
3	0.5	1	8	0.9	4, 9
4	0.8	2	9	0.3	5, 6
5	1.0	2, 3	10	0.5	7, 8

The workers will operate the line for 400 min per day and must produce 300 products per day. A mechanized belt, moving at a speed of 4.0 ft/min, will transport the products between workstations. Because of the variability in the time required to perform the assembly operations, it has been determined that the tolerance time should be equal to 1.5 times the cycle time of the line.

(a) Determine the ideal number of workstations on the line.

(b) Use the ranked positional weights method to balance the line.

(c) Compute the balance delay for your solution in part (b).

(d) Determine the required spacing between assemblies on the conveyor.

(e) Determine the required length of each workstation in order to meet the specifications that have been placed on the design of the line.

6.16. A new small electrical appliance for the home do-it-yourselfer is to be assembled manually on a production flow line. The total job of assembling the product has been divided into minimum rational work elements and these are described in Table P6.16. Also given in this table are tentative time standards as estimated by the industrial engineering department from similar jobs done previously. In the extreme right-hand column of the table are the immediate predecessors established by precedence requirements. The small appliance is to be assembled at the rate of one product per minute off the production line. You are to design the layout of stations along the line so as to meet this production requirement.

Use one of the methods of line balancing presented in Section 6.5 to balance the line as much as possible. How many stations are required? If the production rate is increased or decreased slightly (by not more than 20%), could the balance be improved? What is the percent balance delay? Make a sketch of the flow line layout, showing the positions of stations and operators along the line.

TABLE P6.16   List of Work Elements

No.	Element description	T_e (min)	Immediate predecessors
1	Place frame on workholder and clamp	0.15	—
2	Assemble fan to motor	0.37	—
3	Assemble bracket 1 to frame	0.21	1
4	Assemble bracket 2 to frame	0.21	1
5	Assemble motor to frame	0.58	1,2
6	Affix insulation to bracket 1	0.12	3
7	Assemble angle plate to bracket 1	0.29	3
8	Affix insulation to bracket 2	0.12	4
9	Attach link bar to motor and bracket 2	0.30	4,5
10	Assemble three wires to motor	0.45	5
11	Assemble nameplate to housing	0.18	—
12	Assemble light fixture to housing	0.20	11
13	Assemble blade mechanism to frame	0.65	6,7,8,9
14	Wire switch, motor, and light	0.72	10,12
15	Wire blade mechanism to switch	0.25	13
16	Attach housing over motor	0.35	14
17	Test blade mechanism, light, etc.	0.16	15,16
18	Affix instruction label to cover plate	0.12	—
19	Assemble grommet to power cord	0.10	—
20	Assemble cord and grommet to cover plate	0.23	18,19
21	Assemble power cord leads to switch	0.40	17,20
22	Assemble cover plate to frame	0.33	21
23	Final inspect and remove from workholder	0.25	22
24	Package	1.75	23

chapter 7

Automated Assembly Systems

The term *automated assembly* refers to the use of mechanized and automated devices to perform the various functions in an assembly line or cell. Much progress has been made in the technology of assembly automation in recent years. Some of this progress has been motivated by advances in the field of robotics. Industrial robots are sometimes used as components in automated assembly systems. The applications of robots, including those in assembly operations, are described in Chapter 13. In the current chapter, we study automated assembly as a separate field of automation. Although the manual assembly methods described in Chapter 6 will no doubt be used for many years into the future, significant opportunities for productivity gains exist in the use of automated methods. For the reader interested in pursuing this topic of automated assembly in more detail, there have been several books written in the last few years that we recommend [1,3,9].

It turns out that the product's design has a significant impact on the ease with which its assembly can be automated. We begin our chapter with this topic.

7.1   DESIGN FOR AUTOMATED ASSEMBLY

One of the impediments to automated assembly is that many of the traditional assembly methods described in Chapter 6 evolved when human beings were the only available means of assembling a product. Many of the mechanical fasteners commonly used in industry today almost require the special anatomical and sensory capabilities of human beings. Consider, for example, the use of a screw, a lock washer, and a nut to fasten two sheet metal parts on a partially assembled cabinet. This type of operation is typically accomplished manually at either a single assembly station or on an assembly line. The cabinet is located at the workstation with the two sheet metal parts to be fastened at an awkward position for the operator to reach. The operator picks up the screw, lockwasher, and nut, somehow manipulating them into position on opposite sides of the two parts, and places the lockwasher and then the nut onto the screw. As luck, would have it, the threads of the nut initially bind on the screw threads, so the operator must unscrew slightly and restart the process, using a well-developed sense of touch to ensure that the threads are matching. Once the screw and nut have been tightened with fingers, the operator reaches for the appropriate screwdriver (there are various sizes of screws with different-shaped heads) to tighten the fastener.

This type of manual operation has been used commonly and successfully in industry for many years to assemble products. The hardware required is inexpensive, the sheet metal is readily perforated to provide the matching clearance holes, and the method lends itself to field service. What is becoming very expensive is the manual labor at the assembly workstation required to accomplish the initial fastening. The high cost of manual labor has resulted in a reexamination of assembly technology with a view toward automation. However, automating the assembly operation described above would be very difficult. First, the positions of the holes through which the screw must be inserted are different for each screw, and the position may be difficult for the operator to reach. Second, the screw holes between the two sheet metal parts may not match up perfectly, necessitating the operator to reposition the two parts for a better match. Third, the operator must juggle three separate hardware items (screw, lockwasher, and nut) to perform the fastening operation. Fourth, a sense of touch is required to make sure that the nut is started properly onto the screw thread. Each of these four problems makes automation of the operation difficult. All four problems together make it nearly impossible. As a consequence, attempts at assembly automation have led to an examination of the methods specified by the designer to fasten together the various components of a product.

The first and most general lesson, obvious from the example above, is that the methods traditionally used for manual assembly are not necessarily the best methods for automated assembly. Human beings are the most dexterous and intelligent machines: able to move to different positions in the workstation, able to adapt to unexpected problems and new situations during the work cycle, capable of manipulating and coordinating multiple objects simultaneously, and able to make use of a wide range of senses in performing work. For assembly automation to be achieved, fastening procedures must be devised and specified during product design that do not require all of these human capabilities.

The following are some of the recommendations and principles that can be applied in product design to facilitate automated assembly:

- *Reduce the amount of assembly required.* This principle can be realized during design by combining functions within the same part that were previously accomplished by separate components in the product. The use of plastic molded parts to substitute for sheet metal parts is an example of this principle. A more complex geometry molded into a plastic part might replace several metal parts. Although the plastic part may seem to be more costly, the savings in assembly time probably justify the substitution in many cases.

- *Use modular design.* In automated assembly, increasing the number of separate assembly steps that are done by a single automated system will result in an increase in the downtime of the system. This is demonstrated in a later section of this chapter when we analyze the operation and performance of automated assembly systems. To reduce this effect, Riley [9] suggests that the design of the product be modular, with perhaps each module requiring a maximum of 12 or 13 parts to be assembled on a single assembly system. Also, the subassembly should be designed around a base part to which other components are added [10].

- *Reduce the number of fasteners required.* Instead of using separate screws and nuts, and similar fasteners, design the fastening mechanism into the component design using snap fits and similar features. Also, design the product modules so that several components are fastened simultaneously rather than each component fastened separately.

- *Reduce the need for multiple components to be handled at once.* The preferred practice in automated assembly machine design is to separate the operations at different stations rather than to handle and fasten multiple components simultaneously at the same workstation. (It should be noted that robotics technology is causing a rethinking of this practice since robots can be programmed to perform more complex assembly tasks than a single station in a mechanized assembly system.)

- *Limit the required directions of access.* This principle simply means that the number of directions in which new components are added to the existing subassembly should be minimized. If all of the components can be added vertically from above, this is the ideal situation. Obviously, the design of the subassembly module determines this.

- *Require high quality in components.* High performance of the automated assembly system requires consistently good quality of the components that are added at each workstation. Poor-quality components cause jams in the feeding and assembly mechanisms which cause downtime in the automated system.

- *Implement hopperability.* This is a term that Riley [9] uses to identify the ease with which a given component can be fed and oriented reliably for delivery from the parts hopper to the assembly workhead. One of the major costs in the development of an automated assembly system is the engineering time to devise the means of feeding the components in the correct orientation for the assembly operation. The product designer is responsible for providing the orientation features and other geometric aspects of the components that determine the ease of feeding and orienting the parts.

7.2   TYPES OF AUTOMATED ASSEMBLY SYSTEMS

Assuming that the product design is compatible with automated assembly, there are several different ways to characterize the operation and configuration of the automated assembly system. One way to classify the system is by the type of work transfer system that is used in the system. The types are:

- Continuous transfer system
- Synchronous transfer system
- Asynchronous transfer system
- Stationary base part system   — *workpiece at 1 loc. only + all components brought to it*

The first three types involve the same methods of workpart transport described in Section 4.2. In the stationary base part system, the base part (to which the other components are added) is placed in a fixed location, where it remains during the assembly work.

Another way of classifying automated assembly systems is by their physical configuration. The possible configurations include:

- Dial-type assembly machine
- In-line assembly machine
- Carousel assembly system
- Single-station assembly machine

The *dial-type machine* is shown in Figure 7.1. In the typical application, base parts are loaded onto fixtures or nests that are attached to the circular dial. Components are added and/or fastened at the various workstations located around the periphery of the dial. The dial indexing machine is the most common system in this category. It operates with a synchronous or intermittent motion, where the cycle consists of the process time plus indexing time. Several of the mechanisms describe in Section 4.3 can be used to provide this motion. Although less common, dial-type assembly machines are sometimes designed to use a continuous motion rather than an intermittent motion.

The *in-line assembly machine* consists of a series of automatic workstations located along an in-line transfer system. It is the automated version of the manual assembly line. Continuous, synchronous, or asynchronous transfer systems can be used with the in-line configuration.

The operation of dial-type and in-line assembly systems is similar to the operation of their counterparts described in Chapter 4 for machining (and other processing) operations. Subassemblies at various stages of completion are processed simultaneously at separate workstations. For synchronous transfer of work between stations, the ideal cycle time equals the operation time at the slowest station plus the transfer time between stations. The production rate, at 100% uptime, is the reciprocal of the ideal cycle time. Owing to

FIGURE 7.1   Dial-type assembly machine. (Courtesy of Bodine Corp.)

jams of the components at the workstations and other malfunctions, the system will probably not operate at 100% uptime. We will analyze the operation of these automated assembly systems in a subsequent section of this chapter.

In a sense, the *carousel assembly system* represents a hybrid between the circular flow of work provided by the dial assembly machine and the straight work flow of the in-line system. The carousel configuration is illustrated in Figure 7.2. This type of assembly system can be operated with continuous, synchronous, or asynchronous transfer mechanisms to move the work around the carousel. The carousel configuration with asynchronous transfer of work is often used in partially automated assembly systems. In

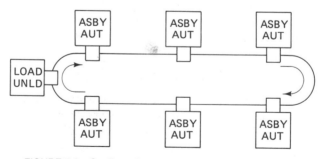

FIGURE 7.2   Configuration of a carousel assembly system.

Chapter 15 we will describe how work-in-process storage is incorporated into the design of the carousel assembly system.

In the *single-station assembly machine,* the assembly operations are performed at a single location (stationary base part system). The typical operation involves the placement of the base part at the workstation where various components are added to the base. The components are delivered to the station by feeding mechanisms, and one or more workheads perform the various assembly and fastening operations. The single-station cell is sometimes selected as the configuration for robotic assembly applications. Parts are fed to the single station and the robot adds them to the base part and performs the fastening operations.

Table 7.1 presents a listing of the possible combinations of work transfer systems and assembly system configurations.

7.3 PARTS FEEDING DEVICES

In each of the configurations described above, a means of delivering the components to the assembly workhead must be designed. In this section we discuss these devices and their operation.

Elements of the parts delivery system

The hardware system that delivers components to the workhead in an automated assembly system typically consists of the following elements:

- *Hopper.* This is the container into which the components are loaded at the workstation. A separate hopper is used for each component type. The components are usually loaded into the hopper in bulk. This means that the parts are randomly oriented initially in the hopper.
- *Parts feeder.* This is a mechanism that removes the components from the hopper one at a time for delivery to the assembly workhead. The hopper and parts feeder are often combined into one operating mechanism. The vibratory bowl feeder, pictured in Figure 7.3, is a very common example of the hopper–feeder combination.

TABLE 7.1   Possible Work Transfer Systems for the Four Assembly Systems Configurations

System configuration	Stationary base part	Work transfer system		
		Continuous	Synchronous	Asynchronous
Dial-type	No	Yes	Yes	No
In-line	No	Yes	Yes	Yes
Carousel	No	Yes	Yes	Yes
Single-station	Yes	No	No	No

FIGURE 7.3   Vibratory bowl feeder. (Courtesy of FMC Corporation, Material Handling Equipment Division.)

   • *Selector and/or orientor.*   These elements of the delivery system establish the proper orientation of the components for the assembly workhead. A selector is a device that acts as a filter, permitting only parts that are in the correct orientation to pass through. Components that are not properly oriented are rejected back into the hopper. An orientor is a device that allows properly oriented parts to pass through but provides a reorientation of components that are not properly oriented initially. Several selector and orientor schemes are illustrated in Figure 7.4. Selector and orientor devices are often combined and incorporated into one hopper–feeder system.
   • *Feed track.*   The preceding elements of the delivery system are usually located some distance from the assembly workhead. A feed track is used to transfer the components from the hopper and parts feeder to the location of the assembly workhead, maintaining proper orientation of the parts during the transfer. There are two general categories of feed tracks: gravity and powered. The gravity feed track is most common. In this type the hopper and parts feeder are located at an elevation that is above the elevation of the workhead. The force of gravity is used to deliver the components to the workhead. The powered feed track uses vibratory action, air pressure, or other means to force the parts to travel along the feed track toward the assembly workhead.

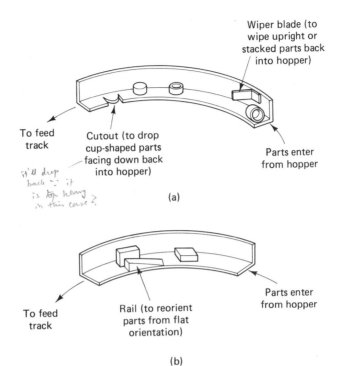

(handwritten notes near cutout label: "it'll drop back in it is top heavy in this case?")

FIGURE 7.4   (a) Selector and (b) orientor devices used with component feeders in automated assembly systems.

- *Escapement and placement device.*   The purpose of the escapement device is to remove components from the feed track at time intervals that are consistent with the cycle time of the assembly workhead. The placement device physically places the component in the correct location at the workstation for the assembly operation by the workhead. These elements are sometimes combined into a single operating mechanism. In other cases, they are two separate devices. Several types of escapement and placement devices are pictured in Figure 7.5.

The elements of the parts delivery system are illustrated schematically in Figure 7.6. A parts selector is illustrated in the diagram. Improperly oriented parts are fed back into hopper. In the case of a parts orientor, improperly oriented parts are reoriented and proceed to the feed track. A more detailed description of the various elements of the delivery system is provided in reference [3].

One of the recent developments in the technology of parts feeding and delivery systems is the programmable parts feeder [5,7]. The programmable parts feeder is capable of feeding components of varying geometries with only a few minutes required to make the adjustments (change the program) for the differences. This type of feeder would possess the flexibility to be used in batch production assembly systems. Most parts feeders are designed as fixed automated systems for high-production assembly.

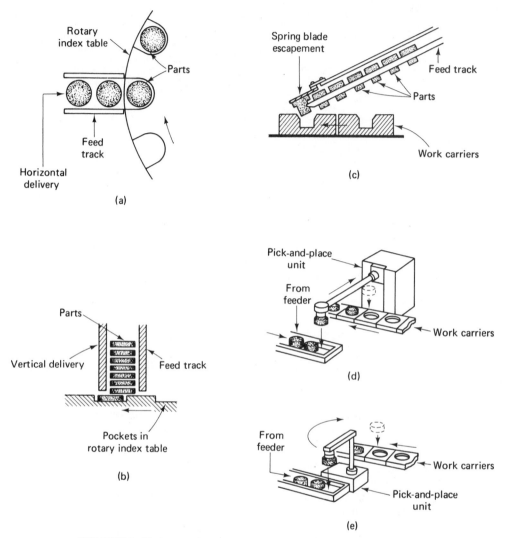

FIGURE 7.5   Various escapement and placement devices used in automatic assembly systems: (a) horizontal and (b) vertical device for placement of parts onto dial indexing table; (c) escapement of rivet-shaped parts actuated by work carriers; (d) and (e) two types of pick-and-place mechanism. (Reprinted from Gay [4].)

Quantitative analysis of the delivery system operation

The parts feeding mechanism is capable of removing parts from the hopper at a certain rate, f. These parts are assumed to be in random orientation initially, and must be presented to the selector or orientor to establish the correct orientation. In the case of the selector,

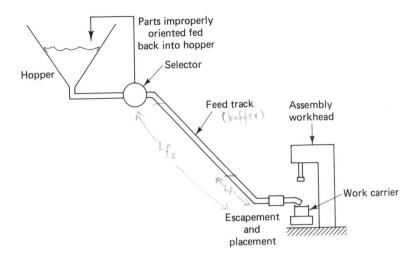

FIGURE 7.6   Elements of the parts delivery system at an assembly workstation.

a certain proportion of the parts will be correctly oriented initially and these will be allowed to pass through. The remaining proportion, which are incorrectly oriented, will be rejected back into the hopper. In the case of the orientor, the parts that are incorrectly oriented will be reoriented, resulting ideally in a 100% rate of parts passing through the orientor device. In many delivery system designs, the functions of the selector and the orientor will be combined. Let us define θ to be the proportion of components that pass through the selector–orientor process and are correctly oriented for delivery into the feed track. Hence the effective rate of delivery of components from the hopper into the feed track will be $f\theta$. The remaining proportion, $(1 - \theta)$, will be recirculated back into the hopper. Obviously, the delivery rate $f\theta$ of components to the workhead must be sufficient to keep up with the cycle rate of the assembly machine.

Assuming that the delivery rate of components $f\theta$ is greater than the cycle rate R_c of the assembly machine, a means of limiting the size of the queue in the feed track must be established. This is generally accomplished by placing a sensor (e.g., limit switch, optical sensor, etc.) near the top of the feed track, which is used to turn off the feeding mechanism when the feed track is full. This sensor is referred to as the high-level sensor, and its location defines the active length L_{f2} of the feed track. If the length of a component in the feed track is L_c, the number of parts that can be held in the feed track is $n_{f2} = L_{f2}/L_c$. The length of the components must be measured from a point on a given component to the corresponding point on the next component in the queue to allow for possible overlap of parts. The value of n_{f2} is the capacity of the feed track.

Another sensor is placed along the feed track at some distance from the first sensor and is used to restart the feeding mechanism again. Defining the location of this low-level sensor as L_{f1}, the number of components in the feed track at this point is $n_{f1} = L_{f1}/L_c$.

The rate at which the quantity of parts in the buffer will be reduced when the high-level sensor is actuated $= R_c$, where R_c is the theoretical cycle rate of the assembly machine. On average, the rate at which the quantity of parts will increase upon actuation of the low-level sensor is $f\theta - R_c$. However, the rate of increase will not be uniform due to the random nature of the feeder–selector operation. Accordingly, the value of n_{f1} must be made large enough to virtually eliminate the probability of a stockout after the low-level sensor has turned on the feeder.

EXAMPLE 7.1

The cycle time for a given assembly workhead = 0.2 min. The parts feeder has a feed rate = 20 components/min. The probability that a given component fed by the feeder will pass through the selector is $\theta = 0.3$. The number of parts in the feed track corresponding to the low-level sensor is $n_{f1} = 6$. The capacity of the feed track is $n_{f2} = 18$ parts.

(a) Determine how long it will take for the supply of parts in the feed track to go from n_{f2} to n_{f1}.

(b) Determine how long it will take on average for the supply for parts to go from n_{f1} to n_{f2}.

Solution:

(a) The rate of depletion of parts in the feed track, starting from n_{f2}, will be $R_c = 1/0.2 = 5$ parts/min. The time to deplete is

$$\frac{18 - 6}{5} = 2.4 \text{ min}$$

(b) The rate of parts increase in the feed track, once the low-level sensor has been reached, is $f\theta - R_c = (20)(0.3) - 5 = 6 - 5 = 1$ part/min. The time to go from n_{f1} to n_{f2} is

$$\frac{18 - 6}{1} = 12 \text{ min}$$

7.4 ANALYSIS OF MULTISTATION ASSEMBLY MACHINES

In this section we examine the operation and performance of automated assembly machines that have several workstations and use a synchronous transfer system. The types include the dial indexing machine, many in-line assembly systems, and certain carousel systems. The measures of performance are production rate, uptime efficiency, and cost.

The analysis of an automated assembly machine with multiple stations shares much in common with the upper-bound approach used for metal machining transfer lines from Chapter 5. Some modifications in the analysis must be made to account for the fact that components are being added at the various workstations in the assembly system. The general operation of the assembly system is pictured in Figure 7.7. In developing the equations that govern the operation of the system, we shall follow the general approach suggested by Boothroyd and Redford [2].

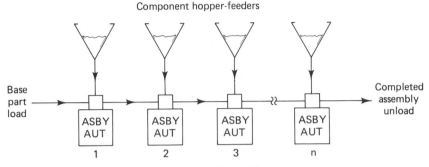

FIGURE 7.7   Multistation assembly machine.

We assume that the typical operation occurring at a workstation of an assembly machine is one in which a component is added or joined in some fashion to an existing assembly. The existing assembly consists of a base part plus the components assembled to it at previous stations. The base part is launched onto the line either at or before the first workstation. The components that are added must be clean, uniform in size and shape, of high quality, and consistently oriented. When the feed mechanism and assembly workhead attempt to join a component that does not meet these specifications, the station can jam. When this occurs, it can result in the shutdown of the entire machine until the fault is corrected. Thus, in addition to the other mechanical and electrical failures that interrupt the operation of a flow line, the problem of defective components is one that specifically plagues the operation of an automatic assembly machine. This is the problem we propose to deal with in this section.

The assembly machine as a game of chance

Defective parts are a fact of manufacturing life. Defects occur with a certain fraction defective rate, q. In the operation of an assembly workstation, q can be considered as the probability that the next component is defective. When an attempt is made to feed and assemble a defective component, the defect might or might not cause the station to jam. Let m equal the probability that a defect will result in the malfunction and stoppage of the workstation. Since the values of q and m may be different for different stations, we subscript these terms as q_i and m_i, where $i = 1, 2, \ldots, n$, the number of stations on the assembly machine.

Considering what happens at a particular workstation, station i, there are three possible events that might occur when the feed mechanism attempts to feed the component and the assembly device attempts to join it to the existing assembly:

1. The component is defective and causes a station jam.
2. The component is defective but does not cause a station jam.
3. The component is not defective.

The probability of the first event is the product of the fraction defective rate for the station, q_i, multiplied by the probability that a defect will cause the station to stop, m_i. This product is the same as the term p_i of Section 5.2, the probability that a part will jam at station i. For an assembly machine,

$$p_i = m_i q_i \tag{7.1}$$

In this case where the component is defective and causes a station jam, the defective component will be cleared and the next component will be allowed to feed and be assembled. We assume that this next component is not defective—the probability of two consecutive defects is very small, equal to q^2.

The second possible event, when the component is defective but does not cause a station jam, has a probability given by

$$(1 - m_i)q_i$$

With this outcome, a bad part is joined to the existing assembly, perhaps rendering the entire assembly defective.

The third possibility is obviously the most desirable. The probability that the component is not defective is equal to the proportion of good parts:

$$1 - q_i$$

The probabilities of the three possible events must sum to unity.

$$m_i q_i + (1 - m_i)q_i + (1 - q_i) = 1 \tag{7.2}$$

For the special case where $m_i = m$ and $q_i = q$ for all i, Eq. (7.2) reduces to

$$mq + (1 - m)q + (1 - q) = 1 \tag{7.3}$$

To determine the complete distribution of possible outcomes that can occur on an n-station assembly machine, we can multiply the terms of Eq. (7.2) together for all n stations:

$$\prod_{i=1}^{n} [m_i q_i + (1 - m_i)q_i + (1 - q_i)] = 1 \tag{7.4}$$

In the special case of Eq. (7.3), where all m_i are equal and all q_i are equal, Eq. (7.4) becomes the multinomial expansion

$$[mq + (1 - m)q + (1 - q)]^n = 1 \tag{7.5}$$

Expansion of Eq. (7.4) or (7.5) will reveal the probabilities for all possible sequences of events which can take place on the assembly machine. Unfortunately, the number of terms in the expansion of Eq. (7.4) becomes very large for a machine with more than two stations. The exact number of terms is equal to 3^n, where n is the number of stations. For an eight-station line, the number of terms is equal to 6561, each term representing the probability of one of the 6561 possible sequences on the assembly machine.

Measures of performance

Fortunately, we are not required to calculate every term to make use of the concept of assembly machine operation provided by Eqs. (7.2) and (7.4). One of the characteristics of performance that we might want to know is the proportion of assemblies that contain one or more defective components. Two of the three terms in Eq. (7.2) represent events that result in the addition of good components at a given station. The first term is $m_i q_i$, which indicates a line stop but also means that a defective component has not been added to the assembly. The other term is $(1 - q_i)$, which means that a good component has been added at the station. The sum of these two terms represents the probability that a defective component will not be added at station i. Multiplying these probabilities for all stations, we get the proportion of acceptable product coming off the line, P_{ap}.

$$P_{ap} = \prod_{i=1}^{n} (1 - q_i + m_i q_i) \tag{7.6}$$

If this is the proportion of assemblies with no defective components, the proportion of assemblies that contain at least one defect is given by

$$P_{qp} = 1 - \prod_{i-1}^{n} (1 - q_i + m_i q_i) \tag{7.7}$$

In the case of equal m_i and equal q_i, these two equations become, respectively,

$$P_{ap} = (1 - q + mq)^n \tag{7.8}$$

$$P_{qp} = 1 - (1 - q + mq)^n \tag{7.9}$$

The proportions provided by Eq. (7.6) or (7.8) give the "yield" of the assembly machine, certainly one important measure of the machine's performance. The proportions of assemblies with one or more defective components, given by Eq. (7.7) or (7.9), must be considered a liability of the machine's operation. Either these assemblies must be identified through an inspection process and possibly repaired, or they will become mixed in with the good assemblies. The latter possibility would lead to undesirable consequences when the assemblies are placed in service.

In addition to the proportions of good and bad assemblies as measures of performance for an assembly machine, we are also interested in the machine's production rate, proportions of uptime and downtime, and average cost per unit produced.

To calculate production rate we must first determine the frequency of downtime occurrences per cycle, F. If each station jam results in a machine downtime occurrence, F can be found by taking the expected number of station jams per cycle. Making use of Eq. (7.1), this value is given by

$$F = \sum_{i=1}^{n} p_i = \sum_{i=1}^{n} m_i q_i \qquad \text{(7.10)}$$

If all p_i are equal and all m_i are equal, Eq. (7.10) becomes

$$F = nmq \qquad \text{(7.11)}$$

The average production time per assembly is therefore given by

$$T_p = T_c + \sum_{i=1}^{n} m_i q_i T_d \qquad \text{(7.12)}$$

where $\qquad\qquad T_c$ = ideal cycle time

$\qquad\qquad\qquad T_d$ = average downtime per occurrence

For the case of equal m_i and equal q_i,

$$T_p = T_c + nmqT_d \qquad \text{(7.13)}$$

From the average production time per assembly, we obtain the production rate from Eq. (5.3), repeated here for convenience:

$$R_p = \frac{1}{T_p}$$

However, it must be remembered that unless $m_i = 1$ for all stations, the production of assemblies will include some units with one or more defective components. Accordingly, the production rate should be corrected to give the rate of output of assemblies that contain no defects. We shall call this R_{ap}, the rate of production of acceptable product. By combining Eqs. (5.3) and (7.6), we obtain

$$R_{ap} = \frac{\prod_{i=1}^{n} (1 - q_i + m_i q_i)}{T_p} = \frac{P_{ap}}{T_p} \qquad \text{(7.14)}$$

Using Eq. (7.8) rather than Eq. (7.6), we get the corresponding rate of production when m_i are all equal and q_i are all equal:

$$R_{ap} = \frac{(1 - q + mq)^n}{T_p} \qquad (7.15)$$

Hence, Eq. (5.3) provides the average production cycle rate for an assembly machine, which includes production of both good and bad product. Equations (7.14) and (7.15) give values of average production rate for good product only.

The line efficiency is calculated as the ratio of ideal cycle time to average production time. This is the same as Eq. (5.5), except that average production time, T_p, is given by Eq. (7.12) or (7.13). Using Eq. (7.13) as an illustration,

$$E = \frac{T_c}{T_p} = \frac{T_c}{T_c + nmqT_d}$$

The proportion of downtime, D, is the average downtime per cycle divided by the average production time. For example, for the case of equal m_i and equal q_i, the value of D would be given by

$$D = \frac{nmqT_d}{T_p} = \frac{nmqT_d}{T_c + nmqT_d} \qquad = 1 - E$$

No attempt has been made to correct either the line efficiency E, or the proportion downtime D, for the yield of good assemblies. We are treating the assembly machine efficiency and the quality of units produced as separate issues in the computation of E and D.

ie ?
using
Tap = Rap
instead of Tp

The cost per assembly produced, on the other hand, must take account of the output quality. Therefore, the general cost formula, given by Eq. (5.8), must be amended to include a correction for yield plus any additional costs such as inspection to identify defective assemblies. As an illustration, the correction for yield of good product would be incorporated into the cost formula as follows:

$$C_{pc} = \frac{C_m + C_L T_p + C_t}{(1 - q + mq)^n} = \frac{C_m + C_L T_p + C_t}{P_{ap}} \qquad (7.16)$$

here, this can be taken
as cost of any equip.
parts which have to be
periodically replaced
due to wear + tear
(apportioned to each unit)

where the cost terms in the numerator were defined in Section 5.1. The C_m term includes the costs of the base part and all components added by the assembly system. The denominator would tend to increase the cost of the assembly. Thus, as the quality of individual components deteriorates, this results in an increased average cost per assembly produced.

It is appropriate to conclude this listing of equations on assembly machine performance with some examples. In addition to the traditional ways of indicating line performance (e.g., production rate, proportion uptime, cost per unit), we see an additional dimension of performance in the form of the yield. While the yield of good product is an important issue in any automated production line, we see that it can be explicitly included in the formulas for assembly machine performance by means of q and m.

EXAMPLE 7.2

A 10-station in-line assembly machine has a 6-s ideal cycle time. The base part is automatically loaded prior to the first station, and components are added at each of the stations. The fraction defect rate at each of the 10 stations is $q = 0.01$, and the probability that a defect will jam is $m = 0.5$. When a jam occurs, the average downtime is 2 min. Determine the average production rate, the yield of good assemblies, and the uptime efficiency of the assembly machine.

Solution:

The average production cycle time is

$$T_p = 0.1 + (10)(0.5)(0.01)(2.0) = 0.2 \text{ min}$$

The production rate is therefore

$$R_p = \frac{60}{0.2} = 300 \text{ assemblies/h}$$

The yield is given by Eq. (7.8):

$$P_{ap} = (1 - 0.01 + 0.5 \times 0.01)^{10} = 0.9511$$

This is the proportion of assemblies coming off the machine that contain no defective parts. Therefore, the proportion of assemblies that contain one or more defects is

$$P_{qp} = 1 - 0.9511 = 0.0489$$

The efficiency of the assembly machine is

$$E = \frac{0.1}{0.2} = 0.50 = 50\%$$

EXAMPLE 7.3

Let us examine how the performance measures in Example 7.2 are affected by variations in q and m. First, for $m = 0.5$, determine the production rate, yield, and efficiency for three levels of q: $q = 0$, $q = 0.01$, and $q = 0.02$. Second, for $q = 0.01$, determine the production rate, yield, and efficiency for three levels of m: $m = 0.2$, $m = 0.5$, and $m = 0.8$. Computations similar to those in Example 7.2 provide the following results:

q	m	Production rate (assemblies/h)	Yield	Efficiency (%)
0	0.5	600	1.0	100
0.01	0.5	300	0.9511	50
0.02	0.5	200	0.9044	33.33
0.01	0.2	429	0.9228	71.43
0.01	0.5	300	0.9511	50
0.01	0.8	231	0.9802	38.46

It seems appropriate to discuss the results of Example 7.3. The effect of component quality, as indicated in the value of q, is predictable. As the fraction defect rate increases, meaning that component quality gets worse, all three measures of performance suffer. Production rate drops, the yield of good product gets lower, and the proportion uptime decreases.

The effect of m, the probability that a defect will jam the workhead and cause the assembly machine to stop, is less obvious. At low values of m (e.g., $m = 0.2$) for the same component quality level ($q = 0.01$), the production rate and machine efficiency are higher, but the yield of good product is lower. Instead of interrupting the assembly machine operation and causing downtime, defective components are passing through the assembly process to become part of the final product. As the value of m increases, production rate and machine efficiency drop, but the yield increases.

In Chapter 4, we discussed two types of control, instantaneous control and memory control. The memory control scheme is particularly appropriate for automated assembly machine operation. With memory control, the assembly machine is provided with logic that identifies when a defective component is encountered, but it does not stop the machine. Instead, it remembers the position of the assembly that is affected by the defect, locking it out from additional assembly operations at subsequent workstations, and rejects the assembly after the last station. By contrast, instantaneous control stops the assembly machine when a defect (or other malfunction) occurs. With the introduction of the variable m, we are now in a position to compare the performance of the two control types.

EXAMPLE 7.4

The two types of control are to be compared on the same automated assembly machine used in Examples 7.2 and 7.3. The fraction defect rate is $q = 0.01$. Under ideal conditions, instantaneous control will result in a value of $m = 1.0$, meaning that every defective component causes the assembly machine to stop. Similarly, memory control will result in a theoretical value of $m = 0$.

Let us add cost data to our example. Suppose that the cost of the components is $0.02 per component at each of the 10 stations and $0.10 for the base part. The total component cost is therefore $0.10 + 10($0.02) = $0.30 per unit. We will assume that these cost data include an allowance for the fraction of defective components. However, it does not include an allowance for final products that might be spoiled during assembly by the inclusion of defective components. In other words, it does not consider the yield of good product from the assembly machine. The cost to operate the assembly machine using instantaneous control is $60/h or $1.00/min. Because of its greater complexity, the cost of operating the memory control is $1.10/min. Other costs are negligible.

Solution:

We will compute the average production time, yield, and cost for instantaneous control first.

$$T_p = 0.1 + (10)(1.0)(0.01)(2) = 0.3 \text{ min}$$

$$P_{ap} = (1 - 0.01 + 1 \times 0.01)^{10} = 1.0$$

Hence, the cost per assembly produced can be determined.

$$C_{pc} = 0.30 + 1.00(0.3) = \$0.60/\text{assembly}$$

Next, the same performance measures for memory control.

$$T_p = 0.1 + (10)(0)(0.01)(2) = 0.10 \text{ min}$$

$$P_{ap} = (1 - 0.01 + 0 \times 0.01)^{10} = 0.9044$$

The cost per assembly is

$$C_{pc} = \frac{0.30 + 1.10(0.10)}{0.9044} = \$0.45/\text{assembly}$$

Although the cost of components is higher, the operating costs are reduced because of no downtime, and the resulting cost per assembly is significantly lower. Memory control has the clear cost advantage in this example.

In practice, the theoretical values of *m* will not be realized for the two control types. With instantaneous control, a portion of the defective components will slip through undetected to become included in the final product, so that the actual value of *m* will be less than 1.0. With memory control, there will be cases of line stops resulting from defective components jamming the machine in such a way that it cannot continue operation. Hence, the actual value of *m* under memory control will be greater than the theoretical value of zero. These realities were ignored in Example 7.4.

7.5 ANALYSIS OF A SINGLE-STATION ASSEMBLY MACHINE

The single-station assembly machine can be pictured as shown in Figure 7.8. We assume a single workhead, with several components feeding into the station to be assembled. Let us use *n* to represent the number of distinct assembly elements that are performed on the machine. Each element has an element time, T_{ei}, where $i = 1, 2, \ldots, n$. The ideal cycle time for the single-station assembly machine is the sum of the individual

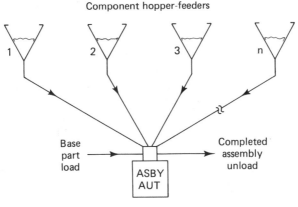

FIGURE 7.8   Single-station assembly machine.

element times of the assembly operations to be performed on the machine, plus the handling time to load the base part into position and unload the completed assembly. We can express this ideal cycle time as

$$T_c = T_h + \sum_{i=1}^{n} T_{ei} \qquad (7.17)$$

here there is no stn.-stn. transfer time since all processes are done at the same stn.

where T_h is the handling time.   *this may be considered negligible for a flow line since parts are auto. transported--*

Many of the assembly elements involve the addition of a component to the existing subassembly. As in our analysis of the multiple-station assembly system, each component type has a certain fraction defect rate, q_i, and there is a certain probability that a defective component will jam the workstation, m_i. When a jam occurs, the assembly machine stops, and it takes an average T_d to clear the jam and restart the system. The inclusion of downtime resulting from jams in the machine cycle time gives

$$T_p = T_c + \sum_{i=1}^{n} q_i m_i T_d \qquad (7.18)$$

For elements that do not include the addition of a component, the value of $q_i = 0$. This might occur, for example, when a fastening operation is performed on a component added during a previous element.

For the special case of equal q and equal m values for all components added, Eq. (7.18) becomes

$$T_p = T_c + nmqT_d$$

Determination of yield (the proportion of assemblies that contain no defective components) for the single-station assembly machine makes use of the same equations as for the multiple-station systems. Uptime efficiency is computed as $E = T_c/T_p$ using the values of T_c and T_p from Eqs. (7.17) and (7.18).

EXAMPLE 7.5

A single-station assembly machine performs five work elements to assemble four components to a base part. The elements are listed below, together with the fraction defect rate and probability of a jam for each of the components added.

Element	Description	Time (s)	q	m
1	Add gear	4	0.02	1.0
2	Add spacer	3	0.01	0.6
3	Add gear	4	0.015	0.8
4	Add gear and mesh	7	0.02	1.0
5	Fasten	5	0	—

The time to load the base part is 3 s and the time to unload the completed assembly is 4 s, giving a total load/unload time of $T_h = 7$ s. When a jam occurs, it takes an average of 1.5 min to clear the jam and restart the machine. Determine the production rate, the yield, and the uptime efficiency of the assembly machine.

Solution:

The ideal cycle time of the assembly machine is

$$T_c = 7 + (4 + 3 + 4 + 7 + 5) = 30 \text{ s} = 0.5 \text{ min}$$

Adding the average downtime due to jams yields

$$T_p = 0.5 + (0.02 \times 1.0 + 0.01 \times 0.6 + 0.015 \times 0.8 + 0.02 \times 1.0)(1.5)$$

$$= 0.5 + 0.087 = 0.587 \text{ min}$$

The production rate is

$$R_p = \frac{60}{0.587} = 102.2 \text{ assemblies/h}$$

The yield of good product is

$$P_{ap} = (1.0)(0.996)(0.997)(1.0) = 0.993$$

and the uptime efficiency is

$$E = \frac{0.5}{0.587} = 0.8518 = 85.18\%$$

As our analysis suggests, increasing the number of elements in the assembly machine cycle results in a higher cycle time, therefore decreasing the production rate of the machine. Accordingly, applications of the single-station assembly machine are usually limited to lower-volume, lower-production rate situations. For higher production rates, one of the multistation assembly systems is generally preferred.

REFERENCES

[1] ANDREASEN, M. M., S. KAHLER and T. LUND, *Design for Assembly,* IFS (Publications) Ltd., Bedford, England, and Springer-Verlag, Berlin, 1983.

[2] BOOTHROYD G., and A. H. REDFORD, *Mechanized Assembly,* McGraw-Hill Publishing Co., Ltd., London, 1968.

[3] BOOTHROYD G., C. POLI, and L. E. MURCH, *Automatic Assembly,* Marcel Dekker, Inc., New York, 1982.

[4] GAY, D. S., "Ways to Place and Transport Parts," *Automation,* June 1973.

[5] GOODRICH, J. L., and G. P. MAUL, "Programmable Parts Feeders," *Industrial Engineering,* May 1983, pp. 28–33.

[6] GROOVER, M. P., M. WEISS, R. N. NAGEL, and N. G. ODREY, *Industrial Robotics: Technology, Programming, and Applications,* McGraw-Hill Book Company, New York, 1986, Chapter 15.

[7] MACKZKA, W. J., "Feeding the Assembly System," *Assembly Engineering,* April 1985, pp. 32–34.

[8] MURCH,L. E., and G. BOOTHROYD, "On–Off Control of Parts Feeding," *Automation,* August 1970, pp. 32–34.

[9] RILEY, F. J., *Assembly Automation,* Industrial Press, Inc., New York, 1983.

[10] SCHWARTZ, W. H. "Robots Called to Assembly," *Assembly Engineering,* August 1985, pp. 20–23.

[11] Syntron (FMC Corporation), *Vibratory Parts Feeders* (Bulletin 400672), Homer City, Pa. 1966.

[12] Syntron (FMC Corporation Materials Handling Equipment Division), *Syntron Parts Handling Equipment,* Catalog No. PHE-10, Home City, Pa., 1984.

PROBLEMS

7.1. A feeder–selector device at one of the stations of an automated assembly machine has a feed rate $f = 25$ parts/min and provides a throughput of one part in four ($\theta = 0.25$). The ideal cycle time of the assembly machine is 10 s. The low-level sensor on the feed track is set at 10 parts, and the high-level sensor is set at 20 parts.

(a) How long will it take for the supply of parts to be depleted from the high-level sensor to the low-level sensor once the feeder–selector device is turned off?

(b) How long will it take for the parts to be resupplied from the low-level sensor to the high-level sensor, on average, after the feeder–selector device is turned on?

(c) What proportion of the time that the assembly machine is operating will the feeder–selector device be turned on? Turned off?

7.2. Do Problem 7.1 but use a feed rate $f = 32$ parts/min. Note the importance of tuning the feeder–selector rate to the cycle rate of the assembly machine.

7.3. A dial indexing machine has six stations that perform the following assembly operations to the base part (also given are element times, and q and m values for the components added):

Station	Description	Element time (s)	q	m
1	Add part A	4	0.015	0.6
2	Fasten part A	3	—	—
3	Assemble part B	5	0.01	0.8
4	Add part C	4	0.02	1.0
5	Fasten part C	3	—	—
6	Assemble part D	6	0.01	0.5

The indexing time for the dial table is 2 s. When a jam occurs, it requires 1.5 min to release the jam and put the machine back in operation. Determine the production rate for the assembly machine, the yield of good product (final assemblies containing no defective components), and the proportion uptime of the system.

7.4. An eight-station assembly machine has an ideal cycle time of 6 s. The fraction defect rate at each of the 8 stations is $q = 0.015$ and the system operates using the instantaneous control strategy. When a breakdown occurs, it takes 1 min, on average, for the system to be put back into operation. Determine the production rate for the assembly machine, the yield of good product (final assemblies containing no defective components), and the proportion uptime of the system.

7.5. Solve Problem 7.4 but assuming that memory control is used rather than instantaneous control. The other data are the same.

7.6. Solve Problem 7.4 only assuming that $m = 0.6$ for all stations. Other data are the same.

7.7. A single-station assembly machine is to be considered as an alternative to the dial indexing machine in Problem 7.3. Use the data given in the table of Problem 7.3 to determine the production rate, the yield of good product (final assemblies containing no defective components), and the proportion uptime of the system. The handling time to load the base part and unload the finished assembly is 7 s and the downtime averages 1.5 min every time a component jams. Why is the proportion uptime so much higher than in the case of the dial indexing machine in Problem 7.3?

7.8. A six-station automatic assembly machine has an ideal cycle time of 12 s. Downtime occurs for two reasons. First, mechanical and electrical failures of the workheads occur with a frequency of once per 50 cycles. Average downtime for these causes is 3 min. Second, defective components also result in downtime. The fraction defect rate of each of the six components added to the base part at the six stations is $q = 2\%$. The probability that a defective component will cause a station jam is $m = 0.5$ for all stations. Downtime per occurrence for defective parts is 2 min. Determine the yield of assemblies that are free of defective components, the proportion of assemblies that contain at least one defective component, the average production rate, and the uptime efficiency.

7.9. An eight-station automatic assembly machine has an ideal cycle time of 10 s. Downtime is caused by defective parts jamming at the individual assembly stations. The average downtime per occurrence is 3.0 min. The fraction defect rate is 1.0% and the probability that a defective part will jam at a given station is 0.6 for all stations. The cost to operate the assembly machine is $90.00/h and the cost of components being assembled is $0.60/unit assembly. Ignore other costs.
(a) Determine the yield of good assemblies.
(b) Determine the average production rate of good assemblies.
(c) What proportion of assemblies will have at least one defective component?
(d) Determine the unit cost of the assembled product.

7.10. A synchronous assembly machine has eight stations and must produce at a rate of 400 completed assemblies per hour. Average downtime per jam is 2.5 min. When a breakdown occurs, all subsystems (including the feeder) stop. The frequency of breakdowns of the machine is once every 50 parts. One of the eight stations is an automatic assembly operation that uses a feeder–selector. The components fed into the selector can have any of five possible orientations, each with equal probability, but only one of which is correct for passage into the feed track to the assembly workhead. Parts rejected by the selector are fed back into the hopper. What minimum rate must the feeder deliver components to the selector during system uptime in order to keep up with the assembly machine?

7.11. An automated assembly machine has four workstations. The first station presents the base part for the assembly, and the other three stations add parts to the base. The ideal cycle time for the machine is 15 s and the average downtime when a jam results from a defective part is 3.0 min. The fraction defective rates and probablities that a defective part will jam the station are given in the following table.

Workstation	Part identification	q	m
1	Base	0.01	1.0
2	Bracket	0.02	1.0
3	Pin	0.03	1.0
4	Retainer	0.04	0.5

Quantities of 100,000 for each of the bases, brackets, pins, and retainers are used to stock the assembly line for operation.
(a) Determine the proportion of good product to total product coming off the line.
(b) Determine the production rate of good product coming off the line during steady-state operation.
(c) With the quantities of components given above, determine the total number of final assemblies that will be produced. Of the total, how many will be good product, and how many will be products that contain at least one defective component?
(d) Of the number of defective assemblies determined in part (c), how many will have defective base parts? How many will have defective brackets? How many will have defective pins? How many will have defective retainers?

7.12. A six-station automatic assembly machine has an ideal cycle time of 6 s. At stations 2 through 6, parts feeders deliver components to be assembled to a base part which is added at the first station. Each of stations 2 through 6 is identical and the five components are identical. That is, the completed product consists of the base part plus the five components. The base parts have zero defects, but the other components are defective at a rate q. When an attempt is made to assemble a defective component to the base part, the machine stops ($m = 1.0$). It takes an average of 2.0 min to make repairs and start the machine up after each stoppage. Since all components are identical, they are purchased from a supplier who can control the fraction defect rate very closely. However, the supplier charges a premium for better quality. The cost per component is determined by the following equation:

$$\text{cost per component} = 0.1 + \frac{0.0012}{q}$$

where q is the fraction defect rate. Cost of the base part is 20 cents. Accordingly, the total cost of the base part and the five components is

$$\text{product material cost} = 0.70 + \frac{0.006}{q} \qquad = .2 + 5\left(.1 + \frac{.0012}{q}\right)$$

The cost to operate the automatic assembly machine is $150.00/h. The problem facing the production manager is this: As the component quality decreases (q increases), the downtime increases which drives production costs up. As the quality improves (q decreases), the material cost increases because of the price formula used by the supplier. To minimize total cost, the optimum value of q must be determined. Determine by analytical methods (rather than trial and error) the value of q that minimizes the total cost per assembly. Also determine the associated cost per assembly and production rate. (Ignore other costs.)

7.13. A six-station dial indexing machine is designed to perform four automatic assembly operations at stations 2 through 5 after a base part has been manually loaded at station 1. Station 6 is the unload station. Each of the assembly operations involves the attachment of a component to the existing base. At each of the four assembly stations, a hopper–feeder is used to deliver components to a selector device which separates components that are improperly oriented and drops them back into the hopper. The system was designed with the following operating parameters for stations 2 through 5.

Station	Assembly process time (s)	Feeder rate, f	Selector, θ	Defect rate, q	Jam rate, m
2	4	32	0.25	0.010	1.0
3	7	20	0.50	0.005	0.6
4	5	20	0.20	0.020	1.0
5	3	15	1.0	0.010	0.7

It takes 2 s to index the dial from one station position to the next. When a component jam occurs, it takes an average of 2 min to release the jam and restart the system. Line stops due to mechanical and electrical failures of the assembly machine are not significant and can be neglected in this problem. The foreman said that the system was designed to produce at a certain hourly rate, which takes into account the jams resulting from defective components. However, the actual delivery of finished assemblies is far below that designed production rate. Analyze the problem and determine the following:

(a) The designed average production rate that the foreman alluded to.

(b) The proportion of assemblies coming off the system that contain one or more defective components.

(c) The problem that limits the assembly system from achieving the expected production rate.

(d) The production rate that the system is actually achieving. State any assumptions that you make in determining your answer.

part **III**

Numerical Control Production Systems

Electronics and computer technologies have had a significant influence on the control function in manufacturing. One important example of the application of these technologies in production systems is numerical control. Numerical control (NC) uses a program of instructions that is electronically transmitted to the production equipment to regulate its function and operation. In the following three chapters we discuss numerical control and its programming.

In Chapter 8 we present the fundamental concepts and operating principles of NC. What are the components of an NC system, and how do they work? This chapter also discusses the variety of applications of numerical control in automated manufacturing systems. These applications include metalworking, electronics assembly, drafting, and others.

Chapter 9 is concerned with the programming of NC systems. In metalworking, specifically metal machining applications, the programming procedure is called part programming because the purpose of the NC application is to machine a part. The two principal methods of part programming in metalworking are manual part programming and computer-assisted part programming. Manual part programming requires the programmer to write the machining instructions in a very low level language. In computer-assisted part programming, a high-level computer language is used. One of the most familiar languages in NC is called APT (for Automatically Programmed Tooling). We provide a somewhat detailed description of the APT language. Other methods of NC part programming include the use of interactive computer graphics on a CAD/CAM (computer-aided design/computer-aided manufacturing) system.

The original NC controllers were hard-wired electronic units. Today, numerical control technology is implemented by means of computers. The terms given to this implementation include computer numerical control (CNC) and direct numerical control (DNC). Chapter 10 discusses these computerized manufacturing systems. We also discuss adaptive control machining, which is a control area related to NC.

chapter **8**

Numerical Control

Most of the automated flow lines discussed earlier are examples of fixed automation. Programmable automation, on the other hand, is designed to accommodate variations in product configuration. Its principal applications are in low- and medium-volume situations, primarily in a batch production mode. One of the most important examples of programmable automation, certainly in discrete metal parts manufacturing, is numerical control.

8.1 WHAT IS NUMERICAL CONTROL?

Numerical control (NC) is a form of programmable automation in which the processing equipment is controlled by means of numbers, letters, and other symbols. The numbers, letters, and symbols are coded in an appropriate format to define a program of instructions for a particular workpart or job. When the job changes, the program of instructions is changed. The capability to change the program is what makes NC suitable for low- and medium-volume production. It is much easier to write new programs than to make major alterations of the processing equipment.

The applications of numerical control range over a wide variety of processes. We divide the applications into two categories in this chapter: (1) machine tool applications such as drilling, milling, turning, and other metalworking; and (2) non–machine tool applications, such as assembly, drafting, and inspection. We discuss these applications in Sections 8.5 and 8.6. The common operating principle of NC in all of these applications is control of the relative position of a tool or processing element with respect to the object (e.g., the workpart) being processed.

Basic components of NC

A numerical control system consists of the following three basic components:

1. Program of instructions
2. Machine control unit
3. Processing equipment

The general relationship among the three components is illustrated in Figure 8.1. The program is fed into the control unit, which directs the processing equipment accordingly.

The *program of instructions* is the detailed step-by-step commands that direct the processing equipment. In its most common form, the commands refer to positions of a machine tool spindle with respect to the worktable on which the part is fixtured. More advanced instructions include selection of spindle speeds, cutting tools, and other functions. The program is coded on a suitable medium for submission to the machine control unit. The most common medium in use over the last several decades has been 1-in.-wide punched tape. Because of the widespread use of the punched tape, NC is sometimes called "tape control." However, this is a misnomer in modern usage of numerical control. Coming into use more recently have been magnetic tape cassettes and floppy diskettes. The programming is done by a person called the part programmer, and we discuss the part programming task in Chapter 9.

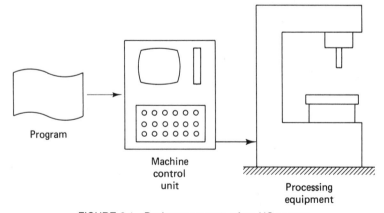

Program

Machine
control
unit

Processing
equipment

FIGURE 8.1   Basic components of an NC system.

The *machine control unit* (MCU) consists of the electronics and control hardware that read and interpret the program of instruction and convert it into mechanical actions of the machine tool or other processing equipment. We discuss the functions and operation of the machine control unit in Section 8.4.

The *processing equipment* is the third basic component of an NC system. It is the component that performs useful work. In the most common example of numerical control, one that performs machining operations, the processing equipment consists of the work-table and spindle as well as the motors and controls needed to drive them.

Historical perspective

The development of numerical control owes much to the U.S. Air Force and the early aerospace industry. The first development work in the area of numerical controls is attributed to John Parsons and an associate named Frank Stulen at Parsons Corporation in Traverse City, Michigan. Parsons was a contractor for the Air Force during the 1940s. The original NC concept involved the use of coordinate positional data contained on punched cards to define the surface contours of helicoptor blades. After development work by Parsons and his colleagues, the idea was presented to the Wright-Patterson Air Force Base in 1948. The initial Air Force contract was awarded to Parsons in June 1949, and a contract was subsequently awarded to the Servomechanism Laboratories at the Massachusetts Institute of Technology to develop the prototype NC machine tool.

This first NC machine was developed by retrofitting a conventional tracer mill with rudimentary numerical controls. The prototype successfully performed simultaneous control of three axes of motion using punched binary tape. The machine was demonstrated at MIT in March 1952.

The machine tool builders gradually began initiating their own development projects to introduce commercial NC products. Also, certain companies in the aerospace industry began to devise numerical control machines to satisfy their own production needs. The Air Force continued its encouragement of NC development by sponsoring additional research at MIT to design a part programming language that could be used for controlling NC machine tools. This research resulted in the development of the APT (Automatically Programmed Tooling) language. The objective of the APT research was to provide a means by which the part programmer could communicate the machining instructions to the machine tool in simple English-like statements. Although the APT language was sometimes criticized as being too large for many of the computers of the time (early and mid-1960s), it nevertheless stands as a major accomplishment in programmable automation. The language is still widely used in industry today, and most other more recent part programming languages are based on APT concepts.

8.2 COORDINATE SYSTEM AND MACHINE MOTIONS

To program the NC processing equipment, it is necessary to establish a standard axis system by which the relative positions of the tool with respect to the work can be specified.

Coordinate system in NC

Using an NC drill press as an example, the drill spindle is in a fixed horizontal position, and the table is moved relative to the spindle. However, to make things easier for the part programmer, the viewpoint is adopted that the workpiece is stationary while the tool is moved relative to it. Accordingly, the numerical control coordinate system is defined with respect to the machine tool table.

Two axes, x and y, are defined in the plane of the table, as shown in Figure 8.2. The z-axis is perpendicular to this plane and movement in the z direction is controlled by the vertical motion of the spindle. The positive and negative directions of motion of tool relative to table along these axes are as shown in Figure 8.2. NC drill presses are classified as either two-axis or three-axis machines, depending on whether or not they have the capability to control the z-axis.

A numerical control milling machine and similar machine tools (boring mill, for example) use an axis system similar to that of the drill press. However, in addition to the three linear axes, these machines may possess the capacity to control one or more rotational axes. Three rotational axes are defined in NC: the a, b, and c axes. These axes are used to specify angles about the x, y, and z axes, respectively. To distinguish positive from negative angular motions, the "right-hand rule" can be used. Using the right hand with the thumb pointing in the positive linear axis direction ($x,y,$ or z), the fingers of the hand are curled to point in the positive rotational direction. This is illustrated in Figure 8.2.

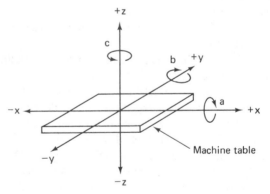

FIGURE 8.2   Machine tool coordinate system for NC.

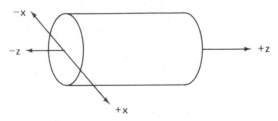

FIGURE 8.3 x- and z-axes for NC turning.

For turning operations, two axes are normally all that are required to command the movement of the tool relative to the rotating workpiece. The z-axis is the axis of rotation of the workpart, and the x-axis defines the radial location of the cutting tool. This arrangement is illustrated in Figure 8.3.

Fixed zero versus floating zero

The purpose of the coordinate system is to provide a means of locating the tool in relation to the workpiece. Depending on the type of NC machine, the part programmer may have several options for specifying the location. One of these options depends on whether the machine has a fixed zero or a floating zero.

In the case of fixed zero, the origin is always located at the same position on the machine table. Usually, the position is the southwest corner (lower left-hand corner) of the table and all locations must be defined by positive x and y coordinates relative to that fixed origin.

The second and more common feature on modern NC machines allows the machine operator to set the zero point at any position on the machine table. This feature is called *floating zero*. The part programmer is the one who decides where the zero point should be located. The decision is based on part programming convenience. For example, the workpart may be symmetrical and the zero point should be established at the center of symmetry. The location of the zero point is communicated to the machine operator. At the beginning of the job, the operator moves the tool under manual control to some "target point" on the table. The target point is some convenient place on the workpiece or table for the operator to position the tool. For example, it might be a predrilled hole in the workpiece. The target point has been referenced to the zero point by the part programmer. In fact, the programmer may have selected the target point as the zero point for tool positioning. When the tool has been positioned at the target point, the machine operator presses a "zero" button on the machine tool console, which tells the machine where the origin is located for subsequent tool movements.

With fixed-zero systems, the part programmer and machine operator must reference the job to the machine's permanent zero point. This is a less convenient arrangement.

Absolute versus incremental positioning

Another option sometimes available to the part programmer is to use either an absolute system of tool positioning or an incremental system. *Absolute positioning* means that the tool locations are always defined in relation to the zero point. If a hole is to be drilled at a spot that is 8 in. above the x-axis and 6 in. to the right of the y-axis, the coordinate location of the hole would be specified as $x = +6.000$ and $y = +8.000$. By contrast, *incremental positioning* means that the next tool location must be defined, with reference to the previous tool location. If in the previous drilling example, the previous hole had been drilled at an absolute position of $x = +4.000$ and $y = +5.000$, the incremental position instructions would be specified as $x = +2.000$ and $y = +3.000$ in order to move the drill to the desired spot. Figure 8.4 illustrates the difference between absolute and incremental positioning.

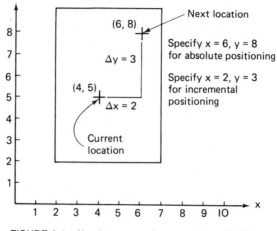

FIGURE 8.4   Absolute versus incremental positioning.

8.3   TYPES OF NC SYSTEMS

The NC system must possess a means of controlling the relative movement of the tool with respect to the work. There are three types of motion control used in numerical control:

1. Point-to-point
2. Straight cut
3. Contouring

The three types are listed in order of increasing level of control sophistication.

Point-to-point NC

Point-to-point (PTP) is also sometimes called a positioning system. In PTP, the objective of the machine tool control system is to move the cutting tool to a predefined location. The speed or path by which this movement is accomplished is not important in point-to-point NC. Once the tool reaches the desired location, the machining operation is performed at that position.

NC drill presses are a good example of PTP systems. The spindle must first be positioned at a particular location on the workpiece. This is done under PTP control. Then, the drilling of the hole is performed at that location, the tool is moved to the next hole location, and so on. Since no cutting is performed between holes, there is no need for controlling the relative motion of the tool and workpiece between hole locations. On positioning systems, the speeds and feeds used by the machine tool are often controlled by the operator rather than by the NC tape. Figure 8.5 illustrates the point-to-point type of control.

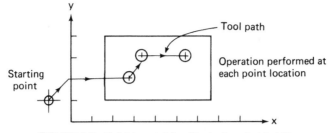

FIGURE 8.5   Point-to-point (positioning) control in NC.

Positioning systems are the simplest machine tool control systems and are therefore the least expensive of the three types. However, for certain processes such as drilling operations and spot welding, PTP is perfectly suited to the task and any higher level of control would be unnecessary.

Straight-cut NC

Straight-cut control systems are capable of moving the cutting tool parallel to one of the major axes at a controlled rate suitable for machining. It is therefore appropriate for performing milling operations to fabricate workpieces of rectangular configurations. With this type of NC system it is not possible to combine movements in more than a single axis direction. Therefore, angular cuts on the workpiece would not be possible. An example of a straight-cut operation is shown in Figure 8.6.

An NC machine tool capable of performing straight-cut movements is also capable of point-to-point movements.

Contouring NC

Contouring is the most complex, the most flexible, and the most expensive type of machine tool control. It is capable of performing both PTP and straight-cut operations. In addition, the distinguishing feature of contouring NC systems is their capacity for simultaneous

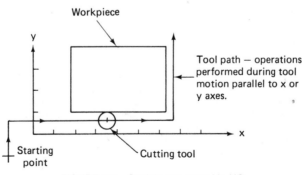

FIGURE 8.6   Straight-cut control in NC.

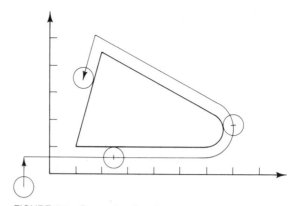

FIGURE 8.7   Contouring (continuous path) control in NC.

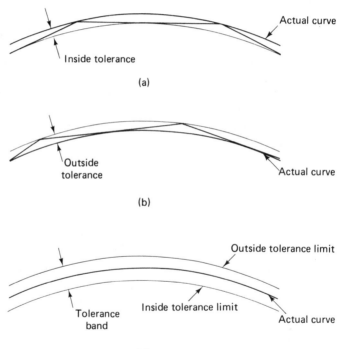

Actual curve

Inside tolerance

(a)

Outside
tolerance

Actual curve

(b)

Outside tolerance limit

Inside tolerance limit

Tolerance
band

Actual curve

(c)

FIGURE 8.8   Approximation of a curved path in NC by a series of straight-line
segments. The accuracy of the approximation is controlled by the tolerance between the actual curve and the maximum deviation of the straight-line segments.
In (a), the tolerance is defined on the inside of the curve. In (b), the tolerance is
defined on the outside of the curve. In (c), the tolerance is defined on both the
inside and outside of the desired curve.

control of more than one axis movement of the machine tool. The path of the cutter is continuously controlled to generate the desired geometry of the workpiece. For this reason, contouring systems are also called continuous-path NC systems. Straight or plane surfaces at any orientation, circular paths, conical shapes, or most any other mathematically definable form are possible under contouring control. Figure 8.7 illustrates the versatility of continuous-path NC. Milling and turning operations are common examples of the use of contouring control.

For the mathematically oriented reader, it might be useful to distinguish between PTP, straight-cut, and contouring in the following way. Consider a two-axis control system, where the table is moved in the xy plane. With point-to-point systems, control is achieved over the x and y coordinates. With straight-cut systems, control is provided for either dx/dt or dy/dt, but only one at a time. With contouring systems, both of the rates dx/dt and dy/dt can be controlled simultaneously. In order to cut a straight path at some angle, the relative values of dy/dt and dx/dt must be maintained in proportion to the tangent of the angle. In order to machine along a curved path, the values of dy/dt and dx/dt must continually be changed so as to follow the path. This is accomplished by breaking the curved path into very short straight-line segments that approximate the curve. Then, the tool is commanded to machine each segment in succession. What results is a machined outline that closely approaches the desired shape. The maximum error between the two can be controlled by the length of the individual line segments as illustrated in Figure 8.8.

The reader can easily imagine the complexity involved when more than two axes movements must be controlled by a contouring system. Some NC machine tools possess the capability to simultaneously control five axes to achieve the desired machined surface.

8.4   THE MCU AND OTHER COMPONENTS OF THE NC SYSTEM

The machine control unit is the NC controller that reads the program and runs the processing equipment (e.g., the machine tool). In this section some of the operating details of the MCU and other components of an NC system are discussed. It should be noted that nearly all modern controls for NC systems are designed around microprocessors. The term *computer numerical control* (CNC) is used to identify these systems, as opposed to conventional numerical control (NC). We describe CNC in Chapter 10; our comments in the present section deal with numerical control operating features that relate both to conventional NC and CNC.

Tape reader

The tape reader is an electrical–mechanical device for winding and reading the punched tape containing the program of instructions. The punched tape format consists of eight parallel tracks of holes along its length. The presence or absence of a hole in a certain position represents bit information, and the entire collection of holes constitutes the NC program. The programming aspects of numerical control are presented in Chapter 9.

There are several techniques used in NC tape readers to sense the hole pattern in the tape. These techniques include:

- *Photoelectric cells.* The reading head shines light at the tape as it is fed through the mechanism, and photoelectric cells behind the tape are activated by the presence of holes in the tape. The arrangement of photoelectric cells corresponds to the hole tracks in the tape.
- *Electrical contact fingers.* In this technique, the reading head consists of a series of eight mechanical fingers or brushes that protrude through the holes in the punched tape. Each finger completes an electrical contact on the opposite side of the tape when a hole is present. In this manner, bit information is read into the MCU.
- *Vacuum method.* In this method, the reading head consists of a series of vacuum sensors that indicate the presence or absence of holes in the tape track positions. The vacuum method derives from the technique used on old player pianos to read the punched paper rolls.

Of the three methods, the use of photoelectric cells has come into dominance. The other methods are slower and less reliable compared to the photoelectric cell technique.

Position and motion control in an NC system

The data read into the MCU through the tape reader define machine table positions corresponding to the axes of the machine tool. Each axis is equipped with a drive unit, such as a dc servomotor, stepping motor, or hydraulic actuator. Using either the dc motor or stepping motor to illustrate, the drive unit is connected to the table by means of a leadscrew, as shown in Figure 8.9. Rotation of the motor causes the leadscrew to turn, which results in linear movement of the table. The pitch of the leadscrew (i.e., distance between successive threads) determines the distance traveled by the table on each revolution of the motor.

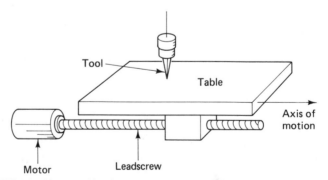

FIGURE 8.9 Motor and leadscrew arrangement used to drive a machine tool axis.

The axis positioning system may be designed as either an open-loop or a closed-loop system. The difference between the two is in the absence or presence of feedback measurements to verify the axis positions of the machine tool table. Schematic diagrams of the two types are illustrated in Figure 8.10.

As shown in the figure, an open-loop NC system is one that does not use feedback signals to indicate the table position to the controller unit. Open-loop NC systems typically make use of stepping motors. The *stepping motor* is a motor that is driven and controlled by an electrical pulse train generated by the MCU (or other digital device). Each pulse drives the stepping motor by a fraction of one revolution, called the *step angle*. The allowable step angles on a stepping motor are determined by the relation

$$\alpha = \frac{360}{n_s} \tag{8.1}$$

where the number of step angles n_s on a stepping motor must be an integer value. The angle of rotation of the stepping motor in response to a pulse train is equal to the number of pulses multiplied by the step angle:

$$\text{angle of rotation} = P\alpha \tag{8.2}$$

where P is the number of pulses received by the motor. An alternative way of expressing this relationship is

$$\text{angle of rotation} = f_p t\alpha \tag{8.3}$$

where f_p is the pulse rate (frequency of the pulse train) and t is the duration of the pulse train.

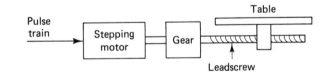

(a)

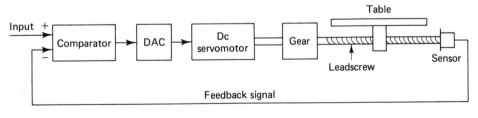

(b)

FIGURE 8.10   (a) Open-loop and (b) closed-loop control in NC.

The rotational speed of the motor can be determined by the following equation:

$$S = \frac{60f_p}{n_s} \qquad (8.4)$$

where S is the rotational speed of the stepping motor.

By controlling the number and rate of pulses to the motor, the position of the table is controlled without the need for feedback sensors. One of the disadvantages of the stepping motor as the drive unit for an NC system is the possible loss of one or more pulses when the motor is operating under load. This results in a loss in accuracy of the table position. Accordingly, stepping motors are used on NC systems in which the load is relatively small. Point-to-point drilling and most of the nonmachining applications of NC are cases where stepping motors can be used to good advantage.

EXAMPLE 8.1

To illustrate the operation of an NC positioning system, let us suppose that the shaft of a stepping motor is connected directly to the *x*-axis leadscrew of the machine table. The pitch of the leadscrew is 3.0 mm. The number of step angles on the stepping motor is 200.

(a) Determine how closely the position of the table can be controlled, assuming that there are no mechanical errors in the positioning system.

(b) What is the required frequency of the pulse train and the corresponding rotational speed of the stepping motor in order to drive the table at a travel rate of 100 mm/min?

Solution:

(a) The motor position can be controlled to 200 increments corresponding to the number of step angles. One revolution of the motor provides a table movement of 3.0 mm, which corresponds to the pitch of the leadscrew. Therefore, the table position can be controlled in increments of

$$\frac{3.0}{200} = 0.015 \text{ mm}$$

This equates to about 0.0006 in.

(b) To drive the table at 100 mm/min (about 3.94 in./min), there must be $100/3.0 = 33.333$ rotations of the leadscrew per minute. The pulse rate must therefore be

$$f_p = (200 \text{ pulses/rev})(33.333 \text{ rotations/min})/(60 \text{ s/min})$$

$$= 111.11 \text{ pulses/s}$$

Owing to the direct connection between the motor and the leadscrew, the rotational speed of the stepping motor is equal to the rev/min rate of the leadscrew, which is 33.333 rev/min. Let us check this with Eq. (8.4):

$$S = \frac{60(111.11)}{200} = 33.33 \text{ rev/min}$$

As illustrated in Fig. 8.10(b), a closed-loop system uses position sensors attached to the machine tool table to measure its position relative to the input value for the axis. Any difference between the input value and the measured value is used to drive the system toward a zero difference. The analysis of closed-loop systems (also called feedback control systems) is discussed in Chapter 19.

The function of the feedback loop in a numerical control system is to assure that the table and workpart have been properly located with respect to the tool. Closed-loop NC systems generally use dc servomotors or hydraulic actuators, although hydraulic actuators are becoming less common in machine tool drive systems.

Various feedback sensor devices are used in NC. One common type is the *optical encoder,* which is also used as a component for position feedback in an industrial robot. The operation of an optical encoder is illustrated in Figure 8.11. The basic device consists of a light source, a photodetector, and a disk that is connected (usually through a gear reduction box) to the rotating shaft whose angular position is to be measured. The light source and the photodetector are located on opposite sides of the disk. The disk has a series of openings through which the light source can be seen by the photosensor. As the disk rotates, the openings cause the light source to be seen as a series of flashes, the number of flashes per revolution corresponding to the number of openings in the disk. The photodetector emits an electrical signal equal to the number of flashes, which are in turn counted by the MCU. It should be noted that some optical encoders are more sophisticated than the one we describe here.

We can define relationships for the optical encoder which are similar to those used for the stepping motor. The angle between the openings in the disk is given by

$$\alpha = \frac{360}{n_d} \tag{8.5}$$

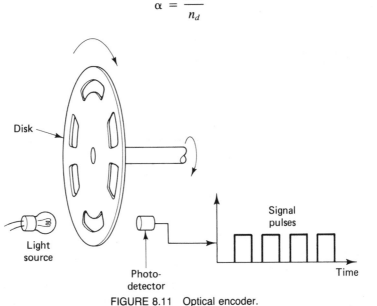

FIGURE 8.11   Optical encoder.

where n_d represents the number of openings in the encoder disk. The angle of rotation measured by the encoder is equal to the number of light pulses (converted to electrical pulses) sensed through the rotating disk. This can be summarized as

$$\text{angle of rotation} = P\alpha \tag{8.6}$$

This measured angle of rotation can be used to determine the linear position of an NC machine table axis by taking into account the pitch of the leadscrew driving the table and the gear reduction between the encoder shaft and the leadscrew. The feed rate of the table can also be determined using an equation similar to Eq. (8.4).

The series of pulses that are generated by the optical encoder is compared with the input position command, and the error is used to control a dc servomotor, which in turn drives the machine table. A digital-to-analog converter (DAC) is required to convert the digital signal used in the typical MCU into a continuous analog power signal to the drive motor. Closed-loop NC systems are generally more appropriate for processes that generate a significant load during operation. Most metal-cutting machine tool applications such as milling and turning are in this category.

Accuracy and repeatability

Two of the important features of a numerical control system are its accuracy and repeatability. The accuracy of an NC system is related to its control resolution. The term *control resolution* refers to the MCU's capability to divide the range of a given axis movement into closely spaced points that can be identified by the controller. This is a function of factors such as the controller's bit storage capacity, the NC drive system (e.g., the number of step angles for a stepping motor), and the capability of the feedback sensor (e.g., the number of pulses generated per revolution by an optical encoder). Let us consider the case where the bit storage capacity is the determining factor in the control resolution. If n represents the number of bits for an axis, the number of control points is given by

$$\text{number of control points} = 2^n$$

The control resolution is therefore defined as the distance between adjacent control points, and can be determined by

$$\text{CR} = \frac{\text{range of axis movement}}{2^n} \tag{8.7}$$

Accuracy is a measure of the control system's capacity to position the machine table at a desired location, which is defined by a set of axis coordinate values. If we consider only one axis for clarity of explanation, a worst-case situation would be for the desired location to lie directly between two adjacent control points. The definition of accuracy assumes this worst-case situation and adds the mechanical errors that result from gear backlash, leadscrew play, deflection of machine components, and similar inaccuracies in the mechanical positioning system. It is appropriate to consider the mechanical errors as forming a statistical distribution about a particular control point. For a linear axis such as a machine tool slide, we will assume that the distribution is normal with a constant variance over the range of the axis movement. If this is the case, we can picture the control resolution and mechanical errors as shown in Figure 8.12. Nearly all (99.74%) of the error is included within ± 3.0 standard deviations of the normal distribution. Hence, we can establish the following definition of *accuracy:*

$$\text{accuracy} = \frac{CR}{2} + 3 \text{ (std. dev. of mech. error)} \tag{8.8}$$

The definition of accuracy is pictured in Figure 8.12.

Repeatability is defined in terms of the ability of the control system to return to a given location that was previously programmed into the controller. Repeatability affects the capacity of the NC machine tool to produce parts that do not vary in machined dimensions from one part to the next. Repeatability errors have as their principal source the mechanical errors mentioned earlier. We can therefore define

$$\text{repeatability} = \pm 3(\text{std. dev. of mech. error})$$

$$= 6(\text{std. dev. of mech. error}) \tag{8.9}$$

Our definition of repeatability is illustrated in Figure 8.12. Because its structure is very rigid, a machine tool can be built to achieve very high repeatability, well under 0.001 in.

EXAMPLE 8.2

A two-axis NC control system used as an x-y positioning table has a bit storage capacity of 12 bits for each axis. Both x and y axes have a range of 15 in. The mechanical accuracy of the machine table can be characterized by a normal distribution with standard deviation = 0.0003 in. for both

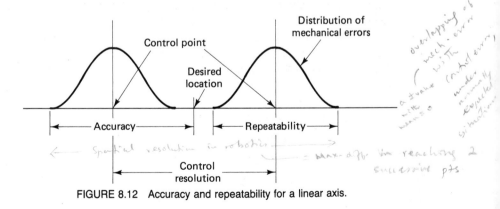

FIGURE 8.12 Accuracy and repeatability for a linear axis.

axes. Determine (a) the control resolution, (b) the accuracy, and (c) the repeatability of the NC system.

Solution:

(a) The control resolution is determined by

$$CR = \frac{15.0 \text{ in.}}{2^{12}} = \frac{15}{4096} = 0.00366 \text{ in.}$$

(b) The accuracy is defined as

$$\text{accuracy} = \frac{0.00366}{2} + 3(0.0003) = 0.00273 \text{ in.}$$

(c) The repeatability, by our definition, is

$$\text{repeatability} = 6(0.0003) = 0.0018 \text{ in.}$$

Interpolation schemes

Our discussion thus far has focused on control issues related to point-to-point positioning. Let us consider one of the important aspects of contouring: interpolation. The cutter paths that a contouring-type NC system is required to generate involve circular arcs and other smooth nonlinear shapes. Some of these shapes can be defined mathematically by relatively simple geometric formulas (e.g., the equation for a circle); others cannot be defined mathematically except by approximation. In any case, a fundamental problem in generating these shapes with NC is that they are continuous while NC is digital. To cut along a circular path, the circle must be divided into a series of straight-line segments as explained in Section 8.3. If the programmer were required to specify the end points for each of the line segments, the programming task would be extremely tedious and fraught with errors. Also, the punched tape would be extremely long because of the large number of points in the program. To ease the burden, interpolation routines have been developed that calculate the intermediate points the cutter must follow in order to generate a particular mathematically defined or approximated path.

There are a number of interpolation schemes that have been developed to deal with the various problems that are encountered in generating a smooth continuous path with a contouring-type NC system. They include:

1. Linear interpolation
2. Circular interpolation
3. Helical interpolation
4. Parabolic interpolation
5. Cubic interpolation

Each of these interpolation procedures permits the programmer (or operator) to generate machine instructions for linear or curvilinear paths, using a relatively few input parameters. The interpolation module in the MCU performs the calculations and directs the tool along the path.

Linear interpolation is the most basic and is used when a straight-line path is to be generated in continuous-path NC. Two-axis and three-axis linear interpolation routines are sometimes distinguished in practice, but conceptually they are the same. The programmer is required to specify the beginning point and end point of the straight line, and the feed rate that is to be followed along the straight line. The interpolator computes the feed rates for each of the two (or three) axes in order to achieve the specified feed rate.

Linear interpolation for creating a circular path would be quite inappropriate because the programmer would be required to specify the line segments and their respective end points that are to be used to approximate the circle. *Circular interpolation* schemes have been developed that permit the programming of a path consisting of a circular arc by specifying the following parameters of the arc: the coordinates of its end points, the coordinates of its center, its radius, and the direction of the cutter along the arc. The tool path that is created consists of a series of straight-line segments, but the segments are calculated by the interpolation module rather than the programmer. The cutter is directed to move along each line segment one by one in order to generate the smooth circular path. A limitation of circular interpolation is that the plane in which the circular arc exists must be a plane defined by two axes of the NC system.

Helical interpolation combines the circular interpolation scheme for two axes described above with linear movement of a third axis. This permits the definition of a helical path in three-dimensional space.

Parabolic and *cubic interpolation* routines are used to provide approximations of free-form curves using higher-order equations. They generally require considerable computational power and are not as common as linear and circular interpolation. Their applications are concentrated in the automobile industry for fabricating dies for car body panels styled with free-form designs that cannot accurately and conveniently be approximated by combining linear and circular interpolations.

8.5 MACHINE TOOL APPLICATIONS

The most common application of numerical control is for machine tool control. This was the first application of NC and is today the most important commercially. In this section we discuss the machine tool applications of NC with emphasis on metal machining.

The machining process

Machining is a manufacturing process in which the geometry of the work is changed by removing excess material. The material is removed by means of the relative motion between a cutting tool and the workpiece. By controlling the action of the tool against the work, the desired geometry is created. Machining is generally considered to be the most versatile production process because it can be used to create a wide variety of shapes and surface finishes on the part. Yet it can be performed at relatively high production rates to achieve low-cost finished products. We first encountered the machining process in our discussion of transfer lines and related systems in Chapter 4. We have need in our present discussion of numerically controlled machine tools to examine the process more closely.

There are five basic types of machining processes: turning, drilling, milling, shaping and planing (usually considered as one category), and grinding. The configurations of the five processes, and the general shapes of the tools used, are shown in Figure 8.13.

For each of the five machining processes, there are certain parameters, called cutting conditions, that are used to control the process and to achieve the desired results. These parameters are typically called the speed, feed, and depth of cut. (There is some variation

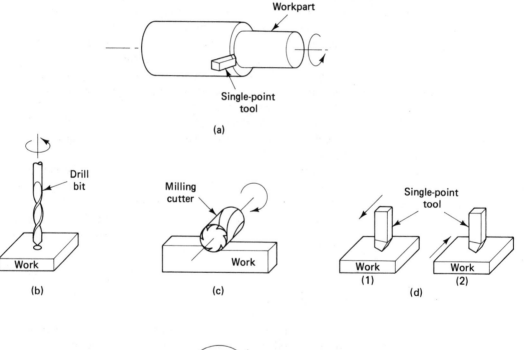

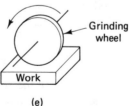

FIGURE 8.13 Five basic machining processes: (a) turning; (b) drilling; (c) milling; (d) shaping (1) and planing (2); (e) grinding.

in the terminology for the grinding process.) These cutting conditions are illustrated in Figure 8.14 for a turning operation. The speed is the relative velocity of the tool with respect to the work surface. Units of surface feet per minute (sfpm) or meters per minute (m/min) are typically used to measure the cutting speed. For cutting tools that rotate, it is sometimes more convenient to refer to the rotational speed in rev/min. The feed is represented by the lateral displacement of the cutting tool relative to the work on each pass or revolution of the tool. Typical units used are in./rev or in./pass. A related term applicable in most machining operations is feed rate, which is the lateral travel rate of the tool expressed in in./min. The depth of cut is the distance the tool penetrates below the original surface of the work, usually measured in units of inches or millimeters.

For milling and drilling it is often necessary to convert from surface speed to spindle rotation speed (and vice versa). Letting S represent the spindle speed in rev/min and V the cutting speed in sfpm,

$$S = \frac{12V}{\pi D} \tag{8.10}$$

where D is the diameter of the cutter in inches. The same formula can be used to compute the spindle speed in a turning operation, given the surface speed, if we let D be the diameter of the cylindrical workpiece rather than the cutter.

Also in a machining operation involving rotation (of the tool or work), feed expressed in in./rev might have to be converted to feed rate in inches per minute. The conversion formula is

$$f_r = Sf \tag{8.11}$$

where f_r is the feed rate in in./min and f is the feed in in./rev. The feed rate corresponds to the travel rate used in Example 8.1, so we now see how the NC machine table travel rate is related to the machining operation.

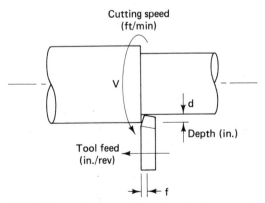

FIGURE 8.14   Cutting conditions for a turning operation.

In a milling operation, the feed must sometimes be determined from the chip load on one tooth of the cutter. Suppose, for example, that a milling cutter has six teeth and each tooth cuts a 0.002-in.-wide chip on its travel into the work. This chip width taken by the milling cutter is called the chip load. The feed is determined as

$$f = \text{(number of teeth on the cutter)(chip load)}$$

where f is the feed in in./rev. For the cutter with six teeth, the feed = (6 teeth)(0.002 in.) = 0.012 in./rev.

The three cutting conditions speed, feed, and depth determine the rate at which metal is removed during machining. This is called the metal removal rate (MRR):

$$\text{MRR} = 12Vfd \qquad (8.12)$$

where $V = $ cutting speed, sfpm

$f = $ feed, in./rev

$d = $ depth, in.

The factor 12 is used to convert the cutting speed from ft/min to in./min. Units of cubic inches per minute (in.^{3}/min) are used for MRR.

Equation (8.12) is most applicable for a turning operation. For a milling or drilling operation some adjustments must be made. For example, for a drilling operation, MRR would most conveniently be calculated by multiplying the area of the drill by the feed rate (in./min). For a milling operation, the most convenient way to calculate MRR is by using the feed rate in in./min and multiplying by the cross-sectional area of the cut (depth × width).

The time required to accomplish the cutting operation is important in determining production rate. This is the time T_m referred to in Eq. (2.8). In most machining operations it can be determined from the formula

$$T_m = \frac{L}{f_r} \qquad (8.13)$$

where L is the length of the workpiece in the direction of feed travel. The value of L usually includes a small distance at the beginning and end of the cut to allow for overtravel. This distance is small enough that it will be neglected in our calculations.

With NC machine tools it is required that the MCU be capable of maintaining the desired cutting conditions in order to properly control the machining process. It is also necessary that the part programmer be sufficiently knowledgeable in these parameters to specify appropriate values for them in the program.

EXAMPLE 8.3

The cutting conditions for a turning operation performed on an NC machine tool are: cutting speed = 400 sfpm, feed = 0.010 in./rev, and depth = 0.100 in. The workpiece diameter = 3.00 in. and its length = 10.0 in. Determine the rotational speed, the feed rate, metal removal rate, and the time to travel from one end of the workpiece to the other.

Solution:

The rotational speed is given by Eq. (8.10):

$$S = \frac{12(400)}{(3.142)(3.0)} = 509.3 \text{ rev/min}$$

The feed rate is given by Eq. (8.11):

$$f_r = 509.3(0.010) = 5.093 \text{ in./min}$$

Metal removal rate can be calculated from Eq. (8.12):

$$MRR = 12(400)(0.010)(0.100) = 4.80 \text{ in.}^3/\text{min}$$

Time to travel the 10-in. length can be determined from Eq. (8.13) by dividing the length by the feed rate:

$$T_m = \frac{10.0}{5.093} = 1.96 \text{ min}$$

Machine tool technology for NC

Each of the five machining processes is carried out on a machine tool designed to perform that process. Turning is performed on a lathe, drilling is done on a drill press, milling on a milling machine, and so on. There are several different types of grinding operations with a corresponding variety of machines to perform them. Numerical control machine tools have been designed for nearly all of the machining processes. The list includes:

- Drill presses
- Milling machines, vertical spindle and horizontal spindle
- Turning machines, both horizontal axis and vertical axis
- Horizontal and vertical boring mills
- Profiling and contouring mills
- Surface grinders and cylindrical grinders

In addition to the machining process, NC machine tools have also been developed for other metalworking processes. These machines include:

- Punch presses for sheet metal hole punching
- Presses for sheet metal bending

The introduction of numerical control has had a pronounced influence on the design and operation of machine tools. One of the effects of NC has been that the proportion of time spent by the machine cutting metal under program control is significantly greater than with manually operated machines. This causes certain components, such as the spindle, drive gears, and feed screws, to wear more rapidly. These components must be designed to last longer on NC machines. Second, the addition of the electronic control unit has increased the cost of the machine, therefore requiring higher equipment utilization. Instead of running the machine on only one shift, which was the convention with manually operated machines, NC machines are often operated two or even three shifts to obtain the required payback. Also, the NC machines are designed to reduce the time consumed by the nonprocessing elements in the operation cycle, such as loading and unloading the workpart, and changing tools. Third, the increasing cost of labor has altered the relative roles of the operator and the machine tool. Consider the role of the human operator. Instead of being the highly skilled worker who controlled every aspect of the part production, the tasks of the operator have been reduced to part loading and unloading, tool changing, chip clearing, and the like. In this way, one operator can often run two or three automatic machines. The role and functions of the machine tool have also changed. NC machines are designed to be highly automatic and capable of combining several operations in one setup that formerly required several different machines. These changes are best exemplified by a new type of machine that did not exist prior to the advent and development of numerical control: the machining center.

The machining center, developed in the late 1950s, is a machine tool capable of performing several different machining operations on a workpart in one setup under program control. The machining center is capable of milling, drilling, reaming, tapping, boring, facing, and similar operations. In addition, the features that typically characterize the NC machining center include the following:

- *Automatic tool-changing capability.* A variety of machining operations means that a variety of tools is required. The tools are contained on the machine in a tool magazine or drum. When a tool needs to be changed, the tool drum rotates to the proper position, and an automatic tool changing mechanism, operating under program control, exchanges the tool in the spindle and the tool in the drum.
- *Automatic workpart positioning.* Most machining centers have the capability to rotate the job relative to the spindle, thereby permitting the cutting tool to access four surfaces of the part.
- *Pallet shuttle.* Another feature is that the machining center has two (or more) separate pallets that can be presented to the cutting tool. While machining is being performed with one pallet in position in front of the tool, the other pallet is in a safe location away from the spindle. In this way, the operator can be unloading the finished part from the prior cycle and fixturing the raw workpart for the next cycle while machining is being performed on the current workpiece.

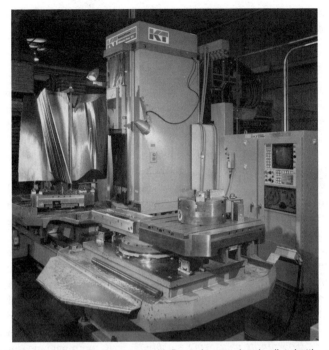

FIGURE 8.15   NC machining center with five-axis control and pallet shuttle, showing complex workpart being machined. (Courtesy of Kearney & Trecker Corp.)

Machining centers are classified as vertical or horizontal. The descriptor refers to
the orientation of the machine tool spindle. A vertical machining center has its spindle
on a vertical axis relative to the worktable, and a horizontal machining center has its
spindle on a horizontal axis. This distinction generally results in a difference in the type
of work that is performed on the machine. A vertical machining center is typically used
for flat work that requires tool access from the top. A horizontal machining center is used
for cube-shaped parts where tool access can best be achieved on the sides of the cube.
An example of an NC horizontal machining center, capable of many of the features
described above, is shown in Figure 8.15.

The success of the machining center has resulted in the development of similar
machine tools for other metalworking processes. One example is the turning center,
designed as a highly automated and versatile machine tool for performing turning, facing,
drilling, threading, and related operations.

8.6   OTHER APPLICATIONS

The operating principle of numerical control, described in Section 8.1, is to control the
relative position of a tool or other processing element with respect to the work. That
same operating principle is applied to various other processes in addition to machining

and pressworking. However, the applications are not always referred to by the term NC. Some of the machines and equipment utilizing NC-type controls include:

- *Electrical wire-wrap machines.* These machines, pioneered by Gardner Denver Corporation, are used to wrap and string wires on the back pins of electrical wiring boards to establish connections between components on the front of the board. The program of coordinate positions that define the back panel connections is determined from design data and fed to the wire-wrap machine. This type of equipment has been used by computer firms and other companies representing the electronics industry.
- *Component insertion machines.* This equipment is used to position and insert components on an *x-y* plane, usually a flat board or panel. The program specifies the *x*- and *y*-axis positions in the plane where the components are to be located. Component insertion machines find extensive applications for inserting semiconductor chips (and other components) into printed circuit boards. They are also used for similar insertion-type assembly operations.
- *Drafting machines.* Automated drafting machines serve as one of the important output devices for a CAD/CAM (computer-aided design/computer aided manufacturing) system. The designs of a product and its components are developed on the CAD/CAM system, working through the various design iterations on the graphics monitor rather than on a mechanical drafting board. When the design is sufficiently finalized for presentation, the output is plotted on the drafting machine, basically a high-speed *x-y* plotter.
- *Coordinate measuring machines.* A coordinate measuring machine (CMM) is an inspection machine used for measuring or checking dimensions on a part. The CMM has a probe that can be manipulated in three axes and identifies when contact is made

FIGURE 8.16   NC laser cutting machine. (Courtesy of Wiedemann Division, Warner & Swasey/A Cross & Trecker Company.)

against the part surface. The location of the probe tip is determined by the CMM control unit, thereby indicating some dimension on the part. Many coordinate measuring machines are programmed to perform automated inspections using NC. We will discuss the CMM in more detail in Chapter 18.

• *Flame cutting, plasma arc cutting, laser cutting, and similar machines.* These are machine tools designed to achieve relative movement in two axes between a worktable and the cutting head (e.g., a gas or plasma arc torch or a laser beam) to perform cutting operations on plate and sheet metal. The cutting path typically involves curved and irregular outlines that cannot be accomplished economically on a conventional shearing press. Movement of the torch relative to the work is usually done by numerical controls. Figure 8.16 illustrates a laser cutting machine.

Additional applications of numerical control include tube bending, cloth cutting, knitting, riveting, and filament winding.

8.7 ECONOMICS OF NC

There are a number of reasons why NC systems are being adopted so widely by the metalworking industry. It has been estimated that 75% of manufacturing is carried out in lost sizes of 50 or less. As indicated above, these small lot sizes are the typical applications for NC. Following are the advantages of numerical control when it is utilized in these small production quantities:

1. *Reduced nonproduction time.*   Numerical control cannot change the basic metal-cutting process, but it can increase the proportion of time the machine is engaged in cutting metal. It accomplishes this decrease in nonproductive time by means of fewer setups, less setup time, reduced workpiece handling time, automatic tool changes on some machines, and so on.
2. *Reduced fixturing.*   NC requires simpler fixtures because the positioning is done by the NC program rather than the fixture or jig.
3. *Reduced lead time.*   Jobs can be set up more quickly with NC.
4. *Greater manufacturing flexibility.*   NC adapts better to changes in jobs, production schedules, and so on.
5. *Easier to accommodate engineering design changes on the workpiece.*   Instead of making alterations in a complex fixture, the program can be altered.
6. *Improved accuracy and reduced human error.*   NC is ideal for complicated parts where the chances of human mistakes are high.

Where is NC most appropriate?

It is clear from the advantages listed above that NC is appropriate only for certain parts, not all parts. The general characteristics of jobs for which NC is most appropriate are the following:

Proposed Equipment: _____

I. Required Investment

1. Installed cost of proposed equipment $ _____
2. Disposal value of any equipment retired _____
3. Capital required in absence of proposed equipment _____
4. Total investment released or avoided (2 + 3) _____
5. Net investment required (1 − 4) _____

II. Effect of Investment on Operating Costs

	A. Savings	B. Losses
6. Direct machine operator labor	____	____
7. Programming costs	____	____
8. Inspection costs	____	____
9. Indirect labor	____	____
10. Fringe benefits	____	____
11. Tooling (expendable tools)	____	____
12. Tool setting	____	____
13. Fixtures	____	____
14. Supplies (cutting fluids, etc.)	____	____
15. Maintenance	____	____
16. Scrap and rework	____	____
17. Downtime (excluding maintenance)	____	____
18. Power	____	____
19. Floor space released or added	____	____
20. Property taxes, insurance	____	____
21. Workpart handling	____	____
22. Inventory (storage, insurance, etc.)	____	____
23. Safety — estimate if applicable	____	____
24. Flexibility — estimate a value	____	____
25. Other factors specific to proposal	____	____
26. Totals (sum 6 through 25)	A. ____	B. ____
27. Net gain (26A–26B)	____	$ ____

III. Effect of Investment on Revenues

	A. Gains	B. Losses
28. From change in product quality	____	____
29. From change in volume of output	____	____
30. Totals (28 + 29)	A. ____	B. ____
31. Net gain (30A − 30B)	$ ____	

IV. Other Factors Related to Proposed Equipment

32. Estimated service life = _____ years
33. Estimated salvage value $ ____
34. Depreciation method: _____
35. Rate of return = _____ %

FIGURE 8.17   NC machine economic analysis form.

1. Parts are processed frequently and in small to medium lot sizes.
2. Part geometry is complex.
3. Close tolerances must be held on the workpart.
4. Many operations must be performed on the part in its processing.
5. Much metal needs to be removed (for machining applications).
6. Engineering design changes are likely.
7. It is an expensive part where mistakes in processing would be costly.
8. Parts require 100% inspection.

In order to justify that a job be processed by NC, it is not necessary that the job possess every one of these attributes. However, the more of these characteristics that are present, the more likely that the part is a good application for numerical control.

Economic analysis of an NC machine investment

There are two aspects of the economic analysis that will be discussed briefly here. The first deals with the introduction of numerical control into the plant. The second is concerned with the justification of a particular NC machine tool.

For an all-conventional machine shop deciding on the possible introduction of numerical control, the decision should be based on whether NC will meet the needs of the shop better than current methods. Determining how appropriate numerical control is for a given machine shop (or pressworking plant) should include consideration of the preceding list of job characteristics for which NC is appropriate. If the shop processes a high proportion and/or number of parts that fit these characteristics, then numerical control is suitable. Once the decision is made to proceed with NC, a substantial commitment is required by the company management. Introducing NC requires the training of machine operators, part programmers, computer specialists, maintenance personnel, and shop supervision. The involvement of nearly all shop personnel in some way or other is required to make the installation a success.

The second aspect of economic analysis deals with the justification of an individual NC machine tool. The methods for evaluating an investment proposal were presented in Chapter 3. Although different companies have their own ways of deciding on capital equipment proposals, the typical factors that should be included are presented in the NC machine economic analysis form presented in Figure 8.17. This form was based on information in references [2] and [4], as well as our discussion in Chapter 3.

REFERENCES

[1] Childs, J. J., *Numerical Control Part Programming*, Industrial Press, Inc., New York, 1973.

[2] DeVries, M. F., "Two Case Studies of the Investment Justification for N/C Machinery Using the MAPI Method," *Educational Module*, Manufacturing Productivity Educational Committee, Purdue University, West Lafayette, Ind., 1977.

[3] GROOVER, M. P., and E. W. ZIMMERS, Jr., *CAD/CAM: Computer-Aided Design and Manufacturing*, Prentice-Hall, Inc., Englewood Cliffs, N.J., 1984.

[4] GROOVER, M. P., T. ONITIRI, and C. MARSHALL, "A Point Scoring System for Decisions on Numerical Control Part Programming," *Technical Paper MS77-295*, Society of Manufacturing Engineers, Dearborn, Mich., 1977.

[5] JABLONOWSKI, J., "What's New in Machining Centers," Special Report 763, *American Machinist*, February 1984, pp. 95–114.

[6] KOREN, Y., *Computer Control of Manufacturing Systems*, McGraw-Hill Book Company, New York, 1983, Chapters 1–6.

[7] MASON, F., and N. B. FREEMAN, "Turning Centers Come of Age," Special Report 773, *American Machinist*, February 1985, pp. 97–116.

[8] *Modern Machine Shop 1985 NC/CAM Guidebook*, Gardner Publications, Inc., Cincinnati, Ohio, January 1985.

[9] PRESSMAN, R. S., and J. E. WILLIAMS, *Numerical Control and Computer-Aided Manufacturing*, John Wiley & Sons, Inc., New York, 1977.

PROBLEMS

8.1. Two stepping motors are used in an NC system to drive the leadscrews for *x-y* positioning. The range of each axis is 10.0 in. The shaft of the motors are connected directly to the leadscrews. The pitch of each leadscrew is 0.1 in. The number of step angles on the stepping motor is 150.

(a) How closely can the position of the table be controlled, assuming that there are no mechanical errors in the positioning system?

(b) What are the required pulse train frequencies and the corresponding rotational speeds of each stepping motor in order to drive the table at 10 in./min in a straight line from point (0, 0) to point (5, 8)?

8.2. A stepping motor is to be used for an NC positioning system. The motor will be connected to a leadscrew whose pitch is 0.125 in., and the leadscrew will drive the table. The control resolution for the table is specified as 0.0005 in. Determine:

(a) The number of step angles required to achieve the specified control resolution.

(b) The size of each step angle in the motor.

(c) The linear travel rate of the motor at a pulse frequency of 200 pulses/s.

8.3. A dc servomotor is used to drive one of the table axes of an NC milling machine. The motor is coupled directly to the leadscrew for the axis, and the leadscrew has 5 threads/in. The optical encoder attached to the leadscrew emits 500 pulses per revolution of the leadscrew. The motor rotates at a normal speed of 300 rev/min. Determine the following:

(a) The control resolution of the system, expressed in linear travel distance of the table axis.

(b) The frequency of the pulse train emitted by the optical encoder when the servomotor operates at full speed.

(c) The travel rate of the table at normal rev/min rate of the motor.

8.4. A two-axis NC system used to control a machine tool table uses a bit storage capacity of 16 bits in its control memory for each axis. The range of the x-axis is 20 in. and the range of the y-axis is 16 in. The mechanical accuracy of the machine table can be represented by a normal distribution with standard deviation = 0.0001 in. for both axes. Determine for each axis: (a) the control resolution, (b) the accuracy, and (c) the repeatability of the NC system.

8.5. Stepping motors will be used to drive the two axes of an insertion machine used for electronic assembly. A printed circuit board is mounted on the table, which must be positioned accurately for reliable insertion of components into the board. The range of each axis is 18.0 in. The leadscrew used to drive each of the two axes has a pitch of 0.10 in. The inherent mechanical errors in the table positioning can be characterized by a normal distribution with standard deviation = 0.0002 in. If the required accuracy for the table is 0.0016 in., determine:
(a) The number of step angles that the stepping motor must have.
(b) How many bits are required in the control memory for each axis to uniquely identify each control position.

8.6. A turning operation is to be performed on an NC lathe. The cutting conditions are: cutting speed = 500 sfpm, feed = 0.008 in./rev, and depth = 0.125 in. The workpiece diameter = 4.00 in. and its length = 15.0 in. Determine (a) the rotational speed of the workbar, (b) the feed rate, (c) the metal removal rate, and (d) the time to travel from one end of the part to the other.

8.7. An end milling operation will be performed on an NC machining center. The total length of travel is 25.0 in. along a straight-line path to cut a particular workpiece. Cutting conditions are: cutting speed = 125 sfpm and chip load = 0.003 in. The end milling cutter has two teeth and its diameter = 0.50 in. Given these conditions, determine the feed rate and the time to complete the cut.

8.8. In Problem 8.7, the axis corresponding to the feed rate uses a dc servomotor as the drive unit and an optical encoder as the feedback sensing device. The motor is geared to the leadscrew with a 10:1 reduction (10 turns of the motor for each turn of the leadscrew). If the leadscrew has a pitch = 0.200 in. and the optical encoder emits 400 pulses per revolution, determine the rotational speed of the motor and the pulse rate of the encoder in order to achieve the feed rate indicated.

8.9. A numerical control drill press drills four 0.250-in. holes at four locations on a flat aluminum plate in a production work cycle. Although the plate is only 0.50 in. thick, the drill must travel a full 1.0 in. at each hole location to allow for clearance above the plate and breakthrough of the drill on the underside of the plate. The cutting conditions are: speed = 75 sfpm and feed = 0.005 in./rev. The hole locations are:

Hole number	x-coordinate	y-coordinate
1	1.0	1.0
2	1.0	3.0
3	3.0	3.0
4	3.0	1.0

The drill starts out at point (0, 0) and returns to the same position after the work cycle is completed. The travel rate of the table in moving from one coordinate position to another is 10 in./min. Owing to the effects of acceleration and deceleration, and the time required for the control system to achieve final positioning, a time loss of 0.1 min is experienced at each stopping position of the table. Assume that all moves are made in a manner similar to that shown in Figure 8.5, which is typical for a point-to-point NC system. If loading and unloading the plate takes 1.0 min, determine the time required for the work cycle.

chapter **9**

NC Part Programming

NC part programming is concerned with the planning and documentation of the sequence of processing steps to be performed on a numerical control machine. It is usually accomplished by a person whose title is part programmer. The planning portion of part programming requires a knowledge of machining (or other processing technology for which the NC machine is designed) as well as geometry and trigonometry. The sequence of processing steps in NC involves a series of movements of the processing head with respect to the machine table and workpart. In this chapter we discuss the various approaches used in NC part programming.

The documentation portion of part programming involves the input medium that is used to transmit the program of instructions to the NC controller unit (the MCU). The most common input medium in use over the last 30 years is 1-in.-wide punched tape. This medium and the data format in which the instructions are conveyed to the MCU are discussed in Section 9.1. Recently, other ways of entering the program to the MCU have been developed. The use of magnetic tape and floppy disks have been growing in popularity since they represent more modern storage technologies for numerical control. The advantage of these input media is their much higher data density. For example, one floppy diskette is capable of storing the equivalent of several thousand feet of punched tape.

In addition, techniques for transmitting the program directly from a central computer to the individual machines in the factory have been introduced. This form of program input is called *direct numerical control* (DNC). We discuss DNC in Chapter 10.

9.1   PUNCHED TAPE AND TAPE FORMAT

In this section we examine the details of the punched tape and how it is coded to contain the part program. Except for the physical form of the coding (punched holes), many of our comments on the program formatting and coding apply equally well to other forms of input media such as diskettes and magnetic tape.

The NC tape

The punched tape used for NC is 1 in. wide. It is standardized as shown in Figure 9.1 by the Electronics Industries Association (EIA), which has been responsible for many of the important standards in the NC industry. The tape can be made out of several materials. Paper tape is common. Although its cost is low, it is not durable and therefore not appropriate for repeated use. Stronger tape materials suitable for higher production use include Mylar-reinforced paper, Mylar-coated aluminum, and certain plastics. Paper is often used for the initial preparation and testing of the part program. Then, a production

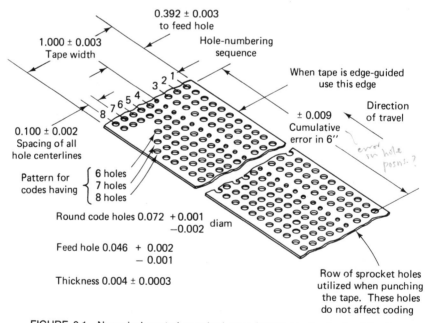

FIGURE 9.1   Numerical control punched tape format as standardized by the Electronics Industries Association (EIA). (Reprinted from Childs [1].)

tape is duplicated out of one of the more durable materials for shop floor use. The punched paper tape is retained as the master copy.

Holes are punched in the tape using a tape punch machine. Tape preparation is accomplished either manually or using the computer. In the manual method, the tape punch machine operates in conjunction with a typewriter-like machine, early versions of which were called Flexowriters. Each character typed on the Flexowriter is converted to a set of hole patterns in the punched tape. With the computer method, the tape punch machine is controlled by the computer according to high-level instructions that have been prepared by the part programmer. The end result with either the manual or the computer method is the same: a punched tape representing commands to operate the NC machine. The punched tape is fed through the tape reader of the MCU using one of the reading techniques described in Section 8.4.

Tape coding

As shown in Figure 9.1, there are eight regular columns of holes running in the lengthwise direction of the tape. There is also a ninth column of holes between the third and fourth regular columns. However, these are smaller and are used as sprocket holes for feeding the tape.

Figure 9.1 shows a hole present in nearly every position of the tape. However, the coding of the tape is provided by either the presence or absence of a hole in the various positions. Because there are two possible conditions for each position—either the presence or absence of a hole—this coding system is called the binary code. It uses the base 2 number system, which can represent any number in the more familiar base 10 or decimal system.

In the binary system, there are only two numbers, 0 and 1. The meaning of successive digits in the binary system is based on the number 2 raised to successive powers. The first digit is 2^0, the second digit is 2^1, the third is 2^2, and so on. The value of 2^0 is 1, $2^1 = 2$, $2^2 = 4$, $2^3 = 8$, and so on. The two numbers, 0 or 1, in the successive digit positions indicate either the presence or absence of the value. Table 9.1 shows how the binary system is used to represent numbers in the decimal system.

For example, the decimal number 5 is represented in the binary system by 0101. The conversion from binary to decimal systems makes use of the following type of computation:

$$1 \times 2^0 + 0 \times 2^1 + 1 \times 2^2 + 0 \times 2^3$$
$$= 1 \times 1 + 0 \times 2 + 1 \times 4 + 0 \times 8 = 5$$

The reader can see from Table 9.1 that four digits are required in the binary system to represent any of the single-digit numbers in the decimal system. Yet there are eight regular columns of holes in the standard NC punched tape. The reason eight columns are needed on the tape is because there are other symbols that must be coded on the tape besides numbers. Alphabetical letters, plus and minus signs, and other symbols are also

TABLE 9.1
Comparison of Binary
and Decimal Number
Systems

Binary	Decimal
0000	0
0001	1
0010	2
0011	3
0100	4
0101	5
0110	6
0111	7
1000	8
1001	9

needed in NC tape coding. The standard EIA tape coding is shown in Figure 9.2. Eight columns provide more than enough binary digits to define any of the required symbols. In fact, the fifth-column position is used exclusively as a check, called *parity,* on the correctness of the tape. The way the parity check works is this: The NC tape reader is designed to read an odd number of holes across the width of the tape. Whenever the particular number or symbol being punched calls for an even number of holes, an extra hole is punched in column 5, hence making the total an odd number. For example, the decimal number 5 uses a punched hole in columns 1 and 3, an even number of holes. Therefore, a parity hole would be added. The decimal number 7 already uses an odd number of holes (columns 1, 2, and 3), so a parity hole is not needed. The parity check helps to assure that the tape punch mechanism has perforated a complete hole in all required positions. If the tape reader counts an even number of holes in the tape, it would signal the operator that a parity error had occurred.

How instructions are formed

A binary digit is called a *bit.* It has a value of 0 or 1 depending on the absence or presence of a hole in a certain row and column position on the tape. (Columns of hole positions run lengthwise along the tape. Row positions run across the tape.) Out of a row of bits, a *character* is made. A character is a combination of bits, which represents a letter, number, or other symbol. A *word* is a collection of characters used to form part of an instruction. Typical NC words are *x*-position, *y*-position, cutting speed, and so on. Out of a collection of words, a *block* is formed. A block of words is a complete NC instruction. Using an NC drilling operation as an example, a block might contain information on the *x* and *y* coordinates of the hole location, the speed and feed at which the cut should be run, and perhaps even a specification of the cutting tool.

To separate blocks, an end-of-block (EOB) symbol is used (in the EIA standard, this is a hole in column 8). The tape reader feeds the data from the tape into the buffer in blocks. That is, it reads in a complete instruction at a time.

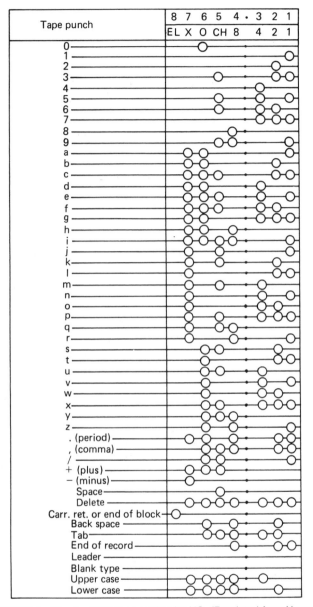

FIGURE 9.2   Standard EIA tape coding for NC. (Reprinted from Howe [3].)

NC words

Following is a list of the different types of words used in the formation of a block. Not every NC machine uses all the words. Also, the manner in which the words are expressed will differ between machines. By convention, the words in a block are given in the order below:

SEQUENCE NUMBER (N-WORDS). This is used to identify the block.

PREPARATORY WORK (G-WORDS). This word is used to prepare the controller for instructions that are to follow. For example, the word g02 is used to prepare the NC controller unit for circular interpolation along an arc in the clockwise direction. The preparatory word is needed so that the controller can correctly interpret the data that follow it in the block. Some typical examples of g-words are given in Table 9.2.

COORDINATES (X-, Y-, AND Z-WORDS). These give the coordinate positions of the tool. In a two-axis system, only two of the words would be used. In a four- or five-axis machine, additional a-words and/or b-words would specify the angular positions.

Although different NC systems use different formats for expressing a coordinate, we will adopt the convention of expressing it in the familiar decimal form: for example, x-7.235 or y-0.500. Some formats do not use the decimal point in writing the coordinate. The + sign to define a positive coordinate location is optional. The negative sign is, of course, mandatory.

FEED RATE (F-WORD). This specifies the feed rate in a machining operation. Units are inches per minute (in./min) by convention.

CUTTING SPEED (S-WORD). This specifies the cutting speed of the process, the rate at which the spindle rotates. Units are revolutions per minute (rev/min). In a machining operation it is usually desirable for the tool engineer to specify the speed in terms of the

TABLE 9.2   Some Common g-Words

Code	Preparatory function
g00	Used with contouring systems to prepare for a point-to-point operation.
g01	Linear interpolation in contouring systems.
g02	Circular interpolation, clockwise.
g03	Circular interpolation, counterclockwise.
g04	Dwell.
g05	Hold until operator restarts.
g08	Acceleration code, causes machine to accelerate smoothly.
g09	Deceleration code, causes machine to decelerate smoothly.
etc.	

relative surface speed of the tool and work. The units would be feet per minute (ft/min). It is therefore necessary for the part programmer to make the conversion from using the machining process equations given in Chapter 8.

TOOL SELECTION (T-WORD).   This word would only be needed for machines with a tool turret or automatic tool changer. The t-word specifies which tool is to be used in the operation. For example, t05 might be the designation of a $\frac{1}{2}$-in. drill bit in turret position 5 on an NC turret drill.

MISCELLANEOUS FUNCTION (M-WORD).   The m-word is used to specify certain miscellaneous or auxiliary functions which may be available on the machine tool. Of course, the machine must possess the function that is being called. A partial but representative list of miscellaneous functions is given in Table 9.3. The miscellaneous function is the last word in the block. To identify the end of the instruction, an end-of-block (EOB) symbol is punched on the tape.

Tape formats

The organization of words within blocks is called the *tape format*. Three tape formats seem to enjoy the most widespread use:

1. Word address format
2. Tab sequential format
3. Fixed block format

The tape format refers to the method of writing the words in a block of instruction. Within each format there are variations because of differences in machining process, type of machine, features of the machine tool, and so on.

TABLE 9.3   Some Typical m-Words

Code	Miscellaneous function
m00	Stops the machine; operator must restart.
m03	Start spindle in clockwise direction.
m04	Start spindle in counterclockwise direction.
m05	Stop spindle.
m06	Execute tool change, either automatically or manually. Does not include selection of tool, which is done by t-word or by the operator. If operator changes tool, he or she must restart machine.
m07	Turn coolant on.
m09	Turn coolant off.
m13	Start spindle in clockwise direction and turn coolant on.
m14	Start spindle in counterclockwise direction and turn coolant on.
m30	End-of-tape command, which tells tape reader to rewind the tape.

WORD ADDRESS FORMAT.   In this format, a letter precedes each word and is used to identify the word type and to address the data to a particular location in the controller unit. The x-prefix identifies an *x*-coordinate word, an s-prefix identifies spindle speed, and so on. The standard sequence of words for a two-axis NC system is

n-word

g-word

x-word

y-word

f-word

s-word

t-word

m-word

EOB

However, since the type of word is designated by the prefix letter, the words can be presented in any sequence. Also, if a word remains unchanged from the previous block or is not needed, it can be deleted from the block.

TAB SEQUENTIAL FORMAT.   This tape format derives its name from the fact that words are listed in a fixed sequence and separated by depressing the tab key (TAB) when typing the manuscript on a Flexowriter. The TAB symbol in the EIA standard is coded as 01111100 (holes in columns 2 through 6) on the tape. Since the words are written in a set order, no address letter is required. The order of words within the block follows the previously mentioned standard. If a word remains the same as in the previous block, it need not be retyped. However, the TAB code is required to maintain the sequence of the words.

FIXED BLOCK FORMAT.   This is the least flexible and probably the least desirable of the three formats. Not only must the words in each block be in identical sequence, but the characters within each word must be the same length and format. If a word remains the same from block to block, it must nevertheless be repeated in each block.

EXAMPLE 9.1

In an NC drilling operation, two holes must be drilled in sequence at the following coordinate locations:

$$\text{Hole 1: } x = 2.000 \; y = 2.500$$

$$\text{Hole 2: } x = 4.000 \; y = 2.500$$

No prepatory or miscellaneous words are required. Tooling is changed manually, so no t-word is required. The holes are to be drilled to $\frac{1}{2}$-in. diameter at 75 sfpm and 0.005 in./rev. Write the two instruction blocks in each of the three tape formats.

Solution:

First we must convert the surface speed to spindle rotational speed in rpm using Eq. (8.8)

$$S = \frac{75 \text{ ft/min}}{0.5 \, \pi \text{ in./rev}} \, (12 \text{ in./ft}) = 573 \text{ rev/min}$$

Now to convert 0.005 in/rev into in./min, multiply by spindle speed as given in Eq. (8.9):

$$f_r = (0.005 \text{ in./rev}) \, (573 \text{ rev/min}) = 2.87 \text{ in./min}$$

There are five words to be coded on the NC tape for each hole:

	Hole 1	*Hole 2*
n-word	001	002
x-word	2.000	4.000
y-word	2.500	2.500
f-word	2.87	2.87
s-word	573	573

In the word address format, the two statements would read

n001 x2.000 y2.500 f2.87 s573 EOB
n002 x4.000 EOB

In the tab sequential format, the two blocks would be

001 TAB 2.00 TAB 2.50 TAB 2.87 TAB 573 EOB
002 TAB 4.00 TAB TAB TAB EOB

We are using TAB and EOB to denote the codes for the tab key and end-of-block (carriage return) on the Flexowriter. In the fixed block format, the two blocks would be

001 +02.000 +02.500 2.87 573 EOB
002 +04.000 +02.500 2.87 573 EOB

Now that we have considered the manner in which the NC tape is coded and the type of data that must be provided to the numerical control system, let us next examine the part programmer's place in the procedure.

9.2 METHODS OF NC PART PROGRAMMING

The tape can be prepared for submission to the MCU using any of several different methods of NC part programming. NC programming represents one of the elements in the broader procedure called *process planning*. We defined process planning in Chapter

2 as a function of manufacturing engineering in which the sequence of individual production operations for making the part are planned. We assume here that a portion of the processing is to be done on one or more NC machines. For those machines, the program must be prepared.

The part programming methods include a variety of procedures ranging from highly manual to highly automated:

1. Manual part programming
2. Computer-assisted part programming
3. Manual data input
4. NC programming using CAD/CAM
5. Computer-automated part programming

In *manual part programming*, the processing instructions are documented on a form called a part program manuscript. The manuscript is a listing of the positions of the tool relative to the workpiece that the machine must follow in order to perform the processing. The listing may also include other commands such as speeds, feeds, tooling, and so on. A punched tape is then prepared directly from the manuscript.

In *computer-assisted part programming*, much of the tedious computational work required in manual programming is performed by the computer. For complex workpart geometries or jobs with many processing steps, use of the computer results in significant savings in the part programmer's time. When computer-assisted part programming is used, the programmer prepares the set of processing instructions in a high-level computer language. For complex jobs, this computer language is much easier to use than the lower-level coding required in manual part programming. The high-level language commands are interpreted by the computer, and the required calculations and data processing are accomplished to prepare the NC program for the tape reader (or other input device).

Manual data input (MDI) is a procedure in which the NC program is entered directly into the MCU at the site of the processing machine. Consequently, the use of the punched tape is avoided, and the programming procedure is simplified to permit machine operators rather than part programmers to do the programming.

NC part programming using CAD/CAM is an advanced form of computer-assisted part programming in which an interactive graphics system equipped with NC programming software is used to facilitate the part programming task. The term *CAD/CAM* means computer-aided design and computer-aided manufacturing. In this method the programmer works on a CAD/CAM workstation to enter the machining commands. The actions indicated by the commands are displayed on the graphics monitor, which provides visual feedback to the programmer. Also, certain portions of the programming cycle are automated by the NC programming software to reduce the total programming time required.

Computer-automated part programming extends the notion of automating certain portions of the NC part programming procedure to its logical conclusion. It automates the complete part programming task using software that is capable of making logical and even quasi-intelligent decisions about how the part should be machined.

We shall describe these various methods of part programming in the following sections of this chapter.

9.3 MANUAL PART PROGRAMMING

In manual programming, the part programmer specifies the machining instructions on a form called a *manuscript*. Manuscripts come in various forms, depending on the machine tool and tape format to be used. For example, the manuscript form for a two-axis point-to-point drilling machine would be different than one for a three-axis contouring machine. Three representative manuscript forms are illustrated in Figure 9.3.

As mentioned, the manuscript is a listing of the relative tool and workpiece locations. It also includes other data, such as preparatory commands, miscellaneous instructions, and speed/feed specifications, all of which are needed to operate the machine under tape control. The manuscript is designed so that the NC tape can be typed directly from it on a Flexowriter or similar tape-punch device.

We shall divide manual programming jobs into two categories: point-to-point jobs and contouring jobs. Except for complex workparts with many holes to be drilled, manual programming is ideally suited for point-to-point applications. On the other hand, except for the simplest milling and turning jobs, manual programming can become quite time-consuming for applications requiring continuous-path control of the tool. Accordingly, we shall only concern ourselves with manual part programming for point-to-point operations in this chapter. Manual contour programming requires such tedious and detailed calculations that the space needed for the topic would be more than is warranted by the basic purpose of this book, which is to survey the field of automated manufacturing systems. Contouring is much more appropriate for computer-assisted part programming (Sections 9.4 and 9.5).

The basic method of manual part programming for a point-to-point application is best demonstrated by means of an example.

EXAMPLE 9.2

Suppose that the part to be programmed is a drilling job. The engineering drawing for the part is presented in Figure 9.4. Three holes are to be drilled at a diameter of 31/64 in. The close hole size tolerance requires reaming to 0.500 in. diameter. Recommended speeds and feeds are given[1] as follows:

	Speed (ft/min)	Feed (in/rev)
0.484-in.-diameter drill	75	0.006
0.500-in.-diameter reamer	50	0.010

[1]Recommended cutting speeds and feeds could be obtained from machinability data handbooks.

NC Part Programming Manuscript
Two-Axis PTP or Contouring Machine
Word Address Format

Part No. _____   Date _____

Part Name _____   Prepared by _____

n-WORD	g-WORD	x-WORD	y-WORD	f-WORD	s-WORD	t-WORD	m-WORD	EOB	COMMENTS

NC Part Programming Manuscript
Two-Axis Point-to-Point Machine
Tab Sequential Format

Part No. _____   Date _____

Part Name _____   Prepared by _____

SEQUENCE NO.	TAB/EOB	x-COORD	TAB/EOB	y-COORD	TAB/EOB	m-WORD	TAB/EOB	COMMENTS

NC Part Programming Manuscript
Two-Axis Point-to-Point Machine
Fixed Block Format

Part No. _____   Date _____

Part Name _____   Prepared by _____

SEQUENCE NO.	x-COORD	y-COORD	m-WORD	COMMENTS

FIGURE 9.3 Three part programming manuscript forms: word address format, tab sequential format, and fixed block format.

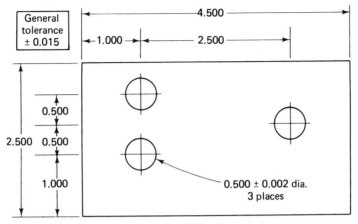

FIGURE 9.4   Part print for Example 9.2.

The NC drill press uses the tab sequential tape format. Drill bits are manually changed by the machine operator, but speeds and feeds must be programmed on the tape. The machine has the floating-zero feature and absolute positioning.

The first step in preparing the part program is to define the axis coordinates in relation to the workpart. We assume that the outline of the part has already been machined before the drilling operation. Therefore, the operator can use one of the corners of the part as the target point. Let us define the lower left-hand corner as the target point and the origin of our axis system. The coordinates are shown in Figure 9.5 for the example part. The x and y locations of each hole can be seen in the figure.

The machine settings for speed and feed must next be determined. For the drill, the spindle speed would be computed from Eq. (8.8):

$$S = \frac{12(75)}{0.484\pi} = 592 \text{ rev/min}$$

The feed rate is determined from Eq. (8.9):

$$f = 592(0.006) = 3.55 \text{ in./min}$$

Similarly, for the reaming operation,

$$S = 382 \text{ rev/min}$$
$$f = 3.82 \text{ in./min}$$

The completed manuscript would appear as in Figure 9.6. The first line shows the x and y coordinates at the zero point. The machine operator would insert the tape and read this first block into the system. (A block of instruction corresponds generally to one line on the manuscript form.) The

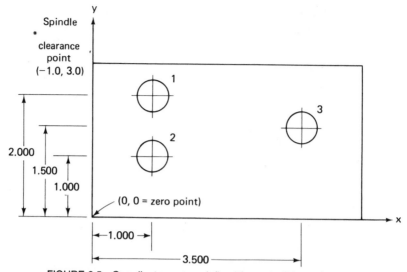

FIGURE 9.5   Coordinate system defined for part of Example 9.2.

tool would then be positioned over the target point on the machine table. The operator would then press the zero buttons to set the machine.

The next line on the manuscript is RWS, which stands for rewind–stop. This signal is coded into the tape as holes in columns 1, 2, and 4. The symbol stops the tape after it has been rewound. The last line on the tape contains the m30 word, causing the tape to be rewound at the end of the machining cycle.

Other m-words used in the program are m06, which stops the machine for an operator tool change, and m13, which turns spindle and coolant on. Note in the last line that the tool has been removed from the work area to allow for changing the workpiece.

9.4   COMPUTER-ASSISTED PART PROGRAMMING

The workpart of Example 9.2 was relatively simple. It was a suitable application for manual programming. Most parts machined on NC systems are considerably more complex. In the more complicated point-to-point jobs and in contouring applications, manual part programming becomes an extremely tedious task and subject to error. In these instances it is much more appropriate to employ the high-speed digital computer to assist in the part programming process. Many part programming language systems have been developed to automatically perform most of the calculations which the programmer would otherwise be forced to do. This saves time and results in a more accurate and more efficient part program.

NC part programming manuscript
Two-axis point-to-point drill press
tab sequential format (obj. posn.)

Part No. EXAMPLE 8.2   Date 4/4/79

Part Name HOLE PLATE   Prepared by MPG

Seq. No.	Tab EOB	x-COORD	Tab EOB	y-COORD	Tab EOB	Feed	Tab EOB	Speed	Tab EOB	m-WORD	Tab EOB	Comments
00 RWS	TAB	0.0	TAB	0.0	EOB							ZERO
01	TAB	1.0	TAB	2.0	TAB	3.55	TAB	592	TAB	13	EOB	DRILL 1
02	TAB		TAB	1.0	EOB							DRILL 2
03	TAB	3.5	TAB	1.5	TAB							DRILL 3
04	TAB	-1.0	TAB	3.0	TAB					06	EOB	TOOL CHG
05	TAB	3.5	TAB	1.5	TAB	3.82	TAB	382	TAB	13	EOB	REAM 3
06	TAB	1.0	TAB	1.0	EOB							REAM 2
07	TAB		TAB	2.0	EOB							REAM 1
08	TAB	-1.0	TAB	3.0	TAB					06	EOB	TOOL CHG
09	TAB		TAB	3.0	TAB		TAB		TAB	30	EOB	REWIND & CHG. PART

for zeroing

symbol which stops tape when rewinding

FIGURE 9.6 Part program manuscript for Example 9.2

243

The part programmer's job

The difference in the part programmer's job between manual programming and computer-assisted programming is this: With manual programming, a manuscript is used which is formatted so that the NC tape can be typed directly from it. With computer-assisted part programming, the machining instructions are written in English-like statements of the NC programming language, which are then processed by the computer to prepare the tape. The computer automatically punches the tape in the proper tape format for the particular NC machine.

When utilizing one of the NC programming languages, part programming can be summarized as consisting basically of two tasks:

1. Defining the geometry of the workpart
2. Specifying the tool path and/or operation sequence

Let us now consider these two tasks in computer-assisted part programming. Our frame of reference will be for a contouring application, but the concepts apply for a positioning application as well.

WORKPART GEOMETRY DEFINITION. No matter how complicated the workpart may appear, it is composed of basic geometric elements. Using a relatively simple workpart to illustrate, consider the component shown in Figure 9.7. Although somewhat irregular in overall appearance, the outline of the part consists of intersecting straight lines and a partial circle. The holes in the part can be expressed in terms of the center location and radius of the hole. Nearly any component that can be conceived by a designer can be described by points, straight lines, planes, circles, cylinders, and other mathematically defined surfaces. It is the part programmer's task to enumerate the component elements out of which the workpart is formed. Each geometric element must be identified and the dimensions and location of the element explicitly defined. Using the APT pro-

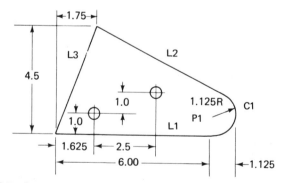

FIGURE 9.7 Sample part to illustrate how it is composed of basic geometric elements such as points, lines, and circles.

gramming language as an example, the following statement might be used to define a point:

$$P1 = POINT/6.0, 1.125,0$$

The point is identified by the symbol P1 and is located at $x = 6.0$, $Y = 1.125$, and $z = 0$.

Similarly, a circle in the x-y plane might be defined by the APT statement

$$C1 = CIRCLE/CENTER, P1, RADIUS, 1.125$$

The center of circle C1 is P1 (previously defined) and the radius is 1.125.

The various geometric elements in the drawing of Figure 9.7 would be identified in a similar fashion by the part programmer.

TOOL PATH CONSTRUCTION   After defining the workpart geometry, the programmer must next construct the path that the cutter will follow to machine the part. This tool path specification involves a detailed step-by-step sequence of cutter moves. The moves are made along the geometry elements which have previously been defined. To illustrate, using Figure 9.7 and the APT language, the following statement could be used to command the tool to make a left turn from line L2 onto line L3:

$$GOLFT/L3, PAST, L1$$

This assumes the tool was previously located at the intersection of lines L2 and L3 and had just finished a cut along L2. The statement directs the tool to cut along L3 until it just passes line L1.

By using statements similar to the above, the tool can be directed to machine along the workpart surfaces, to go to point locations, to drill holes at those point locations, and so on. In addition to geometry definition and tool path specification, the part programmer also provides other commands to the NC system. However, let us await Section 9.5, where we will consider a wide range of possible APT statements.

The computer's job

The computer's job in computer-assisted part programming consists of the following steps:

1. Input translation
2. Arithmetic calculations
3. Cutter offset computation
4. Postprocessor

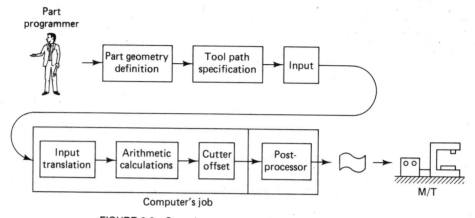

FIGURE 9.8 Steps in computer-assisted part programming.

The sequence of these steps and their relationships to the part programmer and the machine tool are illustrated in Figure 9.8.

INPUT TRANSLATION.   The part programmer enters the program using the APT or other language. The input translation component converts the coded instructions contained in the program into computer-usable form, preparatory to further processing.

ARITHMETIC CALCULATIONS.   The arithmetic calculations unit of the system consists of a comprehensive set of subroutines for solving the mathematics required to generate the part surface. These subroutines are called by the various part programming language statements. The arithmetic unit is really the fundamental element in the part programming package. This unit frees the programmer from the time-consuming geometry and trigonometry calculations to concentrate on the workpart processing.

CUTTER OFFSET COMPUTATION.   When we described the second task of the part programmer as that of constructing the tool path, we ignored one basic factor: the size of the cutting tool. The actual tool path is different from the part outline. This is because the tool path is the path taken by the center of the cutter. It is at the periphery of the cutter that machining takes place.

The purpose of the cutter offset computation is to offset the tool path from the desired part surface by the radius of the cutter. This means that the part programmer can define the exact part outline in his geometry statements. Thanks to the cutter offset calculation provided by the programming system, he need not concern himself with this task. The cutter offset problem is illustrated in Figure 9.9.

POSTPROCESSOR.   As we have noted previously, NC machine tool systems are different. They have different features and capabilities. They use different NC tape formats. Nearly all of the part programming languages, including APT, are designed to be general-purpose languages, not limited to one or two machine tool types. Therefore,

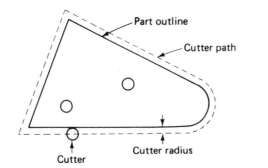

FIGURE 9.9   Cutter offset problem in part programming.

the final task of the computer in computer-assisted part programming is to take the general instructions and make them specific to a particular machine tool system. The unit that performs this task is called a *postprocessor*.

The postprocessor is really a separate computer program that has been written to prepare the punched tape for a specific machine tool. The input to the postprocessor is the output from the other three components: a series of cutter locations and other instructions. This is referred to as the CLFILE or CLDATA (CL stands for cutter location). The output of the postprocessor is the NC tape written in the correct format for the machine on which it is to be used.

NC part programming languages

Probably over 100 NC part programming languages have been developed since the initial MIT research on NC programming systems in 1956. Most of the languages were developed to serve particular needs and machines and have not survived the test of time. However, a good number of languages are still in use today. In this subsection we review some of those which are generally considered important.

APT (AUTOMATICALLY PROGRAMMED TOOLS).   The APT language was the product of the MIT developmental work on NC programming systems. Its development began in June 1956, and it was first used in production around 1959. Today it is the most widely used language in the United States. Although first intended as a contouring language, modern versions of APT can be used for both positioning and continuous-path programming and continuous-path programming in up to five axes.

AUTOSPOT (AUTOMATIC SYSTEM FOR POSITIONING TOOLS).   This was developed by IBM and first introduced in 1962 for PTP programming. Today's version of AUTOSPOT can be used for contouring as well.

SPLIT (SUNDSTRAND PROCESSING LANGUAGE INTERNALLY TRANSLATED).   This is a proprietary system intended for Sundstrand's machine tools. It can handle up to five axis positioning and possesses contouring capability as well. One of the unusual features of SPLIT is that the postprocessor is built into the program. Each machine tool uses its own SPLIT package, thus obviating the need for a special postprocessor.

COMPACT II.   This is a package available from Manufacturing Data Systems, Inc. (MDSI), a firm based in Ann Arbor, Michigan. The NC language is similar to SPLIT in many of its features. MDSI leases the COMPACT II system to its users on a time-sharing basis. The part programmer uses a remote terminal to feed the program into one of the MDSI computers, which in turn produces the NC tape.

ADAPT (ADAPTATION OF APT).   Several part programming languages are based directly on the APT program. One of these is ADAPT, which was developed by IBM under Air Force contract. It was intended to provide many of the features of APT but to utilize a significantly smaller computer. ADAPT is not as powerful as APT, but can be used to program for both positioning and contouring jobs.

EXAPT (EXTENDED SUBSET OF APT).   This was developed in Germany starting around 1964 and is based on the APT language. There are three versions: EXAPT I—designed for positioning (drilling and also straight-cut milling), EXAPT II—designed for turning, and EXAPT III—designed for limited contouring operations. One of the important features of EXAPT is that it attempts to compute optimum feeds and speeds automatically.

9.5   THE APT LANGUAGE

In this section we present some of the fundamental principles of computer-assisted part programming using APT. The reader will certainly not become an expert part programmer after completing this introduction. Our objectives are much less ambitious. What we hope to accomplish is merely to demonstrate the English-like statements of APT and to show how they can be formulated to command the cutting tool through its sequence of machining operations.

APT is not only an NC language; it is also the computer program that performs the calculations to generate cutter positions based on APT statements. We will not concern ourselves with the internal workings of the computer program. Instead, we will concentrate on the language that the part programmer must use.

APT is a three-dimensional system that can be used to control up to five axes. We will limit our discussion to the more familiar three axes, x, y, and z, and exclude rotational coordinates. APT can be used to control a variety of different machining operations. We will cover only drilling and milling applications. There are over 400 words in the APT vocabulary. Only a small (but important) fraction will be covered here.

To program in APT, the workpart geometry must first be defined. Then the tool is directed to various point locations and along surfaces of the workpart to carry out the machining operations. The viewpoint of the part programmer is that the workpiece remains stationary and the tool is instructed to move relative to the part.

There are four types of statements in the APT language:

1. *Geometry statements*. These define the geometric elements that comprise the workpart. They are also sometimes called definition statements.
2. *Motion statements*. These are used to describe the path taken by the cutting tool.
3. *Postprocessor statements*. These apply to the specific machine tool and control system. They are used to specify feeds and speeds and to actuate other features of the machine.
4. *Auxiliary statements* These are miscellaneous statements used to identify the part, tool, tolerances, and so on.

Geometry statements

When the tool motions are specified, their description is in terms of points and surfaces. Therefore, the points and surfaces must be defined before tool motion commands can be given.

The general form of an APT geometry statement is this:

$$\text{symbol} = \text{geometry type/descriptive data} \qquad (9.1)$$

An example of such a statement is

$$P1 = POINT/5.0, 4.0, 0.0 \qquad (9.2)$$

The statement is made up of three sections. The first is the symbol used to identify the geometric element. A symbol can be any combination of six or fewer alphabetic and numeric characters. At least one of the six must be an alphabetic character. Also, although it may seem obvious, the symbol cannot be one of the APT vocabulary words. Some examples may help to show what is permissible as a symbol, and what is not permissible:

PZL	Permissible
PABCDE	Permissible
PABCDEF	No; too many characters
123789	No; must have alphabetic character
POINT	No; APT vocabulary word
P1.2	No; only alphabetic and numeric characters are allowed

The second section of the geometry statement is an APT vocabulary word that identifies the type of geometry element. Besides POINT, other geometry elements in the APT vocabulary include LINE, PLANE, and CIRCLE.

The third section of the geometry statement is the descriptive data that define the element precisely, completely, and uniquely. These data may include quantitative dimensional and positional data, previously defined geometry elements, and other APT words.

The punctuation used in the APT geometry statement is illustrated in the example, Eq. (9.2). The statement is written as an equation, the symbol being equated to the surface type. A slash separates the surface type from the descriptive data. Commas are used to separate the words and numbers in the descriptive data.

There are a variety of ways to specify the different geometry elements. The Appendix at the end of this chapter presents a dictionary of APT vocabulary words as well as a sampling of statements for defining the geometry elements we will be using: points, lines, circles, and planes. The reader may benefit from the examples below.

TO SPECIFY A POINT. In addition to listing the x, y, and z coordinates of the point, it can also be defined by the intersection of two lines:

$$P2 = POINT/INTOF, L1, L2$$

In the descriptive data, INTOF stands for "intersection of." This is followed by the symbols for the two lines.

Other methods for defining a point are given in the Appendix under "POINT."

TO SPECIFY A LINE. The easiest way to specify a line is by two points through which the line passes:

$$L3 = LINE/P3, P4$$

The part programmer may find it convenient to define a new line parallel to another line which has previously been defined. One way of doing this is:

$$L4 = LINE/P5, PARLEL, L3$$

This states that the line L4 must pass through point P5 and be parallel (PARLEL) to line L3.

TO SPECIFY A PLANE. A plane can be defined by specifying three points through which it passes:

$$PL1 = PLANE/P1, P4, P5$$

It can also be defined as being parallel to another plane, similar to the previous line parallelism statement.

$$PL2 = PLANE/P2, PARLEL, PL1$$

Plane PL2 is parallel to plane PL1 and passes through point P2.

To SPECIFY A CIRCLE.   A circle can be specified by its center and its radius.

$$C1 = CIRCLE/CENTER, P1, RADIUS, 5.0$$

The two APT descriptive words are used to identify the center and radius. The orientation of the circle perhaps seems undefined. By convention, it is a circle located in the x-y plane.

GROUND RULES.   There are several rules that must be followed in formulating an APT geometry statement:

1.   The coordinate data must be specified in the order x,y,z. For example, the statement

$$P1 = POINT/5.0, 4.0, 0.0$$

is interpreted by the APT program to mean a point at $x = 5.0$, $y = 4.0$, and $z = 0.0$.
2.   Any symbols used as descriptive data must have been previously defined. For example, in the statement

$$P2 = POINT/INTOF, L1, L2$$

the two lines L1 and L2 must have been previously defined. In setting up the list of geometry statements, the APT programmer must be sure to define symbols before using them in subsequent statements.
3.   A symbol can be used to define only one geometry element. The same symbol cannot be used to define two different elements. For example, the following sequence would be incorrect:

$$P1 = POINT/1.0, 1.0, 1.0$$

$$P1 = POINT/2.0, 3.0, 4.0$$

4.   Only one symbol can be used to define any given element. For example, the following two statements in the same program would render the program incorrect:

$$P1 = POINT/1.0, 1.0, 1.0$$

$$P2 = POINT/1.0, 1.0, 1.0$$

5.   Lines defined in APT are considered to be of infinite length in both directions. Similarly, planes extend indefinitely and circles defined in APT are complete circles.

Motion statements

APT motion statements have a general format, just as the geometry statements do. The general form of a motion statement is

$$\text{motion command/descriptive data} \qquad (9.3)$$

An example of a motion statement is

$$\text{GOTO/P1} \qquad (9.4)$$

The statement consists of two sections separated by a slash. The first section is the basic motion command, which tells the tool what to do. The second section is comprised of descriptive data, which tell the tool where to go. In the example statement above, the tool is commanded to go to point P1, which has been defined in a preceding geometry statement.

At the beginning of the motion statements, the tool must be given a starting point. This point is likely to be the target point, the location where the operator has positioned the tool at the start of the job. The part programmer keys into this starting position with the following statement:

$$\text{FROM/TARG} \qquad (9.5)$$

The FROM is an APT vocabulary word which indicates that this is the initial point from which others will be referenced. In the statement above, TARG is the symbol given to the starting point. Any other APT symbol could be used to define the target point. Another way to make this statement is

$$\text{FROM/} -2.0, \ -2.0, \ 0.0$$

where the descriptive data in this case are the $x, y,$ and z coordinates of the target point. The FROM statement occurs only at the start of the motion sequence.

It is convenient to distinguish between PTP movements and contouring movements when discussing the APT motion statements.

POINT-TO-POINT MOTIONS.   There are only two basic PTP motion commands: GOTO and GODLTA. The GOTO statement instructs the tool to go to a particular point location specified in the descriptive data. Two examples are

$$\text{GOTO/P2}$$

$$\text{GOTO/2.0, 7.0, 0.0}$$

In the first statement, P2 is the destination of the tool point. In the second statement, the tool has been instructed to go to the location whose coordinates are $x = 2.0$, $y = 7.0$, and $z = 0$.

The GODLTA command specifies an incremental move for the tool. For example, the statement

$$GODLTA/2.0, 7.0, 0.0$$

instructs the tool to move from its present position 2 in. in the x-direction and 7 in. in the y-direction. The z-coordinate remains unchanged.

The GODLTA command is useful in drilling and related operations. The tool can be directed to a particular hole location with the GOTO statement. Then the GODLTA command would be used to drill the hole, as in the following sequence:

$$GOTO/P2$$

$$GODLTA/0, 0, -1.5$$

$$GODLTA/0, 0, +1.5$$

EXAMPLE 9.3

Example 9.2 was a PTP job which was programmed manually. Let us write the APT geometry and motion statements necessary to perform the drilling portion of this job. We will set the plane defined by $z = 0$ about $\frac{1}{4}$ in. above the part surface. The part will be assumed to be $\frac{1}{2}$ in. thick.

$$P1 = POINT/1.0, 2.0, 0$$

$$P2 = POINT/1.0, 1.0, 0$$

$$P3 = POINT/3.5, 1.5, 0$$

$$P0 = POINT/-1.0, 3.0, +2.0$$

$$FROM/P0$$

$$GOTO/P1$$

$$GODLTA/0, 0, -1.0$$

$$GODLTA/0, 0, +1.0$$

$$GOTO/P2$$

$$GODLTA/0, 0, -1.0$$

$$GODLTA/0, 0, +1.0$$

$$GOTO/P3$$

$$GODLTA/0, 0, -1.0$$

$$GODLTA/0, 0, +1.0$$

$$GOTO/P0$$

This is not a complete APT program because it does not contain the necessary auxiliary and postprocessor statements. However, the statement sequence demonstrates how geometry and motion statements can be combined to command the tool through a series of machining steps.

CONTOURING MOTIONS.   Contouring commands are somewhat more complicated because the tool's position must be continuously controlled throughout the move. To accomplish this control, the tool is directed along two intersecting surfaces as shown in Figure 9.10. These surfaces have very specific names in APT:

1. *Drive surface.* This is the surface (it is pictured as a plane in Figure 9.10) that guides the side of the cutter.
2. *Part surface.* This is the surface (again shown as a plane in Figure 9.10) on which the bottom of the cutter rides. The reader should note that the "part surface" may or may not be an actual surface of the workpart. The part programmer must define this plus the drive surface for the purpose of maintaining continuous path control of the tool.

There is one additional surface that must be defined for APT contouring motions:

3. *Check surface.* This is the surface that stops the movement of the tool in its current direction. In a sense, it checks the forward movement of the tool.

There are several ways in which the check surface can be used. This is determined by APT modifier words within the descriptive data of the motion statement. The three main modifier words are TO, ON, and PAST, and their use with regard to the check surface is shown in Figure 9.11. A fourth modifier word is TANTO. This is used when the drive surface is tangent to a circular check surface, as illustrated in Figure 9.12. In this case the cutter can be brought to the point of tangency with the circle by use of the TANTO modifier word.

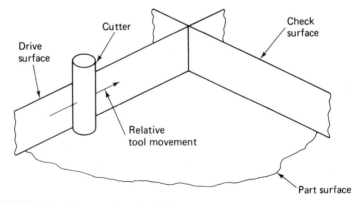

FIGURE 9.10   Three surfaces in APT contouring motions which guide the cutting tool.

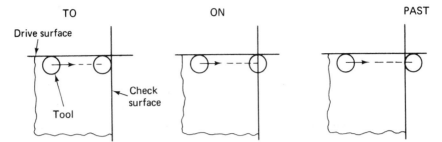

FIGURE 9.11 Use of APT modifier words in a motion statement: TO, ON, and PAST. TO moves the tool into initial contact with check surface. ON moves tool until tool center is on check surface. PAST moves tool just beyond check surface.

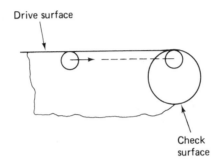

FIGURE 9.12 Use of APT modifier word TANTO. TANTO moves tool to point of tangency between two surfaces, at least one of which is circular.

The APT contour motion statement commands the cutter to move along the drive and part surfaces and the movement ends when the tool is at the check surface. There are six motion command words:

GOLFT   GOFWD   GOUP
GORGT   GOBACK   GODOWN

Their interpretation is illustrated in Figure 9.13. In commanding the cutter, the programmer must keep in mind where it is coming from. As the tool reaches the new check surface, does the next movement involve a right turn or an upward turn or what? The tool is directed accordingly by one of the six motion words.

To begin the sequence of motion commands, the FROM statement, Eq. (9.5), is used in the same manner as for PTP moves. The statement following the FROM statement defines the initial drive surface, part surface, and check surface. The sequence is of the following form:

FROM/TARG

GO/TO, PL1, TO, PL2, TO, PL3

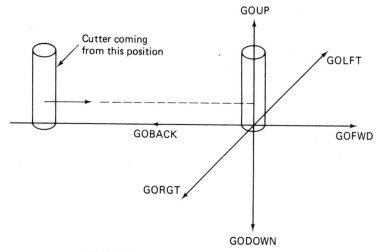

FIGURE 9.13   Use of APT motion commands.

The symbol TARG represents the target point where the operator has set up the tool. The GO command instructs the tool to move to the intersection of the drive surface (PL1), the part surface (PL2), and the check surface (PL3). The periphery of the cutter is tangent to PL1 and PL3, and the bottom of the cutter is on PL2. This cutter location is defined by use of the modifier word TO. The three surfaces included in the GO statement must be specified in the order: drive surface first, part surface second, and check surface last.

Note that the GO/TO command is different from the GOTO command. GOTO is used only for PTP motions. GO/TO is used to initialize the sequence of contouring motions.

After initialization, the tool is directed along its path by one of the six command words. It is not necessary to repeat the symbol of the part surface after it has been defined. For instance, consider Figure 9.14. The cutter has been directed from TARG to the intersection of surfaces PL1, PL2, and PL3. It is desired to move the tool along plane PL3. The following command would be used:

GORGT/PL3, PAST, PL4

This would direct the tool to move along PL3, using it as the drive surface. The tool would continue until past surface PL4, which is the new check surface. Although the part surface (PL2) may remain the same throughout the motion sequence, the drive surface and check surface are redefined in each new command.

Let us consider an alternative statement to the above which would accomplish the same motion but would lead to easier programming:

GORGT/L3, PAST, L4

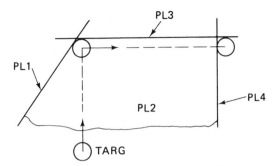

FIGURE 9.14   Initialization of APT contouring motion sequence.

We have substituted lines L3 and L4 for planes PL3 and PL4, respectively. When looking at a part drawing, such as Figure 9.7, the sides of the part appear as lines. On the actual part, they are three-dimensional surfaces, of course. However, it is usually more convenient for the part programmer to define these surfaces as lines and circles rather than planes and cylinders. Fortunately, the APT computer program allows the geometry of the part to be defined in this way. Hence, the lines L3 and L4 in the foregoing motion statement are treated as the drive surface and check surface. This substitution can only be made when the part surfaces are perpendicular to the x-y plane.

EXAMPLE 9.4

We will write the APT geometry and motion statements for the workpart of Figure 9,7, which is repeated in Figure 9.15 with coordinate axes given.

$$P0 = POINT/0, - 1.0, 0$$
$$P1 = POINT/6.0, 1.125, 0$$

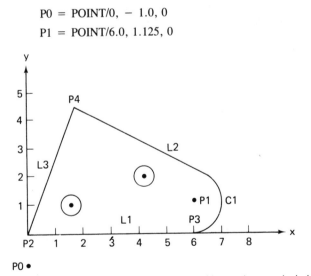

FIGURE 9.15   Workpart from Figure 9.7 redrawn with x and y axes included for Example 9.4.

P2 = POINT/0, 0, 0

P3 = POINT/6.0, 0, 0

P4 = POINT/1.75, 4.5, 0

L1 = LINE/P2, P3

C1 = CIRCLE/CENTER, P1, RADIUS, 1.125

L2 = LINE/P4, LEFT, TANTO, C1

L3 = LINE/P2, P4

PL1 = PLANE/P2, P3, P4

FROM/P0

GO/TO, L1, TO, PL1, TO, L3

GORGT/L1, TANTO, C1

GOFWD/C1, PAST, L2

GOFWD/L2, PAST, L3

GOLFT/L3, PAST, L1

GOTO/P0

The reader may have questioned the location of the part surface (PL1) in the APT sequence. For this machining job, the part surface must be defined below the bottom plane of the workpiece in order for the cutter to machine the entire thickness of the piece. Therefore, the part surface is really not a surface of the part at all. Example 9.4 raises several other questions: How is the cutter size accounted for in the APT program? How are feeds and speeds specified? These and other questions are answered by the postprocessor and auxiliary statements.

Postprocessor statements

To write a complete part program, statements must be written that control the operation of the spindle, the feed, and other features of the machine tool. These are called *postprocessor statements*. Some of the common postprocessor statements that appear in the Appendix at the end of the chapter are:

COOLNT/	RAPID
END	SPINDL/
FEDRAT/	TURRET/
MACHIN/	

The postprocessor statements, and the auxiliary statements in the following sub-section, are of two forms: either with or without the slash (/). The statements without the slash are self-contained. No additional data are needed. The APT words are the slash require descriptive data after the slash. These descriptions are given for each word in the Appendix.

Auxiliary statements

The complete APT program must also contain various other statements, called *auxilliary statements*. These are used for cutter size definition, part identification, and so on. The following APT words used in auxiliary statements are defined in the Appendix to this chapter:

CLPRNT \INTOL/

CUTTER/ OUTTOL/

FINI PARTNO

The offset calculation of the tool path from the part outline is based on the CUTTER/ definition. For example, the statement

CUTTER/.500

would instruct the APT program that the cutter diameter is 0.500 in. Therefore, the tool path must be offset from the part outline by 0.250 in.

EXAMPLE 9.5

We are now in a position to write a complete APT program. The workpart of Example 9.4 will be used to illustrate the format of the APT program.

We will assume that the workpiece is a plain low-carbon steel plate, cut out in the rough shape of the part outline. The tool is a two-flute, $\frac{1}{2}$-in.-diameter, high-speed-steel end-milling cutter. Typical cutting conditions might be recommended as follows: cutting speed = 75 ft/min and feed = 0.002 in./twin.

From Eq. (8.8) the spindle speed should be

$$S = \frac{12(75)}{\pi(0.5)} = 573 \text{ rev/min}$$

The feed rate can be computed as

$$f = 573(0.002)(2) = 2.29 \text{ in./min}$$

Figure 9.16 presents the program with correct character spacing identified at the top as if it were to be keypunched onto computer cards.

Column				
1	6	8	10	72

```
PARTNO              EXAMPLE PART
                    MACHIN/MILL, 1    — indicates which m/c of hence which
                    CLPRNT  — to print out calculated cutter center loc[post proc. tra
                    INTOL/.001    } specifies tol. for calculating interpolation s
                    OUTTOL/.001
                    CUTTER/.500
PO          =       POINT/0, −1.0, 0
P1          =       POINT/6.0, 1.125, 0
P2          =       POINT/0, 0, 0
P3          =       POINT/6.0, 0, 0
P4          =       POINT/1.75, 4.5, 0
L1          =       LINE/P2, P3
C1          =       CIRCLE/CENTER, P1, RADIUS, 1.125
L2          =       LINE/P4, LEFT' TANTO, C1
L3          =       LINE/P2, P4
PL1         =       PLANE/P2, P3, P4
                    SPINDL/573
                    FEDRAT/2.29    indicates where motion start (for calc.)
                    COOLNT/ON
                    FROM/PO          ON
                    GO/TO, L1, TO, PL1, TO, L3
                    GORGT/L1, TANTO, C1
                    GOFWD/C1, PAST, L2
                    GOFWD/L2, PAST, L3
                    GOLFT/L3, PAST, L1
                    RAPID  — to set a high feed rate (non-cutting motion)
                    GOTO/PO
                    COOLNT/OFF
                    FINI  should be present at end of prog.
```

FIGURE 9.16   APT program for Example 9.5.

9.6 MANUAL DATA INPUT

Manual and computer-assisted part programming are methods requiring a relatively high degree of formalistic documentation and procedure. There is a substantial lead time required to write the part program (either using the manuscript or the computer language code), punch the tape, and validate the program. At least two persons are involved, the programmer and the machine operator. A potential method of simplifying the procedure is to have the machine operator perform the task of programming at the site of the machine tool. This is called *manual data input* (MDI) because the operator manually enters the programming data and commands into the machine control unit without the need for a punched tape. The intermediate step of preparing the punched tape, which adds to the job changeover time, is not required. MDI is being offered with growing frequency in the machine tool industry.

Communication between the operator-programmer and the system is accomplished using a CRT (cathode ray tube) display monitor and alphanumeric keyboard. Entering the programming commands into the controller is typically done using a menu-driven procedure in which the operator responds to questions posed by the NC system about the job to be processed. The sequence of questions is designed so that the operator inputs the part geometry and tool motions in a logical and consistent manner. A computer graphics capability is often included in the MDI programming system to permit the operator to visualize the machining operations on the workpart. A minimum of training in NC part programming is required of the machine operator. The skills needed are the ability to read an engineering drawing of the part and to be familiar with the machining process.

MDI systems are perceived as a way for the small machine shop to introduce NC into its operations without the need to acquire the special NC part programming equipment (e.g., tape punch, possibly a separate computer) and to hire a part programmer. This permits the shop to make a minimal initial investment in order to begin the transition to modern numerical control technology.

The limitation, or potential limitation, on manual data input is the risk of programming errors as the jobs become more complicated. For this reason, MDI has usually been applied for relatively simple parts. Also, since there is no punched tape to document and save the program, the most economical MDI applications are those in which the batch is made only once. Repeat orders necessitate repeating the programming procedure with each order. This limitation can be overcome by attaching a storage device (e.g., tape punch and reader, disk drive, magnetic tape cassette drive) to the controller for saving and reading the desired programs.

An important application note in the use of MDI is to make certain that the NC system does not become an expensive toy that stands idle while the operator is inputting the programming instructions. Efficient use of the system dictates that the programming of the next part be performed while the current part is being machined. This reduces the changeover time from one job to the next.

9.7 NC PART PROGRAMMING USING CAD/CAM

The term *CAD/CAM system* typically refers to a computer interactive graphics system equipped with software to accomplish certain functions in design and manufacturing. We discuss CAD/CAM in Chapter 23. One of the possible functions that can be performed on a CAD/CAM system is NC part programming. In this method of part programming, a portion of the procedure usually done by the part programmer is instead done by the computer. Recall that the two tasks of the part programmer in computer-assisted programming are defining the part geometry and specifying the tool path. Advanced CAD/CAM systems have the capability to automate portions of both of these tasks.

Geometry definition using CAD/CAM

A fundamental objective of CAD/CAM is to integrate the design engineering and manufacturing engineering functions. Certainly, one of the important functions in design is the design of the individual components of the product. In the use of a CAD/CAM system, a computer graphics model of each part is developed by the designer and stored in the CAD/CAM data base. That model contains all of the geometric, dimensional, and material specifications for the part.

When the same CAD/CAM system, or a system that has access to the same CAD/CAM data base in which the part model resides, is used to perform NC part programming, it makes little sense to recreate the geometry of the part during the programming procedure. Instead, the programmer has the capability to retrieve the part geometric model from storage, and to use that model to construct the appropriate cutter path. The significant advantage of using CAD/CAM in this way is that it eliminates one of the time-consuming steps in the computer-assisted part programming procedure: geometry definition. After the part geometry has been recalled, the usual procedure is to label the geometric elements that will be used during part programming. These labels are the variable names (symbols) given to the various lines, circles, and surfaces of the part. Most systems have the capacity to automatically label the geometry elements of the part (except the points), and to display the labels on the monitor. The programmer can then refer to those labeled elements during construction of the tool path.

If the NC programmer does not have access to the data base, the geometry of the part must be developed. This is done by using the same interactive graphics techniques that the product designer would use to design the part. Points are defined in a coordinate system using the computer graphics system, lines and circles are defined from the points, surfaces are defined, and so on, to construct a geometric model of the part. The advantage of using the interactive graphics system over geometry definition in computer-assisted part programming is that the programmer receives immediate visual verification of the definitions being created. This tends to improve the speed and accuracy of the geometry definition process.

Tool path generation using CAD/CAM

The second task of the NC programmer in computer-assisted part programming is tool path specification. The first step in specifying the tool path is to select the cutting tool for the operation. Most CAD/CAM systems have tool libraries that can be called by the programmer to identify what tools are available in the tool crib. The programmer decides which of the available tools would be most appropriate for the operation under consideration and specifies it for the tool path. This permits the tool diameter and other dimensions to be entered automatically for tool offset calculations. If the desired cutting tool is not available in the library, an appropriate tool can be specified by the programmer. It then becomes part of the library for future use.

The next step is to describe the tool path. There are differences in capabilities of the various CAD/CAM systems which result in different approaches for generating the tool path. The most basic approach involves the use of the interactive graphics system to enter the motion commands one by one, similar to computer-assisted part programming. Individual statements in APT or other part programming language are entered, and the CAD/CAM system provides an immediate graphic display of the resulting command, thereby providing validation of the program.

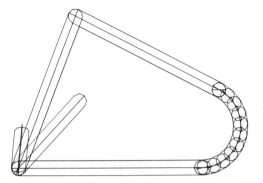

FIGURE 9.17   Cutter path generated automatically by CAD/CAM system. Reprinted by permission from Mikell P. Groover, Emory W. Zimmers, *CAD/CAM: Computer-Aided Design and Manufacturing*, (Englewood Cliffs, NJ: Prentice-Hall, Inc., 1984), p. 200.

A more advanced approach for generating tool path commands is to use one of the automatic software routines that might be available on the CAD/CAM system. These routines have been developed for common machining cycles such as profile milling around the outside periphery of a part, milling a pocket in a part, some surface contouring, and certain point-to-point operations. These are designed as subroutines in the NC programming package that can be called and the required parameters given to execute the machining cycle. Figure 9.17 illustrates one of these automatic machining cycles used in NC programming with interactive graphics.

9.8   COMPUTER-AUTOMATED PART PROGRAMMING

In the CAD/CAM approach to NC part programming, several aspects of the procedure have been automated. In the future, it should be possible to automate the complete NC part programming procedure. We are referring to this fully automated procedure as computer-automated part programming. Given the geometric model of a part that has been defined during product design, the computer-automated system would possess sufficient logic and decision-making capability to accomplish NC part programming with no human assistance.

This can most readily be done for certain NC processes that involve well-defined, relatively simple part geometries. Examples are in point-to-point operations such as NC drilling, wire-wrap machines, and electronic component assembly machines. In these processes, the program consists basically of a series of locations in an x-y coordinate system where work is to be performed (e.g., holes to be drilled, wires to be attached, or components to be inserted). These locations are determined by data that are generated during design of the product. The design data can be processed to generate the NC program for the particular system.

NC contouring systems will be capable of the same level of automation. Automatic programming of this type is closely related to computer-automated process planning (CAPP), which is discussed in Chapter 24.

REFERENCES

[1] CHILDS, J. J., *Numerical Control Part Programming,* Industrial Press, Inc., New York, 1973.

[2] GROOVER, M. P., and E. W. ZIMMERS, Jr., *CAD/CAM: Computer-Aided Design and Manufacturing,* Prentice-Hall, Inc., Englewood Cliffs, N.J., 1984, Chapter 8.

[3] HOWE, R. E., Editor, *Introduction to Numerical Control in Manufacturing,* Society of Manufacturing Engineers, Dearborn, Mich., 1969.

[4] Illinois Institute of Technology Research Institute, *APT Part Programming,* McGraw-Hill Book Company, New York, 1967.

[5] *Modern Machine Shop 1985 NC/CAM Guidebook,* Gardener Publications, Inc., Cincinnati, Ohio, January 1985, Chapter 4.

[6] OGOREK, M., "Interactive Graphics and Conversation Programming," *Manufacturing Engineering,* January 1985, pp. 75–76.

[7] PRESSMAN, R. S., and J. E. WILLIAMS, *Numerical Control and Computer-Aided Manufacturing,* John Wiley & Sons, Inc., New York, 1977.

[8] ROBERTS, A. D., and R. C. PRENTICE, *Programming for Numerical Control Machines,* 2nd ed., McGraw-Hill Book Company, Gregg Division, New York, 1978.

PROBLEMS

9.1. A drilling operation is to be carried out using a $\frac{1}{4}$-in.-diameter high-speed steel (HSS) drill. The work material is a machinable grade of aluminum. Recommended cutting speed is 400 sfpm and recommended feed rate is 0.003 in./rev. Convert these recommendations into machine tool speed and feed: rev/min and in./min, respectively.

9.2. The same work material as in Problem 9.1 is to be milled with a $\frac{3}{4}$-in.-diameter four-flute end milling cutter. Recommendations are cutting speed = 400 ft/min and feed = 0.003 in./turn. Convert these values to rev/min and in./rev.

9.3. A cast-iron workpiece is to be face-milled on an NC machine using cemented carbide inserts. The cutter has 16 teeth and is 5 in. in diameter. The recommended cutting speed is 250 ft/min. The recommended feed is 0.002 in./turn. Convert these to rev/min and in./min for use by the machine tool.

9.4 A part program is to be written to drill the holes in the workpart of Figure P9.4. The part is $\frac{3}{8}$ in. thick.

(a) Define the x and y axes for the job.

(b) Write the part program manuscript (manual part programming) using the word address format and an absolute position system. The words that must be specified for the particular NC drill press are n-, x-, y-, and m-words. The speed and feed are manually set by the operator.

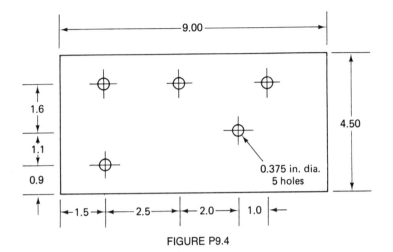

FIGURE P9.4

9.5. Solve Problem 9.4 except that speed and feed specifications must be included in the program (n-, x-, y-, f-, s-, and m-words must be given). Assume that the tool material is HSS and the work material is aluminum so that the cutting conditions would be as determined in Problem 9.1.

9.6. Solve Problem 9.4 except use the tab sequential format rather than word address format.

9.7. Solve Problem 9.5 except use the tab sequential format.

9.8. Solve Problem 9.4 except use the fixed block format.

9.9. The part in Figure P9.9 is to be drilled on a turret-type NC drill press. The $\frac{3}{8}$-in.-diameter holes (4) are to be drilled with a $\frac{23}{64}$-in.-diameter drill and reamed to final size. All tooling is HSS. The turret on the drill press has six positions, but only three are required for this operation sequence. The part is $\frac{3}{8}$ in. thick.
(a) Designate the three tools for turret positions t01, t02, and t03.
(b) Define the *xy* coordinate system.

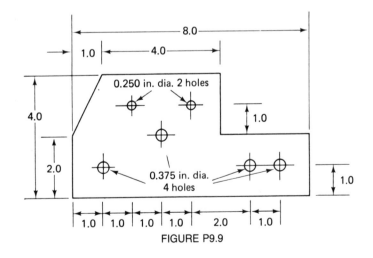

FIGURE P9.9

(c) Write the part program manuscript using the word address format and absolute positioning. The following words must be specified in the program for the particular drill press: n-, x-, y-, t-, and m-words. Cutting conditions are set by the operator.

9.10. Solve Problem 9.9 but the f- and s-words must be included. Recommended cutting conditions are as follows:

$$\text{For drilling:}\quad \text{speed} = 75 \text{ ft/min}$$

$$\text{feed} = 0.004 \text{ in./rev}$$

$$\text{For reaming:}\quad \text{speed} = 50 \text{ ft/min}$$

$$\text{feed} = 0.008 \text{ in./rev}$$

9.11. Write the APT part program to perform the drilling in Problem 9.5.

9.12. Write the APT part program to solve Problem 9.10. — use MACROS... (see hdout for explan

9.13. The outline of the part in Figure P9.13 is to be machined in an end-milling operation. Write the APT geometry statements that define the part outline. Do not consider the two ⅜-in. holes. They will be used for clamping the part during machining.

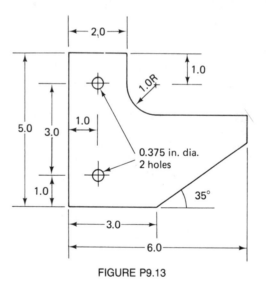

FIGURE P9.13

9.14. Write the complete APT program for the part of Problem 9.13. The postprocessor call statement is MACHIN/TURDRL, 02. The cut will be made with a ¾-in.-diameter end mill. Speed = 500 rev/min; feed = 4.0 in./min. Inside tolerance on the circular approximation is 0.001 in. No outside tolerance is allowed.

9.15. The outline of the cam shown in Figure P9.15 is to be milled using a two-flute, ½-in.-diameter end mill.
(a) Write the geometry statements in APT to define the part outline.
(b) Write the motion statement sequence using the geometry elements defined in part (a).

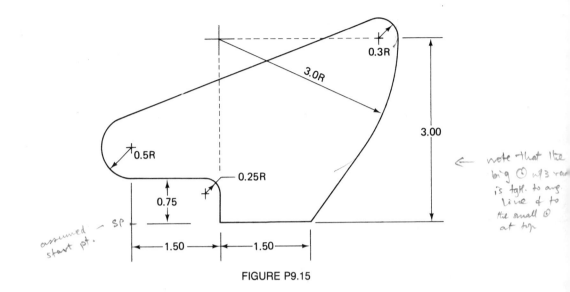

FIGURE P9.15

(c) Write the complete APT program. Inside and outside tolerances should be 0.0005 in. Feed rate = 3 in./min; speed = 500 rev/min. Postprocessor call statement is MACHIN/MILL, 01. Assume that the rough outline for the part has been obtained in a bandsaw operation. Ignore clamping problems with this part.

9.16. The part outline of Figure P9.16 is to be milled in two passes with the same tool. The tool is a 1-in.-diameter end mill. The first cut is to leave 0.050 in. of stock on the part outline. The second cut will take the part to size. Write the APT geometry and motion statements to perform the two passes.

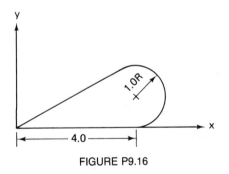

FIGURE P9.16

9.17. The top surface of a large cast iron plate is to be face-milled flat. The area to be machined is 15 in. wide and 27 in. long. The cutter to be used and the machining conditions are as described in Problem 9.3. Sketch the part surface in relation to an assumed set of axes. Write the APT program to complete the job. The postprocessor call statement is MACHIN/MILL, 05. Use a coolant for this job.

APPENDIX: APT WORD DEFINITIONS

ATANGL: At angle (descriptive data). Indicates that the data that follow represent a specified angle. Angle is given in degrees. *See* LINE.

CENTER: Center (descriptive data). Used to indicate the center of circle. *See* CIRCLE.

CIRCLE: Circle (geometry type). Used to define a circle in the *x-y* plane. Methods of definition:

1. By the coordinates of the center and the radius (see Figure A9.1).

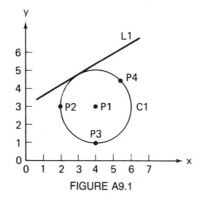

FIGURE A9.1

C1 = CIRCLE/CENTER, 4.0, 3.0, 0.0, RADIUS, 2

C1 = CIRCLE/4.0, 3.0, 0.0, 2.0

2. By the center point and the radius (see Figure A9.1).

C1 = CIRCLE/CENTER, P1, RADIUS, 2.0

3. By the center point and tangent to a line (see Figure A9.1).

C1 = CIRCLE/CENTER, P1, TANTO, L1

4. By three points on the circumference (see Figure A9.1).

C1 = CIRCLE/P2, P3, P4

5. By two intersecting lines and the radius (see Figure A9.2).

C2 = CIRCLE/XSMALL, L2, YSMALL, L3, RADIUS, .375

C3 = CIRCLE/YLARGE, L2, YLARGE, L3, RADIUS, .375

other ways of defining are also possible (w/ diff. modifiers)

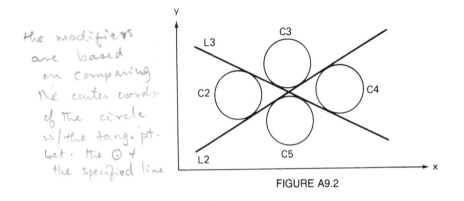

the modifiers
are based
on comparing
the center words.
of the circle
w/the tang. pt.
bet. the ⊙ +
the specified line

FIGURE A9.2

C4 = CIRCLE/XLARGE, L2, YLARGE, L3, RADIUS, .375

C5 = CIRCLE/YSMALL, L2, YSMALL, L3, RADIUS, .375

CLPRINT: Cutter location print (auxiliary statement). Can be used to obtain a computer printout of the cutter location sequence on the NC tape.

COOLNT: Coolant (postprocessor statement). Turns coolant on, off, and actuates other coolant options that may be available. Examples:

COOLNT/ON   COOLNT/OFF

COOLNT/FLOOD   COOLNT/MIST

CUTTER: Cutter (auxiliary statement). Defines cutter diameter to be used in tool offset computations. The statement

CUTTER/1.0

defines a 1.0-in.-diameter milling cutter. Cutter path would be offset from part outline by one-half the diameter.

END: End (postprocessor statement). Used to stop the machine at the end of a section of the program. Can be used to change tools manually. Meaning may vary between machine tools. To continue program, a FROM statement should be used.

FEDRAT: Feed rate (postprocessor statement). Used to specify feet rate in inches per minute.

FEDRAT/6.0

FINI: Finish (auxiliary statement). Must be the last word in the APT program. Used to indicate the end of the complete program.

FROM: From the tool starting location (motion startup command). Used to specify the starting point of the cutter, from which other tool movements will be measured. The starting point is specified by the part programmer and set up by the machine operator. Methods of specification:

1. By a previously defined starting point (TARG).

$$FROM/TARG$$

2. By the coordinates at the starting point.

$$FROM/-1.0, -1.0, 0.0$$

GO: Go (motion startup command in contouring). Used to bring the tool from the starting point against the drive surface, part surface, and check surface. In the statements

$$GO/TO, L1, TO, PL1, TO, L2$$

$$GO/PAST, L1, TO, PL1, ON, L2$$

the initial drive surface is the line L1, the part surface is PL1, and the initial check surface is L2.

GODLTA: Go delta (PTP motion command). Instructs the tool to move in increments as specified from the current tool location. In the statement

$$GODLTA/2.0, 3.0, -4.0$$

the tool is instructed to move 2.0 in. in the x-direction, 3.0 in. in the y-direction, and -4.0 in. in the z-direction from its present position.

GOBACK: Go back (contour motion command). Instructs the tool to move back relative to its previous direction of movement. In the statement

$$GOBACK/PL5, TO, L1$$

the tool is instructed to move in the opposite general direction relative to its previous path. It moves on the drive surface PL5 until it reaches L1. The part surface has been specified in a previous GO statement.

In specifying the motion command the part programmer must pretend to be riding on top of the cutter and must give the next move (GOBACK, GOFWD, GOUP, GODOWN, GORGT, GOLFT) according to the tool's preceding motion. Also, the motion command should indicate the largest direction component. For example, if the next tool move was both forward and to the left, the motion command (GOFWD vs. GOLFT) would be determined by whichever direction component was larger (see Figure 9.13).

GODOWN: Go down (contour motion command). *See* GOBACK.

GOFWD: Go forward (contour motion command). *See* GOBACK.

GOLFT: Go left (contour motion command). *See* GOBACK.

GORGT: Go right (contour motion command). *See* GOBACK.

GOTO: Go to (PTP motion command). Used to move the tool center to a specified point location. Methods of specification:

1.   By using a previously defined point. GOTO/P1

2.   By defining the coordinates of the point.

$$GOTO/2.0, 5.0, 0.0$$

GOUP: Go up (contour motion command). *See* GOBACK.

INTOF: Intersection of (descriptive data). Indicates that the intersection of two geometry elements is the specified point. *See* POINT.

INTOL: Inside tolerance (auxiliary statement). Indicates the allowable tolerance between the inside of a curved surface and any straight-line segments used to approximate the curve (see Figure A9.3).

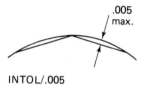

INTOL/.005

FIGURE A9.3

LEFT: Left (descriptive data). Used to indicate which of two alternatives, left or right, is desired. *See* LINE.

LINE: Line (geometry type). Used to define a line that is interpreted by APT as a plane perpendicular to the *xy* plane. Methods of definition:

1.   By the coordinates of two points (see Figure A9.4).

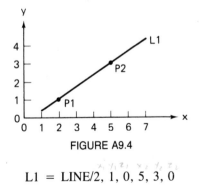

FIGURE A9.4

$$L1 = LINE/2, 1, 0, 5, 3, 0$$

2.   By two points (see Figure A9.4).

$$L1 = LINE/P1, P2$$

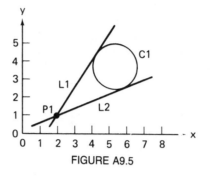

FIGURE A9.5

3. By a point and tangent to a circle (see Figure A9.5).

$$L1 = LINE/P1, LEFT, TANTO, C1$$

$$L2 = LINE/P1, RIGHT, TANTO, C1$$

    The descriptive words LEFT and RIGHT are used by looking from the point toward the circle.

4. By a point and the angle of the line to the *x*-axis or another line (see Figure A9.6).

$$L3 = LINE/P1, ATANGL, 20 \; [X AXIS]$$

$$L4 = LINE/P1, ATANGL, 30, L3$$

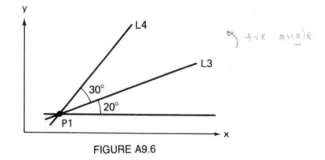

FIGURE A9.6

5. By a point and being parallel to or perpendicular to another line (see Figure A9.7).

$$L5 = LINE/P2, PARLEL, L3$$

$$L6 = LINE/P2, PERPTO, L3$$

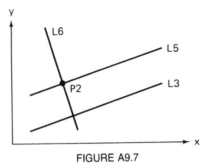

FIGURE A9.7

6. By being tangent to two circles (see Figure A9.8).

L7 = LINE/LEFT, TANTO, C3, LEFT, TANTO, C4

L8 = LINE/LEFT, TANTO, C3, RIGHT, TANTO, C4

L9 = LINE/RIGHT, TANTO, C3, LEFT, TANTO, C4

L10 = LINE/RIGHT, TANTO, C3, RIGHT, TANTO, C4

other ways of defn can be used (looking from the other ⊙)

The descriptive words LEFT and RIGHT are used by looking from the first circle written toward the second circle. For example, another way to specify L7 would be

L7 = LINE/RIGHT, TANTO, C4, RIGHT, TANTO, C3

MACHIN: Machine (postprocessor statement). Used to specify the machine tool and to call the postprocessor for that machine tool. In the statement

MACHIN/MILL, 1

the MILL identifies the machine tool type and 1 identifies the particular machine and postprocessor. The APT system then calls the specified postprocessor to prepare the NC program for that machine.

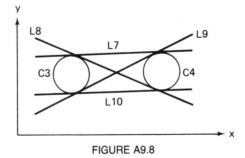

FIGURE A9.8

ON: On (motion modifier word). One of four motion modifier words—the others are TO, PAST, and TANTO—to indicate the point on the check surface where the tool motion is to terminate (see Figure A9.9).

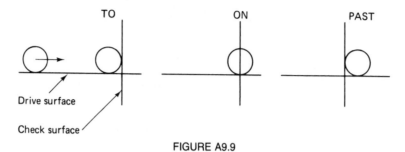

FIGURE A9.9

OUTTOL: Outside Tolerance (auxiliary statement). Indicates the allowable tolerance between the outside of a curved surface and any straight-line segments used to approximate the curve (see Figure A9.10).

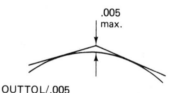

FIGURE A9.10

NOTE: The INTOL and OUTTOL statements can be used together to indicate allowable tolerances on both inside and outside of the curved surface (see Figure A9.11).

INTOL/.0025

OUTTOL/.0025

PARLEL: Parallel (descriptive data). Used to define a line or plane as being parallel to another line of plane. *See* LINE *and* PLANE.

PARTNO: Part number (auxiliary statement). Used at start of program to identify

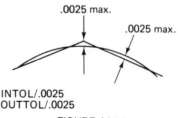

FIGURE A9.11

the part program. PARTNO must be typed in columns 1 through 6 of the first computer card in the deck.

PARTNO MECHANISM PLATE 47320

PAST: Past (motion modifier word). *See* ON.

PERPTO: Perpendicular to (descriptive data). Used to define a line or plane as being perpendicular to some other line or plane. *See* LINE and PLANE.

PLANE: Plane (geometry type). Used to define a plane.

Methods of definition:

1.   By three points that do not lie on the same straight line (see Figure A9.12).

PL1 = PLANE/P1, P2, P3

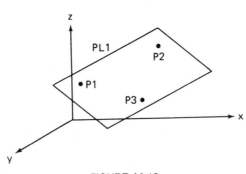

FIGURE A9.12

2.   By a point and being parallel to another plane, (see Figure A9.13).

PL2 = PLANE/P4, PARLEL, PL1

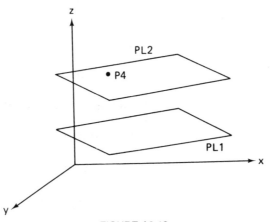

FIGURE A9.13

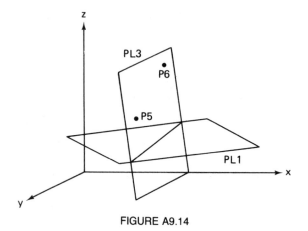

FIGURE A9.14

3.   By two points and being perpendicular to another plane (see Figure A9.14).

$$PL3 = PLANE/PERPTO, PL1, P5, P6$$

POINT: Point (geometry type). Used to define a point.
Methods of definition:
    1.   By the x, y, and z coordinates (see Figure A9.15).

$$P1 = POINT/3.0, 1.5, 0.0$$

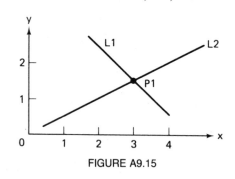

FIGURE A9.15

2.   By the intersection of two lines (see Figure A9.15).

$$P1 = POINT/L1, L2$$

                                    INTOF, ↑ *(annotation)*

3.   By the intersection of a line and a circle (see Figure A9.16)

                                    or YSMALL

$$P2 = POINT/YLARGE, INTOF, L3, C1$$

$$P3 = POINT/XLARGE, INTOF, L3, C1$$

                                   or YSMALL

                                   (qualifier)

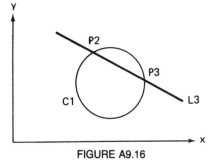

FIGURE A9.16

Any of the descriptive words—XLARGE, XSMALL, YLARGE, YSMALL—can be used to indicate the relative position of the point. For example, for point P2, YLARGE or XSMALL could be used. For point P3, YSMALL or XLARGE could be used.

    4. By two intersecting circles (see Figure A9.17).

$$P4 = POINT/YLARGE, INTOF, C1, C2$$

$$P5 = POINT/YSMALL, INTOF, C1, C2$$

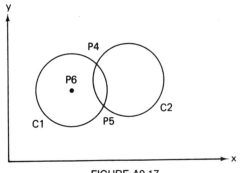

FIGURE A9.17

    5. By the center of a circle:

$$P6 = POINT/CENTER, C1$$

    RADIUS: Radius (descriptive data). Used to indicate the radius of a circle. *See* CIRCLE.

    RIGHT: Right (descriptive data). *See* LEFT *and* LINE.

    TANTO: Tangent to (two uses: descriptive data and motion modifier word).

    1. As descriptive data, it is used to indicate tangency of one geometry element to another. *See* CIRCLE *and* LINE.

    2. As a motion modifier word, it is used to indicate that the tool motion is to terminate at the point of tangency between the drive surface and the check surface (see Figure A9.18). *only, bet· a circle and a line or another ⊙ (or curve?)*

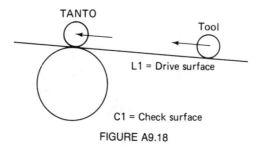

FIGURE A9.18

TO: To (motion modifier word). *See* ON.

TURRET: Turret (postprocessor statement). Used to specify a turret position on a turret lathe or drill or to call a specific tool from an automatic tool changer. Example: TURRET/T30.

XLARGE: In the positive *x*-direction (descriptive data). Used to indicate the relative position of one geometric element with respect to another when there are two possible alternatives. *See* CIRCLE and POINT.

XSMALL: In the negative *x*-direction (descriptive data). *See* XLARGE.

YLARGE: In the positive *y*-direction (descriptive data). *See* XLARGE.

YSMALL: In the negative *y*-direction (descriptive data). *See* XLARGE.

chapter 10

DNC, CNC, and Adaptive Control

The development of numerical control was a significant achievement in batch and job shop manufacturing, from both a technological and a commercial viewpoint. There have been several enhancements and extensions of NC technology, including:

1. Direct numerical control
2. Computer numerical control
3. Adaptive control

Direct numerical control (DNC) and computer numerical control (CNC) represent a marriage between computer technology and NC technology. Direct numerical control was introduced in the mid to late 1960s, and computer numerical control systems were commercially offered during the early 1970s. *Direct numerical control* involves the use of a large central computer to direct the operations of a number of separate NC machines. One of the principal functions of the central computer in DNC is to download the NC part programs to the individual machines as required.

Advances in computer technology over the years have resulted in smaller, less costly, yet more powerful computers. In NC, the result of this trend toward miniaturization was that it became economical for one computer (a minicomputer or a microcomputer) to be used to control each machine tool. This new configuration came to be called *computer numerical control*. By definition, CNC denotes a numerical control system that uses a dedicated, stored-program computer to perform some or all of the basic NC control functions.

Work on the development of adaptive control machining was initiated around 1962. Just as the U.S. Air Force had sponsored much of the original research on numerical control, it also provided financial support for the initial research and development on adaptive control. In our present context, the term *adaptive control* has come to denote a machining system that measures one or more process variables (e.g., cutting force, temperature, horsepower) and regulates feed and/or speed to compensate for undesirable changes in the process variables. Its objective is to optimize the machining process, something that NC alone cannot accomplish.

These three extensions of numerical control are discussed in this chapter. We begin by examining some of the limitations of conventional NC that motivated the search for improvements on the basic technology.

10.1 PROBLEMS WITH CONVENTIONAL NC

There are a number of problems inherent in conventional NC which have motivated machine tool builders to seek improvements in the basic NC system. Among the difficulties encountered in using conventional numerical control machines are the following:

1. *Part programming mistakes.* In preparing a punched tape, part programming mistakes are common. The mistakes can be either syntax or numerical errors, and it is not uncommon for three or more passes to be required before the NC tape is correct. Another related problem in part programming is to achieve the optimum sequence of processing steps. This is mainly a problem in manual part programming. Some of the computer-assisted part programming languages provide aids to achieving the best operation sequence.

2. *Punched tape.* Another problem is the tape itself. Paper tape is especially fragile, and its susceptibility to wear and tear causes it to be an unreliable NC component for repeated use on the shop floor. More durable tape materials, such as Mylar and aluminum foil, are utilized to help overcome this difficulty. However, these materials are relatively expensive.

3. *Tape reader.* The tape reader that interprets the punched tape is generally acknowledged among NC users to be the least reliable hardware component of the system. When a breakdown is encountered on an NC machine, the maintenance personnel usually begin their search for the problem with the tape reader.

4. *Controller.* The conventional NC controller unit is hard-wired. This means that its control features cannot be easily altered to incorporate improvements into the unit.

5. *Management information.* The conventional NC system cannot provide timely information on operational performance to management. Such information might include piececounts, machine breakdowns, and tool changes.

      6. *Nonoptimal speeds and feeds*. The function of conventional NC is to control the position of the tool relative to the work. There is no attempt to optimize the speeds and feeds during the machining process. Consequently, the part programmer must plan the cutting conditions conservatively, and this reduces productivity.

      It was with these problems in mind that the machine tool builders and control systems designers worked to develop DNC, CNC, and adaptive control.

10.2 DIRECT NUMERICAL CONTROL

Direct numerical control can be defined as a manufacturing system in which a number of machines are controlled by a computer through direct connection and in real time. The tape reader is omitted in DNC, thus relieving the system of its least reliable component. Instead of using the tape reader, the part program is transmitted to the machine tool directly from the computer memory. In principle, one computer can be used to control more than 100 separate machines. (One commercial DNC system during the 1970s boasted a control capability of up to 256 machine tools.) The DNC computer is designed to provide instructions to each machine tool on demand. When the machine needs control commands, they are communicated to it immediately.

      Figure 10.1 illustrates the general DNC configuration. The system consists of four components.

1. Central computer
2. Bulk memory, which stores the NC part programs
3. Telecommunication lines
4. Machine tools

The computer calls the part program instructions from bulk storage and sends them to the individual machines as the need arises. It also receives data back from the machines. This two-way information flow occurs in real time, which means that each machine's requests for instructions must be satisfied almost instantaneously. Similarly, the computer

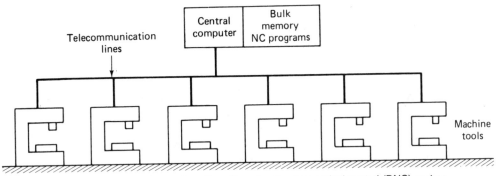

FIGURE 10.1 General configuration of a direct numerical control (DNC) system.

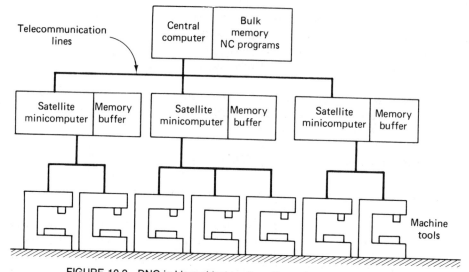

FIGURE 10.2   DNC in hierarchical configuration using satellite computers.

must always be ready to receive information from the machines and to respond accordingly. The remarkable feature of the DNC system is that the computer is servicing a large number of separate machine tools, all in real time.

Depending on the number of machines and the computational requirements that are imposed on the computer, it is sometimes necessary to make use of satellite computers, as shown in Figure 10.2. These satellites are smaller computers, and they serve to take some of the burden off the larger central computer. Each satellite controls several machines. Groups of part program instructions are received from the central computer and stored in buffers. They are then dispensed to the individual machines as required. Feedback data from the machines are also stored in the satellite's buffer before being collected at the central computer.

Two types of DNC

There have been two alternative system configurations by which the communication link is established between the control computer and the machine tool in DNC. One is called a behind-the-tape reader system; the other configuration makes use of a specialized machine control unit.

BEHIND-THE-TAPE READER (BTR) SYSTEM.   In this arrangement, pictured in Figure 10-3, the computer is linked directly to the regular NC controller unit. The replacement of the tape reader by the telecommunication lines to the DNC computer is what gives the BTR configuration its name. The connection with the computer is made between the tape reader and the controller unit—behind the tape reader.

Except for the source of the command instructions, the operation of the system is

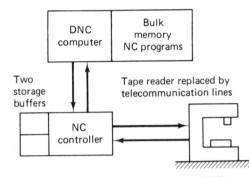

FIGURE 10.3   DNC with behind the tape reader (BTR) configuration.

very similar to conventional NC. The controller unit uses two temporary storage buffers to receive blocks of instructions from the DNC computer and convert them into machine actions. While one buffer is receiving a block of data, the other is providing command instructions to the machine tool.

SPECIAL MACHINE CONTROL UNIT.   The other strategy in DNC is to eliminate the regular NC controller altogether and replace it with a special machine control unit. The configuration is illustrated in Figure 10.4. This special MCU is a device that is specifically designed to facilitate communication between the machine tool and the computer. One area where this communication link is important is in circular interpolation of the cutter path. The special MCU configuration achieves a superior balance between accuracy of the interpolation and fast metal removal rates than is generally possible with the BTR system.

The advantage of the BTR configuration is that its cost is less, since only minor changes are needed in the conventional NC system to bring DNC into the shop. BTR systems do not require the replacement of the conventional control unit by a special MCU. However, this BTR advantage is a temporary one, since virtually all NC machines are sold with computer numerical control (CNC), to be discussed in the next section. The CNC controller serves the same purpose as a special MCU when incorporated into a DNC system.

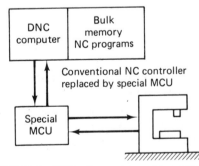

FIGURE 10.4   DNC with special machine control unit.

Advantages of DNC

The advantages typically cited for DNC systems are as follows:

1. Time sharing—the control of more than one machine by the computer.
2. Greater computational capability for such functions as circular interpolation.
3. Remote computer location—the computer is located in a computer-type environment.
4. Elimination of tapes and tape reader at the machine for improved reliability.
5. Elimination of hardwired controller unit on some systems.
6. Programs stored as cutter location data can be post-processed for whatever suitable machine is assigned to process the job.

One obvious question concerning DNC is this: What happens if the computer breaks down? The answer is that production stops. In practice, this has not turned out to be too much of a problem simply because the central computer is so much more reliable than the conventional NC machines.

10.3 COMPUTER NUMERICAL CONTROL

Since the introduction of DNC, there have been dramatic advances in computer technology. The physical size and cost of a digital computer has been significantly reduced at the same time that its computational capabilities have been substantially increased. In numerical control, the result of these advances has been that the large hard-wired MCUs of conventional NC have been replaced by control units based on the digital computer. Initially, minicomputers were utilized in the early 1970s. As further miniaturization occurred in computers, minicomputers were replaced by today's microcomputers.

Computer numerical control is an NC system using a dedicated microcomputer as the machine control unit. Because a digital computer is used in both CNC and DNC, it is appropriate to distinquish between the two types of system. There are three principal differences:

1. DNC computers distribute instructional data to, and collect data from, a large number of machines. CNC computers control only one machine, or a small number of machines.

2. DNC computers occupy a location that is typically remote from the machines under their control. CNC computers are located very near their machine tools.

3. DNC software is developed not only to control individual pieces of production equipment, but also to serve as part of a management information system in the manufacturing sector of the firm. CNC software is developed to augment the capabilities of a particular machine tool.

The general configuration of a computer numerical control system is pictured in Figure 10.5. As illustrated in the diagram, the controller has a tape reader for initial entry of a part program. In this regard, the outward appearance of a CNC system is similar to that of a conventional NC machine. However, the way in which the program is used in CNC is different. With a conventional NC system, the punched tape is cycled through the tape reader for each workpart in the batch. The MCU reads in a block of instructions on the tape, executing that block before proceeding to the next block. In CNC, the entire program is entered once and stored in computer memory. The machining cycle for each part is controlled by the program contained in memory rather than from the tape itself.

Control algorithms contained in the computer convert the part program instructions into actions of the machine tool (or other processing equipment). Certain functions are carried out by hard-wired components in the MCU. For example, circular interpolation calculations are often performed by hard-wired circuits rather than by stored program. Also, a hardware interface is required to make the connections with the machine tool servosystems.

CNC control features

In Section 8.4 the important features and functions of the machine control unit in numerical control were described. CNC has made possible additional features beyond what is normally found in a conventional hard-wired MCU. Some of these features include the following:

• *Storage of more than one part program.* With improvements in computer technology, many of the newer CNC controllers have a large enough capacity to store more than a single program. This translates into the capability to store either one very large program or several small and medium-sized programs.

• *Use of diskettes.* There is a growing use of floppy disks for part programs in manufacturing. The capacity of an 8-in. diskette is the approximate equivalent of 8000 ft of punched tape. Because of this more modern storage technology, many CNC controllers have the optional capability to read in programs stored on disks as well as punched tape.

• *Program editing at the machine tool site.* To deal with the mistakes in part programming, CNC systems permit the program to be edited while it is in computer memory. Hence, the process of testing and correcting the program can be done entirely

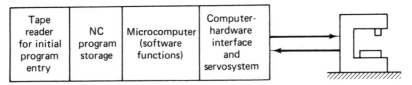

FIGURE 10.5   General configuration of a computer numerical control (CNC) system.

at the machine site rather than returning to the programming office in the shop to make the tape corrections. In addition to part program corrections, editing can also be done to optimize the cutting conditions of the machining cycle. After correcting and optimizing the program, a tape punch can be connected to the CNC controller in order to obtain a revised version of the tape for future use.

• *Fixed cycles and programming subroutines.* The increased memory capacity and the ability to program the control computer in CNC provides the opportunity to store frequently used machining cycles in memory that can be called by the part program. Instead of writing the instructions for the particular cycle into every program, a code is written into the program to indicate that the cycle should be executed. Some of these cycles require the definition of certain parameters in order to execute. An example is a bolt hole circle, in which the diameter of the bolt circle, the spacing of the bolt holes, and other parameters must be specified. In other cases, the particular machining cycle used by the shop would not require parameter definition.

• *Interpolation.* Some of the interpolation schemes described in Chapter 8 are normally executed only on a CNC system because of the computational requirements. Linear and circular interpolation are often hard-wired into the control unit. Helical, parabolic, and cubic interpolations are usually executed in a stored program algorithm.

• *Positioning features for setup.* Setting up the machine tool for a certain job involves installing and aligning the fixture on the machine tool table. This must be accomplished so that the machine axes are aligned with the workpart. The alignment task can be facilitated using certain features that are made possible by software options in a CNC system. *Position set* is one of these features. With position set, the operator is not required to position the fixture on the machine table with extreme accuracy. Instead, the machine tool axes are referenced to the location of the fixture by using a target point or set of target points on the work or fixture.

• *Cutter length compensation.* This is similar to the preceding feature but applies to tool length and diameter. In older-style controls, the cutter dimensions had to be set very precisely in order to agree with the tool path defined in the part program. Other methods for ensuring accurate tool path definition have been incorporated into newer CNC controls. One method involves manually entering the actual tool dimensions into the MCU. These actual dimensions may differ from those originally programmed. Compensations are then automatically made in the computed tool path. Another more recent innovation is to use a tool length sensor built into the machine. In this method, the cutter is mounted in the spindle and brought into contact with the sensor to measure its length. This measured value is then used to correct the programmed tool path.

• *Diagnostics.* Many modern CNC machines possess an on-line diagnostics capability which monitors certain aspects of the machine tool and MCU operation to detect malfunctions or signs of impending malfunctions. When a malfunction is detected, or measurements indicate that a breakdown is about to occur, a message is displayed on the controller's CRT monitor. Depending on the seriousness of the malfunction, the system can be stopped or maintenance can be scheduled for a nonproduction shift. Another use of the diagnostics capability is to help the repair crew determine the reason for a breakdown of the machine tool. One of the biggest problems when a machine failure occurs is often in diagnosing the reason for the breakdown. By monitoring and analyzing its own operation, the system can determine and communicate the reason for the failure.

• *Communications interface.* With the trend toward interfacing and networking in plants today, most modern CNC controllers are equipped with a standard communications interface to allow the particular machine tool to be linked to other computers and computer-driven devices.

Advantages of CNC

Compared to conventional NC, CNC offers additional flexibility and computational capability. New system options can be incorporated into the CNC controller simply by reprogramming the unit. The advantages of computer numerical control over conventional NC are summarized here:

1. *The part program tape and tape reader are used only once to enter the program into memory.* This results in improved reliability, since the tape reader is commonly considered the least reliable component of a conventional NC system.

2. *Tape editing at machine site.* The NC tape can be optimized during tape tryout at the site of the machine tool.

3. *Greater flexibility.* The most significant advantage over conventional NC is CNC's flexibility. New options can be added to the system easily and at relatively low cost.

4. *Metric conversion.* CNC can accommodate conversion of tapes prepared in units of inches into the international system of units.

5. *Total manufacturing system.* CNC is more compatible with the use of a total manufacturing information system.

Considering this last point, what we will no doubt see in the future is more integration of CNC and DNC. The CNC computer will be used for machine tool control while management/manufacturing information about the performance of the process will be channeled to a central computer.

10.4 ADAPTIVE CONTROL MACHINING

One of the principal reasons for using numerical control (including DNC and CNC) is that NC reduces the nonproductive time in manufacturing. This is accomplished through a reduction in the following elements, which constitute a significant portion of total production time:

1. Workpiece handling
2. Setup of the job.
3. Lead times between receipt of an order and production

4. Tool changes
5. Operator delays

Because these nonproductive elements are reduced relative to total production time, a larger proportion of the machine tool's time is spent in actually machining the workpart. Although NC has a significant effect on downtime, it can do relatively little to reduce the in-process time compared to a conventional machine tool. The most promising answer for reducing the in-process time lies in the use of adaptive control (sometimes abbreviated AC). Whereas numerical control guides the sequence of tool positions or the path of the tool during machining, adaptive control determines the proper speeds and/or feeds during machining as a function of variations in such factors as work-material hardness, width or depth of cut, air gaps in the part geometry, and so on. Adaptive control has the capability to respond to and compensate for these variations during the process. Numerical control does not have this capability. Accordingly, adaptive control should be utilized in applications where the following conditions are found:

1. The in-process time consumes a significant portion of the total production time.
2. There are significant sources of variability in the job for which adaptive control can compensate. In essence, adaptive control adapts speed and/or feed to these variable conditions.

Our discussion of adaptive control in this section will be limited to its application in the machining process. We treat adaptive control strategies at a more general level in Chapter 20.

Adaptive control defined

For a machining operation, the term *adaptive control* denotes a control system that measures certain output process variables and uses these to control speed and/or feed. Some of the process variables that have been used in adaptive control machining systems include spindle deflection or force, torque, cutting temperature, vibration amplitude, and horsepower. In other words, nearly all the metal-cutting variables that can be measured have been tried in experimental adaptive control systems. The motivation for developing an adaptive machining system lies in trying to operate the process more efficiently. The typical measures of performance in machining have been metal removal rate and cost per volume of metal removed.

The chronological development of machining adaptive control has been interesting. Starting in the early 1960s, the Bendix Research Laboratories began their attempts to develop an adaptive controller that could be used for metal machining and other processes. This work was sponsored by the U.S. Air Force. At about the same time, Cincinnnati Milacron also initiated work on a similar system. What they both found was that it was extremely difficult to develop practical systems that could measure the true performance of the machining process. The reason was the general inability to measure the important process variables accurately in a machine shop environment. They also found that these initial systems were very expensive. Consequently, the adaptive control machines that were finally put into operation were somewhat less sophisticated (and less expensive) than the research adaptive systems developed earlier. The difference between the practical AC systems and the earlier research AC systems prompted the definition of two distinct forms of adaptive control for machining.

ADAPTIVE CONTROL OPTIMIZATION (ACO). These systems are represented by the early Bendix research on adaptive control machining. In this form of adaptive control, an index of performance is specified for the system. This performance index should be a measure of overall process performance, such as production rate or cost per volume of metal removed. The objective of the adaptive controller is to optimize the index of performance by manipulating speed and/or feed in the operation.

ADAPTIVE CONTROL CONSTRAINT (ACC). These are represented by the systems that were ultimately employed in production. In this form of adaptive control, constraint limits are imposed on the measured process variables. The objective of the adaptive controller is to manipulate speed and/or feed to maintain the measured variables at or below their constraint limit values.

Current-day adaptive control machining systems generally fall into the second category—adaptive control constraint systems. Basically, most ACO systems attempt to maximize the ratio of work material removal rate to tool wear rate. In other words, the index of performance is

$$IP = \text{a function of } \frac{MRR}{TWR}$$

where
$$MRR = \text{material removal rate}$$
$$TWR = \text{tool wear rate}$$

The trouble with this performance index is that TWR cannot be readily measured on-line with today's measurement technology. Hence, the IP above cannot be monitored during the process. Eventually, sensors will be developed to a level at which the true process performance can be measured on-line. When this occurs, adaptive control optimization systems will become more prominent.

It was stated previously that AC should be applied in situations in which there are significant sources of process variability. Let us consider why a machining operation might be an attractive candidate for applying adaptive control.

Sources of variability in machining

The following are the typical sources of variability in machining where adaptive control can be most advantageously applied. Not all of these sources of variability need be present to justify the use of AC. However, it follows that the greater the variability, the more suitable the process will be for using adaptive control.

1. *Variable geometry of cut in the form of changing depth or width of cut.* In these cases, feed rate is usually adjusted to compensate for the variability. This type of variability is often encountered in profile milling or contouring operations.

2. *Variable workpiece hardness and variable machinability.* When hard spots or other areas of difficulty are encountered in the workpiece, either speed or feed is reduced to avoid premature failure of the tool.

3. *Variable workpiece rigidity.* If the workpiece deflects as a result of insufficient rigidity in the setup, the feed rate must be reduced in order to maintain accuracy in the process.

4. *Tool wear.* It has been observed in research that as the tool begins to dull, the cutting forces increase. The adaptive controller will typically respond to tool dulling by reducing the feed rate.

5. *Air gaps during cutting.* The workpiece geometry may contain shaped sections where no machining needs to be performed. If the tool were to continue feeding through these so-called air gaps at the same rate, time would be lost. Accordingly, the typical procedure is to increase the feed rate, by a factor of two or three, when air gaps are encountered.

These sources of variability present themselves as time-varying and, for the most part, unpredictable changes in the machining process. We shall now examine how adaptive control can be used to compensate for these changes.

A typical adaptive control system

A typical practical application of AC is in profile or contour milling jobs on a numerical control machine using feed as the controlled variable, and spindle deflection (to measure force) or horsepower, or both, as measured variables. It is common to attach an adaptive controller to an NC machine tool. Numerical control machines are a natural starting point for AC because of two reasons. First, NC machine tools possess the required servomotors on the table axes to accept automatic control. Second, the usual kinds of machining jobs for which NC is used possess the sources of variability that make AC feasible. Several large companies have retrofitted their NC machines to incorporate AC capabilities. In fact, one company called Macotech Corporation in Seattle specializes in retrofitting for other companies.

The control strategy is of the ACC type rather than ACO type: constraint limits are established for the measured process variables. For example, if cutter deflection is the measured variable, the value of the maximum spindle deflection which the particular cutter and machine tool spindle can withstand is calculated. This value becomes the operating level of spindle deflection. Maximum production rates are obtained by running the machine at the highest feed rate consistent with this force level. Since force is dependent on such factors as depth and width of cut, the end result of the control action is to maximize metal removal rates within the limitations imposed by existing cutting conditions.

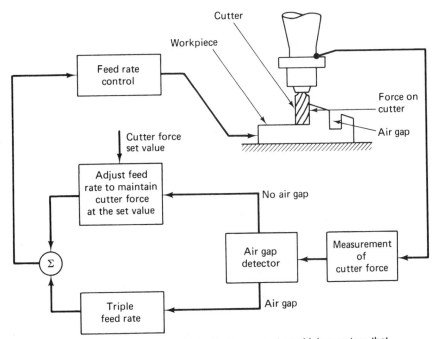

FIGURE 10.6 Configuration of typical adaptive control machining system that uses cutter force as the measured process variable.

Figure 10.6 presents a schematic diagram of the adaptive control machining system. It operates on the principle of maintaining a constant cutter force during the machining operation. When the force increases due to increased workpiece hardness or depth or width of cut, the feed rate is reduced to compensate. When the force decreases, owing to decreases in the foregoing variables or air gaps in the part, feed rate is increased to maximize the rate of metal removal.

Figure 10.6 shows the presence of an air gap override feature which monitors the cutter force and determines if the cutter is moving through air or through metal. This is usually sensed by means of a low threshold value of cutter force. If the actual cutter force is below this threshold level, the controller assumes that the cutter is passing through an air gap. When an air gap is sensed, the feed rate is doubled or tripled to minimize the time wasted traveling across the air gap. When the cutter reengages metal on the other side of the gap, the feed reverts back to the cutter force mode of control.

More than one process variable may be measured in an adaptive control machining system. Originally, attempts were made to employ three measured signals in the Bendix system: temperature, torque, and vibration. The Macotech system has used both cutter load and horsepower generated at the machine motor. The purpose of the power sensor is to protect the motor from overload when metal removal rate is constrained by spindle horsepower rather than spindle force.

Benefits of adaptive control in machining

A number of potential benefits accrue to the user of an adaptive control machine tool. The advantage gained will depend on the particular job under consideration. There are obviously many machining situations for which adaptive control cannot be justified.

1. *Increased production rates.* Productivity improvement was the motivating force behind the development of adaptive control machining. On-line adjustments to allow for variations in work geometry, material, and tool wear provide the machine tool with the capability to achieve the highest metal removal rates that are consistent with existing conditions. This capability translates into more parts per hour. Given the right application, adaptive control will yield significant gains in production rate compared to conventional

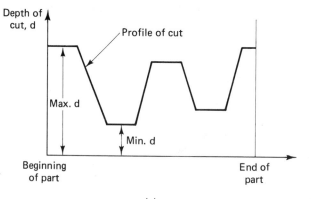

(a)

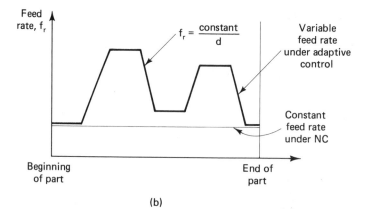

(b)

FIGURE 10.7 Illustration of adaptive control production rate benefit: (a) profile of a surface to be milled showing variation in depth of cut; (b) alternative feed rates with numerical control and adaptive control. Higher feed rate with adaptive control reduces time of cut by approximately 33%.

TABLE 10.1 Comparison of Metal-Cutting Times—Conventional NC versus Low-Cost Retrofitable Adaptive Control (LCRAC)

	Metal-cutting time (min)			
	NC *time*	*LCRAC* *time*	*Savings*	*Percent*
Aluminum				
Phase I	21	18	3	14
Phase II	83	49	34	41
Phase III	381	248	133	37
Total aluminum	485	315	170	35%
Steel				
Phase I	289	202	87	30
Phase II	102	75	27	26
Phase III	1151	731	400	35
Total steel	1542	1028	514	33%
Titanium				
Phase I	182	113	66	36
Phase II	72	37	34	48
Phase III	338	168	170	50
Total titanium	591	318	273	46%
Program total	2618	1661	957	37%

Source: Reference [15].

machining or numerical control. The potential for improvement in production rate is illustrated in Figure 10.7.

　　2. *Increased tool life*. In addition to higher production rates, adaptive control will generally provide a more efficient and uniform use of the cutter throughout its tool life. Because adjustments are made in the feed rate to prevent severe loading of the tool, fewer cutters will be broken.

　　3. *Greater part protection*. Instead of setting the cutter force constraint limit on the basis of maximum allowable cutter and spindle deflection, the force limit can be established on the basis of work size tolerance. In this way, the part is protected against an out-of-tolerance condition and possible damage.

　　4. *Less operator intervention*. The advent of adaptive control machining has transferred the control of the process even further out of the hands of the operator and into the hands of management via the part programmer.

　　5. *Easier part programming*. A benefit of adaptive control which is not so obvious concerns the task of part programming. With ordinary numerical control, the programmer must plan the speed and feed for the worst conditions that the cutter will encounter. He or she may have to try out the program several times before being satisfied with the choice of cutting conditions. In adaptive control part programming, the selection of feed is pretty much left to the controller unit rather than to the part programmer. The constraint limit on force, horsepower, or other variable must be determined according to the particular job and cutter used. However, this can often be calculated from known parameters for the programmer by the system software. In general, the part programmer's task requires

a much less conservative approach than for numerical control. Less time is needed to generate the tape for a job, and fewer tryouts are necessary.

Several years ago a study was conducted for the U.S. Air Force to quantitatively evaluate the advantages of adaptive control over conventional NC machining [15]. The test was performed using a low-cost retrofitable adaptive control (LCRAC) system whose control mode was similar to that described earlier in this section as a typical AC system. The study was divided into three sequential stages, each of which compared the AC system against conventional NC. Different test parts and machines were used in the three stages. Parts were made of aluminum, steel, and titanium. Table 10.1 is taken from the report and shows the overall savings from adaptive control to be 37%. When adaptive control machining is applied to appropriate jobs, the economic savings can be substantial.

10.5 CURRENT TRENDS IN NC

It seems appropriate to summarize these three chapters on numerical control by discussing some of the current trends in the technology and what the future might hold.

The direct numerical control systems that were marketed in the late 1960s and early 1970s were extremely expensive. Their high cost, combined with an unfavorable economic climate at that time, caused businessmen to resist the temptation to plunge into the new DNC technology. Also, the DNC systems available then were somewhat rigid in terms of management reporting formats and hardware requirements. The more recent advent of CNC systems, together with lower-cost computers and improvements in software, have resulted in the development of hierarchical computer systems in manufacturing. In these hierarchical systems, CNC computers have direct control over the production machines and report to satellite computers, which in turn report to other computers, and so on. There are advantages to this hierarchical approach over the DNC packages that were offered around 1970. The common theme in these advantages is flexibility. The information system can be tailored to the specific needs and desires of the firm. This contrasts with many of the early DNC systems, in which the reporting formats were fixed, in some cases providing more data than management wanted and in other cases omitting details that management needed. Another advantage of the hierarchy approach is the ability to gradually build the system instead of implementing the entire DNC configuration all at once. This piece-by-piece installation of the computer-integrated manufacturing system is a more versatile and economic approach. It permits changes and corrections to be made more easily as the system is being built. It also allows the company to spread the cost of the system over a longer time period and to obtain benefits from each subsystem as it is installed. The hierarchical computer arrangement embraces the DNC philosophy, which is to provide useful reports on production operations to management in real time. One might say that DNC has not really been replaced by this new approach; it has simply altered its physical form.

The evolution of the hierarchical control configuration, in which the machine tool MCUs are connected to a central plant computer and the controllers are themselves CNC units, has an architecture very similar to direct numerical control. To distinguish this configuration from direct numerical control, the term *distributed numerical control* is used. The difference is simply in the presence of the CNC controllers in the hierarchy to replace the hard-wired MCU. Today, distributed numerical control represents the generally accepted approach for central computer control of NC machine tools. In present usage, the initials DNC refer to this more modern control configuration.

Improvements in machine tool technology have enhanced the concept of the NC machining center to include the use of large capacity part storage systems connected to the machine tool. These part storage systems represent an extension of the pallet shuttles described in Section 8.5. The storage system may contain a dozen or more part positions together with a transfer mechanism for loading and unloading the parts at the machine spindle. This permits the storage system to be loaded with raw parts at the beginning of a work shift and for these parts to be machined in sequence during the shift with no human operators in attendance. After each part is completed it is placed back in the storage system. The name given to this type of operation is *untended machining*. The Japanese have exploited the use of untended machining to allow production to be accomplished overnight with no operators present. The term *unmanned machining* is also used sometimes in reference to this mode of operation.

Another development in DNC and CNC is the flexible *manufacturing system* (FMS). An FMS is a group of NC machine tools or other automated workstations connected together by a materials handling and storage system and controlled by a computer. It represents an attempt to combine the flexibility of NC with the efficiency of automated flow lines. Flexible manufacturing systems are discussed in Chapter 17.

Finally, a technology related to numerical control is robotics. Industrial robotics borrows much of the control technology of NC but assumes an entirely different anatomical form to accomplish work that is traditionally performed by human beings. The following three chapters focus on the subject of industrial robotics.

REFERENCES

[1] BURGAM, P. M., "Two Tools for the Eighties: Machining Centers and Adaptive Control," *Manufacturing Engineering,* May 1984, pp . 56–60.

[2] GROOVER, M. P., "A New Look at Adaptive Control," *Automation,* April 1973, pp. 60–63.

[3] GROOVER, M. P., "Adaptive Control and Adaptive Control Machining," *Educational Modules,* MAPEC, Copyright Purdue Research Foundation, 1977.

[4] GROOVER, M. P., and E. W. ZIMMERS, Jr., *CAD/CAM: Computer-Aided Design and Manufacturing,* Prentice-Hall, Inc., Englewood Cliffs, N.J., 1984, Chapter 9.

[5] HARRINGTON, J., *Computer Integrated Manufacturing,* Industrial Press, Inc., New York, 1973.

[6] HATSCHEK, R. L., "NC Diagnostics," Special Report 744, *American Machinist,* February 1984, pp. 95–114.

[7] MATHIAS, R. A., "Adaptive Control for the Eighties," *Technical Paper MS80-242*, Society of Manufacturing Enginners, Dearborn, Mich., 1980.

[8] MATHIAS, R. A., "Determining Where Adaptive Control Can Most Benefit Your Machining Operations," *Technical Paper MS81-272*, Society of Manufacturing Engineers, Dearborn, Mich., 1981.

[9] *Modern Machine Shop 1985 NC/CAM Guidebook*, Gardner Publications, Inc., Cincinnati, Ohio, January 1985, Chapter 2.

[10] NASTALI, W. F., "Machine Controls: Smarter Than Ever," *Manufacturing Engineering*, January 1986, pp. 46–49.

[11] OGOREK, M., "CNC Standard Formats," *Manufacturing Engineering*, January 1985, pp. 43–45.

[12] PRESSMAN, R. S., and J. E. WILLIAMS, *Numerical Control and Computer-Aided Manufacturing*, John Wiley & Sons, Inc., New York, 1977, Chapter 10.

[13] SCHAFFER, G. H., "Getting the Most out of DNC," *American Machinist*, July 1985, pp. 83–85.

[14] SMITH, D. N., and L. EVANS, *Management Standards for Computer and Numerical Controls*, The University of Michigan Press, Ann Arbor, Mich., 1977.

[15] WHETHAM, W. J., "Low Cost Adaptive Control Unit Manufacturing Methods," *Technical Report AFML-TR-73-263*, Manufacturing Technology Division, Air Force Materials Laboratory, Air Force Systems Command, November 1973.

PROBLEMS

10.1. Discuss the probable suitability of adaptive control in each of the following machining situations:

(a) Drilling a series of 10-mm-diameter holes in aluminum. Each hole is to be 20 mm deep.

(b) Peripheral milling at a depth of cut of 3.0 mm across a steel bar of rectangular cross section. The steel is C1020. The dimensions of the bar are: length = 1.0 m, cross section 50 mm by 90 mm.

(c) End milling a cast-iron casting where there are several flats to be milled at various depths of cut. The casting is a gearbox housing for a piece of earthmoving machinery.

10.2. A milling cut is to be taken across a workpiece that is 500 mm long. The average depth of cut along this length is 5 mm and the maximum depth is 8 mm. If the job is machined using NC, the feed rate must be set according to worst-case conditions for the maximum depth throughout the entire length. But if the job is done using adaptive control, the feed rate will be adjusted throughout the 500-mm length for differences in depth of cut. The feed rate will be changed in an inverse relationship to depth as provided by the following equation:

$$f = \frac{10}{d}$$

where f = feed rate, mm/s

d = depth of cut, mm

Hence, the feed rate using NC would be 1.25 mm/s throughout the entire length. The feed rate under adaptive control would average 2 mm/s but would vary, reaching as low a value as 1.25 mm/s when the depth was 8 mm. Determine how long the job would take to mill under each of the two alternatives: NC versus adaptive control.

10.3. A workpiece is to be machined in an end-milling operation. Thirty separate cuts are to be made on the piece, at various depths of cut. The accompanying table gives the number of cuts made at each depth, together with the cumulative length of cut at each depth.

Number of cuts	Depth of cut (mm)	Total length of cut (mm)
7	3	400
5	10	200
12	5	250
6	1	150
29	Air gaps	600

The air gaps occur both as a result of the workpiece geometry and when the tool is being positioned for the next cut.

If the workpiece is machined using NC, the feed rate would be set to allow for worst-case conditions (depth of cut = 10 mm). A feed rate of 1 mm/s would be used throughout the piece, including the air gaps.

If the workpiece is machined using adaptive control, the feed rate would be changed throughout the sequence of cuts according to depth. The control system monitors cutting force at the cutter and adjusts feed inversely with force as provided in the following equation:

$$f = \frac{1000}{F_c}$$

where f = feed rate, mm/s

   F_c = cutter force, newtons (N)

   1000 = cutter force set value for this cutter

The cutting force F_c is assumed to vary directly with depth of cut as follows:
$$F_c = 100d$$

where d is depth of cut in millimeters. During air gaps the control system is programmed to feed the cutter at 15 mm/s.

(a) Determine how long the job would take to machine using NC.

(b) Determine how long the job would take to machine using adaptive control.

(c) What are the percent savings in time, adaptive control versus NC?

(d) Assume that the NC system could be programmed to account for the presence of air gaps so that the cutter could feed through air at 15 mm/s. How would this affect the total machining time under NC? (*Note:* In your computations for this problem, ignore the effects of machine tool dynamics.)

10.4. In Problem 10.2 or 10.3, explain how an increase in the variability of depth of cut gives adaptive control the advantage over NC. If there were no variation in depth throughout the workpiece in these problems, would there be any advantage in using adaptive control?

10.5. An existing NC machine is being considered as a retrofit candidate for adaptive control. Retrofitting will cost $20,000. It is estimated that there will be a 37% average savings in machining time using adaptive control compared to the existing NC machining time. This estimate is based on the U.S. Air Force LCRAC Report [15]. The NC machine is currently operated three shifts—6000 h/yr. Time on the machine costs $25/h. The average job performed on this machine takes 100 h to complete and has a revenue value to the company of $3000/job. Of the 100/h/job, 60% represents nonproductive time, including setups, workpiece changing, and so on. The AC retrofitting will have no effect on this nonproductive time. The remaining average 40 h/job is machining time. The average programming cost per job is $300. It is estimated that there will be no change in programming cost per job if the retrofit is made.

(a) How much profit per job, if any, is the company currently making on the NC machine? Ignore any consideration of overhead costs not included in the data given above.

(b) Determine the increase in the number of jobs that can be run on the machine if the NC machine is retrofitted with adaptive control.

(c) Will the AC retrofit pay for itself in the first year of operation?

part **IV**

Industrial Robotics

Closely related to numerical control is the field of industrial robotics. Robotics is another example of programmable automation in production systems. In numerical control, a program of instructions is used to control the relative movement of machine tool axes. A robot also requires a program to control and coordinate the movement of its axes. The difference is that a robot has a mechanical arm that moves rather than a set of machine tool slides. This part of the book consists of three chapters which are concerned with the technology, programming, and applications of industrial robots.

Chapter 11 is devoted to robotics technology. How are robots constructed (robot anatomy)? How do they work (controls)? What are they capable of doing (accuracy, repeatability, speed, load-carrying capacity)? In Chapter 11 we also consider some of the related technical issues such as the robot's hands (called "end effectors") and sensors that are required to enable the robot to perform useful work.

Chapter 12 deals with the programming of robots. Robot programming involves the "teaching" of the work cycle to the robot. The work cycle consists of the motions and other actions that the robot must do to accomplish a given application. These motions and actions are usually repeated in exactly the same way every cycle. The teaching of the work cycle can be done in several ways, and we discuss the methods in this chapter. Some of the methods are very much like computer programming.

A robot program frequently requires control not only of the robot itself, but the other pieces of equipment that work together with the robot in the production cell. Controlling the various components of the workcell is referred to as workcell control. In Chapter 12 we discuss the topic of workcell control and how it is accomplished in robot programming.

In Chapter 13 we survey the variety of applications of industrial robots. These applications include material handling, machine loading, spot welding, spray painting, and assembly. We also examine the characteristics of potential applications that tend to support the use of industrial robots.

chapter 11

Robotics Technology

An industrial robot is a general-purpose, programmable machine possessing certain anthropomorphic characteristics. In present-day robots, the most obvious anthropomorphic characteristic is the robot's mechanical arm, which is used for performing various industrial tasks. Less obvious humanlike characteristics are the robot's capability to make decisions, respond to sensory inputs, and communicate with other machines. These capabilities permit robots to perform a variety of useful tasks in industry. Typical robot applications include spot welding, material transfer, machine loading, spray painting, and assembly.

The definition of an *industrial robot* given by the Robotics Industries Association (RIA) is the following:

> An industrial robot is a reprogrammable, multifunctional manipulator designed to move materials, parts, tools, or special devices through variable programmed motions for the performance of a variety of tasks.

According to this definition, robots can be classified as programmable automation.

11.1   ROBOT ANATOMY

The manipulator of an industrial robot is constructed of a series of joints and links. Robot anatomy deals with the types and sizes of these joints and links and other aspects of the manipulator's physical construction.

Joints and links

A joint of an industrial robot is similar to a joint in the human body; it provides relative motion between two parts of the body. Each joint provides the robot with a so-called *degree of freedom* (d.o.f.) of motion. In nearly all cases, only 1 d.o.f. is associated with a joint. Future robots may be designed with joints having more than 1 degree of freedom each. Robots are often classified according to the total number of degrees of freedom they possess. Connected to each joint are two links, one which we call the *input link,* the other called the *output link*. Links are considered to be the rigid components of the robot. The purpose of the joint is to provide controlled relative movement between the input link and the output link.

Nearly all industrial robots have mechanical joints that can be classified into one of five types. They include two types that provide linear motion and three types that provide rotary motion. These joint types are illustrated in Figure 11.1 and are based on a scheme described in reference [5]. The five joint types are:

1.   *Linear joint*.   The relative movement between the input link and the output link is a linear sliding motion, with the axes of the two links being parallel. We refer to this as a *type L joint*.

2.   *Orthogonal joint*.   This is also a linear sliding motion, but the input and output links are perpendicular to each other during the move. This is a *type O joint*.

3.   *Rotational joint*.   This type provides a rotational relative motion of the joints, with the axis of rotation perpendicular to the axes of the input and output links. This is a *type R joint*.

4.   *Twisting joint*.   This joint also involves a rotary motion, but the axis of rotation is parallel to the axes of the two links. We call this a *type T joint*.

5.   *Revolving joint*.   In this joint type, the axis of the input link is parallel to the axis of rotation of the joint, and the axis of the output link is perpendicular to the axis of rotation. We refer to this as a *type V joint* (V from the "v" in revolving).

Each of these joint types has a range over which it can be moved. A typical range for a linear joint may be from several inches to several feet. The three types of joints which involve rotary motion may have a range as small as a few degrees or as large as several complete turns.

Most robots are mounted on a stationary base on the floor. We shall refer to that base and its connection to the first joint as link O. It is the input link to joint 1, the first in the series of joints used in the construction of the robot. The output link of joint 1 is

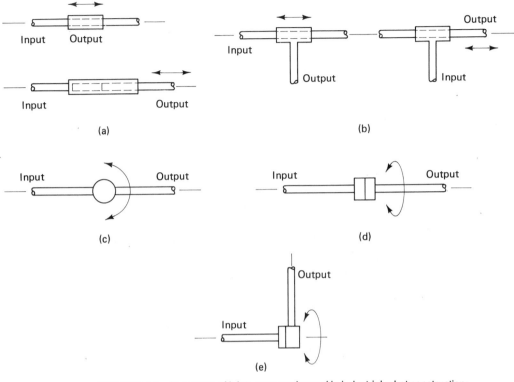

FIGURE 11.1 Five types of joints commonly used in industrial robot construction: (a) two forms of linear joint—type L; (b) two forms of orthogonal joint—type 0; (c) rotational joint—type R; (d) twisting joint—type T; (e) revolving joint—type V.

link 1. Link 1 is the input link to joint 2, whose output link is link 2, and so on. This joint–link numbering scheme is pictured in Figure 11.2.

A typical robot manipulator can be divided into two sections: a body-and-arm assembly, and a wrist assembly. There are usually 3 degrees of freedom associated with the body-and-arm, and either 2 or 3 degrees of freedom usually associated with the wrist. At the end of the manipulator's wrist is an object that is related to the task that must be accomplished by the robot. For example, the object might be a workpart that is to be loaded into a machine, or a tool that is manipulated to perform some process. The body-and-arm of the robot is used to position the object and the robot's wrist is used to orient the object.

To establish the position of the object, the body-and-arm must be capable of moving the object in any of the following three directions:

1. Vertical motion (z-axis motion)
2. Radial motion (in-and-out or y-axis motion)
3. Right-to-left motion (x-axis motion or swivel about a vertical axis on the base)

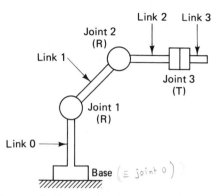

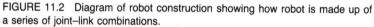

FIGURE 11.2 Diagram of robot construction showing how robot is made up of a series of joint–link combinations.

Depending on the types of joints used to construct the body-and-arm, there are a variety of different ways to accomplish these motions. We examine the various joint combinations in the following subsection.

To establish the orientation of the object, we can define 3 degrees of freedom for the robot's wrist. The following is one possible configuration for a 3 d.o.f. wrist assembly:

1. *Roll.* This d.o.f. can be accomplished by a T-type joint to rotate the object about the arm axis.

2. *Pitch.* This involves the up-and-down rotation of the object, typically done by means of a type R joint.

3. *Yaw.* This involves right-to-left rotation of the object, also accomplished typically using an R-type joint.

These definitions are illustrated in Figure 11.3. To avoid complications in the pitch and yaw definitions, the wrist roll should be assumed in its center position. To illustrate the

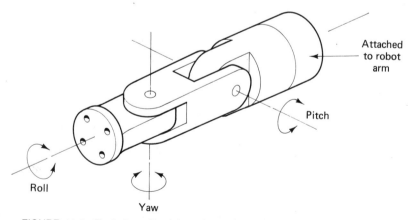

FIGURE 11.3 Typical configuration of a 3-degree-of-freedom wrist assembly showing roll, pitch, and yaw.

possible confusion, a type R joint which provides an up-and-down rotation if the wrist roll is in its center position would provide a right-to-left rotation if the roll position were 90° from the center.

We can use the letter symbols for the five joint types (i.e., L, O, R, T, and V) to define a joint notation system for the robot manipulator. In this notation system, the manipulator is described by the joint types that make up the body-and-arm assembly, followed by the joint symbols that make up the wrist. For example, the notation TLR:TR represents a 5-d.o.f. manipulator whose body-and-arm is made up of a twisting joint (joint 1), a linear joint (joint 2), and a rotational joint (joint 3). The wrist consists of two joints, a twisting joint (joint 4) and a rotational joint (joint 5). A colon separates the body-and-arm notation from the wrist notation.

Common robot configurations

Given the five types of joint defined above, there are $5 \times 5 \times 5 = 125$ different combinations of joints that can be used to design the body-and-arm assembly for a 3-d.o.f. robot manipulator. This does not even consider variations in design within the individual joint types (e.g., sizes, ranges of motion, orientation, etc.), or that the body-and-arm might have more than or fewer than three joints. It is somewhat remarkable, therefore, that there are only about five basic configurations commonly available in commercial industrial robots. These five configurations are:

1. *Polar configuration.* This configuration has a TRL notation. A sliding arm (type L joint) is actuated relative to the body, which can rotate about both a vertical axis (type T joint) and a horizontal axis (type R joint). This configuration is pictured in Figure 11.4.

2. *Cylindrical configuration.* This robot configuration consists of a vertical column, relative to which an arm assembly can be moved up and down. The end-of-arm can be moved in and out relative to the axis of the column. This configuration can be realized structurally in several ways. The possibilities include TLO and LVL. The first of these constructions is illustrated in Figure 11.5.

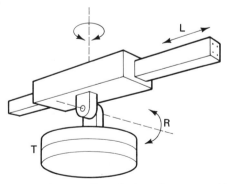

FIGURE 11.4   Polar coordinate body-and-arm assembly (TRL).

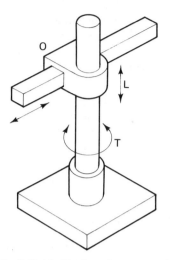

FIGURE 11.5   Cylindrical body-and-arm assembly (TLO).

    3.   *Cartesian coordinate robot.*   Other names for this configuration include rectilinear robot and *x-y-z* robot. As shown in Figure 11.6, it is composed of three sliding joints, two of which are orthogonal. The sketch in the figure shows a LOO notation. Another possible notation is OLO.

    4.   *Jointed-arm robot.*   This robot has the general configuration of a human arm. Its arm has a shoulder joint and an elbow joint, and the arm can be swiveled about the

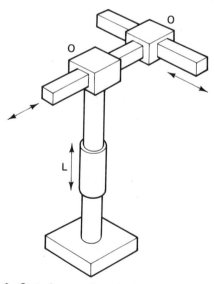

FIGURE 11.6   Cartesian coordinate body-and-arm assembly (LOO).

base. Possible configurations for this type include TRR and VVR. The TRR type is pictured in Figure 11.7.

5. *SCARA.* SCARA is an acronym for Selective Compliance Assembly Robot Arm. This is similar to the jointed arm robot except that the shoulder and elbow rotational axes are vertical. This means that the arm can be constructed to be very rigid in the vertical direction, but compliant in the horizontal direction. This permits the robot to perform insertion tasks (for assembly) in a vertical direction where some side-to-side adjustment may be needed to mate the two parts properly. One possible notation for a SCARA would be VRO, as indicated in Figure 11.8.

The SCARA robot is unique in that it typically does not have a separate wrist assembly. As indicated in our description, it is used for insertion-type assembly operations in which the insertion is made from above. Accordingly, the orientation requirements are minimal and the wrist is therefore not needed. Rotational orientation of the object to be inserted about a vertical axis is sometimes required, and an additional rotation joint is provided for this purpose. This can be indicated by the notation VROT.

The other four body-and-arm configurations possess wrist assemblies that almost

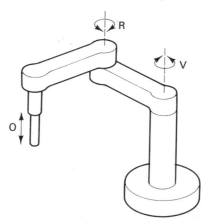

— all joints here have a rotary motion

FIGURE 11.7   Jointed-arm body-and-arm assembly (TRR).

FIGURE 11.8   SCARA body-and-arm assembly (VRO).

always consist of combinations of rotational joints of types R and T. Typical wrist configurations include TR and TRR. The TRR configuration is illustrated in Figure 11.3.

Work volume

The *work volume* of the manipulator is defined as the envelope or space within which the robot can manipulate the end of its wrist. It is sometimes referred to by the term *work envelope*. Work volume is determined by the number and types of joints in the manipulator (body-and-arm and wrist), the physical size of the joints and links, and the ranges of the various joints.

The shape of the work volume depends largely on the type of robot configuration. A polar configuration tends to have a partial sphere as its work volume; a cylindrical robot has a cylindrical work envelope; and a Cartesian coordinate robot has a rectangular work space.

11.2   ROBOT CONTROL SYSTEMS

The actions of the individual joints must be controlled in order for the manipulator to perform a desired motion cycle. In this section we survey the types of drive systems and the associated control systems used in robotics.

Drive systems

The joints are moved by actuators powered by a particular form of drive system. Common drive systems used in robotics are electric drive, hydraulic drive, and pneumatic drive. Electric drive systems make use of electric motors as joint actuators (e.g., dc servomotors and stepping motors, the same general types of motors used in numerical control machine tools discussed in Chapter 8). Hydraulic and pneumatic drive systems use devices such as linear pistons and rotary vane actuators to accomplish the motion of the joint.

Pneumatic drive is typically reserved for smaller robots used in simple material transfer applications. Both electric drive and hydraulic drive are used on more sophisticated industrial robots. Electric drive systems are becoming more prevalent in commercially available robots. They are more readily adaptable to computer control, the predominant technology used today for robot controllers. Electric drive robots are relatively accurate compared to hydraulically powered robots. By contrast, the advantages of hydraulic drive include greater speed and strength.

The type of drive system, actuators, position sensors (and speed sensors if used), and feedback control systems for the joints determine the dynamic response characteristics of the manipulator. The speed with which the robot can achieve a programmed position and the stability of its motion are two important characteristics of dynamic response in robotics. The speed of response is important because it influences the robot's cycle time. This will determine the production rate in the robot application. The *stability* of the robot refers to the amount of overshoot and oscillation that occurs in the robot motion as it attempts to reach a certain location. More oscillation in the motion is an indication of less stability. The problem is that robots with greater stability are inherently slower in their response.

Types of robot control

Control over each joint is achieved by means of the types of feedback controls that are described in Part VIII. A microprocessor-based controller is commonly used today in robotics as the control system hardware. The controller is organized in a hierarchical structure as indicated in Figure 11.9, so that each joint has its own feedback control system, and a supervisory controller coordinates the combined actuations of the joints and sequences the motions according to the sequence of the robot program.

According to the level of sophistication of the robot controller, it can be classified into one of the following four categories [5]:

1. *Limited-sequence robot.* This is the most elementary control type and can be utilized only for simple motion cycles, such as pick-and-place operations (i.e., picking an object up at one location and placing it at another location). It is usually implemented by setting limits or mechanical stops for each joint and sequencing the actuation of the joints to accomplish the cycle. Feedback loops are sometimes used to indicate that the particular joint actuation has been accomplished so that the next step in the sequence can be initiated. However, there is no servo control to accomplish precise positioning of the joint. Many pneumatically driven robots are limited-sequence robots.

2. *Playback robot with point-to-point control.* Playback robots represent a more sophisticated form of control than limited-sequence robots. In these systems, the controller has a memory for recording not only the sequence of the motions in a given work cycle, but also the locations that are associated with each element of the motion cycle. These locations and their sequence are programmed into memory, and subsequently played back during the operation. It is this playback feature that gives the control type its name. In point-to-point (PTP) control, individual positions of the robot arm are recorded into memory. These positions are not limited to the mechanical stops set for each joint as in

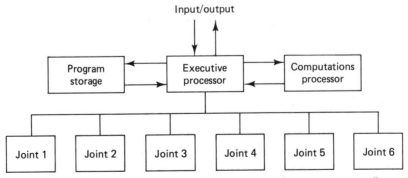

FIGURE 11.9 Hierarchical control structure of a robot microcomputer controller.

the case of limited-sequence robots. Feedback control is used during the motion cycle to ascertain that the individual joints have achieved the desired locations defined in the program.

3. *Playback robot with continuous-path control.* These robots have the same playback capability as the previous type; however, the number of individual locations that can be recorded into memory is far greater than for point-to-point. This means that the points constituting the motion cycle can be spaced very closely together, which permits the robot to accomplish a smooth continuous motion. In PTP, only the final location of the individual motion elements are controlled; the path taken by the arm to reach the final location is not controlled. In a continuous-path motion, the movement of the arm and wrist is controlled during the motion. Servo control is used to maintain continuous control over the position and speed of the manipulator. A playback robot with continuous-path control has the inherent capacity for PTP control as well.

4. *Intelligent robots.* Industrial robots are becoming more and more intelligent. In this context, an intelligent robot is one that exhibits behavior that makes it seem intelligent. Some of the characteristics that make a robot appear intelligent include the capacity to interact with its environment, make decisions when things go wrong during the work cycle, communicate with human beings, make computations during the motion cycle, and operate in response to advanced sensor inputs such as machine vision. In addition, these robots possess the playback capability for either PTP or continuous path control. These features require a relatively high level of computer control and an advanced programming language in order to input the decision-making logic and other "intelligence" into memory.

In Chapter 12 we consider how these various categories of robot control systems are programmed. Let us next consider robot accuracy and repeatability, which are closely associated with the control issue.

11.3 ACCURACY AND REPEATABILITY

The capacity of the robot to position and orient the end of its wrist with accuracy and repeatability is an important control attribute in nearly all industrial applications. Some assembly applications require that objects be located with a precision of only 0.002 to 0.005 in. Other applications, such as spot welding, usually require accuracies of 0.020 to 0.040 in. Let us examine the question of how a robot is able to move its various joints to achieve accurate and repeatable positioning. There are several terms that must be defined in the context of this discussion:

1. Control resolution
2. Accuracy
3. Repeatability

These terms have the same basic meanings in robotics that they have in numerical control as defined in Chapter 8. In robotics, the characteristics should be defined at the end of the wrist and in the absence of any object held or attached at the wrist.

Control resolution refers to the capability of the robot's controller and positioning system to divide the range of the joint into closely spaced points that can be identified by the controller. These are called *addressable points* because they represent locations to which the robot can be commanded to move. Recall from Chapter 8 that the capability to divide the range into addressable points is a function of the controller's bit storage capacity for that joint. If n is the number of bits devoted to a particular joint, the number of addressable points in that joint's range of motion is given by

$$\text{number of addressable points} = 2^n$$

The control resolution is therefore defined as the distance between adjacent addressable points. This can be determined as

$$CR = \frac{\text{joint range}}{2^n}$$

This equation considers only a single joint of the robot. A related term in robotics is the *spatial resolution,* which combines the control resolution with the mechanical errors in the joint and associated links. The mechanical errors arise from such factors as gear backlash, deflection of the links, hydraulic fluid leaks, and a variety of other sources. If we characterize the mechanical errors by a normal distribution, as we did in Chapter 8, spatial resolution is defined in terms of the standard deviation as

$$SR = CR + 6(\text{std. dev. of mech. error})$$

The complete spatial resolution for the manipulator would include the effect of all of the joints, combined with the effect of their mechanical errors. For a multiple-degree-of-freedom robot, the spatial resolution will vary depending on where in the work volume the wrist end is positioned. The reason for this is that certain joint combinations will tend to magnify the effect of the control resolution and the mechanical errors. For example, for a polar configuration robot (TRL) with its linear joint fully extended, any errors in the R or T joints will be larger than when the linear joint is fully retracted.

Accuracy is a measure of the robot's ability to position the end of its wrist at a desired location in the work volume. By the same reasoning used to define accuracy in our discussion of numerical control,

$$\text{accuracy} = \frac{CR}{2} + 3(\text{std. dev. of mech. error})$$

In terms of the spatial resolution, accuracy can be defined as

$$\text{accuracy} = \frac{SR}{2}$$

Repeatability is a measure of the robot's ability to position its end-of-wrist at a previously taught point in the work volume. Each time the robot attempts to return to the programmed point it will return to a slightly different position. Repeatability errors have as their principal source the mechanical errors previously mentioned. Therefore, as in NC,

$$\text{repeatability} = \pm 3(\text{std. dev. of mech. error})$$

Control resolution, accuracy, and repeatability are illustrated in Figure 8.12. In the figure the distribution is shown as having a single dimension. Robots move in three-dimensional space, and the distribution of repeatability errors is therefore three-dimensional. In three dimensions we can conceptualize the normal distribution as a sphere whose center (mean) is at the programmed point and whose radius is equal to 3 standard deviations of the repeatability error distribution. For conciseness, repeatability is usually expressed in terms of the radius of the sphere (e.g., ± 0.030 in.). Some of today's small assembly robots have repeatability values that are as low as ± 0.002 in.

EXAMPLE 11.1

One of the joints of a certain industrial robot is a type L joint with a range of 0.5 m. The bit storage capacity of the robot controller is 10 bits for this joint. The mechanical errors form a normally distributed random variable about a given taught point. The mean of the distribution is zero and the standard deviation is 0.06 mm. The errors will be assumed to be isotropic (the same in all directions). Determine the control resolution, the spatial resolution, the accuracy, and the repeatability for this robot.

Solution:

The number of addressable points in the joint range is $2^{10} = 1024$. The control resolution is therefore

$$CR = \frac{0.50 \text{ m}}{1024} = 0.4883 \text{ mm}$$

This is approximately 0.0192 in. The spatial resolution is the sum of the control resolution and the mechanical errors.

$$SR = CR + 6(\text{std. dev. of mech. error})$$

$$= 0.4883 + 6(0.06) = 0.8483 \text{ mm } (0.0334 \text{ in.})$$

The accuracy = one/half the spatial resolution.

$$\text{accuracy} = \frac{0.8483}{2} = 0.42415 \text{ mm } (0.0167 \text{ in.})$$

Repeatability is defined as ± 3 standard deviations:

$$\text{repeatability} = 3 \times 0.06 = 0.18 \text{ mm}$$

The repeatability is ± 0.18 mm (0.0071 in.), or a total of 6 standard deviations = 0.36 mm.

In reality, the shape of the error distribution will not be a perfect sphere in three dimensions. In other words, the errors will not be isotropic as assumed in the example. Instead, the radius will vary because the associated mechanical errors will be different in certain directions than others. The mechanical arm of a robot is more rigid in certain directions, and this rigidity influences the errors. Also, the so-called sphere will not remain constant in size throughout the robot's work volume. As with spatial resolution it will be affected by the particular combination of joint positions of the manipulator. In some regions of the work volume the repeatability errors will be larger than in other regions. We take these imperfections in our repeatability definition into account by assuming that worst-case conditions apply for defining repeatability.

Accuracy and repeatability have been defined above as static parameters of the manipulator. However, these precision parameters are affected by the dynamic operation of the robot. Such characteristics as speed, payload, and direction of approach will affect the robot's accuracy and repeatability [9].

11.4 OTHER SPECIFICATIONS

Repeatability is a specification that is often cited in the marketing literature of robot firms. Other specifications that should be mentioned are speed and load-carrying capacity.

The speed of movement of an industrial robot is an important factor in determining work cycle time. The upper speed of a large robot might be as high as 2 m/s. The speed can be programmed into the work cycle so that different portions of the cycle are carried out at different velocities. What is sometimes more important than speed is the robot's capability to accelerate and decelerate in a controlled manner. In many work cycles, much of the robot's movement is performed in a confined area of the work volume; hence, the robot never achieves its top-rated velocity. In these cases, nearly all of the motion cycle is engaged in acceleration and deceleration rather than in constant speed.

Other factors that influence the speed of the motion cycle are the weight (mass) of the object that is being manipulated and the precision with which the object must be located at the end of a given move.

The load-carrying capacity of the robot is dependent on its physical size and construction and by the force and power that can be transmitted to the end of the wrist. The weight-carrying capacity of commercial robots ranges from about 1 lb to approximately 2000 lb. Medium-sized robots designed for typical industrial applications have capacities in the range 25 to 100 lb.

One factor that should be kept in mind when considering load-carrying capacities is that robots usually work with tools or grippers attached to their wrists. Grippers are designed to grasp and move objects about the workcell. The net load-carrying capacity of the robot is obviously reduced by the weight of the gripper. If the robot is rated at a 25-lb capacity and the weight of the gripper is 10 lb, the net weight-carrying capacity is reduced to 15 lb.

11.5   END EFFECTORS

The tools and grippers mentioned in the preceding section are called end effectors. An *end effector* is defined as the special device that attaches to the manipulator's wrist to enable the robot to accomplish a specific task. Because of the wide variations in tasks that are performed by industrial robots, the end effector must usually be custom engineered and fabricated for a specified job. In the case of a gripper the part shape and size will vary for different applications; this will influence the design of the gripper.

Tools and grippers are the two general categories of end effectors used in robotics. Tools are used in applications where the robot must perform some processing operation on the workpart. The robot therefore manipulates the tool relative to a stationary or slowly moving object (e.g., workpart, subassembly, etc.). Examples of the tools used as end effectors by robots to perform processing applications include:

- Spot welding gun
- Arc welding tool
- Spray painting gun
- Rotating spindle for drilling, routing, grinding, etc.
- Assembly tool (e.g., automatic screwdriver)
- Heating torch
- Water-jet cutting tool

In each case the robot must not only control the relative position of the tool with respect to the work as a function of time, it must also control the operation of the tool. For this purpose, the robot must be able to transmit control signals to the tool for starting, stopping, and otherwise regulating its actions.

Grippers are end effectors used to grasp and manipulate objects during the work cycle. The objects are usually workparts that are moved from one location to another in the cell. Machine loading and unloading applications fall into this category. Other objects that can be handled by grippers include tools. When tools are held by grippers rather than being attached directly to the wrist end, it is because more than one tool is to be manipulated during the work cycle. The gripper takes the form of a fast-change toolholder for quickly fastening and unfastening the various tools used during the cycle.

Examples of grippers used as end effectors in industrial robot applications include the following:

- Mechanical grippers, in which the part is held between mechanical fingers and the fingers are mechanically actuated

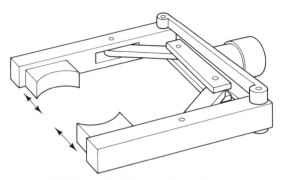

FIGURE 11.10   Robot mechanical gripper.

- Vacuum grippers, in which suction cups are used to hold flat objects
- Magnetized devices, for holding ferrous parts
- Adhesive devices, where an adhesive substance is used to hold a flexible material such as fabrics

A mechanical gripper design is illustrated in Figure 11.10. Some principles and considerations in the design of robot grippers are presented in references 3 and 5.

Some of the innovations and advances in end effector technology include double grippers (two gripper devices for two workparts on one end effector), interchangeable fingers that can be used on one gripper mechanism, quick-change grippers (and tools, as mentioned previously), sensory feedback capabilities in the fingers, and multiple-fingered configurations [6]. Standard end effector products are beginning to become commercially available, thus reducing the need to custom-design the gripper for each separate robot application.

11.6   SENSORS IN ROBOTICS

Sensors used in industrial robotics can be classified into two categories, although the same types of sensors might be used in both categories. The two classes are sensors that are internal to the robot and sensors that are external to the robot.

Sensors internal to the robot are those used for controlling position and velocity of the various joints. These sensors form a feedback control loop with the robot controller. Typical sensors used to control the position of the robot arm include potentiometers and optical encoders. To control the speed of the robot arm, tachometers of various types are used.

Sensors external to the robot are used to coordinate the operation of the robot with the other equipment in the cell. The term *workcell control* is used in reference to these sensor applications. We discuss workcell control in Chapter 12. In many cases these external sensors are relatively simple devices such as limit switches that determine whether a part has been positioned properly in a fixture, or to indicate that a part is ready to be picked up at a conveyor. Other situations require more advanced sensor technologies, including the following:

- *Tactile sensors.* These sensors are used to determine whether contact is made between the sensor and another object. Tactile sensors can be divided into two types in robotics applications: touch sensors and force sensors. *Touch sensors* are those that indicate simply that contact has been made with the object. *Force sensors* are used to indicate the magnitude of the force with the object. This might be useful in a gripper to determine the magnitude of the force being applied to grasp an object.
- *Proximity sensors.* These indicate when an object is close to the sensor. When this type of sensor is used to indicate the actual distance of the object, it is called a *range sensor.*
- *Machine vision and optical sensors.* Vision and other optical sensors can be used for various purposes. *Optical sensors* such as photocells and other photometric devices can be utilized to detect the presence or absence of objects, and are often used for proximity detection. *Machine vision* is used in robotics for inspection, parts identification, guidance, and other uses. In Chapter 18 we provide a more comprehensive discussion of machine vision and optical sensors relative to their uses in automated inspection systems.
- *Miscellaneous sensors.* This category includes other types of sensors that might be used in robotics, including devices for measuring temperature, fluid pressure, fluid flow, electrical voltage, current, and various other physical properties.

In Section 22.2, we present a general discussion of sensors as hardware devices used in computer control systems.

REFERENCES

[1] CONIGLIARO, L., "The Robot Industry," *American Machinist,* May 1985, pp. 134–136.

[2] CRAWFORD, K. R., "Designing Robot End Effectors," *Robotics Today,* October 1985, pp. 27–29.

[3] ENGELBERGER, J. F., *Robotics in Practice,* AMACOM (American Management Association), New York, 1980.

[4] GROOVER, M. P., and E. W. ZIMMERS, Jr., *CAD/CAM: Computer-Aided Design and Manufacturing,* Prentice-Hall, Inc., Englewood Cliffs, N.J., 1984, Chapter 10.

[5] GROOVER, M. P., M. WEISS, R. N. NAGEL, and N. G. ODREY, *Industrial Robotics: Technology, Programming, and Applications,* McGraw-Hill Book Company, New York, 1986.

[6] KEHOE, E. J., "The Expanding Repertoire of Robotics End Effectors," *Robotics Today,* December 1984, pp. 35–36.

[7] KORAM, Y., *Robotics for Engineers,* McGraw-Hill Book Company, New York, 1985.

[8] SNYDER, W. E., *Industrial Robotics—Computer Interfacing and Control,* Prentice-Hall, Inc., Englewood Cliffs, N.J., 1985.

[9] STAUFFER, R. N. "Robot Accuracy," Special Report, *Robotics Today,* April 1985, pp. 43–49.

[10] STAUFFER, R. N., "Advancements in Robot Design," *Robotics Today,* August 1985, pp. 17–20.

[11] TOEPPERWEIN, L. L., M. T. Blackman, et al., "ICAM Robotics Application Guide," *Technical Report AFWAL-TR-80-4042,* Vol. II, Material Laboratory, Air Force Wright Aeronautical Laboratories, Ohio, April 1980.

PROBLEMS

11.1. Based on the notation scheme for defining manipulator configurations (discussed in the text in Section 11.1), make sketches similar to the one in Figure 11.2 of the following robots:
(a) TRT
(b) VVR
(c) VROT

11.2. Based on the manipulator notation scheme, sketch the following robots using diagrams similar to the one in Figure 11.2:
(a) TRL
(b) OLO
(c) LVL

11.3. Based on the robot configuration notation scheme discussed in Section 11.1 make sketches similar to the one in Figure 11.2 of the following robots:
(a) TRT:R
(b) TVT:TR
(c) RR:T

11.4. Discuss and, where possible, sketch the work volumes of the robot configurations for each of the three configurations given in Problem 11.1.

11.5. Using the robot configuration notation scheme discussed in Section 11.1, write the configuration notations for some of the robots in your laboratory or shop.

11.6. Describe the differences in orientation capabilities and work volumes for a :TR and a :RT wrist assembly. Use sketches as needed.

11.7. The linear joint (type L) of a certain industrial robot is actuated by a piston mechanism. The length of the joint when fully retracted is 25 in. and when fully extended is 39 in. If the robot's controller has an 8-bit storage capacity, determine the control resolution for this robot.

11.8. In Problem 11.7 the mechanical errors associated with the linear joint form a normal distribution in the direction of the joint actuation with standard deviation = 0.003 in. Determine the spatial resolution, the accuracy, and the repeatability for the robot.

11.9. The revolving joint (type V) of an industrial robot has a range of 240° of rotation. The mechanical errors in the joint and the input/output links can be described by a normal distribution with its mean at any given addressable point, and a standard deviation of 0.25°. Determine the number of storage bits required in the controller memory so that the accuracy of the joint is as close as possible to, but less than, its repeatability. Use 6 standard deviations as the measure of repeatability.

11.10.   A cylindrical robot has a T-type wrist axis that can be rotated a total of five rotations (each rotation is a full 360°). It is desired to be able to position the wrist with a control resolution of $\frac{1}{2}$° between adjacent addressable points. Determine the number of bits required in the binary register for that axis in the robot's control memory.

11.11.   One axis of a RRL robot is a linear slide with a total range of 36 in. The robot's control memory has a 10-bit capacity. It is assumed that the mechanical errors associated with the arm are normally distributed with a mean at the given taught point and an isotropic standard deviation of 0.10 mm. Determine:

(a) The control resolution for the axis under consideration.

(b) The spatial resolution for the axis.

(c) The defined accuracy.

(d) The repeatability.

11.12.   A TLR robot has a rotational joint (type R) whose output link is connected to the wrist assembly. Considering the design of this joint only, the output link is 25.00 in. long, and the total range of rotation of the joint is 40°. The spatial resolution of this joint is expressed as a linear measure at the wrist, and is specified to be ±0.020 in. It is known that the mechanical inaccuracies in the joint result in an error of ±0.018° of rotation, and it is assumed that the output link is perfectly rigid so as to cause no additional errors due to deflection.

(a) With the given level of mechanical error in the joint, show that it is possible to achieve the spatial resolution specified.

(b) Determine the minimum number of bits required in the robot's control memory in order to obtain the spatial resolution specified.

chapter 12

Robot Programming

To do useful work, a robot must be programmed to perform its motion cycle. A *robot program* can be defined as a path in space to be followed by the manipulator, combined with peripheral actions that support the work cycle. Examples of the peripheral actions include opening and closing the gripper, performing logical decision making, and communicating with other pieces of equipment in the robot cell. Just as in numerical control, there are several different ways to program a robot.

In this chapter we discuss the methods by which robot programming is accomplished. We also examine a related issue called workcell control. In industrial applications, robots must operate with other machines, material handling devices, and even human beings (sometimes). A means of coordinating the activities of the different equipment must be established. This is done using workcell control.

12.1 TYPES OF PROGRAMMING

A robot is programmed by entering the programming commands into its controller memory. Four methods of entering the commands can be distinguished:

1.   Manual setup
2.   Leadthrough programming
3.   Computerlike robot programming languages
4.   Off-line programming

The manual setup method is associated with limited-sequence robots. These robots are programmed by setting limit switches and mechanical stops to control the end points of their motions. The sequence in which the motions occur is regulated by a sequencing device (e.g., a stepping switch). This device determines the order in which each joint is actuated to form the complete motion cycle. Setting the stops and switches and wiring the sequencer is more of a manual setup of the robot rather than a programming method.

Today and in the foreseeable future, nearly all industrial robots have digital computers as their controllers together with compatible storage devices as their memory units. Leadthrough programming and robot language programming are the two methods most commonly used today for entering the commands into computer memory. Leadthrough programming dates back to the early 1960s before computer control was prevalent. These methods are used today for computer-controlled robots. Leadthrough programming involves teaching of the task by moving the manipulator through the required motion cycle. Leadthrough programming is sometimes called "teach by showing."

The use of computer-type programming languages became an appropriate programming method as digital computers took over the control function in robotics. Their use has been stimulated by the increasing complexity of the tasks that robots are being called on to perform, with the concomitant need to embed logical decisions into the robot work cycle. These computerlike programming languages are really on-line/off-line methods of programming, because the robot must still be taught its locations using the leadthrough method.

Off-line programming is a teach method whose applications are very limited today but will grow in the future. The trouble with the leadthrough method and the current language programming techniques is that the robot must be taken out of production for a certain length of time in order to accomplish the programming. The advantage offered by true off-line programming is that new robot programs could be prepared on a computer and downloaded to the robot without interrupting its production. It is likely that some form of graphical computer simulation will be used to validate the programs that are developed off-line.

Leadthrough methods, computerlike robot languages, and off-line programming are the topics of the following three sections.

12.2 LEADTHROUGH PROGRAMMING

Leadthrough programming requires the operator to move the robot arm through the desired motion path during a teach procedure, thereby entering the program into the controller memory. There are two methods of performing the leadthrough teach procedure:

1. Powered leadthrough
2. Manual leadthrough

The difference between the two is the manner in which the manipulator is moved through the motion cycle.

Powered leadthrough is commonly used as the programming method for playback robots with point-to-point control. It involves the use of a teach pendant (hand-held control box) which has toggle switches or contact buttons for controlling the movement of the manipulator joints. Figure 12.1 illustrates the important components of a teach pendant. Using the toggle switches or buttons, the programmer power drives the robot arm to the desired positions, in sequence, and records the positions into memory. During subsequent playback, the robot moves through the sequence of positions under its own power.

Manual leadthrough is convenient for programming playback robots with continuous path control in which the continuous path is an irregular motion pattern such as in spray painting. This programming method requires the operator to physically grasp the

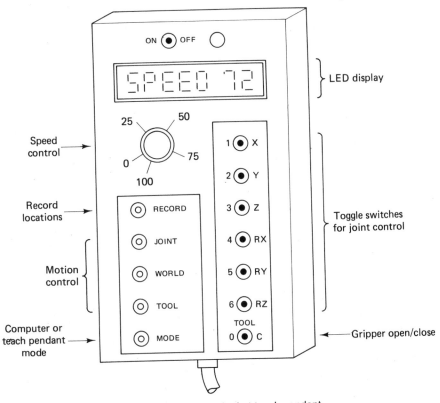

FIGURE 12.1   Typical robot teach pendant.

end-of-arm or tool attached to the arm and manually move through the motion sequence, recording the path into memory. Because the robot arm itself may have significant mass and would therefore be difficult to move, a special programming device often replaces the actual robot for the teach procedure. The programming device has a similar joint configuration to the robot, and it is equipped with a trigger handle (or other control switch), which is activated when the operator wishes to record motions into memory. The motions are recorded as a series of closely spaced points. During playback, the path is recreated by controlling the actual robot arm through the same sequence of points.

It is instructional to survey the important capabilities of the leadthrough programming methods. Our survey will focus principally on the features of powered leadthrough and the use of a teach pendant to enter the programming commands. Powered leadthrough is the most common programming method in industry at this time.

Motion Programming

The leadthrough methods provide a very natural way of programming motion commands into the robot controller. In manual leadthrough the operator simply moves the arm through the required path to create the program. In powered leadthrough the operator uses a teach pendant to drive the manipulator. The teach pendant is equipped with a toggle switch or a pair of contact buttons for each joint. By activating these switches or buttons in a coordinated fashion for the various joints, the programmer moves the manipulator to the required positions in the work space.

Coordinating the individual joints with the teach pendant is sometimes an awkward way to enter motion commands to the robot. For example, it is difficult to coordinate the individual joints of a jointed-arm robot (TRR configuration) to drive the end-of-arm in a straight-line motion. Therefore, many of the robots using powered leadthrough provide two alternative methods for controlling movement of the manipulator during programming, in addition to individual joint controls. With these methods the programmer can control the robot's wrist end to move in straight-line paths. The names given to these alternatives are (1) world coordinate system, and (2) tool coordinate system. Both systems make use of a Cartesian coordinate system. In the *world coordinate system,* the origin and frame of reference are defined with respect to some fixed position and alignment relative to the robot base. This arrangement is illustrated in Figure 12.2(a). In the *tool coordinate system,* shown in Figure 12.2(b), the alignment of the axis system is defined relative to the orientation of the wrist faceplate (to which the end effector is attached). In this way, the programmer can orient the tool in a desired way and then control the robot to make linear moves in directions parallel or perpendicular to the tool.

The world coordinate system and the tool coordinate system are useful only if the robot has the capacity to move its wrist end in a straight-line motion, parallel to one of the axes of the coordinate system. Straight-line motion is quite natural for a Cartesian coordinate robot (LOO configuration), but unnatural for robots with any combination of rotational joints (types R, T, and V). To accomplish straight-line motion for manipulators with these types of joints requires a linear interpolation process to be carried out by the robot's controller. In *straight-line interpolation,* the control computer calculates the se-

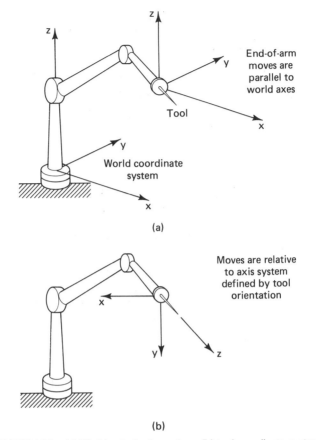

End-of-arm
moves are
parallel to
world axes

Tool

World coordinate
system

(a)

Moves are relative
to axis system
defined by tool
orientation

(b)

FIGURE 12.2 (a) World coordinate system; (b) tool coordinate system.

quence of addressable points in space that the wrist end must move through to achieve a straight-line path between two points.

There are other types of interpolation that the robot can use. More common than straight-line interpolation is joint interpolation. When a robot is commanded to move its wrist end between two points using *joint interpolation*, it actuates each of the joints simultaneously at its own constant speed such that all the joints start and stop at the same time. The advantage of joint interpolation over straight-line interpolation is that there is usually less total motion energy required to make the move. This may mean that the move could be made in slightly less time. It should be noted that in the case of a Cartesian coordinate robot, joint interpolation and straight-line interpolation result in the same motion path.

Still another form of interpolation is that which is used in manual leadthrough programming. In this case the robot must follow the sequence of closely spaced points that are defined during the programming procedure. In effect, this is an interpolation process for a path that usually consists of irregular smooth motions.

The speed of the robot is controlled by means of a dial or other input device located on the teach pendant and/or the main control panel. Certain portions of the program should be performed at high speeds (e.g., moving parts over substantial distances in the workcell), while other parts of the program require low-speed operation (e.g., moves that require high precision in placing the workpart). Speed control also permits a given program to be tried out at a safe slow speed, and then for a higher speed to be used during production.

Interlocks

Interlocks are a means of interfacing the robot with external devices to regulate the sequence of the program and to coordinate the activities in the cell. The interface permits control signals to flow back and forth between the robot controller and the external devices. There are two types of interlocks: input interlocks and output interlocks.

Input interlocks are signals that originate at an external device (e.g., a limit switch, sensor, machine tool) and are transmitted to the robot controller. They have the effect of either interrupting the regular execution of the program or indicating that normal execution of the program should proceed. For example, an input interlock would be used by a machine tool to communicate to the robot that the machining cycle has been completed and that the robot should unload the machine.

Output interlocks are signals sent from the robot controller to some external device (e.g., machine tool, conveyor). They are used to control the operation of the external device and to coordinate its operation with that of the robot. For example, an output interlock would be utilized to signal a machine tool to begin its automatic cycle after the robot has loaded it.

Interlocks can be set up to regulate the operation of playback robots programmed by means of leadthrough techniques. The input/output connections are made at the back panel of the robot controller, and a method is provided to synchronize the operation of these interlocks with the program. In most cases, the interlocks used with playback robots are simple on/off signals rather than analog signals. We examine interlocks in more detail using the WAIT and SIGNAL comands in Section 12.3.

Advantages and disadvantages

The advantage offered by the leadthrough methods is that they can be readily learned by shop personnel. Programming the robot by moving its arm through the required motion path is a logical way for someone to teach the work cycle. It is not necessary for the programmer to possess a background in computer programming. The robot languages described in the next section, especially the more advanced languages, are more easily learned by someone whose background includes computer programming.

There are several inherent disadvantages of the leadthrough programming methods [3]. First, normal production that requires use of the robot must be interrupted during the leadthrough programming procedures. In other words, leadthrough programming results in downtime of the robot cell or production line. The economic consequence of this is that the leadthrough methods must be used for relatively long production runs and are inappropriate for small batch sizes.

Second, the teach pendant used with powered leadthrough and the programming devices used with manual leadthrough are limited in terms of the decision-making logic that can be incorporated into the program. It is much easier to write logical instructions using the computerlike robot languages than the leadthrough methods.

Third, since the leadthrough methods were developed before computer control became common for robots, these methods are not readily compatible with modern computer-based technologies such as CAD/CAM, manufacturing data bases, and local communications networks. The capability to readily interface the various computer-automated subsystems in the factory for transfer of data is considered a requirement for achieving computer-integrated manufacturing.

12.3 ROBOT LANGUAGES

The introduction of textual programming languages for robots has provided the opportunity for performing certain important functions that leadthrough programming cannot readily accomplish. These functions include:

- Enhanced sensor capabilities, including the use of analog as well as digital inputs and outputs
- Improved output capabilities for controlling external equipment
- Program logic control far beyond the capabilities of leadthrough methods
- Computations and data processing similar to computer programming languages
- Communications with other computer systems

There are a variety of commercially available robot languages, including VAL II (by Unimation-Westinghouse), AML (IBM Corp.), RAIL (Automatix Inc.), HELP (General Electric), and others. In this section we review some of the capabilities of these current-generation robot programming languages. Many of the language statements will be taken from actual robot programming languages; in other cases, examples are used that do not derive directly from any single language. A more comprehensive treatment of the robot languages is provided in reference 3.

Motion programming

Motion programming with today's robot languages requires a combination of textual statements and leadthrough techniques. Accordingly, this method of programming is sometimes referred to by the name *on-line/off-line programming*. The textual statements are used to describe the motion, and the leadthrough methods are used to define the position and orientation of the robot during and/or at the end of the motion. To illustrate, the basic motion statement is

MOVE P1

which commands the robot to move from its current position to a position and orientation defined by the variable name P1. The point P1 must be defined, and the most convenient way to define P1 is to use either powered leadthrough or manual leadthrough to place the robot at the desired point and record that point into memory. Statements such as

HERE P1

or

LEARN P1

are used in the leadthrough procedure to indicate the variable name for the point. What is recorded into the robot's control memory is the set of joint positions or coordinates used by the controller to define the point. For example, the aggregate

⟨40.236, 25.088, 16.500, 0.0, 0.0, 0.0⟩

could be utilized to represent the joint positions for a six-jointed manipulator. The first three values (40.236, 25.088, 16.500) give the joint positions of the body-and-arm, while the last three values (0.0, 0.0, 0.0) define the wrist joint positions.

There are variations of the MOVE statement. These include the definition of straight-line interpolation motions, incremental moves, approach and depart moves, and paths. In the VAL II language, the statement

MOVES P1

denotes that the move is to be made using straight-line interpolation. The suffix S on MOVE designates straight-line motion.

An incremental move is one whose end point is defined relative to the current position of the manipulator rather than the absolute coordinate system of the robot. For example, suppose that the robot is presently at a point defined by the joint coordinates ⟨40.236, 25.088, 16.500, 0.0, 0.0, 0.0⟩, and it is desired to move joint 4 (corresponding to a twisting motion of the wrist) from 0.0 to 12.500. The AML language uses the following form of statement to accomplish this move:

DMOVE (4, 12.5)

The new joint coordinates of the robot would therefore be given by ⟨40.236, 25.088, 16.500, 12.500, 0.0, 0.0⟩. The prefix D is interpreted as delta, so DMOVE represents a delta move.

Approach and depart statements are useful in material handling operations. The approach statement moves the gripper from its current position to within a certain distance of the pickup (or drop-off) point, and than a MOVE statement is used to position the end effector at the pickup point. After the pickup is made, a depart statement is used to move the gripper away from the point. The following statements illustrate the sequence:

APPROACH P1, 70 MM

MOVE P1

(actuate gripper)

DEPART 70 MM

The final destination is point P1, but the APPROACH command moves the gripper to a safe distance (70 mm) above the point. This might be useful to avoid obstacles such as other parts in a tote pan. The orientation of the gripper at the end of the APPROACH move is the same as that defined for the point P1, so that the final MOVE P1 is really a spatial translation of the gripper. This permits the gripper to be moved directly to the part for grasping.

A path in a robot program is a series of points connected together in a single move. The path is given a variable name, as illustrated in the following statement:

DEFINE PATH123 = PATH(P1,P2,P3)

This is a path that consists of points P1, P2, and P3. The points are defined in the manner described above. A MOVE statement is used to drive the robot through the path.

MOVE PATH123

The speed of the robot is controlled by defining either a relative velocity or an absolute velocity. The following statement represents the case of relative velocity definition:

SPEED 75

When this statement appears within the program it is typically interpreted to mean that the manipulator should operate at 75% of the initially commanded velocity in the statements that follow in the program. The initial speed is given in a command that precedes the execution of the robot program. For example,

SPEED 75 IPS

EXECUTE PROGRAM1

indicates that the program named PROGRAM1 is to be executed by the robot, and that the commanded speed during execution should be 75 in./s.

Interlock and sensor commands

The two basic interlock commands used for industrial robots are WAIT and SIGNAL. The WAIT command is used to implement an input interlock. For example,

WAIT 20, ON

would cause program execution to stop at this statement until the input signal coming into the robot controller at port 20 was in an "on" condition. This might be used to cause the robot to wait for the completion of an automatic machine cycle in a loading and unloading application.

The SIGNAL statement is used to implement an output interlock. This is used to communicate to some external piece of equipment. For example,

SIGNAL 10, ON

would switch on the signal at output port 10, perhaps to actuate the start of an automatic machine cycle.

Both of the examples above indicate on/off signals. Some robot controllers possess the capacity for controlling analog devices that operate at various levels. Suppose that it were desired to turn on an external device that operates on variable voltages in the range 0 to 10 V. The command

SIGNAL 10, 6.0

is typical of a control statement that might be used to output a voltage level of 6.0 V to the device from controller output port 10.

All of the interlock commands above represent situations where the execution of the statement occurs at the point in the program where the statement appears. There are other situations in which it is desirable for an external device to be monitored continuously for any change that might occur in the device. This might be useful, for example, in safety monitoring where a sensor is set up to detect the presence of human beings who might wander into the robot's work volume. The sensor reacts to the presence of the human beings by signaling the robot controller. The following type of statement might be used for this case:

REACT 25, SAFESTOP

This command would be written to monitor input port 25 continuously for any changes in the incoming signal. If and when a change in the signal occurs, regular program execution is interrupted and control is transferred to a subroutine called SAFESTOP. This subroutine would presumably stop the robot from further motion or would cause some other safety action to be taken.

End effectors are devices which, although they are attached to the wrist of the manipulator, are actuated very much like external devices. Special commands are usually written for controlling the end effector. In the case of grippers, the basic commands are

OPEN and CLOSE

which cause the gripper to actuate to fully open and fully closed positions, respectively. Greater control over the gripper is available in some sensored and servo-controlled hands. For grippers which have force sensors that can be regulated through the robot controller, a command such as

CLOSE 5.0 LB

controls the closing of the gripper until a 5-lb force is encountered by the gripper fingers. A similar command used to close the gripper to a given opening width is

CLOSE 1.0 INCH

A special set of statements is often required to control the operation of tool type end effectors such as spot welding guns, arc welding tools, spray painting guns, and powered spindles (for drilling, grinding, etc.). Spot welding and spray painting controls are typically simple binary commands (e.g., open/close and on/off), and these commands would be similar to those used for gripper control. In the case of arc welding and powered spindles, a greater variety of control statements is needed to control feed rates and other parameters of the operation.

Computations and program logic

Many of the current-generation robot languages possess capabilities for performing computations and data-processing operations that are similar to computer programming languages. Most present-day robot applications do not require a high level of computational power. As the complexity of robot applications grows in the future, it is expected that these capabilities will be better utilized than at present.

Many of today's applications of robots require the use of branches and subroutines in the program. Statements such as

GO TO 150

and

IF (logical expression) GO TO 150

are used to cause the program to branch to some other statement in the program (e.g., to statement number 150 in the illustrations above).

A subroutine in a robot program is a group of statements that are to be executed separately when called from the main program. In a preceding example, the subroutine SAFESTOP was named in the REACT statement for use in safety monitoring. Other uses of subroutines include making calculations or performing repetitive motion sequences at a number of different places in the program. Rather than write the same steps several times in the program, the use of a subroutine is more efficient.

12.4 SIMULATION AND OFF-LINE PROGRAMMING

Off-line programming permits the robot program to be prepared at a remote computer terminal and downloaded to the robot controller for execution. In true off-line programming there would be no need to physically locate the positions in the workspace for the robot as required with present textual programming languages. The programming procedure would be similar to the off-line procedures used in NC part programming (Chapter 9). The significant advantage of true off-line programming is that the downtime for reprogramming would be minimized, thus permitting the robot to continue in production uninterrupted.

The off-line programming procedures being developed and commercially offered use a graphical simulation on a CAD/CAM system. Examples of current available CAD/CAM simulation packages that can be used for off-line robot programming include PLACE [4] (McDonnell Douglas Manufacturing Industry Systems Company), Robographix (Computervision Corporation), Robot-SIM (General Electric Calma Company), and ROBO-CAM [2] (Silma, Inc.).

The PLACE system is one of the more widely used of the simulation packages. The acronym PLACE stands for Positioner Layout and Cell Evaluation. It is a computer graphics model builder that is used to construct a three-dimensional model of a robot cell for evaluation and off-line programming. The cell might consist of the robot, machine tools, conveyors, and other hardware. PLACE permits these components of the cell to be displayed on the graphics monitor and for the robot to perform its work cycle in animated computer graphics. Figure 12.3 illustrates the PLACE graphics simulator.

The associated software module used to write the robot program is called COMMAND. The motion sequences for the robot are developed using the PLACE and COMMAND modules. After the program has been developed using the simulation procedure, it is then converted into the textual language corresponding to the particular robot employed in the cell. This is a step in the off-line programming procedure that is equivalent to postprocessing in NC part programming.

In the current commercial off-line programming packages, some adjustment must be performed to account for geometric differences between the three-dimensional model in the computer system and the actual physical cell. For example, the position of a machine tool in the physical layout might be slightly different than in the model used to do the off-line programming. For the robot to reliably load and unload the machine, it must have an accurate location of the load/unload point recorded in its control memory.

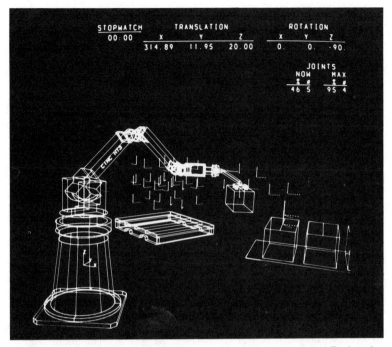

FIGURE 12.3   PLACE graphics simulator. (Courtesy of Mechanical Engineering CAD Laboratory, Lehigh University.)

The PLACE system allows for these adjustments in position to be made by means of a module called ADJUST. This module is used to calibrate the three-dimensional computer model by substituting location data from the actual cell for the approximate values developed in the original PLACE model. The disadvantage with calibrating the cell is that time is lost in performing this procedure.

In future programming systems, the off-line procedure described above will probably be augmented by means of a machine vision system (and other sensors) located in the cell. The vision and sensor systems would be used to update the three-dimensional model of the workplace and thus avoid the necessity for the calibration step in current off-line programming methods. The term sometimes used to describe these future programming systems in which the robot possesses accurate knowledge of its three-dimensional workplace is *world modeling*.

Associated with the concept of world modeling is the use of very high-level language statements, in which the programmer would specify a task to be done without giving details of the procedure used to perform the task. Examples of this type of statement might be

ASSEMBLE PRINTING MECHANISM TO BRACKET

or

WELD UPPER PLATE TO LOWER PLATE

The statements are void of any reference to points in space or motion paths to be followed by the robot. Instead, the three-dimensional model residing in the robot's control memory would identify the locations of the various items to be assembled or welded. The future robot would possess sufficient intelligence to figure out its own sequence of motions and actions for performing the task indicated.

12.5 WORKCELL CONTROL

Industrial applications of robots almost always involve other pieces of equipment, such as machine tools, conveyors, sensors, and fixtures, in addition to the robot itself. Each piece of equipment performs some function in the cell, and for the cell to perform properly, all of these functions must be sequenced and coordinated with the actions of the robot. The function of workcell control is to provide this sequencing and coordination of the cell components.

Several of the programming commands discussed earlier in this chapter relate to workcell control. Examples include input and output interlocks (very important functions in workcell control), sensor commands, the REACT statement, and programming logic statements (e.g., IF . . . GO TO . . .).

Workcell control is accomplished by a control unit called the *workcell controller*. In most applications, the robot's controller serves as the workcell controller. A number of input and output ports are included on the back panel of the robot controller to permit electrical connections to be established with the other cell components. Control commands, interlocks, sensor data, and other similar signals enter and leave the controller through these input/output ports. The sequencing and coordination of the signals is done by means of the robot program, using commands such as SIGNAL, WAIT, and REACT.

In some robot applications, the robot controller is inadequate as the workcell control unit. These applications include situations where the robot lacks sufficient input/output capacity to deal with the number of input/output signals that must be coordinated, or where there are multiple robots in the cell (e.g., a robot spot welding line for car bodies). In these cases, a programmable controller or small computer is used as the workcell controller. These control units download commands to the robots (to activate portions of the robot programs) and other components in the cell in order to accomplish the workcell control function.

The workcell controller performs several important functions in the robot installation. The functions can be divided into three categories, as suggested by Thomas [7]:

1. Sequence control
2. Operator interface
3. Safety monitoring

Sequence control

Sequence control is the basic function of the workcell controller. It is concerned with regulating the sequence of activities in the cell. The sequence is determined not only by controlling the activities as a function of time; it is also determined by using interlocks to ensure that certain elements of the work cycle are completed before other elements are started. For example, consider a robot machine loading and unloading application. Input/output interlocks in sequence control are used for purposes such as the following:

- Making sure that the part is at the pickup location before the robot attempts to grasp it
- Ensuring that the part is properly loaded into the machine before the processing cycle begins
- Indicating to the robot that the machine cycle is completed and the part is ready for unloading

Additional functions within the scope of sequence control include logical decision making, computations, and control of irregular elements that must occur with a certain frequency.

Decisions associated with the work cycle are typically determined according to the value of an input interlock. For example, consider a robot cell designed to process two or more different types of parts. Depending on which part is presented, the robot activates one of several alternative work cycles contained in its program. A sensor scheme would have to be devised to distinguish between the various types of parts, and to input an interlock signal to the controller to activate the correct work cycle for the part presented. This example illustrates the type of elementary decision making used in workcell control.

Computations are sometimes required to support a robot work cycle. For example, determining the location of a point in space to which the robot should move its gripper might require a computation to be made. Programs for palletizing operations are most efficiently written by calculating the positions of the pickup or dropoff points in the container, especially if the number of such positions is relatively large.

Irregular elements in the work cycle are elements that occur with a frequency of once every so many cycles (e.g., once every 10 cycles). Reasons for an irregular element in a work cycle include tool changes that must be accomplished after a certain number of parts have been processed, and exchanging pallets or other containers that hold a certain number of parts.

Operator interface

A means for the operator to interact with the robot cell must be provided. Reasons for establishing the operator interface include the following:

- Programming the robot.
- Participation in the work cycle by a human operator. The human being and the robot each perform a portion of the work in the cell. The human being typically

accomplishes tasks that require judgment or sensory capabilities that the robot does not possess. Certain assembly operations fit this category.

- Data entry by the human operator. The data might simply be the part identification so that the correct work cycle can be used by the robot. In other cases, alphanumeric data (e.g., part dimensions) must be provided.
- Emergency stopping of the cell activities.

There are a number of ways to provide the operator interface: teach pendant, control panel of the robot controller, alphanumeric keyboard and CRT monitor, and emergency stop buttons located in the cell. Alternatives that might be considered include automatic bar code readers and voice input of data.

Another important reason for operator interaction with the robot cell is for stopping the work cycle due to emergency conditions. The emergency might result from a malfunction of the robot (or other equipment in the cell), or from a human worker inadvertently intruding into the cell space. Under these circumstances, it would be desirable to stop the action in the cell to prevent harm to either equipment or people. An emergency stop button in the workcell is provided for this purpose.

Safety monitoring

Emergency stopping of the robot cycle requires that an alert operator be present to notice the emergency and take positive action to interrupt the cycle. Safety emergencies are not always so convenient as to occur when an alert operator is present. A more automatic and reliable means of protecting the cell equipment and people who might wander into the work zone is called *safety monitoring*.

Safety monitoring (the term *hazard monitoring* is also sometimes used) is a workcell control function in which sensors are used to monitor the status and activities of the cell and to detect the unsafe or potentially unsafe conditions. We discussed this function in Chapter 4 in relation to the operation of a transfer line. Its purpose in a robot cell is the same.

Various sensors can be used to implement a safety monitoring system in a robot cell. These sensors include simple limit switches that detect whether the movement of a particular component has occurred correctly, temperature sensors, pressure sensitive floor mats, light beams combined with photosensitive sensors, and machine vision systems.

The safety monitoring system is programmed to respond to the various hazard conditions in different ways. These responses might include one or more of the following: complete stoppage of the cell activity, slowing down the robot speed to a safe level (when human beings are present), warning buzzers to alert maintenance personnel of a safety hazard in the cell, and specially programmed subroutines to permit the robot to recover from a particular unsafe event. This last response is an example of programming for automated systems that is called error detection and recovery. We discuss this topic in more detail in Chapter 22.

REFERENCES

[1]   AUTOMATIX INC., *RAIL Software Reference Manual,* Document No. MN-RB-07, Rev. 5.00, October 1983.

[2]   CRAIG, J. J., "Anatomy of an Off-Line Programming System," *Robotics Today,* February 1985, pp. 45–47.

[3]   GROOVER, M. P., M. WEISS, R. N. NAGEL, and N. G. ODREY, *Industrial Robotics: Technology, Programming, and Applications,* McGraw-Hill Book Company, New York, 1986, Chapters 8, 9, 11, 17.

[4]   HOWIE, P., "Graphic Simulation for Off-Line Robot Programming," *Robotics Today,* February 1984, pp. 63–66.

[5]   SCHREIBER, R. R., "How to Teach a Robot," *Robotics Today,* June 1984, pp. 51–56.

[6]   TAYLOR, R. H., P. D. SUMMERS, and J. M. MEYER, "AML: A Manufacturing Language," *The International Journal of Robotics Research,* Fall 1982, pp. 19–41.

[7]   THOMAS R., "Designing Controls for Robotics Work Cells," *Industrial Engineering,* May 1983, pp. 34–39.

[8]   UNIMATION, INC., *Programming Manual—User's Guide to VAL II* (398T1), Version 1.1, August 1984.

[9]   WATERBURY, R., "Software Animates Assembly Workcells," *Assembly Engineering,* March 1985, pp. 16–23.

PROBLEMS

The following problems require access to industrial robots and their associated programming manuals in a laboratory setting.

12.1.   The setup for this problem requires a felt-tipped pen mounted to the robot's end-of-arm (or held securely in the robot's gripper). Also required is a thick piece of cardboard, mounted on the surface of the work table. Pieces of plain white paper will be pinned or taped to the cardboard surface. The exercise is the following: Program the robot to write your initials on the paper with the felt-tipped pen.

12.2.   As an enhancement of Problem 12.1, consider the problem of programming the robot to write any letter that is entered at the alphanumeric keyboard. Obviously, a textual programming language is required to accomplish this exercise.

12.3.   The apparatus required for this problem consists of two blocks of wood or plastic that can be grasped by the robot gripper. The blocks should be of two different colors. In the workplace setup, the blocks are placed at specific positions (call the positions A and B on either side of a center location (call it position C). The robot should be programmed to do the following: (1) Pick up the block at position A and place it at the central position C. (2) Pick up the block at position B and place it at position A. (3) Pick up the block at position C and place it at position B. (4) Repeat steps 1, 2, and 3 continually.

12.4.   The apparatus for this exercise consists of a cardboard box and a dowel about 4 in. long held in the robot's gripper (any straight, thin cylinder will suffice, e.g., pen, pencil, etc.).

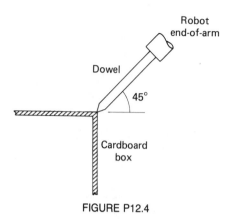

FIGURE P12.4

The dowel is intended to simulate a continuous arc welding torch, and the edges of the cardboard box are intended to represent the seams that are to be welded. The programming exercise is the following: With the box oriented with one of its corners pointing toward the robot, program the robot to weld the three edges that lead into the corner. The dowel (welding torch) must be continuously oriented at a 45° angle with respect to the edge being welded (see Figure P12.4).

12.5. This exercise is intended to simulate a palletizing operation. The apparatus includes: six wooden (other materials will work) cylinders approximately $\frac{3}{4}$ in. in diameter and 3 in. in length, and a 1-in.-thick wooden block approximately 3 in. by 4.5 in. The block is to have six holes of diameter $\frac{7}{8}$ in. drilled in it as illustrated in Figure P12.5. The wooden cylinders represent workparts and the wooden block represents a pallet. (As an alternative to the wooden block, the layout of the pallet can be sketched on a plain piece of paper attached to the worktable). The programming exercise is the following: Using the powered leadthrough programming method, program the robot to pick up the parts from a fixed position on the worktable and place them into the six positions in the pallet. The fixed position on the table might be a stop point on a conveyor. (The student may have to place the parts at the position manually if a real conveyor is not available.)

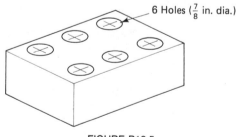

FIGURE P12.5

12.6. This is the same as Problem 12.5, except that a robot programming language should be used and the position of the pallet should be defined by calculating their *x* and *y* coordinates by whatever method is available in the particular programming language used.

12.7. Repeat Problem 12.5 but in the reverse order, to simulate a depalletizing operation.

12.8. This exercise is intended to simulate a machine loading and unloading operation and to make use of interlocks. The apparatus required is a metal block, a nest (fixture) designed to accept the block (the nest should have a limit switch at its center designed to sense the presence of the part), and a position (call it M to represent the machine location) on the worktable. The limit switch should be connected to one of the input ports of the robot so that it can signal the presence of the part. The programming exercise is the following: Program the robot to (1) pick up the part when the part is placed in the nest by the student, (2) transfer the part to a location M, (3) wait 10 s to simulate the processing of the part, and (4) remove the part from position M and place it on an outgoing conveyor—a convenient location from which the student can retrieve the part.

chapter **13**

Robot Applications

Robots are being used in a wide field of applications in industry. In this chapter we discuss these various applications. In the first section we examine some of the general characteristics of work situations that tend to promote the use of robots. In the second section we describe the various workcell designs that are typically used in robot installations. The most common robot applications are described in the remaining sections. Almost all industrial robots today are applied in manufacturing operations.

13.1 CHARACTERISTICS OF ROBOT APPLICATIONS

One of the earliest installations of an industrial robot was around 1961 in a die casting operation [3]. The robot was used to unload the casted parts from the die casting machine. The typical environment around a die casting machine is not pleasant for human beings because of the heat and fumes that are emitted by the casting process. It seemed quite logical to use a robot in this type of work environment in place of a human operator.

The work environment is one of several characteristics that should be considered when selecting a robot application. The general characteristics of an industrial work situation which have tended to promote the substitution of a robot for human labor are the following:

1. *Hazardous work environment for human beings.* When the work environment is unsafe, unhealthful, hazardous, uncomfortable, or otherwise unpleasant for people, this is a reason to consider an industrial robot for the work. In addition to die casting, there are many other work situations that are hazardous or unpleasant for human beings, including forging, spray painting, continuous arc welding, and spot welding. Industrial robots have been utilized in all these applications.

2. *Repetitive work cycle.* A second characteristic that promotes the use of robotics is a repetitive work cycle. If the sequence of elements in the cycle is the same and the elements consist of relatively simple motions, a robot is usually capable of performing the work cycle with greater consistency and repeatability than a human worker. Greater consistency and repeatability are usually manifested as higher product quality than that which can be achieved in a manual operation.

3. *Difficult handling for human beings.* If the task involves the handling of parts or tools that are heavy or otherwise difficult to manipulate, it is likely that an industrial robot is available that can perform the operation. Parts or tools that are too heavy for human beings to handle conveniently are well within the load-carrying capacity of a large robot.

4. *Multishift operation.* In manual operations requiring second and third shifts, substitution of a robot will provide a much faster financial payback than a single-shift operation. Instead of replacing one worker, the robot replaces two or three workers.

5. *Infrequent changeovers.* Most batch or job shop operations require a changeover of the physical workplace between one job and the next. The time required to make the changeover is nonproductive time since parts are not being made. In an industrial robot application, not only must the physical setup be changed, but the robot must be reprogrammed, thus adding to the downtime. Consequently, robots have traditionally been easier to justify for relatively long production runs where changeovers are infrequent. In the future, when off-line robot programming becomes technically more feasible, it will be possible to reduce the time required to perform the reprogramming procedure. This will permit shorter production runs to become more economical.

6. *Part position and orientation are established.* Most robots in today's industrial applications are without vision capability. Their capacity to pick up an object during each work cycle relies on the fact that the part is in a known position and orientation. A means of presenting the part to the robot at the same location each cycle must be engineered.

These characteristics might be used as checklist of features to look for in a work situation in order to determine if a robot application is feasible.

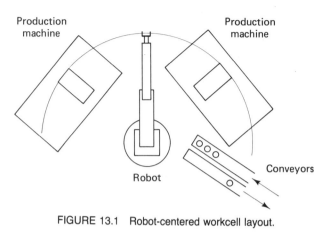

FIGURE 13.1   Robot-centered workcell layout.

13.2   ROBOT CELL DESIGN

As indicated in Chapter 12, industrial robot applications usually involve several pieces of hardware in addition to the robot. These other hardware components include conveyors, pallets, machine tools, fixtures, and so on. In some applications, several robots must be integrated into a single workcell. It is important that the equipment in the cell be organized into an efficient layout. There are three basic types of workcell layout [6]:

1.   Robot-centered cell
2.   In-line robot cell
3.   Mobile robot cell

In the *robot-centered cell,* the robot is located at the approximate center of the workcell, and the other pieces of equipment are arranged around it. The layout is illustrated in Figure 13.1. This type of cell layout is suited to installations in which there is a single robot servicing one or more production machines. Machine loading and unloading applications are examples of this case.

The *in-line robot cell* is an arrangement in which one or more robots are located along an in-line conveyor or other material transport system. The work is organized so that parts are presented to the robots by the transport system, and each robot performs some processing or assembly operation on each part. The arrangement is shown in Figure 13.2. As indicated in the diagram, there are usually multiple robots in this cell layout. The in-line robot cell design is typified by the welding lines used to spot-weld car bodies in the automotive industry.

Any of the various types of workpart transport systems described in Chapter 4 (i.e., continuous, intermittent, and asynchronous) can be used to move the parts along the flow

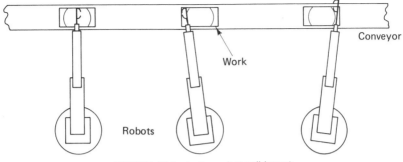

FIGURE 13.2   In-line robot cell layout.

line. The most common type is the intermittent transfer system. It presents the part to each robot in a precise location and orientation at regular time intervals. The asynchronous system offers the same position and orientation feature, but the timing varies according to the cycle-time requirements of each station. The benefit of the asynchronous transfer system is that it permits each robot to work somewhat independently by providing a queue of workparts to accumulate in front of each workstation. If one robot breaks down and the breakdown can be repaired in relatively short time, the rest of the line can continue to operate.

The continuous transfer system presents special problems for the robot because the parts are not held stationary during the processing. Instead, the robot must perform its work cycle as the parts move past on the conveyor. This requires the robot to be capable of tracking the part as it moves along. The term *tracking* means that the robot must maintain the position and orientation of its end effector during the work cycle relative to the moving part rather than relative to some fixed coordinate system. Robot tracking of the parts is accomplished either by moving the robot along a path that is parallel to (and at the same speed as) the conveyor during processing, or by endowing the robot with sufficient computational capability to continuously adjust its arm-and-wrist joints to maintain a fixed orientation with the part as it moves past. Sensors are required to continuously identify the position of the part and relay these data to the robot controller in order to maintain the required positional relationship.

The third category of robot cell layout is the *mobile robot cell*. One possible conceptualization of this cell layout is presented in Figure 13.3. In this arrangement, the robot is provided with a means of being transported within the cell to perform various tasks at different locations. The transport mechanism consists of either a floor-mounted or overhead rail system that allows the robot to be moved along a linear path. The mobile robot cell is appropriate in installations where the robot must service more than one workstation (e.g., a production machine), and the workstations cannot be located around the robot in a robot-centered cell arrangement. One possible reason why the robot would have to relocate itself is that the workstations are geographically separated by distances greater than the robot's reach capacity.

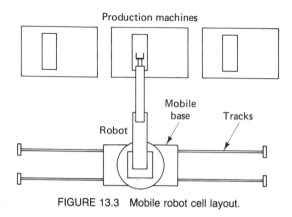

FIGURE 13.3   Mobile robot cell layout.

13.3   TYPES OF ROBOT APPLICATIONS

As indicated in the introduction to this chapter, almost all of the current applications of industrial robots are in manufacturing. The applications can usually be classified into the following three categories:

1.   Material handling
2.   Processing operations
3.   Assembly and inspection

At least some of the work characteristics discussed in Section 13.1 must be present in any of these application categories in order to make the installation of a robot technically and economically feasible.

Most companies require an economic analysis to be performed to justify the investment in the robot cell. The justification of a robot cell is sometimes difficult when conventional methods of investment analysis are used. Accordingly, the analysis should include the effects of inventory reduction, quality improvement, capacity, and other factors discussed in Chapter 3 that are often neglected in the traditional economic analysis.

13.4   MATERIAL HANDLING APPLICATIONS

Material handling applications are those in which the robot moves materials or parts from one location and orientation to another. To accomplish the transfer, the robot is equipped with a gripper type end effector. The gripper must be designed to handle the specific part or parts to be moved in the application. Included within this category are the following cases:

1. Material transfer
2. Machine loading and/or unloading

In nearly all material handling applications, the parts must be presented to the robot in a known position and orientation. This requires some form of material handling device to deliver the parts into the workcell in this defined position and orientation. Future robots, equipped with appropriate sensors, may be able to deal with random entry of parts into the cell, but this is not common in today's applications.

Material transfer

These applications are ones in which the primary purpose of the robot is to pick up parts at one location and place them at a new location. In many cases, a reorientation of the part is desired in the relocation. The basic application in this category is the relatively simple pick-and-place operation, where the robot picks up a part and deposits it at a new location. Transferring parts from one conveyor to another is an example. The requirements of the application are modest; a low-technology robot, (e.g., limited-sequence type) is usually sufficient. Only two, three, or four joints are required for most of the applications. Pneumatically powered robots are often used.

A more complex example of material transfer is palletizing. These are applications in which the robot must retrieve parts or other objects from one location (e.g., a position on a conveyor) and deposit them into a pallet or other container in an ordered arrangement. A typical pallet arrangement is illustrated in Figure 13.4. Although the pickup point is the same for every cycle, the deposit location is different for each part. This adds to the degree of difficulty of the task. Either the robot must be taught each position in the pallet using the powered leadthrough method, or it must compute the location based on the dimensions of the pallet and the center distances between the parts (in both x and y directions). For pallets that hold many parts, the leadthrough programming method can be laborious.

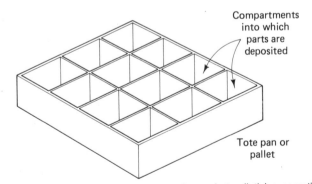

Compartments
into which
parts are
deposited

Tote pan or
pallet

FIGURE 13.4 Typical part arrangement for a robot palletizing operation.

Other applications that are similar to palletizing include depalletizing (removing parts from an ordered arrangement in a pallet and placing them at one specific location), stacking operations (placing flat parts on top of each other, such that the vertical location of the drop-off position is continuously changing with each cycle), and insertion operations (where the robot inserts parts into the compartments of a divided carton).

Machine loading and/or unloading

In machine loading and/or unloading applications, the robot transfers parts into and/or from a production machine. The three possible cases are:

- *Machine loading.* This is the case in which the robot loads parts into the production machine, but the parts are unloaded from the machine by some other means.
- *Machine unloading.* In this case, the raw materials are fed into the machine without using the robot. The unloading of the finished parts is accomplished by the robot.
- *Machine loading and unloading.* This case involves both loading of the raw workpart and unloading of the finished part by the robot.

The robot-centered cell is most commonly used for this application category. The workcell consists of one or more production machines, the robot, and a material handling mechanism for delivering parts into and/or out of the cell. The mobile robot cell is another less common configuration for implementing machine loading/unloading operations.

Industrial robot applications of machine loading and/or unloading include the following processes:

- *Die casting.* The robot unloads parts from the die casting machine. Peripheral operations sometimes performed by the robot include dipping the parts into a water bath for cooling.
- *Plastic molding.* Plastic molding is a robot application similar to die casting. The robot is used to unload molded parts formed in the injection molding machine.
- *Metal machining operations.* The robot is used to load the raw blanks into the machine tool and unload the finished parts from the machine. The change in shape and size of the part before and after machining often presents a problem in end effector design.
- *Forging.* The robot is typically used to load the raw hot billet into the die, hold it during the forging blows, and remove it from the forge hammer. The hammering action and the risk of damage to the die or end effector are significant technical problems. Forging and related processes are difficult as robot applications because of the severe conditions under which the robot must operate.
- *Pressworking.* Human operators work at considerable risk in sheet metal pressworking operations because of the action of the press. Robots are used as substitutes for the human workers to reduce the danger. In these applications, the robot loads the blank into the press, the stamping operation is performed, and the part falls out the back of the machine into a container. In high production runs, pressworking operations can be mech-

anized by using sheetmetal coils instead of individual blanks. These operations require neither human beings nor robots to participate directly in the process.

   • *Heat treating.*   These are often relatively simple operations in which the robot loads and/or unloads parts from a furnace.

   One of the practical problems often encountered when a robot is used to tend a production machine is the difference in cycle time between the robot and the machine. The problem is that the cycle time of the machine may be relatively long compared to the robot's cycle time. It may take only 20 s to load the machine, but several minutes are required for the machine to process the part. In these cases, it is appropriate for one robot to tend more than a single production machine. The following example is a case study of a machining workcell that illustrates this problem in robot loading and unloading applications.

EXAMPLE 13.1

Figure 13.5 shows an overhead view of a robot cell in which parts are loaded and unloaded at two turning centers. The cell also includes an automatic gaging station. Parts are delivered to the workcell in pallets on a conveyor. A Cincinnati Milacron robot retrieves parts from the conveyor and loads them first into the first machine and then into the second machine. Between the two machines and after the second machine, the parts are inspected at the gaging station. Loading and

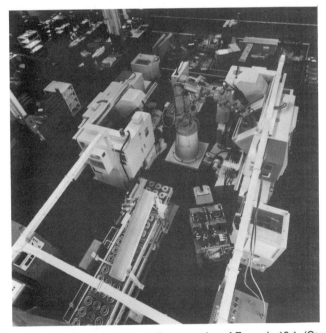

FIGURE 13.5   Machine loading/unloading operation of Example 13.1. (Courtesy of Cincinnati Milacron.)

unloading of the turning centers is done from the rear rather than the front of the machines. This permits access by human beings to the front of the machine tools.

13.5 PROCESSING OPERATIONS

Processing applications are those in which the robot performs a processing operation on the part. A distinguishing characteristic of this category is that the robot is equipped with some type of tool as its end effector. To perform the process, the robot must manipulate the tool relative to the part during the work cycle. In some processing applications, more than a single tool must be used during the work cycle. In these instances, either a gripper or a quick-change mechnism is used to exchange the tools during the work cycle.

Examples of industrial robot applications in the processing category include spot welding, continuous arc welding, spray painting, various machining and other rotating spindle processes, and others.

Spot welding

Spot welding is a metal joining process in which two sheet metal parts are fused together at localized points of contact. Two copper-based electrodes are used to squeeze the metal parts together and apply a large electrical current across the contact point to cause the fusion to occur. The electrodes, together with the mechanism that actuates them, constitute the welding gun in spot welding.

Because of its widespread use in the automobile industry for car body fabrication, spot welding represents one of the most important applications of industrial robots today [3]. The end effector is the spot welding gun used to pinch the car panels together and perform the resistance welding process. The welding gun used for automobile spot welding is typically very heavy. Prior to the use of robots in this application, human workers performed the operation, and the heavy welding tools were difficult for the workers to manipulate accurately. As a consequence, there were many instances of missed welds, poorly located welds, and other defects, resulting in overall low quality of the finished product. The use of industrial robots in this application has dramatically improved the consistency with which the welds are made.

The types of robots used for spot welding are usually large, with sufficient payload capacity to wield the heavy welding gun. Five or six axes are generally needed to achieve the positioning and orientation required. Playback robots with point-to-point control are used, and the programming is accomplished using the powered leadthrough method. Jointed arm and polar coordinate robots are the most common anatomies in the automobile spot welding lines. In-line robot cell layouts with 20 to 30 robots are typical.

EXAMPLE 13.2

The Chrysler LeBaron GTS and Dodge Lancer models are made at Chrysler Corporation's Sterling Heights (Michigan) assembly plant. The car bodies are welded together using 99 industrial robots which apply a total of 1021 spot welds [4]. A number of different robot manufacturers are represented

FIGURE 13.6 Spot-welding operation on the automobile body line of Example 13.2. (Courtesy of Chrysler Corp.)

at the plant, including Cincinnati Milacron, Prab, and Unimation. Figure 13.6 shows a portion of the respot line, where 56 Cincinnati Milacron T3-776 robots perform approximately 900 of the spot welds to the car bodies.

Continuous arc welding

Continuous arc welding is used to provide continuous welded joints rather than individual welds at specific contact points as in spot welding. The resulting joint in arc welding is substantially stronger than in spot welding. Since the weld is continuous, it can be used to make airtight pressure vessels and in other fabrication applications where strength and continuity are required. There are various forms of continuous arc welding, but they all follow the general description given here.

The work conditions are not good for human beings who work at the arc welding process. Welders must wear a face helmet to protect their eyes against the ultraviolet radiation that is emitted by the arc welding process. The helmet window is dark enough to shield the ultraviolet, but so dark that the worker cannot see through the window unless the arc is on. High electrical current is used in the welding process, and this creates a hazard for the welder. Finally, there is the obvious danger from the high temperatures in the process, high enough to melt the steel, aluminum, or other metal that is being welded. A significant amount of hand–eye coordination is required by human welders to make sure that the arc follows the desired path with sufficient accuracy to make a good weld. This, together with the conditions described above, results in a high level of worker fatigue. Consequently, the welder is only accomplishing the welding process for perhaps 20 to 30% of the time. This percentage is called the "arc-on" time, the proportion of time during the shift when the welding arc is on and performing the process. To assist the welder, a second worker is usually present at the work site to set up the parts to be welded and perform other similar chores in support of the welder. This second worker is called the fitter.

Because of these conditions in manual arc welding, automation is used where technically and economically feasible. For welding jobs that involve long continuous joints and are accomplished repetitively, mechanized welding machines have been designed to perform the process. These machines are used for long, straight sections and regular round parts. Examples of these welding jobs include presssure vessels, tanks, and pipes.

Industrial robots are also used to automate the continuous arc welding process. The economics of robot arc welding at the current state of technology indicate that the application should involve a relatively long production run. One possible workplace arrangement for these applications is illustrated in Figure 13.7. The cell consists of the robot, the welding apparatus (power unit, controller, welding tool, and wire feed mechanism), and a fixture that positions the components for the robot. The fixture might be mechanized with several degrees of freedom so that it can present different portions of the work to the robot for welding. For greater productivity, a double fixture is often used so that a human helper can be unloading the completed job and loading the components for the next work cycle while the robot is simultaneously welding the present job.

The robot used in arc welding jobs must be capable of continuous path control. Programming is typically done by one of the leadthrough methods. Jointed arm and Cartesian coordinate robots are frequently used in arc welding applications. The robot should have five or six axes. If it does not, the fixture used to hold the parts during welding should possess several degrees of freedom to establish the required geometric relationship between the robot and the work. The fixture must be designed specifically for the job. Programming for arc welding is also costly. Therefore, most applications require a large batch size to justify the robot cell. In the future, as quick-change fixtures are developed and the programming effort is reduced, shorter production runs will be possible in robot arc welding applications.

Spray painting

Spray painting is the most common example of a more general class of robot applications called spray coating. The latter term suggests the broader range of possible applications, which includes painting. The spray coating process makes use of a spray gun directed at the object to be coated. Fluid (e.g., paint) flows through the nozzle of the spray gun to be dispersed and applied over the surface of the object.

The work environment for human beings who perform this process is filled with health hazards. These hazards include noxious fumes in the air, risk of flash fires, and

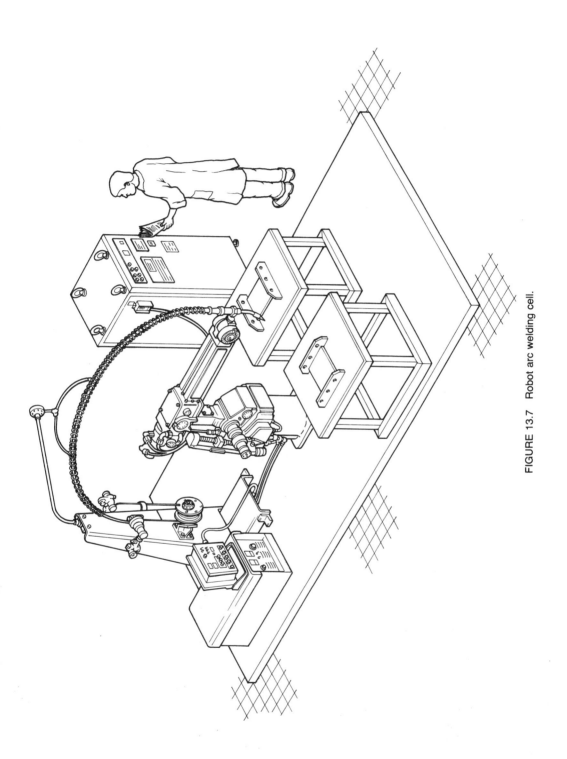

FIGURE 13.7　Robot arc welding cell.

noise from the spray gun nozzle. The environment is also believed to pose a carcinogenic risk for the workers. Largely because of these hazards, robots are being used with increasing frequency for spray coating tasks.

The robot applications include spray coating of appliances, automobile car bodies, engines, and other parts, spray staining of wood products, and spraying of porcelain coatings on bathroom fixtures. The cell layout is typically an in-line configuration in which the work flows past the robot. The robot must be capable of continuous path control to accomplish the smooth motion sequences required in spray painting. The most convenient programming method is manual leadthrough. Jointed arm robots seem to be the most common anatomy for this application. The robot must possess a long reach in order to access the areas of the workpart to be coated in the application.

The use of industrial robots for spray coating applications offers a number of benefits, in addition to protecting workers from a hazardous environment. These other benefits include greater uniformity in the application of the coating than people can accomplish, reduced use of paint (less waste), lower needs for ventilating the work area since human beings are not present during the process, and greater productivity.

Other processing applications

Spot welding, arc welding, and spray coating are the most familiar processing applications of industrial robots today. The list of industrial processes that are being performed by robots is continually growing. Among these processes are the following:

- *Drilling, routing, and other machining processes.* These applications use a rotating spindle as the end effector. Mounted in the spindle chuck is the particular cutting tool. One of the problems with this application is the high cutting forces that are encountered in machining. The robot must be strong enough to withstand these cutting forces and maintain the required accuracy of the cut.
- *Grinding, wire brushing, and similar operations.* These operations also use a rotating spindle to drive the tool (grinding wheel, wire brush, polishing wheel, etc.) at high rpm rates to accomplish finishing and deburring operations on the work.
- *Waterjet cutting.* This is a relatively recent application in which a pressurized stream of water (as high as 60,000 psi) is forced through a small nozzle (from 0.003 to 0.012 in. in diameter) at high speed (approximately 3000 ft/s) to cut plastic sheets, fabrics, cardboard, and other materials with precision. The end effector is the water-jet nozzle which is directed over the desired cutting path by the robot.
- *Laser cutting.* The function of the robot in this application is similar to its function in water-jet cutting. The laser tool is attached to the robot as its end effector. Laser beam welding is a similar possible application for robots.
- *Riveting.* Some work has been done in using robots to perform riveting operations in sheet metal fabrication. A riveting tool with a feed mechanism for feeding the rivets is mounted on the robot's wrist. The function of the robot is to place the riveting tool at the proper hole and actuate the device.

FIGURE 13.8   Robotic water-jet cutting operation of Example 13.3. (Courtesy of GMF Robotics Corp.)

EXAMPLE 13.3

This example involves two processing operations, routing and water-jet cutting. The operations are located at the Adrian (Michigan) plant of Chevrolet Division of General Motors Corp. Two fuel tank shields are thermally formed out of a single 0.195-in. polyethelene sheets and presented to a workcell consisting of four GMF model S-360 robots. The first two robots use routing tools as their end effectors to cut 12 holes and slots in the parts. The second two robots use water jets to divide the part into the two fuel tank shields and to trim around the periphery of the shields. The workcell is pictured in Figure 13.8.

13.6   ASSEMBLY AND INSPECTION

Assembly and inspection are growing application areas for industrial robotics. In some respects, they are hybrids of the previous two robot application categories: material handling and processing. Assembly and inspection applications can involve both the handling of materials and the manipulation of a tool. For example, assembly operations typically involve the addition of components to build the product, which requires material handling. In some cases, the fastening of the components requires a tool to be used by the robot (e.g., staking, welding, driving a screw). Similarly, some robot inspection operations require that parts be manipulated and other applications require that an inspection tool be manipulated.

Assembly and inspection are traditionally labor-intensive activities in industry. They are also highly repetitive and often boring. For these reasons, they are logical candidates for robotic applications. However, assembly work typically involves diverse and some-times difficult tasks, often requiring adjustments to be made in parts that do not quite fit together. A sense of feel is often required to achieve the close fitting of parts that is required. Inspection work requires high precision and patience, and human judgment is often needed to determine whether a product is within quality specifications or not. Because of these complications in both types of work, the application of robots has not been easy. Nevertheless, the potential rewards are so great that substantial efforts are being made to develop the necessary technologies to achieve success in these applications.

Assembly

As indicated in Chapter 6, the assembly process involves the addition of two or more parts to form a new entity, called a subassembly (or assembly). The new subassembly is made secure by fastening the two or more parts together using mechanical fastening techniques (e.g., screws, nuts, rivets, etc.), joining processes (e.g., welding, brazing, and soldering), or adhesives. We have already seen how robots can be used in welding processes, and these applications are often considered separately from mechanical as-sembly applications, as we have separated them in this chapter.

Because of its economic importance, automated methods have been applied to assembly operations. In high production of relatively simple products (e.g., pens, me-chanical pencils, cigarette lighters, and garden hose nozzles), fixed automation is used as described in Chapter 7. Robots are usually at a disadvantage in these high-production situations because they cannot perform as quickly as the fixed automation systems.

The most appealing area for the application of industrial robots for assembly is in the production of a mixture of similar products or models in the same workcell or assembly line. Examples of these kinds of products include electric motors, small appliances, and various other small mechanical and electrical products. In these examples, the basic configuration of the different models is the same, but there are variations in size, geometry, options, and other features. These types of products are often made in batches on manual assembly lines. However, the pressure to reduce inventories has made mixed-model assembly lines more attractive. Robots can be used to substitute for some or all of the manual workstations on these lines.

What makes robots useful in these assembly applications is their capability to execute programmed variations in the work cycle to accommodate different assembly configu-rations. One of the pioneering development projects in this area was performed by Westinghouse Electric Corp., with support from the National Science Foundation [2]. The project was called the "Adaptable-Programmable Assembly System" (APAS), and it involved the design of a flexible automated line for assembly of small electric motors. The assembly line consisted of six workstations, four of which used robots to perform their respective assembly operations. The partially completed motors were held on in-dividual pallet fixtures and transferred between stations by a roller conveyor system. The conveyor system was arranged in a complete loop for return of the pallets after the completed motors were unloaded. Table 13.1 provides some basic details about the functions at each workstation on the line.

TABLE 13.1 Workstation Details for the Adaptable-Programmable
Assembly System (APAS)

Workstation	Functions and operations performed
1	Loading operation. Motor base part (called an endbell) presented to robot, which loads onto pallet fixture. Vision system used to identify motor model and for location prior to robot pickup.
2	Buffer and transfer station.
3	Robot performs insertion operation of three components into endbell.
4	Caps pressed on sides of endbells. Several other parts assembled. Automatic screwdrivers used.
5	Parts feeder delivers parts to pickup location. Robot retrieves parts and performs assembly to endbell.
6	Machine vision system inspects endbell assembly for missing components and other irregularities. Based on vision data, robot sorts motors by model.

The APAS Project demonstrated the technological feasibility of the concept of flexible automated assembly. In addition, the importance of designing the product for automated assembly was identified. The types of assembly techniques that are specified by the product design can make a significant difference between whether a robot or other automated mechanism is capable of performing the assembly operation reliably and quickly. Finally, another lesson learned in the APAS project was that inspection of the product must be done periodically during assembly to ensure that components have been properly mated and fastened.

Industrial robots used for the types of assembly operations described here are typically small, with light load capacities. An internal study at the General Motors Corporation during the 1970s had indicated that a large proportion of assembly tasks require a robot capable of lifting parts that weigh 5 lb or less [7]. The most common configurations are jointed arm, SCARA (Selectively Compliant Assembly Robot Arm), and Cartesian coordinate. Programming is often done using a textual programming language together with powered leadthrough to teach locations in the workcell. Accuracy requirements in assembly work are often more demanding than in other robot applications, and some of the more precise robots in this category have repeatabilities as close as ± 0.002 in. In addition to the robot itself, the requirements of the end effector are often demanding. The end effector may be required to perform multiple functions at a single workstation in order to reduce the number of robots that are required on the line. Examples of these multiple functions include handling more than one part geometry, and performing both as a gripper and an automatic assembly tool.

Inspection

The topic of automated inspection is considered in more detail in Chapter 18. The purpose in the present section is to survey briefly how robots are applied in inspection work.

Inspection tasks that are performed by industrial robots can usually be divided into the following two cases:

1. The robot performs loading and unloading tasks to support an inspection or testing machine. This case is really a machine loading and unloading operation, except that the machine is an inspection machine. The robot picks parts (or assemblies) that enter the cell, loads and unloads them to carry out the inspection process, and places them at the cell output. In some cases, the inspection may result in a parts sorting operation that the robot must perform. Depending on the quality level, the robot puts the parts in different containers or on different exit conveyors.

2. The robot manipulates an inspection device, such as a mechanical probe, to test the product. This case is similar to a processing operation described in Section 13.5 in which the end effector attached to the robot's wrist is the inspection probe. To perform the process, the part must be presented at the workstation in the correct position and orientation, and the robot manipulates the inspection device as required.

The workcell of Example 13.1 includes an inspection operation of the first type. The robot presents machined parts to a gaging station to inspect for size. The gaging station can be seen in the lower right portion of Figure 13.5.

As suggested in the previous discussion of the APAS Project, there is often a need in automated production and assembly systems to inspect the work that is supposed to be done. These inspections accomplish the following types of checks: making sure that a given process has been completed, ensuring that parts have been added in the assembly as specified, and identifying flaws in raw materials and finished parts.

REFERENCES

[1] BEHUNIAK, J. A., "Planning the Successful Robot Application," *Robotics Today,* Summer 1981, pp. 36–37.

[2] CAPTOR, N., B. MILLER, B. D. OTTINGER, A. J. RIGGS, L. M. TOMKO, and M. C. CULVER, "Adaptable-Programmable Assembly Research Technology Transfer to Industry," *Final Report,* NSF Grant ISP 78-18773, January 1983.

[3] ENGELBERGER, J. F., *Robotics in Practice,* AMACOM (American Management Association), New York, 1980.

[4] FREEMAN, N. B., "Better Ways to Build LeBarons," *American Machinist,* September 1985, pp. 73–76.

[5] GROOVER, M. P., and E. W. ZIMMERS, Jr., *CAD/CAM: Computer-Aided Design and Manufacturing,* Prentice-Hall, Inc., Englewood Cliffs, N.J., 1984, Chapter 11.

[6] GROOVER, M. P., M. WEISS, R. N. NAGEL, and N. G. ODREY, *Industrial Robotics: Technology, Programming, and Applications,* McGraw-Hill Book Company, New York, 1986, Chapters 11, 13–16.

[7] JABLONOWSKI, J., "Robots That Assemble," Special Report 739, *American Machinist,* November 1981, pp. 175–190.

[8] OWEN, T., *Assembly with Robots,* Prentice-Hall, Inc., Englewood Cliffs, N.J., 1985.

[9] RAIA, E., "Cold Cuts," *High Technology,* December 1985, pp. 58–59.

[10] "Robotics in Metalworking," Special Report 776, *American Machinist,* May 1985, pp. 105–136.

[11] SCHWARTZ, W. H., "Robots Called to Assembly," *Assembly Engineering,* August 1985, pp. 20–23.

PROBLEMS

Some of the following problems are based on the concepts and analysis methods presented in Chapters 2 and 3.

13.1. A robot performs a loading and unloading operation for a machine tool. The work cycle consists of the following sequence of activities:

Activity	Time(s)
1. Robot picks part from incoming conveyor and loads into fixture on machine tool.	5.5
2. Machining cycle (automatic).	33.0
3. Robot reaches in, retrieves part from machine tool and deposits it onto exit conveyor.	4.8
4. Move back to pickup position.	1.7

The activities are performed sequentially as listed. Every 30 workparts, the cutting tools in the machine must be changed. This irregular cycle takes 3.0 min to accomplish. The uptime efficiency of the robot is 97%; and the uptime efficiency of the machine tool is 98%, not including interruptions for tool changes. These two efficiencies are assumed not to overlap (i.e., if the robot breaks down, the cell will cease to operate, so the machine tool will not have the opportunity to break down, and vice versa). Downtime results from electrical and mechanical malfunctions of the robot, machine tool, and fixture. Determine the hourly production rate, taking into account the lost time due to tool changes and the uptime efficiency.

13.2. Suppose that a double gripper were used instead of the single gripper indicated in Problem 13.1. The activities in the cycle would be changed as follows:

Activity	Time(s)
1. Robot picks raw part from incoming conveyor in one gripper and awaits completion of machining cycle. This activity is performed simultaneously with machining cycle.	3.3
2. At completion of previous machining cycle, robot reaches in, retrieves finished part from machine, loads raw part into fixture, and moves a safe distance from machine.	5.0
3. Machining cycle (automatic).	33.0
4. Robot moves to exit conveyor and deposits part. This activity is performed simultaneously with machining cycle.	3.0
5. Robot moves back to pickup position. This activity is performed simultaneously with machining cycle.	1.7

Steps 1, 4, and 5 are performed simultaneously with the automatic machining cycle. Steps 2 and 3 must be performed sequentially. The same tool change statistics and uptime efficiencies are applicable. Determine the hourly production rate when the double gripper is used, taking into account the lost time due to tool changes and the uptime efficiency.

13.3. Since the robot's portion of the work cycle requires much less time than the machine tool in Problem 13.1, the possibility of installing a cell with two machines is being considered. The robot would load and unload both machines from the same incoming and exit conveyors. The machines would be arranged in a robot-centered cell layout, so that distances between the fixture and the conveyors are the same for both machines. Thus, the activity times given in Problem 13.1 are valid for the two-machine cell. The machining cycles would be staggered so that the robot would be servicing only one machine at a time. The tool change statistics and uptime efficiencies in Problem 13.1 are applicable. Determine the hourly production rate for the two-machine cell. The lost time due to tool changes and the uptime efficiency should be accounted for. Assume that if one of the two machine tools is down, the other machine can continue to operate, but if the robot is down, the cell operation is stopped.

13.4. Determine the hourly production rate for a two-machine cell as in Problem 13.3, but the robot is equipped with a double gripper as in Problem 13.2. Assume that the activity times from Problem 13.2 apply here.

13.5. The arc-on time is a measure of efficiency in an arc welding operation. As indicated in our description of the arc welding process in Section 13.5, typical arc-on times in manual welding range between 20 and 30%. Suppose that a certain welding operation is currently performed using a welder and a fitter. Production requirements are steady at 500 units per week. The fitter's job is to load the component parts into the fixture and clamp them in position for the welder. The welder then welds the components in two passes, stopping to reload the welding rod between the two passes. Some time is also lost each cycle for repositioning the welding rod on the work. The fitter's and welder's activities are done sequentially, with times for the various elements as follows:

Fitter: Load and clamp parts	4.2 min
Welder: Weld first pass	2.5 min
Reload weld rod	1.8 min
Weld second pass	2.4 min
Repositioning time	2.0 min
Delay time between work cycles	1.1 min

Because of fatigue, the welder must take a 20-min rest at midmorning and midafternoon, and a 40-min lunch break around noon. The fitter joins the welder in these rest breaks. The nominal time of the work shift is eight hours, but the last 20 min of the shift is nonproductive time for cleanup at each workstation.

A proposal has been made to install a robot welding cell to perform the operation. The cell would be set up with two fixtures, so that the robot could be welding one job (the set of parts to be welded) while the fitter is unloading the previous job and loading the next job. In this way, the welding robot and the human fitter could be working simultaneously rather than sequentially. Also, a continuous wire feed would be used rather than individual welding rods. It has been estimated that the continuous wire feed must be changed only once every 40 parts and the lost time will be 20 min to make the wire change. The times for the various activities in the regular work cycle are as follows:

Fitter: Load and clamp parts	4.2 min
Robot: Weld complete	4.0 min
Repositioning time *for weld rod*	1.0 min — *assume automatically done by what?*
Delay time between work cycles `	0.3 min

A 10-min break is taken by the fitter in the morning and another in the afternoon, and 40 min is taken for lunch. Cleanup time at the end of the shift is 20 min. In your calculations, assume that the proportion uptime of the robot will be 98%. Determine the following:

(a) The arc-on times (expressed as a percentage, using the 8-h shift as the base) for the manual welding operation and the robot welding station.

(b) The hourly production rate on averge throughout the 8-h shift for the manual welding operation and the robot welding station.

13.6. In Problem 13.5 dealing with the welding operation, the following cost data are applicable:

Hourly rate of welder (includes fringes) = $16.00

Hourly rate of fitter (icludes fringes) = $14.00

Fixture, welding rod costs = nil

Purchase cost of robot = $80,000

Cost of welding apparatus (power unit,

   controller, wire feed unit, etc.) = $25,000

Fixture cost (two fixtures) = $30,000

Other engineering and installation costs = $40,000

Hourly rate of fitter (includes fringes) = $14.00

Power and operating costs = $1.00 per hour

Second-shift differential = $0.30 per hour — *ie, $14.30/hr for 2nd shift (different) personnel*

Overtime paid at 1.5 normal rate — *ie, if the same person works*

Assume a 3-year analysis period using a 30% rate of return. Salvage costs of the robot and welding apparatus will be $35,000 at the end of the 3 years.

(a) How would you organize the manual production operation to meet the weekly demand requirements? (How many cells? How many shifts?)

(b) How would you organize the robot welding operation to meet the weekly demand requirements? (How many cells? How many shifts?)

(c) Determine the equivalent uniform annual costs for the two alternatives defined in parts (a) and (b). Assume 52 weeks of operation per year.

(d) Compute the respective unit costs of product for the two alternatives.

part V

Material Handling and Storage

One of the five basic functions that must be carried out in production is material handling and storage. We briefly discussed this topic in Chapter 2 (Section 2.3). In Part V we describe the material handling and storage function in greater depth. The scope of material handling and storage extends well beyond the factory. Problems in the handling and storing of materials arise in warehousing, distribution, retailing, inventory control, postal services, airport baggage handling, and many other areas, as well as manufacturing. Our coverage of the topic will emphasize the applications in automated manufacturing operations.

We divide the subject into two chapters: Chapter 14 on material handling and Chapter 15 on storage. In Chapter 14 we survey the various types of equipment that are used in factory material handling operations. We also examine some of the general principles and analysis methods that are used to design a material handling system. The chapter focuses on two types of handling systems that seem especially suitable for automation in discrete-product manufacturing. The first type are conveyor systems. Conveyors are available in a wide variety of designs. They are generally applied in situations where materials are moved along well-defined routes in high volumes. The second type of handling systems are called automated guided vehicle systems. These systems are more applicable for automation of low- and medium-volume handling situations, where the routing of materials is more individualized. For both conveyors and guided vehicles, quantitative methods for analyzing these systems are developed in the chapter.

In Chapter 15 we consider the material storage problem. We refer to it as a problem because storing materials uses valuable space and consumes investment monies that might better be used elsewhere. We considered these inventory costs in Chapter 3. There is a widely held belief that the storage function can be accomplished more efficiently using automated systems. Our discussion in Chapter 15 focuses on the two principal types of automated storage systems: automated storage and retrieval systems, and mechanized carousel systems. In both cases we provide a description of the systems and the quantitative techniques used to analyze their operation.

We conclude our coverage of material handling and storage with a discussion of the problem of interfacing material handling systems, storage systems, and manufacturing systems. This problem is concerned with the mechanical and information details of transferring materials back and forth between these various systems. These details must be addressed and resolved if a fully automated factory is to be achieved.

chapter **14**

Automated Material Handling

Material handling is an important, yet sometimes overlooked aspect of automation. The cost of material handling is a significant portion of the total cost of production. Estimates of handling cost run as high as two-thirds of the total manufacturing cost [3]. This fraction varies depending on the type and quantity of production and the degree of automation in the material handling function. For a storage and distribution facility the handling function constitutes the overwhelming majority of cost.

We have discussed several types of material handling systems in earlier chapters. These systems include:

- Transfer mechanisms in automated flow lines
- Conveyors used in manual assembly lines
- Parts feeding devices in automated assembly
- Pallet shuttles in NC machining centers
- Industrial robots used for material handling

In these cases the handling function was an integral part of the production system. In the present chapter we examine material handling as a distinct and identifiable topic in automation. The chapter is not intended to provide a comprehensive discussion of material handling. For a more complete treatment of the subject, the reader is referred to any of several books in the list of references [6,18,20]. Consistent with the scope of our text, the coverage here will focus on automated and mechanized handling technologies rather than the more traditional methods that require manual labor. Also, we will emphasize those material handling systems that relate to factory operations.

14.1 THE MATERIAL HANDLING FUNCTION

The purpose of material handling in a factory is to move raw materials, work-in-process, finished parts, tools, and supplies from one location to another to facilitate the overall operations of manufacturing. The handling of materials must be performed safely, efficiently (at low cost), in a timely manner, accurately (the right materials in the right quantities to the right location), and without damage to the materials.

The material handling function is also concerned with material storage and material control. The storage function and some of the important methods for automating it are considered in Chapter 15.

The material control function is concerned with the identification of the various materials in the handling system, their routings, and the scheduling of their moves. In most factory operations, it is important that the origin, current location, and future destination of materials be known. The firm's shop floor control system is generally used to implement this function by maintaining accurate, complete, and current records on all materials in the factory. This control is sometimes augmented by means of an automatic identification system whose purpose is to identify parts as they are moved or stored. We cover shop floor control and automatic identification systems in Chapter 25.

14.2 TYPES OF MATERIAL HANDLING EQUIPMENT

There is a great variety of material handling equipment available commercially. The equipment can be divided into the six categories presented in Table 14.1. The first three categories are almost always manually operated devices. The basic designs for much of the equipment in these categories has remained the same for many decades.

Categories 4 and 5 are considered within the domain of automated systems, both because they are themselves highly mechanized and/or automated, and because they are used in automated production systems. As indicated in Table 14.1, conveyors can be either gravity driven or powered. Both types, but especially the powered conveyors, are frequently used as components in automated systems of material movement and storage. Conveyor systems are typically associated with high production where the flow of materials

TABLE 14.1 Types of Material Handling Equipment

1. *Hand trucks*—platforms with wheels for manual movement of items, unit loads, and bulk materials. Examples include wheelbarrows, dollies, two-wheeled trucks, four-wheeled trucks, hand-lift or manually operated forklift trucks.
2. *Powered trucks*—powered vehicle with platform for mechanized movement of items, unit loads, and bulk materials. Driven by human beings, powered by battery, gasoline, or propane gas. Examples include walkie trucks (where operator walks with vehicle for steering), riding trucks, forklift trucks, sideloaders, tractor-trailer trains, and industrial crane trucks.
3. *Cranes, monorails, and hoists*—handling devices, usually manually operated, designed for lifting, lowering, and transporting heavy objects. Examples include bridge cranes, gantry cranes, jib cranes, overhead monorails, hand and powered hoists.
4. *Conveyors*—large family of handling devices, often mechanized, sometimes automated, designed to move materials between specific locations over a fixed path, generally in large quantities or volumes. Examples include gravity conveyors (chutes, rollers) and powered conveyors (rollers, belt, chain, overhead, in-floor tow, and cart-on-track).
5. *Automated guided vehicle systems* (AGVS)—battery-powered, automatically steered vehicles designed to follow defined pathways. Some are capable of automatically loading and unloading unit loads. Usually interfaced with other automated systems to achieve full benefits of integrated automation. Examples include driverless trains, pallet trucks, and unit load carriers.
6. *Other handling equipment*—miscellaneous category to cover the many other kinds of hardware that are used for material handling. Examples include:
   Industrial robots and other parts manipulators
   Dial indexing tables
   Transfer mechanisms used in automated flow lines
   Elevators
   Parts feeding and delivery devices
   Pipelines
   Containers (pallets, baskets, tote pans, etc.)
   Highway tractor-trailers
   Railway trains
   Cargo aircraft
   Ships, barges, and other marine vessels

Source: Compiled from references 6, 18, 20.

is along a fixed path. An automated guided vehicle system (AGVS) represents a more versatile means of moving materials automatically. An AGVS is suitable in applications where different materials must be moved from various load points to various unload points. The AGVS therefore holds the promise of being a suitable means of automating the material handling function in batch production and even job shops. We discuss and analyze conveyors and AGV systems in Sections 14.5 and 14.6.

Another way of classifying handling equipment is according to its attributes and characteristics. These characteristics include whether the system is manually operated or automated, mobile or fixed in position, and so on. A list of most of these important attributes is presented in Table 14.2.

Material handling equipment is usually assembled into systems. These systems must be specified and configured for the particular application. The design of the system depends

TABLE 14.2   Attributes and Characteristics by Which to Classify Material Handling
Equipment and Systems

1. *Manual* (hand truck)
     (vs.)
   Mechanized (powered forklift truck, powered conveyor)
     (vs.)
   Automated and computer-controlled (AGVS)
2. *Mobile* (forklift truck)
     (vs.)
   Fixed-in-position (conveyor, bridge crane)
3. *Floor mounted* (roller conveyor)
     (vs.)
   Overhead (overhead hook conveyor, bridge crane)
4. *Fixed route* (conveyor)
     (vs.)
   Programmable routing (AGVS)
5. *One-directional flow* (powered belt conveyor)
     (vs.)
   Flow in multiple directions (some AGV systems)
6. *Discrete items or loads* (forklift trucks, AGVS)
     (vs.)
   Continuous (belt conveyor, pipeline)
7. *Multiple items per carrier* (hook conveyor using baskets)
     (vs.)
   Single items per carrier (hook conveyor for single items)
8. *Delivery-only* (AGVS)
     (vs.)
   Delivery-and-storage systems (some conveyor systems)
9. *Single pickup station* and *single drop-off station*
     (vs.)
   Multiple pickup stations and *multiple drop-off stations*
10. *Pickup and drop-off at the same station*
     (vs.)
   Pickup and drop-off stations separate
11. *Equal rates of loading and unloading*
     (vs.)
   Unequal rates of loading and unloading
12. *Placement of items on the handling system*
   Continuous placement
     (vs.)
   Uniformly spaced discrete placement
     (vs.)
   Randomly spaced discrete placement

on the parts, materials, or products to be handled, the quantities to be moved, the distances of the moves, the type of production system that the handling equipment will serve, and other factors, including the available budget. In the following section we survey some of the analysis concepts and techniques that should be considered when planning an automated material handling system.

14.3 ANALYSIS FOR MATERIAL HANDLING SYSTEMS

The planning for a material handling system must begin with an analysis of the materials to be moved. In this section we discuss the various material characteristics and how they affect the handling system. We then consider some of the quantitative relationships and principles that are common to nearly all material handling systems.

Consideration of material and movement conditions

One obvious characteristic by which to classify a material is according to its physical form: solid, liquid, or gas. A second characteristic is whether the material is to be moved in bulk or as individual pieces. Still a third characteristic is whether the material is to be moved in some form of container (e.g., drums for liquids, tanks for gases, tote pans for individual solid parts, bags for granular solids). The design of the material handling system is influenced by these types of factors. If the material under consideration is a liquid, and it is to be moved in bulk over a long distance, a pipeline should be given serious consideration. But this handling method would be quite inappropriate for moving the liquid if it is contained in drums. For purposes of handling, materials can be classified by the physical characteristics presented in Table 14.3, suggested by a classification scheme of Muther and Haganas [18].

TABLE 14.3 Characteristics of Materials

Category	Measures or descriptors
Physical form	Solid
	Liquid
	Gas
Size	Length, width, and height
	Volume
Weight	Weight per piece
	Weight per unit volume
Shape	Long and FLat
	Round
	Square
Risk of damage	Fragile
	Brittle
	Sturdy
Safety risk	Explosive
	Toxic
	Corrosive
Condition	Hot
	Wet
	Dirty
	Sticky

In addition to these characteristics of the material, there are other factors to consider in analyzing the system requirements. These other factors relate to the movement and handling conditions rather than the material itself. They include:

- The quantity of material to be moved
- The rate of flow required
- The scheduling of the moves
- The route by which the materials are to be moved
- Miscellaneous factors

The quantity of material moved will influence the type of handling system that should be used. If large quantities of material must be handled, a dedicated handling system should be considered. If the quantity is small, the handling equipment must be shared with other items moved. Related to quantity is the rate of flow of the materials. The flow rate is measured in such units as pieces per hour, tons per hour, and cubic feet per day.

Scheduling relates to the timing of the material movement. Whether the materials must be moved continuously, in batches, or one at a time has an effect on the type of handling method used. The urgency of the moves (e.g., rush jobs) affects the cost of a move. Seasonality is also a factor in this category. If the product is seasonal and is handled only 6 months of the year, it would be difficult to justify an automated handling system dedicated to that product, because the system would be idle the other 6 months.

Routing factors include the length or distance of the move and the conditions that exist along the route. Given that other variables remain constant, the cost of handling is directly related to the distance of the move: The longer the move distance, the greater the cost. Conditions along the route include temperature and humidity (which may affect the materials moved), whether a portion of the move is outdoors, whether the path is straight-line or involves many turns, changes in elevation, floor surface condition, traffic congestion, and the presence or absence of people along the same path as the handling system.

Miscellaneous factors include the possible need to keep batches separate to meet government regulations or for other record-keeping purposes, whether the handling involves movement of materials between floors of the building, the numbers of load and unload stations, and whether manual or automatic loading and unloading is used in the system.

Material handling analysis techniques

There are several approaches that can be used to represent the material handling problem for visualization and analysis purposes. Tabular and graphical techniques are quite helpful for visualizing the moves, and quantitative approaches can be useful for determining material flow rates, operation times, and other aspects of performance in material handling.

One of the techniques for displaying information about the material flow is the *from–to chart,* illustrated in Tables 14.4 and 14.5. The from–to chart is similar to a *gives* 'flow rate' in parts (or unit of material) per unit time

— per hr:

TABLE 14.4 From–To Chart Showing Number of Deliveries Required between Different Stations in a Layout

From:	To:				
	1	2	3	4	5
1	0	9	5	6	0
2	0	0	0	0	9
3	0	0	0	2	3
4	0	0	0	0	8
5	0	0	0	0	0

TABLE 14.5 From–To Chart Showing Distances between Different Stations in a Layout[a]

From:	To:				
	1	2	3	4	5
1	0	200	400	700	NA
2	NA	0	NA	NA	300
3	NA	NA	0	300	600
4	NA	NA	NA	0	300
5	100	NA	NA	NA	0

[a]Distances shown in feet. "NA" indicates that the distances are not applicable to this layout.

mileage chart on a road map. As indicated in the tables, the left-hand vertical column lists the origination points from which trips are made, and the horizontal row at the top of the chart lists the destination points. The chart is organized for possible material flows in both directions between the set of load/unload points in the layout. The from–to chart is quite versatile in that it can be used to represent various parameters of the material flow problem. These parameters include the number of deliveries between points (Table 14.4), the distances between from–to points (Table 14.5), and the volume or volume rate of product flowing between various locations in the layout.

Muther and Haganas [18] suggest several graphical techniques for visualizing the moves, including mathematical plots and flow diagrams of different types. The *flow diagram* provides information about the movement of materials and the corresponding origination and destination points of the moves. In this diagram, the origination and destination points are represented as nodes and the material flows are depicted by arrows between the points. The nodes might represent production departments between which parts must be moved, or they might be distinct load and unload stations within a facility. An example of one possible construction of a flow diagram is presented in Figure 14.1. This flow diagram portrays the same information as given in the from–to chart of Table 14.4. We indicate the rates of material flow near the tips of the arrows on the diagram. For greater visual impact, the quantities or rates of materials moved can be shown in the flow diagram by using arrows of different colors or multiple lines to represent various levels of traffic.

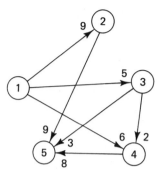

FIGURE 14.1   Flow diagram showing material flow between different loading and unloading stations. Nodes represent load or unload station; arrows with numbers indicate material flow rates.

Certain quantitative measures and equations can be defined to help in analyzing material handling problems. As indicated previously, the rate of flow of the materials can be measured in units such as pieces per hour, tons per hour, and so on, depending on the types of materials moved. Let us use the symbol R_f to represent this flow rate, assuming whatever units are appropriate for the material involved. This flow rate applies to the movement over a certain distance, L_d (length of a delivery), in the factory or warehouse. The product of these two parameters gives a measure of what Muther and Haganas call the transport work, TW, where

$$TW = R_f L_d \qquad (14.1)$$

The units for TW are simply the flow rate units (e.g., pieces/h) multiplied by the appropriate distance measure (e.g., ft). Hence, TW has units such as pieces-ft/h.

The flow rates might be different between origin and destination points, and the distances involved may be different. We can aggregate these various deliveries to determine the total transport work (TTW) by summing the individual values of TW for each delivery:

$$TTW = \Sigma\, R_f L_d \qquad (14.2)$$

where the summation is carried out over all the deliveries that must be accomplished. TTW provides a measure of the total requirements that must be satisfied by the material handling system. That is, the handling system must be capable of performing the amount of transport work indicated by TTW.

EXAMPLE 14.1

To illustrate the concept of the total transport work, let us determine the TTW value for the data shown in the from–to charts of Tables 14.4 and 14.5. If we interpret Table 14.4 to represent the number of parts per hour that must be moved, TTW is calculated to be the sum of the individual elements in Table 14.4 multiplied by the corresponding elements in Table 14.5.

$$\text{TTW} = 9 \times 200 + 5 \times 400 + 6 \times 700 + 2 \times 300 + 9 \times 300 + 3 \times 600 + 8 \times 300$$

$$= 15{,}500 \text{ parts-ft/h}$$ — @ 100% efficiency, w/no 'empty' movement included — given / ideal / theor. cap. reqd.

Because of lost time and inefficiencies in the operation of the material handling system, it must be designed for a greater capacity than that given by TTW. Reasons for the losses and inefficiencies during operation of the system include loading and unloading time, return trips with no loads, system downtime for maintenance and repair, traffic congestion, scheduling problems, and others.

To explain some of these losses, let us begin by examining the typical delivery cycle. The actual delivery involves the movement of the handling system carrier (e.g., forklift truck, overhead conveyor hook, AGV) over the distance between the origination point and the destination point, L_d. If we let V_c represent the speed of the handling system (the subscript c might represent conveyor, carrier, cart, etc.) the time of the delivery is L_d/V_c. This is considered as productive time of the handling system. In addition to this delivery time, each delivery may also involve a loading and unloading operation, and these operations often require time that takes away from the available time for transporting materials. Let us combine the loading and unloading activities into the single term T_h (the subscript h represents handling time).

After the delivery is completed, the carrier leaves the unload station to move to the next pickup location. The carrier usually departs the unload station empty. In most material handling systems, much of the time of the carriers is spent traveling without a load, and this time must be considered an inefficiency of the handling system. It is often possible to measure or estimate the length of travel that the handling system moves empty. For example, in a closed-loop conveyor that picks up parts at one location and drops them at another location, the empty travel distance can readily be measured as the length of the return loop in the conveyor system. From this, the empty traveling time can be determined. If the distance of the empty move is given by L_e, the empty traveling time is L_e/V_c. This assumes no stops along the route to the next pickup point.

In addition to losses from handling time and empty traveling time, other inefficiencies in the material handling system include traffic congestion, poor scheduling, and others. These inefficiencies are sometimes defined by a term called the *traffic factor* [2]. We can express the traffic factor as F_t. For handling systems in which the losses of this type are negligible, the traffic factor has a value of 1.0. For other systems, such as an AGVS, where there can be significant vehicle congestion, the traffic factor might be 0.85 or less. We discuss the reasons for this AGVS traffic congestion in Section 14.6.

As a result of all these reasons for inefficiencies, the material handling system will not operate 100% of the time accomplishing the transport work defined by Eq. (14.2). The various losses can be incorporated into a measure of efficiency for a material handling system, as follows:

$$E_h = \frac{L_d/V_c}{L_d/V_c + T_h + L_e/V_c} F_t \tag{14.3}$$

here, L_d, L_e etc. are avg. values $\left(\text{ie. } L_d = \frac{\Sigma L_d}{\# del.}, \text{ etc.} \right)$

where E_h is the overall efficiency of the handling system. Depending on the type of material handling system, some of the terms in the denominator of the efficiency equation may be absent or may require special interpretation.

The material handling system must be planned with due consideration given to this efficiency. Conceptually, the system must be designed to accomplish an amount of transport work given by

$$\text{required handling system capacity} = \frac{\text{TTW}}{E_h} \tag{14.4}$$

The units on this required capacity are the same units as TTW (e.g., piece-ft/h). Determining a precise and realistic measure of E_h is difficult, since the values of the terms in Eq. (14.3) and the resulting value of efficiency depend not only on the design of the handling system, but also on the way the system is operated and managed.

14.4 DESIGN OF THE SYSTEM

Determining the required capacity of the handling system depends on the particular type of equipment that is to be installed. A conveyor system has application features that are different from cranes, forklift trucks, or automated guided vehicle systems. In the current section we discuss some of the design factors that must be considered during the planning of a material handling system.

Effect of plant layout

Plant layout is an important factor influencing the design of a material handling system. The plant can be classified as either new (not yet constructed) or existing. In the case of a new facility, the design of the handling system should be considered as part of the layout design. If this is done, there is greater opportunity to create a layout that optimizes the material flow in the building and utilizes the most appropriate type of handling system. In the case of an existing facility, there is less latitude in the design of the material handling system. There are usually constraints than inhibit the realization of optimum flow patterns in the building.

The layout should provide the following information for use in the design of the handling system:

- Locations where materials must be picked up (load stations)
- Locations where materials must be delivered (unload stations)
- Possible routes between these locations
- Distances that must be traveled to move materials
- Flow patterns, opportunities to combine deliveries, possible places where congestion might occur

- Total area of the facility and areas within specific departments in the layout
- Arrangement of equipment in the layout

Each of these items of information has an influence on the type of equipment that is selected and the way the equipment is installed to form the material handling system.

In Chapter 2 we described the conventional types of plant layout used in manufacturing: fixed-position layout, process layout, and product-flow layout. The different layout types influence the selection of the material handling system. In the case of a fixed-position layout, the product is large and heavy and therefore remains in a single location during most of its fabrication. Heavy components and subassemblies must be moved to the product. Handling systems used for these moves in fixed-position layouts are large and often mobile. Cranes, hoists, and trucks are common in this situation.

In process layouts, there is a variety of product manufactured and the quantities made per product are medium or small. The handling system must be flexible and programmable (if automated) to deal with the variations. Considerable in-process inventory is usually one of the characteristics of this type of manufacturing, and the handling (and storage) system must be capable of holding this inventory. Hand trucks and forklift trucks (moving pallet loads of parts) are commonly used in process-type layouts. Work-in-progress is often stored on the factory floor near the next-scheduled machines. Because of their capacity to be programmed, automated guided vehicles are likely to become much more common in future factories because they represent a versatile means of handling the various load configurations in medium- and low-volume production.

Finally, the product-flow layout usually involves the production of a standard (or nearly identical types of) product in relatively high volumes. The handling system typically exhibits the following characteristics: fixed installation, fixed route, and mechanized or automated. It is often a delivery and storage system (to reduce the effects of downtime between production areas along the line of product flow). Conveyor systems are often used to transport the product in product-flow layouts. Delivery of component parts for stocking at the various workstations along the flow path in assembly plants is accomplished by trucks and similar unit load vehicles.

Principles of material handling

Certain principles have been developed and documented over the years to provide guidance in the design of a materials handling system. Probably the best known of these principles are those in the list of 20 Principles of Material Handling adopted in June 1966 by the College-Industry Committee on Material Handling Education (sponsored by The Material Handling Institute, Inc., and the International Material Management Society). These 20 principles are presented in most standard references on material handling [6,19,20]. We have borrowed from this list of 20 and revised it to compile the principles presented in Table 14.6. Our list is intended more specifically as a guide in the planning of an automated handling system.

One of the most important of the principles is the unit load principle. According

TABLE 14.6   Principles of Material Handling

Unit load principle. Materials to be moved should be aggregated into a larger unit size, and the unit
size should be the same for all materials. The materials are typically placed on a pallet or other
standard-sized container for convenience in handling. The materials and container are referred to as
the unit load. The unit load should be as large as practical.

Avoid partial loads. Transport the full unit load whenever possible rather than partial loads. Load the
material handling equipment to its maximum safe limit.

Shortest distance principle. Movements of materials should be over the shortest distances possible.
Realization of this principle generally depends on the plant layout design.

Straight-line flow rule. The material handling path should be in a straight line from point of
origination to point of destination. This rule is consistent with the shortest distance principle.

Minimum terminal time principle. Movement of a unit load consists of the move time plus the time
required for loading, unloading, and other activities that do not involve actual transport of the
materials. Minimize these nonmove times.

Gravity principle. Use gravity to assist the movement of materials to the extent possible, at the same
time giving consideration to safety and risk of product damage.

Carry loads both ways. The handling system should be designed and scheduled, to the extent
possible, to carry loads in both directions. Return trips with empty loads are wasteful.

Mechanization principle. Manual handling of materials should be avoided. The handling process
should be mechanized where possible to increase efficiency and economy.

Systems principle. Integrate the materials handling system with other systems in the facility,
including receiving, inspection, storage, production and assembly, packaging, warehousing,
shipping, and transportation.

Systems flow principle. Integrate the flow of material with the flow of information in handling and
storage systems. The information for each item moved should include identification, origination
(pickup) point, and destination point.

Part orientation principle. In automated production systems, the orientation of the workpart should
be established and maintained throughout the material handling process.

Source: Compiled from reference [19] and several other sources.

to the unit load principle, it is desirable to collect a number of individual items into a
single load that can be transported with fewer separate deliveries than the individual
items. The items are usually placed in a container (e.g., tote pan, basket, pallet or pallet
box, etc.), and the handling system is designed to move the container. The dramatic
impact that the unit load principle has on the design of the handling system can be seen
by examining its effect on Eq. (14.4). Let n_p be the number of individual parts or items
in the unit load. For most material handling systems, this would equate to the capacity
of each carrier in the system. Then

$$\text{required handling system capacity} = \frac{\text{TTW}}{n_p E_h} \qquad (14.5)$$

The units of this quantity become unit loads-ft/h. The required capacity of the handling
system can be reduced substantially by taking advantage of the unit load principle and
making the value of n_p as large as possible. The other principles of material handling are

also important, but none has quite as significant an impact on the system's delivery capacity as the unit load principle.

Selection of the material handling equipment must be done so that the resulting system satisfies the requirements of the handling problem. In concept, the equipment listed in Section 14.2 must be specified to match the problem analyzed by the methods in Section 14.3 using the design considerations presented in this section.

Let us turn our attention now to two types of handling systems that are appropriate for automation.

14.5 CONVEYOR SYSTEMS

A conveyor system is used when materials must be moved in relatively large quantities between specific locations over a fixed path. Most conveyor systems are powered to move the loads along the pathways; other conveyors use gravity to cause the load to travel from one elevation in the system to a lower elevation. With respect to the characteristics listed in Table 14.2, conveyors have the following attributes:

- They are generally mechanized, and sometimes automated.
- They are fixed-in-position to establish the paths.
- They can be either floor mounted or overhead.
- They are almost always limited to one-directional flow of materials.
- They generally move discrete loads, but certain types can be used to move bulk or continuous loads.
- They can be used for either delivery-only or delivery-plus-storage of items.

A common feature of powered conveyor systems is that the driving mechanism is built into the conveyor path itself. The individual carriers (if carts or other load receptacles are used) are not individually powered.

Types of conveyors

Within the attributes listed above, many varieties of hardware are available. The major types of conveyors are the following:

- *Roller conveyors*.   This is a very common form of conveyor system. The pathway consists of a series of tubes (rollers) that are perpendicular to the direction of travel, as illustrated in Figure 14.2. The rollers are contained in a fixed frame which elevates the pathway above floor level from several inches to several feet. Flat pallets or tote pans carrying unit loads are moved forward as the rollers rotate. Roller conveyors can be either powered or gravity types. The powered types are driven by any of several different mechanisms; belts and chains are common. The gravity types are arranged so that the pathway is along a downward slope sufficient to overcome rolling friction. Roller conveyors can be used for delivering loads between manufacturing operations, delivery to and from storage,

FIGURE 14.2   Roller conveyor. (Courtesy of Jervis B. Webb Co.)

and distribution applications. Automated systems of conveyors are useful for merging and sorting operations.

- *Skate-wheel conveyors.* These are similar in operation to the roller conveyors. However, instead of rollers, skate wheels rotating on shafts connected to the frame are used to roll the pallet or tote pan or other container along the pathway. The applications of skate-wheel conveyors are similar to those for roller conveyors, except that the loads must generally be lighter since the contacts between the loads and the conveyor are much more concentrated.

- *Belt conveyors.* This type is available in two common forms: flat belts for pallets, parts, or even certain types of bulk materials; and troughed belts for bulk materials. Materials are placed on the belt surface and travel along the moving pathway. The belt is made into a continuous loop so that half of its length can be used for delivering materials, and the other half is the return run (usually empty). The belt is supported by a frame that has rollers or other supports spaced every few feet. At each end of the conveyor (where the belt loops back) are driver rolls (pulleys) that power the belt.

- *Chain conveyors.* Chain conveyors are made of loops of endless chain in an over-and-under configuration around powered sprockets at the ends of the pathway. There may be one or more chains operating in parallel to form the conveyor. The chains travel along channels that provide support for the flexible chain sections. Either the chains slide along the channel or they use rollers to ride in the channel. The loads generally ride along the top of the chain; in some cases, a pusher bar projects up between two parallel chains to push (or pull) the load along a track rather than having the load ride directly on the chain itself.

- *Slat conveyors.* The slat conveyor uses individual platforms, called slats, that are connected to a continuously moving chain. Although its drive mechanism is the powered chain, it operates much like a belt conveyor. Loads are placed on the flat surface of the slats and are transported along with them. Straight-line flows are common in slat conveyor systems. However, because of the chain drive and the capability to alter the chain direction using sprockets, the conveyor pathway can have turns in its continuous loop.

- *Overhead trolley conveyors.* A trolley in material handling is a wheeled carriage running on an overhead rail from which loads can be suspended. A trolley conveyor consists of multiple trolleys, usually equally spaced along the rail system by means of an endless chain or cable. The chain or cable is attached to a drive wheel that supplies power to the system. The path is determined by the configuration of the rail system; it has turns and changes in elevation to form an endless loop. Suspended from the trolleys are hooks, baskets, or other receptacles to carry the loads. The trolley conveyor is shown in Figure 14.3.

FIGURE 14.3 Overhead trolley conveyor. (Courtesy of Jervis B. Webb Co.)

Overhead trolley conveyors are often used in factories to move parts and assemblies between major production departments. They can be used both for delivery and storage purposes.

- *In-floor towline conveyors.* These conveyors make use of wheeled carts powered by means of moving chains or cables located in trenches in the floor. The chain or cable is called the towline—hence the name of the conveyor system. An example is presented in Figure 14.4. The pathways of the conveyor system are defined by the trench and cable system; switches between powered pathways are possible in the towline system to achieve some flexibility in the handling routes. The carts use hardened steel pins (dowels) that project below the floor surface into the trench to engage the chain for towing. The pin can be pulled out of the trench to disengage the cart (for loading, unloading, accumulation of

FIGURE 14.4 In-floor towline conveyor used in an automated manufacturing system to move truck transmission parts between machine tools. (Courtesy of Kearney & Trecker Corp.)

parts, etc., off the main pathway). Towline systems are used for moving unit loads in plants and warehouses.

- *Cart-on-track conveyors.* These conveyor systems use individual carts riding on a two-railed track contained in a frame that places the track a few feet above floor level. The carts are not individually powered; instead, they are driven by means of a rotating tube that runs between the two rails. Owing to the use of the rotating tube, these conveyor systems are sometimes called spinning tube conveyors. A drive wheel, attached to the bottom of the cart and set at an angle to the rotating tube, rests against it and drives the cart forward. The operation of the conveyor system is illustrated in Figure 14.5. The cart speed is controlled by regulating the angle of contact between the drive wheel and the spinning tube. When the drive wheel is perpendicular to the tube, the cart does not move. As the angle is increased toward 45°, the speed increases. One of the advantages of the cart-on-track systems compared to many other conveyor systems is that the carts can achieve relatively high accuracies of position. This permits their use for positioning work during production. Applications of cart-on-track systems

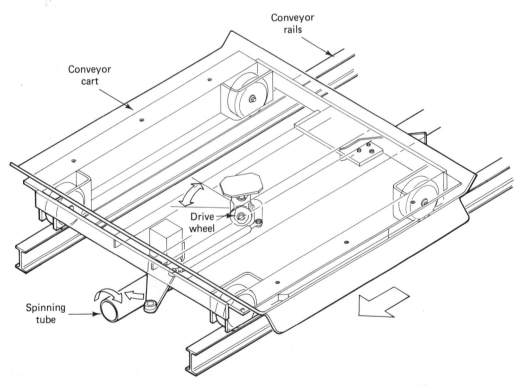

FIGURE 14.5   Diagram showing operation of cart-on-track conveyor. (Courtesy of SI Handling Systems Inc.)

have included robotic spot welding lines and mechanical assembly systems. The latter application is depicted in Figure 14.6.

- *Other types.* There are other types of conveyors, perhaps of lesser importance for our purposes in automation. The other types include chutes, ramps, tubes, screw conveyors, vibrating systems, and vertical-lift conveyors.

Routing and other functions

Conveyor system pathways can be designed to operate in a single direction or in a continuous closed loop for two-way flow. The single-direction conveyors are used to transport loads one way from an origination point to a destination point. These systems are suitable when there is no need to return the pallet or carrier to the loading station. Examples of conveyor types that lend themselves to this one-direction flow are roller,

FIGURE 14.6 Cart-on-track conveyor system used with assembly robot. (Courtesy of SI Handling Systems Inc.)

skate wheel, belt, chain, and all gravity conveyors. Continuous-loop conveyor systems are used for a two-way flow of loads or where it is necessary to return the empty carriers from the unload station back to the loading station. Loop conveyors are also used for temporary storage of work-in-process in production systems. Types of conveyors suited to this configuration include overhead trolley, cart-on-track, and towline conveyors.

It is possible to construct branches, spurs, and sidings into the conveyor pathway. To incorporate these alternate routings into the conveyor system, a divergence in the pathway must be provided. The purpose of using alternative paths is to permit different routings for different loads moving in the system. In nearly all conveyor systems, it is possible to build switches, turntables, shuttles, or other mechanisms to achieve this path divergence. Examples of conveyors that use these types of mechanisms include towline, cart-on-track, and certain overhead trolley systems. In some systems a push-pull mechanism or other device is required at the divergence point to actively move the load from the current pathway onto the new pathway. Examples of conveyor systems that utilize this type of active device to achieve divergence are roller and belt conveyors.

Some conveyors are designed to operate as asynchronous or "power-and-free" systems. As explained in Chapter 4, asynchronous handling allows independent movement of each cart or pallet in the system. Reasons for using asynchronous conveyors include: to accumulate loads, for temporary storage (buffer storage), to allow for differences in production rates between adjacent processing areas, to smooth production when cycle times are variable at different workstations along the conveyor, and to accommodate different conveyor speeds along the pathway. Conveyor systems that can be readily engineered to operate as power-and-free handling systems include cart-on-track, overhead trolley systems, and roller conveyors.

Quantitative relationships and analysis of conveyor systems

Certain basic quantitative measures and equations govern the operation of conveyor systems. Most of these equations are based on the physical relationship between time, distance, and velocity. We have previously defined V_c to be the velocity of the conveyor (ft/min), R_f to be the rate of flow of parts (parts/h) moving along the pathway (this is the same as the feed rate of the conveyor that we encountered in Chapter 6), and E_h to be the efficiency of the handling system.

SINGLE DIRECTION CONVEYOR. Consider the simple case of a single-direction conveyor system (e.g., roller conveyor) with a single load station at the upstream end and a single unload station at the downstream end, separated by a distance L_d. The configuration is schematically shown in Figure 14.7. Carriers or pallets are loaded at one end and unloaded at the other end. The time required to move the carriers from the load station to the unload station is L_d/V_c. The carrier flow rate for the conveyor is limited by the time required to load the conveyor, T_L. The carrier or pallet flow rate cannot be greater than the reciprocal of this loading time. The limitation can be expressed as follows:

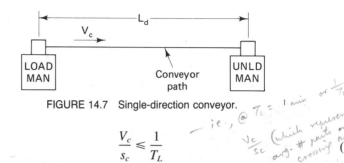

FIGURE 14.7   Single-direction conveyor.

$$\frac{V_c}{s_c} \le \frac{1}{T_L} \qquad (14.6)$$

where s_c is the spacing between carriers. The time required to unload the conveyor, T_u, must be equal to or less than the loading time. If the unload time were greater than the load time, the conveyor speed would have to be reduced, or unremoved loads would be dumped onto the floor at the downstream end of the line.

If we assume that each carrier can hold n_p parts, the flow rate of parts on the conveyor system will be

$$R_f = \frac{n_p V_c}{s_c} \le \frac{n_p}{T_L} \qquad (14.7)$$

According to our definition of handling system efficiency, this type of system will have a relatively high efficiency since there will be no traffic congestion along the conveyor, no empty carts making return trips, and the conveyor does not stop for loading and unloading.

CONTINUOUS LOOP CONVEYOR.   Next consider a continuous closed-loop conveyor (e.g., an overhead trolley conveyor). The complete loop is divided into two portions: the delivery (forward) loop and the return loop, as shown in Figure 14.8. Let us assume that the parts are transported in carriers or containers that are equally spaced at a separation of s_c and fixed to the conveyor. Each carrier holds n_p parts on the delivery trip (the forward loop) and no parts on the return trip. The distance of the delivery loop is L_d, and the distance of the return loop (traveling empty) is L_e. The total length of the conveyor

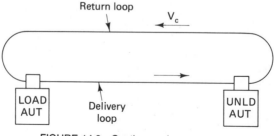

FIGURE 14.8   Continuous loop conveyor.

loop is therefore $L_d + L_e$. The time required to travel the complete loop is $(L_d + L_e)/V_c$. Let n_c represent the number of carriers in the system. It must be true that

$$n_c = \frac{L_d + L_e}{s_c} \tag{14.8}$$

However, since only those carriers on the forward loop contain parts, the total number of parts in the system at any one time (assuming all containers on the forward loop are loaded) is given by

$$\text{total parts in system} = \frac{n_p L_d}{s_c} = \frac{n_p n_c L_d}{L_d + L_e} \tag{14.9}$$

The parts feed rate of the system is again given by $R_f = n_p V_c/s_c$.

RECIRCULATING CONVEYOR. The preceding conveyor model assumes that parts loaded at one end of the loop are unloaded at the other end. That is, no accumulation of parts in the return loop is permitted; the purpose of the return loop is simply to send the empty pallets back for reloading. This method of operation overlooks one of the important opportunities offered by a closed-loop conveyor: to provide for both storage as well as delivery of parts. In providing a storage function, the conveyor system can be used to accumulate parts to smooth out the effects of changes in rates of loading and unloading the conveyor. These rates might represent production rates in different assembly departments in the factory. The problems in operating such a recirculating conveyor system are (1) that no empty carriers may be immediately available at the loading station when needed; and (2) no loaded carriers may be immediately available at the unloading station when needed.

Recirculating conveyors of the type described here have been analyzed by Kwo [7,8], Mayer [11], and Muth [14–16]. We summarize the results of Kwo in the paragraphs below.

According to Kwo's analysis, there are three basic principles that should be used in the design of a closed-loop, recirculating conveyor with one loading station and one unloading station. These principles are the following:

1. *Speed rule.* This principle states that the speed at which the conveyor is operated must be within a certain permissible range. The speed is figured in terms of the number of carriers per unit time (i.e., V_c/s_c). The lower limit on the speed range is determined by the loading and unloading rates at the respective stations, as follows: V_c/s_c should be greater than or equal to the required loading rate or the unloading rate, whichever is greater. The upper limit on the range is determined by the capabilities of the material handlers to handle the materials that are being loaded and unloaded (usually defined by T_L and T_u), and the technological upper limits on speed that are imposed by the conveyor design.

2. *Capacity constraint.* The capacity of the conveyor system must be at least equal to the flow rate requirement. It should be greater than the flow rate requirement to accommodate reserve stock and to allow for the time lapse between loading and unloading due to the delivery distance. If we let L represent the total length of the conveyor loop, the conveyor capacity is given by:

$$\text{conveyor capacity} = \frac{n_c n_p V_c}{L} = \frac{n_p V_c}{S_c} \qquad (14.10)$$

3. *Uniformity principle.* This principle states that parts (loads) should be uniformly loaded throughout the conveyor. This means that there will be no sections of the conveyor in which every carrier is full while there are other sections of the conveyor that are virtually empty. The reason for the uniformity principle is to avoid unusually long waiting times at the load or unload stations for empty or full carriers (respectively) to arrive.

EXAMPLE 14.2

A recirculating conveyor has a total length of 500 ft. Its speed is 100 ft/min and the spacing of part carriers along its length is 25 ft. Each carrier can hold two parts. Robots are used to load and unload the conveyor at its load and unload stations. The time required to load a part is 0.20 min and the unload time is the same. The required loading and unloading rates are both 1.0 part/min.

(a) What is the maximum possible flow rate of parts on the conveyor system?

(b) How many parts could be contained on the conveyor system if every carrier were filled to capacity?

(c) How much time is required for the conveyor to make one complete loop?

(d) Evaluate the conveyor system design with respect to the three principles developed by Kwo.

Solution:

(a) The maximum possible flow rate occurs when every carrier on the conveyor system is filled. This flow rate is given by Eq. (14.7).

$$R_f = (2 \text{ parts/carrier})(100 \text{ ft/min})/(25 \text{ ft/carrier})$$

$$= 8 \text{ parts/min}$$

(b) The total number of carriers = (500 ft)/(25 ft/carrier)

$$= 20 \text{ carriers}$$

The total number of parts, at 2 parts/carrier = 40 parts. (c) At the given speed, it takes (500 ft)/(100 ft/min) = 5.0 min for the conveyor to make a complete loop.

(d) *Speed rule.* The lower limit on the speed range is set by the required loading and unloading rates, which are given as 1 part/min. The upper limit on the speed range is established by the times required to perform the loading and unloading activities. The activity times are equal at 0.20 min, which is equivalent to a rate = 5 parts/min. The conveyor speed = V_c/S_c = 100 ft/min divided by 25 ft/carrier = 4 carriers/min. This value is within the allowable range given by the speed rule.

Capacity constraint. The conveyor capacity is equal to the flow rate, determined in part (a) to be 8 parts/min. Since this is substantially greater than the required delivery rate of 1 part/min, we assume that the capacity constraint is satisfied. Kwo [7,8] provides guidelines for determining the flow rate requirement that should be compared to the conveyor capacity. The total number of parts that can be loaded onto the conveyor is 40, according to the answer for part (b). This provides an alternative measure of the conveyor system capacity.

Uniformity principle. We assume that it is possible to load the conveyor uniformly throughout its length since the loading and unloading rates are equal and since the flow rate capacity is substantially greater than this load/unload rate. Kwo [7,8] defines conditions for checking the uniformity principle, and the reader is referred to those original papers.

The results of Muth [14–16] are somewhat more general than Kwo's, allowing for more than single loading and unloading stations in the conveyor system. Mayer's analysis [11] considers the problem as probabilistic in nature, and he derives several equations for conveyor performance based on the binomial distribution. The interested reader is referred to the original research papers. Also, the results of several of these papers are presented in the book by Tompkins and White [20], and the review paper by Muth and White [17] summarizes much of the research that has been done on conveyor theory.

14.6 AUTOMATED GUIDED VEHICLE SYSTEMS

An automated or automatic guided vehicle system (AGVS) is a materials handling system that uses independently operated, self-propelled vehicles that are guided along defined pathways in the floor. The vehicles are powered by means of on-board batteries that allow operation for several hours (8 to 16 hours is typical) between recharging. The definition of the pathways is generally accomplished using wires embedded in the floor or reflective paint on the floor surface. Guidance is achieved by sensors on the vehicles that can follow the guide wires or paint.

There are a number of different types of AGVS all of which operate according to the preceding description. The types can be classified as follows:

- *Driverless trains.* This type consists of a towing vehicle (which is the AGV) that pulls one or more trailers to form a train. It was the first type of AGVS to be introduced and is still popular. It is useful in applications where heavy payloads must be moved large distances in warehouses or factories with intermediate pickup and drop-off points along the route. Figure 14.9 illustrates the driverless-train AGVS.

- *AGVS pallet trucks.* Automated guided pallet trucks are used to move palletized loads along predetermined routes. In the typical application the vehicle is backed into the loaded pallet by a human worker who steers the truck and uses its forks to elevate the load slightly. Then the worker drives the pallet truck to the guidepath, programs its destination, and the vehicle proceeds automatically to the destination for unloading. The capacity of an AGVS pallet truck ranges up to 6000 lb, and some trucks are capable of handling two pallets rather than one. A more recent introduction related to the pallet

FIGURE 14.9   AGVS driverless train. (Courtesy of Jervis B. Webb Co.)

FIGURE 14.10   AGVS forklift vehicle. (Courtesy of Portec, Inc.)

truck is the forklift AGV. This vehicle can achieve significant vertical movement of its forks to reach loads on shelves. Figure 14.10 illustrates this vehicle type.

• *AGVS unit load carriers.* This type of AGVS is used to move unit loads from one station to another station. They are often equipped for automatic loading and unloading by means of powered rollers, moving belts, mechanized lift platforms, or other devices. The unit load carrier is pictured in Figure 14.11. Variations of the unit load carrier include light-load AGVs and assembly line AGVs. The light-load AGV is a relatively small vehicle with a corresponding light load capacity (typically 500 lb or less). It does not require the same large aisle width as the conventional AGV. Light-load guided vehicles are designed to move small loads (single parts, small baskets or tote pans of parts, etc.) through plants of limited size engaged in light manufacturing. The assembly line AGVS is designed to carry a partially completed subassembly through a sequence of assembly workstations to build the product. Figure 14.12 shows this AGV type.

AGVS technology is far from mature, and the industry is continually working to develop new systems in response to new application requirements. An example of a new and evolving AGVS design involves the placement of a robotic manipulator on an au-

FIGURE 14.11 AGVS unit load carrier. (Courtesy of Jervis B. Webb Co.)

FIGURE 14.12   AGVS unit load carrier used in automobile assembly plant. (Courtesy of Portec, Inc.)

tomated guided vehicle to provide a mobile robot for performing complex handling tasks at various locations in a plant. These robot-vehicles are seen as being useful in clean rooms in the semiconductor industry.

Applications

Automated guided vehicle systems are used in a growing number and variety of applications. The applications tend to parallel the vehicle types described above. We group the applications into the following five categories:

1. *Driverless train operations.*   These applications involve the movement of large quantities of materials over relatively large distances. For example, the moves are within a large warehouse or factory building, or between buildings in a large storage depot. For the movement of trains consisting of 5 to 10 trailers, this becomes an efficient handling method.

2. *Storage/distribution systems.*   Unit load carriers and pallet trucks are typically used in these applications. These storage and distribution operations involve the movement of materials in unit loads (sometimes individual items are moved) from or to specific locations. The applications often interface the AGVS with some other automated handling or storage system, such as an automated storage/retrieval system (AS/RS) in a distribution

center. The AGVS delivers incoming items or unit loads (contained on pallets) from the receiving dock to the AS/RS, which places the items in storage, and the AS/RS retrieves individual pallet loads or items from storage and transfers them to vehicles for delivery to the shipping dock. When the rates of incoming loads and the outgoing loads are in balance, this mode of operation permits loads to be carried in both directions by the AGVS vehicles, thereby increasing the handling system efficiency.

This type of storage/distribution operation can also be applied in light manufacturing and assembly operations in which work-in-progress is stored in a central storage area and distributed to individual workstations for assembly or processing. Electronics assembly is an example of these types of applications. Components are "kitted" at the storage area and delivered in tote pans or trays by the guided vehicles to the assembly workstations in the plant. Light-load AGV systems are used in these applications.

3. *Assembly-line operations.* AGV systems are being used in a growing number of assembly-line applications, based on a trend that began in Europe. In these applications, the production rate is relatively low (perhaps 4 to 10 min per station in the line) and there are a variety of different models made on the production line. Between the workstations, components are kitted and placed on the vehicle for the assembly operations that are to be performed on the partially completed product at the next station. The workstations are generally arranged in parallel configurations to add to the flexibility of the line. Unit load carriers and light-load guided vehicles are the type of AGVS used in these assembly lines. Figure 14.12 illustrates the application. We discussed this application previously in Section 6.8.

4. *Flexible manufacturing systems.* Another growing application of AGVS technology is in flexible manufacturing systems (FMS). In this application, the guided vehicles are used as the materials handling system in the FMS. The vehicles deliver work from the staging area (where work is placed on pallet fixtures, usually manually) to the individual workstations in the system. The vehicles also move work between stations in the manufacturing system. At a workstation, the work is transferred from the vehicle platform into the work area of the station (usually, the table of a machine tool) for processing. At the completion of processing by that station a vehicle returns to pick up the work and transport it to the next area. AGV systems provide a versatile material handling system to complement the flexibility of the FMS operation.

5. *Miscellaneous applications.* Other applications of automated guided vehicle systems include nonmanufacturing and nonwarehousing applications, such as mail delivery in office buildings and hospital material handling operations. Hospital guided vehicles transport meal trays, linen, medical and laboratory supplies, and other materials between various departments in the building. These applications typically require movement of the vehicles between different floors of the hospital, and hospital AGV systems have the capability to summon and use elevators for this purpose.

Vehicle guidance and routing

There are several functions that must be performed to operate any automated guided vehicle system successfully. These functions are:

1. Vehicle guidance and routing
2. Traffic control and safety
3. System management

We describe these functions in this and the following two subsections.

The term *guidance system* refers to the method by which the AGVS pathways are defined and the vehicle control systems that follow the pathways. As indicated above, there are two principal methods currently in use to define the pathways along the floor: embedded guide wires and paint strips. Of the two types, the guide wire system is the more common in warehouse and factory applications.

In the guide wire method the wires are usually embedded in a small channel cut into the surface of the floor. The channel is typically about $\frac{1}{8}$ in. wide and $\frac{1}{2}$ in. deep. After the guide wires are installed, the channel slot is filled so as to eliminate the discontinuity in the floor surface. An alternative but less permanent way to install the guide wires is to tape them to the floor. A frequency generator provides the guidance signal carried in the wire. The signal is of relatively low voltage (less than 40 V), low current (less than 400 mA), and has a frequency in the range 1 to 15 kHz. This signal level creates a magnetic field along the pathway that is followed by sensors on-board each vehicle. The operation of a typical system is illustrated in Figure 14.13. Two sensors (coils) are mounted on the vehicle on either side of the guide wire. When the vehicle is moving along a course such that the guide wire is directly between the two coils, the intensity of the magnetic field measured by each coil will be equal. If the vehicle strays to one side or the other, or if the guide wire path curves, the magnetic field intensity at the two sensors will be different. This difference is used to control the steering motor, which makes the required changes in vehicle direction to equalize the two sensor signals, thereby tracking the defined pathway.

When paint strips are used to define the vehicle pathways, the vehicle possesses an optical sensor system that is capable of tracking the paint. The strips can be taped, sprayed, or painted on the floor. One system uses a 1-in.-wide paint strip containing fluorescent particles that reflect an ultraviolet (UV) light source on the vehicle. An on-board sensor detects the reflected light in the strip and controls the steering mechanism

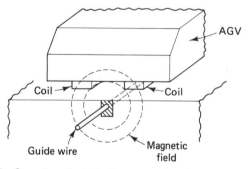

FIGURE 14.13 Operation of a typical sensor system that uses two coils to track the magnetic field of the guide wire.

to follow it. The paint guidance system is useful in environments where electrical noise would render the guide wire system unreliable or when the installation of guide wires in the floor surface would not be appropriate. One problem with the paint strip guidance method is that the paint strip must be maintained (kept clean and unscratched).

A safety feature used in the operation of most guidance systems is automatic stopping of the vehicle in the event that it accidentally strays more than a few inches (typically 2 to 6 in.) from the guide path. This automatic-stopping feature prevents the vehicle from running wild in the building. Alternatively, in the event that the vehicle is off the guide path (e.g., for manual loading of a pallet truck), it is capable of locking onto the guide wire or paint strip if moved within the same few inches of it. The distance is referred to as the vehicle's *acquisition distance*.

The use of microprocessor controls on-board the vehicles has led to the development of a feature called *dead reckoning*. This term refers to the capability of the vehicle to travel along a route that does not follow the defined pathway in the floor. The microprocessor computes the number of wheel rotations and the operation of the steering motor required to move along the desired path. Dead reckoning might be employed by the vehicle to cross a steel plate in the factory floor (where guide wires cannot be installed), or to depart from the guide path for positioning at a load/unload station. At the completion of the dead-reckoning maneuver, the vehicle is programmed to return to within the acquisition distance of the guide path to resume normal guidance control.

Routing in an AGVS is concerned with the problem of selecting among alternative pathways available to a vehicle in its travel to a defined destination point in the system. A typical guided vehicle layout, one that exploits the capabilities of modern AGVS technology, contains features such as multiple loops, branches, side tracks, and spurs, in addition to the required pickup and drop-off stations. Vehicles in the system must decide which path to take to reach a defined destination point.

When a vehicle approaches a branching point in which the guide path splits into two (or more) directions, a decision must be made as to which path the vehicle should take. This is sometimes referred to as a *decision point* for the vehicle. There are two methods used in commercial AGV systems to permit the vehicle to decide which path to take:

1. Frequency select method
2. Path switch select method

In the *frequency select method,* the guide wires leading into the two separate paths at the branch have different frequencies. As the vehicle enters the decision point, it reads an identification code on the floor to identify its location. Depending on its programmed destination, the vehicle selects one of the guide paths by deciding which frequency to track. This method requires a separate frequency generator for each frequency that is used in the guide path layout. This usually means that two or three generators are needed in the system. Additional channels must often be cut into the floor with the frequency select method to provide for bypass channels where only the main channel needs to be powered for vehicle tracking.

The *path switch select method* uses a single frequency throughout the guide path layout. In order to control the path of a vehicle at a decision point, the power is switched off in all branches except the one on which the vehicle is to travel. To accomplish routing by the path switch select method, the guide path layout must be divided into blocks that can be independently turned on and off by means of controls mounted on the floor near their respective blocks. These control units are operated by the vehicles as they move in the various blocks. As a vehicle enters a decision point, it activates a floor-mounted switching device connected to the control unit for the relevant block. The control unit activates the desired guidepath and turns off the alternative branch or branches.

Traffic control and safety

The purpose of traffic control for an AGVS is to prevent collisions between vehicles traveling along the same guide path in the layout. This purpose is usually accomplished by means of a control system called the *blocking system*. The term "blocking" suggests that a vehicle traveling along a given guide path is in some way prevented from hitting any vehicle ahead of it. There are several means used in commercial AGV systems to accomplish blocking. They are:

1. On-board vehicle sensing
2. Zone blocking

On-board vehicle sensing and zone blocking are often used in combination to implement a comprehensive blocking system.

On-board vehicle sensing (sometimes called *forward sensing*) involves the use of some form of sensor system to detect the presence of vehicles and carts ahead on the same guide wire. The sensors used on commercial guided vehicles include optical sensors and ultrasonic systems. When the on-board sensor detects an obstacle (e.g., another guided vehicle) in front of it, the vehicle stops. When the obstacle is removed, the vehicle proceeds. Assuming that the sensor system is 100% effective, collisions between vehicles are avoided and traffic is controlled. Unfortunately, the effectiveness of forward sensing is limited by the capability of the sensor system to detect vehicles in front of it on the guide path. Since the sensors themselves are most effective in detecting obstacles directly ahead of the vehicle, these systems are most appropriate on layouts that contain long stretches of straight pathways. They are less effective at turns and convergence points where forward vehicles may not be directly in front of the sensor.

The concept of *zone control* is simple. The AGVS layout is divided into separate zones, and the operating rule is that no vehicle is permitted to enter a zone if that zone is already occupied by another vehicle. The length of a zone is sufficient to hold one vehicle (or a train in driverless train systems) plus an allowance for safety and other considerations. These other considerations include the number of vehicles in the system, the size and complexity of the layout, and the objective of minimizing the number of separate zone controls. When one vehicle occupies a given zone, any trailing vehicle is not allowed into that zone. The leading vehicle must proceed into the next zone before the trailing vehicle can occupy the given zone. By controlling the forward movement of vehicles in the separate zones, collisions are prevented and traffic in the overall system is controlled. The concept is illustrated in Figure 14.14 in its simplest form. More complicated zone control schemes separate any two vehicles by a blocked zone.

One means of implementing zone control is to use separate control units for each zone. These controls are mounted along the guide path and are actuated by the vehicle in the zone. When a vehicle enters a given zone, it activates the block in the previous (upstream) zone to block any trailing vehicle from moving forward and colliding with the present vehicle. As the present vehicle moves into the next (downstream) zone, it activates the block in that zone and deactivates the block in the previous zone. In effect, zones are turned on and off to control vehicle movement by the blocking system.

In addition to avoiding collisions between vehicles, a related objective is the safety of human beings who might be located along the route of the vehicles traveling in the system. There are several devices that are usually included on an automatic guided vehicle to achieve this safety objective. One of the safety devices is an obstacle-detection sensor located at the front of each vehicle. This is often the same on-board sensor as that used in the blocking system to detect the presence of other vehicles located in front of the sensor. The sensor can detect not only other vehicles, but also people and obstacles in the path of the vehicle. These obstacle-detection systems are usually based on optical, infrared, or ultrasonic sensors. The vehicles are programmed either to stop when an obstacle is sensed ahead of it, or to slow down. The reason for slowing down is that the sensed object may be located off to the side of the vehicle path, or directly ahead of the vehicle beyond a turn in the guide path. In either of these cases, the vehicle should be permitted to proceed at a slower (safer) speed until it has passed the object or rounded the turn.

Another safety device included on virtually all commercial AG vehicles is an emergency bumper. This bumper is prominent in several of our figures, especially Figures 14.9 and 14.11. The bumper surrounds the front of the vehicle and protrudes ahead of it by a distance which can be a foot or more. When the bumper makes contact with an object, the vehicle is programmed to brake immediately. Depending on the speed of the vehicle, its load, and other conditions, the braking distance will vary from several inches to several feet. Most vehicles are programmed to require manual restarting after an obstacle encounter has occurred with the emergency bumper.

Other safety devices on the vehicles include warning lights (blinking or rotating lights) and/or warning bells. These devices alert people that the vehicle is present.

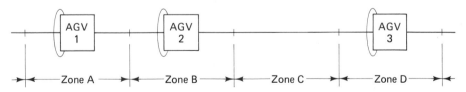

FIGURE 14.14 · Zone control to implement blocking system. Zones A, B, and D are blocked. Zone C is free. Vehicle 2 is blocked from entering zone A by vehicle 1. Vehicle 3 is free to enter zone C.

Finally, another safety feature that prevents runaway vehicles is the inherent operating characteristic of the guidance system: If the vehicle strays by more than a few inches from the defined path, the vehicle is programmed to stop.

System management

Managing the operations of an AGVS deals principally with the problem of dispatching vehicles to the points in the system where they are needed (e.g., to perform pickups and deliveries) in a timely and efficient manner. The system management function depends on reliable operation of the other system functions discussed above (guidance, routing, traffic control). There are a number of methods used in commercial AGV systems for dispatching vehicles. These methods are generally used in combination to maximize responsiveness and effectiveness of the overall system. The dispatching methods include:

- On-board control panel
- Remote call stations
- Central computer control

Each guided vehicle is equipped with some form of control panel for the purpose of manual vehicle control, vehicle programming, and other functions. Most commercial vehicles have the capacity to be dispatched by means of this control panel to a given station in the AGVS layout. Dispatching with an on-board control panel represents the lowest level of sophistication among the possible methods. Its advantage is that it provides the AGVS with flexibility and responsiveness to changing demands on the handling system. Its disadvantage is that it requires manual attention.

The use of remote call stations is another method that allows the AGVS to respond to changing demand patterns in the system. The simplest form of call station is a press button mounted near the load/unload station. This provides a signal to any passing vehicle to stop at the station in order to accomplish a load transfer operation. The vehicle might then be dispatched to the desired location by means of the on-board control panel.

More sophisticated call stations consist of control panels mounted near the various stations along the layout. This method permits a vehicle to be stopped at a given station, and its next destination to be programmed from the remote call panel. This represents a more automated approach to the dispatching function and is useful in AGV systems that are capable of automatic loading and unloading operations.

Both of the call station methods described here involve a human interface with the AGVS at the load/unload station. It is also possible to automate the call function at an automatic load/unload station. One example is an automated production workstation that receives raw materials and sends completed parts by means of the AGVS. The workstation is interfaced with the AGVS to call for vehicles as needed to perform the loading and unloading procedures.

In large factory and warehouse systems involving a high level of automation, the AGVS servicing the factory or warehouse must also be highly automated to achieve efficient operation of the entire production–storage–handling system. Central computer control is used to accomplish automatic dispatching of vehicles according to a preplanned schedule of pickups and deliveries in the layout and/or in response to calls from the various load/unload stations in the system. In this dispatching method, the central computer issues commands to the vehicles in the system concerning their destinations and operations to perform. To accomplish the dispatching function, the central computer must possess real-time information about the location of each vehicle in the system so that it can make appropriate decisions concerning which vehicles to dispatch to what locations. Hence, the vehicles must continually communicate their whereabouts to the central controller.

There are differences in the way these central computer dispatching systems operate. One of the differences involves the distribution of the decision-making responsibilities between the central controller and the individual vehicles. At one extreme, the central computer makes nearly all the decisions about routing of vehicles and other functions. The central computer plans out the routes for each vehicle and controls the operation of the guide path zones and other functions. At the opposite extreme, each individual vehicle possesses a substantial decision-making capability to make its own routing selections and to control its own operations. The central computer is still needed to control the overall scheduling and determine which vehicles should go to the various demand points in the system. However, the vehicles themselves decide which routes to take and control their own load transfer operations. Vehicles in this second category are often referred to as "smart" vehicles.

To accomplish the system management function, it is helpful to monitor the overall operations of the AGVS by means of some form of graphics display. Even with central computer control it is still desirable for human managers to be able to see the overall system operations, in order to monitor its general status and to spot problems (e.g., traffic jams, breakdowns, etc.). A CRT color graphics display is often used for these purposes in modern guided vehicle systems.

Another useful tool in carrying out the systems management function is a system performance report for each shift (or other appropriate time period) of AGVS operation. These periodic reports of system performance provide summary information about proportion uptime, downtime, number of transactions (deliveries) made during a shift, and more detailed data about each station and each vehicle in the system. Hard-copy reports containing this type of information permit the system managers to compare operations from shift to shift and month to month to maintain a high level of overall system performance.

Quantitative analysis of AGV systems

It is possible to define the equations that govern the operation of an automated guided vehicle system. Let V_c be the velocity of the cart (vehicle) in the AGVS. We will assume that the vehicle operates at a constant velocity throughout its operation, and ignore the effects of acceleration, deceleration, and other speed differences that might result from the load carried and other factors that would affect speed. The time elements for a typical AGVS delivery would consist of the following: (1) the loading operation at the pickup station and the unloading operation at the drop-off station (we have previously added these elements to obtain T_h, the load handling time), (2) the travel time to the drop-off station (L_d/V_c), and (3) the empty travel time of the vehicle between deliveries (L_e/V_c). Ignoring any effect of traffic congestion, the total time per delivery per vehicle is therefore given by

$$T_v = \frac{L_d}{V_c} + T_h + \frac{L_e}{V_c} \tag{14.11}$$

If there were no losses from traffic congestion, the number of deliveries per hour made by each vehicle could be determined by taking the reciprocal of T_v. However, the traffic losses can have a significant effect on the performance of an automated guided vehicle system. The previously defined traffic factor, F_t, is used to estimate the effect of these losses on system performance. The sources of inefficiency in an AGVS that are accounted for by the traffic factor include blocking of vehicles, waiting at intersections, vehicles waiting in line, poor scheduling, inefficient routing of vehicles, and poor layout of the guide path. Blocking, waiting at intersections, and vehicles waiting in line are affected by the number of vehicles in the system relative to the size of the layout. For example, if there is only one vehicle in the system, no blocking will occur and the traffic factor will be very close to 1. For systems with many vehicles, there will be many instances of blocking and congestion, and the traffic factor will take a lower value. Other factors that affect traffic congestion are scheduling, routing, and AGVS layout. Central computer control, programmed with optimum scheduling algorithms, tends to be more efficient for scheduling and routing than on-board or remote call dispatching. Typical values of the traffic factor for an AGVS range between 0.85 and 1.0 [2].

To estimate the number of deliveries that can be made per hour by a single vehicle, we assume that T_v is given in minutes and the traffic factor is expressed as a decimal fraction:

$$\text{number of deliveries/hour/vehicle} = \frac{60F_t}{T_v} \tag{14.12}$$

Alternatively, using the handling system efficiency E_h, defined in Eq. (14.3), Eq. (14.12) becomes

$$\text{number of deliveries/hour/vehicle} = \frac{60E_h}{L_d/V_c} \tag{14.13}$$

where L_d/V_c is the direct travel time per vehicle for a delivery with no delays or lost time.

The handling system efficiency E_h does not include the losses that result from an

AGVS layout containing long or superfluous pathways that cause the vehicles to travel farther than necessary to reach their destinations.

The total number of vehicles required in the system can be estimated based on the number of deliveries per hour that each vehicle can make and the total number of deliveries that must be made by the system.

$$\text{number of AGVs} = \frac{\text{number of deliveries req'd/hour}}{\text{number of deliveries/hour/vehicle}} \qquad (14.14)$$

If there is a variation in the number of deliveries that must be made by the system from hour to hour, the maximum demand rate is the appropriate value to use in the equation.

EXAMPLE 14.3

It is desired to determine how many vehicles will be required to satisfy demand for a particular AGVS. The system must be capable of making 40 deliveries/h. The following specifies the performance characteristics of the system:

$$\text{vehicle velocity} = 150 \text{ ft/min}$$

$$\text{average distance traveled per delivery} = 450 \text{ ft}$$

$$\text{pick-up time} = 45 \text{ s } (0.75 \text{ min})$$

$$\text{drop-off time} = 45 \text{ s } (0.75 \text{ min})$$

$$\text{average distance traveling empty} = 300 \text{ ft}$$

$$\text{traffic factor} = 0.90$$

Determine the number of vehicles required to satisfy the delivery demand. Also determine the handling system efficiency.

Solution:

The total time per delivery per vehicle is given by

$$T_v = \frac{450}{150} + 0.75 + 0.75 + \frac{300}{150}$$

$$= 3.0 + 1.5 + 2.0$$

$$= 6.5 \text{ min}$$

The number of deliveries per hour per vehicle, according to Eq. (14.12), is

$$\frac{60(0.90)}{6.5} = 8.3077 \text{ deliveries/h/vehicle}$$

Therefore, the number of vehicles required is

$$\frac{40}{8.3077} = 4.81 \text{ vehicles}$$

This value should be rounded up to 5 vehicles.

The handling system efficiency, according to Eq. (14.3), is

$$E_h = \frac{3.0(0.90)}{6.5}$$

$$= 0.4154$$

Using this value in Eq. (14.13) to check the value obtained above using Eq. (14.12), the number of deliveries per hour per vehicle is

$$\frac{60(0.4154)}{3.0} = 8.31 \text{ deliveries/h/vehicle}$$

Determining the average travel distances, L_d and L_e, requires analysis of the particular AGVS layout. For a simple loop layout, determination of these values is usually straightforward. As the complexity of the AGVS layout increases, the problem becomes more difficult. The following examples will illustrate.

EXAMPLE 14.4

The AGVS layout under consideration is the simple loop shown in Figure 14.15, in which loads are picked up by the vehicles automatically at the load station and delivered to the unload station for drop-off. Distances are given on the layout. Determine the delivery distance and the empty travel distance from the layout.

Solution:

Ignoring the effects of slightly shorter distances around the curves at the corners of the loop, the values of L_d and L_e can be readily determined to be 450 ft and 300 ft, respectively. (This might very well be the system considered in Example 14.3).

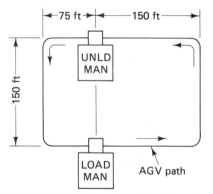

FIGURE 14.15   AGVS loop layout for Example 14.4.

EXAMPLE 14.5

This example uses the from–to charts in Tables 14.4 and 14.5. The layout for the AGVS is presented in Figure 14.16. It includes a load station (station 1) from which raw workparts enter the system for delivery to any of three production workstations (stations 2, 3, and 4). An unload station (station 5) is used to receive the finished parts from the production stations. The load and unload times at stations 1 and 5 are each 0.5 min. Production rates for each workstation are indicated by the delivery requirements in Table 14.4. One complicating factor in the layout is that there must be transshipment of some of the parts between stations 2 and 3. The problem here is to determine the average distance for a delivery, L_d.

Solution:

Table 14.4 shows the number of deliveries that must be made between the various stations. Distances between stations are presented in Table 14.5. These distance values are taken from the drawing of the layout in Figure 14.16. To determine the value of L_d, a weighted average must be calculated based on the distances and corresponding number of trips shown in the from–to charts for the problem.

$$L_d = \frac{9 \times 200 + 5 \times 400 + 6 \times 700 + 2 \times 300 + 9 \times 300 + 3 \times 600 + 8 \times 300}{42}$$

$$= \frac{15{,}500}{42} = 369 \text{ ft}$$

Determination of L_e, the average distance that a vehicle travels empty for each delivery, is more complicated. It depends on the dispatching and scheduling methods that are used to decide how a vehicle should proceed from its last drop-off to its next pickup. If each vehicle were to travel back to the starting point (stations 5 and 1) after

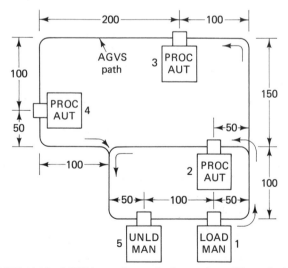

FIGURE 14.16 AGVS layout for production system of Example 14.5.

each drop-off at a production workstation (stations 2, 3, and 4), the distance each vehicle must travel between pickups would be very large. The value of L_e would be significantly greater than L_d, and the resulting efficiency of the handling system would be poor. It is highly desirable, therefore, to minimize the average distance that the vehicle travels empty between pickups in order to improve the overall efficiency of the AGVS layout. If a vehicle can both load a raw workpart and unload a finished part while it is stopped at a given workstation, the empty traveling time for the vehicle will be minimized. Problems 14.14 and 14.15 are concerned with this issue of estimating L_e.

REFERENCES

[1] BOSE, P. P., "Basics of AGV Systems," Special Report 784, *American Machinist and Automated Manufacturing,* March 1986, pp. 105–122.

[2] FITZGERALD, K. R., "How to Estimate the Number of AGVs You Need," *Modern Materials Handling,* October 1985, p. 79.

[3] HARRINGTON, J., *Computer Integrated Manufacturing,* Industrial Press, Inc., New York, 1973, Chapter 7.

[4] KOFF, G. A., "The Basics of AGVS," *Proceedings,* Promat 85, Sessions VII and X, Material Handling Institute, Chicago, Ill., February 1985, pp. 1–18.

[5] KOFF, G. A., and B. BOLDRIN, "Automated Guided Vehicles," in *Materials Handling Handbook,* 2nd ed. (R. A. Kulwiec, Editor), John Wiley & Sons, Inc., New York 1985, pp. 273–314.

[6] KULWIEC, R. A. Editor, *Materials Handling Handbook,* 2nd ed., John Wiley & Sons, Inc., New York, 1985.

[7] KWO, T. T., "A Theory of Conveyors," *Management Science,* Vol. 5, No. 1, 1958, pp. 51–71.

[8] KWO, T. T., "A Method for Designing Irreversible Overhead Loop Conveyors," *Journal of Industrial Engineering,* Vol. 11, No. 6, 1960, pp. 459–466.

[9] MAXWELL, W. L., "Solving Material Handling Design Problems with OR," *Industrial Engineering,* April 1981, pp. 58–69.

[10] MAXWELL, W. L., and J. A. MUCKSTADT, "Design of Automatic Guided Vehicle Systems," *IIE Transactions,* Vol. 14, No. 2, 1982, pp. 114–124.

[11] MAYER, H. E., "An Introduction to Conveyor Theory," *Western Electric Engineer,* Vol. 4, No. 1, 1960, pp. 42–47.

[12] MILLER, R. K., *Automated Guided Vehicle Systems,* Co-published by SEAI Institute, Madison, Ga., and Technical Insights Inc., Fort Lee, N. J. 1983.

[13] MULLER, T., *Automated Guided Vehicles,* IFS (Publications) Ltd., Bedford, England, and Springer-Verlag, Berlin, 1983.

[14] MUTH, E. J., "Analysis of Closed-Loop Conveyor Systems," *AIIE Transactions,* Vol. 4, No. 2, 1972, pp. 134–143.

[15] MUTH, E. J., "Analysis of Closed-Loop Conveyor Systems: the Discrete Flow Case," *AIIE Transactions,* Vol. 6, No. 1, 1974, pp. 73–83.

[16] MUTH, E. J., "Modelling and System Analysis of Multistation Closed-Loop Conveyor," *International Journal of Production Research,* Vol. 13, No. 6, 1975, pp. 559–566.

[17] MUTH, E. J., and J. A. WHITE, "Conveyor Theory: A Survey," *AIIE Transactions,* Vol. 11, No. 4, 1979, pp. 270–277.

[18] MUTHER, R., and K. HAGANAS, *Systematic Handling Analysis,* Management and Industrial Research Publications, Kansas City, Mo., 1969.

[19] The Material Handling Institute, *Basics of Material Handling,* Pittsburgh, Pennsylvania, April 1981.

[20] TOMPKINS, J. A. and J. A. WHITE, *Facilities Planning,* John Wiley & Sons, Inc., New York, 1984, Chapters 6, 15, 16.

PROBLEMS

14.1. The number of deliveries and returns (empty) are indicated in the from–to chart of Table P14.1A, and the corresponding distances are indicated in Table P14.1B. The loading and unloading times at the pickup and drop-off stations are 0.4 min and 0.6 min, respectively. The speed of the handling system = 100 ft/min. From the data provided, determine the following:

(a) The total transport work (TTW) indicated by the two charts.

(b) The efficiency of the handling system, E_h, assuming that the traffic factor = 1.0.

(c) The required handling system capacity, according to Eq. (14.4).

TABLE P14.1A   From–To Chart Showing Number of Moves per Hour between Different Stations In Problem 14.1[a]

	To:			
From:	1	2	3	4
1	0	7D	5D	3D
2	4E	0	0	3D
3	5E	0	0	0
4	6E	0	0	0

[a]Deliveries indicated by D and empty moves indicated by E.

TABLE P141B.   From–To Chart Showing Distances between Different Stations in Problem 14.1[a]

	To:			
From:	1	2	3	4
1	0	150	100	130
2	150	0	NA	80
3	100	NA	0	NA
4	130	NA	NA	0

[a]Distances shown in feet. "NA" indicates that the distances are not applicable to this layout.

14.2. Based on the data provided in Problem 14.1, sketch the flow diagram using a format similar to that of Figure 14.1.

14.3. Assume that four continuously moving loop conveyors are used to accomplish the deliveries indicated in Problem 14.1. The first conveyor moves from station 1 to 2 and returns, the second from station 1 to 3, the third from station 1 to 4, and the fourth from station 2 to 4. In each case, the loading and unloading would be done without stopping the handling system. In effect, the load/unload times would not detract from the efficiency of the handling system as they do in Problem 14.1. Conveyor speed = 100 ft/min.
(a) Determine the total transport work for the four-loop conveyor handling system.
(b) Determine the efficiency of the handling system, E_H.
(c) Determine the total length of the four conveyors used in the handling system. Include forward and return loops in the total.

14.4. Instead of four separate continuously moving loop conveyors as in Problem 14.3, suppose that a single continuously moving loop conveyor (e.g., slat conveyor) is used to accomplish the deliveries in Problem 14.1. The route of the loop conveyor is from 1 to 2 to 3 to 4 to 1. At each station, the pickups and drop-offs will be accomplished as specified in Table P14.1A. As in Problem 14.3, we assume that the loading and unloading times have no impact on the efficiency of the handling system. The distances given in Table P14.1B are applicable, but in addition, the following is given: the distance between stations 2 and 3 is 75 ft and the distance between stations 3 and 4 is 50 ft. Conveyor speed = 100 ft/min.
(a) Determine the total transport work for the single-loop conveyor handling system.
(b) Determine the efficiency of the handling system, E_h.
(c) Determine the total length of the loop conveyor system used in the handling system.
(d) Compared to Problem 14.3, how do you rationalize that the total transport work of the conveyor system has increased, while the total length of the conveyor system has been reduced?

14.5. A roller conveyor moves tote pans in a single direction at a speed of 200 ft/min between the load station and the unload station. The distance between the two stations is 500 ft. The time interval required between loading cycles at the load station is 1.00 min, and the time interval between unloading cycles at the unload station is 0.80 min. The unit load on a tote pan consists of 18 parts. Determine the following:
(a) Total transport work (TTW) for the handling system.
(b) Spacing between tote pan centers flowing on the conveyor system.
(c) Flow rate of parts on the conveyor system.

14.6. In Problem 14.5, if the time interval between unloading cycles at the unload station were 1.25 min instead of 0.80 min, how would this affect the operation of the conveyor system? Determine the effect of this change on the tote pan spacing and the parts flow rate.

14.7. Consider the effect of the unit load principle with respect to Problem 14.5. Suppose that each tote pan were used to hold only one of the parts rather than 18. Determine the total transport work and the flow rate for this case.

14.8. An overhead trolley conveyor is configured as a continuous closed loop. It has a delivery loop of length 250 ft and return loop of length 200 ft. Each hook on the conveyor can hold one part and the hooks are separated by 15 ft. The speed of the conveyor is 125 ft/min.
(a) Determine the total number of parts in the conveyor system and the parts flow rate.
(b) What are the maximum loading and unloading times that are consistent with the operation of the conveyor system?

14.9. A closed-loop conveyor is to be designed to deliver parts from a single load station to a single unload station. The handling system will provide a delivery function only, no storage. The load and unload stations are separated by a distance of 300 ft. It is assumed that the forward loop and the return loop will be of equal lengths. The speed of the conveyor = 150 ft/min. The times required to load parts onto and unload parts from the conveyor at the respective stations are $T_L = T_u = 0.15$ min. The specified flow rate of parts that must be delivered between the two stations is 300 parts/h. Determine the required parameters of the conveyor system that will achieve this flow rate. That is, determine the values for n_c, n_p, and s_c that will work for this problem. The values of n_c and n_p must be integers.

14.10. A recirculating conveyor has a total length of 700 ft. Its speed is 90 ft/min and the spacing of part carriers along its length is 14 ft. Each carrier can hold one part. Automatic machines are used to load and unload the conveyor at its load and unload stations. The time required to load a part is 0.25 min and the unload time is the same. The required loading and unloading rates are both 2.0 parts/min.
(a) What is the maximum possible flow rate of parts on the conveyor system?
(b) How many parts could be contained on the conveyor system if every carrier were filled to capacity?
(c) How much time is required for the conveyor to make one complete loop?
(d) Evaluate the conveyor system design with respect to the three principles developed by Kwo.

14.11. Solve Problem 14.10 except that the carrier spacing = 28 ft rather than 14 ft.

14.12. An automated guide vehicle system has an average travel distance per delivery = 500 ft and an average empty travel distance = 300 ft. The system must make a total of 75 deliveries/h. The load and unload times are both 0.5 min and the speed of the vehicles = 150 ft/min. The traffic factor for the system = 0.85.
(a) Determine the average total time per delivery, the handling system efficiency, and the resulting average number of deliveries per hour for a vehicle.
(b) How many vehicles are required to satisfy the 75 deliveries/h?

14.13. Suppose that an AGVS is used as the material handling system for Problem 14.1. The from–to charts presented in that problem are applicable here. A traffic factor = 0.90 will be assumed. The speed of an AGV in the system is 100 ft/min.
(a) Determine the average total time per delivery, the handling system efficiency, and the resulting average number of deliveries per hour for a vehicle.
(b) How many vehicles are needed to satisfy the indicated deliveries per hour?

14.14. In Example 14.5, suppose that all vehicles must return to stations 5 and 1 after making drop-offs at stations 2, 3, and 4. The AGVS can travel at a speed of 150 ft/min, and the anticipated traffic factor = 0.85. The value of the delivery distance = 369 ft, as determined in Example 14.5, is applicable here.
(a) Complete Tables 14.4 and 14.5 in the format of Tables P14.1A and P14.1B, showing the empty moves and distances.
(b) Determine an estimate of the value of L_e for the layout.
(c) What is the expected efficiency of the handling system under this method of operation?
(d) How many automated guided vehicles will be required to operate the system?

14.15. In Example 14.5, suppose that vehicles can unload finished parts and load raw parts at the same station (stations 2, 3, and 4) so as to minimize the distances the vehicles will be traveling empty. The delivery distance = 369 ft, as determined in Example 14.5.

(a) Complete Tables 14.4 and 14.5 in the format of Tables P14.1A and P14.1B, showing the empty moves and distances.

(b) Determine an estimate of the value of L_e for the layout.

(c) What is the expected efficiency of the handling system under this method of operation?

(d) How many automated guided vehicles will be required to operate the system?

14.16. An AGVS is being planned as part of a flexible assembly system. The system consists of two parallel lines, as illustrated in Figure P14.16. In both lines, a base part is delivered

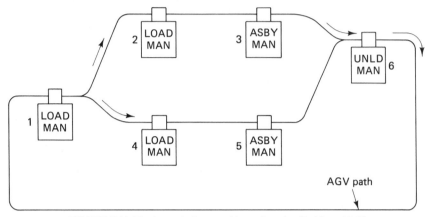

FIGURE P14.16 Layout of assembly system for Problem 14.16.

from station 1 to stations 2 and 4, respectively. At these stations, components are added to a container on the AGV and the AGV then proceeds to the next stations in the line (3 and 5, respectively). The actual assembly of the components is accomplished at these second stations in the lines. From stations 3 and 5, the products move to station 6 for removal from the system. The vehicles remain with the products as they flow through the station sequence. After unloading, the vehicles proceed back to station 1 for reloading. The hourly moves and distances involved are presented in Tables 14.16A and 14.16B. The vehicle speed = 100 ft/min. The cycle times at stations 2 and 3 = 4.0 min each,

TABLE P14.16A From–To Chart Showing Number of Hourly Moves between Different Stations in the Assembly System of Problem 14.16[a]

			To:			
From:	1	2	3	4	5	6
1	0	15L	0	10L	0	0
2	0	0	15L	0	0	0
3	0	0	0	0	0	15L
4	0	0	0	0	10L	0
5	0	0	0	0	0	10L
6	25E	0	0	0	0	0

[a]Loaded vehicles are indicated by L and empty vehicles are indicated by E.

TABLE P14.16B   From–To Chart Showing Distances between Different Stations in Problem 14.16[a]

From:	To:					
	1	2	3	4	5	6
1	0	200	NA	150	NA	NA
2	NA	0	50	NA	NA	NA
3	NA	NA	0	NA	NA	50
4	NA	NA	NA	0	50	NA
5	NA	NA	NA	NA	0	100
6	400	NA	NA	NA	NA	0

[a]Distances shown in feet. "NA" indicates that the distances are not applicable to this layout.

and the cycle times at stations 4 and 5 = 6.0 min each. The loading and unloading times at stations 1 and 6, respectively, are each 1.0 min. Because of the nature of the system, the traffic congestion factor is expected to be 0.80. Determine how many vehicles will be required to operate the system.

chapter **15**

Automated Storage Systems

In Chapter 14 storage was mentioned as one of the functions of material handling. In the present chapter we examine how materials are stored in a factory or warehouse by mechanized and automated methods. Our interest will be more on factory operations rather than warehousing activities. However, the storage concepts and systems we discuss can be applied in both areas. The primary examples of automated storage systems are automated storage/retrieval systems (AS/RS) and carousel storage systems. We begin with some general comments on storage system performance.

15.1 STORAGE SYSTEM PERFORMANCE

The general objective of a storage system is obvious enough: to store materials for a certain period of time. The types of materials that are stored by most manufacturing firms are listed in Table 15.1. Categories 1 through 5 pertain directly to the product, categories 6 and 7 relate to the process, and categories 8 and 9 relate to the overall support of the plant operations. Different storage methods and controls are needed for the various types. Most production plants use manual methods for depositing and retrieving items into and

TABLE 15.1 Types of Materials Typically Stored in a Factory

Type	Description
1. Raw materials	Raw stock to be processed or assembled by factory (e.g., sheet metal, bar stock)
2. Purchased parts	Parts from vendors to be processed or assembled by factory (e.g., castings, purchased components)
3. Work-in-process	Partially completed parts between processing and assembly operations
4. Finished product	Completed product ready to be shipped to customer
5. Rework and scrap	Parts that are out of specification, either to be reworked or scrapped; chips and swarf, other materials that must be discarded by the factory
6. Tooling	Cutting tools, jigs and fixtures, welding rod, other supplies, and tools used in the manufacturing and assembly operations; supplies used in factory (e.g., rags, gloves, helmets, etc.) are usually included in this category
7. Spare parts	Spare parts used to repair machines and equipment in the factory
8. Office supplies	Supplies, paper, paper forms, and other items used in support of plant and company office staff
9. Plant records	Records on product, maintenance records, etc.

from storage. The storage function is generally accomplished in ways that are inefficient and inadequate in terms of control. Automated methods are available to those firms willing to treat the problem of storage with the attention it deserves.

Different companies have different reasons for installing an automated system for storing materials. A list of possible objectives that a company may want to achieve by installing an automated storage system is presented in Table 15.2. An automated storage system represents a significant investment for the firm, and it often necessitates a new and different way of doing business. The performance of the storage system must be sufficient to justify the expense involved. There are a number of performance criteria by which automated storage systems can be measured. These criteria include:

TABLE 15.2 Possible Objectives for Installing an Automated Storage System in a Factory or Warehouse

Increase storage capacity
Increase floor space utilization
Recover space for manufacturing facilities
Improve security and reduce pilferage
Reduce labor cost in storage operations
Increase labor productivity in storage operations
Improve safety in storage function
Improve control over inventories
Increase stock rotation
Improve customer service

Source: Based on a list in reference [5].

- Storage capacity
- System throughput
- Utilization
- Uptime reliability

The *storage capacity* is the total maximum number of individual loads that are expected to be stored. This is determined by the size of the storage system relative to the physical sizes of the items and materials in storage. In a fully automated storage system, materials are generally stored in unit loads that are held in a standard-sized container (pallets, metal or plastic containers, etc.). The standard container can readily be handled, transported, and stored by the storage system and by the automated handling system that may be connected to the storage system. The physical capacity of the storage system should be greater than the actual maximum number of loads that will be held, to provide available empty spaces for materials being entered into the system and to allow for variations in maximum storage requirements.

System throughput can be defined as the number of loads per hour that the storage system can (1) receive and place into storage and (2) retrieve and deliver to the output station. These two activities can be done separately or combined into one cycle. The cycles are referred to as *storage transactions*. The storage system must be designed for the maximum required throughput that will occur during the day. In many factory and warehouse operations, there will be certain periods of the day when the rate of input/output transactions required of the system will be greater than at other times. The system should be designed to handle the maximum rate.

The maximum throughput capacity of the automated storage system will be limited by the time required to perform a storage transaction. The transaction cycle time will involve several time elements. For a storage transaction, the cycle time will consist of the following: time to pick up the load at the input station, time to determine the storage location (the location where the incoming item should be placed), travel time to the storage location, unload time at the storage location, and return travel time. For a retrieval transaction, the cycle time will consist of time to determine the storage location of the item to be retrieved, travel time to the storage location, time to pick the item from storage, return travel time, and unloading time at the output station. There will be variations in the way these elements are performed, depending on the type of storage system. In manual storage procedures, the times for these activities are subject to the variations and motivations of the human workers, and there is a lack of control over the operations. One of the objectives of automating the storage function is to recapture control of the operations.

The throughput capacity will also be limited by the capability of the materials handling system that is interfaced with the storage system. If the handling system is incapable of delivering loads to or removing loads from the storage system at a rate that is compatible with the transaction cycle time, the throughput of the storage system will be adversely affected.

Other performance criteria for a storage system are utilization and uptime reliability. *Utilization* of the storage system is defined as the percentage of time that the system is in use compared to the time it is available. The utilization is expected to vary throughout the day, as requirements vary from hour to hour. It is desirable to design the storage system for relatively high utilization, perhaps in the range 80 to 90%. If the average utilization is too low, the system is probably overdesigned. If the average utilization runs too high, there tends to be no allowance for rush periods or breakdowns of the system.

Uptime reliability is the percentage of time that the system is capable of operating compared to the normally scheduled time of system operation. In Chapter 2 we referred to this operating parameter as availability. Malfunctions of the equipment, both mechanical and electronic (e.g., computer) cause downtime that prevents the system from operating. Some of the reasons for downtime include computer failures, mechanical breakdowns, load jams in the system, improper maintenance, and incorrect procedures by personnel using the system. It is appropriate to design the storage system in such a way that a malfunction of one component or section does not cause the entire system to be down. The reliability of an existing system can be improved by using good preventive maintenance procedures and having repair parts on hand for critical components in the system. Backup procedures should be devised to mitigate the effects of system downtime.

15.2 AUTOMATED STORAGE/RETRIEVAL SYSTEMS

An *automated storage/retrieval system* (AS/RS) is defined by the Materials Handling Institute [5] in the following terms:

> A combination of equipment and controls which handles, stores, and retrieves materials with precision, accuracy, and speed under a defined degree of automation.

AS/R systems are custom-planned for each individual application, and they range in complexity from relatively small mechanized systems that are controlled manually to very large computer-controlled systems that are fully integrated with factory and warehouse operations.

The AS/RS consists of a series of storage aisles that are serviced by one or more storage/retrieval (S/R) machines, usually one S/R machine per aisle. The aisles have storage racks for holding the materials to be stored. The S/R machines are used to deliver materials to the storage racks and to retrieve materials from the racks. The AS/RS has one or more input/output stations where materials are delivered for entry into storage and where materials are picked up from the system. The input/output stations are often referred to as *pickup-and-deposit* (P&D) *stations* in the terminology of AS/R systems. The P&D stations can be manually operated or interfaced to some form of automated handling system, such as a conveyor system or AGVS.

Several important categories of automated storage/retrieval systems can be distinguished. These include:

* *Unit load AS/RS.* This is typically a large automated system designed to handle unit loads stored on pallets or other standard containers. The system is computer-controlled and the S/R machines are automated and designed to handle the unit load containers. A

FIGURE 15.1   Unit load AS/RS. (Courtesy of Eaton-Kenway.)

unit load AS/RS is pictured in Figure 15.1, and a diagram of an AS/RS layout and elevation is presented in Figure 15.2. The unit load system is the generic AS/RS. Other systems described below represent variations on the unit load AS/RS.

   • *Miniload AS/RS.*   This storage system is used to handle small loads (individual parts or supplies) that are contained in bins or drawers within the storage system. The S/R machine is designed to retrieve the bin and deliver it to a P&D station (usually manually operated) at the end of the aisle so that the individual items can be withdrawn from the bins. The bin or drawer is then returned to its location in the system. The miniload AS/R system (Figure 15.3) is generally smaller than the unit load AS/RS and is often enclosed for security of the items stored.

   • *Man-on-board AS/RS.*   The man-on-board (also called *manaboard*) storage/retrieval system represents an alternative approach to the problem of storing and retrieving individual items in the system. Whereas the miniload system delivers the entire bin to the end-of-aisle pick station, the man-on-board system permits the individual items to be picked directly at their storage locations. This offers an opportunity to reduce the transaction time of the system.

   • *Automated item retrieval system.*   These systems are also designed for retrieval of individual items or small unit loads such as cases of product in a distribution warehouse. However, in this system, the items are stored in single-file lanes rather then in bins or drawers. When an item (or case) is to be retrieved, it is released from its lane onto a conveyor for delivery to the pickup station. The supply of items in each lane is generally

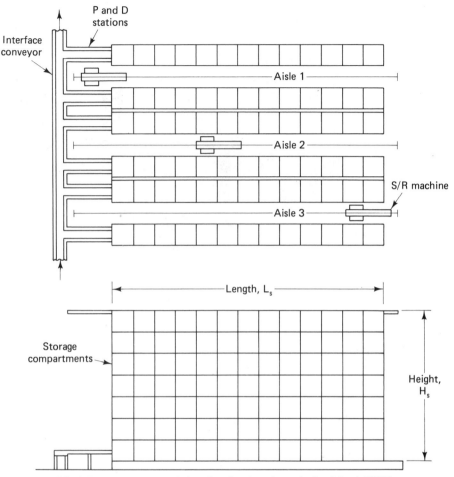

FIGURE 15.2   Layout and elevation drawing of a typical unit load AS/RS.

replenished from the rear of the retrieval system so that there is flow-through of the items, thus permitting first-in/first-out inventory control.

• *Deep-lane AS/RS.*   The deep-lane AS/RS is a high-density unit load storage system that is appropriate when large quantities are to be stored but the number of separate types of material is relatively small. Instead of storing each unit load so that it can be accessed directly from the aisle (as in the conventional unit load system), the deep-lane system stores up to 10 or so loads in a single rack, one load behind the next. Each rack is designed for "flow-through," with input on one side and output on the other side. Loads are picked from one side of the rack system by a special S/R-type machine designed for retrieval, and another special machine is used on the entry side of the rack system for input of loads.

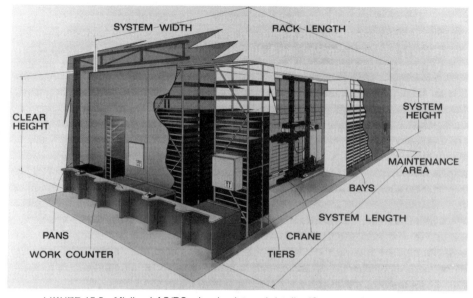

FIGURE 15.3   Miniload AS/RS, showing internal details. (Courtesy of Litton UHS.)

Basic components of an AS/RS

All automated storage/retrieval systems consist of certain basic building blocks, used for nearly all of the AS/RS categories described above. These components are:

1. Storage structure
2. Storage/retrieval (S/R) machine
3. Storage modules (e.g., pallets for unit loads)
4. Pickup-and-deposit stations

The *storage structure* is the fabricated steel framework that supports the loads contained in the AS/RS. The structure must possess sufficient strength and rigidity that it does not deflect significantly due to the loads in storage or other forces on the framework. The individual storage compartments in the structure must be designed to accept and hold the storage modules used to contain the stored materials. Calculating the forces and stresses on alternative welded steel framework designs (i.e., box-frame, cantilever, or other configuration) is a problem made for the specialist in engineering mechanics.

The storage structure may also be used to support the roof and siding of the building in which the AS/RS resides. When used for this purpose there is often a tax advantage because the building (or portions of it) can be depreciated as equipment rather than as building property.

A related function of the storage structure is to support the aisle hardware required to align the S/R machines with respect to the individual storage compartments of the AS/RS. This hardware includes the guide rails at the top and bottom of the structure, as well as the end stops and other features required to help provide safe operation of the S/R machines.

The *S/R machine* (sometimes called a *crane*) is used to accomplish a storage transaction, delivering loads from the input station into storage, or retrieving loads from storage and delivering them to the output station. To perform these transactions, the storage/retrieval machine must be capable of horizontal and vertical travel to align its carriage (which carries the load) with the storage compartment in the storage structure, and it must also pull the load from or push the load into the storage compartment. The S/R machine (Figure 15.4) consists of a rigid upright frame in which is mounted a rail system for vertical motion of the carriage. The upright frame can be either single-masted or double-masted. Wheels are attached at the base of the frame to permit horizontal travel of the frame-and-carriage along a rail system that runs down the length of the aisle. A parallel rail, located at the top of the storage structure, is used to maintain alignment of the frame-and-carriage with respect to the structure.

The carriage consists of some form of shuttle mechanism to deposit loads into and extract loads from their storage compartments. The design of the shuttle system must

FIGURE 15.4   S/R machine used in a miniload AS/RS. (Courtesy of Litton UHS.)

also permit the loads to be transferred from the S/R machine to the P&D station or other material handling interface with the AS/RS. The carriage and shuttle are positioned and actuated automatically in the usual AS/RS. Some S/R machines are equipped for a human operator to ride along on or near the carriage. These machines are used in the man-on-board AS/R systems.

To accomplish the desired motions of the S/R machine, three drive systems are required: Horizontal, vertical, and shuttle. The horizontal drive is capable of speeds up to 500 ft/min along the aisle on modern S/R machines. The vertical or lift speed is limited to around 100 ft/min. These speeds determine the time required for the carriage to travel from the P&D station to a particular location in the storage aisle. Acceleration and deceleration of the S/R machine often have a significant effect in determining travel time over shorter distances.

The *storage modules* are the containers of the stored material. Examples of storage modules include pallets, steel wire baskets and containers, tote pans, storage bins, and special drawers (used in miniload AS/R systems). These modules are generally made to a standard base size that can be handled automatically by the carriage shuttle of the S/R machine. The standard size also permits it to be stored in the storage compartments of the AS/RS structure. The storage modules slide into racks in the compartment that permit convenient entry and extraction of the load by the shuttle.

The *pickup-and-deposit* stations are used to transfer loads to and from the AS/RS. They are generally located at the end of the aisles for access by the S/R machines and the external handling system that brings loads to the AS/RS and takes loads away. The pickup stations and deposit stations may be located at opposite ends of the storage aisle or combined at the same location. This depends on the origination point of the incoming loads and the destination of the output loads. The P&D stations must be designed so that they are compatible with both the S/R machine shuttle and the external handling system. Some of the common methods used to transfer loads out of the AS/RS at the P&D station include manual load/unload, forklift truck, conveyor systems (e.g., roller, cart-on-track, chain), and AGVS.

AS/RS controls

The principal control problem in AS/RS operation is the positioning of the S/R machine within an acceptable tolerance at the storage compartment in the structure for depositing or retrieving a specific load. The locations of materials stored in the system must be determined in order to direct the S/R machine to a particular storage compartment. Each compartment in the AS/RS is identified by a location number, which indicates aisle, horizontal position, and vertical position in the structure. A scheme based on alphanumeric codes can be used for this purpose. Using this location identification scheme, each unit of material that is stored is given an identification code and referenced to a particular location in the storage system. The record of these locations is called the *item location file*. Each time a storage transaction is completed, a record of the transaction must be entered into the item location file.

Given a specified storage compartment to go to, the S/R machine must be controlled to move to that location and position the shuttle for the loading or retrieving operation. One of the positioning methods uses a counting procedure in which the number of bays and levels are counted in the direction of travel (horizontally and vertically) in order to determine position. An alternative to this method is a numerical identification procedure in which each compartment is provided with a highly reflective target with binary-coded location identifications on its face. Optical sensors are used to read the target and position the shuttle for depositing or retrieving a load.

Computer controls and programmable controllers are used to determine the required location and guide the S/R machine to its destination. Computer control permits the physical operation of the AS/RS to be integrated with the supporting information and record-keeping system. Storage transactions can be entered in real time, inventory records can be accurately maintained, system performance can be monitored, and communications can be facilitated with other factory computer systems. These automatic controls can be superseded or supplemented by manual controls when required under emergency conditions or for man-on-board operation of the machine.

Special features

In addition to the basic components of the AS/RS, there are certain other features and components that are often found in these storage systems. These other features include:

- Aisle transfer cars
- Full/empty bin detectors
- Sizing stations
- Load identification stations

Most AS/R systems have one S/R machine per aisle. However, in some systems, even though the number of loads is quite large (thus requiring a large AS/RS), the activity per aisle is relatively low, thus making it difficult to justify a separate S/R machine for each aisle. *Aisle transfer cars* are used in these instances to move S/R machines back and forth between aisles to perform their storage and retrieval functions. The aisle transfer car consists of a rigid frame that accepts the S/R machine and moves it between storage aisles. The car rides on a track that runs along the end of the aisles of the AS/RS.

Full-empty bin detectors are used by the S/R machine carriage to determine the presence or absence of a load in a given storage compartment. The detection schemes are usually based on optical and sonar sensors that bounce light or sound off the load in the compartment. If no load is present, no reflected signal is received back by the sensor. These devices are useful to avoid attempts to enter a load into a compartment that is already full, or to unload a compartment that is empty.

Sizing stations also serve to protect the system by assuring that oversized loads are not entered into the AS/RS. The danger of an oversized load is that the S/R machine would attempt to load it into a compartment that is not large enough, thus possibly causing the load to jam or fall to the ground. The sizing station inspects the length, width, and height of the load. If any of the dimensions exceed the maximum allowable size, the load is moved to a siding for special treatment or resizing.

Load identification stations are used to enter the proper identification data about the load into the computer system to keep track of the location of the load in the AS/RS. The means of identifying the load can be manual, semiautomatic, or automatic. Manual methods involve an operator reading the identification number (or numbers) on the materials (and/or container) and entering them into the system. Bar codes can also be used to identify the load. (We describe how bar code systems work in Chapter 25.) In semiautomatic use of this method, a human operator uses a code-reading wand to scan the bar code and make the identification. The identification can also be accomplished by means of stationary scanning devices that read the bar code as it passes through the identification station.

Applications

Most applications of AS/RS technology have been associated with warehousing and similar distribution operations. A growing number of AS/R systems are being used for storing materials between operations in manufacturing. We can distinguish three application areas for automated storage and retrieval systems:

1. Unit load storage and handling
2. Order picking
3. Work-in-process storage systems

Unit load storage and retrieval applications are represented by the unit load AS/RS and the deep-lane storage systems discussed earlier. These types of applications are commonly found in warehousing for finished goods in a distribution center. Deep-lane systems are applied in the food industry.

Order picking is used to store and retrieve materials in less than full unit load quantities. Miniload, man-on-board, and item retrieval systems are used for this second application area, in which individual items are stored and retrieved.

The third area is a more recent application of automated storage technology, especially germane for the purposes of this book on manufacturing automation. Work-in-process is an important problem in manufacturing, and we devote Section 15.4 to a discussion of it and how automated storage systems can be used to address the problem.

Quantitative analysis

There are several aspects of the AS/RS that are susceptible to quantitative analysis. These include the sizing of the storage structure, the stress and load analysis of the structure, and performance characteristics. Here our interest is in the capacity and operating performance of the AS/RS, and we leave the sizing and structural questions to other books [3,7].

The required height and length of a storage aisle is dependent on how many storage compartments (racks) are arranged vertically and horizontally along the aisle. Let n_v be the number of load compartments to be arranged vertically and n_h be the number of load compartments to be arranged horizontally in the aisle. The total capacity of any storage aisle in an AS/RS (i.e., the total number of unit loads given that every compartment can be filled) is therefore

$$\text{capacity/aisle} = 2n_v n_h \qquad (15.1)$$

under the assumption that loads are stored on both sides of the aisle. If we assume a standard-sized compartment (to accept a standard-sized unit load), the compartment dimensions facing the aisle should be oversized with respect to the unit load dimensions. Let x represent the horizontal dimension of a unit load and y the vertical dimension of a unit load. The height and length of the AS/RS aisle (see Figure 15.2) will therefore be related to the unit load dimensions and quantities as follows [7]:

$$H_s = n_v(y + 10 \text{ in.}) \qquad (15.2)$$
$$L_s = n_h(x + 8 \text{ in.})$$

These dimensions are illustrated in Figure 15.2.

System throughput was defined in Section 15.1 as the number of storage transactions per hour that the AS/RS is capable of accomplishing. The transaction cycle can involve the delivery of a load into storage, or the retrieval of a load out of storage, or both of these activities in one cycle. These possibilities can be divided into two alternative types of transaction cycles: single-command cycles and dual-command cycles. A *single-command cycle* involves either entering a load into storage, or retrieving a load from storage, but not both in one cycle. A *dual-command cycle* involves both entering a load into storage and retrieving a load from storage in the same cycle. The dual-command cycle represents the most efficient way to operate the AS/RS because two loads are handled in one transaction.

Our method of computing the transaction cycle times in these two cases will be based on formulas derived by Bozer and White [1], also described in Tompkins and White [7]. The method assumes the following: randomized storage of loads in the AS/RS [i.e., any compartment (rack) in the storage aisle is equally likely to be selected for a storage or retrieval transaction]; the storage compartments are of equal size; the P&D station is located at the base and at the end of the aisle, constant horizontal and vertical speeds of the S/R machine; and simultaneous horizontal and vertical travel. A statistical approach is used to derive the expected values of the cycle times.

The dimensions of the AS/RS aisle are its length and height, L_s and H_s, as defined previously, and the average horizontal and vertical travel speeds of the S/R machine are

V_h and V_v, respectively. Then the times required to travel horizontally and vertically the full length and height, respectively, of the storage system are given by

$$t_h = \frac{L_s}{V_h}$$

$$t_v = \frac{H_s}{V_v}$$

Using these travel times, the following parameters are defined:

$$T = \max{(t_h, t_v)}$$

$$Q = \min{\left(\frac{t_h}{T}, \frac{t_v}{T}\right)}$$

Using these calculated values, the average single-command transaction time is given by

$$T_{sc} = T\left(\frac{Q^2}{3} + 1\right) + 2T_{pd} \qquad\qquad (15.3)$$

where T_{pd} = shuttle time to perform a pickup or deposit. The average dual-command transaction time is given by

$$T_{dc} = T\left(\frac{4}{3} + 0.5Q^2 - \frac{Q^3}{30}\right) + 4T_{pd} \qquad\qquad (15.4)$$

An example will illustrate the use of these equations.

EXAMPLE 15.1

Consider the operation of a unit load AS/RS that uses an S/R machine for each aisle of the system. The length of the storage aisle is 300 ft and its height is 50 ft. Horizontal and vertical travel speeds of the S/R machine are 400 ft/min and 75 ft/min, respectively. The S/R machine requires 30 s to accomplish a P&D operation. Determine the single-command and dual-command cycle times for the storage system.

Solution:

The values of t_h and t_v are computed as

$$t_h = \frac{300 \text{ ft}}{400 \text{ ft/min}} = 0.75 \text{ min}$$

$$t_v = \frac{50 \text{ ft}}{75 \text{ ft/min}} = 0.667 \text{ min}$$

The parameters T and Q are determined as

$$T = \max(0.75, 0.667) = 0.75 \text{ min}$$

$$Q = \min\left(1.0, \frac{.667}{.75}\right) = 0.8889$$

The single-command transaction cycle time is

$$T_{sc} = 0.75\left(\frac{0.8889^2}{3} + 1\right) + 2(0.50)$$
$$= 1.9475 \text{ min}$$

The dual-command transaction cycle time is

$$T_{dc} = 0.75\left(\frac{4}{3} + 0.5(0.8889)^2 - \frac{.8889^3}{30}\right) + 4(0.50)$$
$$= 3.2786 \text{ min}$$

Transaction cycle-time equations for other AS/RS configurations and operating assumptions are presented in reference 1.

15.3   CAROUSEL STORAGE SYSTEMS

A carousel storage system is a series of bins or baskets fastened to carriers that are connected together and revolve around a long, oval track system. The track system is similar to a trolley conveyor system. Its purpose is to position bins at a load/unload station at the end of the oval. The operation is similar to the powered overhead rack system used by dry cleaners to deliver finished garments to the front of the store.

     The typical operation of the storage carousel is mechanized rather than automated. The load/unload station is manned by a human worker who activates the powered carousel to deliver a desired bin to the station. One or more parts are removed from the bin, and the cycle is repeated. A carousel storage system is illustrated in Figure 15.5. The load/unload station can be automated, and one possible mechanism for this purpose is shown in Figure 15.6.

Configuration and control features

Carousels come in a variety of sizes, ranging between 10 and 100 ft in length of the oval. As the length of the carousel is increased, the storage density increases, but the average transaction time (storage or retrieval) decreases. Accordingly, the typical carousel size ranges perhaps between 30 and 50 ft to achieve a proper balance between these opposing factors.

FIGURE 15.5   Four storage carousels. (Courtesy of White Storage and Retrieval Systems.)

The structure of the carousel consists of welded steel framework that supports the oval track system. The carousel can be either an overhead system (called a top-driven unit) or a floor-mounted system (called a bottom-driven unit). In the top-driven unit a pulley system is mounted at the top of the framework and drives an overhead trolley system. The bins are suspended from the trolleys (carriers). In the bottom-driven unit, the pulley drive system is mounted at the base of the frame, and the carriers ride on a rail in the base. This provides more load-carrying capacity for the carousel storage system. It also eliminates the problem of dirt and oil dripping from the overhead trolley system in top-driven systems. In either top or bottom driven carousels, one or two drive motors are used to power the trolley system.

The design of the individual bins and baskets of the carousel must be compatible with the loads to be stored. Bin widths range between 21 and 30 in., and depths are in the range 14 to 22 in. [8]. Carousel heights are typically 6 to 8 ft, with adjustable shelving used to create openings for the bins or baskets to suit the items that are stored. Standard bins are made from steel wire, which increases the operator's capability to see the contents of the container.

Controls used for modern carousel storage systems range from manual call controls to computer control. Manual controls include the following:

• *Foot pedal control.* This is typically a bidirectional switch that allows the operator at the pick station to rotate the carousel to the desired bin position.

FIGURE 15.6 Automated extractor mechanism consisting of belt conveyor mounted in an elevator, used to store and retrieve tote boxes from a storage carousel. (Courtesy of SPS Technologies, Automated Systems Division.)

- *Hand control.* This type of switch is actuated by hand and is conveniently mounted on an arm that projects from the carousel frame.
- *Keyboard control.* Keyboard control permits a greater variety of control features than the two control types described above. The operator can enter the desired bin position and the carousel is programmed to determine the shortest route to deliver the bin to the pick station. The keyboard also contains controls for bidirectional jogging of the carousel, and emergency stop controls.

Computer controls are implemented using various computer configurations, from microprocessor-based controllers for individual carousels to centralized dedicated minicomputers that control multiple carousels. The features that are provided by means of computer control include the capability to maintain data on bin locations, items in each bin, and inventory control records.

Carousel storage applications

The carousel storage system provides for a relatively high throughput rate and is often an attractive alternative to the miniload AS/RS in the following types of applications:

1. *Storage and retrieval operations.* In certain operations, individual items must be selected from the group of items stored in the bin or basket. Sometimes called "pick and load" operations, this type of procedure is common for order picking of service parts or other items in a wholesale firm, tools in a toolroom, raw materials from a stockroom, and work-in-process in a factory. In small assembly operations such as electronics, carousels are used to accomplish kitting of parts that will be transported to the assembly workstations.

2. *Transport and accumulation.* These are applications in which the carousel is used to transport and/or sort materials as they are stored. One example of this is in progressive assembly operations where the workstations are located around the periphery of a continuously moving carousel and the workers have access to the individual storage bins of the carousel. They remove work from the bins to complete their own respective assembly tasks, then place their work into another bin for the next operation at some other workstation. Another example of transport and accumulation applications is sorting and consolidation of items. Each bin is defined for collecting the items of a particular type or customer. When the bin is full, the collected load is removed for shipment or other disposition.

3. *Unique applications.* These involve specialized uses of carousel storage systems. Examples include electrical testing of components, where the carousel is used to store the item during testing for a specified period of time; and drawer or cabinet storage, in which standard drawer-type cabinets are mounted on the carousel.

Storage carousels are finding an increasing number of applications in manufacturing operations, where its relatively low cost, versatility, and high reliability have been acknowledged. It represents a competitive alternative to the miniload AS/RS and other AS/RS configurations for work-in-progress storage in a manufacturing plant.

Quantitative analysis

The size and capacity of a storage carousel can be determined with reference to Figure 15.7. The individual bins are hung on carriers that revolve around the carousel track. The circumference of the carousel track can be shown to be

$$C = 2(L_s - W_s) + \pi W_s \qquad (15.5)$$

Let the spacing between carriers around the track be given by s_c and the number of carriers be symbolized as n_c. Therefore, it must be true that

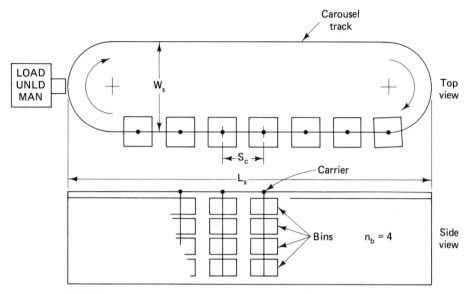

FIGURE 15.7   Layout and elevation drawing of a typical storage carousel.

$$n_c s_c = C \tag{15.6}$$

If the number of separate bins hung from a carrier is n_b, the total number of bins (storage compartments) on the carousel $= n_b n_c$.

The time to perform a transaction can be derived under the following assumptions. First, a transaction cycle consists of either a retrieval or a storage, but not both (i.e., single-command transactions are performed exclusively). Second, the speed of the carousel is constant and symbolized by V_c. Third, random storage is used in the carousel. That is, any point around the carousel is equally likely to be selected for a storage or retrieval transaction. Let us consider a retrieval cycle here. A storage transaction performed under the same assumption of random storage would be equivalent to a retrieval transaction.

The average distance that the carousel must travel in order to move a randomly located bin to the unload station at the end of the carousel depends on whether the carousel revolves in only one direction or in both directions. For the single-direction case, it can be shown that the average travel distance is given by

$$L_r = 0.5C$$

and the corresponding time to complete a retrieval transaction, T_r, is therefore

$$T_r = \frac{0.5C}{V_c} + T_h \tag{15.7}$$

where T_h is the handling time of the picker to remove the item or items from the bin. For the carousel capable of bidirectional travel, the corresponding average travel distance and retrieval transaction time are

$$L_r = 0.25C$$

$$T_r = \frac{0.25C}{V_c} + T_h$$

(15.8)

EXAMPLE 15.2

The oval of a top-driven carousel track has a length = 50 ft and width = 4 ft. The speed of the carousel = 75 ft/min. There are 100 carriers around the carousel, and each carrier has five bins suspended from it. For a single-direction carousel and a bidirectional carousel, compare how long will it take to retrieve 20 parts from the carrier if each part is in a different storage bin and random storage is used in the carousel. Also, determine the spacing between carriers on the carousel. The handling time associated with a retrieval = 20 s.

Solution:

The circumference of the carousel track is

$$C = 2(50 - 4) + 4\pi = 104.57 \text{ ft}$$

For the single-direction carousel, the retrieval of 20 parts would require

$$20T_r = 20 \left(0.5 \times \frac{104.57}{75} + 0.333 \right)$$

$$= 20.61 \text{ min}$$

For a bidirectional carousel, the retrieval time for 20 parts would be

$$20T_r = 20 \left(0.25 \times \frac{104.57}{75} + 0.333 \right)$$

$$= 13.63 \text{ min}$$

The spacing between carriers along the carousel would be

$$s_c = \frac{104.57}{50} = 2.091 \text{ ft}$$

15.4 WORK-IN-PROCESS STORAGE

We discussed the work-in-process problem in Chapter 2 and developed methods for assessing its cost in Chapter 3. Both AS/R systems and carousel systems are finding increased applications for storing work-in-process (WIP) in manufacturing plants. Certain types of conveyor systems (e.g., continuous loop, power-and-free) serve both a delivery and storage function, and therefore might also be included within the category of WIP storage systems. These conveyor systems are typically used in high production rather than batch and job shop production.

The utility of automated (or mechanized) WIP storage systems for batch and job shop manufacturing can best be described by comparing them to the more conventional way of dealing with work-in-process. In most batch production and job shop operations, a typical work cell has several types of work-in-process located in close proximity to it within the factory. The cell is currently processing one order. There are also several orders of parts awaiting processing at the cell. In addition, there may also be one or more orders that have been completed by the cell, waiting to be transported to the next operation. Each order consists of at least one part, sometimes many parts. The work cell described here is probably one of many cells in the factory. It is not unusual for a batch production plant to have hundreds of orders in progress. All of these orders of parts represent work-in-process. The risks and disadvantages of keeping so much work out in the shop include lack of control over the inventory, time spent searching for parts, parts becoming lost, entire orders becoming lost, orders not being processed according to their relative priorities at each work cell, and parts spending more time than necessary in the factory. We considered the time cost of these production inventories in Chapter 3.

Automated WIP storage systems represent a systematic alternative to the unorganized methods that have been the common practice for managing work-in-process in most batch and job shop factories. Some of the reasons that justify the installation of an automated storage system for work-in-process include:

1. *Kitting of parts for assembly*. The storage system is used to store parts for assembly of the product or its subassemblies. When an order for assembly is received, the required components are retrieved from storage, collected into kits, and delivered to the production floor for assembly.

2. *Integral component in a progressive assembly system*. Carousel storage systems are sometimes used as the storage and delivery mechanism in an assembly system. Workstations located around the continuously moving carousel load and unload work from the storage bins during the course of their assembly operations.

3. *Support of just-in-time production*. As we will discuss in Chapter 27, the concept of just-in-time (JIT) production is that parts required for manufacturing should be received immediately before the time they are needed. This results in a great dependency of the factory on its suppliers to deliver the parts at the right time (i.e., just in time). To reduce the risks associated with the JIT approach, some plants have elected to use an AS/RS as a storage buffer for the incoming materials. Although this subverts the objectives of the JIT concept, it reduces some of the risks associated with just-in-time production.

4. *Buffer storage*. An automated storage system can be used as a buffer storage zone between two (or more) processes whose production rates are significantly different. A good example is where a certain process requiring one shift operation to meet demand is used to feed another operation whose production rate is only a fraction of that of the first operation. An in-process buffer is needed to store parts between the two processes.

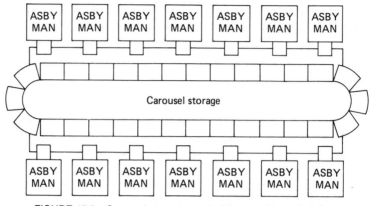

FIGURE 15.8   Carousel storage used with assembly workstations.

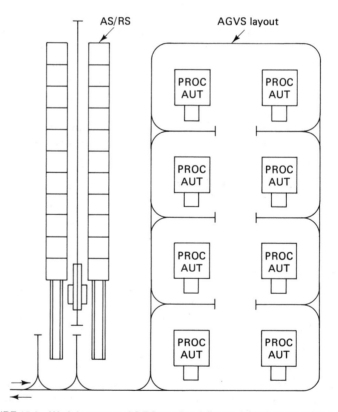

FIGURE 15.9   Work-in-process AS/RS used to deliver unit loads to machine cells
in factory.

5. *Compatible with automatic identification systems.* An AS/RS can be designed to be compatible with an automatic parts identification system such as bar codes.

6. *Greater control and tracking of materials.* The use of an automated WIP storage system provides greater control over WIP. Combined with an automatic identification system, it would permit the locations of all materials in progress to be known.

7. *Support of factory-wide automation.* The use of an automated storage system for work-in-process is considered an essential component in the fully automated factory for batch production. The storage system would be centrally and conveniently located in the factory and would be interconnected to one or more materials handling systems for distribution of parts to the various work cells in the plant.

Several possible configurations of WIP storage systems and their relationship to manufacturing are illustrated in the layout sketches of Figures 15.8 and 15.9. Figure 15.8 shows how a continuously moving storage carousel would be located with respect to its workstations in a mechanized assembly system. Figure 15.9 illustrates a possible arrangement of a WIP AS/RS in a factory. An AGVS might be used to delivery unit loads (e.g., individual parts on pallets or tote pans of parts) to the individual machine cells in a batch production plant.

15.5 INTERFACING HANDLING AND STORAGE WITH MANUFACTURING

We conclude our discussion of materials handling and storage by considering the problems encountered in connecting these various systems to the manufacturing function. These interface problems can be divided into the following two categories:

1. Information interface
2. Mechanical interface

The information interface is concerned with the flow of information that must accompany the movement and storage of materials in the factory. It encompasses the problems of materials identification and tracking, inventory control, production scheduling, and the data communications required to coordinate and control the various systems in the plant. This is one of the major problems addressed by computer-integrated manufacturing, and we defer further discussion until Part IX.

The mechanical interface deals with the problems of transferring parts and loads between storage systems, material handling systems, and production systems. The load transfer function is an integral part of any material handling system. The design of the mechanical interface depends on the type of handling equipment used, the system that is to be interfaced with the handling system, and whether the load/unload procedure is to be done manually or automatically. Our discussion of mechanical interfacing will include two problem areas: (1) positional accuracy of the handling system at the transfer station, and (2) methods of transferring parts or loads to and from the handling system.

Positional accuracy

The accuracy with which the handling system must be positioned at the load transfer station depends on the type of interface. Automatic load transfer requires greater accuracy than does manual loading and unloading. In automatic load transfer, the positional accuracy will determine whether the transfer operation can be accomplished successfully. The following values provide tolerances on stopping accuracies required for different mechanical interfaces [3]:

Interface	Tolerance (in.)
Manual load/unload	± 3
Conveyor/AGVS interface (automatic)	± 1
AS/RS load/unload (automatic)	± 0.25
Machine tool interface (automatic)	± 0.01

Accuracies of ± 0.01 in. are possible with certain types of conveyors and guided vehicles, but they require some type of positive location mechanism to accomplish the accuracy. The design of the locator device is often based on using a tapered pin that seats in a mating hole in the carrier. As the pin is pressed into the hole, it forces the carrier into accurate alignment at the station.

Methods of load transfer

Manual loading and unloading are often used at the mechanical interface. In production systems served by conveyors, human operators perform the loading and unloading functions at their respective workstations. In automated storage systems, the load/unload operations often involve human handling of individual parts for kitting or to make up unit loads.

Certain AGVS operations use manual loading and unloading. In the case of AGVS pallet trucks, loading or unloading a pallet involves positioning the forks into the pallet and lifting them sufficiently to clear the floor. As indicated in Chapter 14, this procedure is typically done manually because the pallets are generally located without enough precision for automatic positioning of the forks. With driverless AGVS trains, the load/unload procedure involves either connecting or disconnecting the coupling mechanism between the trailers and the powered tractor at a side track or spur, or transferring the load between the trailers and some load/unload station. These procedures can be accomplished manually or automatically. Automated procedures are generally preferred to eliminate reliance on the human element in an otherwise automatic system. Automatic techniques have been developed to accomplish the coupling and uncoupling operation between the trailer and the powered vehicle.

Automated methods for transferring loads between mechanical systems include a variety of powered push-pull devices. This type of transfer mechanism is suitable for flat loads (e.g., pallets, tote pans) and where there is low friction between the load and the handling system. Examples of handling systems in this category include cart-on-track carriers, roller conveyors, belt conveyors, slat conveyors, and guided vehicles (or trailer carts) with flat low-friction platforms (e.g., flat surface decks or passive rollers on the AGV). The push-pull mechanisms are installed at the transfer stations and operate by pushing or pulling unit loads between the station platform and the handling system.

Other types of transfer devices used for conveyor systems include lift-and-carry mechanisms. A common way of implementing lift-and-carry transfer is the walking beam mechanism described in Chapter 4. Other mechanisms, including the chain conveyor, are also used. The lift-and-carry devices lift the pallet (or other unit load container) vertically from the main conveyor and transfer it laterally to the unload station. The loading procedure is the reverse of the unloading operation.

Several automatic methods are available for transferring loads to and from AGV unit load carriers. Some of these methods can also be used for loading and unloading trailer carts in driverless trains. The automated techniques include powered roller conveyors or belts on the AGV deck, and powered lift and lower decks.

The use of powered roller conveyors or belts requires alteration of the vehicle deck by installing a powered roller conveyor or continuous belt on the deck. The load/unload stations used with these vehicles also have a powered conveyor or belt at the same elevation as the carrier deck. To accomplish a load transfer, the vehicle positions itself next to the station and the powered conveyor or belts are actuated on both the carrier and the station. This arrangement is illustrated in Figure 15.10.

Unit load carriers with lift and lower platforms require installation of the powered lift mechanism on the deck. The lift/lower mechanism is usually designed for a pallet of a particular standard size. The vehicles are generally used in conjunction with special load/unload stations designed to accept the standard size pallet. The lift/lower carrier and

FIGURE 15.10   AGV equipped with powered roller deck to transfer unit loads from roller conveyor. (Courtesy of Jervis B. Webb Company.)

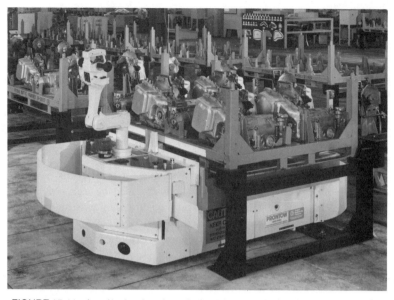

FIGURE 15.11   Load/unload stations designed to accept the standard-sized pallet
from AGV with lift/lower carrier deck. (Courtesy of Jervis B. Webb Company.)

station are pictured in Figure 15.11. In operation, the vehicle drives into the station for
the loading and unloading operation. If the vehicle is to accept a pallet from the station,
the vehicle platform is in the lowered position. With the vehicle located properly at the
station, the platform is raised to lift the pallet from the station for removal and delivery
to the specified destination. If the vehicle is to transfer a load to the station, it enters the
station with its platform in the raised position. After locating itself with respect to the
station, it lowers its platform to bring the pallet to rest on the station.

REFERENCES

[1] Bozer, Y. A., and J. A. White, "Travel-Time Models for Automated Storage/Retrieval
     Systems," *IIE Transactions,* December 1984, pp. 329–338.

[2] Budill, E. J. "Unit Load AS/RS Capabilities and Design Considerations," in *Automated
     Material Handling and Storage* (J. A. Tompkins and J. D. Smith, Editors), Auerbach Pub-
     lishers, Inc. Pennsauken, N.J., 1983.

[3] Kulwiec, R. A., Editor, *Materials Handling Handbook,* 2nd ed., John Wiley & Sons, Inc.,
     New York, 1985.

[4] Rygh, O. B., "Integrating Storage and Manufacturing Functions," paper presented at the Fall
     Industrial Engineering Conference, Toronto, Canada, November 1983.

[5] The Material Handling Institute, *Consideration for Planning and Installing an Automated
     Storage/Retrieval System,* Pittsburgh, Pa., 1977.

[6] The Material Handling Institute, *AS/RS in the Automated Factory,* Pittsburgh, Pa., 1983.

[7] TOMPKINS, J. A., and J. A. WHITE, *Facilities Planning,* John Wiley & Sons, Inc., New York, 1984, Chapters 6, 10, and 11.

[8] WEISS, D. J., "Carousel Systems Capabilities and Design Considerations," in *Automated Material Handling and Storage* (J. A. Tompkins amd J. D. Smith, Editors), Auerbach Publishers, Inc., Pennsauken, N.J., 1983.

PROBLEMS

15.1. A unit load AS/RS must be designed to hold an average of 500 pallets. An allowance of 20% additional storage compartments is to be designed into the storage system for peak-use periods and flexibility. The unit load has dimensions $x = 40$ in., $y = 36$ in., and depth into the storage rack $= 48$ in. It has been determined that the AS/RS will consist of three aisles with one S/R machine per aisle. Because of ceiling height of the existing building, the height of the storage system must be as close to (but not to exceed) 30 ft as possible. Determine the height and length of the aisle in the AS/RS that will satisfy the design specifications.

15.2. The length of an AS/RS is 400 ft and its height is 100 ft. Horizontal and vertical travel speeds are 250 ft/min and 80 ft/min, respectively. The P&D time $= 0.6$ min. Determine the average single-command and dual-command transaction times for the storage system.

15.3. If the times required to travel the length and height of an AS/RS are equal, the storage system is referred to as being "square in time." In Problem 15.2, in which the horizontal speed $= 250$ ft/min, what is the vertical travel speed that will make the system square in time? For this change, determine the expected single-command and dual-command transaction times for the storage system. Comment on any differences between the answers to this problem and Problem 15.2.

15.4. A WIP AS/RS is being designed to serve a production plant. It is anticipated that the storage system will be required to accomplish 30 storage and 30 retrieval transactions per hour. Because of space and cost limitations, a two-aisle system will be installed. Each side of each aisle will hold 8 loads in the vertical direction and 20 loads in the horizontal direction. The P&D time $= 0.4$ min. Each WIP load will be contained on a pallet. The palletized load has dimensions $x = 40$ in., $y = 36$ in., and depth into the storage rack $= 48$ in. Specify what the minimum horizontal and vertical travel speeds must be for the storage system to satisfy the throughput requirements. Assume that only single-command transactions will be used and that the system will be "square in time" as defined as in Problem 15.3.

15.5. In Problem 15.4, assume that all transactions can be accomplished using dual-command cycles instead of single-command cycles. Specify what the minimum horizontal and vertical travel speeds must be for the storage system to satisfy the throughput requirements. Assume that the system will be "square in time" as defined as in Problem 15.3.

15.6. Example 15.1 considers one aisle of an AS/RS. Suppose that the aisle in the example problem were one of five aisles in the storage system. Compute the expected throughput of the AS/RS if it is estimated that the system will have 75% single-command cycles and 25% dual-command cycles.

15.7. (This problem uses concepts and equations from Chapter 14.) An AS/RS is served by an automated guided vehicle system in a highly automated factory. The average delivery time for the AGVS is 5.0 min. There are six vehicles operating in the system at any time, and the traffic factor = 0.90. The three-aisle AS/RS is 200 ft long and 50 ft high. The horizontal and vertical velocities of its S/R machines are 150 ft/min and 75 ft/min, respectively. The interface between the AS/RS and the AGVS consists of three P&D stations, one for each aisle. The P&D time is 0.40 min. Is the design of the AGVS compatible with the design of the AS/RS in terms of throughput? To be conservative, assume that all AS/RS transactions are single-command cycles.

15.8. A mechanized storage carousel has a length of 40 ft and a width of 4.5 ft. The velocity of the carousel = 60 ft/min, and the part handling time at the unload station is 0.40 min. Compute the average time to retrieve a part from the system: (a) Assuming that the system revolves in a single direction. (b) Assuming that the system revolves in both directions.

15.9. A storage system serving an electronics assembly plant consists of three storage carousels, each with its own P&D station. Each carousel has a track that is 60 ft long and 3.5 ft wide. The speed at which the system revolves is 75 ft/min. The P&D handling time is 0.40 min. Determine the throughput rate of the storage system if the storage transactions and retrieval transactions are equally divided during the shift. Assume bidirectional travel of the carousel.

15.10. A WIP carousel storage system is to be designed to serve a mechanical assembly plant. The specifications on the system are that it must have a total of 400 storage bins and a throughput rate of at least 125 storage and retrieval transactions per hour. Two alternative configurations are being considered, a one-carousel system and a two-carousel system. Both systems will use bidirectional travel at a carousel speed = 75 ft/min. For convenience to the picker-operator, the height of the carousel will be limited to five bins (n_b = 5). The standard time for a P&D transaction at the load/unload station = 0.4 min, under the assumption that one part will be picked or stored per bin. If the transaction involves more than one part per bin, the P&D standard time = 0.6 min.

(a) Determine the required length of the one-carousel system if the width of the carousel is given as 4.0 ft and the spacing between carriers = 2.5 ft.

(b) For your answer to part (a), determine the average transaction cycle time and throughput rate, given that 50% of the transactions will involve more than a single component.

(c) Determine the required length of the two-carousel system if the width of the carousel is given as 4.0 ft and the spacing between carriers = 2.5 ft.

(d) For your answer to part (c), determine the average transaction cycle time and throughput rate given that 50% of the transactions will involve more than a single component.

(e) Which configuration better satisfies the design specifications?

15.11. Given your answers to Problem 15.10, it is desired to compare the costs of the two systems. The one-carousel system has an installed cost of $50,000. The two-carousel system has an installed cost of $75,000. The labor cost per picker-operator is $15.00 per hour, including fringe benefits and applicable overhead. The storage systems will be operated 7 hours per day, but the operators are paid for 8 hours per day. The plant operates 250 days per year. Determine the following using a 3-year period for the analysis and a 25% interest rate:

(a) The equivalent uniform annual cost for the two design alternatives. Assume no salvage value at the end of the 3 years.

(b) The average cost per storage/retrieval transaction given that 50% of the transactions will involve more than a single component.

part VI

Group Technology
and Flexible
Manufacturing Systems

Up to this point we have discussed examples of fixed automation (e.g., transfer lines, assembly machines, conveyor systems) and programmable automation (e.g., numerical control, robotics, automated guided vehicle systems). In this part of the book we explore the possibility of flexible automation and what is required to achieve it. Part VI contains two chapters: Chapter 16, on group technology, and Chapter 17, on flexible manufacturing systems. The first chapter sets the stage for our discussion of flexible automation in Chapter 17. However, group technology has important principles and applications of its own.

Group technology is an approach that seeks to identify those attributes of a population that permit its members to be collected into groups, sometimes called families. The members of each particular group possess attributes that are similar. There are usually efficiencies and advantages to be gained from dealing with the population when it is divided into groups. Group technology can be applied to many different areas, including design and manufacturing. Chapter 16 deals mainly with the manufacturing area. We explore the various methods by which manufactured parts can be grouped into families (called part families), including parts classification and coding, and production flow analysis. These methods are described in the chapter. We also examine how the definition of part families can be helpful in designing optimal machine cells for producing the parts.

One type of machine cell that takes advantage of group technology is the flexible manufacturing system. Chapter 17 is concerned with this increasingly popular type of production system. The term *flexible manufacturing system* is derived from the fact that these systems are capable of producing different parts or products without significant downtime for changeover. Hence, they represent examples of flexible automation as we have defined it in Chapter 1. It should be mentioned that there are limitations to the variations among parts made on a flexible manufacturing system; the parts are usually included in a single part family or a small number of part families. What makes the flexible manufacturing system possible is a high level of computer integration of the machines and other components in the cell. In Chapter 17 we explain how this production system operates, describe its components, and classify the different types of systems.

chapter 16

Group Technology

Batch manufacturing is estimated to be the most common form of production in the United States, constituting perhaps 50% or more of the total manufacturing activity. There is a growing need to make batch manufacturing more efficient and productive. Also, there is an increasing trend to achieve a higher level of integration of the design and manufacturing functions in a firm. One of the approaches that is directed at both of these objectives is group technology (GT). In this chapter we discuss group technology, parts classification and coding, and several related topics.

Group technology is a manufacturing philosophy in which similar parts are identified and grouped together to take advantage of their similarities in manufacturing and design. Similar parts are arranged into part families. For example, a plant producing 10,000 different part numbers may be able to group the vast majority of these parts into 50 or 60 distinct families. Each family would possess similar design and manufacturing characteristics. Hence, the processing of each member of a given family would be similar, and this results in manufacturing efficiencies. These efficiencies are achieved by arranging the production equipment into machine groups, or cells, to facilitate work flow. In product design, there are also advantages obtained by grouping parts into families. These advantages lie in the classification and coding of parts.

Parts classification and coding is concerned with identifying the similarities among parts and relating these similarities to a coding system. Part similarities are of two types: *design attributes* (such as geometric shape and size), and *manufacturing attributes* (the sequence of processing steps required to make the part). While the processing steps required to manufacture a part are usually closely correlated with the part's design attributes, this is not always the case. Accordingly, classification and coding systems are often devised to allow for differences between a part's design and its manufacture. The reason for using a coding scheme is to facilitate retrieval for design and manufacturing purposes. In design, for example, a designer faced with the task of developing a new part can use the design-retrieval system to determine if a similar part is already in existence. A simple change in an existing part would be much less time consuming than designing from scratch. In manufacturing, the coding scheme can be used in an automated process planning system.

Group technology and parts classification and coding are closely related. Group technology is the underlying manufacturing concept, but some form of parts classification and coding is usually required in order to implement GT.

16.1   PART FAMILIES

A *part family* is a collection of parts which are similar either because of geometric shape and size or because similar processing steps are required in their manufacture. The parts within a family are different, but their similarities are close enough to merit their identification as members of the part family. Figures 16.1 and 16.2 show two part families. The two parts shown in Figure 16.1 are similar from a design viewpoint but quite different in terms of manufacturing. The 13 parts shown in Figure 16.2 might constitute a parts family in manufacturing, but their geometry characteristics do not permit them to be grouped as a design parts family.

One of the big manufacturing advantages of grouping workparts into families can be explained with reference to Figures 16.3 and 16.4. Figure 16.3 shows a process-type layout for batch production in a machine shop. The various machine tools are arranged

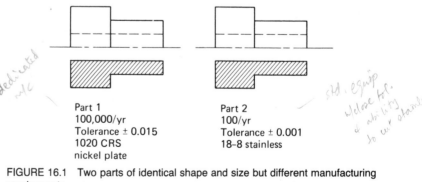

Part 1
100,000/yr
Tolerance ± 0.015
1020 CRS
nickel plate

Part 2
100/yr
Tolerance ± 0.001
18-8 stainless

FIGURE 16.1   Two parts of identical shape and size but different manufacturing requirements.

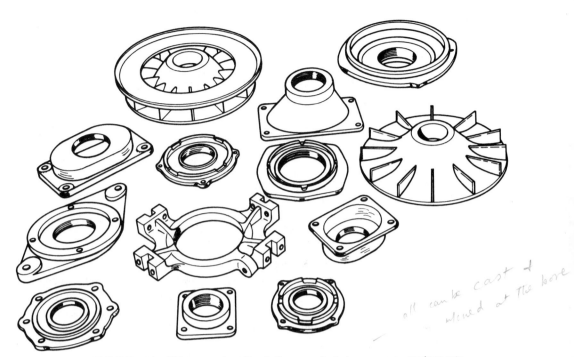

FIGURE 16.2 Thirteen parts with similar manufacturing process requirements but different design attributes.

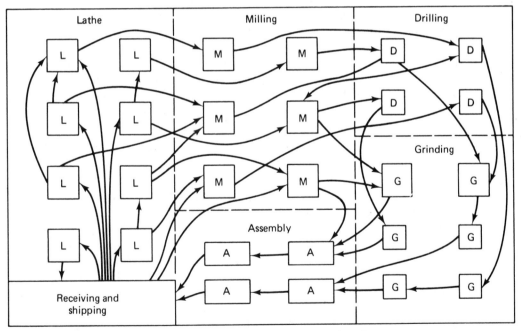

FIGURE 16.3 Process-type layout.

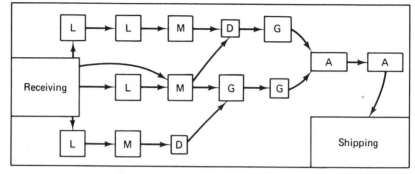

FIGURE 16.4   Group technology layout.

by function. There is a lathe section, milling machine section, drill press section, and so on. During the machining of a given part, the workpiece must be moved between sections, with perhaps the same section being visited several times. This results in a significant amount of material handling, a large in-process inventory, usually more setups than necessary, long manufacturing lead times, and high cost. Figure 16.4 shows a production shop of equivalent capacity, but with the machines arranged into cells. Each cell is organized to specialize in the manufacture of a particular part family. Advantages are gained in the form of reduced workpiece handling, lower setup times, less in-process inventory, and shorter lead times. Some of the manufacturing cells can be designed to form production flow lines, with conveyors used to transport workparts between machines in the cell.

The biggest single obstacle in changing over to group technology from a traditional production shop is the problem of grouping parts into families. There are three general methods for solving this problem. All three methods are time consuming and involve the analysis of much data by properly trained personnel. The three methods are:

1.   Visual inspection
2.   Classification and coding by examination of design and production data
3.   Production flow analysis (PFA)

The *visual inspection* method is the least sophisticated and least expensive method. It involves the classification of parts into families by looking at either the physical parts or their photographs and arranging them into similar groupings. Although this method is generally considered to be the least accurate of the three, one of the first major success stories of GT in the United States made the changeover using the visual method. This was the Langston Division of Molins Machine Company, located in Cherry Hill, New Jersey [8].

The second method involves classifying the parts into families by examining the individual design and/or manufacturing attributes of each part. The classification results in a code number that uniquely identifies the part's attributes. This classification and coding may be carried out on the entire list of active parts of the firm or some sort of sampling procedure may be used to establish the part families. For example, parts produced in the shop during a certain given time period could be examined to identify part family categories. The trouble with any sampling procedure is the risk that the sample may be unrepresentative of the entire population. The method of parts classification and coding seems to be the most commonly used method today. A number of classification and coding systems are described in the literature [4,6,14], and there are several commercially available packages being sold to industrial concerns. We discuss parts classification and coding more thoroughly in Section 16.2.

The third method, *production flow analysis,* makes use of the information contained on route sheets rather than part drawings. Workparts with identical or similar routings are classified into part families. Production flow analysis is discussed in more detail in Section 16.3.

16.2 PARTS CLASSIFICATION AND CODING

As mentioned previously, the three methods of identifying part families all require a significant investment in time and manpower. The most time consuming and complicated of the three methods is parts classification and coding. Many systems have been developed throughout the world, but none has been universally adopted. One of the reasons for this is that a classification and coding system should be custom engineered for a given company or industry. One system may be best for one company while a different system is more suited to another company.

The major benefits of a well-designed classification and coding system for group technology have been summarized as follows by Ham [5]:

1. It facilitates the formation of part families and machine cells.
2. It permits quick retrieval of designs, drawings, and process plans.
3. It reduces design duplication.
4. It provides reliable workpiece statistics.
5. It facilitates accurate estimation of machine tool requirements and logical machine loadings.
6. It permits rationalization of tooling setups, reduces setup time, and reduces production throughput time.
7. It allows rationalization and improvement in tool design.
8. It aids production planning and scheduling procedures.
9. It improves cost estimation and facilitates cost accounting procedures.
10. It provides for better machine tool utilization and better use of tools, fixtures, and manpower.
11. It facilitates NC part programming.

Types of classification and coding systems

Although it would seem from the foregoing list that nearly all departments in the firm can benefit from a good parts classification and coding system, the two main functional areas that use the system are design and manufacturing. Accordingly, parts classification systems fall into one of three categories:

1. Systems based on part design attributes
2. Systems based on part manufacturing attributes
3. Systems based on both design and manufacturing attributes

The types of design and manufacturing workpart attributes that are typically included in classification schemes are listed in Table 16.1. It is clear that there is a certain amount of overlap between the design and manufacturing attributes of a part.

The parts coding scheme consists of a sequence of numerical digits devised to identify the part's design and manufacturing attributes. Coding schemes for parts classification can be of two basic structures:

1. *Hierarchical structure.* In. this code structure, the interpretation of each succeeding symbol depends on the value of the preceding symbols.
2. *Chain-type structure.* In this type of code, the interpretation of each symbol in the sequence is fixed. It does not depend on the value of the preceding symbol.

For example, consider a two-digit code, such as 15 or 25. Suppose that the first digit stands for the general part shape. The symbol 1 means round workpart and 2 means flat rectangular geometry. In a hierarchical code structure, the interpretation of the second digit would depend on the value of the first digit. If preceded by 1, the 5 might indicate

TABLE 16.1   Design and Manufacturing Attributes Typically Included in a Group Technology Classification System

Part design attributes	
Basic external shape	Major dimensions
Basic internal shape	Minor dimensions
Length/diameter ratio	Tolerances
Material type	Surface finish
Part function	

Part manufacturing attributes	
Major process	Operation sequence
Minor operations	Production time
Major dimension	Batch size
Length/diameter ratio	Annual production
Surface finish	Fixtures needed
Machine tool	Cutting tools

some length/diameter ratio, and if preceded by 2, the 5 might be interpreted to specify some overall length. In the chain-type code structure, the symbol 5 would be interpreted the same way regardless of the value of the first digit. For example, it might indicate overall part length, whether the part is rotational or flat rectangular. The advantage of the hierarchical code structure is that more information can be contained in the code. Some parts classification and coding systems use a combination of the hierarchical and chain-type structures.

The number of digits required can range from 6 to 30. Coding schemes that include only design characteristics require fewer digits, perhaps 12 or fewer. Most modern classification and coding systems incorporate both design and manufacturing data into the code. To accomplish this, code numbers with 20 to 30 digits may be needed.

Some of the important classification and coding systems (with emphasis on those in the United States) include the Brisch System (Brisch-Birn, Inc.), CODE (Manufacturing Data Systems, Inc.), CUTPLAN (Metcut Associates), DCLASS (Brigham Young University), MultiClass (OIR—Organization for Industrial Research), and Part Analog System (Lovelace, Lawrence & Co., Inc.).

Two classification and coding systems will be discussed in the following subsections: The Opitz system and MultiClass. The Opitz system is of historical interest because it was one of the first published classification and coding schemes for mechanical parts. MultiClass is a current commercial product offered by OIR, the Organization for Industrial Research.

The Opitz classification system

This parts classification and coding system was developed by H. Opitz of the University of Aachen in West Germany. It represents one of the pioneering efforts in the group technology area and is probably the best known of the classification and coding schemes.

The Opitz coding system uses the following digit sequence:

$$12345 \qquad 6789 \qquad ABCD$$

The basic code consists of nine digits, which can be extended by adding four more digits. The first nine digits are intended to convey both design and manufacturing data. The general interpretation of the nine digits is indicated in Figure 16.5. The first five digits, 12345, are called the "form code" and describe the primary design attributes of the part. The next four digits, 6789, constitute the "supplementary code" which indicates some of the attributes that would be of use to manufacturing (dimensions, work material, starting raw workpiece shape and accuracy). The extra four digits, ABCD, are referred to as the "secondary code" and are intended to identify the production operation type and sequence. The secondary code can be designed by the firm to serve its own particular needs.

The complete coding system is too complex to provide a comprehensive description here. Opitz wrote an entire book on his system [14]. However, to obtain a general idea of how the Opitz system works, let us examine the first five digits of the code, the form code. The first digit identifies whether the part is a rotational or a nonrotational part. It

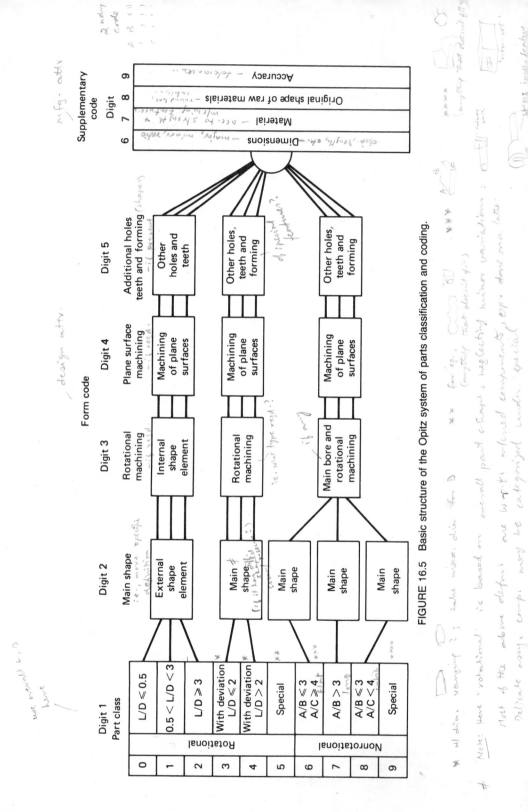

FIGURE 16.5 Basic structure of the Opitz system of parts classification and coding.

Digit 1 — Part class

Code		Part class
	Rotational parts	
0		L/D ≤ 0.5
1		0.5 < L/D < 3
2		L/D ≥ 3
3		
4		
5		
	Nonrotational parts	
6		
7		
8		
9		

Digit 2 — External shape, external shape elements

Code		Description
0		Smooth, no shape elements
	Stepped to one end or smooth	
1		No shape elements
2		Thread
3		Functional groove
	Stepped to both ends	
4		No shape elements
5		Thread
6		Functional groove
7		Functional cone
8		Operating thread
9		All others

Digit 3 — Internal shape, internal shape elements

Code		Description
0		No hole, no breakthrough
	Smooth or stepped to one end	
1		No shape elements
2		Thread
3		Functional groove
	Stepped to both ends	
4		No shape elements
5		Thread
6		Functional groove
7		Functional cone
8		Operating thread
9		All others

Digit 4 — Plane surface machining

Code	Description
0	No surface machining
1	Surface plane and/or curved in one direction, external
2	External plane surface related by graduation around a circle
3	External groove and/or slot
4	External spline (polygon)
5	External plane surface and/or slot, external spline
6	Internal plane surface and/or slot
7	Internal spline (polygon)
8	Internal and external polygon, groove and/or slot
9	All others

Digit 5 — Auxiliary holes and gear teeth

Code		Description
	No gear teeth	
0		No auxiliary hole
1		Axial, not on pitch circle diameter
2		Axial on pitch circle diameter
3		Radial, not on pitch circle diameter
4		Axial and/or radial and/or other direction
5		Axial and/or radial on PCD and/or other directions
	With gear teeth	
6		Spur gear teeth
7		Bevel gear teeth
8		Other gear teeth
9		All others

FIGURE 16.6 Form code (digits 1 through 5) for rotational parts in the Opitz system. Part classes 0, 1, and 2.

441

also describes the general shape and proportions of the part. We will limit our survey to rotational parts possessing no unusual features, those with code values 0, 1, or 2. See Figure 16.5 for definitions. For this general class of workparts, the coding of the first five digits is given in Figure 16.6. An example will demonstrate the coding of a given part.

EXAMPLE 16.1

Given the part design of Figure 16.7 define the "form code" (the first five digits) using the Opitz system.

Solution:

The overall length/diameter ratio, $L/D = 1.5$, so the first digit code $= 1$. The part is stepped on both ends with a screw thread on one end, so the second-digit code would be 5. The third-digit code is 1 because of the through-hole. The fourth and fifth digits are both 0, since no surface machining is required and there are no auxiliary holes or gear teeth on the part. The complete form code in the Opitz system is 15100. To add the supplementary code, we would have to code the sixth through ninth digits with data on dimensions, material, starting workpiece and shape, and accuracy.

MultiClass

MultiClass is a classification and coding system developed by the Organization for Industrial Research. The system is relatively flexible, allowing the user company to customize the classification and coding scheme to a large extent to fit its own products and application. MultiClass can be used for a variety of different types of manufactured product, including machined and sheet metal parts, tooling, electronics, purchased parts, assemblies and subassemblies, machine tools, and other elements. Up to nine different types of components can be included within a single MultiClass software structure.

    MultiClass uses a hierarchical or decision-tree coding structure in which the succeeding digits depend on values of the previous digits. In the application of the system,

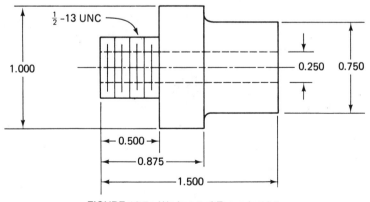

FIGURE 16.7   Workpart of Example 16.1.

TABLE 16.2 First 18 Digits of the Multiclass
Classification and Coding System

Digit	Function
0	Code system prefix
1	Main shape category
2, 3	External and internal configuration
4	Machined secondary elements
5, 6	Functional descriptors
7–12	Dimensional data (length, diameter, etc.)
13	Tolerances
14, 15	Material chemistry
16	Raw material shape
17	Production quantity
18	Machined element orientation

a series of menus, pick lists, tables, and other interactive prompting routines are used to code the part. This helps to organize and provide discipline to the coding procedure.

The coding structure consists of up to 30 digits. The 30 digits are divided into two regions, one provided by OIR and the second designed by the user to meet specific needs and requirements. A prefix precedes the 30 digits and is used to identify the type of part (e.g., a prefix value of 1 indicates machined and sheet metal parts). For a machined part, the coding for the first 18 digit positions (after the prefix) is summarized in Table 16.2.

EXAMPLE 16.2

A rotational part is illustrated in Figure 16.8. Using the MultiClass classification and coding system, the part is coded as illustrated in Figure 16.9.

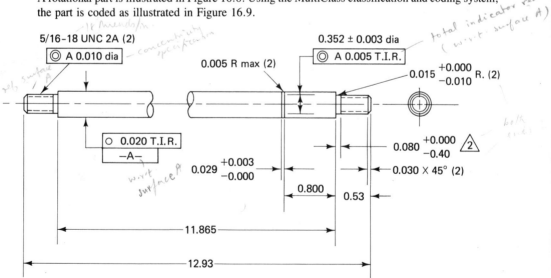

FIGURE 16.8 Workpart of Example 16.2. (Courtesy of OIR, the Organization for Industrial Research.)

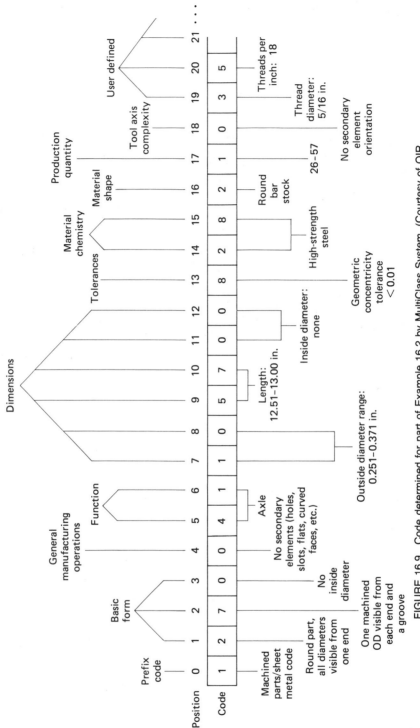

FIGURE 16.9 Code determined for part of Example 16.2 by MultiClass System. (Courtesy of OIR, the Organization for Industrial Research.)

16.3 PRODUCTION FLOW ANALYSIS

Production flow analysis (PFA) is a method for identifying part families and associated groupings of machine tools. It does not use a classification and coding system and it does not use part drawings to identify families. Instead, PFA is used to analyze the operation sequence and machine routing for the parts produced in the given shop. It groups parts with identical or similar routings together. These groups can then be used to form logical machine cells in a group technology layout. Since PFA uses manufacturing data rather than design data to identify part families, it can overcome two possible anomalies. First, parts whose basic geometries are quite different may nevertheless require similar or identical process routings. Second, parts whose geometries are similar may nevertheless require process routings that are quite different. However, the disadvantage of using production flow analysis is that it provides no mechanism for rationalizing the manufacturing routings. It takes the route sheets the way they are, with no consideration being given to whether the routings are optimal or consistent or even logical.

PFA procedure

The procedure in production flow analysis can be organized into the following steps:

1. *Data collection.* The first step in the PFA procedure is to decide on the scope of the study and to collect the necessary data. The scope defines the population of parts to be analyzed. Should all the parts produced in the shop be included in the study, or should a representative sample be selected for analysis? Once the population is defined, the minimum data needed in the analysis are the part number and machine routing (operation sequence) for every part. These data can be obtained from the route sheets. Additional data, such as lot size, time standards, and annual production rate, might be useful for designing machine cells of the desired productive capacity.

2. *Sorting of process routings.* The second step is to arrange the parts into groups according to the similarity of their process routings. For a large number of parts in the study, the only practical way to accomplish this step is to code the data collected in step 1 onto computer cards. One possible format (highly simplified) for these cards is illustrated in Figure 16.10. The format allows space for the part number and a sequence of code

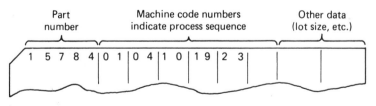

FIGURE 16.10 Card format for organizing process routing data in production flow analysis.

TABLE 16.3 Possible Code Numbers to Indicate Processes and Machines (Highly Simplified)

Process	Code	Process	Code
Cutoff	01	Shaper	13
Lathe	02	Planer	14
Turret lathe	03	Broach	15
Chucker	04	Deburr	16
Drill manual	05	Polish	17
NC drill	06	Buff	18
Mill	07	Clean	19
Bore	08	Paint	20
Grind—surface	09	Paint	20
Grind—surface	09	Plate	21
Grind—exterior cylinder	10	Assemble	22
Grind—interior cylinder	11	Inspect	23
Grind—centerless	12	Package	24

Pack indentification codes

Machine code numbers	A	B	C	D	E	F	G	H	I	J	K	L	M	N	O	P	Q	R	S	T
01	X		X	X	X	X		X				X	X	X	X			X	X	
02		X			X				X	X		X								
03	X			X				X										X	X	X
04					X								X							
05		X						X		X					X			X		
06									X							X				
07		X					X		X	X	X							X	X	
08							X		X											
09							X		X											
10	X				X	X		X				X	X					X		
11	X		X		X							X								
12			X				X						X	X						X
13		X					X										X			
14																				
15		X													X					
16	X	X	X		X	X		X				X	X	X				X	X	X
17								X		X			X							X
18			X						X											
19		X						X				X	X		X	X	X			
20								X							X		X			
21												X	X			X				
22	X		X				X							X						
23	X		X	X			X		X	X	X			X	X					X
24	X			X				X						X						

FIGURE 16.11 PFA chart (highly simplified).

[Handwritten margin annotations: "'family', here?" (pointing to Pack indentification codes); "i.e., pack A consists of all parts requiring the same type of same proces 01, 03 etc"]

446

numbers that identify particular machines in the routing. Table 16.3 presents a list of possible code numbers that might be used (again, highly simplified).

A sorting procedure would be used on the cards to arrange them into "packs." A pack is a group of parts with identical process routings. Some packs will contain only one part number. Each pack is given a pack identification number or letter.

3. *PFA chart.* The processes used for each pack are next displayed graphically on a PFA chart. A simplified version of the PFA chart is shown in Figure 16.11. It is merely a plot of the process code numbers for all the packs that have been determined.

4. *Analysis.* This is the most subjective and most difficult step in production flow analysis, yet it is the crucial step in the procedure. From the pattern of data exhibited in the PFA chart, similar groups must be identified. This can be done by rearranging the data on the original PFA chart into a new pattern which brings together packs with similar routings. One possible rearrangement is shown in Figure 16.12. The different groupings are indicated within blocks. The machines identified together within the blocks of Figure 16.12 would be synthesized into logical machine cells.

Invariably, there will be packs (process routings) that do not fit into similar groupings. These parts can be analyzed to determine if a revised process sequence can be developed which fits into one of the groups. If not, these parts must continue to be manufactured through a conventional process-type plant layout.

Comments on PFA

The weakness of production flow analysis is that the data used in the analysis are derived from production route sheets. The process sequences from these route sheets have been prepared by different process planners, and these differences are reflected in the route sheets. The routings may contain processing steps that are nonoptimal, illogical, and unnecessary. Consequently, the final machine groupings that result from the analysis may be suboptimal. Notwithstanding this weakness, PFA has the virtue of requiring less time to perform than a complete parts classification and coding procedure. It therefore provides a technique that is attractive to many firms for making the changeover to a group technology machine layout.

16.4   MACHINE CELL DESIGN

Whether part families and machine groups have been determined by parts classification and coding or by production flow analysis, the problem of designing the machine cells must be solved. In this section we consider some of the aspects of this important problem in group technology.

The composite part concept

Part families are defined by the fact that their members have similar design and manufacturing attributes. The composite part concept takes this part family definition to its logical conclusion. It conceives of a hypothetical part that represents all of the design

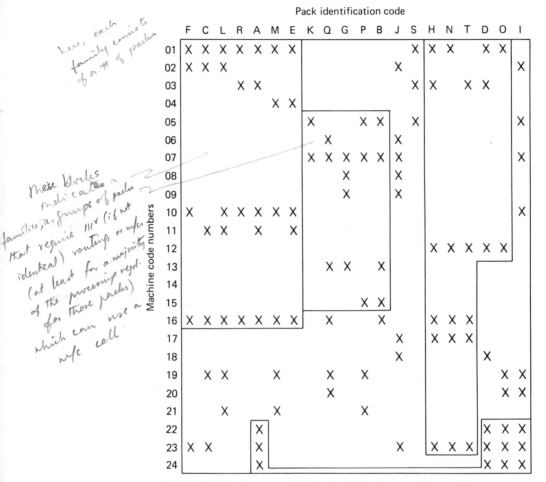

FIGURE 16.12   Rearranged PFA chart, indicating possible machine groups.

and corresponding manufacturing attributes possessed by the various individuals in the family. Such a hypothetical part is illustrated in Figure 16.13. To produce one of the members of the part family, operations are added and deleted corresponding to the attributes of the particular part design. For example, the composite part in Figure 16.13 is a rotational part made up of seven separate design and manufacturing features. These features are listed in Table 16.4.

A machine cell would be designed to provide all seven machining capabilities. The machines, fixtures, and tools would be set up for efficient flow of workparts through the cell. A part with all seven attributes, such as the composite part of Figure 16.13, would go through all seven processing steps. For part designs without all seven features, unneeded operations would simply be omitted.

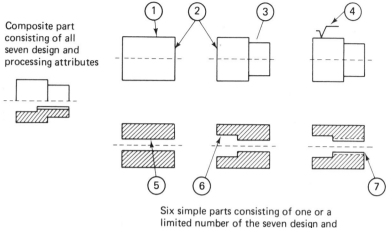

Composite part consisting of all seven design and processing attributes

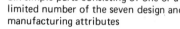

Six simple parts consisting of one or a limited number of the seven design and manufacturing attributes

FIGURE 16.13   Composite part concept.

In practice, the number of design and manufacturing attributes would be greater than seven, and allowances would have to be made for variations in overall size and shape of parts in the part family. Nevertheless, the composite part concept is useful for visualizing the machine cell design problem.

Types of cell designs

The term *cellular manufacturing* is sometimes used to describe the operations of a group technology machine cell. Machine cells can be classified into one of the following categories, according to the number of machines and the degree to which the material flow is mechanized between the machines:

1. Single machine cell
2. Group machine cell with manual handling

TABLE 16.4   Design and Manufacturing Attributes of the Composite Part in Figure 16.13

Number	Design and manufacturing attribute
1	Turning operation for external cylindrical shape
2	Facing operation for ends
3	Turning operation to produce step
4	External cylindrical grinding to achieve specified surface finish
5	Drilling operation to create through hole
6	Counterbore
7	Tapping operation to produce internal threads

3. Group machine cell with semi-integrated handling
4. Flexible manufacturing system (FMS)

As its name indicates, the *single machine cell* consists of one machine plus supporting fixtures and tooling organized to make one or more part families. This type of cell can be applied to workparts whose attributes allow them to be made on one basic type of process, such as turning or milling. For example, the composite part of Figure 16.13 could be produced on a conventional turret lathe with the possible exception of the cylindrical grinding operation (step 4).

The *group machine cell with manual handling* is an arrangement of more than one machine used collectively to produce one or more part families. There is no provision for mechanized parts movement between the machines in the cell. Instead, the human operators who run the cell perform the material handling function. Depending on the size of the parts and the arrangement of the machines in the cell, this function may require the assistance of the regular material handling crew in the shop. The cell is often organized into a U-shaped layout, as shown in Figure 16.14. This layout is considered appropriate when there is a variation in the work flow among the parts made in the cell. It also allows the multifunctional workers in the cell to move easily between machines [13].

The group machine cell with manual handling is sometimes achieved in a conventional process-type layout without rearranging the equipment. This is done simply by assigning certain machines to be included in the machine group, and restricting their work to specified part families. This allows many of the benefits of group technology cellular manufacturing to be achieved without the expense of rearranging equipment in the shop. Obviously, many of the material handling benefits of GT are not realized with this organization.

The *group machine cell with semi-integrated handling* uses a mechanized handling system, such as a conveyor, to move parts between machines in the cell. When the parts made in the cell have identical or nearly identical routings, an in-line layout of machines is considered appropriate. In this case, the machines are laid out along a conveyor to

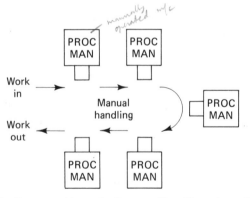

FIGURE 16.14 Group machine cell with manual handling using a U-shaped layout.

match the processing sequence. If the process routings vary, a loop layout is more appropriate since it allows the parts to circulate in the handling system. This permits different processing sequences for the different parts in the system. These two layouts are illustrated in Figure 16.15.

The *flexible manufacturing system* is the most highly automated of the group technology machine cells. It combines automated processing stations with a fully integrated material handling system. Chapter 17 is devoted to this form of automation, and we defer discussion until then.

Determining the best machine arrangement

Determining which type of machine cell to use and the best arrangement of equipment in the cell should be based on work processing requirements. The important factors include:

• *Volume of work to be done by the cell.* This includes the number of parts per year and the amount of work required per part. These factors influence how many machines should be included in the cell, the total cost of operating the cell, and the amount of investment that can be justified to organize and equip the cell.

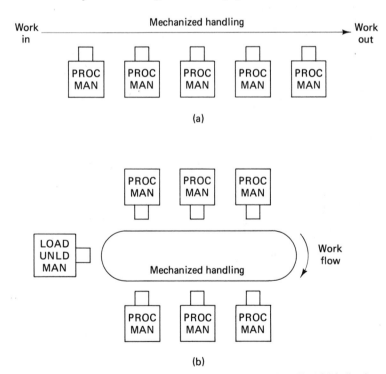

FIGURE 16.15   Group machine cell with semi-integrated handling: (a) in-line layout; (b) loop layout.

• *Variations in process routings of the parts.* This determines the work flow. If all process routings are identical, straight-line flow is appropriate. With significant variations in the routings, a U-shape or loop would be more appropriate.

• *Part size, shape, weight, and other physical attributes.* These factors determine the size and type of material handling and processing equipment that can be used.

A number of methods have been proposed for dealing with the problem of arranging machines in a GT cell. Several of these methods are described in Ham et al. [6]. Also, the production flow analysis technique described in Section 16.3 is helpful in solving a related problem, that of identifying which machines should be in the group.

Let us describe a relatively simple method that is suggested by Hollier [7] and described by Wild [18]. The method makes use of from–to charts, found useful in Chapter 14 for material handling analysis. We can formulate the method as consisting of three steps, as follows:

1. *Develop the from–to chart from part routing data.* The data contained in the chart reflect numbers of part moves between the machines (or workstations) in the cell. Moves into and out of the cell are not included in the chart.

2. *Determine the "to/from ratio" for each machine.* This is accomplished by summing up all of the "to" trips and "from" trips for each machine (or operation). The "to" sum for a machine is determined by adding all the elements in the corresponding column, and the "from" sum for a machine is determined by adding the elements in the corresponding row. For each machine, a "to/from ratio" is formed.

3. *Arrange machines in order of increasing to/from ratio.* The notion is that machines that have a low to/from ratio receive work from few other machines in the cell but distribute work to many machines. Conversely, machines possessing a high to/from ratio receive work more than they distribute it. Therefore, it is logical to place machines with low ratios at the beginning of the work flow, and to put machines with high ratios at the end of the work flow.

An example will illustrate the method.

EXAMPLE 16.3

Suppose that four machines have been identified as belonging in a GT machine cell. An analysis of 50 parts which are processed on these machines provides the following from–to chart (machines are identified by number):

	To:			
From:	1	2	3	4
1	0	5	0	25
2	30	0	0	15
3	10	40	0	0
4	10	0	0	0

Additional information is: 50 parts enter the machine grouping at machine 3, 20 parts leave after processing at machine 1, and 30 parts leave after machine 4. Determine from–to ratios and suggest a logical machine arrangement.

Solution:

Summing up the "from" trips and "to" trips for each machine yields the following:

	To:				
From:	1	2	3	4	"From" sums
1	0	5	0	25	30
2	30	0	0	15	45
3	10	40	0	0	50
4	10	0	0	0	10
"To" sums	50	45	0	40	

The to/from ratios can then be calculated.

Machine	To:	From:	To/from ratio
1	50	30	1.67
2	45	45	1.0
3	0	50	0
4	40	10	4.0

Based on these relative values, the machines in the cell should be arranged

$$3 \rightarrow 2 \rightarrow 1 \rightarrow 4$$

The work flow is mostly in-line; however, there is some back flow of parts which must be considered in the design of any material handling system that might be used by the cell. As a percentage, this back flow constitutes only 15/135 = 11.1% of the total material handling activity. A conveyor might be used for the forward flow between machines, with a less mechanized handling system for the back flow.

It is helpful to use some of the available graphical techniques to help conceptualize the work flow in the cell. The flow diagram, described in Chapter 14, is appropriate in this regard. The flow diagram showing the flow of parts for the machine arrangement in Example 16.3 is presented in Figure 16.16.

Key machine concept

A GT machine cell operates like a manual assembly line in some respects. The concept of line balancing is applicable. It is desirable to spread the workload evenly among the machines in the cell as much as possible. On the other hand, there is typically a certain

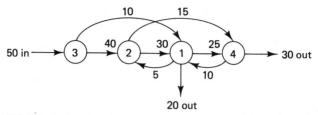

FIGURE 16.16   Flow diagram for machine layout of Example 16.3.

machine in a GT cell (or perhaps two or three machines in a large cell) that is more expensive than the other machines. It is important that the utilization of this expensive machine be high, even if it means that the utilization of the other machines in the cell is relatively low. This expensive machine is referred to as the "key machine." The other machines are referred to as "supporting machines," and they should be organized in the cell to keep the key machine busy. In a sense, the key machine becomes the bottleneck in the system.

Accordingly, there are generally two measures of utilization in a GT cell that are of interest: the utilization of the key machine and of the overall cell. The utilization of the key machine can be measured using the definition in Chapter 2. The utilization of each of the other machines can also be evaluated similarly. The cell utilization is obtained by taking a simple arithmetic average of all the machines in the cell. One of the problems at the end of the chapter serves to illustrate the key machine concept and the determination of utilization.

16.5   BENEFITS OF GROUP TECHNOLOGY

The problems that have prevented the widespread application of group technology in the United States include the following:

The problem of identifying part families among the many components produced by a plant

The expense of parts classification and coding

Rearranging the machines in the plant into the appropriate machine cells

The general resistance that is commonly encountered when changeover to a new system is contemplated

When these problems are solved and group technology is applied, benefits are typically realized in the following areas:

Design

Tooling and setups

Materials handling
Production and inventory control
Process planning
Employee satisfaction

Product design benefits

In the area of product design, the principal benefit derives from the use of a parts classification and coding system. When a new part design is required, the engineer or draftsman can devote a few minutes to figure the code of the required part. Then the existing part designs that match the code can be retrieved to see if one of them will serve the function desired. The few minutes spent searching the design file with the aid of the coding system may save several hours of the designer's time. If the exact part design cannot be found, perhaps a small alteration of the existing design will satisfy the function.

Another advantage of GT is that it promotes design standardization. Design features such as inside corner radii, chamfers, and tolerances are more likely to be standardized with GT.

Tooling and setups

Group technology also tends to promote standardization of several areas of manufacturing. Two of these areas are tooling and setups.

In tooling, an effort is made to design group jigs and fixtures that will accommodate every member of a parts family. Workholding devices are designed to use special adapters which convert the general fixture into one that can accept each part family member.

The machine tools in a GT cell do not require drastic changeovers in setup because of the similarity in the workparts processed on them. Hence, setup time is saved and it becomes more feasible to try to process parts in an order so as to achieve a bare minimum of setup changeovers.

Materials handling

Another advantage in manufacturing is a reduction in the workpart move and waiting time. The group technology machine layouts lend themselves to efficient flow of materials through the shop. The contrast is sharpest when the flow line cell design is compared to the conventional process-type layout (Figures 16.3 and 16.4).

Production and inventory control

Several benefits accrue to a company's production and inventory control function as a consequence of group technology.

Production scheduling is simplified with group technology. In effect, grouping of machines into cells reduces the number of production centers that must be scheduled. Grouping of parts into families reduces the complexity and size of the parts scheduling problem. For those workparts that cannot be processed through any of the machine cells, more attention can be devoted to the control of these parts.

Because of reduced setups and more efficient materials handling within machine cells, manufacturing lead times and work-in-process are reduced. Estimates are that throughput time may be reduced by as much as 60% and in-process inventory by 50% [1].

Process planning

Proper parts classification and coding can lead to an automated process planning system. This topic will be discussed in Section 24.1. Even without an automated process planning system, reductions in the time and cost of process planning can still be accomplished. This is done through standardization. New part designs are identified by their code as belonging to a certain parts family, for which the general process routing is already known.

Employee satisfaction

The machine cell often allows parts to be processed from raw material to finished state by a small group of workers. The workers are able to visualize their contributions to the firm more clearly. This tends to cultivate an improved worker attitude and a higher level of job satisfaction.

Another employee-related benefit of GT is that more attention tends to be given to product quality. Workpart quality is more easily traced to a particular machine cell in group technology. Consequently, workers are more responsible for the quality of work they accomplish. Traceability of part defects is sometimes very difficult in a conventional process-type layout, and quality control suffers as a result.

REFERENCES

[1] Abou-Zeid, M. R., "Group Technology," *Industrial Engineering*, May 1975, pp. 32–39.

[2] Baer, T., "With Group Technology, No One Reinvents the Wheel," *Mechanical Engineering*, November 1985, pp. 60–69.

[3] Black, J. T., "An Overview of Cellular Manufacturing Systems and Comparison to Conventional Systems," *Industrial Engineering*, November 1983, pp., 36–48.

[4] GALLAGHER, C. C., and W. A. KNIGHT, *Group Technology,* Butterworth & Company (Publishers) Ltd., London, 1973.

[5] HAM, I., "Introduction to Group Technology," *Technical Report MMR76-03,* Society of Manufacturing Engineers, Dearborn, Mich., 1976.

[6] HAM, I., K. HITOMI, and T. YOSHIDA, *Group Technology,* Kluwer Nijhoff Publishers, Hingham, Mass., 1985.

[7] HOLLIER, R. H., "The Layout of Multi-product Lines," *International Journal of Production Research,* Vol. 2, No. 1, 1963, pp. 47–57.

[8] HOLTZ, R. D., "GT and CAPP Cut Work-in-process Time 80%," *Assembly Engineering,* Part 1, June 1978, pp. 24–27; Part 2, July 1978, pp. 16–19.

[9] HOUTZEEL, A., "The Many Faces of Group Technology," *American Machinist,* January 1979, pp. 115–120.

[10] HOUTZEEL, A., *Classification and Coding,* Organization for Industrial Research, Inc., Waltham, Mass.

[11] HOUTZEEL, A., "Classification and Coding, Group Technology, Design Retrieval, and Computer Assisted Process Planning," Organization for Industrial Research, Waltham, Mass.

[12] HYER, N. L., and U. WEMMERLOV, "Group Technology and Productivity," *Harvard Business Review,* July–August 1984.

[13] MONDEN, Y., *Toyota Production System,* Industrial Engineering and Management Press, Institute of Industrial Engineers, Norcross, Ga., 1983.

[14] OPITZ, H., *A Classification System to Describe Workpieces,* Pergamon Press Ltd., Oxford, 1970.

[15] OPITZ, A., and H. P. WIENDAHL, "Group Technology and Manufacturing Systems for Medium Quantity Production," *International Journal of Production Research,* Vol. 9, No. 1, 1971, pp. 181–203.

[16] PHILLIPS, R. H., and J. ELGOMAYEL, "Group Technology Applied to Product Design," *Educational Module,* Manufacturing Productivity Educational Committee, Purdue University, West Lafayette, Ind., 1977.

[17] SHUNK, D. L., "Group Technology Provides Means to Realizing CIMS Benefits," *Industrial Engineering,* April 1985, pp. 74–80.

[18] WILD, R., *Mass Production Management,* John Wiley & Sons Ltd., London, 1972, Chapter 8.

PROBLEMS

16.1. Develop the form code (first five digits) in the Opitz system for the part illustrated in Figure P16.1.

16.2. Develop the form code (first five digits) in the Opitz system for the part illustrated in Figure P16.2.

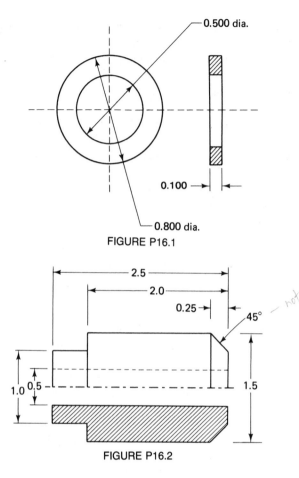

FIGURE P16.1

FIGURE P16.2

16.3. The four machines used to produce a certain family of parts are to be arranged into a GT cell. The from–to data for the parts processed by the machines are as follows:

From:	To:			
	1	2	3	4
1	0	5	0	45
2	0	0	0	0
3	50	0	0	0
4	0	45	0	0

(a) Determine the most logical sequence of machines for these data, according to the to/from ratios.

(b) Construct the flow diagram for the data.

in-line or U-shaped, based on options.

(c) Develop a feasible layout plan for the cell.

(d) Where do parts enter the cell and exit the cell? How many parts in each place?

16.4. Five machines will constitute a GT cell. The from–to data for the machines are as follows:

			To:		
From:	1	2	3	4	5
1	0	10	80	0	0
2	0	0	0	85	0
3	0	0	0	0	0
4	70	0	20	0	0
5	0	75	0	20	0

(a) Determine the most logical sequence of machines for these data, according to the to/from ratios.

(b) Construct the flow diagram for the data.

(c) Develop a feasible layout plan for the cell.

(d) Where do parts enter the cell and exit the cell? How many parts in each place?

16.5. A GT machine cell contains four machines. Machines 1 and 2 are identical and are used to feed machine 3, which is the key machine in the cell. The output of machine 3 feeds into machine 4. The cell is set up to produce a family of five parts (A, B, C, D, and E). The operation times for each part at each machine are given in the following table.

try to maximize util. of key mch.

	Operation time (min.)		
Part	Machines 1 and 2	Machine 3	Machine 4
A	4.0	15.0	10.0
B	15.0	18.0	7.0
C	26.0	20.0	15.0
D	15.0	20.0	10.0
E	8.0	16.0	10.0

A B C D E

The products are to be produced in the ratio 4:3:2:2:1. If the hours worked per week are 35, determine how many of each product will be made by the cell? What are the utilization of the key machine and the utilization of the cell?

16.6. This problem is concerned with the design of a GT cell to machine the components for a certain family of parts. The parts come in several sizes and the cell is to be designed to change over quickly from one size to the next. This will be accomplished using fast-change fixtures and direct numerical control (DNC) to download the NC programs from the plant computer to the CNC machines in the cell. The parts are rotational-type components, so the cell must be able to perform turning, boring, facing, drilling, and cylindrical grinding operations. Accordingly, there will be several machine tools in the cell, of types and numbers to be specified by the designer. To transfer parts between machines in the cell, one or more large robots will be used. The robot to be used has a jointed arm configuration with a reach of 2.0 m. Its base measures 1.0 m. × 1.0 m. The designer may also elect to use a belt or similar conveyor system to move parts within the cell. Any conveyor equipment of this type will be 0.4 m wide. The arrangement of the various pieces of equipment in the cell is the principal problem to be considered.

The raw workparts will be delivered into the machine cell on a belt conveyor to a fixed location so that the robot can pick up each part to start it through the cell. The raw parts are forgings so that the parts are ready for machining. The finished parts must be deposited onto a conveyor that delivers them to the assembly department. The input and output conveyors are 0.4 m wide, and the designer must specify how they enter and exit the cell. The five parts are currently machined by conventional methods in a process-type layout. In the current production method, there are seven machines involved but two of the machines are virtual duplicates. From–to data have been collected for the jobs that are relevant to this problem.

				To:				
From:	1	2	3	4	5	6	7	Parts out
1	0	112	0	61	59	53	0	0
2	12	0	0	0	0	226	0	45
3	74	0	0	35	31	0	180	0
4	0	82	0	0	0	23	5	16
5	0	73	0	0	0	23	0	14
6	0	0	0	0	0	0	0	325
7	174	16	20	30	20	0	0	0
Parts in	25	0	300	0	0	0	75	

The from–to data indicate the number of workparts moved between machines during a typical 40-hour week. The data refer to the five parts considered in the case. The two categories "parts in" and "parts out" indicate parts entering and exiting the seven-machine group. A total of 400 parts on average are processed through the seven machines per week. However, as indicated by the data, not all 400 parts are processed by every machine.

Machines 4 and 5 are identical and assignment of parts to these machines is arbitrary. Average production rate capacity on each of the machines for the particular distribution of this parts family is given in the table below. Also given are the floor space dimensions of each machine in meters. Assume that all loading and unloading operations take place in the center of the machine.

Machine	Operation	Production rate (pc/h)	Machine dimensions (m)
1	Turn O.D.	9	3.5 × 1.5
2	Bore I.D.	15	3.0 × 1.6
3	Face ends	10	2.5 × 1.5
4	Grind O.D.	12	3.0 × 1.5
5	Grind O.D.	12	3.0 × 1.5
6	Inspect	5	Manually done
7	Drill	9	1.5 × 2.5

Operation 6 is currently a manual inspection operation. It is anticipated that this manual station will be replaced by a coordinate measuring machine (CMM). This automated inspection machine will triple the throughput rate from 5 parts per hour for the manual method to 15 parts per hour. The floor space dimensions of the CMM are 2.0 m × 1.6 m. All of the other machines currently listed are to be candidates for inclusion in the new machine cell.

(a) Analyze the problem and determine the most appropriate arrangement of the machines in the cell using the data contained in the from–to chart.

(b) Prepare a layout (top view) drawing of the GT cell, showing the machines, the robot(s), and any other pieces of equipment in the cell. Write a one-page (or less) description of the cell, explaining the basis of your design and why the cell is arranged as it is. (c) Identify any key machine(s) in the cell. Determine the production capacity and the utilization of the cell as you have designed it.

chapter **17**

Flexible Manufacturing Systems

One of the types of machine cell listed in Chapter 16 is the flexible manufacturing system (FMS). An FMS integrates many of the concepts and technologies that we have discussed in previous chapters into one highly automated production system. These concepts and technologies include:

- Flexible automation
- Group technology
- CNC machine tools
- Automated material handling between machines
- Computer control of machines (DNC) and material handling

The first FMS installations in the United States were made around 1967. These initial systems performed machining operations on families of parts using NC machine tools. By 1981, the FMS population had grown to about 25 in the United States, 40 in

Japan, and 50 in Europe [6]. By the beginning of 1985, the number of flexible manu-facturing system installations had reached an estimated 300 worldwide.

In this chapter we define and discuss flexible manufacturing systems: their com-ponents, their operation, their applications, and their significance. In current technology, the FMS represents one of the highest levels of achievement in automated production.

17.1   WHAT IS AN FMS?

A *flexible manufacturing system* consists of a group of processing stations (predominantly CNC machine tools), interconnected by means of an automated material handling and storage system, and controlled by an integrated computer system. What gives the FMS its name is that it is capable of processing a variety of different types of parts simulta-neously under NC program control at the various workstations. The initials FMS are sometimes used to denote the term *flexible machining system*. The machining process is presently the largest application area for FMS technology. However, it seems appropriate to interpret FMS in its broader meaning, allowing for a wide range of possible applications beyond machining.

Components of an FMS

As indicated in our definition above, there are three basic components of a flexible manufacturing system:

1. *Processing stations.* In present-day applications, these workstations are typ-ically computer numerical control (CNC) machine tools that perform machining operations on families of parts. However, flexible manufacturing systems are being designed with other types of processing equipment, including inspection stations, assembly workheads, and sheet metal presses. In Section 17.2 we examine some of the issues involved in selecting the equipment used in these processing stations.

2. *Material handling and storage.* Various types of automated material handling equipment are used to transport the workparts and subassemblies between the processing stations, sometimes incorporating storage into the function. We discuss the FMS material handling systems in Section 17.3.

3. *Computer control system.* Computer control is used to coordinate the activities of the processing stations and the material handling system in the FMS. The computer system is described in Section 17.4.

One additional component in the FMS is human labor. Human beings are needed to manage the operations of the flexible manufacturing system. Functions typically performed by people include loading raw workparts onto the system, unloading finished parts (or assemblies) from the system, changing and setting tools, equipment maintenance and repair, NC part programming, and programming and operating the computer system.

Types of systems

There are various ways to classify flexible manufacturing systems. One classification that is sometimes made in FMS terminology is the difference between a flexible manufacturing system and a manufacturing cell. There is no clear dividing line. Generally, the term *cell* can be used to refer to a machine grouping that consists of either manually operated or automated machines, or combinations of the two. The cell may or may not include automated material handling, and it may or may not be computer controlled. The term "flexible manufacturing system" generally means a fully automated system consisting of automated workstations, automated materials handling, and computer control.

The term *manufacturing cell* is used largely in connection with group technology, but both cells and FMSs rely on a GT approach in their design. A distinction that is sometimes made between a flexible manufacturing cell and a flexible manufacturing system is in the number of machines in the grouping. A grouping of four or more machines is a system, and three or fewer machines constitute a cell. For example, a grouping of several machines served by a robot and capable of processing a family of parts is commonly called a *flexible manufacturing cell*.

A classification in flexible machining systems is based on the part geometry being processed. Machined parts can usually be divided into either of two categories: prismatic or round. Prismatic parts are cubelike and require milling and related machining operations to shape them. Round parts are cylindrical or disk-shaped and require turning and related rotational operations. Production systems are sometimes classified according to whether they make one of the two part geometry types or the other.

Finally, flexible manufacturing systems can be described as being either a dedicated FMS or a random-order FMS. A *dedicated FMS* is used to produce a much more limited variety of part configurations. The geometry differences are minor and the product design is considered stable. Therefore, the machine sequence is identical or nearly identical for all parts processed on the system. This means that a flow line configuration is generally most appropriate, and that the system can be designed with a certain amount of process specialization to make the operations more efficient. Instead of using general-purpose machines, the machines can be designed for the specific processes required to make the limited part family.

The *random-order FMS* is the more appropriate type under the following conditions: the part family is large, there are substantial variations in the part configurations, there will be new part designs produced on the system and engineering changes in parts currently made on the system, and the production schedule is subject to change from day to day. To accommodate these variations, the random-order FMS must be more flexible than the dedicated FMS. It is equipped with general-purpose machines to deal with the variations in product and is capable of processing parts in various sequences (random order). A more sophisticated computer control system is required for this FMS type.

Where to apply FMS technology

Flexible manufacturing systems are considered to fill a gap between high-production transfer lines and low-production NC machines. The relative position of the FMS as a means of production is shown in Figure 17.1. For high volumes and output rates, transfer lines represent the most efficient method. The limitation of the transfer line is that variations in product configuration cannot be readily tolerated. A substantial redesign of the product may render this mode of production obsolete. On the other hand, stand-alone NC and CNC machines can accommodate changes in part configuration, but the production rates are substantially lower and the parts are usually made in batches. In terms of manufacturing efficiency and productivity, a gap exists between the high-production transfer line and the highly flexible NC machines. The solution to this midvolume production problem is the flexible manufacturing system.

In the midvolume range, the advantages of the FMS over stand-alone NC is that the production of several products can be intermixed, and production rates are higher. Instead of batching the products one at a time on an NC machine to meet requirements, the various products can be made simultaneously on the system. The setup time for changeover is minimized with an FMS, so the economic batch size reduces to one at the same time that the average production rate increases. Intermixing of products on the system permits the output rate of each product to be set at its corresponding demand rate. This reduces the work-in-process and final product inventories that are so typical of batch production methods.

The advantage of the flexible manufacturing system over a transfer line is flexibility. The FMS can be used to run a variety of product configurations, whereas the transfer line can produce only one or a limited number of product types.

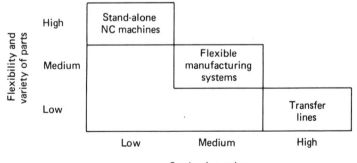

FIGURE 17.1   Application characteristics of flexible manufacturing systems.

17.2 FMS WORKSTATIONS

The processing or assembly equipment used in a flexible manufacturing system depends on the type of work that is accomplished on the system. In a system designed for machining operations, the principal types of processing station are CNC machine tools. However, the FMS concept is being applied to various other processes as well. Following is a list of the types of machines used in FMS workstations.

• *Machining centers.* The CNC machining center was described in Chapter 8. In addition to its use as a highly automated stand-alone machine, it can be used as a component of a flexible manufacturing system. It possesses features that make it very compatible with the FMS approach to production, including automatic tool changing and tool storage, use of palletized workparts, CNC control, and capacity for DNC control.

• *Head changers.* For specialized machining applications involving multiple tool cuts on the workpart, head changers can be used as processing stations in an FMS. A head changer is a special machine tool with the capability to change tool heads, just as a machining center changes single cutters. The tool heads are usually multiple-spindle tool modules that can be stored on a rack or drum located on or near the machine. They are used to perform simultaneous multiple drilling and related machining operations on a workpart. Higher production rates can be achieved than when the operations are performed one at a time. Because of the high cost of the tooling involved, head changers are useful only where production volume is sufficient to justify the savings in production time.

• *Head indexers.* The head indexer is similar to the head changer except that the tool heads are larger, too large to permit them to be moved between the spindle drive and a tool storage location. Accordingly, instead of exchanging the tool heads to and from storage, the heads are attached semipermanently to an indexing mechanism on the machine tool. In that way, they can be rotated into position to perform the simultaneous machining operations on the part. Eight or more heads can be mounted on the indexing table, and the tool heads can range up to 60 in. in size. The application of head indexers is normally limited to FMS installations involving the processing of specific families of parts. This type of equipment comes in either simplex style (single indexing table) or duplex style (two indexing tables opposing the workpiece). Figure 17.2 illustrates the duplex style.

• *Milling modules.* In some machining systems, the types of operations performed are concentrated in a certain category of machining, such as drilling, milling, or turning. For drilling (and similar operations such as reaming, tapping, etc.), a head changer or head indexer is often appropriate for maximizing the production rates. For milling, special milling machine modules can be used to achieve higher production levels than a machining center is capable of. The milling module can be vertical spindle, horizontal spindle, or multiple spindle.

• *Turning modules.* For turning operations, special turning modules can be designed for the FMS. In conventional turning, the workpiece is rotated against a tool that

FIGURE 17.2 Duplex head indexer used in an FMS. Each tool head performs multiple spindle operations simultaneously. (Courtesy of Kearney & Trecker Corp.)

is held in the machine and fed in a direction parallel to the axis of work rotation. Since many of the parts made on an FMS are held in a pallet fixture throughout processing on the FMS, the turning module must be designed to rotate the single-point tool around the work. This type of turning module is illustrated in Figure 17.3.

• *Assembly workstations.* Some flexible manufacturing systems include assembly within the scope of their operations. Indeed, flexible automated assembly systems are being developed to replace manual labor in the assembly of products typically made in batches [4,21]. Industrial robots are usually considered to be most appropriate as the automated workstations in these flexible assembly systems. They can be programmed to perform tasks with variations in sequence and motion pattern to accommodate the different product styles made on the system.

• *Inspection stations.* Inspection can be incorporated into a flexible manufacturing system, either by including an inspection operation at a given workstation, or by designating a specific station for inspection. Coordinate measuring machines, special inspection probes that can be used in a machine tool spindle, and machine vision represent three possible methods of performing inspection on an FMS. Inspection has been found to be particularly important in flexible assembly systems to ensure that components have been properly added at the workstations as specified. We examine the topic of automated inspection in more detail in Chapter 18, where the notion of a flexible automated inspection system is introduced.

FIGURE 17.3 Turning module used on an FMS. Turning head has four tool positions. (Courtesy of Kearney & Trecker Corp.)

• *Sheet metal processing machines.* The flexible system concept is being adapted to the sheet metal fabrication processes [23]. The processing workstations consist of pressworking operations such as punching, shearing, and certain bending and forming processes.

• *Forging stations.* Flexible systems are being developed to automate the forging process [20]. Forging is traditionally a very labor intensive manufacturing activity. The workstations in the system consist principally of the heating furnace, the forging press, and a trimming station.

Flexible manufacturing systems that illustrate the use of several of these types of workstations are discussed in application case studies in Section 17.7.

17.3 MATERIAL HANDLING AND STORAGE SYSTEM

The second major component of an FMS is its material handling and storage system. This section discusses the functions of the handling system, the types of FMS layout, and the types of handling equipment typically used in an FMS.

Functions of the handling system

The material handling and storage system in a flexible manufacturing system should perform the following functions:

1. *Random, independent movement of workparts between workstations.* This means that parts must be capable of moving from any one machine in the system to any other machine. This allows the system to achieve various processing sequences on the different machines in the cell, and to make substitutions when certain machines are busy.

2. *Handle a variety of workpart configurations.* For prismatic parts, this is usually accomplished by using pallet fixtures in the handling system. The fixture is located on the top face of the pallet and is designed to accommodate different part configurations by means of common components, quick-change features, and other devices that permit a rapid buildup of the fixture for a given part. The base of the pallet is designed for the material handling system. For rotational parts, industrial robots are often used to load and unload the turning type machine tools, and to transfer parts between workstations.

3. *Temporary storage.* The number of parts in the FMS typically exceeds the number of parts actually being processed. In this way, each machine can have a queue of parts waiting to be processed. This helps to increase machine utilization.

4. *Convenient access for loading and unloading workparts.* The handling system must provide a means to load and unload parts from the FMS. This is often accomplished by having one or more load/unload stations in the system. Manual operators are used to build up the pallet fixtures, load the parts, and unload the finished parts when processing has been completed.

5. *Compatible with computer control.* The handling system must be capable of being controlled directly by the computer to direct it to the various workstations, load and unload stations, and so on.

FMS layout configurations

The handling system establishes the FMS layout. The types of layout configurations commonly found in today's flexible manufacturing systems can be divided into the following five categories, as suggested by a classification presented in reference [9]:

1. In-line
2. Loop
3. Ladder
4. Open-field
5. Robot-centered cell

The *in-line* configuration is illustrated in Figure 17.4. It is most appropriate for systems in which the parts progress from one workstation to the next in a well-defined sequence with no back flow. The operation of this type of system is very similar to a transfer line, described in Chapter 4. Work always flows in one direction, as shown in Figure 17.4(a). Depending on the flexibility and storage features of the handling system it is possible to accommodate back flow of work on the system. One possible arrangement for doing this is shown in Figure 17.4(b), in which a secondary work handling system is provided at each workstation.

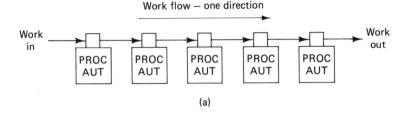

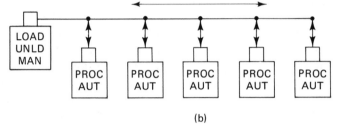

FIGURE 17.4 In-line FMS layout: (a) basic in-line configuration with one directional work flow; (b) in-line with transfer at workstations to allow back flow on primary handling system.

The basic *loop* configuration is shown in Figure 17.5. Parts usually flow in one direction around the loop with the capability to stop at any station. The load/unload station(s) are typically located at one end of the loop. A secondary handling system is shown at each workstation to permit parts to move without obstruction around the loop. The Ingersoll-Rand FMS described in our first application example and illustrated in Figure 17.5 uses a loop configuration.

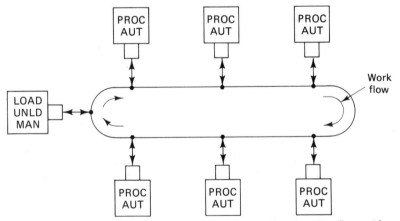

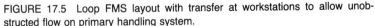

FIGURE 17.5 Loop FMS layout with transfer at workstations to allow unobstructed flow on primary handling system.

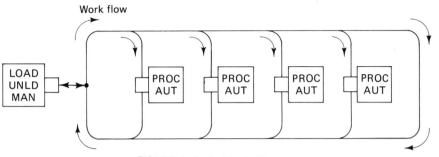

FIGURE 17.6   Ladder FMS layout.

The *ladder* configuration is an adaptation of the loop, as shown in Figure 17.6. It contains rungs on which workstations are located. The rungs increase the possible ways of getting from one machine to the next. This reduces the average travel distance, thereby reducing the transfer time between workstations.

The *open-field* layout is also an adaptation of the loop configuration. It consists of loops, ladders, and sidings organized to achieve the desired processing requirements. This layout type is generally appropriate for the processing of a large family of parts. The number of different machine types may be limited, and parts are routed to different workstations depending on which one becomes available first. Examples of the open field layout are shown in Figures 17.9 and 17.10.

Finally, the *robot-centered cell* is a relatively new form of flexible system in which one or more robots are used as the material handling system. We described the robot-centered cell in Chapter 13, and the configuration is illustrated in Figure 13.1. Industrial robots can be equipped with grippers that make them well suited for the handling of rotational parts. FMS layouts designed around robots as the material handling system are therefore used to process cylindrical or disk-shaped parts.

Material handling equipment

The types of material handling equipment that have been used to transfer parts between stations in an FMS include: roller conveyors, cart-on-track conveyors, and other types of conveyor systems; in-floor towline carts; automated guided vehicle systems; and industrial robots. All of these handling systems have been discussed in previous chapters. They constitute what is sometimes called the *primary material handling system* in the FMS. The primary handling system establishes the basic form of the layout configurations described in the preceding subsection. The types of material handling equipment typically utilized for the five FMS layouts are summarized in Table 17.1.

In addition to the primary handling system, many FMS installations make use of a *secondary handling system*. The secondary handling system is located at each workstation and is used to transfer work from the primary system to the machine tool or other processing station. Its function is to position and locate the parts with sufficient accuracy and repeatability at the workstation for processing. Buffer storage of parts may also be provided at each workstation by the secondary system.

TABLE 17.1   Material Handling Systems Typically Used for
the Five FMS Layouts

Layout configuration	Typical material handling system
1. In-line	Conveyor system, shuttle system
2. Loop	Conveyor system
3. Ladder	Conveyor system, AGVS,
4. Open field	AGVS, in-floor towline carts
5. Robot-centered cell	Industrial robot(s)

In some FMS installations, the secondary handling system is not included. All of the positioning and registration requirements at the individual stations are satisfied by the primary work handling system.

The primary material handling system is sometimes supported by an automated storage system such as an automated storage/retrieval system. A good illustration of storage in an FMS is described in reference [13]. The FMS is integrated with an AS/RS, and the S/R machine serves the work handling function for the workstations as well as delivering parts to and from the storage racks. The layout of the FMS is shown in Figure 17.7.

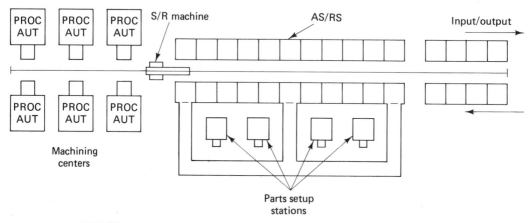

FIGURE 17.7   Layout of FMS incorporating AS/RS for handling and storage of work.

17.4   COMPUTER CONTROL SYSTEM

The operation of a flexible manufacturing system is computer controlled. In this section the functions of the computer, the data files needed to carry out these functions, and typical kinds of reports generated by the computer are described.

Computer functions

The functions performed by the FMS computer control system can be grouped into the following eight categories:

1. *Control of each workstation.* In a fully automated FMS, the individual processing or assembly stations generally operate under some form of computer control. For a machining system, CNC is used to control the individual machine tools.

2. *Distribution of control instructions to workstations.* Some form of central intelligence is also required to coordinate the processing at the individual stations. In a machining FMS, part programs must be downloaded to the machines, and DNC is used for this purpose. The DNC system stores the programs, allows entering and editing of programs as needed, and performs the other DNC functions described in Chapter 10.

3. *Production control.* This function includes decisions on part mix and rate of input of the various parts onto the system. These decisions are based on data entered into the computer, such as desired production rate per day for the various parts, numbers of raw workparts available, and number of applicable pallets.[1] The computer performs its production control function by routing an applicable pallet to the load/unload area and providing instructions to the operator to load the desired raw part. A *data entry unit* (DEU) is located in the load/unload area for communication between the operators and the computer.

4. *Traffic control.* The term *traffic control* refers to the regulation of the primary workpiece transport system which moves parts between workstations. This control is effected by dividing the transport systems into zones. A zone is a section of the primary transport system (towline chain, conveyor, etc.) which is individually controlled by the computer. By allowing only one cart or pallet to be in a zone, the movement of each individual workpart is controlled. The traffic controller operates the switches at branches and merging points, stops workparts at machine tool loading points, and moves parts to operator load/unload stations. Traffic control is very similar to the AGVS zone control discussed in Section 14.6.

5. *Shuttle control.* This is concerned with the regulation of the secondary part handling systems at each machine tool. Each shuttle system must be coordinated with the primary handling system, and it must also be synchronized with the operations of the machine tool it serves.

6. *Work handling system monitoring.* The computer must monitor the status of each cart and/or pallet in the primary and secondary handling systems as well as the status of each of the various workpart types in the system.

7. *Tool control.* Monitoring and control of cutting tool status is an important feature of a FMS computer system. There are two aspects to tool control: accounting for the location of each tool in the FMS and tool-life monitoring.

The first aspect of tool control involves keeping track of the tools at each station

---

[1]The term *applicable pallet* refers to a pallet that is fixtured to accept a workpart of the desired type.

on the line. If one or more tools required in the processing of a particular workpart are not present at the workstation specified in the part's routing, the computer control system will not deliver the part to that station. Instead, it will determine an alternate machine to which the part can be routed, or it will temporarily "float" the part in the handling system. In the second case, the operator is notified via the data entry unit what tools are required in which workstation. The operator then manually loads the tools and notifies the computer accordingly. Any type of tool transaction (e.g., removal, replacement, addition) must be entered into the computer to maintain effective tool control.

The second aspect of tool control is tool-life monitoring. A tool life is specified to the computer for each cutting tool in the FMS. A file is kept on the machining time usage of each tool. When the cumulative machining time reaches the life for a given tool, the operator is notified that a replacement is in order.

8. *System performance monitoring and reporting.* The FMS computer can be programmed to generate various reports desired by management on system performance. The types of reports are discussed later in this subsection.

These computer functions can be accomplished by any of several computer configurations. One computer can be used for all components of the FMS, or several different computers can be used. Up to three levels are practical in a given manufacturing system. CNC would be used for control of each individual machine tool. DNC would be appropriate for distribution of part programs from a central control room to the machines. A third control level would concern itself with production control, the operation of the work handling system, tool control, and generation of management reports.

FMS data files

To exercise control over the FMS, the computer system relies on data contained in computer storage files. The principal data files required for a flexible manufacturing system are of the following six types:

1. *Part program file.* The part program for each workpart processed on the system is maintained in this file. For any given workpart, a separate program is required for each station that performs operations on the part.

2. *Routing file.* This file contains the list of workstations through which each workpart must be processed. It also contains alternate routings for the parts. If a machine in the primary routing is down for repairs or there is a large backlog of work waiting for the machine, the computer will select an alternate routing for the part to follow.

3. *Part production file.* A file of production parameters is maintained for each workpart. It contains data relative to production rates for the various machines in the routing, allowances for in-process inventory, inspections required, and so on. These data are used for production control purposes.

4. *Pallet reference file*. A given pallet is fixtured only for certain parts. The pallet reference file is used to maintain a record of the parts that each pallet can accept. Each pallet in the FMS is uniquely identified and referenced in this file.

5. *Station tool file*. A file is kept for each workstation, identifying the codes of the cutting tools stored at that station. This file is used for tool control purposes.

6. *Tool-life file*. This data file keeps the tool-life value for each cutting tool in the system. The cumulative machining time of each tool is compared with its life value so that a replacement can be made before complete failure occurs.

System reports

Performance data collected during monitoring of the FMS can be summarized into the following types of reports:

1. *Utilization reports*. These are reports that summarize the utilization of individual workstations as well as overall average utilization for the FMS.

2. *Production reports*. Management is interested in the daily and weekly quantities of parts produced from the FMS. This information is provided in the form of production reports which list the required schedule together with actual production completions. One possible format for the production report is illustrated in Figure 17.8.

3. *Status reports*. Line supervision can call for a report on the current status of the system at any time. A status report can be considered an instantaneous "snapshot" of the present condition of the FMS. Of interest to supervision would be status data on workparts, machine utilization, pallets, and other system operating parameters.

4. *Tool reports*. These reports relate to various aspects of tool control. Reported data might include a listing of missing tools at each workstation. Also, a tool-life status report can be prepared at the start of each shift, similar to the one illustrated in Figure

```
              PART SUMMARY
               SHIFT 1                     PAGE 01  02/13           17:35:44
                        02/13  09:28  TO  02/13  17:35      8.1 HRS.
                    P/S         SCHED.  COMPL.   DIFF.         PCT.

                268923      1       7        6       -1         -14.3
                268923      2       7        9        2          28.6
                268315      1       7        8        1          14.3
                268315      2       7        8        1          14.3
                268315      3       7        7        0           0.0
                267171      1       7        5       -2         -28.6
                267171      2       7        9        2          28.6
```

FIGURE 17.8 Production shift report, indicating FMS performance. (Reprinted from *Understanding Manufacturing Systems* [19].)

TOOL LIFE STATUS FOR STATION 3   PAGE 01   07/16   11:40'22

TOOL NUMBER	EST. LIFE	ACT. USE	PCT. OF EST.
00003	500.0	600.6	120.1
00165	50.0	3.0	6.0
00166	200.0	3.0	1.5
00173	91.5	22.0	24.0
10011	800.0	0.0	0.0
10014	135.0	3.9	2.9
10017	225.0	236.0	104.9
10020	300.0	59.0	19.7
10021	115.0	59.0	51.3
10023	210.0	0.0	0.0
10025	142.0	118.0	83.1
10027	100.0	0.0	0.0
10032	300.0	0.0	0.0
10034	999.0	0.0	0.0
10035	320.0	112.0	35.0
10036	380.0	1188.7	312.8
10037	35.0	85.0	242.9
10056	600.0	6.0	1.0
10057	400.0	118.0	29.5
10061	400.0	472.0	118.0
10062	350.0	472.0	134.9
10064	65.0	91.0	140.0

FIGURE 17.9   Tool life status report for one machine tool in an FMS. (Reprinted from *Understanding Manufacturing Systems* [19].)

17.9. This list shows that several of the tools have been used well beyond their anticipated lives and are in need of replacement.

17.5 PLANNING THE FMS

The purchase and implementation of a flexible manufacturing system represents a major investment and commitment by the user company. It is important that the installation of the system be preceded by a thorough procedure of planning and design. The factors described in Section 16.4 are applicable in the planning of a fully automated FMS. As outlined in that section, these factors include:

1. *Volume of work to be produced by the system.* The amount of production planned for the FMS determines how many machines will be required in the system and the type of material handling equipment that would be used.
2. *Variations in process routings.* If the variations in process sequence are minimal, an in-line flow is most appropriate, perhaps approaching the configuration of a transfer line. As product variety increases, the loop and open-field layouts become can-

didates. If there is significant variation in the processing, a ladder layout becomes attractive.

3. *Physical characteristics of the workparts.* The size and weight of the parts determine the size of the machines used at the workstations and the type of material handling system used. Prismatic or cube-shaped parts are generally handled using pallet fixtures that are moved by conveyor, towcart, or AGVS. Robots might be most appropriate for relatively small round parts. Large rotational components that are too heavy for a robot would have to be palletized.

In addition to these factors, there are other factors that should be considered during planning. Klahorst [7] presents a useful list of considerations and rules of thumb that we borrow from and paraphrase to continue our list.

4. *Part families defined according to product commonality.* The definition of part families to be processed on the FMS should not be selected only on the basis of part design similarity; product commonality should also influence the selection of which parts are to be made on the system. The term *product commonality* means different components used on the same product. Many of the successful FMS installations are designed to accommodate part families defined by this criterion.

5. *FMS manpower requirements.* To keep the FMS running smoothly, Klahorst recommends the following manpower ratios for a machining-type system:

- One part loader/unloader for each five machines.
- One tool setup person for every 10 machines to exchange tools in the tool storage magazines. This assumes that the FMS does not have an automated tool-changing system beyond the use of tool drums at each machine tool. Duties may include building up the pallet fixtures for different part designs.
- One utility worker for each 10 machines. The utility worker performs minor repairs and maintenance, and other technical duties to keep the system operating.
- One system manager per FMS.

In addition, part programmers and computer operators are needed. The FMS personnel staff is responsible for an expensive system of equipment. The appropriate personnel must be identified for these staff positions, and they must be provided with proper training. Consideration must be given to these requirements during FMS planning.

6. *Appropriate production volume range: 5000 to 75,000 parts per year.* If annual production volume lies below this range, an FMS is likely to be an expensive alternative. If production volume is above this range, a more specialized production system (i.e., a transfer line) should probably be considered.

7. *Minimum number of machines per FMS: four.* To justify the expense of the computer control system and the automated handling system, four machines in the FMS is considered to be a minimum. Below that level, a GT cell or stand-alone CNC machining center should be considered.

8. *Minimum normal tolerance on work in an FMS: ±0.002.*   The use of pallet fixtures and the material handling system introduces additional positioning errors beyond those of a stand-alone machine tool. Consequently, an FMS cannot achieve close tolerances as well as a single machine. If part tolerances are closer than ±0.002, a stand-alone machining center should be easily capable of that level of accuracy; an FMS will require special processing considerations (e.g., inspection probes, precision boring heads, etc.) to achieve such a tolerance.

17.6   ANALYSIS METHODS FOR FLEXIBLE MANUFACTURING SYSTEMS

The quantitative analysis of flexible manufacturing systems can be accomplished using a number of different mathematical modeling techniques. The models can be divided into several categories:

1. *Static or deterministic models.*   These are quantitative production system models similar to ones presented in Chapter 2. They are used to provide gross estimates of such system parameters as production throughput, capacity, and utilization. They do not permit adequate evaluation of operating characteristics such as the buildup of queues and other dynamics which can impair the performance of the production system. Consequently, the static and deterministic models tend to overestimate the FMS performance.

2. *Queueing models.*   These models are based on the mathematical theory of queues. They permit the inclusion of certain dynamic characteristics (notably, queues), but only in a general way and for relatively simple system configurations. The performance measures that are calculated are usually average values for the steady-state operation of the production system. Examples of queueing models for flexible manufacturing systems are described in references 16 and 18.

3. *Computer simulation.*   Discrete-event simulation on a digital computer offers the most flexible approach for modeling a flexible manufacturing system. The computer model can be constructed to more closely resemble the details of a complex FMS operation than what is possible with either static or queueing models. Characteristics such as layout configuration, number of pallet shuttles in the system, and production scheduling rules can be incorporated into the FMS simulation model. Some of the available simulation languages applicable to FMS modeling include GPSS/H (Wolverine Software Corp.), SIMAN (Systems Modeling Corp.), and SLAM and MAP/1 (Pritsker & Associates). Examples of simulation modeling for flexible manufacturing systems are documented in references 12 and 15.

Among the list of references at the end of the chapter, we have attempted to provide the titles that indicate some of the significant work in the modeling of flexible manufacturing systems. Two good literature reviews are contained in papers by Buzacott and Shanthikumar [3] and Wilhelm and Sarin [22].

17.7   APPLICATIONS AND BENEFITS

The concept of flexible automation is applicable to a wide variety of manufacturing operations. The full potential of this technology has not yet been realized. In this section some of the important FMS applications are reviewed and the benefits are summarized.

FMS applications

Machining is the most common example of current FMS installations. Other applications are growing and include assembly, sheet metal pressworking, and forging. In this section, some of the applications are examined using case studies to illustrate. Our first three examples are machining installations.

EXAMPLE 17.1

One of the first FMS installations in the United States was at the Roanoke, Virginia, plant of the Tool and Hoist Division of Ingersoll-Rand Company. The system was installed by Sundstrand in 1970. It consists of two five-axis OM-3 Omnimil Machining Centers, two four-axis Machining Centers, and two four-axis OD-3 Drilling Machines. The machines are equipped with 60-tool drums and automatic tool changers and pallet changers. A powered roller conveyor system is used for the primary and secondary workpart handling systems. Three operators plus foreman run the line three shifts. Up to 140 different part numbers can be run on the system. Part-size capability ranges up to a 3-ft cube. Production quantities for the various part numbers processed on the line range from 12 per year up to 20,000 per year. Cast-iron and aluminum castings are machined on the

FIGURE 17.10   Overview of the Ingersoll-Rand FMS in Roanoke, Virginia, described in Example 17.1. (Courtesy of White-Sundstrand Machine Tool, Inc.)

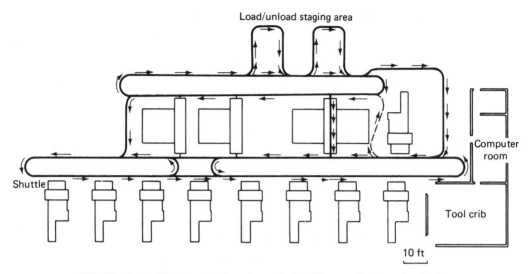

FIGURE 17.11 FMS layout at Avco-Lycoming in Williamsport, Pennsylvania, described in Example 17.2. (Reprinted from "Our FMS Will Do the Work of 67 Conventional Machine Tools" [10].)

line, including hoist cases, motor cases, and so on. A view of the system is presented in Figure 17.10.

EXAMPLE 17.2

A more recent FMS was designed and installed by Kearney & Trecker Corporation at the Avco-Lycoming plant in Williamsport, Pennsylvania. The system is used to machine aluminum crankcase halves for aircraft engines. The layout is an open-field type and is illustrated in Figure 17.11. The handling of workparts between machines is performed by an in-floor towline cart system with a total of 28 pallet carts. The system contains 12 machine tools: one duplex multispindle head indexer (shown in Figure 17.2), two simplex head indexers, and nine machining centers.

EXAMPLE 17.3

A flexible manufacturing system installed at Vought Aerospace in Dallas, Texas, by Cincinnati Milacron is shown in Figure 17.12. The system is used to machine approximately 600 different aircraft components. The FMS consists of eight CNC horizontal machining centers plus inspection modules. Part handling is accomplished by an automated guided vehicle system using four vehicles. Loading and unloading of the system is done at two stations. These load/unload stations consist of storage carousels which permit parts to be stored on pallets for subsequent transfer to the machining stations by the AGVS. The system is capable of processing a sequence of single, one-of-a-kind parts in a continuous mode, permitting a complete set of components for the aircraft to be made efficiently without batching.

Several attempts have been made to apply flexible automation concepts to assembly operations. One example is the adaptable-programmable assembly system (APAS), de-

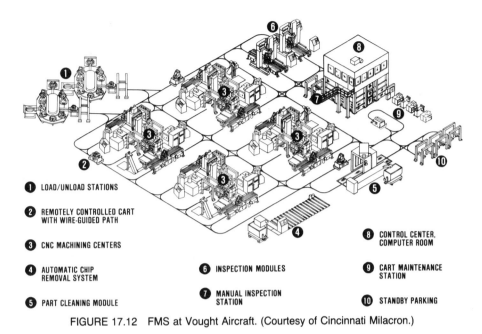

1. LOAD/UNLOAD STATIONS

2. REMOTELY CONTROLLED CART
   WITH WIRE-GUIDED PATH

3. CNC MACHINING CENTERS

4. AUTOMATIC CHIP
   REMOVAL SYSTEM

5. PART CLEANING MODULE

6. INSPECTION MODULES

7. MANUAL INSPECTION
   STATION

8. CONTROL CENTER,
   COMPUTER ROOM

9. CART MAINTENANCE
   STATION

10. STANDBY PARKING

FIGURE 17.12   FMS at Vought Aircraft. (Courtesy of Cincinnati Milacron.)

scribed in Section 13.6. The following example illustrates a flexible assembly system that makes minimal use of industrial robots.

EXAMPLE 17.4

An FMS for assembly installed by Allen-Bradley Company is reported in reference [21]. The "flexible automated assembly line" produces motor starters in 125 model styles. The line boasts a 1-day manufacturing lead time on lot sizes as low as 1 and production rates of 600 units per hour. The system consists of 26 workstations which perform all assembly, subassembly, testing, and packaging required to make the product. The stations are linear and rotary indexing assembly machines with pick-and-place robots performing certain handling functions between the machines. One hundred percent automated testing at each step in the process is used to achieve very high quality levels. The flexible assembly line is controlled by a system of Allen-Bradley programmable logic controllers.

Pressworking and forging are two other manufacturing processes in which efforts are being made to develop flexible automated systems. References 20 and 23 describe the FMS technologies involved. The following example illustrates the development efforts in the pressworking area.

EXAMPLE 17.5

The term *flexible fabricating system* (FFS) is sometimes used in connection with systems that perform sheet metal pressworking operations. One FFS concept by Wiedemann is illustrated in Figure 17.13. The system is designed to unload sheet metal stock (at right in figure), feed it through

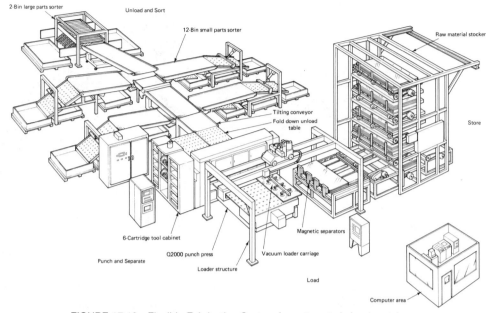

2-Bin large parts sorter

Unload and Sort

12-Bin small parts sorter

Raw material stocker

Tilting conveyor

Fold down unload table

Store

6-Cartridge tool cabinet

Q2000 punch press

Punch and Separate

Loader structure

Vacuum loader carriage

Magnetic separators

Load

Computer area

FIGURE 17.13   Flexible Fabricating System for automated sheet metal processing. (Courtesy of Wiedemann Division, Warner & Swasey/A Cross & Trecker Company.)

the punch press operations, and separate the finished parts (upper left of figure), all under computer control.

FMS benefits

When properly applied, flexible manufacturing systems provide a number of benefits and advantages over alternative methods of production, including:

• *Higher machine utilization.*   Flexible manufacturing systems achieve a higher average utilization than machines in a conventional batch production machine shop (process-type layout). More efficient work handling, off-line setups, and better scheduling contribute to FMS machine utilization of 80% or more. This compares to about 50% for the conventional organization of batch work.

• *Reduced work-in-progress.* Because different parts are processed together rather than separately in batches, the number of parts being processed at any moment tends to be less than in a batch production mode.

• *Lower manufacturing lead times.*   Closely correlated with reduced work-in-process is the time spent in process by the parts. This means faster customer deliveries.

• *Greater flexibility in production scheduling.*   In the random-order FMS, the capability exists to make adjustments in the production schedule from one day to the next, and to respond to rush orders and special customer requests.

- *Higher labor productivity.* The higher production rate capacity of the FMS and its lower reliance on direct labor means that the productivity per labor hour is significantly greater than with conventional production methods.

REFERENCES

[1] BEVANS, J. P., "First, Choose an FMS Simulator," *American Machinist,* May 1982, pp. 143–145.

[2] BUZACOTT, J. A., "Modeling Automated Manufacturing Systems," *Proceedings,* 1983 Annual Industrial Engineering Conference, Louisville, Ky. May 1983, pp. 341–347.

[3] BUZACOTT, J. A., and J. G. SHANTHIKUMAR, "Models for Understanding Flexible Manufacturing Systems," *AIIE Transactions,* December 1980, pp. 339–349.

[4] CAPTOR, N., B. MILLER, B. D. OTTINGER, A. J. RIGGS, L. M. TOMKO, and M. C. CULVER, "Adaptable-Programmable Assembly Research Technology Transfer to Industry," *Final Report,* NSF Grant ISP 78-18773, January 1983.

[5] GROOVER, M. P., and E. W. ZIMMERS, *CAD/CAM: Computer-Aided Design and Manufacturing,* Prentice-Hall, Inc., Englewood Cliffs, N.J., 1984, Chapter 20.

[6] JABLONSKI, J., "Reexamining FMSs," Special Report 774, *American Machinist,* March 1985, pp. 125–140.

[7] KLAHORST, H. T., "How to Plan Your FMS," *Manufacturing Engineering,* September 1983, pp. 52–54.

[8] *KT's World of Manufacturing Systems,* Kearney & Trecker Corporation, Milwaukee, Wis., 1980.

[9] *Modern Machine Shop 1985 NC/CAM Guidebook,* Gardner Publications, Inc., Cincinnati, Ohio, January 1985, Chapter 10.

[10] "Our FMS Will Do the Work of 67 Conventional Machine Tools," *Production,* April 1978, pp. 66–69.

[11] RANKY, P., *The Design and Operation of FMS,* IFS (Publications) Ltd., Bedford, England, and North-Holland Publishing Company, Amsterdam, 1983.

[12] ROLSTON, L. J., "Modeling Flexible Manufacturing Systems with MAP/1," *Proceedings,* First ORSA/TIMS Special Interest Conference on Flexible Manufacturing Systems, University of Michigan, Ann Arbor, August 1984, pp. 199–204.

[13] "S/R Machine Delivers Directly to Machine Tools," *Modern Materials Handling,* February 1985, pp. 56–57.

[14] SAUL, G., "Flexible Manufacturing System Is CIM Implemented at the Shop Floor Level," *Industrial Engineering,* June 1985, pp. 35–39.

[15] SCRIBER, T. J., "The Use of GPSS/H in Modeling a Typical Flexible Manufacturing System," *Proceedings,* First ORSA/TIMS Special Interest Conference on Flexible Manufacturing Systems, University of Michigan, Ann Arbor, August 1984, pp. 168–182.

[16] SOLBERG, J. J., "CAN-Q User's Guide," *Report 9 (Revised),* NSF Grant APR74-15256, Purdue University, School of Industrial Engineering, West Lafayette, Ind., 1980.

[17] SURI, R., "An Overview of Evaluative Models for Flexible Manufacturing Systems," *Proceedings,* First ORSA/TIMS Special Interest Conference on Flexible Manufacturing Systems, University of Michigan, Ann Arbor, August 1984, pp. 8–15.

[18] SURI, R., and R. R. HILDEBRANT, "Modeling Flexible Manufacturing Systems Using Mean Value Analysis," *Journal of Manufacturing Systems,* Vol. 3, No. 1, 1984, pp. 27–38.

[19] *Understanding Manufacturing Systems* (A Series of Technical Papers), Vol. I, Kearney & Trecker Corporation, Milwaukee, Wis.

[20] VACCARI, J. A., "Forging in the Age of the FMS," Special Report 782, *American Machinist,* January 1986, pp. 101–108.

[21] WATERBURY, R., "FMS Expands into Assembly," *Assembly Engineering,* October 1985, pp. 34–37.

[22] WILHELM, W. E., and S. C. SARIN, "Models for the Design of Flexible Manufacturing Systems," *Proceedings,* 1983 Annual Industrial Engineering Conference, Louisville, Ky. May 1983, pp. 564–574.

[23] WINSHIP, J. T., "Flexible Sheetmetal Fabrication," Special Report 779, *American Machinist,* August 1985, pp. 95–106.

part VII

Quality Control and Automated Inspection

In recent years the issue of quality control has become a national topic of conversation in the United States. The Japanese automobile industry has demonstrated that high-quality cars can be manufactured at relatively low cost. This combination of high quality and low cost is a contradiction of conventional wisdom in America, where we have always believed that better quality is obtained only at higher cost. The lower cost of cars built in Japan can be explained partially by the lower labor rates of Japanese workers compared to their counterparts in the United States. But there are other factors operating as well. A well-developed work ethic and orientation toward quality have been trained into the Japanese workers, which has made their workmanship admired throughout the world. In addition, design features have been incorporated into the Japanese car which reduce the labor content and improve the reliability and quality of the product. Finally, significant attention is paid to the use of statistical quality control procedures during manufacturing to ensure high quality.

The economic impact of automobile imports from overseas has not gone unnoticed in Detroit (and elsewhere in the United States). There has been a renewed interest in improving quality in the automotive industry (and in nearly all other industries) as a result of foreign competition. This new interest has been demonstrated in advertising slogans (at the time of writing, these slogans include: "Quality is Job One" at Ford, and "Nobody sweats the details like GM"). It has also taken form in new technologies to improve quality and to monitor it. The present part of the book is concerned with some of these new technologies in quality control.

Part VII contains only one chapter; it is concerned with the aspects of quality control that are most directly related to automation. The chapter is entitled "Automated Inspection and Testing." The discussion examines the principles of automated inspection and the important sensor technologies that are used to implement it. These techniques are sometimes divided into two categories: contact inspection and noncontact inspection. As our principal example of contact inspection, we describe the coordinate measuring machine, which uses a touch probe to measure physical dimensions of a part. In the category of noncontact inspection, we consider machine vision to be a most important technology which will be used extensively in the future for automated inspection. Machine vision and several other sensor techniques that do not directly touch the product are described.

chapter 18

Automated Inspection and Testing

Inspection and testing activities represent one of the five basic functions in manufacturing, as discussed in Section 2.3. They are included within the scope of what is called *quality control* (QC). Through the use of inspection and testing procedures, QC is concerned with the problems of detecting poor quality in manufactured product and taking corrective action to eliminate it.

Inspection and testing are traditionally accomplished using manual methods that are time consuming and costly. Consequently, manufacturing lead time and product cost are increased without adding any real value. Another of the major disadvantages of these manual QC methods is that they are performed after the process. Therefore, if bad products have been made, it is too late to correct the defect(s) during regular processing. Parts already manufactured that do not meet specified quality standards must either be scrapped or reworked at additional cost.

New approaches to the quality control function are emerging that are drastically altering the way inspection and testing are performed. These new approaches are based on advanced sensor technologies often combined with computer-based systems to interpret the sensor signals. In addition, new software tools are being developed to automate the operation of complex sensor systems and to statistically analyze the sensor measurements.

In this chapter we examine these modern approaches to quality control, with an emphasis on automating the inspection function.

18.1   INSPECTION AND TESTING

Inspection and testing constitute the operational part of quality control. They are performed before, during, and after manufacturing to ensure that the quality level of the product is consistent with accepted design standards. There are differences between inspection and testing, as described below.

QC inspection

The term *inspection* refers to the activity of examining the product (or its components, or subassemblies, or materials out of which it is made) to determine if it meets specified design standards. The design standards are defined by the product designer, and for mechanical products they relate to factors such as dimensions, surface finish, and appearance. The objective of the inspection procedure is either:

1. To take actual measurements of the values of the specified product characteristics.
2. Simply to check whether or not the specified characteristics meet the design standards.

In the first case, the factor (e.g., diameter of a turned part) is measured using an appropriate measuring instrument. For example, instruments for measuring diameter include micrometers, calipers, or even a simple linear scale. In the second case, a device called a *gage* is compared to the part to determine whether the quality characteristic of the product matches that of the gage. For example, a *go/no-go gage* might be used to check the part diameter. The gage is designed so that if the part diameter is below a certain size it will pass through the gage opening. The gage opening is therefore set at the upper acceptable size limit of the design specification.

The advantage of measuring the part characteristic is that data can be collected about its actual value. The data might be recorded over time and used to observe trends in the process making the part. It might even be used to make adjustments in the process so that future parts are produced with dimensions that are closer to the nominal design value. When a part dimension is simply checked with a go/no-go gage, all that is known is whether the part is acceptable, and perhaps whether it is too big or too small.

On the other hand, the advantage of gaging a part is that it can be done more quickly and therefore at lower cost. Measuring the quality characteristic is usually a more involved procedure and therefore takes more time. Whether measurement or gaging is done, inspection procedures are used at various stages during the manufacture of a product or part. Inspections are also performed on incoming raw materials to decide whether the materials should be accepted from the vendor.

QC testing

Whereas inspection is used to assess the quality of the product relative to design specifications, *testing* is a term in quality control that is generally used relative to the functional aspects of the product: Does it operate the way it is supposed to operate? Will it continue to operate for a reasonable period of time? Will it operate in environments of extreme temperature and humidity? And so on. Accordingly, QC testing is a procedure in which the item being tested (i.e., product, subassembly, part) is observed during actual operation or under conditions that might be present during operation. For example, a product might be tested by operating it for a certain period of time to determine whether it functions properly. If the product passes the test, it is approved for shipment to the customer. As another example, a part, or the material out of which the part is to be made, might be tested by subjecting it to a stress load that is equivalent to or greater than the load anticipated during normal operation.

Sometimes the testing procedure used on an item is damaging or destructive to the item. To ensure that the majority of the items (e.g., raw materials or finished products) are of satisfactory quality, a limited number of the items are sacrificed. However, the expense of destructive testing is significant enough that great efforts are made to devise methods that do not result in the destruction of the item. These methods are referred to as nondestructive testing (NDT) and nondestructive evaluation (NDE).

Another type of testing procedure involves not only testing the product to see that it functions properly, but also requires an adjustment or calibration of the product that depends on the outcome of the test. During the testing procedure, one or more operating variables of the product are measured, and adjustments are made in certain inputs that influence the performance of the operating variables. For example, in testing certain appliances with heating elements, if the measured temperature is too high or too low after a specified time, adjustments can be made in the control circuitry (e.g., changes in potentiometer settings) to bring the temperature within the acceptable operating range.

As indicated in the introduction, both inspection and testing are usually performed using manual labor. The work is often boring and monotonous, yet the need for precision and accuracy is very high. Hours are sometimes required to measure the important dimensions of only one workpart. Because of the time and expense involved in inspection work, statistical procedures are used to reduce the need to inspect every part. These procedures fall within a field of study called statistical quality control.

18.2 STATISTICAL QUALITY CONTROL

In *statistical quality control* (SQC), inferences are made about the quality of an item (e.g., product, subassemblies, components, or materials) based on a sample taken from the population of the items. The sample consists of one or more items drawn at random from the population. Each item in the sample is inspected (or tested) for certain quality characteristics of interest. In the case of a manufactured part, these characteristics relate to the process or processes just completed. For example, a cylindrical part may be inspected for diameter immediately following the turning operation that generated the diameter.

Our discussion in this section will emphasize the methods that are commonly used in traditional SQC (when inspection and testing are performed manually). However, most of the concepts and principles are directly applicable when automated inspection and testing are utilized. Also, throughout our discussion in this chapter, we will emphasize inspection; however, many of the concepts presented apply as well to quality testing.

Variations in manufacturing

In any manufacturing operation there is variability which is manifested in the products made by the operation. In a machining operation, the machined parts may appear to be identical, but close inspection will reveal that there are differences in the corresponding dimensions from one part to the next. These manufacturing variations can be divided into two categories: random and assignable.

Random variations result from many causes: factors such as human variability in adjusting the production equipment, variations in the raw materials used, machine vibration, and so on. Individually, these causes do not amount to much, but collectively the resulting errors can be significant enough to cause trouble unless they are within the tolerances allowed for the part.

Random variations typically form a statistical distribution which is *normal*, that is, the output of the process will have a tendency to cluster about the mean value, in terms of any of the product's quality characteristics (e.g., length, diameter, etc.). There will be a large proportion of the population of parts that will be centered around the mean, and fewer and fewer parts away from the mean. When the only variations in the process are these random variations, the process is said to be in *statistical control*. This type of process variability will continue as long as the process is operating normally. It is when the process deviates from this normal operating condition that variations of the second type begin to appear.

Assignable variations are those which indicate an exception from normal operating conditions. Something has occurred in the process that is not within the normal range accounted for by random variations. Reasons for assignable variations include operator error, defective raw material, tool failure, and machine malfunction. Assignable variations in manufacturing usually betray themselves by causing the output to deviate from the normal statistical distribution for the process.

Process capability

The term *process capability* refers to the normal variations inherent in the manufacturing process output when the process is in statistical control. By definition, the process capability equals 6 standard deviations (± 3 standard deviations), under the assumptions that the process output is normally distributed, that it is in statistical control, and that steady-state operation has been achieved. The ± 3 standard deviations are sometimes called the *natural tolerance limits* of the process. Under the assumptions of our process capability definition, it can be shown statistically that 99.73% will fall within ±3.0 standard deviations of the mean.

The design tolerances specified for the product must be compatible with the process capability. It serves no useful purpose to specify tolerances of ±0.001 in. on a certain dimension if the process that is selected has a process capability significantly greater than ±0.001 in. Either the tolerance should be widened (if design functionality permits) or a different manufacturing process should be selected (if one is available). Ideally, the specified tolerance should be equal to or greater than the natural tolerance limits. If this cannot be done, a sorting procedure must be incorporated into the manufacturing sequence to inspect every unit of product and to separate those units that meet specifications from those that do not.

Control charts

It is the objective of SQC to identify when the process has gone out of statistical control, thus indicating that some corrective action should be taken. There are a number of statistical tools that have been developed for use in SQC. The two principal techniques are acceptance sampling and control charts. *Acceptance sampling* is a technique in which a sample is taken from a batch of parts and a decision is made whether to accept or reject the batch on the basis of the quality of the sample. It can be used to decide whether to accept a batch of raw materials from a vendor. Or it can be used to decide whether or not to ship a batch of product to a customer. Acceptance sampling is also used to inspect parts that are between steps in the manufacturing process.

A *control chart* is a technique for plotting the measured values of certain characteristics of the process output over time to determine if the process remains in statistical control. Control charts are most appropriately applied to monitor the critical processes in high- and midvolume production plants. The general form of the control chart is illustrated in Figure 18.1. The chart consists of three horizontal lines (lines that are

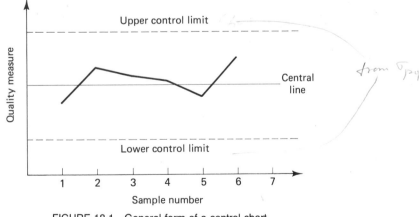

FIGURE 18.1   General form of a control chart.

constant over time): a central line, an upper control limit (UCL), and a lower control limit (LCL). The central line corresponds to the mean of the process output. It represents the expected nominal value of the output. The upper and lower control limits indicate extreme statistical values of the process. If any measured values of the output are plotted outside these limits, it is an indication that the process is no longer in statistical control; and that an investigation should be undertaken to determine the reason for the out-of-control condition. This condition is illustrated in Figure 18.2.

The natural tolerance limits (± 3 standard deviations) are usually used to define the upper and lower control limits in control charts. Accordingly, for a sample drawn at random from a process to have a mean that lies above the UCL or below the LCL would be extremely unlikely (probability $= 0.0027$) if the process were in statistical control.

There are several types of control charts used in industry for statistical quality control. They all have the same general form shown in Figure 18.1. The types include:

- $\overline{X}$ *chart*. This control chart is used to plot the average measured value of a certain quality characteristic for each of a series of samples taken from the production process. It indicates how the process mean is varying over time.
- *R chart*. In this control chart, the range of each sample is plotted. The R chart monitors the variability of the process and indicates whether the variability changes over time.
- *p chart*. This chart is used to plot the percentage (p for percent) of defectives in the sample. If the percent defectives suddenly increases beyond the UCL, the process is out of statistical control.
- *c chart*. Here the number or count (c for count) of defects in the sample are plotted as a function of time.

With regard to our previous discussion on inspection procedures (measurement versus gaging), the $\overline{X}$ chart and R chart require that the quality characteristic of interest

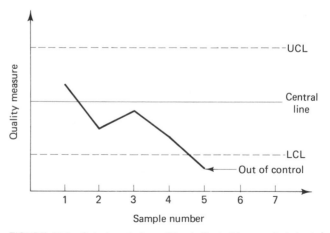

FIGURE 18.2   Out-of-control condition indicated in a control chart.

be measured during the inspection process. The p chart and c chart simply require a determination of whether each part is defective or how many defects there are in the sample. The details of how these charts are set up, as well as other statistical techniques and equations used in SQC calculations, can be found in texts on quality control, such as references [4] and [12].

18.3 AUTOMATED INSPECTION PRINCIPLES AND METHODS

When SQC inspection and testing are carried out manually, the sample size is often small compared to the size of the population. The sample size may only represent 1% or fewer of the number of parts made in a high-production run. Certainly in destructive testing procedures, it is desirable to make the sample size as small as possible. Owing to this fact that only a portion of the items in the population are measured, there is a risk in any SQC sampling procedure that errors will occur and that defective parts will slip through. One of the objectives in statistical quality control is to define the expected risk, that is, to determine the average fraction defect rate that will pass through the sampling inspection procedure over the long run, under the assumption that the manufacturing process remains in statistical control. The frequency with which samples are taken, the sample size, and the permissible quality levels are three important factors that affect the level of risk involved. But the fact remains that something less than 100% good quality must be tolerated as a price that is paid for using statistical sampling procedures.

In principle, the only way to achieve 100% good quality is to use 100% inspection. By this approach, theoretically, only good-quality parts will be allowed to pass through the inspection procedure. However, when 100% inspection is done manually, two problems occur. The obvious problem is the expense involved. Instead of dividing the cost of inspecting the sample over the number of parts in the production run, the inspection cost per piece is applied to every part in the batch. The inspection cost can sometimes exceed the cost of making the part. In addition, in 100% manual inspection, there is almost always an error rate associated with the procedure. The error rate depends on the complexity and difficulty of the inspection task and how much judgment is required by the human inspector. The error rate is due to two sources: the inherent errors of the measurement procedure (we discuss measurement errors in Section 18.4), and mistakes by the operator resulting from fatigue and other factors. This error rate means that a certain number of poor-quality parts will be accepted and that a certain number of good-quality parts may be rejected. Therefore, 100% inspection using manual methods is no guarantee of 100% good-quality product.

100% automated inspection

Automation of the inspection process offers an opportunity to overcome the two problems associated with 100% manual inspection. *Automated inspection* is defined here as the automation of one or more of the steps involved in the inspection procedure. It can involve a number of alternative approaches: automated presentation of parts by an automated handling system with a human operator still performing the actual inspection process (e.g., visually examining the parts for flaws), manual loading of parts into an automatic inspection machine, or a completely automated inspection system in which parts presentation and inspection are both performed automatically.

The full potential of automated inspection is best achieved when it is integrated into the manufacturing process, when a 100% inspection procedure is adopted, and when the results of the procedure lead to some positive action relative to the process. The positive actions can be of two forms:

1. *Feedback* data to the preceding manufacturing processes that are responsible for the quality characteristics being evaluated or gaged in the inspection operation. The purpose of the feedback is to allow compensating adjustments to be made in the processes to improve quality. If the measurements from the automated inspection indicate that the output of the process is beginning to drift toward the high side of the tolerance (e.g., due to tool wear), corrections can be initiated in the input parameters to bring the output back to the nominal value. In this way, average quality is maintained within a smaller variability range than is possible with sampling inspection methods. In effect, the process capability is improved.

2. *Sortation* of the parts according to quality level: acceptable versus unacceptable quality. There may be more than two levels of quality appropriate for the process (e.g., acceptable, reworkable, and scrap). The sortation procedure may be an integral part of the inspection operation, or it may require a separate sorting operation that is regulated according to feedforward data from the inspection.

Off-line and on-line inspection

The timing of the inspection procedure in relation to the manufacturing process is an important consideration in quality control. Three alternative situations can be distinguished:

1. Off-line inspection
2. On-line/in-process inspection
3. On-line/postprocess inspection

The three types are illustrated in Figure 18.3. An *off-line inspection,* shown in part (a) of the figure, is performed away from the manufacturing process, and there is generally a delay between processing and inspection. Most manual inspections fall into this category. Factors that tend to promote the use of off-line inspection include: when the process capability is well within the specified design tolerance; for high-production runs with short cycle times; under stable processing conditions with relatively small risk of significant assignable variations in the output; and when the cost of inspection is high relative to the cost of a few detective parts. Since it is typically performed manually, off-line

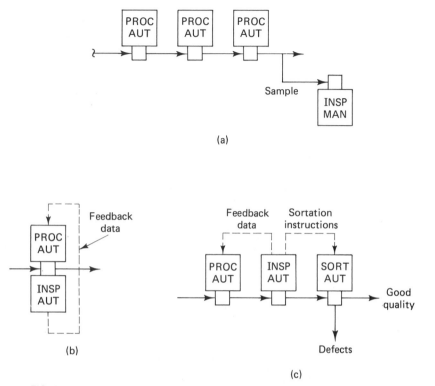

FIGURE 18.3 Three alternatives in the timing of inspection: (a) off-line; (b) on-line/in-process; (c) on-line/post-process.

inspection usually involves a statistical sampling procedure. The disadvantage of off-line inspection is that the parts have already been made by the time any poor quality is detected.

The alternative to off-line inspection is on-line inspection. This is an inspection procedure that is performed as the parts are being made, either as an integral step in the processing or assembly operation, or immediately afterward. The two on-line procedures can be distinguished as on-line/in-process and on-line/postprocess. The two cases are illustrated in Figure 18.3(b) and (c).

On-line/in-process inspection is achieved by performing the inspection procedure during the manufacturing operation. As the parts are being made, the inspection procedure is measuring or gaging the parts simultaneously. The benefit of in-process inspection is that it may be possible to influence the operation that is making the current part, thereby correcting a potential quality problem before the part is completed. When on-line/in-process inspection is performed manually, it means that the worker who is performing the manufacturing process is also performing the inspection procedure. The Japanese are said to use this approach in their manually operated production lines. For automated manufacturing systems, this on-line inspection method is typically done on a 100% basis using automated sensor methods. Technologically, automated on-line/in-process inspection is usually difficult and expensive to implement. As an alternative, on-line/postprocess procedures are often used.

With *on-line/postprocess inspection,* the measurement or gaging procedure is accomplished immediately following the production process. Even though it follows the process, it is still considered an on-line method because it is integrated with the manufacturing workstation and the results of the inspection can immediately influence the production operation. The limitation of on-line/postprocess inspection is that the part has already been made, and it is therefore impossible to make corrections that will influence its processing. The best that can be done is to influence the production of the next part. If the results of the on-line inspection produce no action, either to feed back data for process compensation or to provide sortation instructions, off-line inspection might as well be utilized instead of on-line technologies.

On-line/postprocess inspection can be performed as either a manual or an automated procedure. When accomplished manually, it is done using a sampling procedure or on a 100% basis (with all of the risks associated with 100% manual inspection). When automated, it is typically performed on a 100% basis. Whether manual or automated, SQC techniques are useful for analyzing the results of the inspection procedure.

Distributed inspection and final inspection

In *distributed inspection,* several inspection stations are located along the line of flow of work in a factory, placed strategically at critical points in the manufacturing sequence. A distributed inspection system identifies any defective product as soon as possible to permit some action to be taken in response to the quality problem: either correction of the process or sortation of the defects from the line (or both). The goal of this inspection strategy is to prevent further cost from being added to defective products. This is especially relevant in assembled products where many components are combined into a single unit that cannot easily be taken apart. If one defective component would render the assembly defective, it is obviously better to catch the defect before it is assembled. These situations are found in electronics manufacturing operations. Printed circuit board (PCB) assembly is a good illustration. An assembled PCB may consist of 100 or more electronic components that have been soldered to the base board. If only one of the components is defective, the entire board may be useless unless repaired at substantial additional cost. For example, suppose that 100 components are assembled, and that each component has a 1% defect rate; the probability that the assembly will contain no defects is given by $(1 - 0.01)^{100} = (0.99)^{100} = 0.366$. In these types of cases, it is important to discover and remove the defects from the production line before further processing or assembly are accomplished. One hundred percent on-line automated inspection is most appropriate in these situations.

Another strategy, sometimes considered to be an alternative to distributed inspection, is *final inspection.* The final inspection approach involves one comprehensive inspection and testing procedure on the product immediately before shipment to the customer. The notion behind this approach is that it will be more efficient and less expensive, from an inspection viewpoint, to perform all of the inspection tasks at one location rather than distribute them throughout the plant. Final inspection is also more appealing to the customer because, logically, it offers the greatest protection against poor quality.

Most quality-conscious manufacturers combine the two strategies in their operations. Distributed inspection will be used for certain operations in the plant that warrant the approach (i.e., high defect rate, to prevent added costs in subsequent operations), and final inspection will be used to ensure that the highest possible quality goes to the customer.

18.4 SENSOR TECHNOLOGIES FOR AUTOMATED INSPECTION

Modern automated inspection procedures are typically carried out by sensors that are controlled by and/or communicate data to digital computers. In some cases an appropriate interface must be designed to provide for this control and communication.

Types of sensors

There are a variety of sensor technologies available for automated inspection. We divide the possibilities into two broad categories:

1. Contact inspection methods
2. Noncontact inspection methods

Contact inspection involves the use of a mechanical probe or other device that makes contact with the object being inspected. The purpose of the probe is to measure or gage the object in some way. By its nature, contact methods are usually concerned with some physical dimension of the part. Accordingly, contact inspection methods are used predominantly in the mechanical manufacturing industries (e.g., machining and other metal working, plastic molding, etc.). Three methods of automated contact inspection that represent the high end of the technology spectrum are:

1. Coordinate measuring machines
2. Flexible inspection systems
3. Inspection probes

Coordinate measuring machines are discussed in Section 18.5 and the other two methods are discussed in Section 18.6.

Noncontact inspection methods do not involve direct contact with the product. Instead, a sensor is located at a certain distance from the object to measure or gage the desired features. The potential advantages offered by noncontact inspection include lower inspection times and avoidance of damage to the part that might occur from contacting it. Contact inspection procedures usually require special handling and positioning of the parts, whereas noncontact methods can often be accomplished on the production line without the need for special handling. Also, the noncontact inspection processes are inherently faster as a general rule. The reason is that contact inspection procedures require positioning of the contacting probe against the part, which is time consuming. Most of the noncontact methods use a stationary probe that does not need repositioning for every part. Lower inspection times means that 100% inspection becomes more feasible with noncontact sensing methods.

There are numerous sensor technologies used in noncontact inspection. They can be classified as either optical or nonoptical. Prominent among the *optical* inspection methods is machine vision, but other optical techniques are also commonly used in automated inspection. *Nonoptical* inspection sensors include electrical field techniques, radiation techniques, and ultrasonics. We discuss these noncontact inspection sensor technologies in Sections 18.7 through 18.9.

Measurement errors

There are sources of error in any measuring system. The terms accuracy and precision are often used in this connection. A measuring system that has high *accuracy* is one in which the measurement will contain no systematic positive or negative errors about the true value. On the other hand, high *precision* means that the measurement will be made with little or no random variability or noise in the measured value. The distinction between accuracy and precision in measurement is illustrated in Figure 18.4. As suggested in the figure, measurement errors are often assumed to be normally distributed. If a measuring system has perfect accuracy, the mean of the measured value is coincident with the parameter being measured. Perfect precision means that the standard deviation of the measuring system is zero. Therefore, a measurement system with perfect accuracy and perfect precision will measure with no error. Unfortunately, perfection in measurement, as in everything else, is not possible.

The errors introduced by the measuring process in automated inspection must be matched either to the design tolerance of the item being inspected or to the process capability of the manufacturing operation that is making the item. If the design tolerance has not been set at the process capability, the tolerance is generally the more important of the two criteria to use. Stout [21] recommends that the errors in the inspection mea-

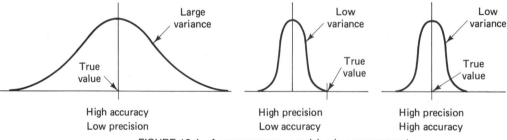

FIGURE 18.4   Accuracy versus precision in measurement.

surement system should not be more than 10% of the tolerance. In the context of our discussion on accuracy and precision, this is interpreted to mean that the accuracy of the measuring system should be within 10% of the tolerance value, and that its precision (defined as ± 3 standard deviations $= 6$ standard deviations) should also be within 10% of the tolerance.

18.5 COORDINATE MEASURING MACHINES

A *coordinate measuring machine* (CMM) consists of a contact probe and a means of positioning the probe in three-dimensional space relative to the surfaces and features of a workpart. The probe is not merely positioned relative to the part; its location can be accurately and precisely recorded to obtain dimensional data concerning the part geometry. A commercially available coordinate measuring machine is shown in Figure 18.5. In this section we discuss the construction features of a CMM, the control and programming of

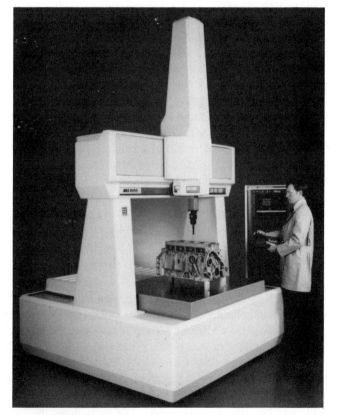

FIGURE 18.5 Coordinate measuring machine. (Reproduced by permission of Sheffield Measurement Division.)

the machine, the types of measurements it can make, the advantages of the CMM over manual inspection, and some of the trends in the technology.

CMM construction

In the construction of a coordinate measuring machine, the probe is fastened to some type of structure that allows movement of the probe relative to the part. The part is located on a worktable that is usually connected to the structure. There are several different physical configurations for achieving the motion of the probe, including the following common types:

- *Cantilever construction.* In the cantilever configuration, pictured in Figure 18.6(a), the probe is attached to a vertical quill that moves in a z-axis direction relative to a horizontal arm that overhangs the worktable. The quill can also be moved along the length of the arm to achieve y-axis motion, and the arm can be moved relative to the worktable to achieve x-axis motion. The advantages of this construction are the convenient access to the worktable and its relatively small floor space requirements [15]. Its disadvantage is lower rigidity than some of the other CMM constructions.
- *Bridge construction.* The bridge configuration, shown in Figure 18.6(b), is the most common type used in industry. Instead of a cantilevered arm to achieve the y-axis movement of the probe, the arm is supported on both ends like a bridge. This construction provides greater inherent rigidity, and its advocates claim that this makes the bridge construction more accurate than the cantilevered CMM.
- *Column construction.* This construction, shown in Figure 18.6(c), is similar to the construction of a machine tool. Instead of achieving the relative motion exclusively by moving the probe, the column-type CMM obtains x-axis and y-axis relative motion by moving the worktable. The probe quill is moved vertically along a rigid column to obtain the z-axis motion.
- *Gantry construction.* This construction is generally intended for inspecting large objects. As illustrated in Figure 18.6(d), the x- and y-axis motions are achieved by a construction similar to a gantry crane. The probe quill (z-axis) moves relative to the horizontal arm extending between the two rails of the gantry.

In all of these constructions, special design features are used to build high accuracy and precision into the frame. These features include low-friction air bearings, installation mountings to isolate the CMM and reduce vibrations in the factory from being transmitted through the floor, and various schemes to counterbalance the overhanging arm in the case of the cantilever construction [15].

One of the most important aspects in the design of a CMM is the probe. Most common today are "touch-trigger" probes, which use a highly sensitive electrical contact that emits a signal when the end of the probe is deflected from its neutral position in the slightest amount. Immediately upon contact the coordinate positions of the probe are recorded by the CMM controller. Any limited overtravel of the probe quill due to mo-

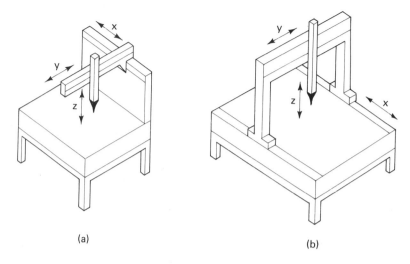

(a)   (b)

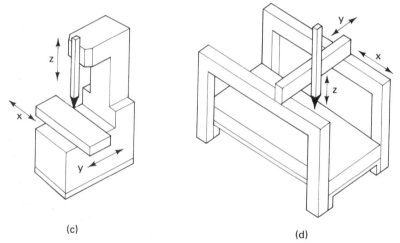

(c)   (d)

FIGURE 18.6 Four types of CMM construction: (a) cantilever; (b) bridge; (c) column; (d) gantry.

mentum is neglected by the CMM. After the probe has been separated from the contact surface, it returns to the neutral position.

Operation and programming

The positioning of the probe relative to the part can be accomplished either manually or under computer control. The methods of operating and controlling a coordinate measuring machine can be classified as follows [15]:

1. Manual control
2. Manual computer-assisted
3. Motorized computer-assisted
4. Direct computer control

In the *manual control* method, the human operator physically moves the probe along the machine's axes to make contact with the part and record the measurements. The probe is designed to be free-floating to permit easy movement along the coordinate axes. The measurements are proved on a digital readout, which the operator can record either manually or automatically (paper printout). Any calculations on the data (e.g., calculating the center and diameter of a hole) must be made by the operator. The *manual computer-assisted* CMM provides some level of computer data processing and computational capability for performing these calculations. The types of data processing and computations range from simple conversions between U.S. customary units and metric, to more complicated geometry calculations such as determining the angle between two planes. The probe is still free-floating to permit the operator to bring it into contact with the desired part surfaces.

The *motorized computer-assisted* CMM uses a motor drive to power the probe along the machine axes under the operator's guidance. A joystick or similar device is typical as the means of controlling the motion. Features such as low-power stepping motors and friction clutches are utilized to reduce the effects of collisions between the probe and the part. The motor drive can be disengaged to permit the operator to physically move the probe as in the manual control method.

The *direct computer control* CMM operates like a CNC machine tool. It is motorized, and the movements of the coordinate axes are controlled by the computer. The computer also performs the various data-processing and calculation functions, and compiles a record of the measurements made during inspection. The direct computer-controlled machine is a highly automated inspection machine that operates under program control.

There are two principal methods of programming the direct computer control CMM. In one method, programming is accomplished by a manual leadthrough method, similar to the robot programming technique of the same name. The operator leads the CMM probe through the various motions, indicating the points and surfaces that are to be measured, and records these into the control memory. During regular operation, the CMM controller plays back the program to complete the inspection procedure.

The other method of programming is accomplished in the manner of conventional NC part programming. The program is prepared off-line and then downloaded to the CMM controller for execution. The programming statements for a computer-controlled CMM include motion commands, measurement commands, and report formatting commands. The motion commands are used to direct the probe to a desired inspection location, in the same way that a cutting tool is directed in a machining operation. The measurement statements are used to control the measuring and inspection functions of the machine, calling the various data processing and calculation routines into play. Finally, the formatting statements permit the specification of output reports to document the inspection.

Measurement capabilities

The basic measurement of the coordinate measuring machine is the definition of the x-, y-, and z-axis coordinate values where contact is made with the surface of a part. Incorporating computer control and its associated software into the operation of the CMM provides opportunities for accomplishing much more sophisticated measurements and inspections. Presented in Table 18.1 are some of these measuring capabilities.

CMM benefits and trends

The principal advantages of using coordinate measuring machines over manual inspection methods are [15]:

- *Productivity.* Because of the automated techniques included in the operation of a CMM, inspection procedures are speeded and labor productivity is improved. A direct computer-controlled CMM is capable of accomplishing many of the measurement tasks listed in Table 18.1 in one-tenth the time needed for manual techniques.
- *Flexibility.* A CMM is a general-purpose machine that can be used to inspect a variety of different part configurations with minimal changeover time. In the case of the direct computer-controlled machine, where the programming is performed off-line, the changeover time only involves making the physical setup.

TABLE 18.1 Measurement and Inspection Capabilities Made Possible by Computer and Software in a CMM

Dimensions. A dimension of a part can be determined by taking the difference between the two surfaces defining the dimension.

Hole location and diameter. By measuring three points around the surface of a circular hole, the "best-fit" center coordinates of the hole and its diameter can be computed.

Cylinder axis and diameter. This is similar to the preceding problem except that the calculation deals with an outside surface rather than an internal (hole) surface.

Sphere center and diameter. By measuring four points on the surface of a sphere, the best-fit center coordinates and the radius (or diameter) can be calculated.

Definition of a plane. Based on a minimum of three contact points on a plane surface, the best-fit plane is determined.

Flatness. By measuring more than three contact points on a supposedly plane surface, the deviation of the surface from a perfect plane can be determined.

Angle between two planes. The angle between two planes can be found by defining each of two planes using the plane definition method above, and calculating the angle between them.

Parallelism between two planes. This is an extension of the previous function. If the angle between two planes is zero, the planes are parallel. The degree to which the planes deviate from parallelism can be determined.

Angle and point of intersection between two lines. Given two lines known to intersect (e.g., two edges of a part that meet in a corner), the point of intersection and the angle between the lines can be determined based on two points measured for each line (a total of four points).

- *Reduced operator error.*   Automating the inspection procedure has the obvious effect of reducing human errors in measurements and setups.
- *Greater inherent accuracy and precision.*   A coordinate measuring machine is inherently more accurate and precise than the manual surface plate methods of inspection traditionally used.

The technology of the coordinate measuring machine is evolving toward greater computer sophistication. The trends include increased functional capabilities of CMM systems. Examples are computer graphic display of the inspection results, on-line data analysis with connections back to the manufacturing process, and three-dimensional contour analysis of surfaces such as cams and other complex shapes. Another trend is toward more user-friendly features, which make the CMM easier to program and easier to use. Ultimately, it should be possible to program the CMM based on the part model contained in the CAD/CAM data base, in a manner similar to NC part programming with CAD/CAM.

Finally, another future development is likely to be automated loading/unloading of the coordinate measuring machine. At the time of this writing, most CMM operations still require manual loading and unloading of parts from the measuring table. Future operations are likely to include automatic loading and unloading of the workpart.

18.6   OTHER CONTACT INSPECTION METHODS

The technology of coordinate measuring machines has spawned other contact inspection methods. In this section we discuss two of these extensions: flexible inspection systems and inspection probes.

Flexible inspection systems

The flexible inspection system (FIS) takes the versatility of the CMM a step further. In concept, the FIS is related to a CMM the way an FMS is related to a machining center. A *flexible inspection system* is defined as a highly automated inspection workcell consisting of one or more CMMs and other types of inspection equipment, plus the parts handling systems needed to move parts into, within, and out of the cell. Robots might be used to accomplish some of the parts handling tasks in the system. As with the flexible manufacturing system, all of the components of the FIS are controlled by an integrated computer system.

An example of a prototype flexible inspection system at Boeing Aerospace Company has been reported by Schaffer [19]. The layout of the system is shown in Figure 18.7. The system consists of two direct computer-controlled CMMs, a robotic inspection station, an automated storage system, and a storage-and-retrieval cart that interconnects the various components of the cell. A staging area for loading and unloading pallets into and out of the cell is located immediately outside the FIS. The purpose of the project was to demonstrate the feasibility of a multistation automated inspection station capable of dealing with a variety of part configurations and inspection procedures. The coordinate measuring

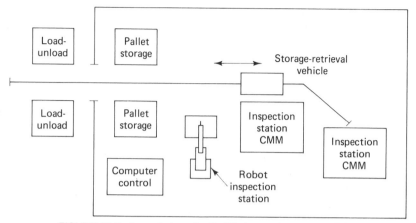

FIGURE 18.7   Layout plan of a flexible inspection system (FIS).

machines in the cell perform dimensional inspection based on programs prepared off-line. The robotic station in the cell is equipped with an ultrasonic inspection probe to check skin thicknesses of hollow wing sections for one of Boeing's aerospace products.

Inspection probes

In recent years there has been a significant growth in the use of tactile probes as on-line inspection systems for machine tool applications. These probes are mounted in holders, inserted into the machine tool spindle, stored in the tool drum, and handled by the automatic tool changer in the same way that cutting tools are exchanged. When mounted in the spindle, the machine tool is controlled very much like a CMM. Sensors in the probe determine when contact has been established with the part surface. Signals from the sensor are transmitted by any of several different means (e.g., direct electrical connection, induction-coil, infrared data transmission, etc.) to the controller, which performs the required data processing to interpret and utilize the signal.

Touch-sensitive probes are sometimes referred to as in-process inspection devices, but by our definitions they are on-line/postprocess devices because they are employed immediately following the machining operation rather than during cutting. However, these probes are sometimes used between machining steps in the same setup: for example, to establish a datum reference either before or after initial machining so that subsequent cuts can be accomplished with greater accuracy.

Some of the other calculation features of machine-mounted inspection probes are similar to the capabilities of computer-assisted CMMs. The features include determining the centerline of a cylindrical part or a hole, and determining the coordinates of an inside or outside corner.

One of the controversial aspects of machine-mounted inspection probes is the fact that the same machine tool that is making the part is also performing the inspection. The argument is that certain inherent errors in the cutting operation will also be manifested in the probe measuring operation. In practice, however, the use of these devices has proved to be effective in improving quality and saving time in expensive off-line inspection operations.

18.7 MACHINE VISION

Machine vision can be defined as the acquisition of image data, followed by the processing and interpretation of this data by computer for some useful application. Machine vision is a rapidly growing technology, with its principal applications in industrial inspection. In this section we examine how they work and their applications in QC inspection and other areas.

Vision systems are classified as being either two-dimensional or three-dimensional. Two-dimensional systems view the scene as a two-dimensional image. This is quite adequate for many industrial applications since many situations involve a two-dimensional scene. Examples include dimensional measuring and gaging, verifying the presence of components, and checking for features on a flat (or semiflat) surface. Other applications require three-dimensional analysis of the scene, and three-dimensional vision systems are required for this purpose. At the time of this writing, the technology of three-dimensional vision is still developing, and the number of such systems installed in industry is small compared to two-dimensional systems. Our discussion will be in the context of the simpler two-dimensional systems, although many of the techniques used for two-dimensional systems are also applicable in three-dimensional vision work.

The operation of a machine vision system can be divided into the following three functions:

1. Image acquisition and digitization
2. Image processing and analysis
3. Interpretation

These functions and their relationships are illustrated schematically in Figure 18.8.

Image acquisition and digitization

Image acquisition and digitization is accomplished using a video camera and a digitizing system to store the image data for subsequent analysis. The camera is focused on the subject of interest and an image is obtained by dividing the viewing area into a matrix of discrete picture elements (called *pixels*), in which each element has a value that is proportional to the light intensity of that portion of the scene. The intensity value for each pixel is converted into its equivalent digital value by an analog-to-digital converter (ADC). (Analog-to-digital conversion techniques are discussed in Chapter 22.) The operation of viewing a scene consisting of a simple object that contrasts substantially with

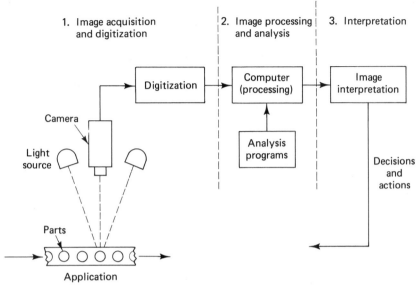

FIGURE 18.8   Basic functions of a machine vision system.

its background, and dividing the scene into a corresponding matrix of picture elements, is depicted in Figure 18.9.

The figure illustrates the probable image obtained from the simplest type of vision system, a binary vision system. In *binary vision,* the light intensity of each pixel is ultimately reduced to either of two values, white or black, depending on whether or not the light intensity exceeds a given threshold level. A more sophisticated vision system is capable of distinguishing and storing different shades of gray in the image. This is called a *gray-scale system.* This type of system can determine not only an object's outline and area characteristics, but also its surface characteristics, such as texture and color. Gray-scale vision systems typically use 4, 6, or 8 bits of memory. Eight bits corresponds to $2^8 = 256$ intensity levels, which is generally more levels than the video camera can really distinguish, and certainly more than the human eye can discern.

Each set of pixel values is referred to as a *frame.* Each frame, consisting of the set of digitized pixel values, is stored in a computer memory device called a *frame buffer.* The process of reading all the pixel values in a frame is performed with a frequency of 30 times per second (typical in the United States; 25 times per second in European vision systems).

Two types of cameras are used in machine vision applications: vidicon cameras (the type used for television) and solid-state cameras. *Vidicon cameras* operate by focusing the image onto a photoconductive surface and scanning the surface with an electron beam to obtain the relative pixel values. Different areas on the photoconductive surface have different voltage levels corresponding to the light intensities striking the areas. The electron beam follows a well-defined scanning pattern, in effect dividing the surface into a large number of horizontal lines and reading the lines from top to bottom. Each line is in turn divided into a series of points. The number of points on each line, multiplied by the number of lines, gives the dimensions of the pixel matrix, as shown in Figure 18.9. During the scanning process, the electron beam reads the voltage level of each pixel.

Solid-state cameras operate by focusing the image onto a two-dimensional array of very small, finely spaced photosensitive elements. The photosensitive elements form the matrix of pixels shown in Figure 18.9. An electrical charge is generated by each element according to the intensity of light striking the element. The charge is accumulated in a storage device consisting of an array of storage elements corresponding one-to-one

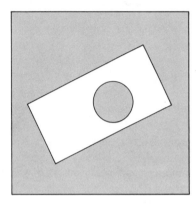

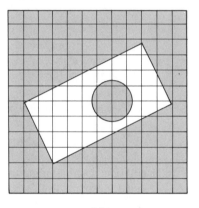

(a)   (b)

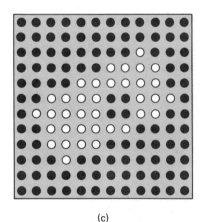

(c)

FIGURE 18.9   Dividing the image into a matrix of picture elements, where each element has a light-intensity value corresponding to that portion of the image: (a) the scene; (b) 12 × 12 matrix of picture elements superimposed on the scene; (c) picture element intensity values for the scene, either black or white.

with the photosensitive picture elements. These charge values are read sequentially in the data-processing and analysis function of machine vision.

The solid-state camera has several advantages over the vidicon camera in industrial applications. It is physically smaller and more rugged, and the image produced is more stable. The vidicon camera suffers from distortion that occurs in the image of a fast-moving object because of the time lapse associated with the scanning electron beam as it reads the pixel levels on the photoconductive surface. The relative advantages of solid-state cameras have resulted in their growing dominance in machine vision systems. One popular type of solid-state camera is the charge-coupled-device (CCD) camera.

Typical pixel arrays are 128×128, 256×256, and 512×512 picture elements. In vision technology at the time of this writing, vidicon cameras typically possess a higher number of picture elements than do solid-state cameras. The resolution of the vision system—its ability to sense fine details and features in the image—is dependent on the number of picture elements used. The more pixels that are designed into the vision system, the higher its resolution. However, the cost of the camera increases as the number of pixels is increased. Even more important, the time required to read the picture elements and process the data sequentially increases as the number of pixels grows. The following example illustrates the problem.

EXAMPLE 18.1

A certain video camera has a 256×256 pixel matrix. Each pixel must be converted from an analog signal to the corresponding digital signal by an ADC. The A-to-D conversion process takes $0.1~\mu s$ (0.1×10^{-6} s) to complete. Assuming no lost time in moving between pixels, how long will it take to collect the image data for one frame, and is this time compatible with processing at the rate of 30 frames/s?

Solution:

There are $256 \times 256 = 65{,}536$ pixels to be scanned and converted. The total time to complete the analog-to-digital conversion process is

$$(65{,}536 \text{ pixels})(0.1 \times 10^{-6} \text{ s}) = 0.00655 \text{ s}$$

At a processing rate of 30 frames/s, the processing time for each frame is 0.0333 s. This is significantly larger than the 0.00655 s required to perform analog-to-digital conversion. There would be a certain time loss between pixels (e.g., as the scanning electron beam moved between lines), but this would be relatively small in comparison to the ADC process.

Another important aspect of machine vision is lighting. The scene viewed by the vision camera must be well illuminated, and the illumination must be constant over time. This almost always requires that special lighting be installed for a machine vision application rather than relying on ambient lighting. There are numerous ways to illuminate the scene. One way to classify the possibilities is according to the location of the light source: front lighting, back lighting, and side lighting. The three light source locations

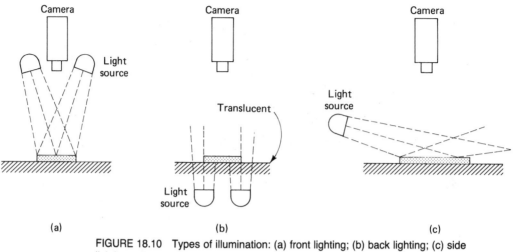

FIGURE 18.10 Types of illumination: (a) front lighting; (b) back lighting; (c) side lighting.

are shown in Figure 18.10. In *front lighting,* the light source is located on the same side of the object as the camera. This produces a reflected light from the object, which allows inspection of surface features such as the printing on a label, and surface patterns such as the solder lines on a printed circuit board. In *back lighting,* the light source is placed behind the object being viewed by the camera. This creates a dark silhouette of the object, which contrasts sharply with the light background. This type of lighting can be used for binary vision systems to inspect for part dimensions and to distinguish between different part outlines. *Side lighting* causes irregularities in an otherwise plane smooth surface to cast shadows which can be identified by the vision system. This can be used to inspect for defects and flaws in the surface of an object or material.

Image processing and analysis

The second function in the operation of a machine vision system is image processing and analysis. As indicated by the preceding example, the amount of data that must be processed and analyzed is significant. The data for each frame must be analyzed within the time required to complete one scan ($\frac{1}{30}$s). A number of techniques have been developed for analyzing the image data in a machine vision system. One category of techniques in image processing and analysis is called *segmentation*. Segmentation techniques are intended to define and separate regions of interest within the image. Two of the common segmentation techniques are thresholding and edge detection. *Thresholding* involves the conversion of each pixel intensity level into a binary value, representing either white or black. This is done by comparing the intensity value of each pixel with a defined threshold value. If the pixel value is greater than the threshold, it is given the binary bit value of white, say 1. If less than the defined threshold, it is given the bit value of black, say 0. Reducing the image to binary form by means of thresholding usually simplifies the subsequent problem of defining and identifying objects in the image. *Edge detection* is concerned with determining the location of boundaries between an object and its surroundings in an image. This is accomplished by identifying the contrast in light intensity that exists between adjacent pixels at the borders of the object. A number of software algorithms have been developed for following the border around the object.

Another set of techniques in image processing and analysis that normally follows segmentation is that of *feature extraction*. Most machine vision systems define an object in the image by means of the object's features. Some of the features of an object include the area of the object; length, width, or diameter of the object; perimeter; center of gravity; and aspect ratio. Feature extraction methods are designed to determine these features based on the object's area and its boundaries (using thresholding, edge detection, and other segmentation techniques). For example, the area of the object can be determined by counting the number of white (or black) pixels that make up the object. The object's length can be found by measuring the distance (in terms of pixels) between the two extreme opposite edges of the part.

Interpretation

For any given application, an interpretation of the image must be accomplished based on the extracted features. The interpretation function is usually concerned with recognizing the object, a task termed *object recognition* or *pattern recognition*. The objective in this task is to identify the object in the image by comparing it to predefined models or standard values. Two commonly used interpretation techniques are template matching and feature weighting. *Template matching* is the name given to various methods that attempt to compare one or more features of an image with the corresponding features of a model or template stored in computer memory. The most basic template matching technique is one in which the image is compared, pixel by pixel, with a corresponding computer model. Within certain statistical tolerances, the computer determines whether or not the image matches the template. One of the technical difficulties of this method is the problem of aligning the part in the same position in front of the camera, to allow the comparison to be made without complications in image processing.

Feature weighting is a technique in which several features are combined into a single measure by assigning a weight to each feature according to its relative importance in identifying the object. The score of the object in the image is compared with the score of an ideal object residing in computer memory to achieve proper identification.

Machine vision applications

The reason for interpreting the image is to achieve some practical objective in an application. Machine vision applications in manufacturing divide into four categories:

1. Inspection
2. Part identification

3. Visual guidance and control
4. Safety monitoring

By far, quality control *inspection* is the biggest category. Some estimates are that inspection (measurement and gaging) constitutes as much as 90% of machine vision applications [18]. Machine vision installations in industry perform a variety of automated inspection tasks, most of which are either on-line/in-process or on-line/postprocess. The applications are almost always in mass production, where the time required to program and set up the vision system can be spread over many thousands of units. One hundred percent inspection is done almost exclusively. Typical industrial inspection tasks include the following:

- *Dimensional measurement.*   These applications involve determining the size of certain dimensional features of parts or products usually moving at relatively high speeds along a moving conveyor. The machine vision system must compare the features (dimensions) with the corresponding features of a computer-stored model and determine the size value.
- *Dimensional gaging.*   This is similar to the preceding except that a gaging function rather than a measurement is performed.
- *Verification of the presence of components in an assembled product.*   Machine vision has proved to be an important element in flexible automated assembly systems. (see Section 13.6).
- *Verification of hole location and number of holes in a part.*   Operationally, this task is similar to the preceding.
- *Identification of flaws and defects on the surface of a part or material.*   Flaws and defects in a surface often reveal themselves as a change in reflected light. The vision system can identify the deviation from an ideal model of the surface.
- *Identification of flaws in a printed label.*   The defect can be in the form of a poorly located label or poorly printed text, numbering, or graphics on the label.

Part identification applications are those in which the vision system is used to recognize and perhaps distinguish parts so that some action can be taken. The applications include counting different parts flowing past along a conveyor, part sorting, and character recognition. *Visual guidance and control* involves applications in which a vision system is teamed with a robot or similar machine to control the movement of the machine. Examples of these applications include seam tracking in continuous arc welding, part positioning and/or reorientation, and bin picking. A *safety monitoring* application of machine vision is one in which the vision system is used to monitor the operation of a production cell. Its purpose is to detect irregularities which indicate a condition that is hazardous to equipment or people working in the cell. It can also be used to detect human intruders who might be at risk by wandering into the cell (e.g., a robot cell).

18.8   OTHER OPTICAL INSPECTION METHODS

Machine vision is a well-publicized technology, perhaps because it is similar to one of the important human senses. Its potential for applications in industry is substantial. However, there are other optical sensing techniques used for inspection. Our discussion will provide a survey of these techniques.

Scanning laser systems

The unique feature of laser measuring systems is that they use a coherent beam of light that can be projected with minimum diffusion. Owing to this feature, lasers have been used in a number of industrial processing and measuring applications. High-energy laser beams are used for welding and cutting of materials, while low-energy lasers are utilized in various measuring and gaging situations.

The scanning laser device falls into the latter category. A schematic diagram of the device is pictured in Figure 18.11. It makes use of a laser beam that is deflected by a rotating mirror to produce a beam of light that can be focused to sweep past an object. A photodetector on the far side of the object senses the light beam except for the period during the sweep when it is interrupted by the object. This period can be timed with great accuracy and related to the size of the object in the path of the laser beam. The scanning laser beam device can complete its measurement in a very short time cycle. Hence, the scheme can be applied in high-production on-line/postprocess inspection and gaging. A microprocessor-based system counts the time interruption of the scanning laser beam as its sweeps past the object, makes the conversion from time to a linear dimension, and signals other equipment to make adjustments in the manufacturing process and/or activate

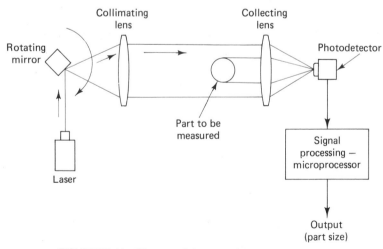

FIGURE 18.11   Diagram of the scanning laser technique.

a sortation device on the production line. Applications of the scanning laser technique include rolling mill operations, wire extrusion, and some machining and grinding processes.

Linear array devices

The operation of a linear array for automated inspection is simple. The device consists of a light source that emits a planar sheet of light directed at an object. On the opposite side of the part is a linear array of closely spaced photodiodes. The sheet of light is blocked by the object, and this blocked light is measured by the photodiode array to indicate the object's dimension of interest. A schematic diagram showing a typical arrangement of a linear array device is presented in Figure 18.12.

The linear array measuring scheme has the advantages of simplicity, accuracy, and speed. It has no moving parts and is claimed to possess a resolution as small as 50 millionths of an inch [20]. It can complete a measurement in a much smaller time cycle than either a machine vision system or the scanning laser beam technique.

Optical triangulation techniques

Triangulation techniques are based on the trigonometric relationships of a right triangle. The techniques are used for range finding, that is, to determine the distance or range of an object from two known points. Use of the principle in an optical measuring system is explained with reference to Figure 18.13. A light source (typically a laser) is used to focus a narrow beam at an object to form a spot of light on the object. A linear array of photodiodes or other position-sensitive optical detector is used to determine the location of the spot. The angle A of the beam directed at the object is fixed and known, and so is the distance L between the light source and the photosensitive detector. Accordingly, the range R of the object from the baseline defined by the light source and the photo-

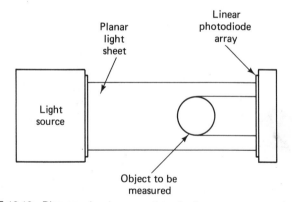

FIGURE 18.12 Diagram showing operation of a linear array measuring device.

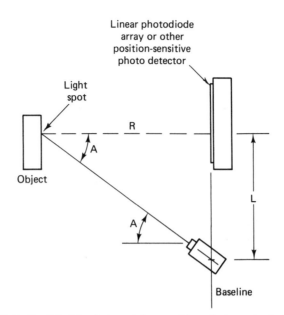

FIGURE 18.13   Principle of triangulation used in optical sensing technique.

sensitive detector in Figure 18.13 can be determined as a function of the angle from trigonometric relationships.

A variation of the conventional triangulation computation can be used to determine surface contours of parts. A planar sheet of highly focused light is directed against the surface of the object at a certain known angle, as illustrated in Figure 18.14, resulting

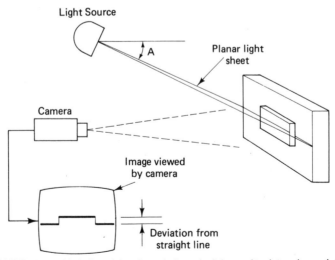

FIGURE 18.14   Variation of the triangulation principle used to determine variations in surface contour.

in the formation of a bright line where the beam intersects the surface. An optical sensor or vision camera is positioned so that its line of sight is perpendicular to the surface of the object. In this orientation, the sheet of light will cause any variations from the general plane of the part to appear as deviations from a straight line along the part. The distance of any deviation from the straight line can be determined by optical measurement, and the corresponding elevation of the surface from the plane can be calculated using trigonometry.

18.9 OTHER NONCONTACT INSPECTION METHODS

In addition to noncontact optical inspection methods, there are also a variety of nonoptical techniques used for inspection tasks in manufacturing. Examples include sensor techniques based on electrical fields, radiation, and ultrasonics. In this section we briefly review these technologies as they might be used for inspection. More details are provided in references [7] and [14].

Under certain conditions, *electrical fields* can be created by an electrically active probe and are affected by an object in the vicinity of the probe. Examples of these fields include reluctance, capacitance, and inductance. In the typical application, the object (workpart) is positioned in a defined relation with the probe. By measuring the effect of the object on the electrical field, an indirect measurement or gaging of certain part characteristics can be made, such as dimensional features, thickness of sheet material, and in some cases, flaws (cracks and voids below the surface) in the material.

Radiation techniques utilize X-ray radiation to accomplish noncontact inspection procedures on metals and weld-fabricated products. The amount of radiation absorbed by the metal object can be used to indicate thickness and the presence of flaws in the metal part or welded section. An example is the use of X-ray inspection techniques to measure the thickness of sheet metal product being made in a rolling mill. The inspection is performed as an on-line/postprocess procedure, with information from the inspection used to make adjustments in the opening between rollers in the rolling mill.

Ultrasonic techniques make use of very high frequency sound (greater than 20,000 Hz) for various inspection tasks. Some of the techniques are performed manually, whereas others are automated. One of the automated methods involves the analysis of ultrasonic sound waves that are emitted by a probe and reflected off the object to be inspected. In the setup of the inspection procedure, an ideal test part is placed in front of the probe to obtain a reflected sound pattern. This sound pattern becomes the standard against which production parts are later compared. If the reflected pattern from a given production part matches the standard (within an allowable statistical variation), the part is considered acceptable; otherwise, it is rejected. One technical problem with this technique involves the presentation of the production parts in front of the probe. To avoid extraneous variations in the reflected sound patterns, the parts must always be placed in the same position and orientation relative to the probe.

REFERENCES

[1] ARTLEY, J. W., "Automated Visual Inspection Can Boost Quality Control Affordability," *Industrial Engineering,* December 1982, p. 28–32.

[2] BALLARD, D. H., and C. M. BROWN, *Computer Vision,* Prentice-Hall, Inc., Englewood Cliffs, N. J., 1982.

[3] FARNUM, G. T., "Measuring with Lasers," *Manufacturing Engineering,* February 1986, pp. 47–51.

[4] FEIGENBAUM, A. V., *Total Quality Control,* 3rd ed., McGraw-Hill Book Company, New York 1983.

[5] GEVARTER, W. B., "Machine Vision: A Report on the State of the Art," *Computers in Mechanical Engineering,* April 1983, pp. 25–30.

[6] GROOVER, M. P., "The Changing Nature of Quality Control," *CAD/CAM Technology,* Spring 1983, pp. 21–24.

[7] GROOVER, M. P., and E. W. ZIMMERS, *CAD/CAM: Computer-Aided Design and Manufacturing,* Prentice-Hall, Inc., Englewood Cliffs, N. J., 1984, Chapter 19.

[8] GROOVER, M. P., M. WEISS, R. N. NAGEL, and N. G. ODREY, *Industrial Robotics: Technology, Programming, and Applications,* McGraw-Hill Book Company, New York, 1986, Chapter 7.

[9] HUDSON, D. L., and J. E. TROMBLY, "Developing Industrial Applications for Machine Visions," *Computers in Mechanical Engineering,* April 1983, pp. 18–23.

[10] LAPIDUS, S. N., "New Techniques for Industrial Vision Inspection," *Proceedings,* Third Annual Applied Machine Vision Conference, Chicago, Ill., February 27–March 1, 1984, pp. 4–1 to 4–13.

[11] LEVI, P., "Quality Assurance and Machine Vision for Inspection," in *Methods and Tools for Computer Integrated Manufacturing* (published lecture notes from course on computer integrated manufacturing, September 1983, U. Rembold and R. Dillman, Editors), Springer-Verlag, Berlin, 1984, pp. 329–377.

[12] MONTGOMERY, D. C., *Introduction to Statistical Quality Control,* John Wiley & Sons, Inc., New York, 1985.

[13] RILEY, F. J., *Assembly Automation,* Industrial Press, Inc., New York, 1983, Chapter 8.

[14] SCHAFFER, G. H., "A New Look at Inspection," Special Report 714, *American Machinist,* August 1979, pp. 103–126.

[15] SCHAFFER, G. H., "Taking the Measure of CMMs," Special Report 749, *American Machinist,* October 1982, pp. 145–160.

[16] SCHAFFER, G. H., "Sensors: the Eyes and Ears of CIM," Special Report 756, *American Machinist,* July 1983, pp. 109–124.

[17] SCHAFFER, G. H., "Statistical Quality Control," Special Report 762, *American Machinist,* January 1984, pp. 97–108.

[18] SCHAFFER, G. H., "Machine Vision: A Sense for CIM," Special Report 767, *American Machinist,* June 1984, pp. 101–120.

[19] SCHAFFER, G. H., "Integrated QA: Closing the CIM Loop," Special Report 775, *American Machinist,* April 1985, pp. 137–160.

[20]   Sheffield Measurement Division, Cross & Trecker Corporation, *66 Centuries of Measurement,* Dayton, Ohio, 1984.

[21]   STOUT, K., *Quality Control in Automation,* Prentice-Hall, Inc., Englewood Cliffs, N. J., 1985.

PROBLEMS

18.1.   (This problem requires use of tables of the standard normal distribution, which are not included in this book.) The variation in a critical dimension produced by a certain discrete-product manufacturing process can be characterized by a normal distribution with mean equal to the set point for the process, and standard deviation = 0.002 in.
(a) Determine the natural tolerance limits of the process.
(b) If the actual tolerance specified for the output by the product designer is ±0.005 in., and the process is set at the nominal dimension specified by the product designer, determine the proportion of product that will not meet the specified tolerance.
(c) If the actual tolerance specified for the output by the product designer is ±0.005 in. but the process is set at a value that is 0.001 in. above the nominal dimension specified by the product designer, determine the proportion of product that will not meet the specified tolerance.
(d) Specify the required accuracy and precision of a measuring sensor that might be used in an on-line inspection system for the process. What is the standard deviation that characterizes the measurement distribution?

18.2.   A grinding processes at the APSCIM machine shops is currently considered to be operating within statistical control. One of the important dimensions on the part is its diameter. In a series of six samples, each with 10 parts per sample, the means of the samples were, respectively, 1.5034, 1.5012, 1.5004, 1.5020, 1.4996, and 1.5018 in.
(a) Determine the natural tolerance limits of the process.
(b) Specify the required accuracy and precision of a measuring sensor that might be used in an on-line inspection system.

18.3.   A CCD solid-state camera has a 128 × 128 pixel matrix. The analog-to-digital converter takes 0.25 μs (0.25 × 10⁻⁶ s) to convert the analog charge signal for each pixel into the corresponding digital signal. If there is no time loss in switching between pixels, determine the following:
(a) How much time is required to collect the image data for one frame?
(b) Is the time determined in part (a) compatible with the processing rate of 30 frames/s?

18.4.   The pixel count on the photoconductive surface of a vidicon camera is 512 × 512. Each pixel is converted from an analog voltage signal to the corresponding digital signal by an analog-to-digital converter. The conversion process takes 0.1 μs (0.1 × 10⁻⁶ s) to complete. In addition to the ADC process, it takes 2 μs to move from one horizontal line of pixels to the one below. Given these times, how long will it take to collect and convert the image data for one frame? Can this be done 30 times per second?

18.5.   A scanning laser device, similar to the one shown in Figure 18.12, is to be used to measure the diameter of shafts that are ground in a centerless grinding operation. The part has a diameter of 0.475 in. with a tolerance of ±0.002 in. The four-sided mirror of the scanning laser beam device rotates at 250 rev/min. The collimating lens focuses 30° of the sweep of the mirror into a swath which is 1.000 in. wide. It is assumed that the light beam moves at a constant speed across this swath. The photodetector and timing circuitry is capable of resolving time units as fine as 100 ns(100×10^{-9} s). This resolution should be equivalent to no more than 10% of the tolerance band (0.004 in.).

(a) Determine the interruption time of the scanning laser beam for a part whose diameter is equal to the nominal size.

(b) How much of a difference in interruption time is associated with the tolerance of ±0.002 in.?

(c) Is the resolution of the photodetector and timing circuitry sufficient to achieve the 10% rule on the tolerance band?

18.6. Triangulation computations are to be used to determine the distance of parts moving on a conveyor. The setup of the optical measuring is as illustrated in Figure 18.14. The angle between the beam and the surface of the part is 25°. Suppose that for one given part passing on the conveyor, the baseline distance is 6.55 in., as measured by the linear photosensitive detection system. What is the distance of this part from the baseline?

18.7. A planar sheet of light is focused on a surface in the manner illustrated in Figure 18.15. The angle that the light sheet makes with the nominal surface of the part is 30°. At this angle, the intersection line that the light sheet makes with the surface deviates 0.055 in. from a nominal straight line when viewed by a vision camera from a position normal to the surface. How much of a change in surface elevation is this equivalent to?

part **VIII**

Control Systems

Control is an essential ingredient in any automated production system. Transfer lines, numerical control, industrial robots, material handling, and flexible manufacturing systems all require some form of control to ensure their successful operation. In this part of the book we examine the various types of controls available for use in automated production systems. For purposes of organization, we divide these controls into four categories: conventional linear feedback control (analog controls), optimal control (which optimizes some economic performance objective), sequence control (logic control and other forms of on/off control commonly used in industrial control systems), and computer process control (which uses the digital computer for controlling manufacturing operations).

In Chapter 19 we present an introductory treatment of linear feedback control. The need for this type of control arises in many physical processes, including industrial production processes. The theory and analysis of linear control systems rely on mathematical models that are formulated as linear ordinary differential equations. Our discussion of these models includes the definition of transfer functions and block diagrams. The models can be analyzed by various techniques, and the root-locus method is presented to illustrate these analysis techniques. The final section in this chapter covers design principles for linear control systems.

In Chapter 20 we consider the topic of optimal control. The various optimal control strategies can best be implemented by means of digital computer controllers because they generally involve considerable computations and data processing to achieve the control objective. The strategies include optimal control, adaptive control, and on-line search techniques, all of which are discussed in Chapter 20.

In Chapter 21 we deal with another form of control used widely in industry: sequence control. We encountered sequence control previously in our discussion of transfer lines and robotic work cells. Sequence control is concerned with co-ordinating the timing and sequencing of activities that take place in an automated production system. The term *industrial logic control* is sometimes used to refer to the sequence control functions discussed in this chapter. An important device used in this type of process control is the programmable logic controller, and we describe these controllers in Chapter 21.

Chapter 22 is concerned with computer process control. There are a number of different ways in which the computer can be interfaced with industrial processes, and the various methods are examined in this chapter. The computer can be installed merely to observe the manufacturing process (process monitoring) or to both observe and regulate the production operations (process control). We con-sider both possibilities in this chapter. We also examine the important implemen-tation issues in computer process monitoring and control: interfacing the computer to the manufacturing process, levels of computer control, interrupts, error detection and recovery, and system malfunction diagnostics.

chapter 19

Linear Feedback Control Systems

Most industrial processes are characterized by variables that are analog and continuous. Before digital computers were used for process control in industrial plants, analog devices were used. Indeed, the development of analog controllers represented a major advance in automation. Many of the concepts and strategies used in conventional analog control are used today in computer control (direct digital control in particular).

The analysis of analog controllers and the processes with which they operate are based on the use of linear differential equations. Such equations constitute the foundation for linear control theory. The theory of linear controls is concerned with the analysis of systems that can be modeled by linear ordinary differential equations. Examples of the use of differential equations can be drawn from nearly every technical field. These include mechanical systems (spring–mass–damper), electrical circuits, (resistance–inductance–capacitance circuits), chemical reactions, thermal systems (the Fourier equation in heat transfer), hydraulic systems (fluid power mechanisms), and many others. We consider some of these examples in this chapter.

Linear differential equations are preferred over nonlinear ones because they are generally much easier to solve. Unfortunately, real-life physical relationships are not always linear. Nevertheless, enough of the real world obeys linearity that linear control theory is a powerful tool in the study of process control.

19.1 PROCESS MODEL FORMULATION

Types of models

One of the first steps in the study and analysis of a physical process (including most industrial processes) is to develop a mathematical model to represent the process. There are two basic methods of formulating a mathematical model of a physical process. The first is to derive analytically the relationship between the process variables of interest. *Analytical models* are obtained based on fundamental assumptions and principles about the phenomenon being studied. An example is the familiar Newton's equation for constant mass (specifically, *Newton's second law*):

$$\text{force} = \text{mass} \times \text{acceleration}$$

Since acceleration is the second derivative of displacement (let y represent displacement), we could express Newton's second law as

$$F = M\frac{d^2y}{dt^2} \tag{19.1}$$

where F is force, M is mass, and $d^2y/dt^2 = $ acceleration. The reader will recognize this as a differential equation. A differential equation is any algebraic equality that contains one or more derivatives.

The second method for formulating a mathematical model of a physical process is to base the model on experimental data collected from observing the process. This is called an empirically derived model or an *empirical equation*. No particular concern is given to the underlying principles about the process. An equation is determined which best fits the observed data. Statistical techniques, such as regression analysis, are often used to find the best equation. An example of an empirical equation that should be familiar to manufacturing people is the *Taylor tool-life equation*:

$$VT^n = C \tag{19.2}$$

where V is the cutting speed, T is the tool life, and n and C are constants in the equation. Taylor developed this equation based on experimental data of cutting speed and corresponding tool life. For a particular tool, work material, and cutting conditions, he found that certain values of n and C in Eq. (19.2) gave the best "fit" to the data.

Mathematical models of physical processes can also be developed by combining the two approaches above. A basic form of the equation is hypothesized from theoretical considerations. Then data are collected from the actual process to determine the most accurate parameter values for the model. This hybrid approach has much merit and is often used in industrial process model formulation.

Let us consider how a mathematical model might be formulated using differential equations. We begin with a relatively simple, yet illustrative example.

Hydraulic system

Figure 19.1 represents a physical system of the type that chemical engineers might have to consider in the design of an industrial flow process. As shown in the drawing, let x_1 represent the flow rate in the tank and x_2 represent the rate of flow out. Appropriate units might be liters per minute. The volume in the tank would be determined by the cross-sectional area of the tank, A (which we assume to be constant throughout the height), and the level of fluid in the tank. We will use the symbol h to symbolize this liquid level (h stands for head).

The "continuity" law specifies for a system such as this one that the flow rate into the tank minus the flow rate out of the tank must equal the rate of liquid volume increase (or decrease) in the tank. This can be expressed in the form of a differential equation:

$$x_1 - x_2 = A\frac{dh}{dt} \tag{19.3}$$

Figure 19.1 shows that the outlet stream is restricted by a valve of resistance R. If the flow through the valve is laminar (rather than turbulent flow), the hydraulic resistance is equal to the head (pressure) divided by the flow rate through the valve. This relationship can be expressed as

$$R = \frac{h}{x_2} \quad \text{or} \quad x_2 = \frac{h}{R} \tag{19.4}$$

By substituting Eq. (19.4) into Eq. (19.3), we can express the differential equation as follows:

$$x_1 - \frac{h}{R} = A\frac{dh}{dt}$$

or

$$AR\frac{dh}{dt} + h = Rx_1 \tag{19.5}$$

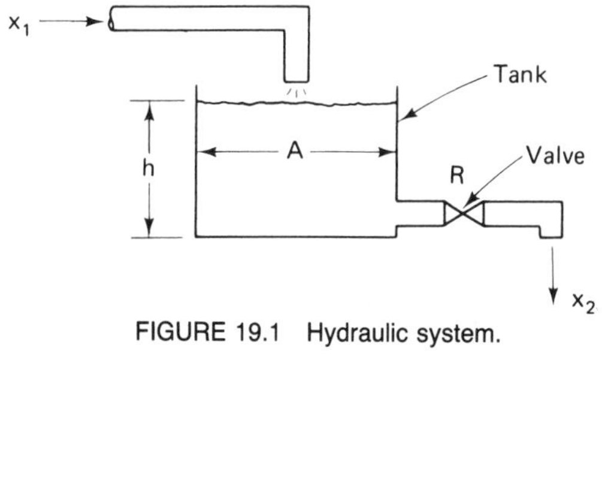

FIGURE 19.1   Hydraulic system.

Equation (19.5) is a first-order linear differential equation. The variable h is the dependent variable in the system and x_1 is the input. Time t is the independent variable. The input can change over time in a variety of ways. For purposes of mathematical analysis, the form of the input can be a step function or some type of oscillation, such as a sine wave. These two possibilities are shown in Figure 19.2. Other idealized mathematical functions can also be used to test the behavior of the system.

Let us consider the response of the hydraulic system to the step input shown in Figure 19.2(a). The solution of Eq. (19.5) would begin with the formulation of the characteristic equation, which is

$$ARs + 1 = 0$$

where s stands for the differential operator. The root of the characteristic equation is

$$s = \frac{-1}{AR}$$

We shall define the term

$$\tau = AR$$

Hence, the complementary function is

$$h_c = C_1 e^{-t/\tau}$$

Since the input to the system is a step function, it is a constant value, X_1, beyond time zero. The steady-state solution to Eq. (19.5) would therefore be a constant whose first derivative is zero.

$$AR(0) + h_p = RX_1$$

$$h_p = RX_1$$

The complete solution would consist of the complementary function plus the particular integral:

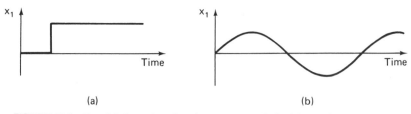

(a)   (b)

FIGURE 19.2   Possible input functions in systems analysis: (a) step function; (b) sine-wave function.

$$h = h_c + h_p = C_1 e^{-t/\tau} + RX_1 \tag{19.6}$$

Since the initial conditions are that $h = 0$ when $t = 0$,

$$0 = C_1(1) + RX_1$$

then

$$C_1 = -RX_1$$

and therefore,

$$h = RX_1(1 - e^{-t/\tau}) \tag{19.7}$$

where RX_1 is specified to be a constant value in this case. The response represented by Eq. (19.7) is shown in Figure 19.3.

In Eq. (19.6), the term RX_1 is called the *steady-state response* of the system. It represents the value that the dependent variable will assume after sufficient time for any transient or startup effects to disappear. The steady-state value is shown in Figure 19.3 as the horizontal line at the level RX_1.

The term $C_1 e^{-t/\tau}$ in Eq.(19.6) is called the *transient solution* or *transient response* of the system. Because of the nature of the function $e^{-t/\tau}$, the transient response will die out as time increases. The term τ is referred to as the *time constant* in the solution of the first-order linear differential equation. Its value depends on the parameters in the equation, in this case $\tau = AR$. Its effect is to determine the length of time taken before the transient effects disappear. To see this effect, consider the term in parentheses in Eq. (19.7):

$$1 - e^{-t/\tau}$$

When $t = \tau$, the output has reached

$$1 - e^{-1} = 0.632$$

of its steady-state value. At $t = 2\tau$, the output has reached

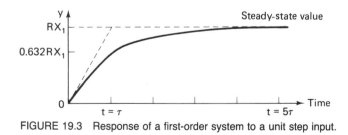

FIGURE 19.3   Response of a first-order system to a unit step input.

$$1 - e^{-2} = 0.865$$

of its final value. When $t = 5\tau$, the output has achieved

$$1 - e^{-5} = 0.993$$

of the final value. It can be seen that the transient solution plays a minor role after $t = 5\tau$. For all practical purposes, the output has completed its response to the step input.

First-order linear differential equations similar to Eq. (19.5) are quite common in modeling physical systems. The parameters of the equations have different physical interpretations, but the basic form of the equation is the same. This mathematical model is a basic building block of many complex physical and industrial processes.

Let us consider another building block, the second-order linear differential equation, by resorting to a familiar mechanical example.

Spring–mass–damper system

Shown in Figure 19.4 is the typical spring–mass–damper arrangement. There are three components, all interrelated to produce a single mechanical system. A mass M is connected to two solid surfaces, by a spring of constant K_s on the one side and a dashpot whose damping coefficient is K_d on the other side. The behavior of the system is characterized by the displacement of the mass, which is symbolized by the variable y.

When the mass is displaced, there are forces introduced that affect the motion of the mass. Thus, the variable y is dynamic; that is, it is a function of time and the function can be expressed in the form of a differential equation. The forces acting on the mass come from three sources. First, as the mass moves, it undergoes acceleration and deceleration. The resulting force is defined by Newton's second law of Eq. (19.1) as

$$M\frac{d^2y}{dt^2}$$

The second force results from the displacement of the spring. As the spring is either stretched or compressed, it exerts a force on the mass that is proportional and opposite

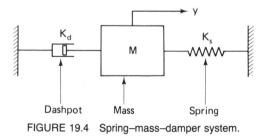

FIGURE 19.4   Spring–mass–damper system.

to the displacement. (There are, of course, limits to this proportionality, but we will assume that the displacement is within those limits.) The force from the spring can be written as

$$K_s y$$

The third force component results from the action of the dashpot. The dashpot is a device that exhibits a tendency to resist motion. It is a frictional device (viscous friction) which gives a force proportional to velocity. Velocity is the first derivative of displacement y, so the damping force can be expressed as follows:

$$K_d \frac{dy}{dt}$$

Assuming that we have considered all the forces on the mass, we can write the equation of motion for the spring–mass–damper system by summing the forces:

$$\sum \text{forces} = M\frac{d^2y}{dt^2} + K_d\frac{dy}{dt} + K_s y = 0 \tag{19.8}$$

This second-order differential equation states that the system is not influenced by any stimuli that are external to itself. Our interest in the application of differential equations to model systems is usually motivated by the presence of some outside stimulus on the system. For example, if an initial displacement x were given to the spring, the differential equation would be written

$$M\frac{d^2y}{dt^2} + K_d\frac{dy}{dt} + K_s y = K_s x \tag{19.9}$$

The system described by Eq. (19.9) is represented in Figure 19.5, in which the displaced end of the spring replaces the fixed wall.

In the equation, the term $K_s x$ is the driving force for the mechanical system. We refer to x as the input to the system, and y is the output that responds to the input. As

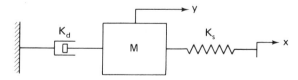

FIGURE 19.5   Spring–mass–damper system with positive displacement given to end of spring.

with the previous first-order example, the form of the input can be a step function or some other more complex motion. For purposes of illustration, the step input is useful, and we will assume that the term $K_s x$ in Eq. (19.9) is of this type.

To solve, the characteristic equation is

$$Ms^2 + K_d s + K_s = 0 \qquad (19.10)$$

where s stands for the differential operator. The two roots to this characteristic equation are

$$s_{1,2} = \frac{-K_d}{2M} \pm \frac{\sqrt{K_d^2 - 4MK_s}}{2M} \qquad (19.11)$$

The motion of the mass, as defined by the variable y, will depend on the relative values of the parameters of the system: M, K_d, and K_s. It turns out that four general outcomes are possible:

1. No damping in the system
2. Underdamped system
3. Critically damped system
4. Overdamped system

Let us consider the conditions that lead to each of these outcomes and what the typical response looks like for each case.

No DAMPING. In this case the damping coefficient, $K_d = 0$ (the dashpot is removed in Figure 19.5). In this case the characteristic equation becomes

$$Ms^2 + K_s = 0$$

and the roots of the equation are

$$s_{1,2} = \pm j\sqrt{\frac{K_s}{M}}$$

where j in this equation means that the roots are imaginary. This means that the behavior of the system is oscillatory and is described by a term called the *natural frequency* of the system. This is symbolized by ω_n, where

$$\omega_n = \sqrt{\frac{K_s}{M}}$$

The solution of Eq. (19.9) assuming x is a step input is

$$y = C_1 \sin\omega_n t + C_2 \cos\omega_n t + X \qquad (19.12)$$

where C_1 and C_2 are constants that depend on initial conditions. The general appearance of this response is shown in Figure 19.6(a).

UNDERDAMPED SYSTEM. If a relatively small amount of damping is present, it means that the square-root value in Eq. (19.11) is imaginary. Then the roots could be rewritten

$$s_{1,2} = -a \pm j\omega_d$$

where

$$a = \frac{K_d}{2M}$$

$$\omega_d = \frac{\sqrt{4MK_s - K_d^2}}{2M}$$

The term ω_d is called the *damped natural frequency* of the underdamped system. The response of y under these conditions would be

$$y = e^{-at}(C_1 \sin\omega_d t + C_2 \cos\omega_d t) + X \qquad (19.13)$$

whose typical shape appears as in Figure 19.6(b).

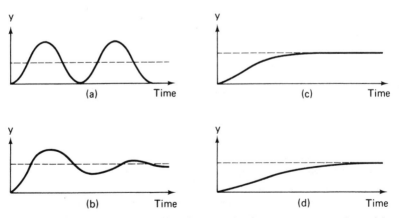

FIGURE 19.6   Possible responses of a second-order system to a step input: (a) no damping; (b) underdamped; (c) critically damped; (d) overdamped.

CRITICALLY DAMPED SYSTEM.   This is the special case that results when

$$K_d^2 = 4MK_s$$

It means that the characteristic equation is

$$s_{1,2} = \frac{-K_d}{2M} \pm 0$$

and the solution of the differential equation in this case is

$$y = C_1 e^{-at} + C_2 t e^{-at} + X \tag{19.14}$$

The shape of this response is shown in Figure 19.6(c). It can be seen that a critically damped system responds to a step input in a relatively short time compared to the other responses shown in Figure 19.6.

OVERDAMPED SYSTEM.   Conditions for the overdamped system occur when

$$K_d^2 > 4MK_s$$

The roots of the characteristic equation are

$$s_{1,2} = -a \pm b$$

where

$$a = \frac{K_d}{2M} \quad \text{as before}$$

$$b = \frac{\sqrt{K_d^2 - 4MK_s}}{2M}$$

The system response in an overdamped case is

$$y = C_1 e^{(-a+b)t} + C_2 e^{(-a-b)t} + X \tag{19.15}$$

and the typical response shape is shown in Figure 19.6(d). There is no oscillation in this response, but the time required for the system to reach a steady-state value is longer than for the critically damped case.

Although the spring–mass–damper system analyzed above seems somewhat academic, its general characteristics are frequently encountered in real life. For example, the suspension system on an automobile is basically a spring–mass–damper mechanical system, although somewhat more complex than that analyzed above. There are other systems and components of systems that exhibit the characteristic of damping and mechanical elasticity. And, of course, all mechanical systems possess mass. The damping and elasticity are not always provided by objects that resemble a dashpot or a spring. For example, a cutting tool will deflect under the force of the machining operation, sometimes causing vibration, which is called "chatter." A rotating shaft that is driven on one end and must transmit motion to the other end will exhibit the characteristics of the idealized spring–mass–damper system.

Concluding comments on modeling

In the two examples of first-order and second-order systems, the constants in the differential equations could be determined by taking measurements on the components of the system. In Eq. (19.5), the value of A could be determined simply by measuring the area of the tank in Figure 19.1. The parameter R could also be estimated by observing the pressure-flow characteristics of the valve. In Figure 19.5 the spring, mass, and damper were treated as separate components so that the values of K_s, M, and K_d could be evaluated for Eq. (19.9). For many physical systems, the parameter values can be determined for the mathematical models simply by measuring the system components.

However, in many other physical situations, the constants in the model cannot be so easily evaluated. In these cases, the parameters must be determined by taking measurements of the behavior of the system responding to some known input. In effect, we deduce the model parameters by empirical means. Most often the general form of the model can be developed from theoretical considerations. Then the constants of the model are evaluated based on observations of the system's performance. There are other occasions when the form of the differential equation cannot be formulated with confidence. When this occurs, the model must be derived on a completely empirical basis. The response data are compared against various hypothesized models, and the model that gives the best agreement is used.

Whatever the situation, mathematical models can be developed to represent the behavior of physical systems. Industrial processes are composed of several interconnected physical systems. By linking together the individual physical systems, the industrial process is constructed. By linking together the equations of the individual systems, the mathematical model of the industrial process is formed. In the next section we consider a convenient method for dealing with this problem of building large process models from their component parts. We also consider how these large models can then be reduced to a basic input/output relationship for the process.

19.2 TRANSFER FUNCTIONS AND BLOCK DIAGRAMS

In this section we develop the concepts of the transfer function and the block diagram. Both are important in the traditional theory of linear control systems.

Transfer functions

The *transfer function* for a linear system or component of a system is defined as the ratio of the output to the input.[1] We will examine how the transfer function is determined for a system component. Then we consider how the transfer function is obtained for an entire system or process.

TRANSFER FUNCTION FOR A SYSTEM COMPONENT. The transfer function for a component or a relatively simple system is obtained as follows:

1. Determine the equation that expresses the behavior of the system. The equation must be linear if it is to be used as an element in a block diagram. It may be a linear differential equation or a linear equation, such as a proportionality relationship.
2. If the equation is a differential equation, write the equation in the differential operator format using the *s*-variable.
3. Rewrite the equation as the ratio of the output to the input.

Several examples will serve to illustrate how this procedure is accomplished. First, consider the hydraulic system of Section 19.1. Equation (19.5) expressed the differential equation for the system:

$$AR\frac{dh}{dt} + h = Rx_1$$

This is rewritten in the *s*-operator notation,

$$ARsh(s) + h(s) = Rx_1(s)$$

or

$$(ARs + 1)h(s) = Rx_1(s)$$

Finally, the ratio of the output over the input is expressed as

$$\frac{h(s)}{x_1(s)} = \frac{R}{ARs + 1} \tag{19.16}$$

which is the transfer function for this system. The original variables h and x_1 are functions of time t. However, when the differential operator notation is used, these variables are

---

[1] To be precise, it is defined as the ratio of the Laplace transform of the output to the Laplace transform of the input, given that all initial conditions are zero. The Laplace transform makes use of the differential operator s, which we explore more fully in the next section.

transformed from functions of t to functions of s. Readers who are familiar with differential equations will recognize s as the Laplace variable.

As a second example, consider the spring–mass–damper system developed in the preceding section. The differential equation was given by Eq. (19.9):

$$M\frac{d^2y}{dt^2} + K_d\frac{dy}{dt} + K_sy = K_sx$$

Using the s-operator format, it is rewritten

$$Ms^2y(s) + K_dsy(s) + K_sy(s) = K_sx(s)$$

or

$$(Ms^2 + K_ds + K_s)y(s) = K_sx(s)$$

The transfer function is obtained from the ratio of output to input:

$$\frac{y(s)}{x(s)} = \frac{K_s}{Ms^2 + K_ds + K_s} \tag{19.17}$$

As a third illustration, consider a proportional relationship in which the input is simply multiplied by some gain factor to obtain the output. Such a relationship is typical of various transducers in which a mechanical displacement or speed is converted into an electrical voltage signal, as shown in Figure 19.7. The basic equation that governs this relationship is

$$e = Kx$$

where e stands for the voltage and x is displacement. The basic input/output relationship is

$$\frac{e(s)}{x(s)} = K \tag{19.18}$$

where the variables are expressed as functions of s, to be consistent with the transfer functions of the other components in the system.

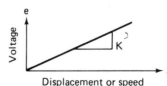

FIGURE 19.7   Proportional relationship.

TRANSFER FUNCTION FOR THE ENTIRE SYSTEM.   The transfer functions for the various components of a system can be grouped together to form the transfer function of the entire system. Its interpretation is the same as for an individual component. It expresses the relationship between the input of the system and its output. The method we will use to determine the system transfer function is block diagram algebra.

Block diagrams

A block diagram is a pictorial method of portraying the interrelationships among components of a physical system or process. It is composed of blocks and arrows between the blocks. The arrows represent the flow of signals or variables. The blocks represent the operations that are performed on the signals. Each block contains a transfer function that defines exactly how the input signal is mathematically transformed into the output signal. Also, signals can be summed together, and one signal can be used as an input to more than a single block.

The basic elements of a block diagram are as follows:

1. *Block.* This represents a given system component and contains the transfer function for the component.
2. *Arrows.* The arrows indicate the direction in which the signals or variables flow. Figure 19.8 shows a block containing a transfer function. The arrows into and out of the block show the input and output of the component.
3. *Summing point.* The summing point is illustrated in Figure 19.9. It can be used to add or subtract signals as shown in Figure 19.9 (a) and (b). More than two signals can flow into a summing point, but only one signal can flow out.
4. *Takeoff point.* The takeoff point permits a variable to be used in more than one place. It is shown in Figure 19.10. The variable is not changed in value

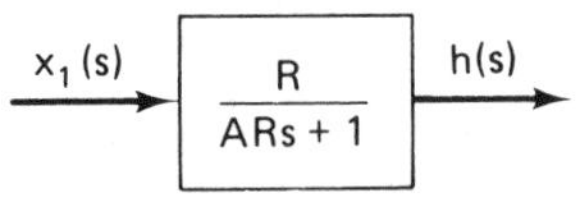

$$x_1(s) \quad \boxed{\frac{R}{ARs + 1}} \quad h(s)$$

FIGURE 19.8   Block diagram symbols: block and arrows (input and output arrows) for Eq. (19.16).

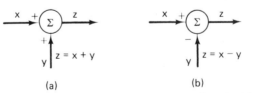

FIGURE 19.9   Block diagram symbols: summing points for (a) addition and (b) subtraction.

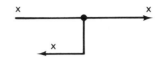

FIGURE 19.10   Block diagram symbols: takeoff point.

when it proceeds through a takeoff point to two or more destinations (blocks and/or summing points).

An example of a block diagram is presented in Figure 19.11. The diagram shows the basic form of a feedback control system with input x and output y. A takeoff point is used to feed the y signal through the block indicated by H. H represents the mathematical operation performed on the y signal. H is the transfer function for the block. The output of block H is subtracted from the input signal x, and the difference is fed into block G. G represents the transfer function that transforms the difference signal into the output y. All the elements of a block diagram—blocks, arrows, summing point, and takeoff point— are present in Figure 19.11.

Figure 19.11 presents an opportunity to define some of the terminology of feedback control systems. In a feedback control system, the controlled variable is compared with the input and any difference between them is used to drive the controlled variable toward its desired value. In Figure 19.11, y is the controlled variable. The feedback system is also referred to as a closed-loop system, since the block diagram takes on the appearance of a closed loop. By contrast, an open-loop system is a system without feedback. In Figure 19.11, G is the forward transfer function and H is the feedback transfer function. The transfer function for the entire feedback control system can be determined from block diagram algebra.

Block diagram algebra

It is possible to take a large complicated block diagram and reduce it to a single block. The single block contains the transfer function for the entire system represented by the original diagram. The process of reducing the diagram is called *block diagram algebra* and is based on traditional algebra.

Let us use the block diagram of Figure 19.11 to illustrate. The signals entering the summing point are the input signal x and the signal Hy. Exiting the summing point is the signal

$$x - Hy$$

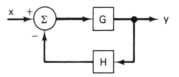

FIGURE 19.11   Block diagram of the basic form of a feedback control system.

This is multiplied by the transfer function G to obtain the output of the system:

$$y = G(x - Hy)$$

$$= Gx - GHy$$

$$y + GHy = Gx$$

$$y(1 + GH) = Gx$$

Writing this as a ratio of y to x gives us

$$\frac{y}{x} = \frac{G}{1 + GH}$$

Hence, we have the transfer function of the feedback control system pictured in Figure 19.11. To be technically correct, we should remember that this ratio is defined using the s-operator notation. Hence, y/x should be $y(s)/x(s)$. The transfer functions G and H may represent complicated expressions in s.

By performing algebraic operations such as the above, various arrangements of blocks, summing points, and takeoff points interconnected by arrows can be reduced to a single block. It is not necessary to proceed through an algebraic manipulation similar to the one above for every block diagram. Instead, certain basic arrangements have been cataloged, and we present some of the more important block diagram equivalences below.

1. *Blocks in series.* These are also called *cascaded blocks* and are pictured in Figure 19.12(a). Components connected in series are equivalent to a single block whose transfer function is the product of the transfer functions of the individual components.

2. *Blocks in parallel.* Components connected in parallel as shown in Figure 19.12(b) are equivalent to a single block whose transfer function is the sum of the individual components' transfer functions.

3. *Elimination of a basic feedback loop.* This is the algebraic reduction for the basic feedback loop of Figure 19.11. The general form is presented in Figure 19.12(c).

4. *Moving a summing point.* In the reduction of a complex block diagram, it is generally desirable to move summing points to the left. This is illustrated in Figure 19.12(d).

5. *Moving a takeoff point.* It is sometimes desirable to move takeoff points to the right in block diagram reduction. This is shown in Figure 19.12(e).

STEPS IN BLOCK DIAGRAM REDUCTION.   The reduction of a large complex block diagram to a single block using the equivalences shown in Figure 19.12 should proceed in the following general sequence:

1. Combine all series block arrangements into single blocks according to Figure 19.12(a).

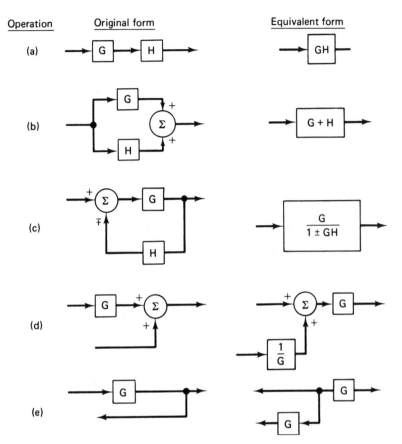

FIGURE 19.12   Basic operations in block diagram algebra: (a) blocks in series;
(b) blocks in parallel; (c) elimination of a feedback loop; (d) moving a summing
point; (e) moving a takeoff point.

2.   Combine all parallel block arrangements into single blocks according to Figure
     19.12(b).
3.   Convert basic feedback loops into equivalent single blocks according to Figure
     19.12(c).
4.   Shift summing points to the left and takeoff points to the right according to
     Figure 19.12(d) and (e).

An example should help to illustrate the use of block diagram algebra in the simplification
of a somewhat complex diagram.

EXAMPLE 19.1

Given the block diagram of Figure 19.13(a), we want to reduce this to a single equivalent block
in order to determine the system transfer function.

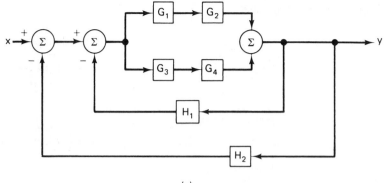

(a)

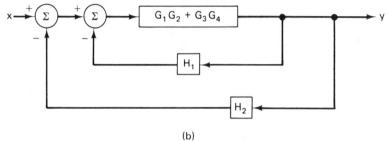

(b)

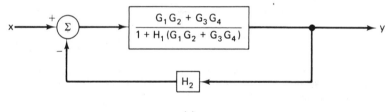

(c)

$$\frac{\dfrac{G_1 G_2 + G_3 G_4}{1 + H_1 (G_1 G_2 + G_3 G_4)}}{1 + H_2 \left[\dfrac{G_1 G_2 + G_3 G_4}{1 + H_1 (G_1 G_2 + G_3 G_4)} \right]}$$

(d)

FIGURE 19.13 Example 19.1 block diagram: (a) initial block diagram; (b) block diagram after series and parallel reduction; (c) block diagram after first feedback loop elimination; (d) transfer function for the system.

540

Solution:

The solution is illustrated in parts (b), (c), and (d) of Figure 19.13. The first step is to combine series blocks, then parallel blocks. This is shown in part (b). Next, the inside feedback loop is converted into an equivalent block, Figure 19.13(c). Finally, the outside feedback loop is eliminated to provide the transfer function for the complete system.

EXAMPLE 19.2

Figure 19.14 presents a sketch of two cascaded tanks. In each tank some chemical reaction takes place by the addition of small traces of ingredients to the basic fluid flowing through the system. Our purpose is to model the physical flow portion of the system rather than the chemical reactions that take place. The flow into the first tank is to be treated as the input and the head (or level) in the second tank is to be considered here as the system output. The problem is to develop the block diagram for the system and then find the transfer function by block diagram algebra.

Solution:

The reader will no doubt notice the similarities between this flow system and the hydraulic example we used to illustrate a first-order linear differential equation. The equations that govern this industrial flow process are the following:

$$x_1 - x_2 = A_1 \frac{dh_1}{dt}$$

$$x_2 = \frac{h_1}{R_1}$$

$$x_2 - x_3 = A_2 \frac{dh_2}{dt}$$

$$x_3 = \frac{h_2}{R_2}$$

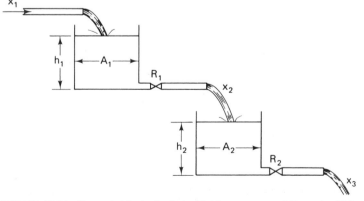

FIGURE 19.14   Cascaded tanks for industrial flow process of Example. 19.2.

$$\text{where } x = \text{various flow rates}$$

$$h = \text{head in each of the tanks}$$

$$R = \text{hydraulic resistance}$$

The first and third equations are differential equations and can be expressed in terms of the differential operator, s.

$$x_1 - x_2 = A_1 s h_1$$

$$x_2 - x_3 = A_2 s h_2$$

From the four equations, the block diagram can be constructed as shown in Figure 19.15(a). Although this system contains feedback loops, the relationship between the input x_1 and the defined output h_2 is basically an open-loop relationship. There is no feedback of the h_2 signal for comparison with the input x_1.

Figure 19.15(b) shows the transfer function for the industrial flow process. This expression could be reduced to a simpler form by algebraic manipulation.

MULTIPLE INPUTS TO THE SYSTEM.   Many physical systems have more than one input. The approach for reducing the block diagram of a system with multiple inputs is to treat each input separately and independently. Following is the procedure:

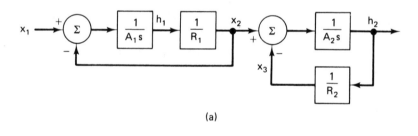

(a)

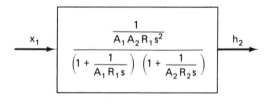

(b)

FIGURE 19.15   Solution to Example 19.2: (a) block diagram of industrial flow process; (b) transfer function determined after block diagram algebra.

1. Set all inputs equal to zero except one.
2. Determine the transfer function by block diagram algebra using that input alone.
3. Repeat steps 1 and 2 for other inputs.
4. Add algebraically the products of transfer functions and their respective inputs to obtain the effect of all inputs acting simultaneously.

We will illustrate this procedure with a simple example.

EXAMPLE 19.3

Consider the control system of Figure 19.16(a), which has two inputs x_1 and x_2. We want to determine the system response y that results from these two inputs.

Solution:

First we consider the case where x_2 is zero and x_1 is nonzero, shown in Figure 19.16(b). The transfer function for this arrangement is presented beneath the block diagram.

The next step is to set $x_1 = 0$ and assume that x_2 is nonzero, as shown in Figure 19.16(c). Again, the transfer function for this system is given below the block diagram.

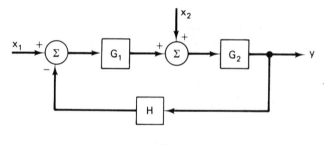

(a)

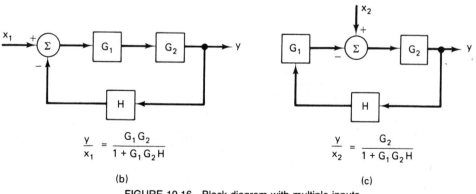

$$\frac{y}{x_1} = \frac{G_1 G_2}{1 + G_1 G_2 H}$$

$$\frac{y}{x_2} = \frac{G_2}{1 + G_1 G_2 H}$$

(b)

(c)

FIGURE 19.16   Block diagram with multiple inputs.

To determine the total system response, simply add the separate response of each input. Each separate response is the input multiplied by its corresponding transfer function.

$$y = \frac{G_1G_2}{1 + G_1G_2H} x_1 + \frac{G_2}{1 + G_1G_2H} x_2$$

EXAMPLE 19.4

Our fourth example of block diagram modeling is a case of multiple inputs and also a more realistic illustration of process modeling than that in Example 19.3. It is based on a research paper of Jaeschke, Zimmerly, and Wu [5]. The paper deals with the use of cutting temperature to control speed in a turning operation. The system measures cutting temperature by means of a tool-chip thermocouple (the two dissimilar metals forming the thermocouple junction are the tool and the chip coming off the workpiece). The voltage signal is amplified and fed back to be compared with a reference voltage. If cutting temperature is too high, speed is reduced. If cutting temperature is below the desired level, speed is increased. A schematic diagram of the control system is shown in Figure 19.17. The authors distinguish between two cases in the operation of the system. The first case is when speed is increasing. The block diagram for this situation is illustrated in Figure 19.18(a). The second case is when speed is decreasing, and the block diagram is shown in Figure 19.18(b). The difference in the two cases is that different components are used in each case. In Figure 19.18(a), the control system, consisting of integrator, amplifier, and Adjusto-Spede unit, must provide a positive torque to increase the cutting speed. In Figure 19.18(b), the cutting torque tends to decrease the speed and the control system components are not brought into action. Hence, two block diagrams must be used to completely describe the behavior of this control system.

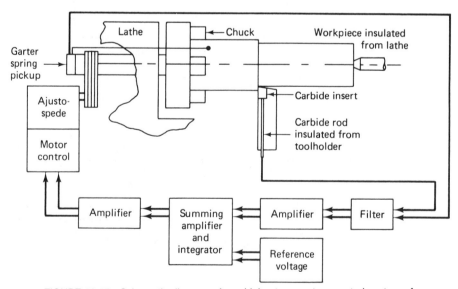

FIGURE 19.17 Schematic diagram of machining temperature control system of Example 19.4.

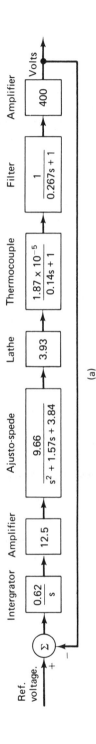

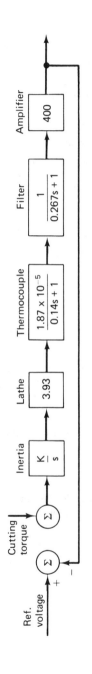

FIGURE 19.18 Two block diagrams for machining temperature control system of Example 19.4: (a) acceleration torques; (b) decelerating torques.

19.3   LAPLACE TRANSFORMS

In previous sections of this chapter we have used the differential operator notation to express a differential equation. The symbol s has been used to represent the mathematical operation of taking the derivative of any dependent variable with respect to time t. In this and the following sections, we will examine more closely the variable s and its association with the Laplace transform to solve differential equations and to analyze linear control problems.

The Laplace transform is used to transform a differential equation which is a function of time t into a corresponding algebraic equation which is a function of the variable s. When this is accomplished, we say that the function has been transformed from the time domain or t-domain into the s-domain. The reason for taking the trouble to transform the problem from the t- to the s- domain is to facilitate the problem's solution. It is usually easier to solve a complicated control system problem by using the Laplace transformation.

The Laplace transform defined

The *Laplace transform* of $f(t)$, where $f(t)$ is a function of time, is defined in the following way:

$$F(s) = \int_0^\infty f(t)e^{-st}dt \tag{19.19}$$

where $F(s)$ is the Laplace transform of $f(t)$ and s is a complex variable defined by

$$s = \sigma + j\omega \tag{19.20}$$

The transformation is, of course, limited to functions $f(t)$ for which the integral according to Eq. (19.19) exists.

EXAMPLE 19.5

Let us illustrate the Laplace transformation given by Eq. (19.19) by means of a simple example. Suppose that we wish to take the Laplace transform of the step function whose constant value is C.

$$f(t) = \begin{cases} C & t \geq 0 \\ 0 & t < 0 \end{cases}$$

Then, by Eq. (19.19),

$$F(s) = \int_0^\infty Ce^{-st}\, dt = \left. \frac{-Ce^{-st}}{s} \right|_0^\infty$$

$$= \frac{-C(0)}{s} - \frac{-C(1)}{s} = \frac{C}{s}$$

The Laplace transform may be determined for a variety of different functions of t, so its application is of great value in control systems analysis.

TABLE OF LAPLACE TRANSFORMS.   To avoid the necessity of performing the integration defined by Eq. (19.19) for every function of t in a particular problem, tables of common Laplace transforms have been prepared. These appear in books of mathematical tables and other references. We present some of the more familiar Laplace transforms in Table 19.1.

The last two entries in the table are the transforms for the first and second derivatives. In writing a differential equation, it is the usual practice to write the dependent variable alone (e.g., y) rather than stating explicitly that it is a function of t [e.g., $y(t)$]. However, when the variable is transformed into the s-domain, we must indicate this by using the form $y(s)$ to show that y is a function of s. We have conformed to this convention in

TABLE 19.1   Common Laplace Transforms

Time function $f(t)$	Laplace transform $F(s)$
Unit step 1	$\dfrac{1}{s}$
Unit ramp t	$\dfrac{1}{s^2}$
Polynomial t^n	$\dfrac{n!}{s^{n+1}}$
Exponential e^{-at}	$\dfrac{1}{s+a}$
Sine wave $\sin \omega t$	$\dfrac{\omega}{s^2 + \omega^2}$
Cosine wave $\cos \omega t$	$\dfrac{s}{s^2 + \omega^2}$
te^{-at}	$\dfrac{1}{(s+a)^2}$
$e^{-at} \sin \omega t$	$\dfrac{\omega}{(s+a)^2 + \omega^2}$
$e^{-at} \cos \omega t$	$\dfrac{s+a}{(s+a)^2 + \omega^2}$
First derivative $\dfrac{dy}{dt}$	$sy(s) - y(t=0)$
Second derivative $\dfrac{d^2y}{dt^2}$	$s^2y(s) - sy(t=0) - \dfrac{dy(t=0)}{dt}$

the last two entries of Table 19.1. The first derivative dy/dt is shown in the left-hand column, where dy/dt is a function of time t. In the right-hand column, the corresponding Laplace transform is written:

$$sy(s) - y(t = 0)$$

The first term contains the differential operator s and the variable $y(s)$, which is now a function of s. The second term is the initial value of y at time $t = 0$.

Similarly, the Laplace transform of the second derivative of y is written

$$s^2y(s) - sy(t = 0) - \frac{dy(t = 0)}{dt}$$

The s^2 in the first term indicates the second derivative. The second term is s multiplied by the value of y at $t = 0$. The third term is the value of dy/dt at time $t = 0$.

EXAMPLE 19.6

Given the initial conditions that $y = 5$ and $dy/dt = 2$ at $t = 0$, write the Laplace transform of the differential equation

$$\frac{d^2y}{dt^2} + 3\frac{dy}{dt} + y = 0$$

Solution:

The Laplace transform of the first term is

$$s^2y(s) - 5s - 2$$

The transform of the second term is

$$3[sy(s) - 5]$$

and the transform of the third term is simply $y(s)$. Hence, the complete Laplace transform of the differential equation above would be developed as follows:

$$s^2y(s) - 5s - 2 + 3sy(s) - 15 + y(s) = 0$$
$$s^2y(s) + 3sy(s) + y(s) - 5s - 17 = 0$$
$$(s^2 + 3s + 1)y(s) = 5s + 17$$
$$y(s) = \frac{5s + 17}{s^2 + 3s + 1}$$

The inverse transformation

In the typical application of Laplace transforms, the differential equation is converted from the time domain to the s-domain. It is then manipulated algebraically into an appropriate solution form. However, to be of value the solution must then be transformed back into the time domain. This procedure is called the *inverse transformation*. It is accomplished by making use again of Table 19.1. In other words, the transformations indicated in Table 19.1 can proceed in either direction.

EXAMPLE 19.7

We shall demonstrate the use of the Laplace transform and the inverse transform in the solution of the following differential equation:

$$\frac{dy}{dt} + 5y = 0$$

where the initial conditions are that $y = 3$ and $dy/dt = 0$ at time $t = 0$.

The Laplace transform would be written:

$$sy(s) - 3 + 5y(s) = 0$$

$$(s + 5)y(s) = 3$$

$$y(s) = \frac{3}{s + 5}$$

Now applying the inverse transform (the fourth entry in Table 19.1), we get the solution for y as a function of time:

$$y = 3e^{-5t}$$

The solution for y has a value of 3.0 when $t = 0$ and decays exponentially toward zero as time increases.

PARTIAL FRACTION EXPANSION. The Laplace transform of the solution to the differential equation is often expressed as the ratio of two polynomials:

$$y(s) = \frac{a_0 + a_1 s + a_2 s^2 + \cdots + a_m s^m}{b_0 + b_1 s + b_2 s^2 + \cdots + b_n s^n} \tag{19.21}$$

The particular polynomial form may not appear as one of the entries in a table of standard Laplace transforms. Hence, it is difficult to directly obtain the inverse transform of $y(s)$. It is therefore desirable to reduce the form of Eq. (19.21) to a more convenient, yet equivalent form. One method of accomplishing this reduction is provided by partial fraction expansions.

The procedure begins by first factoring the denominator of Eq. (19.21), to form

$$y(s) = \frac{a_0 + a_1 s + a_2 s^2 + \cdots + a_m s^m}{(s + r_1)(s + r_2) \cdots (s + r_n)} \qquad (19.22)$$

where $-r, -r_2, \ldots, -r_n$ are the roots of the denominator obtained by setting the denominator equal to zero. It is assumed that it is possible to factor the denominator of Eq. (19.21) into its roots even if some of the roots are imaginary or complex numbers.

The second step in the partial fraction expansion is to write Eq. (19.22) in the following form:

$$y(s) = \frac{C_1}{s + r_1} + \frac{C_2}{s + r_2} + \cdots + \frac{C_n}{s + r_n} \qquad (19.23)$$

We will assume for the moment that each root is distinct. That is, none of the roots are equal.

The third step is to find the values of $C_1, C_2 \ldots, C_n$ in Eq. (19.23). This is accomplished by means of the following set of equations:

$$C_1 = \left. \frac{a_0 + a_1 s + a_2 s^2 + \cdots + a_m s^m}{(s + r_1)(s + r_2) \cdots (s + r_n)} (s + r_1) \right|_{s = -r_1} \qquad (19.24)$$

$$C_2 = \left. \frac{a_0 + a_1 s + a_2 s^2 + \cdots + a_m s^m}{(s + r_1)(s + r_2) \cdots (s + r_n)} (s + r_2) \right|_{s = -r_2} \qquad (19.25)$$

$$\begin{aligned} &\bullet \\ &\bullet \\ &\bullet \end{aligned}$$

$$C_n = \left. \frac{a_0 + a_1 s + a_2 s^2 + \cdots + a_m s^m}{(s + r_1)(s + r_2) \cdots (s + r_n)} (s + r_n) \right|_{s = -r_n} \qquad (19.26)$$

After each of the constants has been determined in Eq. (19.23), the terms in the equation should be in the form of one of the common Laplace transforms. Converting the solution from the s-domain to the t-domain is a straightforward matter involving the inverse transforms in Table 19.1.

EXAMPLE 19.8

To illustrate the partial fraction expansion method, let us use the same basic differential equation from Example 19.7 except that a forcing function equal to a unit step will be on the right-hand side of the equation.

$$\frac{dy}{dt} + 5y = 1$$

where $y = 3$ and $dy/dt = 0$ at $t = 0$.
    The Laplace transform would be written

$$sy(s) - 3 + 5y(s) = \frac{1}{s}$$

$$(s + 5)y(s) = \frac{1}{s} + 3$$

$$= \frac{1 + 3s}{s}$$

$$y(s) = \frac{1 + 3s}{s(s + 5)}$$

The roots of $s(s + 5) = 0$ are $s = 0$ and $s = -5$. We wish to find the equivalent expression:

$$y(s) = \frac{C_1}{s} + \frac{C_2}{s + 5}$$

The values of C_1 and C_2 are obtained by using Eqs. (19.24) and (19.25).

$$C_1 = \frac{1 + 3s}{s(s + 5)}(s)\bigg|_{s=0} = \frac{1 + 3(0)}{0 + 5} = \frac{1}{5}$$

$$C_2 = \frac{1 + 3s}{s(s + 5)}(s + 5)\bigg|_{s=-5} = \frac{1 + 3(-5)}{-5} = \frac{14}{5}$$

Hence,

$$y(s) = \frac{1/5}{s} + \frac{14/5}{s + 5}$$

Using Table 19.1 for the inverse transform, we get

$$y(t) = \frac{1}{5} + \frac{14}{5}e^{-5t}$$

    The method above is appropriate for the case when there are no repeated roots in the denominator of Eq. (19.22). Suppose, upon factoring the denominator, that two of the roots are equal. Let the equal roots be r_1 and r_2. That is, $r_1 = r_2$, so Eq. (19.22) could be written as follows:

$$y(s) = \frac{a_0 + a_1 s + a_2 s^2 + \cdots + a_m s^m}{(s + r_1)^2 (s + r_3) \cdots (s + r_n)} \tag{19.27}$$

In this event, the partial fraction expansion corresponding to Eq. (19.23) is

$$y(s) = \frac{C_1}{(s + r_1)^2} + \frac{C_2}{s + r_1} + \frac{C_3}{s + r_3} + \cdots + \frac{C_n}{s + r_n} \tag{19.28}$$

Evaluation of constants C_3 through C_n involves the same calculation procedure as before. Equations of the form of Eqs. (19.24) through (19.26) would be used. However, to evaluate C_1 and C_2 in Eq. (19.28) for the repeated roots, the following formulas must be used:

$$C_1 = \frac{a_0 + a_1 s + a_2 s^2 + \cdots + a_m s^m}{(s + r_1)^2 (s + r_3) \cdots (s + r_n)} (s + r_1)^2 \Bigg|_{s = -r_1} \tag{19.29}$$

$$C_2 = \frac{d}{ds} \left[\frac{a_0 + a_1 s + a_2 s^2 + \cdots + a_m s^m}{(s + r_1)^2 (s + r_3) \cdots (s + r_n)} (s + r_1)^2 \right]_{s = -r_1} \tag{19.30}$$

EXAMPLE 19.9

The case of repeated roots will be illustrated with the following equation in the s-domain:

$$y(s) = \frac{s + 2}{(s + 3)^2 (s + 1)}$$

The equation is written in the form of partial fractions:

$$y(s) = \frac{C_1}{(s + 3)^2} + \frac{C_2}{s + 3} + \frac{C_3}{s + 1}$$

From Eq. (19.29),

$$C_1 = \frac{s + 2}{(s + 3)^2 (s + 1)} (s + 3)^2 \Bigg|_{s = -3} = \frac{-3 + 2}{-3 + 1} = \frac{1}{2}$$

From Eq. (19.30),

$$C_2 = \frac{d}{ds} \left[\frac{s + 2}{(s + 3)^2 (s + 1)} (s + 3)^2 \right]_{s = -3} = \frac{d}{ds} \left[\frac{s + 2}{s + 1} \right]_{s = -3}$$

$$= \frac{(s + 1) - (s + 2)}{(s + 1)^2} \Bigg|_{s = -3} = \frac{(-3 + 1) - (-3 + 2)}{(-3 + 1)^2} = -\frac{1}{4}$$

and from Eq. (19.26) we can calculate C_3.

$$C_3 = \frac{s + 2}{(s + 3)^2(s + 1)}(s + 1)\bigg|_{s=-1} = \frac{-1 + 2}{(-3 + 1)^2} = \frac{1}{4}$$

Hence, we obtain

$$y(s) = \frac{0.5}{(s + 3)^2} - \frac{0.25}{s + 3} + \frac{0.25}{s + 1}$$

whose inverse transform gives y as a function of time:

$$y = 0.5te^{-3t} - 0.25e^{-3t} + 0.25e^{-t}$$

Equations (19.29) and (19.30) can be extended to cover the general case of any number of repeated roots. However, we will not consider the general case here, preferring to leave this for books whose exclusive concern is with linear control theory. Two repeated roots constitutes the highest number of equal roots we will encounter in this book.

19.4 CONTROL ACTIONS

The block diagram of a conventional feedback control system was illustrated in Figure 19.11. The G-block is the forward transfer function. In a typical process control application the forward transfer function consists of two main components, as illustrated in Figure 19.19. The first is the controller unit, whose transfer function is symbolized by $C(s)$. The second component is the transfer function of the process itself, symbolized by $P(s)$. It is desired to control the output of $P(s)$ by using the appropriate control action $C(s)$. By comparing Figures 19.11 and 19.19, the reader can see that the following relationship is true:

$$G(s) = C(s)P(s) \tag{19.31}$$

The conventional feedback control system compares the system output y with the input x. Since the y signal may be a different type than the input signal (e.g., y is displacement while x is voltage), it may be necessary to use a transducer, represented by $H(s)$, to convert the output signal into a form that is compatible with the input. The summing

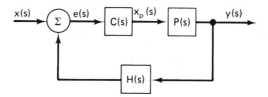

FIGURE 19.19   Block diagram for typical process control application.

block in Figure 19.19 represents the comparison between x and y. Any difference between the two is used as the input to the controller. Thus the actuating signal for $C(s)$ in the block diagram is the difference $e(s) = x(s) - H(s)y(s)$. The particular way in which $C(s)$ manipulates this signal is referred to as the *control action*. The output of the controller is $x_p(s)$, which becomes the input to the process $P(s)$. The controller unit must be designed so that its control action is to correct any deviations from the desired level of the output. The selection of the best control action $C(s)$ depends on the nature of $P(s)$ and $H(s)$.

There are four basic control actions, which are commonly used either alone or in some combination. These are:

1. Proportional control
2. Integral control
3. Derivative control
4. On/off control

We discuss these four basic types in this section and then examine how to select the appropriate control action in the following sections.

Proportional control

In proportional control, the controller output x_p is proportional to the input e. This is expressed in equation form as

$$x_p = Ke$$

where K is the constant of proportionality. For purposes of control system analysis, this can be expressed as a transfer function:

$$\frac{x_p(s)}{e(s)} = K \tag{19.32}$$

The value K is often called the *gain* of the proportional controller.

The relationship between the error signal e and the output signal x_p is shown in Figure 19.20(a). Both signals are shown as a function of time. The nature of this control action is that as long as the error persists, the controller will continue to produce a corrective signal.

Integral control

An alternative form of control action is integral control. In this case, the output of the controller is proportional to the time integral of the actuating signal e. This can be written mathematically as

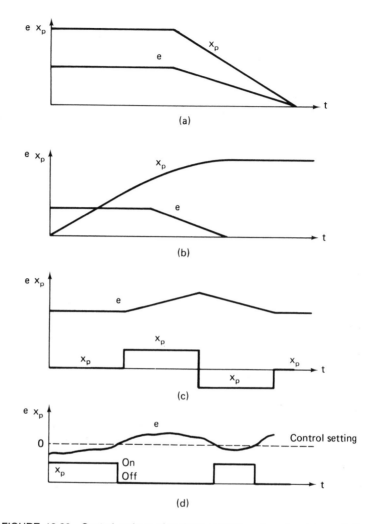

FIGURE 19.20 Control actions of various controllers (e = input to controller, x_p = output of controller): (a) proportional control; (b) integral control; (c) derivative control; (d) on/off control.

$$x_p = K \int e \, dt$$

where K is the gain of the integral controller. Rewriting this in transfer function notation, the integral control action becomes

$$\frac{x_p(s)}{e(s)} = \frac{K}{s} \tag{19.33}$$

The relationship between e and x_p is illustrated in Figure 19.20(b). If the error signal is positive, the correction signal x_p will occur at an increasing rate. The rate of increase will be proportional to the level of the error signal. If the error signal is zero, the signal x_p will be constant. In order for the correction signal x_p to decrease, a negative error e must be present. This results in the tendency for integral control action to overshoot the desired value of the output, which in turn produces an oscillatory response on the part of the process output.

Derivative control

In derivative control, the value of x_p is proportional to the rate of change of e. This can be expressed as follows:

$$x_p = K\frac{de}{dt}$$

where K is the gain of the derivative controller. The corresponding transfer function for the derivative controller is

$$\frac{x_p(s)}{e(s)} = Ks \tag{19.34}$$

The relationship between x_p and e, both plotted over time, is shown in Figure 19.20(c). When the error signal e is steady, the derivative control produces an output signal $x_p = 0$. When e is increasing or decreasing, the controller provides for a signal that is proportional to the rate of increase or decrease. Hence, when e is increasing at a steady rate, x_p is a constant positive value. When e is decreasing at a constant rate, x_p is a negative value.

The disadvantage of derivative control, as illustrated in Figure 19.20(c), is that an error can exist without any corrective action being taken. In the first time interval of Figure 19.20(c), e is a constant positive value. However, it is not until that error signal begins to change that we see the derivative controller coming into action. For this reason, it is not common to use derivative control by itself. Instead, it is generally used in parallel with one of the two previous control actions.

The advantage of derivative control is that it tends to anticipate the occurrence of a deviation from the desired output level. As soon as the e signal deviates from a steady-state level, the derivative control action begins to make a correction.

On/off control or two-position control

In many control systems, it is satisfactory for the controller to operate at either of two levels rather than over a continuous range as in the three preceding control actions. Typically, the two levels are on or off. More generally, this type of control action is referred to as *two-position control*. The reason is that the two levels may be other than on and off. For instance, the controller may operate at either of two constant speeds, or forward/reverse, and so on.

Perhaps the most familiar application of on/off control is in the operation of home heating systems. The controller unit is the thermostat. The occupant of the home sets the thermostat at the desired temperature level. If the actual room temperature is below the thermostat setting, the furnace (or alternative heating unit) is turned on by the thermostat. After a while, the room begins to heat up. When the room temperature finally reaches (or slightly exceeds) the thermostat setting, the furnace is turned off. As the room cools down, the thermostat finally turns the furnace back on. The home heating system cycles back and forth between the on and off positions.

The on/off control action is illustrated in Figure 19.20(d). When the error exceeds the control setting, the controller sets the value of x_p to the "off" value. When e is below the control setting, x_p is set to the "on" position. Recall that e represents the difference between the input x and the feedback signal from y. Accordingly, the control setting will usually be set at a value of zero.

The disadvantage with two-position control is that the controller response cannot be matched to the magnitude of the error signal. The control action is either too much or none at all. Depending on the sensitivity of the system, the controller may potentially cycle back and forth between the two positions at a frequency that is too high. To compensate for this problem, the controller is often provided with two limits. The lower limit may turn the controller on while the upper limit turns it off. In this mode of operation, the controlled variable is regulated within a range of values rather than at one given level. The advantage of the two-position controller is its low cost and simplicity. In many control situations, this type of control action is quite adequate.

On/off control is more cumbersome to analyze by traditional linear control theory because its control action represents a discontinuous function. For this reason, the system must be divided into two problems, one in which the controller is on, the other with the controller off. This was illustrated in Example 19.4. We will examine the use of on/off controls in much greater detail in Chapter 21.

Combinations of control actions

Combinations of the proportional, integral, and derivative actions are frequently used to achieve the desired control over the process. The resulting transfer functions include the following:

1. Proportional plus integral:

$$\frac{x_p(s)}{e(s)} = K_1 + \frac{K_2}{s} \tag{19.35}$$

2. Proportional plus derivative:

$$\frac{x_p(s)}{e(s)} = K_1 + K_3 s \qquad (19.36)$$

3. Proportional, integral, and derivative:

$$\frac{x_p(s)}{e(s)} = K_1 + \frac{K_2}{s} + K_3 s \qquad (19.37)$$

EXAMPLE 19.10

Let us examine the effect of using the three control actions—proportional, integral, and derivative— on the hypothetical process control situation shown in Figure 19.21. The process is represented by the transfer function

$$\frac{5}{s + 2}$$

The feedback transfer function is a proportional gain of 0.1, and the contoller transfer function is represented by $C(s)$. Using block diagram algebra, the system transfer function is determined to be

$$\frac{y(s)}{x(s)} = \frac{5C(s)}{s + 2 + 0.5C(s)}$$

The system transfer function can be obtained for each of the three control actions by substituting the particular controller transfer function $C(s)$ into the equation above. We will use a gain of $K = 2$ for all three control actions.

1. Proportional control: $C(s) = 2.0$

$$\frac{y(s)}{x(s)} = \frac{5(2)}{s + 2 + 1} = \frac{10}{s + 3}$$

2. Integral control: $C(s) = 2/s$

$$\frac{y(s)}{x(s)} = \frac{10/s}{s + 2 + 1/s} = \frac{10}{s^2 + 2s + 1}$$

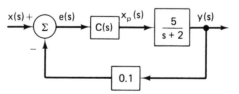

FIGURE 19.21   Block diagram for system of Example 19.10.

3. Derivative control: $C(s) = 2s$

$$\frac{y(s)}{x(s)} = \frac{10s}{s + 2 + s} = \frac{5s}{s + 1}$$

It can be seen that the system transfer functions are quite different for the three different control actions.

We will next examine the effect of a step input of $x = 4.0$ on the system output y. This can be done by multiplying the Laplace transform of the input by the transfer function and then converting the resulting value of $y(s)$ back into the time domain. The transform of the input is $x(s) = 4/s$.

1. For the proportional controller:

$$y(s) = \frac{4}{s} \frac{10}{s + 3} = \frac{40}{s(s + 3)}$$

$$= \frac{13.33}{s} - \frac{13.33}{s + 3}$$

$$y = 13.33(1 - e^{-3t})$$

2. For the integral controller:

$$y(s) = \frac{4}{s} \frac{10}{(s + 1)^2} = \frac{40}{s(s + 1)^2}$$

$$= \frac{40}{s} - \frac{40}{(s + 1)^2} - \frac{40}{s + 1}$$

$$y = 40(1 - te^{-t} - e^{-t})$$

3. For the derivative controller:

$$y(s) = \frac{4}{s} \frac{5s}{s + 1} = \frac{20}{s + 1}$$

$$y = 20e^{-t}$$

The three responses are clearly different. For the proportional control, the value of y quickly reaches a steady-state value of 13.33. In the case of integral control, a steady-state value of $y = 40.0$ is achieved but at a much slower rate than for the proportional control. It should be mentioned that in both of these cases the gain K could be altered to achieve a given steady-state output level for y. For the derivative controller, the steady-state value for y is zero. The three solutions are plotted in Figure 19.22.

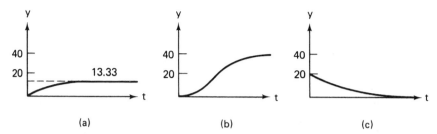

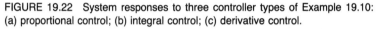

FIGURE 19.22   System responses to three controller types of Example 19.10:
(a) proportional control; (b) integral control; (c) derivative control.

19.5   LINEAR SYSTEMS ANALYSIS

In the preceding sections the presentation has been focused on the modeling of linear
process control systems (linear differential equations and block diagrams) and on one of
the important mathematical tools (Laplace transforms) to facilitate solution of these systems. We have also discussed several control actions (proportional, integral, derivative,
and on/off control) which are commonly used in process control. In this section, our
emphasis shifts from mathematical descriptions of linear control systems to mathematical
analysis and design considerations. The current section covers several preliminary, yet
important topics in systems analysis. In the following section we present the root-locus
method for analyzing linear control systems, and in the last section we are concerned
with the design aspects of systems engineering.

The analysis of any control system must include the following performance characteristics of the system:

1.   *Stability.*   Is the control system stable? If not, how can it be made stable? If
it is stable, there are varying degrees of stability and it is important to know the extent
of system stability.

2.   *Steady-state performance.*   What is the performance of the control system, as
characterized by its output, after the transient response has disappeared? Does the output
achieve some desirable steady-state value?

3.   *Transient performance.*   What is the system's transient response when subjected to a change in input or a disturbance? Does the system respond quickly to a change
in input? Does the system correct itself quickly from the effect of an outside disturbance?
Does the output oscillate and, if so, do the oscillations continue indefinitely?

These are the three principal areas of concern in control systems analysis. In this
chapter we are limiting our discussion to linear systems. The analysis of nonlinear systems
is far more complicated and we leave this to books devoted to the subject [3].

System stability

System stability means that the system response will not tend toward a value of infinity when subjected to a noninfinite input. In a practical control system, an infinite response value would never be reached. Instead, the output would reach some limiting value or the system would self-destruct, whichever happens first. It is important to design the system so that it is stable. Accordingly, it is important in systems analysis to be able to recognize the characteristics of a system which cause instability.

A *stable system* is one in which the transient response decays as time increases. An *unstable system* is one in which the transient response increases as time increases. Two examples of system responses will illustrate the case of instability. In the response

$$y = C - C_1 e^{at} \tag{19.38}$$

the second term will increase (in a negative direction) indefinitely as time t goes to infinity. In the response

$$y = C - e^{at}(C_1 \sin \omega t + C_2 \cos \omega t) \tag{19.39}$$

the second term will oscillate as a result of the sine and cosine terms, but the amplitude of oscillation will increase indefinitely because of the positive exponential term. In each of these equations, the first term represents the steady-state response and the second term represents the transient response.

For each of these hypothetical differential equation solutions, the transient response can be traced back to the characteristic equation. For the solution represented by Eq. (19.38), the characteristic equation in the Laplace domain is

$$s - a = 0 \tag{19.40}$$

so the root of the equation is $s = +a$. If the forcing function in the differential equation is a step input, the resulting solution is of the form given by Eq. (19.38).

For the response indicated in Eq. (19.39), the characteristic equation is

$$s^2 - 2as + (\omega^2 + a^2) = 0$$

or

$$(s - a + j\omega)(s - a - j\omega) = 0 \tag{19.41}$$

for which the roots are

$$s = a - j\omega \quad \text{and} \quad s = a + j\omega$$

Again, a step input to the system would provide a solution, as given in Eq. (19.39).

For Eq. (19.40) the positive root ($s = a$) leads to the unstable solution in Eq. (19.38). In the case of Eq. (19.41), the real part of the complex roots ($s = a - j\omega$ and $s = a + j\omega$) are positive, and this leads to the instability of the solution given in Eq. (19.39). This leads us to the following conclusion:

> For a linear system to be stable, the roots of the characteristic equation must all be negative real numbers or complex numbers with negative real parts.

This statement is true for the first- and second-order systems represented by Eqs. (19.40) and (19.41), and it is also true for higher-order systems as well. For a linear system with 50 roots, the foregoing stability criterion remains valid. Even if only one of the 50 roots is positive and real, the system will be unstable.

Some systems are said to be *marginally stable*. This is the case in which the characteristic equation has complex roots with real parts equal to zero. An example of such a characteristic equation is

$$s^2 + \omega^2 = 0 \tag{19.42}$$

This yields roots $s = \pm j\omega$, and the solution of this system for a step input is

$$y = C + C_1 \sin\omega t + C_2 \cos\omega t \tag{19.43}$$

This solution would continuously oscillate about a mean value of $y = C$. The oscillations would never die out. Accordingly, such a system would be of limited practical value in most situations, because the output never achieves a steady-state constant value. Marginal stability (another name for this is *limited stability*) represents the dividing line between a stable system and an unstable system.

It should be mentioned that it is not always easy to verify system stability by using the negative real root criterion. The source of the difficulty is that the characteristic equation must be factored in order to determine whether the real roots are negative or the complex roots have negative real parts. Factoring the characteristic equation becomes difficult for high-order differential equations. There are other criteria that can be used to assess system stability, but these are beyond the scope of this survey on linear control theory.

Steady-state performance

Assume that it has been determined that the process control system of interest is stable. The next concern in the analysis is to determine the steady-state performance of the system. There is an important theorem in control systems analysis which permits the determination of steady-state response. It is called the *final value theorem* and it uses the Laplace transform of the system output. This allows us to find the steady-state value of a function $f(t)$ without requiring that the inverse transform be determined. There is another theorem, called the *initial value theorem,* which is a companion to the final value theorem. The initial value theorem is not nearly as useful as the final value theorem. However, we present both theorems in the following subsections.

FINAL VALUE THEOREM.   The final value of a function of time, $f(t)$, is the steady-state value and is given by

$$\lim_{t \to \infty} f(t) = \lim_{s \to 0} sF(s) \qquad\qquad (19.44)$$

where $F(s)$ is the Laplace transform of $f(t)$. This assumes that

$$\lim_{t \to \infty} f(t)$$

exists.

INITIAL VALUE THEOREM.   The initial value of a function of time, *f(t),* is given by

$$\lim_{t \to 0} f(t) = \lim_{s \to \infty} sF(s) \qquad\qquad (19.45)$$

Mathematically, the time variable t is assumed to approach zero from a positive position.

EXAMPLE 19.11

Let us illustrate these two theorems by considering the three systems from Example 19.10. Recall that there were three different control units used on the process and that the input to each system was a step function of value 4.0.
   For the system that used the proportional controller, the solution in the s-domain was

$$y(s) = \frac{40}{s(s + 3)}$$

According to the final value theorem, the steady-state solution would be

$$y(t = \infty) = \lim_{s \to 0} \frac{40s}{s(s + 3)} = \frac{40}{0 + 3} = 13.33$$

The initial value theorem yields

$$y(t = 0+) = \lim_{s \to \infty} \frac{40s}{s(s + 3)} = 0$$

For the system using the integral control action

$$y(s) = \frac{40}{s(s + 1)^2}$$

Using the final value theorem,

$$y(t = \infty) = \lim_{s \to 0} \frac{40s}{s(s + 1)^2} = 40$$

From the initial value theorem,

$$y(t = 0+) = \lim_{s \to \infty} \frac{40s}{s(s + 1)^2} = 0$$

Finally, in the case of the derivative controller,

$$y(s) = \frac{20}{s + 1}$$

From the final value theorem,

$$y(t = \infty) = \lim_{s \to 0} \frac{20s}{s + 1} = 0$$

Using the initial value theorem yields

$$y(t = 0+) = \lim_{s \to \infty} \frac{20s}{s + 1} = 20$$

Each of these results agrees with the previous solutions obtained for y in the time domain.

Transient performance

A third characteristic of interest in linear systems analysis is the transient response of the system. There are several properties of the transient response that are of concern in systems analysis.

1. *Response time*. Time required for the system to reach steady state. One property that is sometimes used to characterize this time is called the *settling time*, defined as the time required for the output to achieve within 2% (sometimes 5% is used) of its final value when the system is subjected to a step input. It is generally desirable for the settling time to be as short as possible.

2. *Overshoot*. This response occurs when the output temporarily exceeds the desired steady-state value. The characteristic overshoot is shown in Figure 19.23(a).

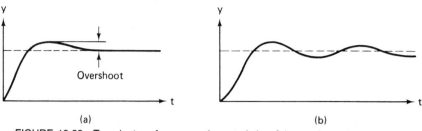

FIGURE 19.23   Transient performance characteristics: (a) overshoot; (b) oscillatory behavior.

Technically, overshoot is defined as the maximum deviation of the response above the steady-state value.

3. *Oscillatory behavior.* Although the system may be stable according to the previous stability criterion, its response may tend to oscillate for an extended period of time. This is considered undesirable. Oscillatory transient response is illustrated in Figure 19.23(b).

To investigate these and other characteristics of the transient behavior, a number of analysis techniques are available. First, the analyst might obtain the solution to the differential equations for the system. This is usually difficult for systems of higher than second order. To aid in solving such systems, the analog computer can be employed. In addition, digital computer programs that simulate the operations of the analog computer have been developed and are commercially available. These "analog simulators" possess many added features not available on most conventional analog computers. Examples of these features are on-off functions, multipliers, dividers, and other special functions. Hence, it is possible to obtain solutions to system models which are nonlinear. Analytical solutions to nonlinear models are often quite difficult to obtain.

It is cumbersome to develop the best design for a control system using the method of direct solution of the differential equation. Designing the system requires trying alternative controller actions (Section 19.4) and different system gains. Each alternative configuration leads to a new differential equation, and each equation must be solved.

Another technique for linear systems analysis which avoids much of this labor is the *root-locus method*. The root-locus method is a graphical technique that analyzes the roots of a system as a function of system gain. It does this without actually solving the differential equation. In addition, the method provides much insight into the stability characteristics and transient behavior of the system. We devote the final two sections of the chapter to a presentation of the root-locus method and how it can be used as an aid in process control design.

19.6   THE ROOT-LOCUS METHOD

In Section 19.2 the basic form of the feedback control system was described (Figure 19.11). The transfer function of this control system was defined as

$$\frac{y(s)}{x(s)} = \frac{G(s)}{1 + G(s)H(s)} \tag{19.46}$$

Even for complicated feedback systems, it is generally possible to reduce the block diagram to the basic form shown in Figure 19.11 so that the transfer function of the type given by Eq. (19.46) can be written.

The essence of the root-locus method is contained in the denominator of the right-hand side of Eq. (19.46). It can be shown that the roots of the characteristic equation for the system must satisfy the equation

$$1 + G(s)H(s) = 0 \tag{19.47}$$

This expression can be rewritten in the form

$$G(s)H(s) = -1 \tag{19.48}$$

where $G(s)H(s)$ is called the *open-loop transfer function*.

$G(s)H(s)$ is, of course, a function of the variable s. In the definition of the Laplace transform in Section 19.3, the variable s was defined as a complex number,

$$s = \sigma + j\omega$$

where σ is the real part of the complex number and ω the imaginary part. Any given value of s can be plotted in a coordinate system defined by the complex plane. In the complex plane, the abscissa is the σ-axis (real axis) and the ordinate is the $j\omega$-axis (imaginary axis).

Referring back to the open-loop transfer function $G(s)H(s)$, the values of s that cause $G(s)H(s) = 0$ are called the *zeros* of $G(s)H(s)$. Also, the values of s that cause $G(s)H(s) = \infty$ are called the *poles* of $G(s)H(s)$. The poles and zeros of a function $G(s)H(s)$ can be plotted in the complex plane on a *pole–zero map*. The location of a pole of $G(s)H(s)$ is indicated on the pole–zero map by a cross ($\times$), and the zero locations are denoted by a circle ($\bigcirc$).

In section 19.4, we showed how the forward transfer function $G(s)$ was composed of a controller unit $C(s)$ and a process $P(s)$ for a typical process control application. Common control actions include proportional control [$C(s) = K$], integral control [$C(s) = K/s$], and derivative control [$C(s) = Ks$], plus combinations of these types. All of these control actions contain a gain factor K. The best value of K must be determined in order to achieve the desired performance from the control system.

Since $G(s)H(s)$ is a function of $C(s)$ and since $C(s)$ contains the gain factor K, this means that the roots which satisfy Eq. (19.47) will vary depending on K. The locations of the roots in the complex plane will change as the value of K is changed. The locus of these roots as a function of the gain K is called the *root locus*, and the associated analysis to determine the loci is called the root-locus method.

How to plot the root locus

To determine the loci of roots for a given function $G(s)H(s)$, there are several rules to follow. We shall present the most fundamental of these rules, which permit the reader to plot the root locus for a limited variety of open-loop transfer functions.

1. *Magnitude requirement.* The basic expression of the magnitude requirement for the root locus is embodied in Eq. (19.48):

$$G(s)H(s) = -1$$

All points on the root locus must satisfy this requirement.

2. *Angular requirement.* An alternative way of expressing Eq. (19.48) in the complex plane is the following:

$$G(s)H(s) = 1\underline{/n180°} \qquad n = \pm 1, \pm 3, \pm 5, \ldots \qquad (19.49)$$

This is the angular requirement that must be satisfied by all points on the root locus. As we shall see later, this does not necessarily mean that all points on the root locus must be on the real axis (σ-axis).

An alternative way of expressing this angular requirement is

$$\sum \theta_z - \sum \theta_p = n180° \qquad n = \pm 1, \pm 3, \pm 5, \ldots \qquad (19.50)$$

where θ_z is the angle between any point on the root locus and the zero, and θ_p the angle made between any point on the root locus and the pole.

3. *Number of loci.* A root-locus plot will have a number of loci, or branches, equal to the number of poles of $G(s)H(s)$.

4. *Symmetry of the root-locus plot.* The root-locus plot will be symmetrical about the real axis (σ-axis).

5. *Starting points and end points.* The loci of roots begin at the poles of $G(s)H(s)$ and end at either the zeros of $G(s)H(s)$ or at infinity. The corresponding values of gain factor K are $K = 0$ at the poles of $G(s)H(s)$ and $K = \infty$ at the zeros of $G(s)H(s)$ or at infinity.

6. *Loci on the real axis.* Branches of the root locus lie on the real axis only to the left of an odd number of poles and/or zeros. For example, if poles existed at -2 and -8 and a zero was located at -5, the root locus would exist on the real axis from -2 to -5, and from -8 to ∞.

7. *Asymptotes.* The branches of the root locus tend toward a set of straight-line asymptotes which begin at a point on the real axis. This point is called the *center of asymptotes* and is symbolized by σ_c. In determining the root-locus plot, it is helpful to compute σ_c by means of the following formula:

$$\sigma_c = \frac{\sum P - \sum Z}{n_p - n_z} \tag{19.51}$$

where P and Z represent the numerical values of the poles and zeros, respectively, and n_p and n_z are the numbers of poles and zeros.

The number of asymptotes emanating from the center of asymptotes, σ_c, is given by the difference between n_p and n_z:

$$\text{number of asymptotes} = n_p - n_z \tag{19.52}$$

Finally, the asymptotes are oriented at different angles with respect to the real axis. The angles will be denoted by the symbol α, where

$$\alpha = \frac{n180°}{n_p - n_z} \qquad n = \pm 1,\ \pm 3,\ \pm 5,\ \dots \tag{19.53}$$

Note that the multiple possible values of n ($\pm 1,\ \pm 3,\ \pm 5,\ \dots$) may allow α to take on more than a single value. Each of the asymptotes has its own angle α.

As an illustration, consider

$$G(s)H(s) = \frac{K(s + 1)}{s(s + 2)(s + 5)}$$

There are three poles and one zero, so there are two asymptotes according to Eq. (19.52). By Eq. (19.51), the center of asymptotes is located at

$$\sigma_c = \frac{(0 - 2 - 5) - (-1)}{3 - 1} = -3.0$$

The angles made by the two asymptotes are given by Eq. (19.53):

$$\alpha = \frac{180}{2},\ \frac{3(180)}{2}$$

That is,

$$\alpha = 90° \text{ and } 270°$$

8. *Breakaway points.* A *breaking point* σ_b is a point on the real axis where two branches of the root locus leave the real axis. A *break-in point* is a point on the real axis where two branches arrive at the real axis. The problem of locating breakaway points and break-in points in the root locus is the same.

The location of a breakaway point (or a break-in point) is found by solving the following equation:

$$\sum^{n_p} \frac{1}{\sigma_b - P} = \sum^{n_z} \frac{1}{\sigma_b - Z} \tag{19.54}$$

The summation process is carried out for the n_p values of P and the n_z values of Z. To illustrate, consider the transfer function

$$G(s)H(s) = \frac{K}{s(s + 5)}$$

To find the breakaway point(s) we must solve for σ_b in Eq. (19.54), which, for this transfer function, is

$$\frac{1}{\sigma_b} + \frac{1}{\sigma_b + 5} = 0$$

The right-hand side is zero because there are no zeros in the transfer function.

$$\sigma_b + 5 + \sigma_b = 0$$

$$2\sigma_b = -5$$

$$\sigma_b = -2.5$$

The branches of the root locus leave the real axis at $\sigma_b = -2.5$.

9. *Departure and arrival angles.* The root locus leaves a complex pole with a certain angle, called the *departure angle*. The angle is measured against a line through the pole parallel to the real axis. Similarly, the root locus arrives at a complex zero with a certain angle, called the *arrival angle*. To plot the root locus accurately, it is necessary to determine the departure and/or arrival angles.

The departure angle for a pole or the arrival angle for a zero can be obtained by applying the angular requirement defined by Eq. (19.50) to a point very close to the pole under consideration. To illustrate, suppose that we wanted to determine the departure angles for the poles of

$$G(s)H(s) = \frac{K}{(s + 1 + j2)(s + 1 - j2)}$$

The poles are illustrated in Figure 19.24. Consider the pole at $-1 + j2$. Pick a sample point near the pole and determine the angles made between that point and all zeros and poles. The angle between the sample point and the pole at $-1 + j2$ is the unknown angle of departure. Since there are no zeros, the application of Eq. (19.50) reduces to

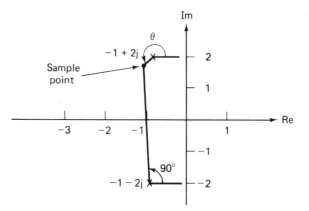

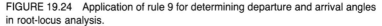

FIGURE 19.24 Application of rule 9 for determining departure and arrival angles in root-locus analysis.

$$\sum \theta_z - \sum \theta_p = 0 - (90° + \theta) = \pm 180°$$

$$90 + \theta = 180°$$

$$\theta = 90°$$

The root-locus branch departs from the upper pole with an angle of 90°. Similarly, the reader can show that the other root-locus branch departs from the lower pole with an angle of $-90°$. This result could also be obtained by symmetry (rule 4).

Several example problems will serve to demonstrate how the foregoing rules are used to construct the root locus for a given transfer function.

EXAMPLE 19.12

Construct the root-locus plot for the open-loop transfer function

$$G(s)H(s) = \frac{K}{(s + 1)(s + 3)(s + 6)}$$

Solution:

From rules 3 and 5, we know that there will be three branches to the root locus, that they will begin at -1, -3, and -6, and that they will all end at infinity. From rule 6, the root locus exists on the real axis between -1 and -3, and between -6 and $-\infty$. The asymptotes can be determined from rule 7. There are $n_p - n_z = 3 - 0 = 3$ asymptotes. Their center of asymptotes is located on the real axis at

$$\sigma_c = \frac{(-1 - 3 - 6) - (0)}{3 - 0} = -3.33$$

The angles made by the asymptotes are given by Eq. (19.53).

$$\alpha = \frac{180}{3}, \frac{3(180)}{3}, \frac{5(180)}{3}$$

$$\alpha = 60°, \ 180°, \ \text{and} \ 300°$$

The breakaway point can be found from Eq. (19.54) of rule 8.

$$\frac{1}{\sigma_b + 1} + \frac{1}{\sigma_b + 3} + \frac{1}{\sigma_b + 6} = 0$$

The solution yields a value of $\sigma_b = -1.88$. Since there are no complex poles or zeros, rule 9 does not apply.

The root locus for this example is plotted in Figure 19.25. Closed-loop poles start at $(-1, -3, -6)$ for $K = 0$ and follow the three branches as K approaches infinity.

EXAMPLE 19.13

Construct the root locus for the open-loop transfer function

$$G(s)H(s) = \frac{K(s + 1)}{(s + 2 - j)(s + 2 + j)}$$

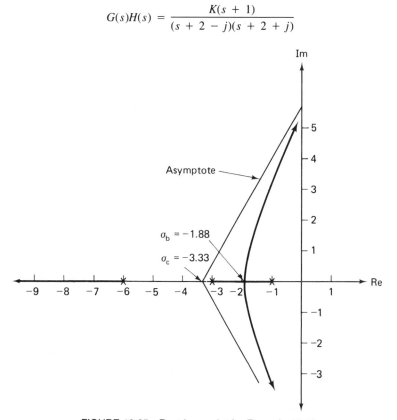

FIGURE 19.25 Root-locus plot for Example 19.12.

Solution:

There are two branches according to rule 3. One branch begins at the pole at $-2 + j$ and the other at $-2 - j$. The branches arrive at the real axis somewhere between -1 and $-\infty$, from rule 5. One branch goes to -1, the other to $-\infty$. To determine the break-in point, rule 8 must be used:

$$\frac{1}{\sigma_b + 2 - j} + \frac{1}{\sigma_b + 2 + j} = \frac{1}{\sigma_b + 1}$$

The solution is $\sigma_b = -2.414$.

Rule 9 provides the method for determining the departure angles from the two complex poles. Picking a sample point near the pole at $-2 + j$, Eq. (19.50) becomes the following:

$$\sum \theta_z - \sum \theta_p = 135 - (90 + \theta) = 180°$$

which leads to an angle of departure

$$\theta = -135° = 225°$$

The root-locus plot for this problem would appear approximately as shown in Figure 19.26.

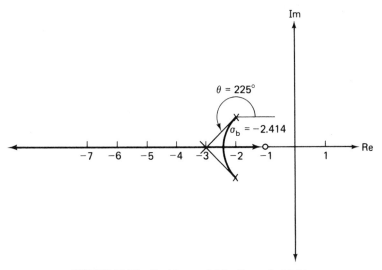

FIGURE 19.26   Root-locus plot for Example 19.13.

19.7 SYSTEM DESIGN

In the design of a process control system, the root-locus method can be used to decide on the system gain for achieving certain desired response characteristics. What makes this possible is that the root-locus plot shows the variation of the poles of the closed-loop system as a function of the gain K. In this section we demonstrate the relationships between the root locus and some of the important system specifications. Then we explore the ways in which the root-locus plot can be utilized to design the system to meet the desired specifications.

Root-locus relationships

There are a number of design objectives that are typically established for a feedback control system. The general criteria of system performance discussed in Section 19.5 are:

1. *Stability of the system*. The system must be stable for a variety of inputs.
2. *Steady-state performance*. The response of the system must achieve the desired value within a certain allowable error.
3. *Transient performance*. This criterion includes such specifications of the system as speed of response, the overshoot of the response, and the oscillatory behavior, which is determined by the system's damping characteristics.

These general criteria are related to many of the dynamic response characteristics we have considered in previous sections of this chapter. For example, to achieve a desired speed of the response, the time constants of the system would have to be set below some specified value. Or, to obtain a desired oscillatory response, the damping characteristics of the system would have to be specified. To ensure against instability, the roots of the system characteristic equation could not be allowed to become positive (positive real parts in the case of complex roots). All these characteristics can be interpreted from the root-locus plot.

First, consider system stability. For the linear feedback system to be stable, all roots of the characteristic equation must have negative values. On the root-locus plot, negative roots, or negative real parts of complex roots, must appear to the left of the imaginary axis. Hence, the regions of stability and instability for a given system are as illustrated in Figure 19.27. For the system to be stable, the gain factor K would have to be specified so that all the roots of the characteristic equation are on the left half of the complex plane.

The speed of response of the system is determined by the largest time constant appearing in the characteristic equation. The interpretation of the time constant τ was given in Section 19.1. On the root-locus plot, lines parallel to the imaginary axis represent lines that have constant $1/\tau$ value. Hence, they can be considered as lines of fixed time constant value. For example, suppose that the following specification were established for a given control system: the maximum allowable time constant must be less than or equal to $\frac{2}{3}$s. In terms of the root locus, this means that all the roots of the system must lie to the left of the line located at $\sigma = -\frac{3}{2} = -1.50$, as shown in Figure 19.27.

Two additional terms were defined in Section 19.1: the undamped natural frequency ω_n, and the damped natural frequency ω_d. Both of these characteristics relate to the oscillatory behavior of the system response. Lines that are parallel to the real axis, as shown in Figure 19.27, are lines of constant ω_d. Constant ω_n values are indicated in the root-locus plot by circles about the origin. This is also illustrated in Figure 19.27. Although

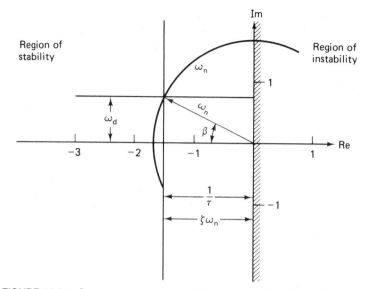

FIGURE 19.27   System design characteristics interpreted on the root-locus plot.

it is not desirable for a system to operate at its natural frequency since this implies no damping, it is nevertheless possible to graphically define the term in the complex plane.

One of the design specifications sometimes used for the damping characteristics of a system is the *damping ratio,* symbolized by the Greek letter ζ. It is defined as the ratio of the actual damping of the system to the damping that would occur if the system were critically damped. Referring back to Eq. (19.11), the damping of a second-order system is characterized by the damping coefficient K_d. In a critically damped second-order system,

$$K_d^2 = 4MK_s$$

or

$$K_d = 2\sqrt{MK_s}$$

Hence, the damping ratio can be defined mathematically as

$$\zeta = \frac{K_d}{2\sqrt{MK_s}} \tag{19.55}$$

When the damping ratio is equal to unity ($\zeta = 1.0$), the system is critically damped. When $\zeta < 1.0$, the system will exhibit an oscillatory response; and when $\zeta > 1.0$, the response will be overdamped and there will be no oscillations.

The damping ratio can be used to relate the damped natural frequency ω_d of the system to its undamped natural frequency ω_n.

$$\omega_d = \omega_n\sqrt{1 - \zeta^2} \qquad (19.56)$$

Also, the natural frequency can be related to the time constant by means of the damping ratio.

$$\frac{1}{\tau} = \zeta\omega_n \qquad (19.57)$$

Hence, vertical lines on the complex plane representing constant $1/\tau$ values also represent constant $\zeta\omega_n$ values.

In the use of the root locus, constant ζ values are displayed as straight lines radiating from the origin. This is shown in Figure 19.27. The angle that relates the inclination of the damping ratio is β, defined as

$$\cos\beta = \zeta \qquad (19.58)$$

It is clear that Eqs. (13.56) through (13.58) do not provide for values of ζ greater than unity.

Root-locus design approaches

The root-locus method provides for two principal approaches to the system design problem. The two approaches are:

1. *Gain factor compensation.* System design specifications can sometimes be satisfied by setting the gain factor to an appropriate value.
2. *Addition of compensating elements.* When gain factor compensation does not achieve the desired results, the appropriate use of compensating elements in the closed-loop system will often improve system performance.

Generally, these approaches can be applied by making the proper selection of the controller (the most common control actions were discussed in Section 13.4) and/or by setting the gain factor to an appropriate value.

Both of the methods will be discussed and illustrated by means of example problems in the following paragraphs.

GAIN FACTOR COMPENSATION.   This is the simpler approach. The objective is to acheive the desired system performance by selecting the best value of the gain factor K. The root-locus plot shows how the system's closed-loop poles vary as a function of K. Hence, the closed-loop poles can be located on the root-locus plot so as to achieve the required specifications by choosing the appropriate K value.

EXAMPLE 19.14

Let us consider the feedback system whose block diagram is presented in Figure 19.28. The closed-loop transfer function for this system is

$$\frac{y(s)}{x(s)} = \frac{G(s)}{1 + G(s)H(s)} = \frac{\dfrac{2K}{(s + 1)(s + 3)(s + 6)}}{1 + \dfrac{K}{(s + 1)(s + 3)(s + 6)}}$$

$$= \frac{2K}{(s + 1)(s + 3)(s + 6) + K}$$

$$= \frac{2K}{s^3 + 10s^2 + 27s + 18 + K}$$

The open-loop transfer function is given by

$$G(s)H(s) = \frac{K}{(s + 1)(s + 3)(s + 6)}$$

The reader may recall that this was the open-loop transfer function for Example 19.12 for which the root-locus plot was given in Figure 19.25.

The specifications for this system are that the maximum value of time constant is $\tau = 0.80$ s (we want a relatively fast response from the system). It is also specified that there is to be no oscillation in the response.

Solution:

The time constant specification of $\tau = 0.80$ means that $1/\tau = 1.25$. To satisfy the design specification, the roots of the characteristic equation must lie on the root-locus plot to the left of $\sigma = -1.25$. Since a nonoscillatory response is required, the roots must all lie on the real axis. From the root-locus plot of Figure 19.25, the breakaway point lies at a value of $\sigma_b = -1.88$. Accordingly, the first root that satisfies the specifications lies on the real axis somewhere in the range $\sigma = -1.25$ to $\sigma_b = -1.88$. The second root lies between $\sigma_b = -1.88$ and $\sigma = -3.0$. And the third root will be on the real axis to the left of the pole at $\sigma = -6.0$.

Let us strive for the most favorable response in terms of speed of response. Our selection of the first root would be a value of $s = -1.88$ so as to minimize the time constant. The time

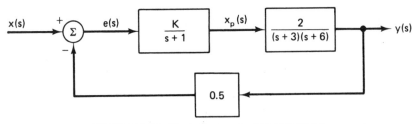

FIGURE 19.28   Block diagram for Example 19.14.

constant $\tau = 1/1.88 = 0.53$ s. To determine the value of K that corresponds to $s_1 = -1.88$, we make use of the magnitude requirement, Eq. (19.48):

$$G(s)H(s) = -1$$

$$\frac{K}{(s_1 + 1)(s_1 + 3)(s_1 + 6)} = -1$$

$$K = -(s_1 + 1)(s_1 + 3)(s_1 + 6)$$

$$= -(-1.88 + 1)(-1.88 + 3)(-1.88 + 6)$$

$$= -(-0.88)(1.12)(4.12)$$

$$= 4.06$$

The second root also lies at the breakaway point $s_2 = -1.88$. The third root has a value to the left of the pole at $\sigma = -6.0$, and must also satisfy the foregoing magnitude requirement when $K = 4.06$:

$$\frac{K}{(s_3 + 1)(s_3 + 3)(s_3 + 6)} = -1$$

$$(s_3 + 1)(s_3 + 3)(s_3 + 6) = -4.06$$

Solving for s_3, we obtain a value for the third root of $s_3 = -6.24$.

Thus, the root-locus analysis has provided a value of $K = 4.06$, which satisfies the design requirements and gives a maximum time constant of $\tau_1 = 0.53$ s, well below the desired 0.80 s specification. The second time constant is also $\tau_2 = 0.53$ s, since both roots were located at the breakaway point. And the third time constant $\tau_3 = 1/6.24 = 0.16$ s.

It would be of instructional value to the reader to relate this solution back to the closed-loop system. Let us determine the response of the system to a step input $x = 5$. The closed-loop transfer function is

$$\frac{y(s)}{x(s)} = \frac{8.12}{s^3 + 10s^2 + 27s + 22.06}$$

We have already determined the roots of the denominator:

$$\frac{y(s)}{x(s)} = \frac{8.12}{(s + 1.88)^2 (s + 6.24)}$$

Multiplying the transfer function by the Laplace transform of the input gives the Laplace transform of the output, $y(s)$:

$$y(s) = \frac{5(8.12)}{s(s + 1.88)^2(s + 6.24)}$$

Using the method of partial fraction expansion, we obtain

$$Y(s) = \frac{C_1}{s} + \frac{C_2}{(s + 1.88)^2} + \frac{C_3}{s + 1.88} + \frac{C_4}{s + 6.24}$$

$$= \frac{1.84}{s} - \frac{4.95}{(s + 1.88)^2} - \frac{1.50}{s + 1.88} - \frac{0.34}{s + 6.24}$$

Table 19.1 provides the inverse transforms to obtain $y(t)$:

$$y(t) = 1.84 - 4.95te^{-1.88t} - 1.50e^{-1.88t} - 0.34e^{-6.24t}$$

EXAMPLE 19.15

Suppose in Example 19.14 that the minimum possible setting of the gain factor was $K = 10$. What will be the effect of this limitation on system performance? Will the system be stable if $K = 10$?

Solution:

According to root-locus rule number 5, the value of K increases as we move farther away from the poles of the root-locus plot. When the value of K was 4.06, two of the roots of the characteristic equation were located at the breakaway point of the root locus. With a value of $K = 10.0$, these two roots will be located on the root locus away from the real axis.

To determine the value of these roots, start with the magnitude requirement, which is an expression of the system characteristic equation,

$$\frac{10}{(s + 1)(s + 3)(s + 6)} = -1$$

or

$$s^3 + 10^2 + 27s + 28 = 0$$

Solving for the roots,

$$s_1 = -1.742 + 1.123j$$

$$s_2 = -1.742 - 1.123j$$

$$s_3 = -6.515$$

The approximate positions can be located in the root-locus plot of Figure 19.25.

Although we will not go through the calculations to determine the response to the same step input used in Example 19.14, we can tell from the roots of the characteristic equation that the response will be oscillatory and slower than in the previous example. The nature of this response is determined by roots s_1 and s_2, which are complex. The imaginary part, $\pm 1.123j$, gives the root its oscillatory behavior while the real part, -1.742, determines the speed of response. The time constant associated with these roots is $\tau = 1/1.742 = 0.57$ s. The time constant associated with root s_3 is $1/6.515 = 0.15$ s.

We can determine the damped natural frequency from the root-locus plot of Figure 19.25. The vertical distance of roots s_1 and s_2 above and below the real axis gives the value of $\omega_d = 1.123$

rad/s. The undamped natural frequency associated with roots s_1 and s_2 is given by the distance between the origin and either of these two points.

$$\omega_n = \sqrt{(1.742)^2 + (1.123)^2} = 2.07 \text{ rad/s}$$

From Eq. (19.56) we can determine the damping ratio for the system:

$$1.123 = 2.07 \sqrt{1 - \zeta^2}$$
$$\zeta = 0.84$$

We can utilize Eq. (19.57) as a check on this value:

$$1.742 = \zeta(2.07)$$
$$\zeta = 0.84$$

Because of the negative real parts of the complex roots s_1 and s_2 and because s_3 is negative and real, the system is stable.

EXAMPLE 19.16

For the same basic system of the two preceding examples, let us determine the limiting gain factor K for which stability will be maintained.

Solution:

We examine the points at which the two root-locus branches cross the imaginary axis. These points will correspond to the two characteristic equation roots of the form

$$s_1, s_2 = 0 \pm j\omega$$

Therefore, we can write two equations with the two unknowns K and ω as follows:

$$(-j\omega)^3 + 10(-j\omega)^2 + 27(-j\omega) + 18 + K = 0$$

and

$$(j\omega)^3 + 10(j\omega)^2 + 27(j\omega) + 18 + K = 0$$

Solving for the two unknowns, we obtain

$$\omega = 5.196$$
$$K = 252$$

Hence, the first two roots will be

$$s_1 = +5.196j$$
$$s_2 = -5.196j$$

The third root will be real and negative and will have a value that satisfies

$$s_3^3 + 10s_3^2 + 27s_3 + (18 + 252) = 0$$

That value is

$$s_3 = -10.0$$

With a gain factor of $K = 252$, the response of the system to a step input will continually oscillate. This results from roots s_1 and s_2, which contain no negative real portions to make the response decay with time.

ADDITION OF COMPENSATING ELEMENTS.   It may not be possible to meet system specifications simply through adjustment of the gain factor K. When this is the case, the desired performance can sometimes be obtained by the addition of a compensating element to the closed-loop system. The purpose of this new element is to change the pole–zero configuration of the root locus into a more desirable form. Basically, the compensating element possesses a transfer function that changes the system transfer function in a beneficial way.

Although there are a number of different objectives in applying compensating elements, we will consider just one type in this survey: cancellation compensation. In this arrangement, the purpose of the compensating element is to cancel one or more of the poles (or zeros) of the existing system. In essence, the new element replaces an undesirable pole (or zero) with a desirable one. This has the consequence of improving overall system performance. Let us examine a hypothetical example to illustrate this general approach.

EXAMPLE 19.17

Figure 19.29 shows the block diagram for a system that must have a time constant of 0.25 min or less (time units in this example are minutes, not seconds).

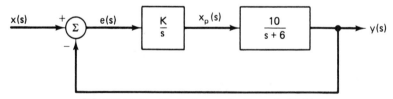

FIGURE 19.29   Block diagram for Example 19.17.

Solution:

The root-locus plot for the system is presented in Figure 19.30. It can be seen that the minimum possible time constant for this system is $\tau = 0.333$ min, which corresponds to the breakaway point $\sigma_b = -3.0$.

To meet system specifications, a compensating element must be added to the system to

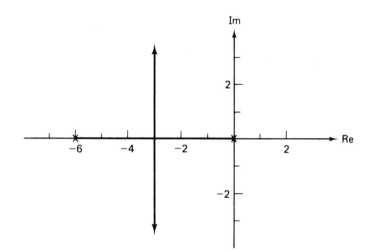

FIGURE 19.30   Root-locus plot for Figure 19.29 of Example 19.17.

change the root-locus plot into a more desirable form. Consider the addition of the following compensating element, as illustrated in Figure 19.31:

$$\frac{s}{s + 2}$$

This new element would change the open-loop transfer function of the system from

$$G(s)H(s) = \frac{10K}{s(s + 6)}$$

into

$$G(s)H(s) = \frac{10K}{s(s + 6)} \frac{s}{s + 2} = \frac{10K}{(s + 6)(s + 2)}$$

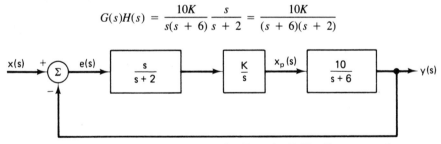

FIGURE 19.31   Revised block diagram for Example 19.17 with compensating element added.

The corresponding root-locus plot would be shifted to the left, as illustrated in Figure 19.32. In this case, a time constant of $\tau = 0.25$ min is possible if the roots of the characteristic equation are both located at $s = -4.0$. The corresponding value of the gain factor can be determined from the magnitude requirement to be $K = 0.4$.

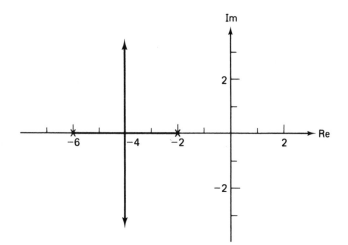

FIGURE 19.32 New root-locus plot for revised block diagram shown in Figure 19.31 of Example 19.17.

REFERENCES

[1] D'Azzo, J. J., and C. H. Houpis, *Linear Control System Analysis and Synthesis,* 2nd Ed., McGraw-Hill Book Company, New York, 1981.

[2] Dorf, R. C., *Modern Control Systems* 2nd ed., Addison-Wesley Publishing Company, Inc., Reading, Mass., 1974.

[3] Gibson, J. E., *Nonlinear Automatic Control,* McGraw-Hill Book Company, New York, 1963.

[4] Harrison, H. L., and J. G. Bollinger, *Introduction to Automatic Controls,* 2nd Ed., Harper & Row Publishers, Inc., New York, 1969.

[5] Jaeschke, J. R., R. D. Zimmerly, and S. M. Wu, "Automatic Cutting Tool Temperature Control," *International Journal of Machine Tool Design Research,* Vol. 7, 1967, pp. 465–475.

[6] Kuo, B. C., *Automatic Control Systems,* 4th ed., Prentice-Hall, Inc., Englewood Cliffs, N.J., 1982.

[7] Raven, F. H., *Automatic Control Engineering,* 3rd ed., McGraw-Hill Book Company, New York, 1978.

PROBLEMS

19.1. A mechanical measuring device used in a certain manufacturing process is believed to possess the response characteristics of a first-order system. That is, the mathematical model for the measuring device is a first-order linear differential equation. Data have been collected over a 20-s period at 5-s intervals on the input to the device, x, the output, y, and the rate of change of the output, dy/dt:

Time (s)	x	y	dy/dt
0	5.3	2.0	0.26
5	5.7	2.2	0.26
10	5.9	2.4	0.22
15	5.4	2.6	0.04
20	4.9	2.5	-0.02

From these data, determine the values of the parameters in the model. Specifically, for the differential equation:

$$A \frac{dy}{dt} + By = x$$

determine the values of A and B that are consistent with these data.

19.2. Solve the differential equation determined in Problem 19.1 for a step input $x = 1.0$ which starts at time $t = 0$. Assume that $y = 0$ at $t = 0$. What is the time constant for the system?

19.3. The speed control unit for operating the spindle on a certain machine tool is being studied to determine its response characteristics. As part of the study, measurements were made of the actual spindle speed in revolutions per second. The input to the control unit is voltage. Given in the table are the collected data when the speed control unit was subjected to a step input of 20 V at time $t = 0$.

Time (s)	Input voltage (V)	Output-spindle speed (rev/s)
0	20	0
0.5	20	3.32
1.0	20	5.23
1.5	20	6.05
2.0	20	6.25
2.5	20	6.21
3.0	20	6.12
4.0	20	6.01
5.0	20	5.99
10.0	20	6.00

(a) Plot the data on a piece of graph paper.

(b) Characterize the response as probably falling into which one of the following categories: (1) first order; (2) second order, no damping; (3) second order, underdamped; (4) second order, critically damped; (5) second order, overdamped.

19.4. For the data of Problem 19.3, determine the appropriate form of the differential equation that could be used as a mathematical model to describe the operation of the speed control unit. What additional data would you need to determine the parameter values in the differential equation?

19.5. Reformulate your answer to Problem 19.2 as a transfer function using the s-differential operator notation.

19.6. Reformulate your general answer to Problem 19.4 as a transfer function using the s-differential operator notation.

19.7. A mechanical device used in a forge press operation has the following differential equation of motion:

$$16.3 \frac{d^2y}{dt^2} + 87.5 \frac{dy}{dt} + 221y = F$$

where F is the forcing function and y represents the response of the device.

(a) Determine the roots of the characteristic equation. Will the response be oscillatory?

(b) Determine the damped natural frequency ω_d.

19.8. Rewrite the following differential equations as transfer functions, where x represents the input and y represents the output of the transfer function:

(a) $5 \frac{dy}{dt} = 2x$

(b) $3 \frac{dy}{dt} + 7y = x$

(c) $\frac{d^2y}{dt^2} + 3 \frac{dy}{dt} + 2.5y = 1.2x$

(d) $\frac{d^2y}{dt^2} + 2 \frac{dy}{dt} + 8y = \frac{dx}{dt} + 3x$

19.9. For the following set of equations, change each equation into its corresponding s-operator equation; then construct the block diagram that relates the three equations.

$$\frac{dz}{dt} + 2z = w$$

$$\frac{dy}{dt} + 7y = 3z$$

$$w = x - 0.3y$$

19.10. Construct the block diagram that combines the following set of equations expressed in the s-notation:

$$w = x - y$$

$$v = w - z$$

$$z(s + 6) = v(s + 2)$$

$$y(s^2 + 6s + 8) = z$$

Let x be the input to the system and y be the output.

19.11. Reduce the block diagrams in Figure P19.11 to a simple transfer function by means of block diagram algebra.

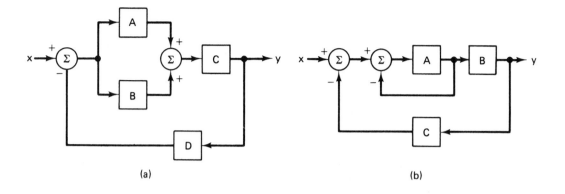

(a) (b)

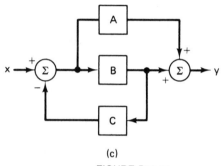

(c)

FIGURE P19.11

19.12. Reduce each of the block diagrams in Figure P19.12 into a single transfer function by means of block diagram algebra.

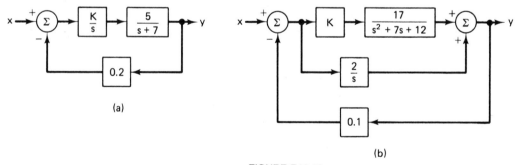

(a)

(b)

FIGURE P19.12

19.13. Reduce the block diagram determined in Problem 19.9 into a single transfer function with x = input and y = output.

19.14. Reduce the block diagram determined in Problem 19.10 into a single transfer function with x = input and y = output. Express this transfer function as a differential equation.

19.15. The following set of equations expresses the relationships that exist for a certain production process:

$$u = x - w$$

$$\frac{Ku}{s} + z = v$$

$$15v = y(s + 6)$$

$$w(s + 8) = 0.3y$$

The two inputs to the process are x and z. The variable y is the process output. Variables u, v, and w are internal to the process.
(a) Construct the overall block diagram for the production process.
(b) Determine the transfer function for input x and output y.
(c) Determine the transfer function for input z and output y.

19.16. In Problem 19.15, if the input x is a step input of value $x = 3.0$ and the input z is a sine-wave function $z = 2 \sin 5t$, write the Laplace transform of the output y. Assume that the initial conditions are zero.

19.17. Given the initial conditions that y and its derivatives are all zero at $t = 0$, write the Laplace transform of the following differential equations:

(a) $\dfrac{d^2y}{dt^2} + 5\dfrac{dy}{dt} + 2y = 8$

(b) $2\dfrac{dy}{dt} + 7y = 3 \sin 3t$

(c) $\dfrac{d^2y}{dt^2} + 8y = 5 \cos t$

(d) $\dfrac{d^2y}{dt^2} + 6\dfrac{dy}{dt} + 8y = 2t$

(e) $7\dfrac{dy}{dt} + 3y = 5 + 2t$

19.18. Expand the following functions of s into partial fractions by the methods of Section 19.3.

(a) $y(s) = \dfrac{3}{s^2 + 7s + 10}$

(b) $y(s) = \dfrac{2s + 1}{s(s^2 + 4s + 3)}$

(c) $y(s) = \dfrac{5s}{s^2 + 8s}$

19.19. Expand the following functions of s into partial fractions by the method of Section 19.3.

(a) $y(s) = \dfrac{s + 1}{(s^2 + 4s + 4)}$

(b) $y(s) = \dfrac{4}{s^2(s + 7)}$

19.20. Find the inverse transform by the methods of Section 19.3 for the following:

(a) $y(s) = \dfrac{1}{s + 1} + \dfrac{2}{s + 3} - \dfrac{1}{s + 2}$

(b) $y(s) = \dfrac{2}{s} + \dfrac{0.1}{s^2} + \dfrac{2}{s + 5}$

(c) $y(s) = \dfrac{5}{s} + \dfrac{2}{s^2 + 4}$

(d) $y(s) = \dfrac{6}{s + 5} + \dfrac{3}{(s + 2)^2}$

(e) $y(s) = \dfrac{3}{s} + \dfrac{2s}{s^2 + 3} - \dfrac{1}{s^2 + 6s + 9}$

19.21. Find the inverse transforms for parts (a) through (c) of Problem 19.18.

19.22. Find the inverse transforms for parts (a) and (b) of Problem 19.19.

19.23. Given the initial conditions $y = 3$ and $dy/dt = 0$ at $t = 0$, write the Laplace transform of the following differential equation:

$$\frac{dy}{dt} + 3y = 4$$

Solve the differential equation by using the inverse transform method.

19.24 Given the initial conditions $y = 0$, $dy/dt = 0$, and $d^2y/dt^2 = 0$, write the Laplace transform of the following differential equation:

$$2\frac{d^2y}{dt^2} + 10\frac{dy}{dt} + 12.5y = 16$$

Solve the differential equation by using the inverse transform method.

19.25. Use the initial value theorem and the final value theorem to determine the values of y at time $t = 0$ and $t = \infty$, respectively, for the following:

(a) $y(s) = \dfrac{5}{s(s + 5)}$

(b) $y(s) = \dfrac{13}{s^2 + 18}$

(c) $y(s) = \dfrac{s + 2}{s(s^2 + 9s + 14)}$

19.26. Consider the process control situation illustrated in Figure 19.21 except that the process has the following transfer function:

$$\frac{4}{s + 5}$$

The feedback transfer function is a proportional gain of 0.2. It is desired to achieve a steady-state response of $y = 50$ when the input x is a step function of value $x = 20$ by selecting the appropriate gain factor K using a proportional control $C(s) = K$. Determine the appropriate value of K that will achieve the desired response value. Plot the response as a function of time on a piece of graph paper.

19.27. Construct the root-locus plots for each of the following open-loop transfer functions:

(a) $G(s)H(s) = \dfrac{K}{(s + 2)(s + 8)}$

(b) $G(s)H(s) = \dfrac{K}{s(s + 2)(s + 8)}$

(c) $G(s)H(s) = \dfrac{K(s + 3)}{s^2(s + 7)}$

(d) $G(s)H(s) = \dfrac{K}{s(s + 1)(s + 3)(s + 4)}$

19.28. Construct the root-locus plots for each of the following open-loop transfer functions:

(a) $G(s)H(s) = \dfrac{K}{(s + 1)(s^2 + 4s + 5)}$

(b) $G(s)H(s) = \dfrac{5K(s + 1)}{s^3 + 5s^2 + 6s}$

19.29. For each of the root-locus plots in Problem 19.27, determine the value of K at which the system becomes unstable if the root-locus plot indicates that instability is possible.

19.30. Assume that the block diagram in Figure P19.30 represents the model for some industrial process (time units are seconds):
(a) Determine the open-loop transfer function for this system.
(b) Determine the closed-loop transfer function for this system.
(c) Plot the root locus for this system.

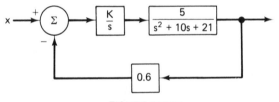

FIGURE P19.30

19.31. Assume that the block diagram in Figure P19.31 represents the model for some industrial process:
(a) Determine the open-loop transfer function for this system.
(b) Determine the closed-loop transfer function for this system.
(c) Plot the root locus.

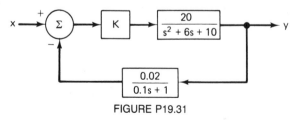

FIGURE P19.31

19.32. Determine the value of K at which the system in Problem 19.30 will become unstable. Also, determine the largest possible value of K for which the system will have no complex roots.

19.33. Consider the industrial process of Problem 19.30. The specifications on this system are that the maximum value of the time constant is to be $\tau = 1.5$ s and that there is to be no oscillation in the response. Is this performance possible to achieve in this system and, if so, what is the corresponding value of the gain factor K?

19.34. Suppose in Problem 19.33 that the minimum possible setting of the gain factor is $K = 4$. What will be the effect of this limitation on system performance? Will the system response be oscillatory if $K = 4$?

19.35. In Example 19.14, the steady-state response for a step input of $x = 5.0$ is $y = 1.84$. Suppose that the desired value of the output is $y = 3.0$.
   (a) Would you recommend that this be achieved by increasing the value of K in the solution to this sample problem? If not, why not?
   (b) How could the desired output of $y = 3.0$ be achieved?

19.36. Consider the industrial process of Problem 19.31. The specification for the system is that the maximum value of the time constant is to be $\tau = 0.40$ s. Determine the value of the gain factor K that achieves this response. Determine the damping ratio for the system. Compute the damped natural frequency for this system.

19.37. Assume that the block diagram in Figure P19.37 represents the model for a certain industrial process.

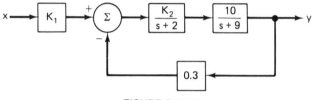

FIGURE P19.37

   (a) Determine the value of the gain factor K_2 that achieves a minimum time constant of $\tau = 0.25$ s. Use the root-locus method.
   (b) It is desired for the steady-state response to be $y = 5.0$ when the input is a step function $x = 2.0$. Determine the value of the gain factor K_1 which achieves this steady-state response.
   (c) Write the equation that expresses y as a function of time when x is a step input of value $x = 2.0$.

chapter 20

Optimal Control

In addition to linear feedback controls, other types of strategies are frequently used in modern industrial control systems. These other strategies are usually aimed at optimizing the performance of the process, in which some economic criterion is used as the measure of performance. In this chapter we examine several of these control strategies:

1. Steady-state optimal control
2. Adaptive control
3. On-line search strategies

To provide a framework for studying these control schemes, let us first consider the technological structure that typifies nearly all manufacturing processes.

20.1 STRUCTURAL MODEL OF A MANUFACTURING PROCESS

Most production operations are characterized by a multiplicity of dynamically interacting process variables. These variables can be cataloged into two basic types, input and output variables. However, there are different kinds of input variables and the same is true for output variables.

First, consider how input variables might be classified:

1. *Controllable input variables*. These are sometimes called *manipulative variables,* because they can be changed or controlled during the process. In a machining operation, it is technologically possible to make adjustments in speed and feed during the operation. Not all machine tools possess this capability. In a chemical process, the controllable input variables may include flow rates, temperature settings, and so on.

2. *Uncontrollable input variables*. Variables that change during the operation but which cannot be manipulated are defined as uncontrollable input variables. In chemical processing, the starting raw chemicals may be an uncontrollable input variable for which compensation must be made during the process. In machining, examples include tool sharpness, work-material hardness, and workpiece geometry. The reader may argue that some of these examples can be controlled. However, from a control systems viewpoint, it is more appropriate to consider them as uncontrollable during the process.

3. *Fixed variables*. A third category of input to the process is the fixed variable. These are conditions of the setup, such as tool geometry and workholding device, which can be changed between operations but not during the operation. Fixed inputs for a continuous chemical process would be tank size, number of trays in a distillation column, and other factors that are established by the equipment configuration.

It should be evident to the reader that the classification of variables will be different for different processes. For example, feed rate may be a controllable variable for one machine tool and a fixed variable for another machine tool. It depends on the capability of the machine.

The other major type of variable in a manufacturing process is the output variable. It is convenient to divide output variables into two types:

1. *Measurable output variables*. The defining characteristic of this first type is that it can be measured on-line during the process. Examples in a machining operation include tool forces, vibration, power, and temperature. Other output variables that cannot be measured on-line, at least not with current sensor technology, are surface finish and tool wear.

2. *Performance evaluation variables*. These are the measures of overall process performance and are usually linked to either the economics of the process or the quality of the product manufactured. Examples of performance evaluation variables in machining are: cost per unit produced, production rate, some given measure of product quality such as surface finish or part size, and so on. Examples in the continuous-process industries include yield, cost per gallon, and cost per ton.

The structural relationships between these different input and output variables are illustrated in Figure 20.1. The measurable output variables are determined by the input variables. The performance of the process, as indicated by the performance evaluation

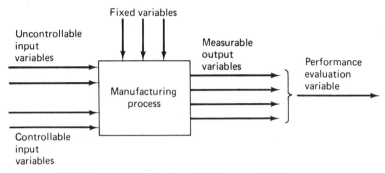

FIGURE 20.1   Structural model of a manufacturing process.

variable, is determined by the measurable output variables. To assess process performance, the performance evaluation variable must be calculated from measurements taken on the output variables.

Within the structural model of a manufacturing process, there are usually constraints or limits on the values the variables can assume. For example, there are practical limits on the rate of flow through a pipe of a given diameter, there is a maximum possible spindle speed for a given machine tool, and there are limits on the forces that can be endured by the moving elements of a piece of processing equipment. These constraints impose limits on the achievement of optimal performance in a manufacturing process.

20.2   STEADY-STATE OPTIMAL CONTROL

The term *optimal control* refers to a large class of control problems. We shall limit its meaning in this discussion to systems whose configuration is open-loop. That is, there is no feedback of data about the process performance used to implement the control strategy. Instead, there is sufficient knowledge about the process, and sufficient reliance that the process will behave in a predictable manner, that performance feedback is assumed to be unnecessary.

The solution to the open-loop optimal control problem must be based on the following well-defined attributes of the process or system:

1. *Performance evaluation variable.* This measure of system performance is also called the objective function, index of performance, or figure of merit. Basically, it represents the overall indicator of process performance that we desire to optimize by solving the optimal control problem. Among the performance objectives typically used in optimal control are cost minimization, profit maximization, production-rate maximization, quality optimization, least-squares-error minimization, and process-yield maximization. These objectives are general and must be specified to suit the particular application.

2. *Mathematical model of the process.* The relationships between the input variables and the objective function (measure of process performance) must be mathematically

defined. The model is assumed to be valid throughout the operation of the process. That is, there are no disturbances that might affect the final result of the optimization procedure. This is why we refer to the problem as steady-state optimal control. The mathematical model of the process may include constraints on some or all of the variables. These constraints limit the allowable region within which the objective function can be optimized.

With these two attributes of the process defined, the solution of the optimal control problem consists of determining the values of the input variables that optimize the objective function. To accomplish this task, a great variety of optimization techniques are available to solve the steady-state optimal control problem. The following list of optimization techniques demonstrates the wide variety of methods that are available. Suitable references to each technique are cited:

> Differential calculus [19]
>
> Lagrange multiplier technique [19]
>
> Linear programming [16,17]
>
> Geometric programming [19]
>
> Dynamic programming [2]
>
> Calculus of variations [6]
>
> The optimum principle [19]

These approaches have all been applied to problems in the class we are calling steady-state optimal control problems. Some of the approaches can be applied manually. Others are more appropriate for computer solution when employed to solve problems of practical size.

It is not feasible (nor is it within the scope of this book) to present all of these techniques in this section. The objective of our discussion on steady-state optimal control is to survey some of the methods listed to demonstrate the general problem area. The interested reader could devote a career to the study of optimization techniques. We have only a few pages to devote.

Use of differential calculus

The steady-state optimal control problem and its solution can be demonstrated by means of the differential calculus. The problem is to solve some function for its maximum or minimum value. Suppose that z is the function of x we wish to maximize.

$$z = f(x) \tag{20.1}$$

It is known that $f(x)$ possesses a maximum and that the function is unimodal—that is, it has but a single peak. Then, to find the value of x that maximizes z, take the partial derivative of z with respect to x and set the derivative equal to zero.

$$\frac{dz}{dx} = 0 \tag{20.2}$$

Solve Eq. (20.2) for x. The application to process control can be illustrated by an example. A minimization problem will be used rather than one in maximization, as above.

EXAMPLE 20.1

The process of interest is shown in Figure 20.2 as a very elementary block diagram. The transfer function for the process is

$$\frac{y(s)}{x(s)} = \frac{50}{s + 10} = \frac{5}{0.1s + 1}$$

which shows that the dynamics of the process are represented by a first-order lag.

The objective function for this process is to minimize z, where z is a least-squares-error function. That is, the objective is to

$$\text{minimize } z = (Y - y)^2$$

where z = objective function

y = output variable of the process

Y = desired steady-state value of y, which we will assume is 20; $Y = 20$

Note that the two attributes of the steady-state optimal control problem are present: the measure of system performance, z, and the mathematical model of the process expressed as the transfer function, $y(s)/x(s)$.

Our concern is with the steady-state solution, so we will use an input x to the process which has a constant value. To achieve this constant value, we will assume a step function input. Hence,

$$x(s) = \frac{x}{s}$$

where x becomes the unknown constant value. Hence,

$$y(s) = \frac{5x}{s(0.1s + 1)}$$

According to the final value theorem [Eq. (19.44)], the steady-state value of y is

$$y(t = \infty) = \lim_{s \to 0} \frac{5xs}{s(0.1s + 1)} = 5x$$

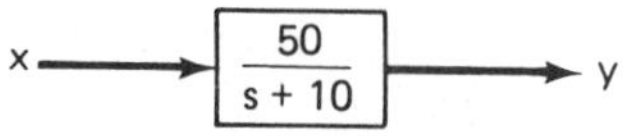

FIGURE 20.2   Process of Example 20.1.

The objective is to

$$\text{minimize } z = (20 - y)^2$$

$$z = (20 - 5x)^2$$

$$z = 400 - 200x + 25x^2$$

This is the specific function of x that was expressed in general form as Eq. (20.1). To find the value of x that minimizes z, Eq. (20.2), is applied.

$$\frac{dz}{dx} = 0 - 200 + 2(25)x = 0$$

$$50x = 200$$

$$x = 4$$

Since x is the independent input variable, we can now set $x = 4$ and thereby minimize the performance criterion. Note that we have done so in an open-loop fashion (no feedback information about y was used in setting $x = 4$).

Stripping the problem to its bare essentials, we have a steady-state process model

$$y = 5x$$

and an objective to make $y = 20$. Given these two pieces of information, it seems quite obvious that x must equal 4. Perhaps the reader perceived this during the statement of the problem. If so, Example 20.1 may have seemed like a rather involved procedure to determine an answer that was obvious from the start. Most optimal control problems are not as simple as this one. What we have attempted to demonstrate here is the general structure of the optimal control problem, not its many potential complexities.

EXAMPLE 20.2

For a second illustration, still using the differential calculus, we borrow an example problem from the book on optimization by Wilde and Beightler [19]. The example is a hypothetical manufacturing plant that produces a certain chemical by means of the five-stage process shown in Figure 20.3. Raw-material gases are mixed with recycled unreacted gases and brought up to operating pressure

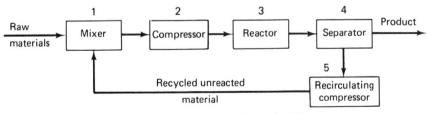

FIGURE 20.3   Process of Example 20.2.

in a compressor. The mixture passes through a reactor, where the chemical product is produced, and is then isolated in the separator stage. The unreacted gases are then returned to the mixing stage by a recirculating compressor. The two variables that control the performance of the process are:

$$x_1 = \text{operating pressure (measured in atmospheres)}$$
$$\text{achieved in the second stage}$$

$$x_2 = \text{recycle ratio, which is the ratio of recirculated}$$
$$\text{unreacted material to raw material entering the process}$$

In the operation of this plant the objective is to minimize the total annual operating cost z. This cost includes direct operating expenses, plant and equipment capital costs, and so on. The influence of x_1 and x_2 on this annual cost can be summarized in the following relationship:

$$z = 1000x_1 + \frac{4(10^9)}{x_1 x_2} + 2.5(10^5)x_2$$

Of course, the annual cost would also be determined by the amount of raw materials, but it is assumed that the plant will produce a certain quantity of final product, so the quantity of raw materials is predetermined.

The differential calculus approach for the two variable process involves taking the partial derivatives of the objective function z with respect to x_1 and x_2 and setting them equal to zero. This provides two equations in two unknowns, x_1 and x_2, which can be solved to find the optimum set of operating conditions.

$$\frac{\partial z}{\partial x_1} = 1000 - \frac{4(10^9)}{x_1^2 x_2} = 0$$

$$\frac{\partial z}{\partial x_2} = -\frac{4(10^9)}{x_1 x_2^2} + 2.5(10^5) = 0$$

Solution of the two equations gives

$$x_1 = 1000 \quad \text{and} \quad x_2 = 4$$

If this were a real problem in process control, the difficult part of its solution would not be in determining the optimal values of the input variables. The difficulty would lie in developing the underlying mathematical model for the process. This difficulty is a common one in process control situations. Great effort and expense are often required to acquire the data necessary to derive an accurate model of a given process.

Linear programming

We conclude the discussion of steady-state optimal control with a technique that is usually associated with the field of operations research rather than control systems. However, the linear programming approach is ideal for large-scale systems where the problem is to allocate limited resources in the pursuit of some linear objective function. The technique can be used either for maximization problems or minimization problems.

All linear programming problems possess the following characteristics:

1. *Linear objective function.* The objective in the problem is to maximize or minimize some linear objective function

$$z = a_1x_1 + a_2x_2 + \ldots + a_nx_n \tag{20.3}$$

2. *Linear constraints.* The optimization of the objective function is constrained by limited resources or other requirements of the problem. These limitations are expressed in the form of linear constraints, which are of three basic types:

a. Less-than-or-equal-to constraints:

$$b_1x_1 + b_2x_2 + \ldots + b_nx_n \leq b_0 \tag{20.4}$$

b. Greater-than-or-equal-to constraints:

$$b_1x_1 + b_2x_2 + \ldots + b_nx_n \geq b_0 \tag{20.5}$$

c. Equal-to constraints:

$$b_1x_1 + b_2x_2 + \ldots b_nx_n = b_0 \tag{20.6}$$

In any given linear programming problem, there may be a mixture of the three types. However, less-than-or-equal-to constraints are usually associated with maximization problems and greater-than-or-equal-to constraints are usually associated with minimization problems.

3. *Nonnegativity requirement.* The solution variables must take on either positive or zero values. Negative values are not allowed.

Within this framework there is a wide variety of different application areas, including problems that fall within our definition of steady-state optimal control. There are also various solution methods that can be applied to the linear programming problem, some of which are appropriate for the digital computer. We shall illustrate the linear programming problem by means of a simple example that contains only two variables. Realistic problems would have many variables. The reason for selecting a two-variable problem is so that the solution can be obtained by a graphical method. Readers interested in pursuing the more powerful approaches, such as the simplex method, should consult a text on operations research [14,16,17].

EXAMPLE 20.3

One of the most familiar problems in linear programming is the "product-mix" problem. Let us construct a fictional manufacturing control problem which involves the use of several limited resources to try to maximize profit. The process under consideration is greatly oversimplified. It

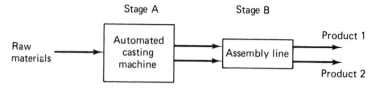

FIGURE 20.4   Manufacturing process of Example 20.3.

consists of two stages, as shown in Figure 20.4. Stage A is an automated casting machine into which flows the raw material, a certain grade of metal. The output of stage A consists of the two base parts for the two products made in this process. The two products will be identified simply by numbers 1 and 2. Stage B is an assembly line where manual operators perform several machining and assembly operations to each of the products.

A profit can be made by the company from either of the two products. As close as the firm's accounting department can figure, the unit profit on product 1 is $10.00 and the unit profit on product 2 is $20.00. Hence, the total profit enjoyed by the company from operating this two-stage manufacturing process is

$$z = 10x_1 + 20x_2$$

where $x_1 =$ number of units of product 1 produced

$x_2 =$ number of units of product 2 produced

The objective, of course, is to maximize the total profit, represented by z.

The production manager is smart enough to realize that profit will not necessarily be maximized simply by manufacturing only product 2. More labor resources are required for each unit of product 2 produced. Following are the constraints on the problem. First, 1 unit of raw material is needed for each unit of product 1, and 1 unit of raw material is needed for each unit of product 2. The total amount of raw material that can be processed through stage A each day is 9 units. This constraint can be expressed mathematically as

$$1x_1 + 1x_2 \leqslant 9$$

Next, there is a labor constraint on the assembly line. One hour of labor is required for each unit of product 1, and 3 labor-hours are required for each unit of product 2. Total labor hours available per day is 15 (two persons at $7\frac{1}{2}$ h each). This can be written

$$1x_1 + 3x_2 \leqslant 15$$

In the graphical method of solving the linear programming problem, these two constraints are plotted as the two lines

$$x_1 + x_2 = 9$$

$$x_1 + 3x_2 = 15$$

The two lines are shown in the graph of Figure 20.5. Since both of the constraints are of the less-than-or-equal-to type, expressed by Eq. (20.4), the area to the left and below these two lines

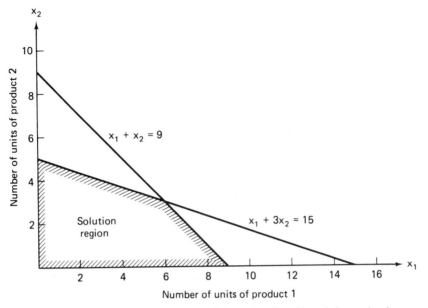

FIGURE 20.5 Two constraints plotted to form the allowable solution region for Example 20.3.

constitutes the allowable region within which the solution must lie. The values of x_1 and x_2 must be positive, so the solution falls within the crosshatched area shown in Figure 20.5.

The objective of the problem is to find the combination of x_1 and x_2 values that maximizes

$$z = 10x_1 + 20x_2$$

To determine this maximum point, a series of constant-profit lines can be drawn on the same graph as the constraints. This is illustrated in Figure 20.6. Constant-profit lines have the same value of z for all combinations of x_1 and x_2 on the line. When the constant-profit lines are superimposed on the constraint region, it can be seen that the optimum point is at $x_1 = 6$ and $x_2 = 3$ when $z = \$120$ per day. No other combination of x_1 and x_2 will yield a higher profit. To test this statement, we might try the largest possible x_2 value ($x_2 = 5$) within the convex polygon that defines the allowable region. If $x_2 = 5$, then $x_1 = 0$, and the profit is

$$z = 10(0) + 20(5) = \$100$$

which is less than the previous value of $z = \$120$ found in the graphical method.

Although this example may be a somewhat trivial problem in linear programming, the L.P. approach has been applied to a significant number of real-life problems. For the interested reader, Whitehouse and Wechsler [17] provide a survey of linear programming application studies.

As indicated by the techniques and examples in this section, problems in steady-state optimal control do not use feedback to check on the value of the objective function. This is assumed to be unnecessary in our definition of steady-state optimal control. We

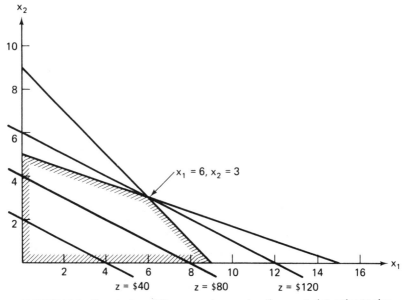

FIGURE 20.6   Constant-profit lines superimposed on the constraint region to give the solution at $x_1 = 6$, $x_2 = 3$, and $z = \$120$.

next turn our attention to control systems whose objective is optimization but whose output must be monitored in order for the objective to be reached. This type of system is referred to as adaptive control.

20.3   ADAPTIVE CONTROL

In Section 10.4, the subject of adaptive control machining was presented as a logical extension of numerical control. Applications of adaptive control are not limited to the machining process. Entire volumes have been written on the subject of adaptive control theory and methodology [4,6]. In this section, we survey some of the principles and techniques, supplementing the discussion with several examples.

Adaptive control has attributes of both feedback systems and optimal control systems. Like a feedback system, measurements are taken on certain process variables. Also like an optimal system, an overall measure of performance is used. In adaptive control, this measure is called the *index of performance* (IP). The feature that distinguishes adaptive control from the other two types is that an adaptive system is designed to operate in a time-varying environment. It is not unusual for a system to exist in an environment that changes over the course of time. If the internal parameters or mechanisms of the system are fixed, as is the case in a feedback control system, the system might operate quite differently in one type of environment than it would in another. For example, the controls of an airplane cause different effects at sea level in subsonic flight than during supersonic flight at an altitude of 60,000 ft. An adaptive control system is designed to compensate for the changing environment by monitoring its performance and altering, accordingly, some aspect of its control mechanism to achieve optimal or near-optimal performance. The term "environment" is used in a most general way and may refer to the normal operation of the process. For example, in a manufacturing process, the changing environment may simply mean the day-to-day variations that occur in tooling, raw materials, air temperature and humidity (if these have any influence on the process operation), and so on.

An adaptive system is different from a feedback system or an optimal system in that it is provided with the capability to cope with this time-varying environment. The feedback and optimal systems operate in a known or deterministic environment. If the environment changes significantly, these systems might not respond in the manner intended by the designer.

On the other hand, the adaptive system evaluates the environment. More accurately, it evaluates its performance within the environment and makes the necessary changes in its control characteristics to improve or, if possible, to optimize its performance. The manner of doing this involves three functions which characterize adaptive control and distinguish it from other modes of control.

Three functions of adaptive control

To evaluate its performance and to response accordingly, the adaptive controller is furnished with the capacity to perform the following three functions: identification, decision, and modification. It may be difficult, in any given adaptive control system, to separate out the components of the system that perform these three functions; nevertheless, all three must be present for adaptation to occur.

    1.   *Identification function.* This involves determining the current performance of the process or system. Normally, the performance quality of the system is defined by some relevant index of performance. The identification function is concerned with determining the current value of this performance measure by making use of the feedback data from the process. Since the environment will change over time, the performance of the system will also change. Accordingly, the identification function is one that must proceed over time more or less continuously. Identification of the system may involve a number of possible measurement activities. It may involve estimation of a suitable mathematical model of the process or computation of the performance index from measurements of process variables. It could include a comparison of the current performance quality with some desired optimal performance.

    2.   *Decision function.* Once the system performance is determined, the next function of adaptive control is to decide how the control mechanism should be adjusted to improve process performance. This decision procedure is carried out by means of a preprogrammed logic provided by the system designer. Depending on the logic, the decision may be to change one or more of the controllable inputs to the process; it may be to alter some of the internal parameters of the controller, or some other decision.

3.   *Modification function.* The third adaptive function is to implement the decision. While the decision function is a logic function, modification is concerned with a physical or mechanical change in the system. It is a hardware function rather than a software function. The modification involves changing the system parameters or variables so as to drive the process toward a more optimal state.

Figure 20.7 illustrates the sequence of the three functions in an adaptive controller applied to a hypothetical process. The process is assumed to be influenced by some time-varying environment. The adaptive system first identifies the current process performance by taking measurements of inputs and outputs. Depending on current performance, a decision procedure is carried out to determine what changes are needed to improve system performance. Actual changes to the system are made in the modification function.

EXAMPLE 20.4

Before proceeding further, let us consider an example to illustrate several of the points presented up to now. First, we want to show the differences among the three types of control: feedback, optimal, and adaptive control. Second, we want to demonstrate the three functions of an adaptive control system: identification, decision, and modification.

This will be a simple numerical example to show how a hypothetical process might be controlled under a number of different circumstances. Consider the process shown in Figure 20.8 with transfer function = 5.0. That is, the output y is related to the process input x_p as

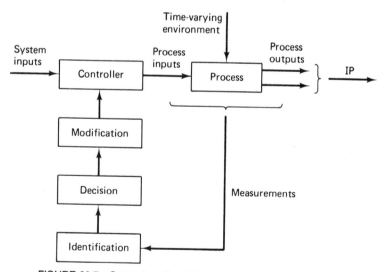

FIGURE 20.7   General configuration of an adaptive control system.

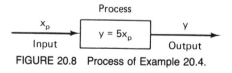

FIGURE 20.8   Process of Example 20.4.

$$y = 5x_p$$

Let us suppose that the desired value of y is 20. According to the foregoing relationship, it is obvious that the value of x must be 4.0 in order for y to equal 20. However, let us see how the problem might be perceived first as a feedback control problem, then as an optimal control problem, and finally as an adaptive control problem. We will ignore the presence of system dynamics. We could easily incorporate time into our model, but in doing so the mathematics would become more complex and we might lose track of our purpose, which is to show the differences between the three control strategies. Therefore, let us consider the problem without including time dynamics.

Solution:

1. *Feedback control.* Using feedback control to regulate the value of y, the block diagram of the system might appear as in Figure 20.9. The value of y is fed back through some "measuring device" which produces a signal one-tenth the value of y. This signal is compared with the system input x, which has a value of 4.0. The difference between the two (the error, e) is fed into the proportional controller, which multiplies the signal with a "gain" of 2.0. The output of the controller is x_p, which drives the process.

By block diagram algebra, the following can be shown:

$$e = x - 0.1y = 4 - 0.1y$$

$$x_p = 2e$$

$$y = 5x_p$$

Therefore,

$$y = (5)(2)(4 - 0.1y) = 40 - y$$

This equation can be solved for y:

$$2y = 40$$

$$y = 20$$

The gain value for each block in the system is set to yield a steady-state value of y at the desired level of 20.

However, we have so far ignored the possibility of a disturbance to the process. Let us

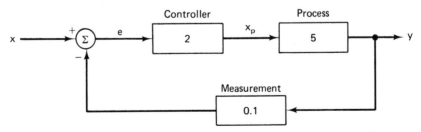

FIGURE 20.9   Feedback control used to regulate output y in Example 20.4.

assume that the process is suddenly disturbed, throwing the output y to a new value of 25. Will the control system respond in such a way as to drive the system back to $y = 20$?

Assuming that the system dynamics do not result in instability, we can show that the tendency will be for y to resume its previous value. If $y = 25$, then

$$e = 4 - 0.1y = 4 - 2.5 = 1.5$$

If $e = 1.5$, then

$$y = (5)(2)e = 15$$

It can be seen that a high value of y will cause the error, e, to be low. When this error signal is fed through the controller and the process, the effect is to reduce the value of y. Similarly, a low value of y will tend to be increased by the system. The system dynamics (time lags and second-order and higher-order effects) will determine the actual response of y over time.

2. *Optimal control.* To solve the example as an optimal control problem, we will assume a least-squares-error objective function:

$$\text{minimize } z = (20 - y)^2$$

The solution of the optimal control problem will consist of substituting the function $y = 5x_p$ into the objective function, differentiating z with respect to x_p, and setting the derivative to zero in order to find the value of x_p that minimizes z:

$$z = (20 - 5x_p)^2$$

$$= 400 - 200x_p + 25x_p^2$$

$$\frac{dz}{dx} = 0 - 200 + 2(25)x_p = 0$$

$$x_p = 4$$

The reader may recall that this is the same problem that was solved in Example 20.1.

3. *Adaptive control.* With this control strategy, the adaptive controller will try to monitor the performance and compensate for changes in environment.

Let us say in our example that the changes in the environment are manifested in an altered value of the process gain. Say that the gain has decreased from a value of 5 to a value of 4. We will now see how ineffective a feedback control system would be when used to try to maintain the value of y at 20. As before,

$$e = x - 0.1y = 4 - 0.1y$$

$$x_p = 2e$$

$$y = 4x_p \qquad \text{(the changed process)}$$

Therefore,

$$y = 8(4 - 0.1y) = 32 - 0.8y$$

$$1.8y = 32$$

$$y = 17.777$$

The steady-state value of y is not maintained at the desired level of 20 by the feedback control strategy.

Under the optimal control policy, where the process was assumed to possess a gain = 5, the optimal value of x_p was determined to be 4.0. Now that the process gain = 4, the value of $x_p = 4$ leads to the following:

$$y = 4x_p = 4(4) = 16$$

Steady-state optimal control, with no provision for monitoring the performance, misses the desired value even more than feedback control.

Let us proceed to see how adaptive control might be employed. The objective function will be the same as in the previous optimal control solution. However, it is termed the index of performance in adaptive control.

$$\text{minimize } z = (20 - y)^2$$

Measurements will be taken of both x_p and y, the input and output of the process, and these signals will be fed back to the adaptive controller. Of course, it may be unnecessary to take actual measurements of the input, since this variable is determined directly by the controller unit.

The adaptive controller, as part of its logic function, will attempt to determine the mathematical function that exists between x_p and y. This represents the identification function of adaptive control. Often, enough is known about the process that a good guess can be made as to the mathematical form of the function. In our case, we will assume that the suggested model form is

$$y = Kx_p$$

Now, using the measured values of x_p and y, the value of K can be calculated. Consistent with our previous discussion, we will assume that the measured values of x_p and y are 4 and 16, respectively. Hence, the calculated value of K would be

$$K = \frac{y}{x_p} = \frac{16}{4} = 4.0$$

Next, the adaptive controller will compute the value of x_p to minimize the index of performance z. This would be the decision function. These computations would be based on the following preprogrammed steps, similar to the solution approach used in optimal control:

$$z = (20 - y)^2 = (20 - Kx)^2$$

$$= 400 - 40Kx + K^2x^2$$

$$\frac{dz}{dx} = 0 - 40\,K + 2K^2x = 0$$

$$2K^2x = 40K$$

$$Kx = 20$$

$$x = \frac{20}{K}$$

From the previous steps, K had been computed to have a value of 4. Accordingly,

$$x_p = 5$$

Finally, as the last step in the adaptive control procedure, a modification would be made in the process input changing its value from 4 to the new value:

$$x_p = 5.0$$

As the process evolves over time and the value of the process gain continues to change unpredictably, the adaptive control system would make either continuous or periodic computations and adjustments in order to maintain the output y at the value of 20. The sequence of activities is displayed in Figure 20.10.

We have considered a most elementary example. Yet it features the principal attribute for which adaptive control is ideally suited: a time-varying, unpredictable environment, manifested in changing values of process gain K. Neither feedback control nor optimal control are capable of providing a satisfactory response in this situation. The adaptive strategy possesses this capability to deal with an ever-changing environment.

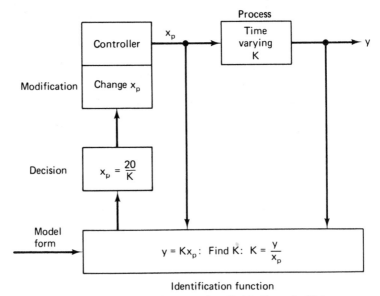

FIGURE 20.10 Adaptive control applied to Example 20.4.

If the process is not subjected to a time-varying and difficult-to-predict environment, a simpler form of strategy (e.g., feedback) would be more appropriate than adaptive control. It is therefore appropriate to examine whether a given process is a feasible candidate for adaptive control by considering whether the process is one that changes over time.

Why process changes occur

The following are several of the primary reasons why process changes might occur over time in an unpredictable manner:

1. *Environmental changes.* Some processes are affected by their environment. For example, some chemical processes are affected by the temperature and relative humidity in the air. Efforts are often made to maintain these conditions at satisfactory values. In other cases, these factors cannot conveniently be controlled so other variables must be altered to compensate.

2. *Changes in raw materials.* It is not difficult to imagine the many possible variations that could occur in raw material inputs to a process. It is virtually impossible to control all the properties that define a material. The variations in properties might have an adverse effect on the operation of the process.

For example, considering a metal machining operation, the variations in raw materials include changes in hardness, strength, microstructure, chemistry, thermal properties, and so on. Each of these factors has an effect on machinability and each can be expected to vary to some extent from workpiece to workpiece or lot to lot. We have not even considered in the list above the possible variations in part size and geometry.

3. *Wear of components.* The moving parts of a piece of production equipment can be expected to wear over time. This will often cause misalignment of the equipment, for which compensating adjustments must be made. In many manufacturing operations, some form of tooling is required which is used up or worn out during the process. Metal cutting is, of course, an example. An adaptive control system can sometimes be used to counteract the effects of wear.

4. *Failure of components.* Worse than the wear of some machine component is the actual failure of the component. This usually means that the entire system breaks down. For example, the final failure of the cutting tool in a machining operation means the process must be stopped and the tool changed. However, there are other systems or processes in which the failure of some minor component does not necessarily shut down the system. A production flow line with parallel stations might be an example. If one of the parallel stations breaks down, the others can maintain production. The throughput of the line may be reduced, but at least the line can be kept running.

In each of the preceding cases, the process has been changed in some manner. The various process changes that can occur over time are reflected as changes in the mathematical model of the process.

Changes in process model

The identification function in adaptive control usually reduces to the problem of determining either the value of the index of performance or the mathematical model that describes the process. Even the index of performance, when it is the object of the identification procedure, is generally based on a mathematical model. For example, the index of performance for a machining process might be cost per cubic inch of metal, which would have to be formulated as a mathematical equation.

It is therefore of importance to consider how the mathematical model of the process can be affected by the changes occurring in the process over time. These effects can be cataloged into three basic types:

1. *Changes in the model coefficients.* In this case we assume that the structure or form of the mathematical model remains accurate, but the constants in the model become altered in value to reflect process changes.

As an illustration, the previous example used the model

$$y = 5x_p$$

to express the relationship between output and input. The change that occurred in the hypothetical process of Example 20.4 was a shift in the value of the process gain from 5 to 4.

2. *Structural changes in model.* This is a more difficult case to deal with because the number of possible model forms is almost endless. Finding the correct form, unless some limitations are placed on the possibilities, would be a very tedious task.

An example of a structural change in the model would be a change from the model

$$y = Bx \qquad \text{as above}$$

to

$$y = A + Bx$$

or

$$y = Bx^n$$

or some other form of equation.

3. *Changes in constraints.* In a practical problem, the variables usually have an allowable range of values. The upper and lower extremes of the range can be expressed as constraints within which the variables must operate. These constraint values represent part of the mathematical model describing the process. As changes occur to the process, these changes may be defined in terms of changes in the constraints.

For example, the amount of torque that a drill bit can sustain without breaking depends on the size of the drill. The torque limit can be expressed as a constraint value. When the drill is changed, a new constraint value becomes applicable.

The identification problem

The previous two subsections have considered some of the possible reasons why a process may change over time, and how these changes might be simulated by changing the mathematical model of the process. If the changes over time are serious enough in terms of process performance, it is appropriate to consider adaptive control as a candidate for controlling the system.

In an adaptive control system the most difficult problem is usually the identification problem. Often, the solution of this problem is individualized. That is, the identification function is performed in a way that is unique for the given process. The types of identification problem can usually be placed in one of two categories:

1. *Where process identification is possible and feasible.* Enough information is known about the process that a mathematical model can be assumed with some reliability. Then, the identification function is concerned with using on-line measurements to determine the parameters of the model. In the more difficult case, the form of the mathematical model must be selected during identification. In any case, once the model and its parameters have been identified, the optimization procedure can be carried out.

2. *Where process identification is not possible or feasible.* In this situation, the process is poorly defined or a model of the process would be too complex. Hence, it is not feasible to make practical use of an assumed mathematical model. It is, however, possible to evaluate or estimate the performance quality of the process by means of measurements taken. Some sort of search procedure is then required to seek out the optimal point at which to operate the process.

We consider methods of identification that fall into the first category in this section. The second category of identification problem, requiring a systematic search procedure, we postpone until Section 20.4.

A variety of techniques have been proposed for solving the identification problem in adaptive control [4,6,13]. Some of these techniques require a fairly high level of mathematical sophistication, and the interested reader is invited to seek out the references cited. Presented in the following subsections are two techniques for process identification:

1. Instantaneous approximation method
2. Regression techniques

These methods are relatively straightforward to use, yet effective in practice.

Instantaneous approximation method

Many model identification techniques rely on observing the system over time in order to incorporate the dynamics of the system into the model. The instantaneous approximation method does not. However, the limitation of the method is that it can estimate only a single parameter in the model. Therefore, it is applicable only to those cases where only one of the process model parameters is expected to fluctuate over time. The other parameters in the model are assumed to remain at relatively constant values.

In this approximation technique, periodic measurements are taken of the input and output variables of the process. The measured values of these variables are inserted into the model of the process, along with the values of all parameters except the one to be estimated.

Then, the model is solved for the missing parameter value. For this method to yield satisfactory results, the model form must be known in advance and all parameter values must be fairly constant except the one to be estimated. Also, the system dynamics, if significant, must be included in the model.

EXAMPLE 20.5

To illustrate the instantaneous approximation method, assume a process whose mathematical model is given by

$$y = A + Bx$$

The process has been studied and it is known that the value of A remains relatively constant at a value of 10, while the value of B seems to fluctuate between 4.0 and 8.0. This variation takes place relatively slowly, but it makes it difficult to control the value of y. It is desired that the value of B be estimated from measurements taken of x and y.

Solution:

If x and y are known from measurements made on the process and the parameter A is assumed at a value of 10, then B can be solved as follows:

$$B = \frac{y - A}{x} = \frac{y - 10}{x}$$

For example, let us say that the values of x and y were measured as $x = 3$ and $y = 25$. Solving the foregoing equation for B yields

$$B = \frac{25 - 10}{3} = \frac{15}{3} = 5.0$$

Having determined B, we have therefore identified the process model.

$$y = 10 + 5x$$

We can now make whatever adjustments are required in the input x to produce the desired result in the output y.

EXAMPLE 20.6

Suppose that the process model included a rate or derivative term, as follows:

$$\frac{dy}{dt} + y = A + Bx$$

where the rate of change of y is expressed as the derivative dy/dt. We assume that the coefficient of this term is unity, but any other value could be assumed also. The instantaneous approximation method might be used to again find the current value of the varying parameter B, as long as all variables can be measured (including the derivative term), and as long as all other parameters in the model except B remain at their assumed values. For example, suppose that the measured variables had values as follows:

$$y = 25$$

$$\frac{dy}{dt} = 6$$

$$x = 3$$

Solving for B, we obtain

$$B = \frac{dy/dt + y - A}{x}$$

$$= \frac{6 + 25 - 10}{3} = 7.0$$

The instantaneous approximation method produces a quick estimate of the unknown parameter value. It is often impractical because of the assumption that all other parameter values are constant and known. Most practical processes are more complex than that.

Regression techniques

One of the several weaknesses of the instantaneous approximation method is that it presumes no error in the variable measurements. If error is present in the measurement of the process variables, the estimation of the unknown parameter value will contain error. Another limitation which was already mentioned is the fact that only one parameter can be approximated. Thus, the preceding method would be quite inadequate where more than one parameter is to be estimated, and where the variable measurements contained noise or error.

Regression techniques can be employed to overcome these problems. To use these methods, the process must be observed over a length of time, with measurements taken periodically of the process variables. A model form for the process must be assumed, but the parameters of the model vary over time. We must assume that the variation in parameter values takes place slowly compared with our procedure of sampling the process and estimating the parameters. After a sequence of values of the process variables has been collected, a regression computation is made to determine the model parameter values at the current time. The whole procedure is repeated at regular intervals, depending on the rate at which the model parameters drift.

METHOD OF LEAST SQUARES.   Regression analysis is typically performed by means of the least-squares technique. To illustrate the method of least squares in the simplest case, suppose that it is desired to determine the linear relationship between some dependent variable y and the independent variable x. Table 20.1 shows seven pairs of x-y values which will be used for illustration purposes. These data may represent the measurements collected from some physical experiment, or the results of a calibration procedure on some sensing instrument, or the sampled data compiled on some manufacturing process. Our interest here is in the data rather than the source from whence they come.

TABLE 20.1   Hypothetical Data to Illustrate the Least-Squares Technique

i	*1*	*2*	*3*	*4*	*5*	*6*	*7*
y_i	0.5	1.2	1.3	1.1	1.8	2.2	2.7
x_i	0.8	1.0	1.5	2.5	3.1	3.6	4.4

The data are plotted in Figure 20.11. The linear relationship between x and y is determined by finding the straight line that best fits the set of data presented in this figure. One way to do this would be to fit the line to the data "by eye." The trouble is, different analysts would probably come up with different lines. To overcome this variation in judgment, statisticians have developed the least-squares criterion. This criterion states

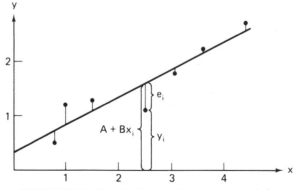

FIGURE 20.11   Data to illustrate least-squares technique.

that the "best fit" is the line that minimizes the sum of the squared errors between data points and the line. To elucidate this statement, the equation for a straight line is

$$y = A + Bx \tag{20.7}$$

where B = a constant representing the slope of the line

A = a constant representing the intercept of the line with the y-axis (at $x = 0$)

One possible line that follows this general equation is shown in Figure 20.11. The vertical distance between the straight line and any given data point (defined by x_i, y_i) is termed the error e_i. That is,

$$e_i = y_i - (A + Bx_i) \tag{20.8}$$

Mathematically expressing the criterion of least squares, the objective is to find values of A and B that

$$\text{minimize} \sum_{i=1}^{n} e_i^2 = \sum_{i=1}^{n} [y_i - (A + Bx_i)]^2 \tag{20.9}$$

where n is the number of points in the data set.

To find the values of A and B that satisfy this objective, the partial derivatives of Eq. (20.9) with respect to A and B can be found and set equal to zero.

$$2 \sum_{i=1}^{n} [y_i - (A + Bx_i)] (-1) = 0$$

$$2 \sum_{i=1}^{n} [y_i - (A + Bx_i)] (-x_i) = 0$$

These equations can be written in a more convenient form by separating the terms being summed as followed:

$$\sum_{i=1}^{n} y_i = An + B \sum_{i=1}^{n} x_i$$

$$\sum_{i=1}^{n} x_i y_i = A \sum_{i=1}^{n} x_i + B \sum_{i=1}^{n} x_i^2 \tag{20.10}$$

Equations (20.10) are called the *normal equations*. By solving these two equations simultaneously, the values of A and B can be computed which provide the "best fit" to the data by the least-squares criterion. The statistically minded reader may find objectionable the use of the symbols A and B in Eq. (20.10), since these are the same symbols used in Eq. (20.7). A and B in Eq. (20.7) represent the true values of the constants in the relationship between x and y. The values calculated from Eq. (20.10) are estimates of these true values based on a sampling of data from the relationship.

EXAMPLE 20.7

The method of least squares will be illustrated by means of the data presented in Table 20.1. To make use of Eqs. (20.10), it is convenient to construct a calculations table similar to the one shown in Table 20.2. In this table, the intermediate computations are performed to collect the terms used in the normal equations. From Table 20.2,

$$\sum_{i=1}^{7} y_i = 10.8 \qquad \sum_{i=1}^{7} x_i = 16.9$$

$$\sum_{i=1}^{7} x_i y_i = 31.68 \qquad \sum_{i=1}^{7} x_i^2 = 52.07$$

Inserting these terms into Eqs. (20.10), we have

$$10.8 = 7A + 16.9B$$

$$31.68 = 16.9A + 52.07B$$

Solving these two equations for A and B, we determine that $A = 0.342$ and $B = 0.497$. The resulting equation is

$$y = 0.342 + 0.497x$$

This equation is shown in Figure 20.11 as the straight line through the data points.

It is usually desirable to examine some of the statistical characteristics of the regression equation which indicate how good the relationship is. Among these characteristics are the sample correlation coefficient and the standard error of estimate.

TABLE 20.2 Calculations Table for Example 20.7

i	y_i	x_i	$x_i y_i$	x_i^2
1	0.5	0.8	0.40	0.64
2	1.2	1.0	1.20	1.00
3	1.3	1.5	1.95	2.25
4	1.1	2.5	2.75	6.25
5	1.8	3.1	5.58	9.61
6	2.2	3.6	7.92	12.96
7	2.7	4.4	11.88	19.36
	10.8	16.9	31.68	52.07

To calculate these two statistics, it is convenient to define several intermediate terms as follows:

$$S_{xx} = n \sum_{i=1}^{n} x_i^2 - \left(\sum_{i=1}^{n} x_i \right)^2 \tag{20.11}$$

$$S_{yy} = n \sum_{i=1}^{n} y_i^2 - \left(\sum_{i=1}^{n} y_i \right)^2 \tag{20.12}$$

$$S_{xy} = n \sum_{i=1}^{n} x_i y_i - \left(\sum_{i=1}^{n} x_i \right) \left(\sum_{i=1}^{n} y_i \right) \tag{20.13}$$

The *sample correlation coefficient* can now be defined as

$$r = \frac{S_{xy}}{\sqrt{S_{xx} S_{yy}}} \tag{20.14}$$

The sample correlation coefficient ranges in value between -1.0 and $+1.0$. It indicates the strength of the linear relationship between the sampled values of x and y. If r is close to $+1.0$, this indicates a strong positive correlation between x and y. If r is close to -1.0, it is an indication that a strong negative linear correlation exists between the two variables. A value of r near zero indicates the absence of any strong correlation.

The *standard error of estimate* can be defined as

$$s_e = \sqrt{\frac{S_{xx} S_{yy} - (S_{xy})^2}{n(n-2)S_{xx}}} \tag{20.15}$$

The s_e statistic for a regression equation gives the average value of the e_i errors. It is not an arithmetic average, but rather a root-mean-square average corrected for the number of degrees of freedom. Although less convenient than Eq. (20.15), an alternative way of defining the standard error of estimate is given by

$$s_e = \sqrt{\frac{\sum_{i=1}^{n} e_i^2}{n-2}} = \sqrt{\frac{\sum_{i=1}^{n} [y_i - (A + Bx_i)]^2}{n-2}} \tag{20.16}$$

The squared term inside the radical sign shows the root-mean-square averaging process. The $n-2$ term is the number of degrees of freedom.

The sign of a "good fit" is when the value of s_e is low relative to the values of y in the data set. If $s_e = 0$, this indicates that the equation fits the data perfectly.

EXAMPLE 20.8

We will demonstrate how these two statistics are calculated by using the data from Example 20.7. From Table 20.2 we have

$$\sum_{i=1}^{7} y_i = 10.8 \qquad \sum_{i=1}^{7} x_i = 16.9$$

$$\sum_{i=1}^{7} x_i y_i = 31.68 \qquad \sum_{i=1}^{7} x_i^2 = 52.07$$

The only additional term we need in order to make the calculations is $\sum_{i=1}^{7} y_i^2$:

$$\sum_{i=1}^{7} y_i^2 = (0.5)^2 + (1.2)^2 + \ldots + (2.7)^2$$

$$= 19.96$$

From Eqs. (20.11) through (20.13)

$$S_{xx} = 7(52.07) - (16.9)^2 = 78.88$$

$$S_{yy} = 7(19.96) - (10.8)^2 = 23.08$$

$$S_{xy} = 7(31.68) - (16.9)(10.8) = 39.24$$

From Eq. (20.14) the sample correlation coefficient is

$$r = \frac{39.24}{\sqrt{(78.88 \times 23.08)}} = 0.9197$$

This is close to $+1.0$ and indicates that the values of x and y are closely correlated. From Eq. (20.15) the standard error of estimate is

$$s_e = \sqrt{\frac{(78.88)(23.08) - (39.24)^2}{7(5)(78.88)}} = 0.3189$$

The average value of y is $10.8/7 = 1.543$. The standard error of estimate is roughly 20% of this average y.

The reader can visually interpret these calculated statistics in Figure 20.11.

MULTIPLE REGRESSION. Most industrial processes are too complex to be modeled by the simple linear relation of Eq. (20.7). There are often two or more input variables which determine the process output variable of interest. Also, the dynamics of the process usually play an important role in its behavior. Accordingly, these additional features of the process must be taken into account in the identification function. If the model is linear (or if it is nonlinear but can be transformed into an equivalent linear form), the least-squares method can be extended to determine the parameters of the model. The regression of some dependent variable y on more than a single independent variable is called *multiple regression*.

To illustrate how multiple regression might be used in process identification, suppose that the model for a certain industrial process is the following:

$$K \frac{dy}{dt} + y = A + Bx_1 + Cx_2$$

where

$$dy/dt = \text{rate of change of the output variable } y$$

$$x_1, x_2 = \text{two process input variables}$$

We can take measurements of all variables, including the derivative term, but there is random noise in each of the signals. We will assume that the noise is normally distributed about the mean value of the variable. In operating the process, we must make routine changes in the inputs x_1 and x_2, and we then observe the effect on the output y and its rate of change dy/dt. One final assumption is this: that the rate at which the model parameters, K, A, B, and C, change is slow relative to our ability to perform the estimating procedure.

To carry out the model identification scheme, we first take measurements of the four variables y, dy/dt, x_1, and x_2 at discrete intervals, making minor changes in x_1 and x_2 to observe the effects on y and dy/dt. This will provide a set of values over time in the format shown in Table 20.3. In effect, we are sampling the process at discrete points in time $(t, t + 1, t + 2, \text{etc.})$. With the data from Table 20.3, the least-squares com-

TABLE 20.3   Data Set Format Used in Multiple Regression Computation

Sampling time	$\dfrac{dy}{dt}$	y	x_1	x_2
t	$\dfrac{dy}{dt}(t)$	$y(t)$	$x_1(t)$	$x_2(t)$
$t + 1$	$\dfrac{dy}{dt}(t + 1)$	$y(t + 1)$	$x_1(t + 1)$	$x_2(t + 1)$
$t + 2$	$\dfrac{dy}{dt}(t + 2)$	$y(t + 2)$	$x_1(t + 2)$	$x_2(t + 2)$
.	.	.	.	.
.	.	.	.	.
.	.	.	.	.
$t + n$	$\dfrac{dy}{dt}(t + n)$	$y(t + n)$	$x_1(t + n)$	$x_2(t + n)$

putation can be performed to determine current estimates of the four parameters, K, A, B, and C.

To carry out the least-squares computations, Eq. (20.17) must be rearranged into the following form:

$$y = A + Bx_1 + Cx_2 - K\frac{dy}{dt}$$

Since the sign of the fourth term will take care of itself in the least-squares calculations, it is more convenient to write this equation as

$$y = A + Bx_1 + Cx_2 + K\frac{dy}{dt} \tag{20.18}$$

Now the dependent variable y can be regressed on x_1, x_2, and dy/dt. Statisticians might object to this on the grounds that the variable dy/dt is not independent of y. Although this objection is valid from a statistical viewpoint, the least-squares method is nevertheless an appropriate and convenient calculation procedure for estimating the unknown parameters in the linear model.

The approach to this problem is similar to the procedure used for the case of $y = A + Bx$. The objective is to minimize the sum of the squared error terms:

$$\text{minimize} \sum_{i=1}^{n} e_i^2 = \sum_{i=1}^{n} \left[y_i - \left((A + Bx_1 + Cx_2 + K\frac{dy}{dt} \right) \right]^2$$

From this the normal equations can be derived by taking the partial derivatives with respect to A, B, C, and K, and setting each equal to zero. The resulting normal equations are:

$$\sum y = nA + B \sum x_1 + C \sum x_2 + K \sum \frac{dy}{dt}$$

$$\sum x_1 y = A \sum x_1 + B \sum x_1^2 + C \sum x_1 x_2 + K \sum x_1 \frac{dy}{dt} \tag{20.19}$$

$$\sum x_2 y = A \sum x_2 + B \sum x_1 x_2 + C \sum x_2^2 + K \sum x_2 \frac{dy}{dt}$$

$$\sum y\frac{dy}{dt} = A \sum \frac{dy}{dt} + B \sum x_1 \frac{dy}{dt} + C \sum x_2 \frac{dy}{dt} + K \sum \left(\frac{dy}{dt}\right)^2$$

The normal equations for other model forms can be derived in the same manner. Problem 20.15 asks the reader to derive the normal equations for the model $y = A + Bx_1 + Cx_2$. Computer software packages are available for the least-squares computations in multiple regression. The reader may therefore ask why we need bother with these manual calculations. The answer is that it is often necessary to program this type of computation into the software used for specific process monitoring and control applications.

EXAMPLE 20.9

Let us proceed through the calculations for the multiple regression case. Suppose that sampled data have been collected for a manufacturing process that can be modeled by an equation of the form of Eq. (20.17). The data are collected and summarized in Table 20.4. The sampling interval is 1 min. The resulting equation for this sampling period (calculated using a computer statistical package) is

$$y = 3.172 + 2.389x_1 + 5.763x_2 - 0.771 \frac{dy}{dt}$$

Rewriting this in the form of Eq. (20.17) yields

$$0.771 \frac{dy}{dt} + y = 3.172 + 2.389x_1 + 5.763x_2$$

The sampling of the process would be repeated at suitable intervals to recalculate the parameter values. In this way, any drift in the parameters would be identified.

EXAMPLE 20.10

The use of regression techniques has increased in the electronics industry in recent years as a consequence of the need for tighter process control in the manufacture of integrated circuits (ICs). One example is the control of the ion implantation process [1]. In the process, ions are produced from a dopant source and implanted into the silicon substrate of the IC wafers. A mass spectrometer is used to select certain species of the ions to be implanted. These ions are used to alter the substrate electrical characteristics. Process control is required to regulate the total charge per unit area, called the total dose (Q_T), which is a function of the ion implantation process. Measurements are obtained of the implanted substrate resistivity (V/I), which characterizes the behavior of the implanter. A

TABLE 20.4 Hypothetical Data Set for Example 20.9

Sampling time (min)	y	x_1	x_2	$\frac{dy}{dt}$
1	22.3	1.1	3.0	1.0
2	23.5	1.2	3.2	1.3
3	24.8	1.2	3.4	1.1
4	25.9	1.3	3.6	1.4
5	26.2	1.3	3.5	0.4
6	26.5	1.4	3.5	0.2
7	26.3	1.4	3.4	0.2
8	25.8	1.3	3.3	0.7

microprocessor-based instrument, sometimes called a dosimeter, is used to accomplish the process control.

To illustrate the use of regression techniques for the process, suppose that a production batch of wafers is to be implanted with phosphorus. The desired substrate resistivity (V/I) is 460 Ω/square. The data in Table 20.5 have been collected from previous test runs of the implanter. The desired dosimeter setpoint must be determined to achieve the desired substrate resistivity. Solving the regression equation for the data in Table 20.5, using V/I as the dependent variable, we find

$$\frac{V}{I} = -2.01 \times 10^{-10} \, Q_T + 1765$$

Rearranging the equation to solve for Q_T, we obtain

$$Q_T = \frac{V/I - 1765}{-2.01 \times 10^{-10}}$$

Accordingly, the set point can be computed for a desired substrate resistivity of 460 Ω/square:

$$Q_T = \frac{460 - 1765}{-2.01 \times 10^{-10}}$$

$$= 6.49 \times 10^{12} \text{ ions/cm}^2$$

There are several aspects of this regression technique that ought to be mentioned. First, the number of data sets required depends on statistical and practical considerations. More data sets will usually give more accurate estimates of the parameter values. Second, a major disadvantage of the regression method discussed here is that the process must be perturbed in order to assess the effects of changes in the controllable input variables. If no changes occurred in x_1 and x_2, the parameter values cannot be estimated. Third, it is important to acknowledge the effects that system dynamics play in the operation of the process. All the significant rate terms should be included in the process model.

TABLE 20.5   Process Data for Example 20.10

Test run	Dosimeter setpoint total dose, Q_T $\times 10^{12}$ ions/ cm^2)	Measured substrate resistivity, V/I (Ω/square)
1	6.31	496
2	6.77	405
3	6.65	427
4	6.43	475
5	6.39	480
6	6.56	446

Practical problems with adaptive control

Although adaptive control is the appropriate way to solve the problem in which the system is confronted with unpredictable environmental changes, there are some difficulties associated with its use. The following discussion explores most of these difficulties, some of which are not exclusively associated with adaptive control but apply to other control systems as well.

1. *Complexity of the system.* Adding an adaptive control loop will increase the complexity of the analysis problem. The use of AC may turn a relatively simple linear system into a complex nonlinear system. Accordingly, this difficulty should be considered and adaptive control should be applied only where it represents the most feasible way of dealing with the problem.

2. *Difficulty with the identification function.* There are several problems associated with the system identification function in adaptive control.

   a. *Definition of index of performance.* The performance of the system can be no better than the measure used to evaluate performance. There are clearly difficulties involved when an attempt is made to characterize the overall performance of a process or system with a single index of performance. Despite these difficulties, the use of adaptive control requires that process performance be combined into one measure. It is therefore important that the index of performance selected be truly representative of overall performance.

   b. *Sensor problems.* One of the biggest problems in applying adaptive control to the machining process is the difficulty in obtaining accurate and reliable measurements of the process variables. Without such measurements, the index of performance cannot be accurately assessed and the process cannot be accurately identified.

   c. *Identification under normal operating conditions.* The identification function should be performed under normal operating conditions. Tests required to identify the process model (transfer function of the process) should not disturb the routine operation of the process. This is often very difficult. Among the model identification methods explored in this section, the regression techniques require that the process be disturbed during the measurement procedure. Also, the search techniques discussed in Section 20.4 require perturbations of the process to carry out the optimum seeking strategy. These disturbances must be considered as costs associated with the identification function. The benefits of adaptive control must more than compensate for these costs.

3. *System stability.* As a consequence of the preceding, the system may become unstable. This means that the system has a tendency to get out of control, possibly to cause damage to itself.

4. *System cost.* The attachment of adaptive control to the process will obviously have a cost. The improvement in process performance must be greater in value than the associated cost.

20.4   ON-LINE SEARCH STRATEGIES

When model identification is infeasible, it may still be possible to make a determination of the index of performance for the process. This can either be done through direct observation of the IP or by calculating the IP from measurements of the process variables that determine its value. Even though we can evaluate the index of performance, the problem still remains that the relationship between the IP and the process inputs is unknown. Therefore, we cannot directly determine the values of these inputs which will optimize the system performance. In this type of situation, we must resort to some form of search procedure.

The general strategy in any of the search techniques is to make adjustments to the controllable input variables and observe the effects on the output variables. Based on the effects, decisions are made to systematically change the inputs so as to improve process performance.

The common search techniques encompass a variety of approaches, ranging from pure trial and error to gradient strategies. The scope of this book restricts us from examining the entire range. We will focus on the gradient strategies. There is little evidence to suggest that these search techniques are widely applied in discrete-parts manufacturing. The applications are more prevalent in the continuous process industries.

Desirable properties of a search strategy

A search strategy is a procedure of logical computations used to adjust the process inputs in order to try to improve the index of performance. By repeating the logical procedure, the search strategy tends to move toward the optimum value of the IP. As mentioned above, there are many different search strategies. One strategy may be appropriate for some search problems and inappropriate for others. Because the nature of the search problem is that we are dealing with an unknown process, it is often difficult to decide in advance which search strategy would work best. The success of the search sometimes reduces to a matter of luck on the part of the programmer selecting the strategy. The general criteria used to judge the effectiveness of a search strategy are the following:

1.   *Speed of arriving at the optimum.* It is desirable for the strategy to arrive at the optimum IP value in the minimum number of steps. In process control, this is especially important when the industrial process is subjected to frequent shifts and a new optimum set of operating conditions must continually be sought.

2.   *Simplicity of the strategy.* This is desirable from the viewpoint of the operating personnel who must supervise the process. If the strategy is complicated, it will be difficult to understand by those using it. This may result in the operator's overriding the strategy. Simplicity of the strategy is also an advantage in programming the strategy on the control computer.

3.   *Capability to deal with difficult or unusual search problems.* Some search strategies work well on certain problems, while other strategies are more suited to other

situations. A desirable search strategy is one that is versatile enough to cope with a variety of different search problems.

4. *Stopping criteria*. When the optimum has been reached, the search should be terminated. Because of the stochastic nature of many manufacturing processes, the optimum is often disguised by the presence of random noise. This makes it difficult to identify the optimum operating conditions. One criterion used to judge a search strategy is its ability to discern this stopping point.

Some basic definitions

In order to explain the operation of any of the search techniques, it is necessary to establish certain basic definitions.

RESPONSE SURFACE.   Perhaps the most fundamental concept required to understand how a search strategy works is the concept of the response surface. A *response surface* is a mathematical relationship of the index of performance (or other dependent variable) as a function of the input variables. For two inputs, x_1 and x_2, the response surface can be plotted very conveniently as shown in Figure 20.12. The plot reads something like a geological survey map. The contour lines are lines of constant IP value. In Figure 20.12, the value of each contour line is identified.

In concept a response surface can be defined mathematically as

$$z = f(x_1, x_2) \tag{20.20}$$

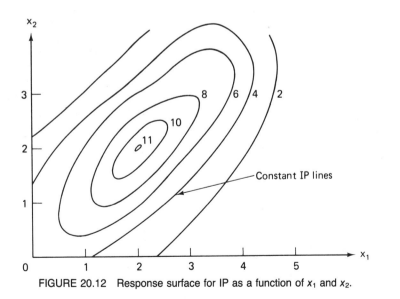

FIGURE 20.12   Response surface for IP as a function of x_1 and x_2.

where

$$z = \text{index of performance or dependent variable}$$

$$x_1, x_2 = \text{inputs or independent variables on which } z \text{ is functionally} \\ \text{dependent}$$

Although a response surface can be mathematically defined in principle, it turns out that this mathematical definition is often very difficult to realize in practice for many industrial processes. In this section we use mathematical functions to define and illustrate certain terms relating to search strategies. However, the reader should recognize that real manufacturing processes cannot often be defined so precisely. If they could, there would be little need to apply search techniques for finding the optimum. We could use the methods of Sections 20.2 and 20.3 to determine optimum operating conditions.

OPTIMUM POINT. The optimum point on a response surface is the combination of x_1 and x_2 values at which the index of performance is optimized. In Figure 20.12 the optimum (maximum) IP value is slightly greater than 11.0 and its location is approximately $x_1 = 2.0$ and $x_2 = 2.0$. For a maximization problem, the optimum point is at the peak or summit of the response surface. For a minimization problem, the optimum point is located at the deepest point in the valley of the response surface.

UNIMODALITY. Search strategies rely on the assumption that the response surface is unimodal. What this means is that there is only one peak in the response surface. The objective of the search strategy is to find that single peak. If more than one peak exists, the strategy might seek out a peak that is not the highest one. Hence, the true optimum point would be neglected.

GRADIENT. Many search strategies are based on the use of gradients. The gradient is a vector quantity whose components are along the axes of the independent variables (x_1 and x_2). The magnitude of each component is equal to the partial derivative of the index of performance with respect to the corresponding independent variable. Our interest will be limited to two independent variables, although the concept of the gradient applies to n-dimensional response surfaces. For two inputs, x_1 and x_2, the components of the gradient are defined as

$$G_{1p} = \left. \frac{\partial z}{\partial x_1} \right|_p$$

$$G_{2p} = \left. \frac{\partial z}{\partial x_2} \right|_p$$

(20.21)

where G_{1p}, G_{2p} = components of the gradient in the x_1 and x_2 directions, respectively; these components must be evaluated at a particular location on the response surface and this location is identified as point p

z = index of performance, a function of x_1 and x_2

The two components add together to form the gradient

$$G_p = iG_{1p} + jG_{2p} \qquad (20.22)$$

where i and j represent unit vectors parallel to the x_1 and x_2 axes. The gradient points in the direction of the steepest slope. Moving in the direction of steepest slope is a reasonable strategy to reach the top of the response surface. This is why many search strategies are based on the use of gradients.

The *magnitude of the gradient* is a scalar quantity given by

$$M_p = \left[\left(\frac{\partial z}{\partial x_1} \bigg|_p \right)^2 + \left(\frac{\partial z}{\partial x_2} \bigg|_p \right)^2 \right]^{1/2} \qquad (20.23)$$

Again, the magnitude of the gradient is defined at a particular point p on the x_1,x_2 surface.

The *direction of the gradient* is a unit vector defined as

$$D_p = \frac{1}{M_p} G_p \qquad (20.24)$$

It is sometimes more convenient to work with the direction of the gradient rather than the gradient itself because the length of the direction vector does not vary. Its length is always 1 unit.

The definitions of gradient, magnitude, and direction given above can all be extended to response surfaces with more than two independent variables. The visualization is more difficult, but the concepts are identical in multidimensional space.

TRAJECTORY. Whether or not the search strategy makes use of gradients to find its way, the trajectory is the sequence of moves followed by the strategy to seek out the optimum. An efficient search will exhibit a fairly straight line trajectory from the starting point to the optimum point.

EXAMPLE 20.11

We will illustrate several of the definitions presented in this subsection. Suppose that the response surface for some hypothetical process is given by

$$Z = 24x_1 + 22x_2 - x_1^2 - 0.5x_2^2$$

The variable z represents perhaps the yield of the process as a function of two inputs, x_1 and x_2. The objective is to maximize the yield. The current operating conditions are at $x_1 = 5$ and $x_2 = 6$. Let us determine the values of the gradient itself, and the magnitude and direction of the gradient.

Solution:

From Eq. (20.21), the components of the gradient are

$$G_{1p} = \frac{\partial z}{\partial x_1}\bigg|_p = 24 - 2x_1 = 24 - 2(5) = 14$$

$$G_{2p} = \frac{\partial z}{\partial x_2}\bigg|_p = 22 - x_2 = 22 - 6 = 16$$

The gradient, according to Eq. (20.22), is

$$G_p = 14i + 16j$$

The magnitude of the gradient is given by Eq. (20.23):

$$M_p = \sqrt{14^2 + 16^2} = 21.26$$

and the direction of the gradient can be determined from Eq. (20.24):

$$D_p = \frac{14i + 16j}{21.26} = 0.658i + 0.753j$$

All of these quantities are defined at the point $p(x_1 = 5, x_2 = 6)$. The terms would have different values at different x_1, x_2 locations.

To demonstrate the usefulness of the gradient in pointing the way toward the optimum, we can determine the actual location of the optimum by the same approach used in Example 20.2. Setting the partial derivatives equal to zero and solving for x_1 and x_2, we obtain

$$\frac{\partial z}{\partial x_1} = 24 - 2x_1 = 0 \qquad x_1 = 12$$

$$\frac{\partial z}{\partial x_2} = 22 - x_2 = 0 \qquad x_2 = 22$$

In Figure 20.13 this optimum point is plotted along with the direction of the gradient at $x_1 = 5$ and $x_2 = 6$. It can be seen that the gradient direction is pointed roughly toward the optimum.

Gradient search strategies

The most familiar gradient search strategy is called the *method of steepest ascent*. This method begins by estimating the gradient at the current operating point. It then moves the operating point to a new position in the direction of the gradient. The gradient is determined again at the new position in anticipation of the next move toward the optimum. The cycle of gradient determination and step move is repeated until the optimum point is achieved.

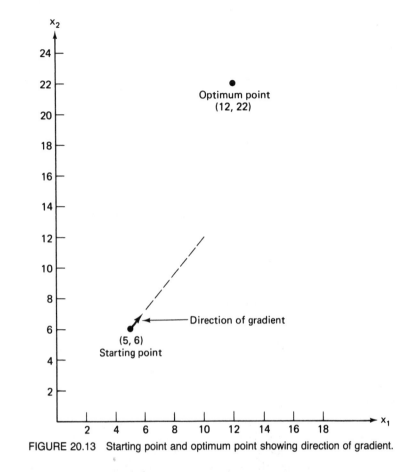

FIGURE 20.13   Starting point and optimum point showing direction of gradient.

DETERMINING THE GRADIENT.   In a practical problem, the mathematical equation for the response surface is not usually known. Accordingly, the gradient cannot simply be found by employing Eq. (20.21). Instead, the slope of the response surface is determined by making several exploratory moves centered around the current operating point. The exploratory moves are arranged in the form of a factorial experiment. That is, a square of experimental points is established around the current operating point, as illustrated in Figure 20.14. At each point the value of the index of performance is determined. Then the gradient components are estimated by means of the following equations:

$$G_{1p} = \frac{(z_2 + z_3) - (z_1 + z_4)}{2\Delta x_1}$$

$$G_{2p} = \frac{(z_2 + z_4) - (z_1 + z_3)}{2\Delta x_2}$$

(20.25)

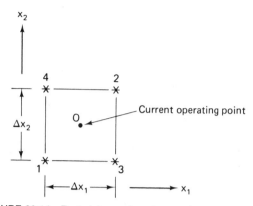

FIGURE 20.14   Factorial experiments to estimate the gradient.

where z_1, z_2, z_3, z_4 = values of the performance index at the four experimental
points

Δx_1 = difference in the independent variable x_1 separating
the experimental points

Δx_2 = difference in the independent variable x_2 separating the
experimental points

The reason for sequencing the exploratory points 1, 2, 3, and 4 as shown in Figure 20.14
is to reduce the effect of any drift in the process. The values of Δx_1 and Δx_2 must be
decided according to two opposing factors. First, Eqs. (20.25) approximate the true partial
derivatives of Eqs. (20.21) more accurately as Δx_1 and Δx_2 become smaller. On the other
hand, if experimental error is present in the measurement of z (and it invariably is present
in most process situations), the separation between experimental points must be large
enough to overcome the effect of the error. Also, the exploratory moves may have to be
repeated to average the errors. Judgment must be used by the analyst in order to decide
on the values of Δx_1 and Δx_2 as well as the number of experimental replications. We
shall leave the statistical analysis of the errors to other volumes, such as Box and Draper
[3], if the reader wishes to pursue the subject.

EXAMPLE 20.12

Let us compare the use of Eqs. (20.25) with Eqs. (20.21) in Example 20.11. The equation for the
response surface was

$$z = 24x_1 + 22x_2 - x_1^2 - 0.5x_2^2$$

The current operating point is $x_1 = 5$ and $x_2 = 6$, which yields $z = 209$. For convenience we
will use $\Delta x_1 = 2$ and $\Delta x_2 = 2$, which means that the four test points and corresponding z values
are:

Test point	x_1	x_2	z
1	4	5	177.5
2	6	7	237.5
3	6	5	205.5
4	4	7	209.5

The components of the gradient are calculated by Eqs. (20.25):

$$G_{1p} = \frac{(237.5 + 205.5) - (177.5 + 209.5)}{2(2)} = 14$$

$$G_{2p} = \frac{(237.5 + 209.5) - (177.5 + 205.5)}{2(2)} = 16$$

From Eq. (20.22) the gradient is

$$G_p = 14i + 16j$$

For this response surface, the set of exploratory moves has provided the exact value of the gradient at the point $x_1 = 5$, $x_2 = 6$.

STEP MOVES.   Exploratory moves are used for the purpose of determining the gradient. Once the gradient has been determined, a step move is made to the new operating point. The step move is taken in the direction of the gradient. The input variables x_1 and x_2 are incremented in proportion to the components of the direction vector.

$$\text{new } x_1 = \text{old } x_1 + C \frac{G_{1p}}{M_p}$$

$$\text{new } x_2 = \text{old } x_2 + C \frac{G_{2p}}{M_p} \qquad (20.26)$$

where C is a scalar quantity that determines the size of the step move. The use of the constant C in Eqs. (20.26) means that the length of the step move is the same for every cycle. This occurs in spite of the fact that the gradient components will change in value both relatively and absolutely with every cycle.

STOPPING CRITERIA.   The search continues until the optimum is reached. At the optimum value of the index of performance, the gradient has a value of zero. It would be sheer coincidence if a step move were to land exactly on the optimum point. A more likely occurrence is for the strategy to "overshoot" the optimum. When this happens, it can be identified by the fact that the next gradient changes direction very abruptly, perhaps heading in roughly the opposite direction from previous step moves.

When the vicinity of the optimum is found, it is usually beneficial to reduce the size of the step move. This is accomplished by reducing the value of the constant C in Eqs. (20.26). In the beginning of the search, a large step size would be used to speed convergence to the optimum. The final resolution of the optimum must be achieved with smaller step moves. A reasonable criterion for stopping the search would be when repeated step moves produce no significant improvement in the index of performance.

EXAMPLE 20.13

Let us continue Example 20.12 through the first two cycles of the method of steepest ascent. We will use a step move of length 5 units. That is, C in Eqs. (20.26) equals 5.

Cycle 1. From Example 20.12, the gradient at the starting point has components

$$G_{1p} = 14 \ and \ G_{2p} = 16$$

The magnitude of the gradient is 21.26. By application of Eqs. (20.26) we get the new operating point:

$$new \ x_1 = 5.0 + (5.0)(0.658) = 8.290$$

$$new \ x_2 = 6.0 + (5.0)(0.753) = 9.765$$

The index of performance can be calculated to be

$$z = 24(8.29) + 22(9.765) - (8.29)^2 - 0.5(9.765)^2 = 331.6$$

This value compares with the IP at the starting point ($x_1 = 5$, $x_2 = 6$):

$$z = 24(5) + 22(6) - (5)^2 - 0.5(6)^2 = 209$$

The search has led us to an improved IP value.

Cycle 2. Since the response surface is mathematically defined for this hypothetical example, we could use either Eq. (20.21) or (20.25). For ease of computation, we will use Eq. (20.21).

$$G_{1p} = 24 - 2x_1 = 24 - 2(8.290) = 7.420$$

$$G_{2p} = 22 - x_2 = 22 - 9.765 = 12.235$$

The magnitude of the gradient $= 14.309$.

$$new \ x_1 = 8.290 + (5.0)\frac{7.420}{14.309} = 10.883$$

$$new \ x_2 = 9.765 + (5.0)\frac{12.235}{14.309} = 14.040$$

The index of performance has a value at this point of $z = 353.1$.

A continuation of the method of steepest ascent produces the trajectory shown in Figure 20.15. The z values are indicated for each step move in the search. The reader will note that after cycle 4 ($x_1 = 11.498$, $x_2 = 23.799$), the search begins to oscillate. The gradient direction changes in cycles 5 and 6, and this is usually a tipoff that the vicinity of the optimum has been located. The reader will also note that the IP does not improve significantly. In fact, it tends to fluctuate in value. The search is stepping back and forth across the optimum. When this happens, the step size should be reduced. This is done in cycle 7 (the length of the step move is reduced from $C = 5.0$ to $C = 1.0$). The result is that the next move brings the search to within a very small error (0.39%) of the optimum IP value.

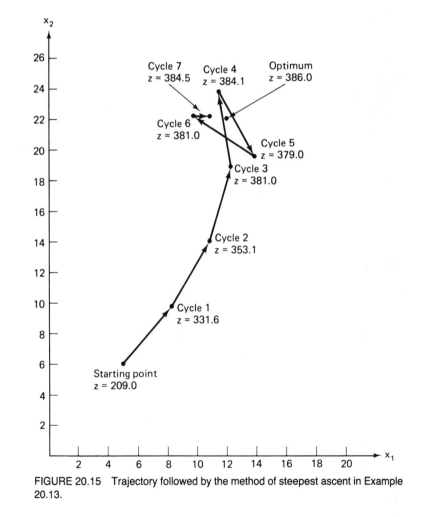

FIGURE 20.15 Trajectory followed by the method of steepest ascent in Example 20.13.

OTHER GRADIENT STRATEGIES. There are other gradient search strategies in addition to the method of steepest ascent. A close cousin is the *optimum gradient method*. The procedure of the optimum gradient method is as follows:

1. The strategy begins with a determination of the index of performance and its gradient at the starting point.
2. A step move is made in the direction of the gradient.
3. The index of performance is determined at the new operating point. If the current index of performance is greater than the previous IP, take another step move in the direction of the previous gradient.
4. Repeat step 3 until no further improvement in IP results. When the current IP is less than the previous IP, determine the gradient at the previous point. Go to step 2 in the procedure.

The advantage of the optimum gradient method is that in most search problems it will not be necessary to make exploratory moves to find the gradient after every step move. Since there is a time and cost associated with each exploratory move, the optimum gradient method will be less time consuming and less expensive to operate in most search problems.

EXAMPLE 20.14

To illustrate how the optimum gradient method works, we will use the response surface from the previous examples in this section.

$$z = 24x_1 + 22x_2 - x_1^2 - 0.5x_2^2$$

Starting from the point $x_1 = 5$, $x_2 = 6$, the gradient was found in Example 20.11 to be

$$G_p = 14i + 16j$$

To compare the optimum gradient method with the method of steepest ascent, the same step-move size of 5 units will be used from Example 20.13. The first step move in the optimum gradient method will be identical to the initial move in the method of steepest ascent (see Example 20.13).

Cycle 1:

$$\text{new } x_1 = 5.0 + 5(0.658) = 8.290$$

$$\text{new } x_2 = 6.0 + 5(0.753) = 9.765$$

At the starting point the index of performance had a value $z = 209$, and after the first move the new IP value is $z = 331.6$. Since the new IP value is greater than the previous one, we take another step move in the same direction (step 3 of the procedure).

Cycle 2:

$$\text{new } x_1 = 8.290 + 5(0.658) = 11.580$$

$$\text{new } x_2 = 9.765 + 5(0.753) = 13.530$$

The new IP value is

$$z = 24(11.58) + 22(13.53) - (11.58)^2 - 0.5(13.53)^2 = 349.9$$

Another step move is taken in the original direction since the IP has been further increased.

Cycle 3:

$$\text{new } x_1 = 11.58 + 5(0.658) = 14.870$$

$$\text{new } x_2 = 13.53 + 5(0.753) = 17.295$$

The corresponding $z = 366.7$.

Cycle 4:

$$\text{new } x_1 = 14.87 + 5(0.658) = 18.16$$

$$\text{new } x_2 = 17.295 + 5(0.753) = 21.06$$

The new IP value is $z = 347.6$.

Since the latest index of performance value is less than the previous value, we go back to the previous point and determine the gradient as provided in step 4 of the procedure. The previous operating point was $x_1 = 14.87$, $x_2 = 17.295$. The gradient components are

$$G_{1p} = 24 - 2(14.87) = -5.74$$

$$G_{2p} = 22 - (17.295) = 4.705$$

The magnitude of the gradient is

$$M_p = 7.422$$

Therefore, using this point ($x_1 = 14.87$, $x_2 = 17.295$) to proceed with our search in the revised direction, we get:

Cycle 5:

$$\text{new } x_1 = 14.87 + 5\left(\frac{-5.74}{7.422}\right) = 11.003$$

$$\text{new } x_2 = 17.295 + 5\left(\frac{4.705}{7.422}\right) = 20.465$$

The index of performance is $z = 383.8$, which is greater than the previous point, where $z = 366.7$.

Cycle 6:

$$\text{new } x_1 = 11.003 + 5(-0.773) = 7.136$$

$$\text{new } x_2 = 20.465 + 5(0.634) = 23.635$$

The corresponding $z = 361.0$. The reduction in index of performance means that we should redetermine the gradient components at the previous point ($x_1 = 11.003$, $x_2 = 20.465$).

$$G_{1p} = 24 - 2(11.003) = 1.994$$

$$G_{2p} = 22 - 20.465 = 1.535$$

$$M_p = 2.516$$

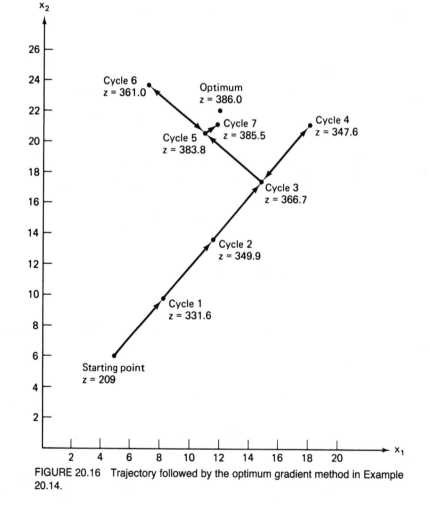

FIGURE 20.16   Trajectory followed by the optimum gradient method in Example 20.14.

The reader might observe that the direction of the gradient has virtually reversed itself from the previous value. This is the signal that the search has overstepped the optimum point. A reduction in the step size is therefore advisable. We shall (arbitrarily) reduce the length of the step move from 5.0 to 1.0 and proceed.

Cycle 7:

$$\text{new } x_1 = 11.003 + 1 \left(\frac{1.994}{2.516} \right) = 11.796$$

$$\text{new } x_2 = 20.465 + 1 \left(\frac{1.535}{2.516} \right) = 21.075$$

The corresponding IP value is $z = 385.5$.

Additional cycles will cause the search to begin to oscillate back and forth across the summit of the response surface.

From Example 20.11 the reader will recall the actual location of the optimum to be at $x_1 = 12$ and $x_2 = 22$. The corresponding IP value is $z = 386$. The optimum gradient method has led us to within 0.13% of the maximum IP on this response surface. Of course, in a real search problem in manufacturing, the true optimum index of performance would not be known.

The trajectory followed by this search procedure is illustrated in Figure 20.16.

REFERENCES

[1] AKIKI, G., "Application of Regression Analysis in Microelectronics Manufacturing," MSE 427 Project, Lehigh University, Bethlehem, Pa., Spring 1985.

[2] BELLMAN, R. E., and S. E. DREYFUS, *Applied Dynamic Programming*, Princeton University Press, Princeton, N.J., 1962.

[3] BOX, G. E. P., and N. R. DRAPER, *Evolutionary Operation*, John Wiley & Sons, Inc., New York, 1969.

[4] DAVIES, W. D. T., *System Identification for Self-Adaptive Control*, Wiley-Interscience, London, 1970.

[5] DRAPER, N. R., and H. SMITH, *Applied Regression Analysis*, John Wiley & Sons, Inc., New York, 1966.

[6] EVELEIGH, V. W., *Adaptive Control and Optimization Techniques*, McGraw-Hill Book Company, New York, 1967.

[7] GROOVER, M. P., "Adaptive Control and Adaptive Control Machining," *Educational Module*, MAPEC, Copyright Purdue Research Foundation, 1977.

[8] HARRISON, T. J. (Editor), *Minicomputers in Industrial Control*, Instrument Society of America, Pittsburgh, Pa., 1978.

[9] IDLESOHN, J. M., "10 Ways to Find the Optimum," *Control Engineering*, June 1964, pp. 97–100.

[10] LEE, T. H., G. E. ADAMS, and W. M. GAINES, *Computer Process Control: Modeling and Optimization*, John Wiley & Sons, Inc., New York, 1968.

[11] PRESSMAN, R. S., and J. E. WILLIAMS, *Numerical Control and Computer-Aided Manufac-turing,* John Wiley & Sons, Inc., New York, 1977.

[12] SAVAS, E. S., *Computer Control of Industrial Processes,* McGraw-Hill Book Company, New York, 1965.

[13] SMITH, C. L. *Digital Computer Process Control,* Intext Educational Publishers, Scranton, Pa., 1972.

[14] TAHA, H. A., *Operations Research, An Introduction,* 3rd ed., Macmillan Publishing Co., Inc., New York, 1982.

[15] TIPNIS, V. A., "Development of Mathematical Models for Adaptive Control Systems," *Proceedings,* 13th Annual Meeting of the Numerical Control Society, March, 1976, Cincinnati, Ohio, pp. 149–156.

[16] WAGNER, H. M., *Principles of Operations Research,* 2nd ed., Prentice-Hall, Inc., Englewood Cliffs, N.J., 1975.

[17] WHITEHOUSE, G. E., and B. L., WECHSLER, *Applied Operations Research,* John Wiley & Sons, Inc., New York, 1976.

[18] WILDE, D. J., *Optimum Seeking Methods,* Prentice-Hall, Inc., Englewood Cliffs, N.J., 1964.

[19] WILDE, D. J., and C. S. BEIGHTLER, *Foundations of Optimization,* 2nd ed., Prentice-Hall, Inc., Englewood Cliffs, N.J., 1979.

PROBLEMS

20.1. Consider some manufacturing or industrial process with which you are familiar. For this process, classify the process variables into the following categories:
   (a) Input variables
       i. Controllable input variables
       ii. Uncontrollable input variables
       iii. Fixed variables
   (b) Output variables
       i. Measurable output variables
       ii. Performance evaluation variables
   Discuss the general effect of each of the input variables on the measurable output variables. (If there is a large number of input variables of the three types, limit your discussion to those variables which are the most important.) How is the performance evaluation variable determined from the measurable output variables?

20.2. For the process considered in Problem 20.1, what are the practical constraints on the values the variables can assume?

20.3. In Problem 20.1, can a mathematical model of the process be determined to express:
   (a) The relationship between the controllable input variables and the measurable output variables?
   (b) The relationship between the measurable output variables and the performance evaluation variable?
   According to your answers to parts (a) and (b) and your knowledge of the process, what type of control strategy would be most appropriate for the process?

20.4. Consider a process similar to the one shown in Figure 20.2, except that the transfer function for the process is given by

$$\frac{y(s)}{x(s)} = \frac{37.2}{s + 5.8}$$

The desired steady-state value of the output y is 10.0. Set up the problem as a steady-state optimal control problem with objective function:

$$\text{minimize } z = (10 - y)^2$$

Solve for the required step input x that will achieve this objective in the steady state.

20.5. The performance of a certain manufacturing process is determined by two input variables, x_1 and x_2. The performance evaluation variable z represents the process yield, which is to be maximized. The relationship between yield z and the two inputs x_1 and x_2 has been determined as follows:

$$z = 0.523 + 0.020x_1 - 0.0012x_1^2 + 0.17x_2 - 0.025x_2^3$$

The constraints on the values of x_1 and x_2 are as follows: $2.2 < x_1 < 14.0, 0.7 < x_2 < 2.0$. Within these constraints, what values of x_1 and x_2 will maximize the yield? What is the maximum yield that can be expected from the process?

20.6. The measurable output variables for a new experimental welding process are y_1 and y_2. These outputs are regulated by means of two inputs to the process, which can be manipulated as desired. The two inputs are x_1 and x_2. The relationships between inputs and outputs are as follows:

$$y_1 = 1.6 + 2.2x_1 + 3.7x_2$$

$$y_2 = 7.1x_2$$

The most appropriate performance evaluation variable, z, for the welding process is the linear speed of the welding head, since this is a measure of the production rate. The objective in the process is to maximize this performance variable. In the research on the process, it has been determined that z is related to the two outputs y_1 and y_2 as follows:

$$z = 3.0y_1 - 0.40y_1^2 + 1.8y_2 - 1.208y_2^2$$

Determine the values of x_1 and x_2 that maximize the welding head speed z.

20.7. The performance z of a process is related to the inputs x_1 and x_2 by the following equation:

$$z = 25x_1 - 2x_1^2 + 41x_2 - 5x_2^2 + 4x_1x_2$$

Find the values x_1 and x_2 that maximize z. What is the optimum z value?

20.8. Solve the following linear programming problem:

$$\text{maximize } z = 10x_1 + 3x_2$$

subject to

$$6x_1 + 4x_2 \leqslant 24$$

$$4x_1 + 8x_2 \leqslant 40$$

$$10x_1 + 2x_2 \leqslant 30$$

$$x_1 \leqslant 0, \; x_2 \leqslant 0$$

20.9. One of the production shops at Special-T Company makes two products, each of which requires three manufacturing operations. The company can sell all it can make of these two products. In fact, it is considering a proposal to increase production capacity. For the time being, however, the constraints on the operations and other data are given in the following table:

Product	Production time required per unit (h/unit)			Cost ($)	Selling Price ($)
	Oper 1	*Oper 2*	*Oper 3*		
1	1.2	2.3	4.5	80	95
2	2.3	6.8	1.9	110	130
Hours available	24.0	32.0	24.0		

(a) Determine the product mix that maximizes profit.
(b) If production capacity were to be increased, to which operations should the additional capacity be allocated? Is there surplus capacity on any operation?

20.10. Assume a process whose mathematical model is given by

$$y = A + Bx$$

The value of A remains constant throughout process operation at $A = 50$. However, the value of B varies through a range from $B = 10$ to 20. In order to optimize the process the value of B must be measured. It has been decided that the instantaneous approximation method is to be used. If y and x can be measured with sufficient accuracy, what is the value of B if $y = 135$ and $x = 5$.

20.11. Assume that a process can be modeled by an equation of the form

$$y = Ax + B/x$$

The value of A remains constant throughout process operation at $A = 32$. However, the value of B fluctuates slowly because of gradual environmental changes.
(a) Use the instantaneous approximation method to determine the value of B if y and x have been recently measured at values $y = 95.0$ and $x = 2.1$.
(b) Using the value of B determined in part (a), determine the value of x that will minimize y, which is a measure of product cost.
(c) What new value of y will result if the change in x from part (b) is implemented?

20.12. Consider the welding process from Problem 20.6. It has been found in applications that the process model is sensitive to variations in work material and atmospheric conditions. The input/output relationships can be modeled by equations of the form

$$y_1 = 1.6 + Ax_1 + 3.7x_2$$

$$y_2 = Bx_2$$

Fortunately, the four variables y_1, y_2, x_1, and x_2 can all be measured during the operation. During the welding of a special high-strength alloy in an enclosed vessel, the following values were measured:

$$y_1 = 4.05 \quad x_1 = 0.91$$

$$y_2 = 0.87 \quad x_2 = 0.13$$

As in Problem 20.6, the objective is to maximize the objective function

$$z = 3.0y_1 - 0.40y_1^2 + 1.8y_2 - 1.208y_2^2$$

(a) From the variable measurements, determine the unknown parameter values, A and B.
(b) What changes should be made in the inputs x_1 and x_2?

20.13. The tool-chip thermocouple is a thermocouple whose two dissimilar metals are the cutting tool and the chip. The cutting temperature in a machining operation can be monitored by measuring the emf output at the tool-chip interface (this interface constitutes the junction of the two dissimilar metals of the thermocouple). It has been proposed to monitor cutting temperature as part of an adaptive control machining system. The data given below were taken during the calibration of the tool-chip thermocouple.

Tool-chip thermocouple (mV)	11.5	12.7	14.0	15.3	17.1	18.2	18.9
Temperature (°C)	552	601	670	742	839	878	930

(a) Use the least-squares method to determine the calibration equation

$$y = A + Bx$$

where y = temperature, °C
    x = emf output of the tool-chip thermocouple, mV

(b) What are the correlation coefficient and the standard error of estimate for the equation?

20.14. The model for a certain component of a manufacturing process is given by

$$y = Ax^n$$

However, the values of A and n are observed to change slowly over time because of unpredictable environmental factors. Determining these two parameters is a necessary condition for control of the process. Both the independent variable x and the dependent variable y can be measured during the operation. Over a 15-min observation period, the following data have been monitored on x and y:

x	50.1	52.0	54.9	57.2	53.8	59.7
y	606	621	642	659	635	675

Determine by the least-squares method the values of A and n in the model above. (*Hint:* By a logarithmic transformation, the equation $y = Ax^n$ can be converted into

$$\ln y = \ln A + n \ln x$$

which has the standard linear equation form for using the least squares.)

20.15. Derive the normal equations for the linear equation

$$y = A + Bx_1 + Cx_2$$

20.16. The process model for a certain component of an industrial operation is

$$K \frac{dy}{dt} + y = A + Bx$$

where the parameters K, A, and B vary over time. During operation, the values of dy/dt, y, and x can all be measured. During a particular 7-min interval the following values have been sampled:

Time	dy/dt	y	x
1	4.0	11.0	3.0
2	3.1	18.2	4.0
3	1.9	22.4	4.5
4	1.0	25.5	4.7
5	-0.2	26.4	4.4
6	-0.9	25.9	4.0
7	-1.0	24.8	3.8

Use the normal equations derived in Problem 20.15 to determine the current values of the parameters K, A, and B in the model above. *Notes:* (1) The same sort of rearrangement of the equation illustrated in Example 20.9 must be used in this problem; (2) the computations must be carried out with a high degree of precision.

20.17. The response surface for the index of performance as a function of two input variables is given by the following equation:

$$z = 25x_1 - 2x_1^2 + 41x_2 - 5x_2^2 + 4x_1x_2$$

(a) Determine the gradient at the point defined by $x_1 = 2$, $x_2 = 2$.

(b) Determine the magnitude of the gradient at the same point.

(c) Determine the direction of the gradient.

20.18. For the same response surface from Problem 20.17, solve for the gradient, the magnitude of the gradient, and the direction of the gradient at the point

$$x_1 = 15, x_2 = 10.$$

20.19. For the same response surface from Problem 20.17, solve for the gradient, the magnitude, and the direction at the point $x_1 = 17.25$, $x_2 = 11.0$.

20.20. The current operating point for a particular long-run machining job is: cutting speed = 200 ft/min (1.016 m/s) and feed rate = 0.010 in./rev (0.254 mm/rev). At these conditions, the unit cost of the operation = $2.00. A series of exploratory moves have been made to determine whether improvements in cutting conditions can be made. The results given in the accompanying table have been recorded (these data represent the averages of several replications).

Speed		Feed		Unit cost
ft/min	m/s	in./rev	mm/rev	
250	1.27	0.012	0.305	$2.22
250	1.27	0.008	0.203	1.96
150	0.762	0.012	0.305	2.01
150	0.762	0.008	0.203	1.78

(a) With data such as these, there is a large difference in the units scale for speed versus the units scale for feed rate. This results in problems during calculation and interpretation of the gradient. To overcome these problems, the data can be coded. The objective of the data coding is to approximately equalize the scale of the two variables, in this case speed and feed. For example, in the U.S. Customary units, the speed in ft/min could be divided by 20 and the feed in in./rev could be multiplied by 1000. The problem is not so severe in the SI units. Here the scale could be leveled by multiplying feed in mm/rev by 4.0. Rewrite the table by coding both the U.S.C. and SI variables as indicated.

(b) Determine the gradient components in either the (coded) U.S.C. or SI units system.

(c) If the step move to be taken in the method of steepest ascent is defined by $C = 2.0$ in Eqs. (20.26), determine the new operating conditions.

20.21. Suppose that the response surface for a certain manufacturing process was defined by the equation

$$z = 17x_1 + 27x_2 - x_1^2 - 0.9x_2^2$$

Determine the approximate optimum operating point using the method of steepest ascent. The starting point of the search should be $x_1 = 2$, $x_2 = 3$, and the step size should be $C = 4.0$.

20.22. Solve Problem 20.21 using the optimum gradient method.

chapter **21**

Sequence Control and Programmable Controllers

In Chapter 19 we discussed control systems in which the process variables are analog—they can take on any value within a range of possible values. In the present chapter we consider control systems in which the variables are binary—they can have either of two possible values, 1 or 0. The values can be interpreted to mean ON or OFF, true or false, object present or not present, high voltage value or low voltage value, and so on, depending on the application. These control systems operate by turning on and off switches, motors, valves, and other devices in response to operating conditions and as a function of time. A list of on/off devices commonly used in industrial control systems is presented in Table 21.1, along with the interpretation of their 0 and 1 values. The input devices are those which send signals to the controller, and the output devices are those which are regulated by the controller.

In previous chapters we have referred to these types of systems as sequence control systems. For example, in the operation of transfer lines and automated assembly machines, sequence control is used to coordinate the various actions of the production system (e.g., transfer of parts, feeding of the machining head, etc.). In our discussion of robot workcell control, sequence control was identified as the principal means of controlling and sequencing the work cycle.

TABLE 21.1 Binary Input and Output Devices

Device	One/zero interpretation
Input	
Limit switch	Contact/no contact
Photodetector	Contact/no contact
Pushbutton switch	On/off
Timer	On/off
Control relay	Contact/no contact
Circuit breaker	Contact/no contact
Output	
Motor	On/off
Alarm buzzer	On/off
Control relay	Contact/no contact
Lights	On/off
Valves	Closed/open
Clutch	Engaged/not engaged
Solenoid	Energized/not energized

A modern controller device used extensively for sequence control today in transfer lines, robotics, process control, and many other automated systems is the programmable logic controller, or simply, programmable controller. In this chapter we discuss some of the important operating principles of sequence control and how programmable controllers are used to implement it.

21.1 LOGIC CONTROL AND SEQUENCING

What we have been referring to as sequence control can be divided into two categories: logic control and sequencing. Both types operate on variables that can take either of two values (e.g., on and off). Both are referred to as switching systems in the sense that they switch their output values on and off during operation.

A *logic control system,* also referred to in the literature as a *combinational system* [8,9], is a switching system whose output at any moment is determined exclusively by the values of the inputs. A logic control system has no memory and does not consider any previous values of input signals in determining the output signal. Neither does it have any operating characteristics which perform as a function of time.

We can borrow an example from robotics to illustrate logic control. Suppose that in a machine loading application, the robot is programmed to pick up a raw workpart from a known stopping point along a conveyor and place it into a forging die. Three conditions must be satisfied to initiate the loading cycle. First, the raw workpart must be at the stopping point; second, the forge press must have completed the process on the previous part; and third, the previous part must be removed from the die. The first condition can be indicated by means of a simple limit switch that senses the presence of the part at the conveyor stop, and transmits an ON signal to the robot controller. The second condition can be indicated by the forge press, which sends an ON signal after it has completed the previous cycle. The third condition might be determined by a photodetector designed to sense the presence or absence of the part in the forging die. When the finished part is removed from the die, an ON signal is transmitted by the photocell. All three of these ON signals must be received by the robot controller in order to initiate the work cycle. Although we have referred to these incoming signals in robotics as input interlocks, they also illustrate logic control. When these input signals have been received by the controller, the robot loading cycle is switched on. No previous conditions or past history are needed.

A *sequencing system* is one that uses internal timing devices to determine when to initiate changes in output variables. Washing machines, dryers, dishwashers, and similar appliances use sequencing systems to time the start and stop of cycle elements. There are many industrial applications of sequencing systems. For example, suppose that an induction heating coil is used to heat a part to the desired temperature in our previous example of a robotics forging application. An induction heating system uses a high-energy source focused on an object to heat it. Rather than use a temperature sensor that might be damaged by the induction coil, the heating cycle could be timed so that enough energy was provided to heat the workpart to the desired temperature. The heating process is sufficiently predictable that a certain duration of time in the induction coil will consistently heat the part to a certain temperature (with minimum variation).

Sequence control, as we are using the term in this book, includes both logic control and sequencing. It provides output signals which are a function of the instantaneous input variables as well as a function of time. In Section 21.2 we describe the basic building blocks of logic control systems, and in Section 21.3 we describe some of the building blocks of sequencing systems.

21.2 LOGIC CONTROL ELEMENTS

The basic elements of logic control systems are the logic gates AND, OR, and NOT. In each case, the logic gate is designed to provide a specified output value based on the values of the input(s). For both inputs and outputs, the values can be either of two levels, the binary values 0 or 1. For purposes of industrial control, we will define 0 (zero) to mean OFF and 1 (one) to mean ON.

The basic elements can be physically realized in a number of different ways, including the use of electromagnetic relays, discrete transistors, fluidic devices, and integrated microelectronic circuits. We will briefly discuss some of these hardware devices to reinforce the reader's understanding of the switching systems. Today, logic control is most commonly implemented by means of programmable controllers and control computers. These controllers rely on microelectronic circuits. Of greater concern in our presentation than the detailed operation of the individual devices is how the controllers are used in production automation and control.

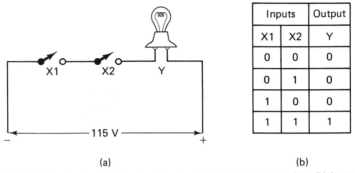

FIGURE 21.1   Logical AND gate: (a) circuit illustrating its operation; (b) its truth table.

The logical AND, OR, and NOT gates

The *logical AND gate* outputs a value of 1 if all of the inputs are 1, and 0 otherwise. Figure 21.1(a) illustrates the operation of a logical AND gate. If both of the switches, X1 and X2 (representing inputs), in the circuit are closed, the lamp Y (representing the output) is on. The truth table is often used to present the operation of logic systems. The *truth table* is a tabulation of all of the combinations of input values to the corresponding logical output values. The truth table for the AND gate is presented in Figure 21.1(b).

The AND gate might be used in an automated production system to indicate that two (or more) actions have been successfully completed, therefore signaling that the next step in the process should be initiated. The interlock system in our previous robot forging example illustrates the AND gate. All three conditions must be satisfied before the loading of the forge is allowed to occur.

The *logical OR gate* outputs a value of 1 if either of the inputs have a value of 1, and 0 otherwise. Figure 21.2(a) shows how the OR gate operates. In this case, the two input signals X1 and X1 are arranged in a parallel circuit, so that if either of the switches

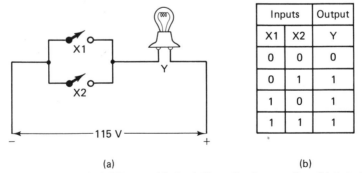

FIGURE 21.2   Logical OR gate: (a) circuit illustrating its operation; (b) its truth table.

is closed, the lamp Y will be on. The truth table for the OR gate is presented in Figure 21.2(b).

A possible use of the OR gate for an automated production system is in a safety monitoring circuit. Suppose that two sensors are utilized to monitor two different safety hazards. When a hazard is present, the sensors emit a positive signal. If either of the safety hazards is present, the operator should be alerted by means of an alarm buzzer. The OR gate could be used to turn on the alarm if either of the sensors signaled a positive hazard.

Both the AND and OR gates can be used with two or more inputs without changing their method of operation. The NOT gate has a single input. The operation of the *logical NOT gate* is as follows: If the input is 1, the output is 0; if the input is 0, the output is 1. Figure 21.3(a) shows a circuit in which the input switch X1 is arranged in parallel with the output so that the voltage flows through the lower path when the switch is closed (thus Y = 0), and through the upper path when the switch is open (thus Y = 1). The truth table for the NOT gate is shown in Figure 21.3(b).

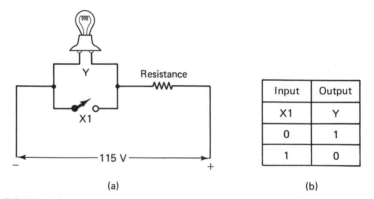

Input	Output
X1	Y
0	1
1	0

(a)   (b)

FIGURE 21.3   Logical NOT gate: (a) circuit illustrating its operation; (b) its truth table.

Various diagramming techniques have been developed to represent the logic elements and their relationships in a given logic control system. The logic network diagram is one of the most common methods. Symbols used in the logic network diagram are illustrated in Figure 21.4. We demonstrate the use of the logic network diagram in several examples at the end of this section.

In addition to the three basic elements, there are two more elements that can be identified for use in combinational switching circuits. These are the NAND and NOR gates. The logical NAND gate is formed by combining an AND gate and a NOT gate in sequence, as shown in Figure 21.5(a). The logic network symbol for the NAND gate and its truth table are presented in parts (b) and (c) of Figure 21.5. The logical NOR gate is formed by combining an OR gate followed by a NOT gate as illustrated in Figure 21.6(a). The logic network symbol and truth table for the NOR gate are presented in Figure 21.6(b) and (c).

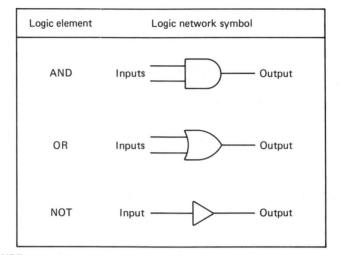

FIGURE 21.4   Symbols for AND, OR, and NOT used in logic network diagrams.

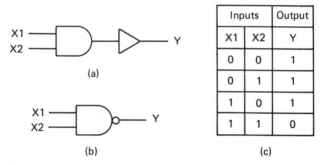

	Inputs		Output
	X1	X2	Y
	0	0	1
	0	1	1
	1	0	1
	1	1	0

FIGURE 21.5   NAND gate: (a) combining AND and NOT gates to form NAND; (b) logic network symbol for NAND; (c) truth table for NAND.

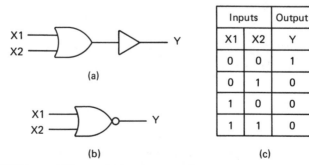

	Inputs		Output
	X1	X2	Y
	0	0	1
	0	1	0
	1	0	0
	1	1	0

FIGURE 21.6   NOR gate: (a) combining OR and NOT gates to form NOR; (b) logic network symbol for NOR; (c) truth table for NOR.

Boolean algebra

The three logic elements AND, OR, and NOT form the foundation for a special algebra that was developed around 1847 by George Boole and which bears his name. Its original purpose was to provide a symbolic means of testing whether complex statements of logic were TRUE or FALSE. It was not until about a century later that Boolean algebra was shown to be useful in digital logic systems. We briefly describe some of the fundamentals of Boolean algebra here, with a minimum of elaboration.

In the notation of Boolean algebra, the AND function is expressed as

$$Y = X1 \cdot X2 \tag{21.1}$$

This is called the *logical product* of X1 and X2. The following list enumerates the results of the AND function for four combinations of two binary variables:

$$0 \cdot 0 = 0$$
$$0 \cdot 1 = 0$$
$$1 \cdot 0 = 0$$
$$1 \cdot 1 = 1$$

The OR function in Boolean algebra notation is given by

$$Y = X1 + X2 \tag{21.2}$$

This is called the *logical sum* of X1 and X2. Enumerating the OR function for the four combinations of binary values, we have

$$0 + 0 = 0$$
$$0 + 1 = 1$$
$$1 + 0 = 1$$
$$1 + 1 = 1$$

The NOT function is referred to as the *negation* or *inversion* of the variable. It is indicated by placing a bar above the variable (e.g., NOT X1 = $\overline{X1}$). To illustrate,

$$\overline{0} = 1$$
$$\overline{1} = 0$$

Note in each of the illustrations above that the results of the Boolean algebra operations agree with the truth tables for these functions previously given.

There are certain laws and theorems of Boolean algebra. We cite them in Table

TABLE 21.2 Laws and Theorems of Boolean Algebra

Commutative law:
$$X + Y = Y + X$$
$$X \cdot Y = Y \cdot X$$

Associative law:
$$X + Y + Z = X + (Y + Z)$$
$$= (X + Y) + Z$$

$$X \cdot Y \cdot Z = X \cdot (Y \cdot Z)$$
$$= (X \cdot Y) \cdot Z$$

Distributive law:
$$X \cdot Y + X \cdot Z = X \cdot (Y + Z)$$
$$(X + Y) \cdot (Z + W) = X \cdot Z + X \cdot W + Y \cdot Z + Y \cdot W$$

Law of absorption:
$$X \cdot (X + Y) = X + X \cdot Y = X$$

De Morgan's laws:
$$\overline{(X + Y)} = \overline{X} \cdot \overline{Y}$$
$$\overline{(X \cdot Y)} = \overline{X} + \overline{Y}$$

Consistency theorem:
$$X \cdot Y + X \cdot \overline{Y} = X$$
$$(X + Y) \cdot (X + \overline{Y}) = X$$

Inclusion theorem:
$$X \cdot \overline{X} = 0$$
$$X + \overline{X} = 1$$

21.2. These laws and theorems can often be applied to simplify logic circuits and reduce the number of elements required to implement the logic, with resulting savings in hardware and/or programming time. The reader is referred to a text that discusses Boolean algebra and related topics for a detailed explanation of these theorems.

Hardware for implementing combinational systems

Among the hardware components used to construct the types of logic control systems described in this section are binary sensors, solenoids, and relays.

Binary sensors can be used as input devices to the controller to indicate either of the two possible states of a certain process variable. The two states might be: presence or absence of a workpart in a fixture, whether or not a machine slide has reached the end of its travel, whether a valve is open or closed, and similar binary conditions. The two possible states are interpreted according to the output signal of the sensor. The output can be either 1 or 0, determined by the presence or absence of the sensor signal (usually a low-voltage signal). Examples of binary sensors are limit switches and photodetector switches (Table 21.1).

A *solenoid* is an electromagnetic actuator that can be used to open and close a valve, electrical contact, or other mechanical device. A schematic diagram of the mechanism is shown in Figure 21.7. The solenoid operates by means of an electrical current flowing through a wire coil to produce a magnetic field within (and around) the coil. The force of the magnetic field is used to pull a metal core toward the center of the coil. A mechanical spring causes the core to be retracted out of the coil when the electrical current is turned off. One of the potential problems with the solenoid described here is that in the event of a power failure, the solenoid becomes deenergized and the spring retracts the core out of the coil. This may result in harmful consequences to the process. A double-acting solenoid is one in which the core can be driven in either direction by reversing the polarity of the coil. If the power fails, the core remains in its current position rather than being driven by a spring to some neutral position.

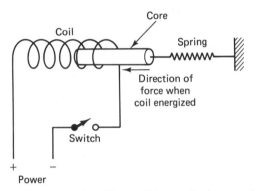

FIGURE 21.7   Solenoid operation. When coil is energized, magnetic field pulls core into coil. When de-energized, spring pulls core out of coil.

An *electromechanical relay* is an electrical switch that can be actuated indirectly by another switch. A diagram of the electromechanical relay is shown in Figure 21.8. Its operation relies on the use of an electromagnetic force generated by a coil similar to the action of the solenoid described above. When the coil is energized, an armature is drawn toward the coil. The armature is attached to a lever arm as indicated in the diagram. The lever arm pushes against one of the contacts, causing it to close against the opposite contact. Owing to the springiness of the contacts, they open when the coil is deenergized.

There are variations in the design of electromechanical relays, and Figure 21.8 is only meant to be a simplified representation. Relays can be designed with normally open contacts (as shown in our diagram) or with normally closed contacts (in which case, the actuation of the relay causes the contacts to open). The electromechanical relay has been a common device in logic controllers, but relay-based controllers are rapidly being replaced by programmable logic controllers.

Let us summarize our discussion of logic control with some examples.

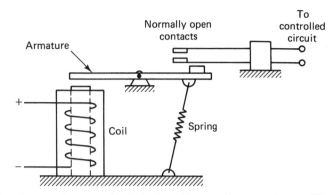

FIGURE 21.8 Electromechanical relay with normally open contacts. When coil is energized, armature is pulled down, causing lever arm to close the contacts. When deenergized, spring pulls lever arm down, separating contacts.

EXAMPLE 21.1

The robot machine loading example described at the beginning of Section 21.2 requires three conditions to be satisfied before the loading sequence is initiated. Determine the Boolean algebra expression and the logic network diagram that represent the operation of this interlock system.

Solution:

Let $X1$ = whether the raw workpart is present at the conveyor stopping point ($X1$ = 1 for present, $X1$ = 0 for not present). Let $X2$ = whether the press cycle for the previous part has completed ($X2$ = 1 for completed, 0 for not completed). Let $X3$ = whether the previous part has been removed from the die ($X3$ = 1 for removed, $X3$ = 0 for not removed). Finally, let Y = whether the loading sequence can be started (Y = 1 for begin, Y = 0 for wait). The Boolean algebra expression is

$$Y = X1 \cdot X2 \cdot X3$$

All three conditions must be satisfied, so the logical AND function is used. All of the inputs $X1$, $X2$, and $X3$ must have values of 1 before Y = 1, hence initiating the start of the loading sequence. The logic network diagram for this interlock condition is presented in Figure 21.9.

FIGURE 21.9 Logic network diagram for robotic machine loading interlock system of Example 21.1.

EXAMPLE 21.2

A pushbutton switch used for starting and stopping electric motors and other powered devices is a common hardware component in an industrial control system. As shown in Figure 21.10(a), it consists of a box with two buttons, one for START and the other for STOP. When the START

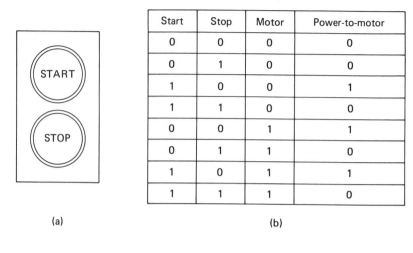

Start	Stop	Motor	Power-to-motor
0	0	0	0
0	1	0	0
1	0	0	1
1	1	0	0
0	0	1	1
0	1	1	0
1	0	1	1
1	1	1	0

(a)   (b)

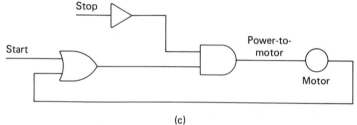

(c)

FIGURE 21.10   (a) Pushbutton switch; (b) its truth table; (c) its logic network diagram.

button is depressed momentarily by a human operator, power is supplied and maintained to the motor (or other load) until the STOP button is pressed. The values of the variables can be defined as follows:

START = 0 normally open contact status

START = 1 when the START button is pressed to contact

STOP = 0 normally closed contact status

STOP = 1 when the STOP button is pressed to break contact

MOTOR = 0 when off (not running)

MOTOR = 1 when on

POWER-TO-MOTOR is the output of the pushbutton switch

POWER-TO-MOTOR = 0 when the contacts are open

POWER-TO-MOTOR = 1 when the contacts are closed

The truth table for the pushbutton is presented in Figure 21.10(b). From an initial motor off condition (MOTOR = 0), the motor is started by depressing the start button (START = 1). If the stop button is in its normally closed condition (STOP = 0), power will be supplied to the motor (POWER-TO-MOTOR = 1). While the motor is running (MOTOR = 1), it can be stopped by depressing the stop button (STOP = 1). The corresponding network logic diagram is shown in Figure 21.10(c).

In a sense, the pushbutton switch of Example 21.2 goes slightly beyond our definition of a pure logic system because it exhibits characteristics of memory. The MOTOR and POWER-TO-MOTOR variables are virtually the same signal. The conditions that determine whether power will flow to the motor are different depending on the motor ON/OFF status. [Compare the first four lines of the truth table with the last four lines in Figure 21.10(b).] It is as if the control logic must remember whether the motor is on or off to decide what conditions will determine the value of the output signal. This memory feature is exhibited by the feedback loop (the lower branch) in the logic network diagram of Figure 21.10(c).

21.3 SEQUENCING ELEMENTS

Many applications in automation require the controller to provide a prescheduled set of ON/OFF control functions for the output variables. The outputs are usually provided in an open-loop fashion, meaning that there is no feedback verification that the control function has actually been executed. Another feature that typifies this mode of control is that the sequence of output signals is usually cyclical; the signals occur in the same repeated pattern within each regular cycle. Timers and counters illustrate this type of control component.

Timers

The basic component used in sequencing applications is the timer. One of the simplest ways to construct a timer is illustrated in Figure 21.11. It consists of a limit switch riding on a rotating cam. The cam is attached through a gear reduction box to the shaft of a

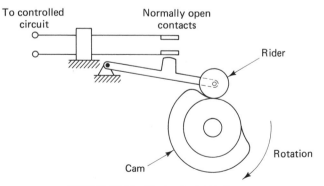

FIGURE 21.11 Mechanical cam timer.

small electric motor. The limit switch opens and closes according to the rise and fall of the cam as it rotates. The design of the cam, and its rotational speed as determined by the motor and gear box, define the on and off schedule of the timer. Timers of this type can be designed to provide a specified delay between the receipt of an input signal and the sending of an output signal. The input signal starts the rotation of the cam, and the delay in the output signal depends on the length of time before the change in height of the cam causes the limit switch to close its contacts.

To control multiple on–off devices, a drum timer can be used. The mechanical *drum timer* has been a commonly used sequencing device whose operation is similar to the mechanical timer described above. Instead of only one cam attached to the rotating

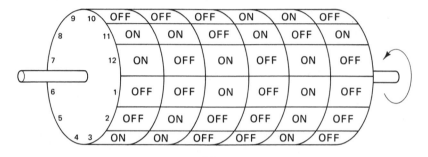

(a)

Output variables

	Y1	Y2	Y3	Y4	Y5	Y6
1	0	0	1	0	1	0
2	0	1	0	0	1	0
3	1	1	0	0	1	0
4	0	1	0	0	1	1
5	0	1	0	0	1	0
6	0	0	0	1	0	0
7	0	0	0	1	0	1
8	0	1	0	1	0	0
9	0	1	0	1	1	0
10	0	0	0	1	1	0
11	1	1	0	1	0	1
12	1	0	1	0	1	0

Timing sequence

(b)

FIGURE 21.12   (a) Cylinder model of a drum timer; (b) matrix of on/off commands around the cylinder.

shaft, a drum consisting of a set of cams is used. A separate limit switch rides on each cam. A constant-speed motor with appropriate gear reduction is used to drive the drum at the desired rotational velocity. As each cam rotates with the drum, it activates the corresponding limit switch according to the location of the high points on the cam. The collection of cams provides a scheduled sequence of ON/OFF controls.

For visualization purposes, we can consider the drum to be a cylinder which is divided into a matrix of on/off commands around its periphery. The cylinder is pictured in Figure 21.12(a) and the corresponding matrix in Figure 21.12(b). The vertical axis of the matrix corresponds to time intervals with each step identified by number. The time intervals are defined to be consistent with the timing requirements of the sequencing application. The durations of the time intervals are determined by the cam shapes representing the different tracks around the cylinder.

The changes in the values of the variables as a function of time for the sequence control system (e.g., drum timer or other ON/OFF controller) can be displayed using a charting technique called a *timing diagram* (the terms *time line diagram* [2] and *timing chart* [9] are also used). The timing diagram is quite simple in concept. The horizontal axis represents time, and the vertical axis consists of a series of plots representing the two possible states of each variable of interest. Figure 21.13 illustrates the timing diagram for the ON/OFF controls depicted in the drum timer matrix of Figure 21.12(b).

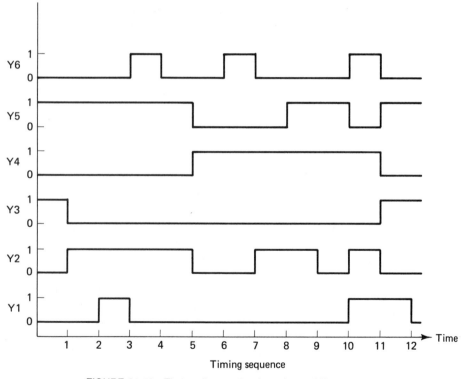

FIGURE 21.13   Timing diagram for drum timer of Figure 21.12.

Where the timing diagram is especially useful is when logic elements and sequencing elements are combined in one control system. In this case, the diagram can be used to help analyze the effects of alternative values of system inputs on the output variables.

Counters

Another device that can be used for sequencing applications is the *counter*. The counter is a mechanical or electronic component used to count a physical quantity (e.g., electrical pulses). Most counters in use today are binary counters which are built using sequential logic gates called flip-flops. Flip-flops are electronic devices that possess memory capability; hence they can be used to store the results of the counting procedure. The instantaneous contents can be displayed or used in some control algorithm.

Counters are frequently used for production applications such as counting the number of products moving down a conveyor. A microswitch, photosensor, or other sensing device can be set up along the production line to detect the presence of products flowing past on the conveyor and to generate an electrical pulse for each unit. The counter then records the number of electrical pulses so that the quantity of units is obtained. This value might be used to simply count the products made during a given time period, or to separate the units into lot sizes suitable for a certain container size (e.g., 12 units per carton) or for some other useful purpose.

Electronic counters can operate in either of two ways: count-up or count-down. The count-up procedure starts at zero and adds to the current value of the count each time another pulse is received. This method might be used, for example, to determine the number of units produced during a certain shift. The count-down method starts with a certain value and subtracts from the total each time a pulse is received. The procedure continues until a value of zero is reached, at which time some action is typically taken, and then the counting procedure starts over. For example, this count-down approach might be used to separate product units into precise quantities suitable for containerizing.

21.4 LADDER LOGIC DIAGRAMS

The logic network diagrams, of the type shown in Figures 21.9 and 21.10(c), are useful for displaying the relationships between combinational logic elements. However, they are inadequate for showing the various input/output variables as a function of time. The timing diagram shows the actions of variables as they change over time, but it is not useful for displaying the logic of the system.

Another diagramming technique that exhibits the logic and, to some extent, the timing and sequencing of the system is the ladder logic diagram. This graphical method also has an important virtue in that it is analogous to the electrical circuits used to accomplish the logic and sequence control. In addition, ladder logic diagrams are familiar to the shop personnel who must construct, test, maintain, and repair the control system.

In a ladder logic diagram, the various logic elements and other components are displayed along horizontal lines or rungs connected on either end to two vertical rails, as illustrated in Figure 21.14. The diagram has the general configuration of a ladder,

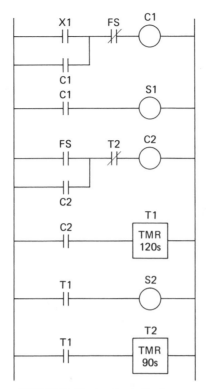

FIGURE 21.14   Ladder logic diagram.

hence its name. The elements and components are contacts (usually representing logical inputs) and loads (representing outputs). The power (e.g., 120 V ac) to the components is provided by the two vertical rails. It is customary in ladder diagrams to locate the inputs to the left of each rung and the outputs to the right.

Symbols used in ladder diagrams for the common logic and sequencing components discussed in the previous sections are presented in Figure 21.15. *Normally open contacts* of a switch or other similar device are symbolized by two short vertical lines along a horizontal rung of the ladder, as in part (a) of the figure. *Normally closed contacts* are shown as the same vertical lines but with a diagonal line across them as in part (b). Both types of contacts are used to represent ON/OFF inputs to the logic circuit. In addition to switches, these inputs include relays, on/off sensors (e.g., limit switches, photodetectors, etc.), and similar binary contact devices.

Output loads such as motors, lights, alarms, solenoids, and other electrical components which are turned on and off by the logic control system are shown as nodes (circles) as indicated in part (c) of Figure 21.15. Timers and counters are symbolized by squares (or rectangles) with appropriate inputs and outputs to properly drive the device as shown in parts (d) and (e). The simple timer requires the specification of the time delay and the input signal that activates the delay. When the input signal is received, the

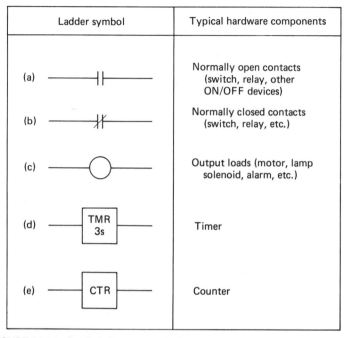

FIGURE 21.15   Symbols for common logic and sequence components in a ladder
logic diagram.

timer waits the specified delay time before switching on the output signal. The timer is
reset (to make it ready for the next delay cycle and set the output back to its initial value)
by turning off the input signal.

There are variations in the way timers operate and we have described perhaps the
simplest possible way in which they work. The operation of drum timers is more involved,
but their operation can be simplified by considering them as a collection of individual
cam timers. Exercise 21.7 considers this problem.

Counters require two inputs. The first is the pulse train (series of on–off signals)
that is counted by the counter. The second is a signal to reset the counter and restart the
counting procedure. Resetting the counter means zeroing the count for a count-up device,
and setting the starting value for a count-down device. The accumulated count is retained
in memory for use if required for the application.

The three basic logic gates (AND, OR, and NOT) can be symbolized in a ladder
logic diagram as illustrated in Figure 21.16. Notice that the NOT symbol is the same as
a normally closed contact, which is the logical inverse of a normally open contact. Several
examples will help in understanding the use of ladder logic diagrams.

EXAMPLE 21.3

Consider the three circuits illustrated in Figures 21.1, 21.2, and 21.3. These are the lamp circuits
used to illustrate the AND, OR, and NOT functions. The three ladder diagrams corresponding to

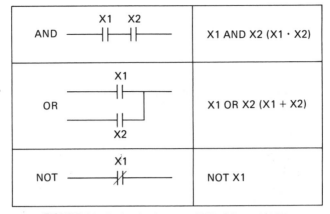

FIGURE 21.16   Logic elements AND, OR, and NOT.

these circuits are presented in Figure 21.17(a), (b), and (c). Note the similarity between the original circuit diagrams and the ladder diagrams shown here.

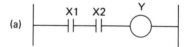

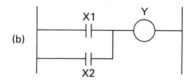

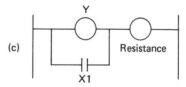

FIGURE 21.17   Three ladder logic diagrams for circuits shown in (a) Figure 21.1, (b) Figure 21.2, and (c) Figure 21.3.

EXAMPLE 21.4

The operation of the pushbutton switch of Example 21.2 can be depicted in a ladder logic diagram. From Figure 21.10, let START be represented by X1, STOP by X2, and MOTOR by Y. The ladder diagram is presented in Figure 21.18. X1 and X2 are input contacts and Y is a load in the diagram. Note how Y serves also as an input contact to provide the POWER-TO-MOTOR connection.

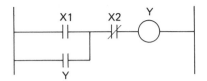

FIGURE 21.18   Ladder logic diagram for the pushbutton switch of Example 21.4.

EXAMPLE 21.5

The operation of a control relay can be readily demonstrated by means of the ladder logic diagram presented in Figure 21.19. As we show in this example, a relay can be used to control on/off actuation of a powered device at some remote location. It can also be used to define alternative decisions in logic control. The diagram in our figure illustrates both uses. The relay is indicated by the load C (for control relay), which controls the on/off operation of two motors (or other types of output loads) Y1 and Y2. When the control switch X is open, the relay is deenergized, thereby connecting the load Y1 to the power lines. In effect, the open switch X turns on motor Y1 by means of the relay. When the control switch is closed, the relay becomes energized. This opens the normally closed contact of the second rung of the ladder and closes the normally open contact of the third rung. In effect, power is shut off to load Y1 and turned on to load Y2.

Example 21.5 illustrates several important features of the ladder logic diagram. First, the same input can be used more than once in the diagram. In our example, the relay contact R was used as an input on both the second and third rungs of the ladder. As we shall see in the following section, this feature of using a given relay contact in several different rungs of the ladder diagram to serve multiple logic functions provides a substantial advantage for the programmable controller over hard-wired control units. With hard-wired relays, separate contacts must be built into the controller for each logic function. A second feature of Example 21.5 is that it is possible for an output (load) on one rung of the diagram to be an input (contact) for another rung. The relay C was the output on the top rung in Figure 21.19, but that output was used as an input elsewhere in the diagram. This same feature was illustrated in the pushbutton ladder diagram of Example 21.4.

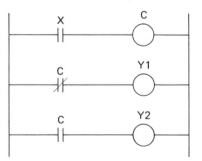

FIGURE 21.19   Ladder logic diagram for the control relay of Example 21.5.

EXAMPLE 21.6

This example is similar to the hydraulic system example shown in Figure 19.1. We examine it in a different way here. Suppose that we have a fluid storage tank as illustrated in Figure 21.20. When the start button X1 is depressed, this energizes the control relay C1. In turn this energizes solenoid S1, which opens a valve, allowing fluid to flow into the tank. When the tank becomes full, the float switch FS closes (the contact is open until the fluid reaches the full level). This opens relay C1, causing the solenoid S1 to be deenergized, thus turning off the in-flow. It also activates timer T1, which provides a 120-s delay for a certain chemical reaction to occur in the tank. At the end of the delay time, the timer energizes a second relay C2 which controls two devices: (1) It energizes solenoid S2, which opens a valve to allow the fluid to flow out of the tank; and (2) it initiates timer T2, which waits 90 s to allow the contents of the tank to be drained. At the end of the 90 s, the timer deenergizes C2 which deenergizes solenoid S2, thus closing the outflow valve. Depressing the start button X1 resets the timers and opens their respective contacts. Construct the ladder logic diagram for the system.

Solution:

The ladder logic diagram is constructed as shown in Figure 21.14.

The ladder logic diagram is an excellent scheme for representing the combinational logic control problems in which the output variables are based directly on the values of the inputs. As indicated by Example 21.6, it can also be used to display sequential control (timer) problems, although the diagram is somewhat more difficult to interpret and analyze for this purpose. At the time of this writing, the ladder diagram represents the principal technique for setting up the control programs in programmable logic controllers.

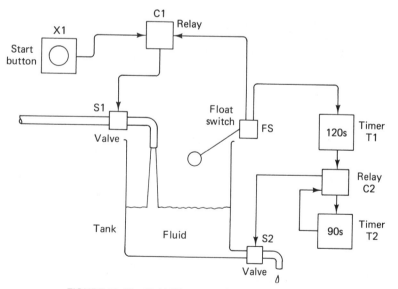

FIGURE 21.20   Fluid filling operation of Example 21.6.

21.5 PROGRAMMABLE LOGIC CONTROLLERS

All of the logic and sequencing functions we have described in the preceding sections can be implemented by means of a programmable logic controller. Instead of using discrete components such as relays, switches, timers, counters, and other separate elements to construct a sequence controller, a programmable controller can be used. A *programmable logic controller* is defined by the National Electrical Manufacturers Association (NEMA) as:

> A digitally operating electronic apparatus which uses a programmable memory for the internal storage of instructions for implementing specific functions such as logic, sequencing, timing, counting, and arithmetic to control, through digital or analog input/output modules, various types of machines or processes.

In essence, the programmable logic controller consists of computer hardware which is programmed to simulate the operation of the individual logic and sequence elements that might be contained in a bank of relays, timers, counters, and other hard-wired components.

We will adopt the initials PLC as an abbreviation for the programmable logic controller. PC is widely used in industry for the programmable controller, but the increasingly popular personal computer is also abbreviated PC. To avoid confusion in our book, we will use PLC exclusively for the programmable controller and PC for the personal computer.

The PLC was introduced around 1969 largely as a result of specifications written by the General Motors Corporation. The automotive industry had traditionally been a large buyer and user of electromechanical relays to control transfer lines, mechanized production lines, and other automated systems. In an effort to reduce the cost of new relays purchased each year, GM prepared the specifications for a "programmable logic controller" in 1968. The requirements included:

- The device must be programmable and reprogrammable.
- It must be designed to operate in an industrial environment.
- It must accept 120-V ac signals from standard pushbuttons and limit switches.
- Its outputs must be designed to switch and continuously operate loads such as motors and relays of 2-A rating.
- Its price and installation cost must be competitive with relay and solid-state logic devices then in use.

Several companies saw a commercial opportunity in the GM initiative and developed various versions of a special-purpose computer we now refer to as the PLC.

There are significant advantages in using a programmable logic controller rather than conventional relays, timers, counters, and other hardware elements. These advantages include:

- Programming the PLC is easier than wiring the relay control panel. We discuss PLC programming in one of the following subsections.
- The PLC can be reprogrammed. Conventional controls must be rewired and are often scrapped instead.
- PLCs take less floor space then relay control panels.
- Maintenance of the PLC is easier, and reliability is greater.
- The PLC can be connected to the plant computer systems more easily than relays can.

The following subsections describe the components, programming, and operation of the PLC. We also survey some of its additional capabilities beyond logic control and sequencing.

Components of the PLC

A schematic diagram of a programmable logic controller is presented in Figure 21.21. The basic components of the PLC are the following:

- Input module
- Output module
- Processor
- Memory
- Power supply
- Programming device

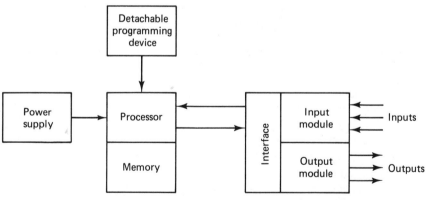

FIGURE 21.21   Diagram of the programmable logic controller.

These components are housed in a suitable cabinet designed for the industrial environment. A commercially available PLC is shown in Figure 21.22.

FIGURE 21.22 Commercially available programmable controller. (Courtesy of Allen-Bradley Company, Industrial Computer Group, Highland Heights, Ohio.)

The input module and output module are the connections to the industrial process that is to be controlled. The inputs to the controller are signals from limit switches, pushbuttons, sensors, and other on/off devices. In addition, as we will describe later, most larger PLCs are capable of accepting signals from analog devices of the type modeled in Chapter 19. The outputs from the controller are on/off signals to operate motors, valves, and other devices required to actuate the process.

The processor is the central processing unit (CPU) of the programmable controller. It executes the various logic and sequencing functions described in Sections 21.2 and 21.3 by operating on the PLC inputs to determine the appropriate output signals. The processor is a microprocessor very similar in its construction to those used in personal computers and other data-processing equipment. Tied to the CPU is the PLC memory, which contains the program of logic, sequencing, and other input/output operations. The memory for a programmable logic controller is specified in the same way as for a computer, and may range from 1K to over 48K of storage capacity. A power supply of 115 V ac is typically used to drive the PLC even though the components of the industrial process that are regulated may have a higher voltage and power rating than the controller itself.

The PLC is programmed by means of a programming device. The programming device (sometimes referred to as a *programmer*) is usually detachable from the PLC cabinet so that it can be shared between different controllers. Different PLC manufacturers provide different devices, ranging from simple teach pendant-type devices, similar to those used in robotics, to special PLC programming keyboards and CRT displays. Figure 21.23 shows one such programming device.

Programming the PLC

Most of the programming methods in use today for PLCs are based on the ladder logic diagram. This diagram has been found to be very convenient for shop personnel who are familiar with circuit diagrams because it does not require them to learn an entirely new programming language. What is required is a means of inputting the program into the PLC memory. There are various approaches for entering and interconnecting the individual logic elements. These include:

FIGURE 21.23   Programming device used for a PLC. (Courtesy of Allen-Bradley Company, Industrial Computer Group, Highland Heights, Ohio.)

1. Entry of the ladder logic diagram
2. Low-level computer-type languages
3. High-level computer-type languages
4. Functional blocks
5. Sequential function chart

The first method involves direct *entry of the ladder logic diagram* into the PLC memory. This method requires the use of a keyboard and CRT with limited graphics capability to display symbols representing the components and their interrelationships in the ladder logic diagram. The symbols are similar to those presented in Figure 21.15. The PLC keyboard device is often designed with keys for each of the individual symbols. Programming is accomplished by inserting the appropriate components into the rungs of the ladder diagram. The components are of two basic types: contacts and coils. Contacts are used to represent input switches, relay contacts, and similar elements. Coils are used to represent loads such as motors, solenoids, relays, timers, counters, etc. In effect, the programmer inputs the ladder logic circuit diagram rung by rung into the PLC memory with the CRT displaying the results for verification.

The second method makes use of a *low-level computer-type language* that parallels the ladder logic diagram. Using the language instructions, the programmer constructs the ladder diagram by specifying the various components and their relationships for each rung. Let us explain this approach by developing an elementary PLC instruction set. As we did in Chapter 12 for robot programming, our PLC "language" will be a composite of various manufacturers' languages, containing perhaps fewer features than most commercially available PLCs. We will assume that the programming device consists of a suitable keyboard for entering the individual components on each rung of the ladder logic diagram. A CRT capable of displaying each ladder rung, and perhaps several rungs that precede it, is useful to verify the program. The command set for our PLC is presented in Table 21.3 with a concise explanation of each command. Let us examine the use of these commands with several examples.

TABLE 21.3   Typical Low-Level Language Instruction Set for a Programmable Logic Controller

STR	Store a new input and start a new rung of the ladder.
AND	Logical AND referenced with the previously entered element. This is interpreted as a series circuit relative to the previously entered element.
OR	Logical OR referenced with the previously entered element. This is interpreted as a parallel circuit relative to the previously entered element.
NOT	Logical NOT or inverse of entered element.
OUT	Output element for the rung of the ladder diagram.
TMR	Timer element. Requires one input signal to initiate timing sequence. Output is delayed by a duration that is specified by the programmer in seconds. Resetting the timer is accomplished by interrupting (stopping) the input signal.
CTR	Counter element. Requires two inputs; one is the incoming pulse train which is counted by the CTR element, the other is the reset signal indicating a restart of the counting procedure.

EXAMPLE 21.7

Using the command set in Table 21.3, write the PLC programs for the three ladder diagrams from Figure 21.17, depicting the AND, OR, and NOT circuits from Figures 21.1, 21.2, and 21.3.

Solution:

Command	Comment
STR X1	Store input X1
AND X2	Input X2 in series with X1
OUT Y	Output Y
STR X1	Store input X1
OR X2	Input X2 parallel with X1
OUT Y	Output Y
STR NOT X1	Store inverse of X1
OUT Y	Output Y

EXAMPLE 21.8

Using the command set in Table 21.3, write the PLC program for the control relay depicted in the ladder logic diagram of Figure 21.19.

Solution:

Command	Comment
STR X	Store input X
OUT C	Output contact relay C
STR NOT C	Store inverse of C output
OUT Y1	Output load Y1
STR C	Store C output
OUT Y2	Output load Y2

The low-level languages are generally limited to the types of logic and sequencing functions that can be defined in a ladder logic diagram. Although timers and counters have not been illustrated in the two preceding examples, some of the problems at the end of the chapter require the reader to make use of them.

High-level computer-type languages are likely to become more common in the future to program the PLC. There are several of these languages that are beginning to be offered commercially, including [6] SYBIL (GTE Sylvania), MCL model APC-2 (Cincinnati Milacron), and Control Statements (Reliance Electric). Most of the available languages use an instruction set that is similar to the BASIC computer language for personal computers. There are additional statements available beyond the normal BASIC set to accomplish the control functions.

The principal advantage offered by the high-level languages for programming the

PLC is their capability to perform data processing and calculations on values other than binary. Ladder logic diagrams and low-level PLC languages are usually quite limited in their ability to operate on signals that are other than ON/OFF types. The capability to perform data processing and computation permits the use of more complex control algorithms, communications with other computer-based systems, display of data on a CRT console, and input of data by a human operator. Another advantage of the higher-level languages is the relative ease with which a printout of a complicated control program can be interpreted by a user. Explanatory comments can be inserted into the program to facilitate the interpretation.

The use of high-level control languages for programming the PLC begins to overlap with our coverage of computer process control in Chapter 22. We discuss some of the issues related to these high-level languages for control programming in Section 22.7.

Functional blocks provide another means of inputting high-level instructions; however, the format in which the instructions are entered is the same as the ladder logic diagram. The instructions are composed of operational blocks. Each block has one or more inputs and one or more outputs. Within the block, certain operations take place on the inputs to transform the signals into the desired outputs. The functional blocks include operations such as timers and counters, control computations using equations (e.g., proportional–integral–derivative control), data manipulation, and data transfer to other computer-based systems. We leave the description of these function blocks to other references, such as reference [6], and operation manuals for commercially available PLC products, such as reference [1].

Other methods for representing the sequencing and logic control problems and for programming the PLC have been developed. One of these is the *sequential function chart* (also called the *Grafcet method*), which graphically displays the sequential functions of an automated system as a series of steps and transitions from one state of the system to the next. The sequential function chart is described in Lloyd [7] and has become a standard PLC programming technique in France for logic control and sequencing. However, its use in the United States is limited at the time of this writing, and for more details on the method, we refer the reader to the reference cited.

How the PLC operates

Referring back to the diagram of the PLC in Figure 21.21, let us consider how the controller operates. As far as the PLC user is concerned, the program steps defined by the ladder logic diagram are executed simultaneously and continuously. In truth, a certain amount of time is required for the PLC processor to step through the program and execute any changes in outputs. First, the inputs to the PLC are sampled by the processor and the contents are stored in memory. Next, the control program is executed. The input values stored in memory are used in the control logic calculations to determine the values of the outputs. Finally, the outputs are updated to agree with the calculated values. This cycle, consisting of reading the inputs, executing the control program, and revising the outputs, is referred to as a *scan*. The time to perform the scan is called the *scan time*, and this depends on the number and complexity of control functions to be performed each cycle. Stating this another way, the scan time depends on the number of rungs in the ladder diagram and the complexity of the logic operations to be carried out on each rung. These times typically vary between 1 and 100 ms [6].

One of the potential problems that can occur during the scan cycle is that the value of an input can change immediately after it has been sampled. Since the program uses the input value that is stored in memory, any output values that are dependent on that input are determined incorrectly. There is obviously a potential risk involved in this mode of operation. However, the risk is minimized because the time between updates is so short that it is unlikely that the output value being incorrect for such a short duration will have a serious effect on the process operation. The risk becomes most significant in processes in which the response times are very fast, and where hazards can occur during the scan time. Some PLCs have special features for making "immediate" updates of output signals when input variables are known to cycle back and forth at frequencies faster than the scan time.

Additional capabilities of the PLC

The logic control and sequencing functions described in Sections 21.2 and 21.3 are perhaps the principal control operations that are accomplished by the PLC. These were the functions for which the programmable controller was originally designed. However, the PLC has evolved to include several capabilities in addition to logic control and sequencing. Some of the important capabilities available on commercial PLCs include:

• *Arithmetic functions.* These functions are addition, subtraction, multiplication, and division. Use of these functions permits more complex control algorithms to be developed than what is possible with conventional logic and sequencing elements.

• *Matrix functions.* Some PLCs have the capability to perform matrix operations on stored values in memory. This capability can be used to compare the actual values of a set of inputs and outputs with the values stored in the PLC memory to determine if some error has occurred [8].

• *Analog control.* The proportional–integral–derivative (PID) control is available on some programmable controllers. These control algorithms have traditionally been implemented on analog controllers. Today the analog control schemes are approximated using the digital computer, either with a PLC or a computer process controller. The approximation of PID control on a digital computer is called *direct digital control* (DDC).

Direct digital control and the other capabilities described in the preceding list are characteristic of the calculations normally performed on a digital computer. Indeed, the evolution of the programmable logic controller is tending to merge with the conventional computer. In Chapter 22 we examine the issues involved in using the computer for process control.

REFERENCES

[1] ALLEN-BRADLEY COMPANY, *PLC-2/30 Programmable Controller, Programming and Operations Manual,* Publication 1772-806, March 1986.

[2] ASFAHL, C. R., *Robotics and Manufacturing Automation,* John Wiley & Sons, Inc., New York, 1985, Chapters 10–12.

[3] DELTANO, D., "Programming Your PC," *Instruments and Control Systems,* July 1980, pp. 37–40.

[4] GENERAL ELECTRIC COMPANY, *Series One Programmable Controller,* Series One Manual, Publication GEK-25375A, February 1984.

[5] GROOVER, M. P., and E. W. ZIMMERS, JR., *CAD/CAM: Computer-Aided Design and Manufacturing,* Prentice-Hall, Inc., Englewood Cliffs, N.J., 1984, Chapter 3.

[6] JONES, C. T., and L. A. BRYAN, *Programmable Controllers,* International Programmable Controls, Inc., An IPC/ASTEC Publication, Atlanta, Ga., 1983.

[7] LLOYD, M., "Graphical Function Chart Programming for Programmable Controllers," *Control Engineering,* October 1985, pp. 73–76.

[8] SCHMITT, N. M., and R. F. FARWELL, *Understanding Electronic Control of Automation Systems,* Texas Instruments, Inc., Dallas, Tex., 1983, Chapters 4, 8.

[9] TAKAHASHI, Y., M. J. RABINS, and D. M. AUSLANDER, *Control and Dynamic Systems,* Addison-Wesley Publishing Company, Inc., Reading, Mass. 1972, Chapter 15.

[10] WILHELM, R. E., *Programmable Controller Handbook,* Hayden Book Company, Inc., Hasbrouck Heights, N.J. 1985.

PROBLEMS

21.1. Write the Boolean logic expression for the pushbutton switch of Example 21.2 using the following symbols: X1 = START, X2 = STOP, Y1 = MOTOR, and Y2 = POWER-TO-MOTOR.

21.2. Draw the timing diagram for the fluid filling and emptying operation of Example 21.6, showing the changes with time of all relevant variables, including the fluid level in the tank.

21.3. Construct the ladder logic diagram for the robot interlock system in Example 21.1.

21.4. In the circuit of Figure 21.1, suppose that a photodetector were used to determine whether the lamp worked. If the lamp does not light when both switches are closed, the photodetector causes a buzzer to sound. Construct the ladder logic diagram for this system.

21.5. Construct the ladder logic diagrams for (a) the NAND gate and (b) the NOR gate.

21.6. Construct the ladder logic diagrams for the following Boolean logic equations:

(a) $Y = (X1 + X2) \cdot X3$

(b) $Y = (X1 + X2) \cdot (X3 + X4)$

(c) $Y = (X1 \cdot X2) + X3$

(d) $Y = X1 \cdot \overline{X2}$

21.7. Show how the ladder logic diagram symbol for the timer (TMR) can be used to provide the ON/OFF controls for output variables Y1 and Y2 for the drum timer of Figure 21.12. Assume that each time unit in the timing sequence axis is 1 s.

21.8. Write the low-level language statements for the robot interlock system in Example 21.1 using the instruction set in Table 21.3.

21.9. Write the low-level language statements for the lamp and photodetector system in Problem 21.4 using the instruction set in Table 21.3.

21.10. Write the low-level language statements for the fluid-filling operation in Example 21.6 using the instruction set in Table 21.3.

21.11. Write the low-level language statement for the four parts of Problem 21.6 using the instruction set in Table 21.3.

21.12. In the fluid-filling operation of Example 21.6, suppose that a sensor (e.g., a submerged float switch) is used to determine whether the contents of the tank have been evacuated, rather than relying on timer T2 to empty the tank.
(a) Construct the ladder logic diagram for this revised system.
(b) Write the low-level language statements for the system using the PLC instruction set in Table 21.3.

21.13. In the manual operation of a sheet metal stamping press, a two-button safety interlock system is often used to prevent the operator from inadvertently actuating the press while his hand is in the die. Both buttons must be depressed to actuate the stamping cycle. In this system, one pressbutton is located on one side of the press while the other button is located on the opposite side. During the work cycle the operator inserts the part into the die and depresses both pushbuttons, using both hands.
(a) Write the truth table for this interlock system.
(b) Write the Boolean logic expression for the system.
(c) Construct the logic network diagram for the system.
(d) Construct the ladder logic diagram for the system.

21.14. An emergency stop system is to be designed for a certain automatic production machine. A single "start" button is used to turn on the power to the machine at the beginning of the day. In addition, there are three "stop" buttons located at different locations around the machine, any one of which can be pressed to immediately turn off power to the machine.
(a) Write the truth table for this system.
(b) Write the Boolean logic expression for the system.
(c) Construct the logic network diagram for the system.
(d) Construct the ladder logic diagram for the system.

21.15. This is similar to Problem 12.8 except that a PLC is used here as the robot cell controller. The cell operates as follows:

1. A human worker places a workpart into a nest.
2. The robot reaches over and picks up the part and places it into an induction heating coil.
3. A time of 10 s is allowed for the heating operation.
4. The robot reaches in and retrieves the part and places it on an outgoing conveyor.

A limit switch XI (normally open) will be used in the nest to indicate part presence. The robot will signal the PLC that the part has been placed into the heating coil using X2. X2 remains energized until the part is removed from the heater. The robot will use X3 to indicate that the part has been placed on the conveyor. (X2 and X3 are output interlocks for the robot but input contacts for the PLC.) Output contact Y1 will be used to signal the robot to execute step 2 of the work cycle. (This is an output contact for the PLC but an input interlock for the robot controller.) Timer T1 will be used to provide the 10 s delay in step 3. Output contact Y2 will be used to signal the robot to execute step 4.

(a) Construct the ladder logic diagram for the system.

(b) Write the low level language statements for the system using the PLC instruction set in Table 21.3.

21.16   A PLC is used to control the sequence in an automatic drilling operation. A human operator loads and clamps a raw workpart into a fixture on the drill press table and presses a start button to initiate the automatic cycle. The drill spindle turns on, feeds down into the part to a certain depth (the depth is determined by limit switch), and then retracts. The fixture then indexes to a second drilling position, and the drill feed-and-retract is repeated. After the second drilling operation, the spindle turns off, and the fixtures moves back to the first position. The worker then unloads the finished part and loads another raw part.

(a) Specify the input/output variables for this system operation and define symbols for them (e.g, X1, X2, C1, Y1, etc.)

(b) Construct the ladder logic diagram for the system.

(c) Write the low-level language statements for the system using the PLC instruction set in Table 21.3.

21.17. An industrial furnace is to be controlled as follows: The contacts of a bimetallic strip inside the furnace close if the temperature falls below the set point, and open when the temperature is above the set point. The contacts regulate a control relay which turns on and off the heating elements of the furnace. If the door to the furnace is opened, the heating elements are temporarily turned off until the door is closed.

(a) Specify the input/output variables for this system operation and define symbols for them (e.g., X1, X2, C1, Y1, etc.)

(b) Construct the ladder logic diagram for the system.

(c) Write the low-level language statements for the system using the PLC instruction set in Table 21.3.

chapter 22

Computer Process Control

In Chapters 19 and 20 we presented some of the important principles of linear control systems and optimal control. In Chapter 21 we continued the presentation with a discussion of logic control and sequencing, and also discussed the implementation of logic controls using programmable controllers. In this final chapter in Part VIII we consider how the digital computer is used in process control.

Computer process control is defined as the use of a stored program digital computer to control an industrial process. By this definition, programmable controllers are included within the scope of computer process control because the processor of a PLC is a stored program digital computer. When originally developed, the PLC for process control was more clearly distinguishable from computer process control than it is today. The capabilities of programmable controllers have evolved so that they can perform much of the data-processing and other functions that were previously reserved for computer control. Our discussion of computer process control in this chapter allows for the possibility that PLCs with sufficient capabilities might be substituted for the digital computer.

In this chapter we consider how the computer is used to perform process control. The first two sections examine some of the hardware issues involved in interfacing the computer to the manufacturing process. This is followed by a discussion of the various strategies used to implement computer process control and the associated programming issues.

22.1   THE COMPUTER–PROCESS INTERFACE

Computers are traditionally used with a variety of peripheral devices, such as CRTs, alphanumeric keyboards, printers, plotters, and so on. These devices are required for data processing and engineering/scientific calculations to enter the programs and data and to output the results. In computer process control applications, a different problem is encountered—the problem of connecting the computer to the manufacturing process. This section examines the characteristics of the data that must be communicated between the process and the computer, as well as the types of input/output capabilities that are required for the communication.

Characteristics of manufacturing process data

For the computer to be used in process monitoring and control, the computer must collect data from the manufacturing operation. If the computer is utilized to control the process directly, data (i.e., commands or instructions) must be communicated to the process. The data flowing back and forth between the computer and the process can be classified into three types:

1.   Continuous analog signals
2.   Discrete binary data
3.   Pulse data or discrete data that are not restricted to binary; in other words, more than two values are possible

The three types are illustrated in Figure 22.1.

CONTINUOUS ANALOG DATA.   A continuous variable is one that assumes a continuum of values over time. The variable is uninterrupted as time proceeds (at least during the cycle of the manufacturing process). An analog variable is one that can take on any value within a certain limited range. The amplitude of the variable is not restricted to a discrete set of values. A continuous analog variable is one that possesses the attributes of both a continuous variable and an analog variable. Most industrial operations, in both discrete-parts manufacturing and the process industries, are characterized by continuous analog variables. Examples are force, temperature, flow rate, pressure, velocity, and so on. All of these variables are continuous with time during the process, and they can take on any of an infinite number of possible values within a certain range. As a practical matter, the number of values is limited only by the capacity of the measuring instrument to distinguish the different levels of the variables.

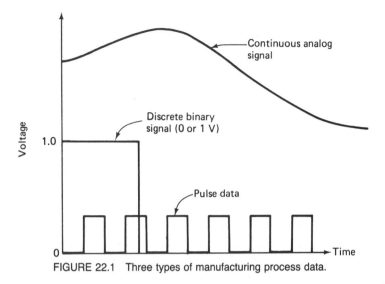

FIGURE 22.1   Three types of manufacturing process data.

DISCRETE BINARY DATA.   As we discussed in Chapter 21, discrete binary data are data that can assume either of two possible values, such as on or off, opened or closed, and so on. Such data might take on the following significance in a manufacturing operation:

> To sense the presence or absence of a workpart at the proper workstation location.
> To indicate whether the power feed drive of a transfer line drill head was working.
> To signal that the flow valve of a chemical process was opened or closed.

PULSE DATA OR DISCRETE DATA.   Pulse data are a train of pulse signals as indicated in Figure 22.1. This type of data is used in digital transducers, such as digital tachometers and turbine flow meters. An electrical pulse train can be used to drive a stepping motor, which is found in a wide variety of computer control applications because of its compatibility with the digital computer. Discrete data are similar to discrete binary data except that the number of possible levels is not limited to two. A prime example of discrete data is piece counts. Pulse data are related to discrete data because the number of pulses in a pulse train can be counted within a certain time interval. Hence, pulse data can be converted into discrete data, and vice versa.

EXAMPLE 22.1

Let us examine the different classes of data that might be found in a metal-cutting NC machine tool application. Examples of continuous analog signals are:

> Cutting force or torque
> Cutting temperature

Velocity of spindle rotation—assumed continuously variable

Feed rate (table speed)—assumed continuously variable

Among the discrete binary data in the operation are:

Workpart in place in the fixture or not

Cutting fluid on or off

Critical dimensions machined within tolerance or not

Machine tool under operator command or automatic cycle

Machine tool operational or broken down (used to tabulate machine utilization)

Examples of pulse data or discrete data that might apply to the application are:

Pulse train to drive stepping motor for x-coordinate table position

Pulse train to drive stepping motor for y-coordinate table position

Pulse train indicating spindle rotational speed to be converted to discrete data for display on operator console

Piece counts (production per shift)

Process data input/output

To implement a system of computer process monitoring and control, the three classes of manufacturing data must be interfaced with the computer. For monitoring the process, a means must be provided for inputting the data to the computer. For process control, a method must be devised for output of command signals from the computer to the process. The general configuration of this computer–process interface is shown in Figure 22.2. There are six categories of interface representing inputs and outputs for the three types of process data. These categories are:

1. Analog-to-digital interface
2. Contact input interface
3. Pulse counters
4. Digital-to-analog interface
5. Contact output interface
6. Pulse generators

Certain types of discrete data can be entered through the data-processing interface (depicted in Figure 22.2), perhaps by manual data entry terminals or CRTs located in the factory.

In the paragraphs that follow, we consider the six categories of interface between the computer and the manufacturing process.

ANALOG-TO-DIGITAL INTERFACE. The continuous analog signals must be converted into digital values in order to be used by the computer. The procedure for making

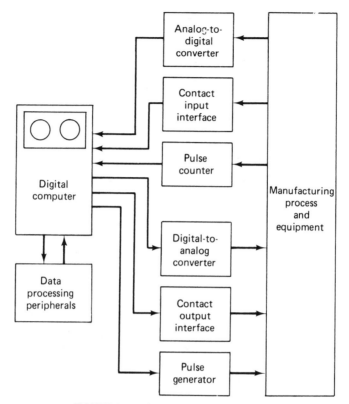

FIGURE 22.2 Computer–process interface.

this conversion typically involves the steps illustrated in Figure 22.3. These steps involve a variety of hardware devices, which can be enumerated as follows:

1. *Transducers*. Transducers are used to measure the continuous analog signals by converting the variable (such as temperature, flow rate, force, etc.) into a more

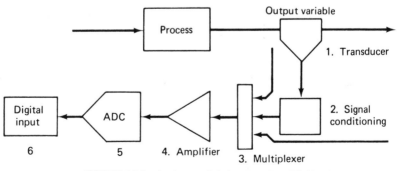

FIGURE 22.3 Analog-to-digital conversion (ADC).

convenient electrical signal (such as voltage or current). Transducers are discussed in more detail in Section 22.2.

2. *Signal conditioning.* The electrical signal leaving the transducer may require conditioning. The reason for this requirement may be that the signal (usually voltage) contains random noise, in which case an RC filter would be used to smooth out the signal. Another reason for signal conditioning is that the transducer output may be of the wrong form. For example, a current signal might need to be converted into a voltage signal.

3. *Multiplexer.* The multiplexer is used to share the analog-to-digital converter (ADC) among many incoming signals. In effect, the multiplexer samples each incoming signal at periodic intervals and sends the signal on to the ADC. Multiplexers will be discussed in Section 22.2.

4. *Amplifiers.* Amplifiers are used to scale the incoming signal either up or down to be compatible with the range of the analog-to-digital converter.

5. *Analog-to-digital converter (ADC).* The function of the ADC is to transform the incoming analog signal into its digital equivalent. The operation of analog-to-digital converters will be explained in Section 22.2.

6. *Digital input.* This is the computer's input/output section and its function is to accept the output of the ADC. A device called a limit comparator is sometimes inserted between the ADC and the input channel. The purpose of the limit comparator is to compare the incoming digitized signal with certain upper and lower limits. As long as the signal is within the limits, the data do not enter the computer. Hence, the advantage of using a limit comparator is that CPU time is required only if the measured variable has strayed outside the desired limits.

CONTACT INPUT INTERFACE. Discrete binary data are read into the computer through the contact input interface. This interface consists of relatively simple contacts that can be either opened or closed to indicate the status of limit switches, motor push-buttons, and valve positions associated with the process. The computer stores in memory the desired status of these contacts and periodically scans the actual status for comparison. The procedure is similar to that used by a programmable logic controller.

PULSE COUNTERS. Some measuring instruments, called digital transducers, generate a series of pulses as their output. Pulse counters are used to convert the pulse train into a digital quantity. This quantity is then entered into the computer through its input channel. We will discuss the operation of pulse counters in Section 22.2.

DIGITAL-TO-ANALOG INTERFACE. The three preceding interfaces have all been concerned with process data inputs to the computer. The digital-to-analog interface is one of three interfaces by which data and commands can be communicated back to the process. This interface converts digital data generated by the computer into a pseudo-analog continuous signal. We refer to this as a pseudo-analog signal because the digital output of the computer can be expressed with only a limited precision, which depends on the word length of the computer. We focus on this problem when we discuss digital-to-analog converters (DACs) in Section 22.2. A "data-hold circuit" is required to maintain the analog signal at the desired level until the next digitized value comes from the computer. A multiplexer is sometimes sandwiched between the DAC and the hold circuit to share the digital-to-analog converter.

CONTACT OUTPUT INTERFACE.   In applications of computer monitoring only, the contact output interface is used to turn on indicator lights and operator alarms. In some applications the computer might be programmed to shut down the process during emergencies through the contact output interface. In computer control applications, this subsystem is used to control solenoids, motors, alarms, and other similar devices. Alarms and indicator lamps can also be operated as in monitoring. The computer can be programmed to control the sequence of activities in the process through this contact output interface.

In the contact output interface, the computer sets the position of the contact in one of two states—on or off. The contact is maintained in that position until changed.

PULSE GENERATORS.   These devices generate a pulse train as specified by the computer. The pulse train is typically used to operate stepping motors. In the pulse train, the pulses are of a certain amplitude and frequency to be compatible with the stepping motor.

22.2 INTERFACE HARDWARE

In the preceding section, the general configuration of the computer–process interface was discussed. We now consider some of the hardware devices that make up this interface.

Sensors and transducers

A *transducer* is a device that converts one type of physical quantity (e.g., temperature, force, velocity, flow rate) into another type (commonly electrical voltage). The reason for making the conversion is that the converted signal can be used or evaluated more conveniently. Transducers are often called *sensors* when they are used to measure the value of a physical quantity. Transducers are of two general types: analog and digital. *Analog transducers* produce a continuous analog signal such as electrical voltage. The signal can be interpreted as the value of the measured variable. To make the interpretation, a calibration procedure is required. The *calibration* of the measuring device establishes the relationship between the variable that is to be measured and the converted output signal (e.g., voltage).

Digital transducers are measuring devices that produce a digital output signal. The digital signal may be in the form of a set of parallel status bits or a series of pulses that can be counted. In either case, the digital signal represents the quantity to be measured. Digital transducers are finding increased utilization because of the ease with which they can be read when used as stand-alone measuring instruments, and because of their compatibility with the digital computer.

Some of the desirable features of transducers and sensors used for process control purposes are the following:

1. *High accuracy.* High accuracy is defined to mean that the measurement will contain no systematic errors about the true value.
2. *High precision.* High precision means that the random variability or noise in the measured value will be low.

Accuracy and precision in measuring systems were explained in our discussion of inspection sensors in Chapter 18.

3. *Wide operating range.* The sensor should possess the attributes of accuracy and precision over a wide range of the physical variable being measured.
4. *Speed of response.* The sensor should be able to respond quickly to changes in the physical variable. Ideally, the time lag would be zero. The sensor must be capable of identifying hazardous operating conditions in the shortest possible time.
5. *Ease of calibration.* The measuring device should be easy to calibrate. It should not be subject to drift during use, which would necessitate frequent recalibrations of the sensor. *Drift* refers to the gradual loss of accuracy between the measured variable and the transduced signal (e.g., millivolts).
6. *High reliability.* The sensor should not be subject to frequent mechanical or electrical failures. It must be capable of operating in extreme environments characteristic of the process (e.g., high temperature, humidity, vibration, pressure, etc.).
7. *Low cost.* The cost to purchase (or fabricate) and install the sensor should be low relative to the worth of the information provided by the sensor.

There are few measuring devices that possess all of these desirable characteristics. A compromise must be made among these various features when selecting a transducer for a particular application. Several of the common sensors and measuring devices used in industrial control systems are listed in Table 22.1. A more detailed listing and discussion of sensors is included in several of the references [1,2,9].

Analog-to-digital converters

An analog-to-digital converter (ADC) is a device that converts an analog signal into digital form. It is sometimes called an encoder. The device that performs the reverse process, called a digital-to-analog converter (DAC), will be discussed in the following subsection.

Analog signals are usually continuous, as illustrated in Figure 22.4. Analog-to-digital conversion consists of three phases:

1. *Sampling.* The continuous signal is periodically sampled to convert it into a series of discrete-time analog signals. This sampling process is illustrated in Figure 22.4.
2. *Quantization.* Each discrete-time analog value must be assigned to one of a finite number of previously defined amplitude levels. These amplitude levels consist of discrete values of voltage ranging over the full scale of the ADC.

TABLE 22.1 Common Sensors and Measuring Devices

Ammeter—meter to indicate electrical current.

Bourdon tube—widely used industrial gage to measure pressure and vacuum.

Chromatographic instruments—laboratory-type instruments used to analyze chemical compounds and gases.

Eddy current sensor—device that produces a magnetic field and induces eddy currents in a conductive object. Used to indicate presence or absence of the object.

Inductance-coil pulse generator—transducer used to measure rotational speed. Output is pulse train.

Infrared sensor—device that measures temperature from the infrared light emitted from the object's surface.

Linear-variable-differential transformer (LVDT)—electromechanical transducer used to measure angular or linear displacement. Output is voltage.

Limit switch—electrical on-off switch that makes contact by depressing a button or lever. Can be used to detect presence of an object.

Manometer—liquid column gage used widely in industry to measure pressure.

Ohmmeter—meter to indicate electrical resistance.

Optical pyrometer—device to measure temperature of an object at high temperatures by sensing the brightness of the object's surface.

Optical encoders—digital pulse generator used to measure rotational displacement and rotational speed.

Orifice plate—widely used flowmeter to indicate fluid flow rates.

Photometric transducers—a class of transducers used to sense light, including phototubes, photodiodes, phototransistors, and photoconductors.

Piezoelectric accelerometer—transducer used to measure vibration. Output is emf.

Pitot tube—laboratory device used to measure flow.

Positive displacement flowmeter—variety of transducers used to measure flow. Typical output is pulse train.

Potentiometer—instrument used to measure voltage.

Pressure transducers—a class of transducers used to measure pressure. Typical output is voltage. Operation of the transducer can be based on strain gages or other devices.

Radiation pyrometer—device to measure temperature by sensing the thermal radiation emitted from the object.

Strain gage—widely used transducer used to indicate torque, force, pressure, and other variables. Output is change in resistance due to strain, which can be converted into voltage.

Thermistor—also called a resistance thermometer; an instrument used to measure temperature. Operation is based on change in resistance as a function of temperature.

Thermocouple—widely used temperature transducer based on the Seebeck effect, in which a junction of two dissimilar metals emits emf related to temperature.

Turbine flowmeter—transducer to measure flow rate. Output is pulse train.

Venturi tube—device used to measure flow rates.

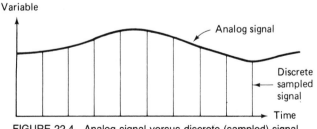

FIGURE 22.4 Analog signal versus discrete (sampled) signal.

3. *Encoding.* The various amplitude levels obtained during quantization must be converted into digital code. This involves the representation of the amplitude level by a sequence of binary digits. The quantization and encoding of a discrete-time analog signal will be explained below when we discuss ADC resolution.

GENERAL CHARACTERISTICS OF AN ADC. In selecting and applying an analog-to-digital converter, the following basic considerations are important:

1. *Sampling rate.* This is the rate at which the continuous analog signal is sampled. Higher sampling rates mean that the continuous waveform of the analog signal can be more closely approximated. When the ADC is used with multiplexing to convert a significant number of process signals, a high sampling rate is desirable because it means that these signals can all be surveyed in a short period of time. In cases where the process variables change slowly, it is not necessary to sample the sensors with high frequency. The upper limit on the sampling rate is imposed by the conversion time of the ADC.

2. *Conversion time.* The conversion time of an ADC is the time interval between when the incoming analog signal is applied and when the digital output value has been established by the quantization process. In short, it is the time required by the ADC to perform its function. Conversion time depends on the type of procedure used to make the conversion (two of these procedures will be discussed below). It also is proportional to the number of bits used to define the value. The number of bits determines the resolution capability of the ADC.

3. *Resolution.* The resolution of an analog-to-digital converter refers to the precision with which the analog signal is evaluated. Since the signal must be represented in binary form, the precision is determined by the number of quantization levels, which in turn is determined by the bit capacity of the ADC and computer. The number of quantization levels is defined by

$$\text{number of quantization levels} = 2^n \tag{22.1}$$

where n is the number of bits. Consistent with our previous usage of the term resolution in this book, we define the *resolution* of an ADC as the full-scale range of the incoming analog signal, divided by the number of quantization levels. That is,

$$\text{resolution} = \frac{\text{full-scale range}}{2^n} \tag{22.2}$$

The resolution is equivalent to the *quantization-level spacing,* the range of each quantization level. It is a measure of the precision of the analog-to-digital converter. To be compatible with the ADC, the incoming analog signal must typically be amplified (either up or down) to a range of 0 to 10 V.

The error that results from the quantization process is called the *quantization error,* and it can be considered analogous to a round-off error in numerical analysis. Using this round-off analogy, the quantization error can be as large as one-half the quantization-level spacing. This can be expressed

$$\text{quantization error} = \pm \frac{1}{2} \text{resolution} \qquad (22.3)$$

Quantization errors can be reduced by increasing the number of bits used in the ADC process.

EXAMPLE 22.2

A continuous-voltage signal is to be converted by an ADC. The maximum possible range of the voltage signal is 0 to 10 V. Two ADCs are being considered for a process control application, one with a 4-bit capacity, the second with an 8-bit capacity. Determine the number of quantization levels, the resolution, and the quantization error for the two alternatives.

Solution:

For the 4-bit capacity, the number of quantization levels, according to Eq. (22.1), is 16. The resolution is given by Eq. (22.2):

$$\text{resolution} = \frac{10}{16} = 0.625 \text{ V}$$

The quantization error is one-half this value, or 0.3125 V.

For the 8-bit A/D converter, the number of quantization levels = 256. The resolution = 0.0391 V, and the quantization error = 0.0195 V.

Clearly, the 8-bit capacity produces a more precise analog-to-digital conversion.

EXAMPLE 22.3

For the 4-bit analog-to-digital converter of Example 22.2, show how a voltage signal of ± 10 V range might be interpreted in binary form.

Solution:

Of the four binary digits, we will use the first to indicate sign: 0 means a negative voltage and 1 means a positive voltage. The three remaining digits will be used to indicate successively increasing quantization levels. Since one binary digit is being used to designate the polarity of the signal, this leaves three digits for quantization of the full-scale 10 V. The quantization-level spacing is therefore $10 \times 2^{-3} = 1.25$ V. The series of bits 1000 might be used to represent the range 0 to 1.25 V and 1001 to represent the range 1.25 to 2.50 V, and so on. The complete range of voltage signal values might be assigned binary numbers according to the following list:

Voltage range (V)	Binary number	Voltage range (V)	Binary number
0 to + 1.25	1000	0 to − 1.25	0000
+ 1.25 to + 2.5	1001	− 1.25 to − 2.5	0001
+ 2.5 to + 3.75	1010	− 2.5 to − 3.75	0010
+ 3.75 to + 5.0	1011	− 3.75 to − 5.0	0011
+ 5.0 to + 6.25	1100	− 5.0 to − 6.25	0100
+ 6.25 to + 7.5	1101	− 6.25 to − 7.5	0101
+ 7.5 to + 8.75	1110	− 7.5 to − 8.75	0110
+ 8.75 to + 10.0	1111	− 8.75 to − 10.0	0111

TYPES OF ADC.   A variety of methods can be used to convert a continuous voltage signal into its digital counterpart. We discuss only two of these methods.

1.   Successive approximation method
2.   Integrating ADC method

The successive approximation method is one of the most common ADC techniques. To convert an electrical voltage into binary code by the successive approximation method, trial voltages are successively compared to the input signal. The general scheme is illustrated in Figure 22.5. Suppose that the input signal to be encoded were 6.8 V. The first trial voltage might be 5.0 V. Comparing the input voltage with the trial voltage yields a "1" if input exceeds trial voltage, and "0" if input is less than trial voltage. Each

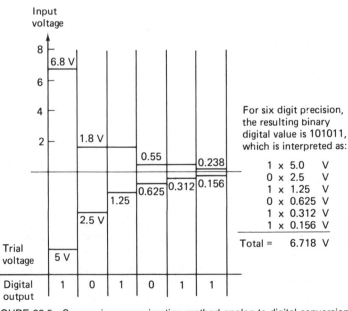

FIGURE 22.5   Successive approximation method analog-to-digital conversion.

subsequent trial voltage is one-half the preceding value. The digital encoded value is developed by this successive comparison process as illustrated in Figure 22.5. The resolution of the encoding procedure depends on the number of bits used to define the value. On the other hand, better resolution leads to increased conversion times. A typical conversion time might be 9 μs for the 6-bit precision shown in Figure 22.5.

There are several types of integrating analog-to-digital converters. All of them operate by converting the input voltage into a time period that can be measured by a counter. We will explain the operation of the simplest of the integrating-type ADCs. This is called the *single-slope converter* and its operation is illustrated in Figure 22.6. The input voltage is compared with a voltage that increases linearly with time (it is a ramp function). A counter is used to measure the time required from the initiation of the comparison voltage until it reaches the value of the input signal. This time is proportional to the incoming voltage from the transducer. The resolution of this ADC method depends on the frequency of the pulse train during the time interval of the comparison and the slope of the comparison ramp voltage. Higher pulse-train frequency and lower ramp slopes provide greater precision in the conversion process. A typical conversion time for 6-bit precision would be about 14 μs. Hence, the single-slope integrating type ADC is somewhat slower than the successive approximation ADC method.

An improved version of the integrating ADC method is the *dual-slope converter*. Its advantage is greater accuracy and less susceptibility to random signal noise. The disadvantage is lower conversion speed.

Digital-to-analog converters

The function performed by a digital-to-analog converter (DAC) is the reverse of the ADC function. The process control computer receives data from the process via the analog-to-digital link, performs its control calculations, and sends commands back to the process. Since the computer operates on digital data and the process variables are continuous analog signals, the DAC is required to provide the communication link from the computer

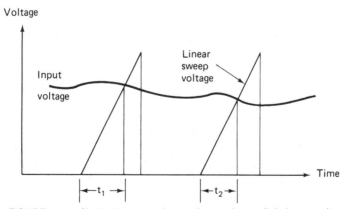

FIGURE 22.6 Single-slope-type integrating analog-to-digital conversion.

back to the process. Digital-to-analog converters may also be required to drive various types of recorders, plotters, and other electronic display units.

The DAC process can be viewed as consisting of two steps:

1. *Decoding.* This involves the conversion of digital data (from the computer) into sampled analog data.
2. *Data holding.* This step transforms the sampled data into a continuous signal (usable by the process or other analog device).

DECODING. The first step in the DAC procedure is to convert the binary digital data into its equivalent sampled analog signal format. This is accomplished by transferring the digital data to a binary register. This register controls a reference voltage source. The level of the output voltage depends on the status of the bits in the register. Each successive bit controls one-half the voltage of the preceding bit. Thus, the output voltage is determined as

$$V_o = V_{ref}[0.5B_1 + 0.25 B_2 + 0.125B_3 + \cdots + (2^n)^{-1} B_n]$$

where V_o = output of the decoding operation

V_{ref} = reference voltage   (22.4)

$B_1, B_2, \ldots, B_n$ = status (0 or 1) of successive bits in the register

DATA HOLDING. The holding device converts sampled data into a continuous analog signal. Data holding is an integral part of the digital-to-analog conversion process. The objective of the data hold is to approximate the envelope formed by the sampled data, as illustrated in Figure 22.7. Data-holding devices are sometimes classified according to the order of the extrapolation calculation used to determine the voltage output between sampling instants. The ideal envelope shown in Figure 22.7 would be a very high order extrapolator. The most common data extrapolator is the zero-order hold. In this case the output voltage between sampling instants is a sequence of step signals, as shown in Figure 22.7. We can express the voltage between sampling instants as a function of time very simply in the following way:

$$V(t) = V_o \tag{22.5}$$

where V_o is the output voltage from Eq. (22.4).

The first-order is less common than the zero-order hold but more closely approximates the true envelope of the sampled data values. With the first-order hold, the voltage $V(t)$ between sampling instants changes with a constant slope determined by the two preceding V_o values. Expressing this mathematically, we have

$$V(t) = V_o + at \tag{22.6}$$

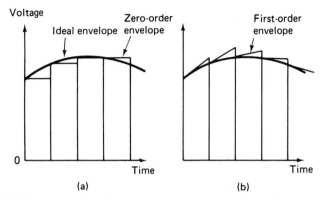

FIGURE 22.7   Data hold function: (a) zero-order hold; (b) first-order hold.

$$a = \frac{V_o - V_o(-\tau)}{\tau} \tag{22.7}$$

where a = rate of change of $V(t)$

τ = time interval between sampling instants

$V_o(-\tau)$ = value of V_o at the preceding sample instant (removed in time by τ)

Both the zero-order hold and the first-order hold are illustrated in Figure 22.7. Hold extrapolators of higher order are not common.

EXAMPLE 22.4

A digital-to-analog converter uses a reference voltage of 100 V and has six-binary-digit precision. In three successive sampling instants 0.5 s apart, the data contained in the binary register are:

Instant	Binary data
1	101000
2	101010
3	101101

Determine the decoder output voltage according to Eq. (22.4). Also, plot the voltage signals as a function of time between sampling instants 2 and 3 using a zero-order hold and a first-order hold.

Solution:

In sampling instant 1, the decoder output voltage is

$$V_o = 100[0.5(1) + 0.25(0) + 0.125(1) + 0.0625(0) + 0.03125(0) + 0.15625(0)]$$

$$= 62.5V$$

Correspondingly, V_o = 65.63 V for instant 2 and V_o = 70.31 V for instant 3.

The zero-order hold between instants 2 and 3 produces a constant voltage of $V(t) = 65.63$ V. The first-order hold produces a steadily increasing voltage. The slope can be determined from Eq. (22.7),

$$a = \frac{65.63 - 62.5}{0.5} = 6.25$$

and from Eq. (22.6),

$$V(t) = 65.63 + 6.25t$$

The solution to this example is displayed in Figure 22.8. Note that the first-order hold is superior in terms of anticipating the value of V_o in the third sampling instant.

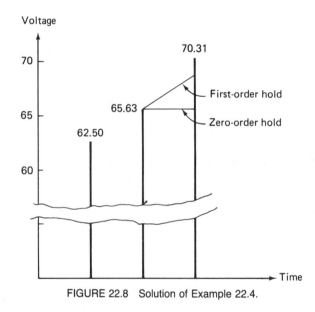

FIGURE 22.8   Solution of Example 22.4.

Multiplexers

The *multiplexer* is a switching device connected in series with each input channel from the process. It is used to time-share the analog-to-digital converter (and associated amplifiers) among the incoming signals. The alternative to the use of the multiplexer is a separate ADC for each transducer. This would be prohibitively expensive for a large installation with many inputs to the computer. Since the process variables need only be sampled periodically anyway, the multiplexer provides a very cost-efficient method of satisfying system design requirements.

A multiplexer consists of a set of switches arranged in the typical configuration shown in Figure 22.9. The switches illustrated in the figure are single-pole, single-throw switches in which a common ground is utilized. This type of multiplexer is called a

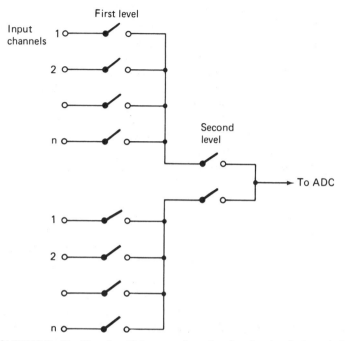

FIGURE 22.9   Traditional multiplexer configuration (two levels, single ended).

single-ended multiplexer. For two incoming leads from each transducer, the switches would be double-pole, single-throw types and the multiplexer is called a *differential multiplexer.* The number of switches on a single multiplexer can range from 16 to more than 1000. To increase the number of input channels which can be connected to a single analog-to-digital converter, the multiplexers can be arranged into more than one level. This is shown in Figure 22.9. Each of the individual input channels can be addressed by the combination of switch positions at the two levels.

The order in which the incoming signals are entered into the ADC can be random or sequential. With the random-order type, the individual input channels are selected as needed by the control computer. With the sequential type, the input channels are sampled in a fixed sequence. The sequential type is less expensive than the random-order multiplexer.

Pulse counters and pulse generators

As described in Section 22.1, some of the data flowing between the computer and the production operation are in the form of a pulse train, as illustrated in Figure 22.1. Certain types of transducers generate a series of pulses which must be read into the computer. The computer must also drive certain control devices (e.g., stepping motors) which respond to a train of pulses. To assist the computer in communicating with these hardware components, pulse counters and pulse generators are employed.

The operation of the *pulse counter* was described in Section 21.3. In that discussion we referred to the device simply as a counter to allow for mechanical as well as electronic counting devices. The most common type of counter today is one that counts electrical pulses. In process control applications, the pulse counter can be used to measure certain continuous physical variables in the process. To illustrate, suppose the rotational speed of a shaft is to be measured at regular intervals. The shaft is connected to an optical encoder (see our description in Section 8.4) which generates a certain number of pulses for each rotation of the shaft. The measurement might be made as follows. At the start of the measuring cycle, a clock is initialized and a register in the counter is loaded with the number of pulses to be counted. As each pulse from the optical encoder is received, the register subtracts one. When the register reaches zero, the clock time is recorded. To determine velocity, the number of pulses is divided by the clock time. Then this value is divided by the number of pulses per revolution of the shaft.

A *pulse generator* is used to generate a pulse train as specified by the computer. There are two ways in which the pulses can be used. The first is where a certain number of pulses are to be generated. For example, the number of pulses might correspond to the desired *x*-coordinate position of an NC machine table. The second case is where a pulse train of a certain frequency is used to drive a stepping motor at a certain rotational speed. The pulse generator performs its function by repeatedly opening and closing a contact, thus providing a sequence of discrete electrical pulses. The amplitude and frequency of the pulses are designed to be compatible with the device to be controlled.

22.3 COMPUTER PROCESS MONITORING

Computer process monitoring is one of the ways in which the computer can be interfaced with the manufacturing process. Computer process monitoring involves the use of the computer to observe the process and associated equipment and to collect and record data from the operation. The computer is not used to directly control the process. Control remains in the hands of human beings, who use the data to guide them in managing and operating the process.

The data that are collected by the computer in process monitoring can generally be classified into three categories:

1. *Process data.*   The input and output variables of the process are monitored to determine the overall status or performance of the operation. When the process variables are found to deviate from previously determined desired values, the computer signals the operator to take corrective action.

2. *Machine tool/equipment data.*   Data can also be collected by the computer which relate to the status of the production machine tools and equipment. This type of data is valuable to help avoid machine breakdowns, to monitor equipment utilization, to determine optimum tool change schedules, to diagnose the cause of equipment breakdowns, and so on.

3. *Product data.* Because of government regulations, the company may be required under law to collect and preserve production data on its products. Computer monitoring of the process is the most convenient and accurate method for fulfilling these requirements. The firm may also want to collect product data for its own uses. Examples of these data include piece counts, production yield, and product quality attributes.

   Collection of data from factory operations can be accomplished by any of several means. Shop data can be entered by workers through manual terminals located throughout the plant, or can be collected automatically by means of limit switches, sensor systems, bar code readers, machine vision, or other devices. The collection and use of production data in factory operations is often called *shop floor control*. We discuss this topic in Chapter 25.

   Computer process monitoring does not constitute a type of computer process control since there is no direct control exercised by the computer over the process. The control is accomplished indirectly, using human beings as the control mechanism.

22.4 TYPES OF COMPUTER PROCESS CONTROL

We can classify the methods of implementing computer process control into the following three categories:

1. Preplanned control
2. Direct digital control
3. Supervisory computer control

The first category is discussed in this section. The other two methods are discussed in the two sections that follow.

Preplanned control

The term *preplanned control* refers to the use of the computer for directing the process or equipment to carry out a predetermined series of operational steps. The control sequence must be developed in advance (programmed) to cover the variety of process conditions that might be encountered. This control strategy often uses feedback control loops to make certain that each step in the operation sequence has been completed before proceeding to the next step. However, in some cases, feedback verification is not required, and the process is controlled in an open-loop fashion. The name "preplanned control" is not universally applied throughout all areas of industry. We are using the term here to denote a variety of computer control schemes in which the defining characteristic is the use of a preprogrammed control cycle.

   Sequence control is one type of preplanned control. As indicated in Chapter 21, sequence control consists of logic control and sequencing. Logic control is a control scheme in which decisions are made and actions are taken in response to events that occur in the production system. The outputs of the controller are determined by the inputs from the production system. A sequencing system uses internal timers to determine when outputs to the production system should be changed. The combination of logic control and sequencing is commonly used to control industrial processes, in particular those consisting of a series of ON/OFF functions. As suggested by our presentation of the topic in Chapter 21, programmable controllers are frequently used to implement this type of control. Digital computers (i.e., minicomputers and microcomputers) can also be used.

The use of digital computers is advantageous in sequence control when other types of calculations are required for the control algorithms, in addition to logic switching and sequencing. The control of an industrial robot and its work cell is a good example of this situation. The control of the work cell involves interlocks that utilize logic control. But in addition, the robot controller must perform a variety of calculations for positioning, determining arm trajectory, interpolation, feedback control, and other functions. Hence, computers (e.g., microcomputers) are typically used as the robot controller.

The control of an automated transfer line or assembly machine is another example where computational and data processing functions may be required in addition to ON/OFF switching. The sequence of powered feed motions at the workstations, parts transfers between stations, on-line automated inspections, and so on, are all performed under sequence control, using either a programmable logic controller or a computer. The computer may be the desired controller for the application if requirements include performing diagnostic analysis in the event of a malfunction, collecting production data for performance records, indicating when tools should be changed, and performing other functions that require the data-processing capabilities of a computer rather than a PLC.

Computer numerical control is another example of preplanned control. CNC was described in Chapter 10. It involves the use of the computer (again, a microcomputer) to direct a machine tool through a series of preprogrammed processing steps.

Program control is a term that is used in the process industries. It involves the application of the computer to start up or shut down a large complex industrial process, or to guide the process through a changeover from one product grade to another. The term also refers to the computer's application in batch processing to control the process through the cycle of processing steps. With program control the objective is usually to direct the process from one operating condition to a new operating condition and to accomplish the transition in minimum time and energy. There are often constraints on this objective, so the control strategy is to determine the optimum values of the process variables at each step.

22.5 DIRECT DIGITAL CONTROL

In tracing the evolution of industrial process control systems, manual regulation of production operations was implemented first. The operator had to determine how well the process was doing by means of his own senses. To help in this task, measuring devices were developed which gave the operator a more definite and accurate picture of the process. The operator was still required to make the necessary adjustments in the input variables to keep the operation running smoothly. The advent of analog control meant that these adjustments could be made automatically, without the human operator getting directly involved in every minor change that had to be made. With analog control, each individual output variable is monitored and changes are made in the corresponding input variable to maintain the output at a desired level. As industrial processes became more and more complex, the number of these control loops grew. In a large, modern industrial plant (e.g., oil refinery, chemical plant, paper mill, etc.), the number of control loops can easily exceed several hundred. When the digital computer was developed, it was only logical to consider the replacement of these analog loops by the computer.

Direct digital control (DDC) involves the replacement of the conventional analog control devices with the digital computer. The regulation of the process is accomplished by the digital computer on a time-shared, sampled-data basis rather than by many individual analog elements, each working in a continuous dedicated fashion. With DDC, the computer calculates the desired values of the input variables, and then these calculated values are applied directly to the process. This direct link between the computer and the process is the reason for the name "direct digital control."

DDC was originally perceived as a more efficient means of carrying out the same types of control actions as the analog elements that it replaced. However, the analog devices were somewhat limited in terms of the mathematical operations that could be performed (proportional control, integral control, derivative control, and combinations of these). The digital computer is considerably more versatile with regard to the variety of control calculations that it can be programmed to perform. Hence, direct digital control offers not only the opportunity for greater efficiency in doing the same job than analog control, it also opens up the possibility for increased flexibility in the type of control action, as well as the option to reprogram the control action should that become desirable.

Analog process control

The three basic types of control action—proportional, integral, and derivative—typically performed by analog controllers were described in Section 19.4. Their mathematical operations were defined by Eqs. (19.32) through (19.34), respectively. These three control actions are often combined into a single equation to provide the necessary degree of regulation over the particular process variable. Equation (19.37) expressed the transfer function for this proportional–integral–derivative control:

$$\frac{x_p(s)}{e(s)} = K_1 + \frac{K_2}{s} + K_3 s \qquad (22.8)$$

This equation can be restated in the time domain as follows:

$$x_p(t) = K_1 e + K_2 \int_0^t e \, dt + K_3 \frac{de}{dt} \qquad (22.9)$$

This general expression for the three-mode control can be used to represent any one of the single control actions simply by setting the appropriate gain factors (K_1, K_2, or K_3) to zero.

The mechanism by which the process variables are altered according to Eq. (22.9) depends on the particular system. If the variable signals are electrical voltages, these electrical signals can be multiplied, integrated, or differentiated by various circuits composed of operational amplifiers. Where the variables are not electrical signals, the mechanical, pneumatic, hydraulic, thermal, and so on, variables can be transduced into electrical form to facilitate the control calculations.

Figure 22.10 illustrates a typical analog control loop for an industrial process. Although the process has multiple inputs and outputs, only one feedback control loop is shown in the figure. The components of the analog loop consist of the transducer (or sensor which measures the output variable), a measuring instrument for displaying the output (not always included in the loop), some means of establishing the set point for the loop (shown as a dial in the figure), a comparator (to compare the set point with the measured output), the analog controller and amplifier, and finally the connection of the process input (servomotor, valve, etc.).

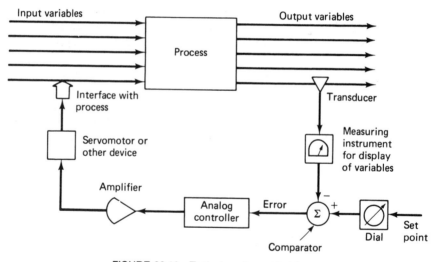

FIGURE 22.10   Typical analog control loop.

Components of DDC

In direct digital control, certain of the elements of the feedback loop are replaced with the digital computer or components that are digitally operated. This results in the configuration shown in Figure 22.11. As the diagram illustrates, some of the control loop components remain unchanged, including the transducers, sensors, and many of the process interface devices. Components that are replaced include the analog controller, recording and display elements, set point dials, and comparator. New components in the

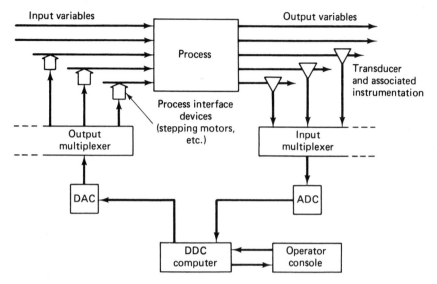

FIGURE 22.11 Components of a direct digital control system.

loop include the digital computer, analog-to-digital and digital-to-analog converters, and multiplexers to share signals from different loops with the same computer.

Control actions in DDC

In analog control, the mathematical operations are performed on continuous analog signals. With direct digital control, these operations must be approximated by finite-difference calculations. The finite-difference approximation of Eq. (22.9) is

$$x_{pn} = K_1 e_n + K_2 \Delta t \sum_{i=0}^{n} e_i + \frac{K_3}{\Delta t} (e_n - e_{n-1})$$

where x_{pn} = value of the process input as determined
by the controller for time period n (22.10)

e_n = value of the error signal at time period n

Δt = sampling interval = $t_n - t_{n-1}$

K_1, K_2, K_3 = constants

As the sampling interval Δt becomes smaller, Eq. (22.10) more closely approximates the continuous function in Eq. (22.9). To put this timing into perspective, suppose that the control computations of Eq. (22.10) required 100 μs (0.0001 s) to complete for each loop. Further, suppose that the DDC computer were required to service 100 control loops. How often would the computer be able to sample each loop? In other words, how long is the sampling interval Δt? The answer is that the computer would be capable of sampling each control loop every $(100)(0.0001 \text{ s}) = 0.01$ s in theory. Some time would be lost by the multiplexer, ADC, and DAC, so the actual sampling interval would be slightly greater than this. Except for processes with extremely short time constants, this sampling interval would be more than adequate.

The practice of simply using the digital computer to imitate the characteristics of analog controllers seems to represent a transitional phase in computer process control. Direct digital control alone is difficult to justify in terms of reduced costs. However, the use of the computer in process control applications can be supported by improvements in the overall performance of the manufacturing operation. It is this problem of overall process improvement and optimization that we address in the following section.

22.6 SUPERVISORY COMPUTER CONTROL

Supervisory computer control denotes a control system in which the computer seeks to optimize some performance objective for the process. The performance objective is sometimes referred to as the objective function or index of performance. Examples of performance objectives in industrial control include maximum production rate, minimum cost per unit of product, maximum yield, and other objectives that pertain to process performance.

Supervisory control represents a higher level of control than preplanned control (e.g., sequence control), direct digital control, or the more conventional analog control. In general, these three types of control systems can be considered to be process-level computer control methods, in that they operate directly on the process. By contrast, supervisory control directs the operation of these process-level control systems. This relationship between supervisory control and the process-level control techniques is illustrated in Figure 22.12.

Control objectives

There are several control objectives or strategies that can be implemented in supervisory computer control. We can classify these strategies as follows:

1. Regulatory control
2. Feedforward control
3. Steady-state optimization
4. Adaptive control
5. Search techniques
6. Other specialized techniques

These control strategies are executed at the supervisory level and implemented through one of the process-level control systems. The selection of the strategy depends on the process and the performance objectives for the process.

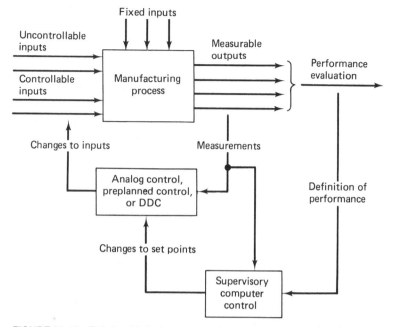

FIGURE 22.12   Relationship between supervisory computer control and process-level computer control.

In *regulatory control,* the objective is to control the process so as to maintain the performance at a certain level, or within a given tolerance band of that level. This would be appropriate in situations where performance is measured in terms of product quality, and it is desired to maintain the product quality at a particular level. In a chemical process, this quality level might be the concentration of the final chemical product. The purpose of supervisory control is to maintain that quality at the desired constant value during the process. To accomplish this purpose, set points are determined for individual feedback loops in the process and other control actions are taken to compensate for disturbances to the process. Regulatory control is analogous to feedback control except that feedback control applies to the individual control loops in the process. We are using the term "regulatory control" to describe a similar control objective for the overall process performance.

The trouble with regulatory control (the same problem exists with a simple feedback control loop discussed in Chapter 19) is that compensating action is taken only after a disturbance has affected the process output. An error must be present in order for any control action to be initiated. The presence of an error means that the output of the process is different from the desired value.

In *feedforward control* the disturbances are measured before they have upset the process, and anticipatory corrective action is taken. In the ideal case, the corrective action compensates completely for the disturbance, thus preventing any deviation from the desired output value. If this ideal can be reached, feedforward control represents an improvement over feedback control.

The essential features of a feedforward control system are illustrated in Figure 22.13. The feedforward control concept can be applied to the individual measurable output variables in the process or to the performance evaluation variable for the entire process. The disturbance is measured and serves as the input to the feedforward control elements. These elements compute the necessary corrective action to anticipate the effect of the disturbance on the process. To make this computation, the feedforward controller contains a mathematical or logical model of the process which includes the effect of the disturbance. Feedforward control by itself does not include any mechanism for checking that the output is maintained at the desired level. For this reason, feedforward control is usually combined with feedback control as pictured in Figure 22.13. The feedforward loop is especially helpful when the process is characterized by long "response times" or "dead times" between inputs and outputs. Feedback controls alone would be unable to make timely corrections to the process.

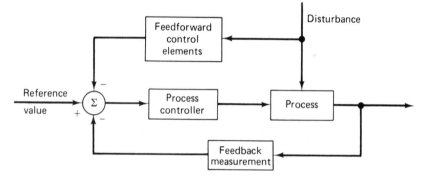

FIGURE 22.13   Feedforward control (combined with feedback control).

Regulatory and feedforward control are implemented at the process level using analog control, DDC, or logic controls, or a combination of these process-level control types.

Steady-state optimal control, adaptive control, and optimum search techniques are the three optimal control strategies discussed in Chapter 20. We shall not discuss these strategies further here except to indicate the merits of implementing them by means of computer control. Since each of these techniques can involve the processing of substantial amounts of data, computer control becomes a logical and often the only practical way to accomplish the strategies.

Other specialized techniques include strategies that are currently evolving in control theory and computer science. Examples are learning systems, expert systems, and other artificial intelligence methods for process control.

22.7 PROGRAMMING FOR COMPUTER PROCESS CONTROL

In this section we are concerned with the issues involved in programming the process control computer. Programming for process control is somewhat different from the conventional programming required for applications in data-processing and engineering calculations. We have dealt with process control programming in previous chapters, although it was not referred to by that name: numerical control part programming in Chapter 9 and robot programming in Chapter 12. In the present section process control is considered in a more generic way.

Requirements of control programming

There are several reasons why computer programming for process monitoring and control is different from programming for data processing and scientific/engineering calculations. The requirements of programming for computer control include the following:

1. *Timer-initiated events.* The computer must be capable of responding to events that are triggered by clock time. An example would be sampled-data values of process variables that must be collected at regular time intervals during process monitoring.

2. *Process-initiated interrupts.* The computer must be able to respond to incoming signals from the process. Depending on the relative importance of these signals, the computer might be required to interrupt its current program of calculations to perform higher-priority functions. A process-initiated interrupt is typically triggered by abnormal operating conditions, which indicates that some corrective control action is needed.

3. *Computer commands to process.* The process-initiated interrupt represents a communication from the process to the computer. This may be sufficient for process monitoring. But for process control, the computer system must have the software capability to direct the various process hardware devices that regulate the process in the desired manner.

4. *System- and program-initiated events.* These are events related to the computer system itself. When several computers are linked together in a computer network, data must be transferred back and forth between the computers. This type of arrangement is common in CIM systems, where different computers occupy different levels in a pyramidal structure. Such an arrangement, called a hierarchical computer system, is discussed in Chapter 26. Communication between computers falls into the category of a system-initiated event. Signals from peripheral devices such as a card reader or printer are also examples of system events. An example of a program-initiated event is when the program calls for data to be printed on some output device (e.g., teletype, CRT, line printer). The system and program events are really no different from the computer operations found in business and engineering applications. In process control, these events generally occupy a relatively low priority compared to process- or timer-initiated events.

5. *Operator-initiated events.*   Also similar to conventional programming, the control system software must be capable of accepting input from operating personnel. This operator input may include any of the following types of items:

Request for printout of certain process variables or status data

New programs or changes in existing programs

Startup instructions or commands which may be part of the process operating routine

Batch number or customer identification data to be associated with a certain production run

The preceding control software requirements can be satisfied by means of a priority interrupt system.

Interrupt system

Computers used for process control are equipped with an interrupt logic system. The purpose of the interrupt system is to permit program control to be switched between different programs or subroutines in response to different priority interrupts. When the interrupt is received, program control suspends execution of the current program and transfers to a predetermined storage location corresponding to the type of interrupt. Meanwhile, the location and status of the interrupted program is remembered so that its execution can be resumed when servicing of the interrupt has been completed.

The various interrupt conditions can be classified as external or internal. External interrupts are triggered by events that are external to the computer system. These include process-initiated interrupts and operator inputs. Internal interrupts are also called system interrupts because they are generated within the system itself. These include timer-initiated events, computer commands to the process, and other system- or program-related events.

PRIORITY INTERRUPT LEVELS.   The reason for using the interrupt system is to make the computer perform more important functions before it performs less important functions. For this reason, the various possible functions that the computer might be called upon to perform are classified according to priority level. A higher-level priority function can interrupt a lower-level function. The system designer must decide what level of priority should be attached to the various computer functions. A typical ranking of priority levels among control functions might be the following:

Priority level	*Computer function*
1 (lowest level)	Operator inputs
2	System interrupts
3	Timer interrupts
4	Commands to process
5 (highest level)	Process interrupts

However, this listing is intended only as a rough guide. There may be different levels of interrupt priority within a certain category listed above. Some process interrupts may be more important than others. Certain system interrupts may take precedence over some of the process interrupts. Also, the computer interrupt system may have more or less than the five levels shown above.

A *single-level interrupt system* has only two modes of operation: normal mode and interrupt mode. The normal mode is interruptible but the interrupt mode is not. This means that overlapping interrupts are serviced on a first come/first served basis. This could lead to hazardous consequences if an important process interrupt was forced to wait in the queue while a series of unimportant operator and system interrupts were serviced.

A *multilevel interrupt system* has more than two operating modes as follows:

Normal mode

Interrupt priority 1—interruptible by priority 2

Interrupt priority 2—interruptible by priority 3

And so on, for as many priority levels as the system has.

Figure 22.14 shows how the computer control system responds to different priority interrupts under the single-level and multilevel interrupt designs. Programming for the multilevel system is somewhat more complicated than for the single-level configuration.

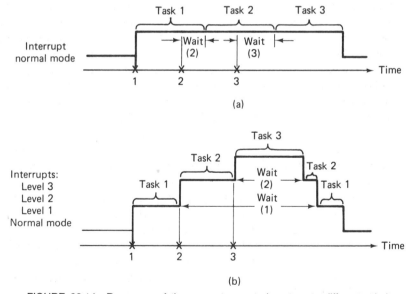

FIGURE 22.14 Response of the computer control system to different priority interrupts: (a) single-level interrupt system; (b) multilevel interrupt system.

However, the additional software expense is of low consequence compared to the risk of upsetting the process when high-priority interrupts are ignored.

REAL TIME CLOCK INTERRUPTS. The timer-initiated interrupts are worthy of special mention. This is one of the most useful features of the control computer system. Timer-initiated events are driven by a real-time clock which basically marks time with the outside world. The real-time clock is a programmable control device that can generate an interrupt signal at regular time intervals. These time intervals can range from 100 μs to several minutes, depending on the capability of the real-time clock.

Some of the uses of the real-time clock in computer control applications are the following:

1. To scan the variables of a manufacturing process at regular sampling intervals.

2. To initiate a recomputation of optimum conditions at which to operate a process. External conditions and raw materials change over time and the operating parameters of the process must be periodically fine-tuned.

3. To output data to the operator's console at various times during the production run.

4. To open and close contacts in sequencing control at appropriate times during the operating cycle.

Error detection and recovery

In the operation of any process control system, there will be hardware malfunctions and unexpected events that occur during process operation. These events typically result in costly delays and loss of product until the problem has been corrected and regular operation restored. In an automated process, human assistance is often required to intervene, diagnose the problem, make the repairs, and restart the system. With the increased use of computer control for manufacturing processes, there is a trend toward using the control computer to detect these malfunctions and unexpected events, and to automatically perform the necessary procedures to restore the system. The term *error detection and recovery* is used when the computer performs these functions.

As indicated by the term, error detection and recovery consists of two phases: error detection and error recovery. The detection of malfunctions and errors in the process requires the use of sensors interfaced with the control computer. Signals from the sensors must be interpreted by the computer system to properly identify that an error has occurred. Errors that occur in the manufacturing process can be classified into one of three categories: random errors, systematic errors, and aberrations. Random errors occur as a result of the normal stochastic nature of the process. These are errors associated with the operation when the process is in statistical control (refer to our discussion of statistical quality control in Section 18.2). Large variations in part dimensions even when the process is in statistical control can cause problems in downstream manufacturing operations. By detecting these deviations on a part-by-part basis, corrective action can be taken in the subsequent processes. Systematic errors are those that result from some assignable cause such as a change in raw material properties or a drift in an equipment setting. These errors usually cause the product to deviate from specifications so as to be unacceptable in quality terms. Finally, the third type of error, the aberrations, results from either an equipment failure or a human mistake. Examples of equipment failures include fracture of a mechanical shear pin, bursts in a hydraulic line, rupture of a pressure vessel, sudden failure of a cutting tool, and so on. Examples of human mistakes include errors in the control program, improper fixturing setups, substitution of the wrong raw materials, and so on.

The difficulty in error detection is to design the appropriate sensor systems and associated interpretive software which is capable of anticipating all of the possible problems that can occur in a given process situation. This task requires a systematic evaluation of the possible cases under each of the three error classifications, and a means of detecting and recognizing the error.

Error recovery is concerned with applying the necessary response to the identified error to bring the system back to normal operation. The problem of designing an error recovery system focuses on devising appropriate strategies and procedures that will either correct or compensate for the variety of errors that can occur in the process. Generally, a specific recovery strategy and procedure must be designed for each different error. The types of strategies can be classified as follows:

1. *Correct at end of current cycle.* This strategy involves adjustments in the operation at the completion of the current work cycle or part. The error for which this response is employed usually has a relatively low urgency level. This type of strategy is most likely associated with random errors in the process.

2. *Correct during cycle.* This generally indicates a higher level of urgency than the preceding type. In this case, the action to correct or compensate for the detected error is initiated immediately. Processes monitored by on-line/in-process inspection systems provide the opportunity for this type of error recovery strategy. Compensating action to deal with the error can be taken as soon as the error is detected.

3. *Stop the process and invoke automatic recovery procedure.* In this case, the error is of a nature that requires the process to be stopped. Depending on the reason, it may be possible for the system to automatically recover from the error without human assistance. An example would be when a tool fails during the cut, and a substitute tool from the machine's tool drum can be used to replace the broken tool. In this situation the system can automatically recover from the error by stopping the current processing step, making the substitution, and resuming the operation.

4. *Stop the process and call for human intervention.* In this case, the error requiring stoppage of the process cannot be resolved through automated procedures. Accordingly, the only recourse is to call for help from a human operator. Considering our example in type 3 above, suppose that a substitute tool were not available in the machine tool storage drum. The only way to recover from the tool failure is for a human operator to intervene and replace the broken tool.

When an error in the process is sensed and identified, an interrupt in the normal program execution is invoked in order to branch to the appropriate recovery subroutine. This is done either at the end of the current cycle (type 1 above) or immediately (types 2, 3, and 4). At the completion of the recovery procedure, program execution reverts back to normal operation.

Malfunctions and errors during processing must be accepted as a fact of life in today's manufacturing environment. Error detection and recovery represents an important area in process control programming for dealing with these problems.

Diagnostics

Modern automated production systems are becoming increasingly complex and sophisticated, thus complicating the problem of maintaining and repairing them. A feature of some computer control systems that is closely related to error detection and recovery is diagnostics. Indeed, in error detection it is usually necessary for some kind of diagnostic analysis to be performed to interpret and classify the sensor signals during process control.

Diagnostics refers to the capabilities of a computer process control system that help identify the source of malfunctions and failures of the system. Three modes of operation are typical of a modern diagnostics subsystem:

1. *Status monitoring.* In the status monitoring mode, the diagnostic subsystem monitors and records the status of key sensors and parameters of the system during normal operation. On request the diagnostics subsystem can display any of these values and provide an interpretation of current system status.

2. *Failure diagnostics.* The failure diagnostics mode is invoked when a malfunction or failure occurs. Its purpose is to interpret the current values of the monitored variables and to review the recorded values preceding the failure so that the cause of the failure can be identified.

3. *Recommendation of repair procedure.* In the third mode of operation the subsystem provides a recommended procedure to the repair crew as to the steps that should be taken to effect repairs. Methods for developing the recommendations are sometimes based on the use of expert systems in which the collective judgments of many repair experts are pooled and incorporated into a computer program using artificial intelligence techniques.

Monitoring the process variables serves two important functions in machine diagnostics: providing information for diagnosing a current failure (failure diagnostics) and providing data to predict a future malfunction. First, when a failure of the equipment has occurred it is usually difficult for the repair crew to determine the reason for the failure and what steps should be taken to make repairs. It is often helpful to reconstruct the events leading up to the failure. The computer is programmed to monitor and record the variables and to draw logical inferences from their values about the reason for the malfunction. This diagnosis helps the repair personnel to make the necessary repairs and to replace the appropriate components. This is especially helpful in electronics repairs, where it is difficult to determine on the basis of a visual inspection which components have failed.

The second function of status monitoring is to identify signs of an impending failure so that the affected components can be replaced before failure actually causes the system to go down. These part replacements can be made during the night shift or other time when the process is not operating, with the result that the system experiences no loss of regular operation.

REFERENCES

[1] DIEFENDERFER, A. J., *Principles of Electronic Instrumentation*, W. B. Saunders Company, Philadelphia, 1972.

[2] DOEBELIN, E. O., *Measurement Systems: Application and Design*, rev. ed., McGraw-Hill Book Company, New York, 1975.

[3] GROOVER, M. P., M. WEISS, R. N. NAGEL, and N. G. ODREY, *Industrial Robotics: Technology, Programming, and Applications*, McGraw-Hill Book Company, New York, 1986, Chapter 11.

[4] REMBOLD, U., M. K. SETH, and J. S. WEINSTEIN, *Computers in Manufacturing*, Marcel Dekker, Inc., New York, 1977.

[5] REMBOLD, U., K. ARMBRUSTER, and W. ULZMANN, *Interface Technology for Computer-Controlled Manufacturing Processes*, Marcel Dekker, Inc., New York, 1983.

[6] SAVAS, E. S., *Computer Control of Industrial Processes*, McGraw-Hill Book Company, New York, 1965.

[7] SCHAFFER, G., "Computers in Manufacturing," *American Machinist*, April 1978, pp. 115–130.

[8] SCHMITT, N. M., and R. F. FARWELL, *Understanding Electronic Control of Automation Systems*, Texas Instruments, Inc., Dallas, Tex., 1983.

[9] SOISSON, H. E., *Instrumentation in Industry*, John Wiley & Sons, Inc., New York, 1975.

PROBLEMS

22.1. A continuous voltage signal is to be converted into its digital counterpart by an analog-to-digital converter. The maximum voltage range is ± 30 V. The ADC has a 12-bit capacity. Determine the number of quantization levels, the resolution, the spacing of each quantization level, and the quantization error for this ADC.

22.2. A voltage signal with a range of 0 to 115 V is to be converted by means of an ADC. Determine the minimum number of bits required to obtain a quantization error of (a) ± 5 V maximum; (b) ± 1 V maximum; (c) ± 0.1 V maximum.

22.3. A digital-to-analog converter uses a reference voltage of 120 V dc and has eight-binary-digit-precision. In one of the sampling instants, the data contained in the binary register are 01010101. If a zero-order hold is used in generating the output signal, determine the voltage output level.

22.4. A DAC uses a reference voltage of 80 V and has 6-bit precision. In four successive 1-s sampling periods, the binary data contained in the output register were 100000, 011111, 011101, and 011010. Determine the equation for the voltage as a function of time between sampling instants 3 and 4 using (a) a zero-order hold; (b) a first-order hold.

22.5. In Problem 22.4, suppose that a second-order hold were to be used to generate the output signal. The equation for the second-order hold is

$$V(t) = V_0 + at + bt^2$$

where V_0 is the starting voltage at the beginning of the time interval. For the binary data given in Problem 22.4, determine the values of a and b that would be used in the equation for the time interval between instants 3 and 4. Compare the first-order and second-order holds in anticipating the voltage at the fourth instant.

part IX

Computer Integrated Manufacturing

The technology that has had the greatest impact on production systems over the last several decades is computer technology. We have seen in Chapter 22 how the computer is used in process control. Examples of computer control discussed in earlier chapters of our book have included computer numerical control, robotics, and flexible manufacturing systems. Although computer process control is certainly important, we would be remiss if we did not acknowledge that there are other applications of computer systems beyond process control in the operations of a manufacturing firm. These applications range from product design to manufacturing planning and control, and include the business operations of the company as well (such as order entry, cost accounting, customer billing, etc.). These various functions constitute the information-processing cycle that occurs in a manufacturing firm (see Figure 2.4). We refer to it as the information-processing cycle because the common denominator that drives these functions is information—information, data, and knowledge. One of the principal roles of the computer in the information-processing cycle is to integrate the different functions—design, manufacturing, and business operations—into a unified, well-coordinated, and smooth-running system. This role of the computer has given rise to the term "computer integrated manufacturing."

In this part of the book we provide a survey of computer integrated manufacturing (CIM). It begins with CAD/CAM. Computer-aided design/computer-aided manufacturing is defined and discussed in Chapter 23. We explain the reasons why design and manufacturing should be and can be treated as a continuous and integrated sequence of activities in the company. The relationship of CAD/CAM and CIM is also examined.

In Chapters 24 and 25 we discuss manufacturing planning and control in the information-processing cycle of CIM. In Chapter 24 we describe several planning steps that are required in manufacturing and how the computer is used to augment or accomplish them. Computer-aided process planning (CAPP) and material requirements planning (MRP) are two principal examples of these planning activities. In Chapter 25 we discuss manufacturing control, in particular those aspects that do not relate to computer process control defined in Part VIII. The chapter is titled "Shop Floor Control and Automatic Identification Techniques." Shop floor control is concerned with monitoring the progress of the production orders as they move through the factory. It is also concerned with comparing the progress to the plans defined in Chapter 24. Automatic identification techniques, such as bar code readers, are being used increasingly to automate shop floor control. We examine these technologies in Chapter 25.

Computer integrated manufacturing can be achieved only by connecting the various computer systems in the firm's information-processing cycle, allowing them and their respective users to communicate with each other. These connections are established by means of computer networks. In Chapter 26 we examine the issues of computer networks in manufacturing.

The book concludes with a view of the future automated factory. In Chapter 27 we attempt to forecast how the various manufacturing technologies, automated production systems, and computerized techniques discussed throughout the book will evolve into the fully automated factory. We also discuss the probable social impact of the factory of the future.

chapter 23

Fundamentals of CAD/CAM

CAD/CAM involves the use of the digital computer to accomplish certain functions in design and production. CAD is concerned with the use of the computer to support the design engineering function, and CAM is concerned with the use of the computer to support manufacturing engineering activities. The combination of CAD and CAM in the term CAD/CAM is symbolic of efforts to integrate the design and manufacturing functions in a firm into a continuum of activities, rather than to treat them as two separate and disparate activities, as they have been considered in the past.

In this chapter we discuss computer-aided design, computer-aided manufacturing, and how CAD/CAM fits within the scope of CIM. For a more detailed discussion of CAD/CAM, we refer the reader to a companion text [1].

23.1 COMPUTER-AIDED DESIGN

Computer-aided design (CAD) can be defined as any design activity that involves the effective use of the computer to create, modify, or document an engineering design. CAD is most commonly associated with the use of an interactive computer graphics system, referred to as a CAD system. The term CAD/CAM system is also used if it supports manufacturing as well as design applications.

There are several important reasons for using a computer-aided design system to support the engineering design function [1]:

1. *To increase the productivity of the designer.* This is accomplished by helping the designer to conceptualize the product and its components. In turn this helps to reduce the time required by the designer to synthesize, analyze, and document the design.

2. *To improve the quality of the design.* The use of a CAD system with appropriate hardware and software capabilities permits the designer to do a more complete engineering analysis and to consider a larger number and variety of design alternatives. The quality of the resulting design is thereby improved.

3. *To improve design documentation.* The graphical output of a CAD system results in better documentation of the design than what is practical with manual drafting. The engineering drawings are superior, and there is more standardization among the drawings, fewer drafting errors, and greater legibility.

4. *To create a manufacturing data base.* In the process of creating the documentation for the product design (geometric specification of the product, dimensions of the components, materials specifications, bill of materials, etc.), much of the required data base to manufacture the product is also created.

The design process

The general process of design is characterized by Shigley [7] as an iterative process which consists of the following six phases:

1. Recognition of need
2. Definition of the problem
3. Synthesis
4. Analysis and optimization
5. Evaluation
6. Presentation

These six design steps, and the iterative nature of the sequence in which they are performed, are depicted in Figure 23.1. Recognition of need involves the realization by someone that a problem exists for which some corrective action can be taken in the form of a design solution. This recognition might mean identifying some defect in a current machine design by an engineer or perceiving of some new product opportunity by a salesperson. Definition of the problem involves a thorough specification of the item to be designed. This specification includes the physical characteristics, function, cost, quality, and operating performance.

Synthesis and analysis are closely related and highly interactive in the design process. Consider the development of a certain product design. Each of the subsystems of the product would be conceptualized by the designer, analyzed, improved through this

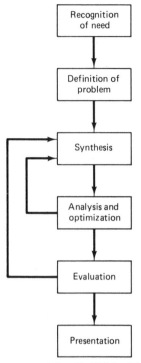

FIGURE 23.1   Design process as defined by Shigley [7]. (Reprinted by permission from Mikell P. Groover and Emory W. Zimmers, *CAD/CAM: Computer-Aided Designs and Manufacturing* (Englewood Cliffs, NJ: Prentice-Hall Inc., 1984), p. 57 [1].)

analysis procedure, redesigned, analyzed again, and so on. The process would be repeated until the design has been optimized within the constraints imposed on the designer. The individual components would be synthesized and analyzed into the final product in a similar manner.

Evaluation is concerned with measuring the design against the specifications established in the problem definition phase. This evaluation often requires the fabrication and testing of a prototype model to assess operating performance, quality, reliability, and other criteria. The final phase in the design procedure is the presentation of the design. Presentation is concerned with the documentation of the design by means of drawings, material specifications, assembly lists, and so on. In essence, documentation means that the design data base is created.

Application of computers in design

A computer-aided design system can beneficially be used in four phases of the design process. The four phases, together with the CAD activity that corresponds to the phase given in parentheses, are [1]:

- Synthesis (geometric modeling)
- Analysis and optimization (engineering analysis)
- Evaluation (design review and evaluation)
- Presentation (automated drafting)

These CAD activities are illustrated in Figure 23.2 as an overlay on the design process of Shigley.

Geometric modeling is concerned with the use of a CAD system to develop a mathematical description of the geometry of an object. The mathematical description, called a *model,* is contained in computer memory. This permits the user of the CAD system to display an image of the model on a graphics terminal and to perform certain operations on the model. These operations include creating new geometric models from basic building blocks available in the system, moving the images around on the screen, zooming in on certain features of the image, and so on. These capabilities permit the

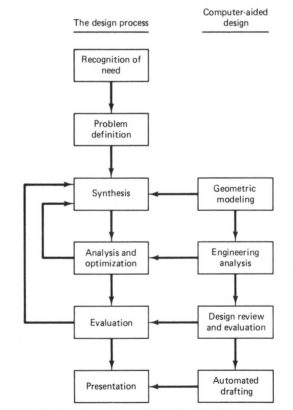

FIGURE 23.2   Design process using CAD. (Reprinted by permission from Mikell P. Groover and Emory W. Zimmers, *CAD/CAM: Computer-Aided Designs and Manufacturing* (Englewood Cliffs, NJ: Prentice-Hall Inc., 1984), p. 59 [1].)

designer to construct a model of a new product (or its components) or to modify an existing model.

There are various types of geometric models used in computer-aided design. One classification distinguishes between two-dimensional and three-dimensional models. Two-dimensional models are best utilized for design problems in two dimensions, such as flat objects and layouts of buildings. In the first CAD systems developed in the early 1970s, two-dimensional systems were used principally as automated drafting systems. They were often used for three-dimensional objects, and it was left to the designer or draftsman to properly construct the various views of the object. Three-dimensional CAD systems are capable of modeling an object in three dimensions. The operations and transformations on the model are done by the system according to user instructions in three dimensions. This is helpful in the conceptualization of the object since the true three-dimensional model can be displayed in various views and from different angles.

Geometric models in CAD can also be classified as being either wire-frame models or solid models. A wire-frame model uses interconnecting lines to depict an object as illustrated in Figure 23.3. Wire-frame models of complicated geometries can become somewhat confusing because all of the lines depicting the shape of the object are usually shown, even the lines representing the other side of the object. Techniques are available for removing these so-called hidden lines, but even with this improvement, wire-frame representation is still often inadequate. Solid models are a more recent development in geometric modeling. In this approach, an object is modeled in solid three dimensions, providing the user with a vision of the object very much like it would be seen in real life. More important for engineering purposes, the geometric model is stored in the CAD system as a three-dimensional solid model, thus providing a more accurate representation of the object. This is useful for calculating certain properties of the object, to perform

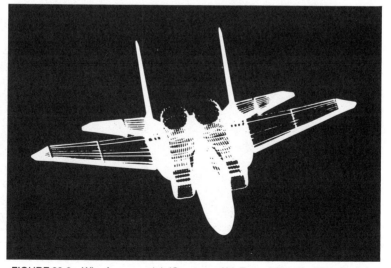

FIGURE 23.3 Wire-frame model. (Courtesy of McDonnell Douglas Manufacturing Industry Systems Company.)

interference checking between mating components in an assembly, and in other engineering computations. A solid model display on a CAD system monitor is shown in Figure 23.4.

Finally, two other features in CAD system models are color and animation. Some CAD systems have color capability rather than only black and white. The value of color is largely to enhance the ability of the user to visualize the object on the graphics screen. For example, the various components of an assembly can be displayed in different colors, thereby permitting the parts to be more readily distinguished. Animation capability permits the operation of mechanisms and other moving objects to be displayed on the graphics monitor.

After a particular design alternative has been developed, some form of engineering analysis must often be performed as part of the design process. The analysis may take the form of stress–strain calculations, heat transfer analysis, or dynamic simulation. The computations required are often quite complex and time consuming, and before the advent of computer-aided design, these analyses were often greatly simplified or even omitted in the design procedure. The availability of software for computer-aided *engineering analysis* on a CAD system greatly increases the designer's ability and willingness to perform a more thorough analysis of a proposed design. Two examples of the software typically offered on CAD systems are mass properties and finite-element analysis. Mass

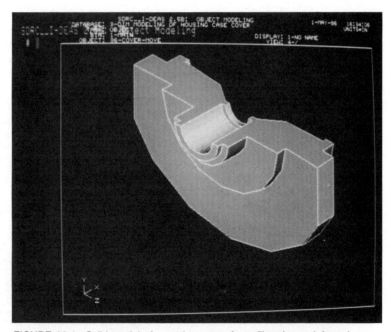

FIGURE 23.4 Solid model of a casing cover for a fiberglass-reinforced pump, displayed on a CAD system. (Courtesy of Computer-Aided Design Laboratory, Lehigh University.)

properties analysis involves the computation of such features of a solid object as its volume, surface area, weight, and center of gravity. Prior to CAD, determination of these properties often required painstaking and time-consuming calculations by the designer. Finite-element analysis is available on most CAD systems to aid in heat transfer, stress–strain, and other engineering computations. Figure 23.5 illustrates a finite-element model (FEM) to analyze stresses in a part design.

Design evaluation and review procedures can be augmented by a computer-aided design system. Some of the CAD features that are helpful in evaluating and reviewing a proposed design include:

- *Automatic dimensioning routines,* which determine precise distance measures between surfaces on the geometric model identified by the user.
- *Interference checking routines,* which identify whether two objects occupy the same space. This is especially helpful in the design of assemblies where it is desired to make sure that there is no interference between components.
- *Kinematics routines,* used to test the operation of mechanical linkages. These systems usually require animation capability.

The fourth area where computer-aided design is useful in the design process is presentation and documentation. CAD systems can be used as *automated drafting machines* to prepare highly accurate engineering drawings quickly. It is estimated that a

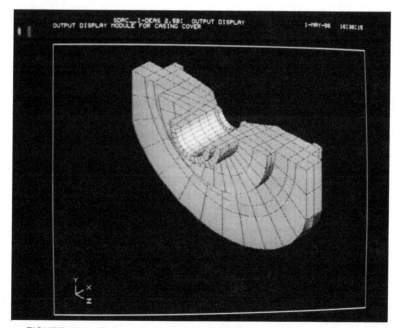

FIGURE 23.5   Finite-element analysis: (a) FEM of part shown in Figure 23.4.

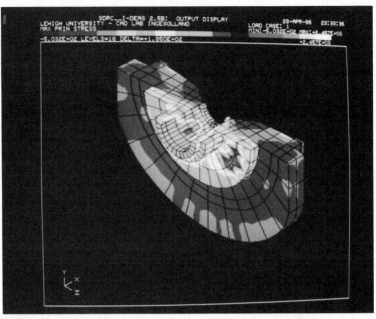

FIGURE 23.5   (b) FEM showing stress contours. (Courtesy of Computer-Aided
Design Laboratory, Lehigh University.)

CAD system increases productivity in the drafting function by about fivefold over manual
preparation of the drawings.

A typical CAD system

A typical commercially available computer-aided design system consists of the following
components:

- One or more design workstations
- Processor
- Secondary storage
- Plotter and/or other output devices

The relationship among the components is illustrated in Figure 23.6. The design workstation is the interface between the CAD system and the user. For the user to accomplish
the various phases of the design process, the workstation must be able to receive input
instructions from the user and to display output data and graphics to the user. Operator
input devices are used for the input functions. The input devices for a CAD system
typically include an alphanumeric keyboard, electronic keypad or other device to input
special graphics functions, and a cursor control device (e.g., a light pen, "mouse,"
joystick, or electronic tablet and "puck"). The graphical design output is accomplished

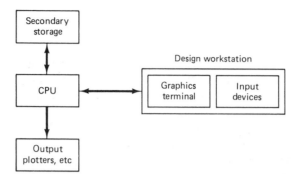

FIGURE 23.6   Configuration of a typical CAD system. (Reprinted by permission from Mikell P. Groover and Emory L. Zimmers, *CAD/CAM: Computer-Aided Designs and Manufacturing* (Englewood Cliffs, NJ: Prentice-Hall, Inc. 1984), p. 80 [1].)

by means of a graphics display monitor. A typical design workstation is shown in Figure 23.7.

The processor is the CAD system computer. A current-day processor for CAD applications uses a 32-bit central processing unit or CPU. The processor performs the mathematical calculations required for geometric modeling, engineering analysis, and other calculations and data-processing functions in computer-aided design. Connected to the processor is a secondary storage for application programs and design data. Also

FIGURE 23.7   CAD design workstation showing function keypad, alphanumeric keyboard, and electronic tablet and puck for cursor control. (Courtesy of Computer Integrated Manufacturing Laboratory, Lehigh University, photo by John Keefe.)

connected to the processor are one or more output devices such as x-y plotters, electrostatic plotters, and similar equipment used for the automated drafting function.

There is a trend in computer-aided design toward small CAD systems in which many of the functions and capabilities of a full computer-aided design system can be accomplished on a personal computer (PC). The PC-based CAD system offers much of the same convenience and user friendliness for design applications that the conventional PC provides for engineering calculations, word processing, and other computer applications. PC-CAD systems can be used as stand-alone systems for small firms that cannot afford a large CAD installation based on a mainframe computer. Or they can be interconnected to a mainframe and to other PC-CAD systems using a local area network. This permits access to the mainframe for applications that require a more powerful computer than the PC, or to exchange data between CAD workstations on the network.

23.2   COMPUTER-AIDED MANUFACTURING

Computer-aided manufacturing (CAM) is defined as the effective use of computer technology in the planning, management, and control of the manufacturing function. With reference back to our model of production in Chapter 1, the applications of CAM can be divided into two broad categories:

1.   Manufacturing planning
2.   Manufacturing control

The two categories represent two different levels of involvement of the computer in the operations of the plant. In the following subsections we briefly discuss these categories.

Manufacturing planning

CAM applications for manufacturing planning are those in which the computer is used indirectly to support the production function, but there is no direct connection between the computer and the process. The computer is used "off-line" to provide information for the effective planning and management of production activities. The following list surveys the important applications of computer-aided manufacturing in this category:

•   *Cost estimating.*   The task of estimating the cost of a new product has been simplified in most industries by computerizing several of the key steps required to prepare the estimate. The computer is programmed to apply the appropriate labor and overhead rates to the sequence of planned operations for the components of new products. The program then sums the individual component costs from the engineering bill of materials to determine the overall product cost.

•   *Computer-aided process planning (CAPP).*   Process planning is concerned with the preparation of route sheets which list the sequence of operations and work centers required to produce the product and its components. CAPP systems are available today to prepare these route sheets. We discuss computer-aided process planning in Chapter 24.

  • *Computerized machinability data systems.* One of the problems in operating a metal-cutting machine tool is determining the speeds and feeds that should be used to machine a given workpart. Computer programs have been written to recommend the appropriate cutting conditions to use for different materials. The calculations are based on data that have been obtained either in the factory or laboratory which relate tool life to cutting conditions. These machinability data systems are described in reference [1].

  • *Computer-assisted NC part programming.* The subject of part programming for numerical control was discussed in Chapter 9. For complex part geometries, computer-assisted part programming represents a much more efficient method of generating the control instructions for the machine tool than manual part programming.

  • *Development of work standards.* The time study department has the responsibility for setting time standards on direct labor jobs performed in the factory. Establishing standards by direct time study can be a tedious and time-consuming task. There are several commercially available computer packages for setting work standards. These computer programs use standard time data that have been developed for basic work elements that comprise any manual task. By summing the times for the individual elements required to perform a new job, the program calculates the standard time for the job. These packages are discussed in reference [1].

  • *Computer-aided line balancing.* Finding the best allocation of work elements among stations on an assembly line is a large and difficult problem if the line is of significant size. Computer programs such as COMSOAL and CALB (discussed in Chapter 6) have been developed to assist in the solution of this problem.

  • *Production and inventory planning.* The computer has found widespread use in many of the functions in production and inventory planning. These functions include maintenance of inventory records, automatic reordering of stock items when inventory is depleted, production scheduling, maintaining current priorities for the different production orders, material requirements planning, and capacity planning. We discuss some of these planning activities in Chapter 24.

Manufacturing control

The second category of CAM applications is concerned with developing computer systems for implementing the manufacturing control function, as described in Chapter 2. Manufacturing control is concerned with managing and controlling the physical operations in the factory. Process control, quality control, shop floor control, and process monitoring are all included within the scope of this function.

  We discussed process control in Part VIII—in particular, computer process control in Chapter 22. The applications of computer process control are pervasive today in automated production systems. They include transfer lines, assembly systems, numerical control, robotics, material handling, and flexible manufacturing systems. All of these topics have been covered in earlier chapters.

Shop floor control refers to production management techniques for collecting data from factory operations and using the data to help control production and inventory in the factory. Computerized factory data collection techniques and computer process monitoring represent the preferred means of implementing a shop floor control system today. We discuss shop floor control and computerized factory data collection systems in more detail in Chapter 25.

23.3 COMPUTER INTEGRATED MANUFACTURING

The term *computer integrated manufacturing* (CIM) is often used interchangeably with CAD/CAM. The terms are closely related; however, CIM is interpreted to possess a slightly broader meaning than CAD/CAM. In this section we attempt to define the meaning and scope of CAD/CAM and CIM.

CAD/CAM

As described in our introduction, computer-aided design and computer-aided manufacturing are concerned principally with the engineering functions in design and manufacturing, respectively. Product design, engineering analysis, and documentation of the design (e.g., drafting) represent engineering activities in the design function. Process planning, NC part programming, and many other activities associated with CAM represent engineering activities in manufacturing. The CAD/CAM systems developed during the 1970s and early 1980s were designed primarily to address these types of engineering problems. In addition, CAM has evolved to include many other functions in manufacturing, such as material requirements planning, production scheduling, computer production monitoring, and computer process control.

It should also be noted that CAD/CAM denotes an integration of design and manufacturing activities by means of computer systems. The method of manufacturing a product is a direct function of its design. With conventional procedures practiced for so many years in industry, engineering drawings were prepared by design draftsmen and then used by manufacturing engineers to develop the process plan (i.e., the route sheets). The activities involved in designing the product were separated from the activities associated with process planning. Essentially, a two-step procedure was employed. This was time consuming and involved duplication of effort by design and manufacturing personnel. With CAD/CAM, a direct link is established between product design and manufacturing engineering. It is the goal of CAD/CAM not only to automate certain phases of design and certain phases of manufacturing, but also to automate the transition from design to manufacturing. In the ideal CAD/CAM system, it is possible to take the design specification of the product as it resides in the CAD data base and convert it into a process plan for making the product, this conversion being done automatically by the CAD/CAM system. A large portion of the processing might be accomplished on a numerically controlled machine tool. As part of the process plan, the NC part program would be generated automatically by CAD/CAM. The CAD/CAM system would then download the NC program directly to the machine tool by means of a telecommunications network. Hence, under this arrangement (which is certainly within the capabilities of today's CAD/CAM technology), product design, NC programming, and physical production can all be implemented by computer.

Computer integrated manufacturing

Computer integrated manufacturing includes all of the engineering functions of CAD/CAM, but it also includes the business functions of the firm as well. The ideal CIM system applies computer technology to all of the operational functions and information processing functions in manufacturing from order receipt, through design and production, to product shipment (refer back to Section 2.4). Some writers even suggest that it includes service and field support after the sale [2]. The scope of computer integrated manufacturing, compared with the more limited scope of CAD/CAM, is depicted in Figure 23.8.

The CIM concept is that all of the firm's operations related to the production function are incorporated in an integrated computer system to assist, augment, and/or automate the operations. The computer system is pervasive throughout the firm, touching all activities that support manufacturing. In this integrated computer system, the output of one activity serves as the input to the next activity, through the chain of events that starts

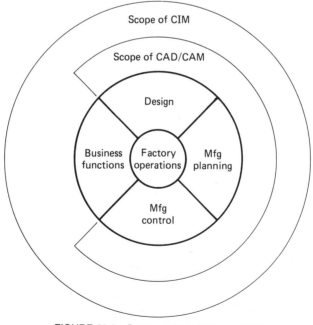

FIGURE 23.8 Scope of CAD/CAM and CIM.

with the sales order and culminates with shipment of the product. The components of the integrated computer system, and their relationship to our model of manufacturing, are illustrated in Figure 23.9. Customer orders are initially entered by the company's sales force into a computerized order-entry system. The orders contain the specifications describing the product. The specifications serve as the input to the product design department. New products are designed on a CAD system. The components that comprise the product are designed, the bill of materials is compiled, and assembly drawings are prepared. The output of the design department serves as the input to manufacturing engineering, where process planning, tool design, and similar activities are accomplished to prepare for production. Many of these manufacturing engineering activities are supported by the CIM computer system: Process planning is performed using computer-aided process planning, and tool design is done on a CAD system, making use of the product model generated during product design. The output from manufacturing engineering provides the input to production planning and control, where material requirements planning and scheduling is performed using the computer system. And so it goes, through

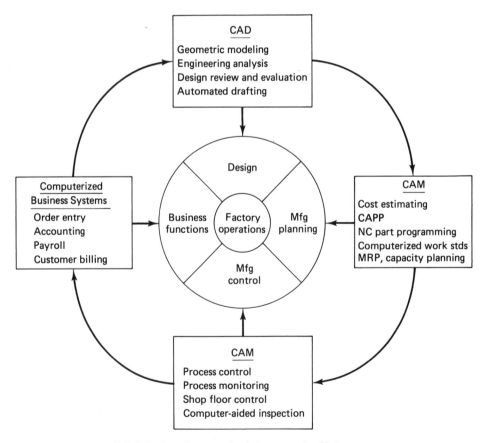

FIGURE 23.9 Computerized elements of a CIM system.

each step in the manufacturing cycle. Full implementation of CIM results in the automation of the information flow through every aspect of the company's organization.

REFERENCES

[1] GROOVER, M. P., and E. W. ZIMMERS, JR., *CAD/CAM: Computer-Aided Design and Manufacturing,* Prentice-Hall, Inc., Englewood Cliffs, N.J., 1984.

[2] GUNN, T., "The CIM Connection," *Datamation,* February 1, 1986, pp. 50–58.

[3] HARP, J., "CAD/CAM: Back to Basics," *Manufacturing Engineering,* October 1985, pp. 61–63.

[4] KROUSE, J. K., "Engineering without Paper," *High Technology,* March 1986, pp. 38–46.

[5] *Machine Design,* CAD/CAM Reference Issue, October 17, 1985.

[6] *Modern Machine Shop 1985 NC/CAM Guidebook,* Gardner Publications, Inc., Cincinnati, Ohio, January 1985, Chapter 8.

[7] SHIGLEY, J. E., and L. D. MITCHELL, *Mechanical Engineering Design,* 4th ed., McGraw-Hill Book Company, New York, 1983.

[8] WILLIAMSON, D., "CAD/CAM: Plotting the Impact of Shakeout," *Manufacturing Engineering,* October 1985, pp. 67–69.

chapter **24**

Computerized Manufacturing Planning Systems

In Section 23.2 we presented a list of manufacturing planning activities that can be implemented by computer. Some of the activities fall within the scope of process planning and production planning, and in the current chapter we consider some of the computer-aided systems that are used to support these functions.

Process planning involves the preparation and documentation of the plans for manufacturing the products. Computer-aided process planning (CAPP) is a means of implementing this planning function by computer. Many of the functions in production management also involve planning activities. Material requirements planning (MRP) and capacity planning are examples of these activities. In the modern practice of production management, these are considered to be components of a highly integrated production management system that is implemented by computer. We discuss the production planning activities in this chapter.

24.1 COMPUTER-AIDED PROCESS PLANNING

Computer-aided process planning represents the link between design and manufacturing in a CAD/CAM system. As described in Chapter 2, process planning is concerned with

724

determining the sequence of processing and assembly steps that must be accomplished to make the product. The processing sequence is documented on a form called a *route sheet*. The route sheet typically lists the production operations, machine cells or workstations where each operation is performed, fixtures and tooling required, and the standard time for each task.

During the last decade or so, there has been much interest in automating the task of process planning by means of CAPP systems. The shop-trained people who are familiar with the details of machining and other processes are gradually retiring, and these people will be unavailable in the future to do process planning. An alternative way of accomplishing this function is needed, and CAPP systems are providing this alternative.

Computer-aided process planning systems are designed around two approaches. These approaches are called:

1. Retrieval CAPP systems
2. Generative CAPP systems

Retrieval CAPP systems

Retrieval-type computer-aided process planning systems, also called *variant CAPP systems,* are based on the principles of group technology and parts classification and coding (Chapter 16). With these systems, a standard process plan (route sheet) is stored in computer files for each part code number. The standard route sheets are based on current part routings in use in the factory, or on an ideal plan that is prepared for each family. The development of the data base of these process plans requires substantial effort.

In use, a retrieval CAPP system operates as illustrated in Figure 24.1. The user begins by deriving the GT code number for the component for which the process plan is to be determined. One of the parts classification and coding methods discussed in Chapter 16 might be used for this purpose. With this code number, a search is made of the part family file to determine if a standard route sheet exists for the given part code. If the file contains a process plan for the part, it is retrieved and displayed for the user. The standard process plan is examined to determine whether any modifications are necessary. It might be that although the new part has the same code number, there are minor differences in the processes required to make the part. The user edits the standard plan accordingly. It is this capacity to alter an existing process plan that gives the retrieval system its other name: variant CAPP system.

If the file does not contain a standard process plan for the given code number, the user may search the computer file for a similar or related code number for which a standard route sheet does exist. Either by editing an existing process plan, or by starting from scratch, the user writes the route sheet for the new part. This route sheet becomes the standard process plan for the new part code number.

The process planning session concludes with the process plan formatter, which prints out the route sheet in the proper format. The formatter may call

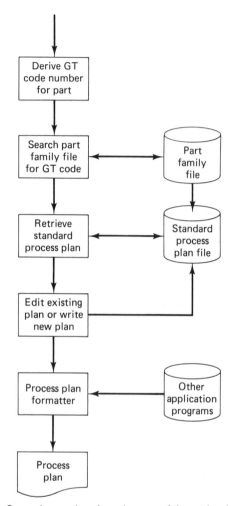

FIGURE 24.1 General procedure for using one of the retrieval computer-aided process planning systems.

other application programs into use: for example, to determine machining conditions for the various machine tool operations in the sequence, to calculate standard times for the operations (e.g., for direct labor incentives), or to compute cost estimates for the operations.

One of the commercially available retrieval CAPP systems is MultiCapp, from OIR, the Organization for Industrial Research. It is an on-line computer system that permits the user to create new plans, or retrieve and edit existing process plans, as we have explained above. An example of a route sheet representing the output from the MultiCapp system is shown in Figure 24.2.

ORGANIZATION FOR INDUSTRIAL RESEARCH, INC. FACILITY – F1								
PART NUMBER: PROB.15.10.1			LAST FOUR ORDERS			MINIMUM QTY	DUE DATES	PRI #
			S/O #	PRJ #	QTY			
PART NAME: DRIVER, VLV GUIDE								
PLNG REV: 1 1 DWG REV: C			4-232	SD122	4000	3500	12-8X	1
PLANNER: FRED SAMBERA								

CHANGE APPROVALS & DATE				CODE #1: 1-3300-07-234901-5-0516-0000000000000				
	#1	#2	#3	CODE #2: 5-2120-3654-22-01				
MFG		A3		CODE # 3: 6-4032-417				
ENG		E1	E2					
Q/A		Q2		START: 08/15/8X	T.O.T.D.: 4000	T.R.DOC: 1		

MATERIAL REQUIRED:
SPECIAL INSTRUCTIONS:

OPER NO	MACH TOOL	OPERATION DESCRIPTION—ASSY INSTRUCTIONS	TIMES		OPERATOR STAMP
			S/U	RUN	
0010	1258	SET-UP 3/4 DIA COLLET PADS SET TURRET STOP TO HOLD 4.5 LENGTH ROUGH TURN .5 DIA TO .532 DIA + .01 − .01 ROUGH TURN .375 DIA TO .39 + .01 − .01 HOLD 1.625 LENGTH FINISH TURN .500 DIA + OR − .005 FINISH TURN .375 DIA + OR − .005 HOLD 1.625 CUT-OFF TO 5-7/8 LENGTH	1.7	.40	
0020	1258	S/U COLLET HOLD ON .500 DIA ROUGH TURN .437 DIA AND FORM 30 DEG ANG. FINISH TURN .437 DIA + OR − .005 AND FORM 30 DEG ANG HOLD 1.75 DIM + OR − .015 FACE TO 5 3/4 LENGTH + OR − 1/16 BURR SHARP CORNERS	1.5	.15	
0030	9401	HARDEN, HEAT AT 1550 DEG. F. − OIL QUENCH AT 120 DEG. F.	.25	.50	
0040	9401	STRAIGHTEN TO .005 T.I.R.	.10	.25	
0050	9401	TEMPER AT 400 DEG. F. MIN. TC 46-50 R.C. FOR ONE HOUR	.25	0.05	
0060	9805	INSPECT HEAT TREAT - 46-50 R.C.	.10	.15	
0070	9201	CHROME PLATE	.27	.05	
0080	4102	S/U THRU FEED GRIND DD TO .5100	.375	.06	
0090	9805	INSPECT ALL DIMENSIONS PER PRINT	.10	.15	

FIGURE 24.2 Route sheet prepared by The MultiCapp System. (Courtesy of OIR, the Organization for Industrial Research.)

Generative CAPP systems

Generative CAPP systems represent an alternative approach to automated process planning. Instead of retrieving and editing an existing plan contained in a computer data base, a generative system creates the process plan based on logical procedures similar to the procedures a human planner would use. In a fully generative CAPP system, the process sequence would be planned without human assistance and without a set of predefined standard plans.

The problem of designing a generative CAPP system is considered part of the field of expert systems, a branch of artificial intelligence. An *expert system* is a computer program that is capable of solving complex problems that normally require a human being who has years of education and experience. Process planning fits within the scope of that definition.

There are several ingredients required in a fully generative process planning system. First, the technical knowledge of manufacturing and the logic that is used by successful process planners must be captured and coded into a computer program. In an expert system as it would be applied to process planning, the knowledge and logic of the human process planners is incorporated into a so-called "knowledge base." The generative CAPP system would then use that knowledge base to solve process planning problems (i.e., create route sheets).

The second ingredient in generative process planning is a computer-compatible description of the part to be produced. This description contains all of the pertinent data and information needed to plan the process sequence. Two possible ways of providing this description are: (1) the geometric model of the part that is developed on a CAD system during product design, and (2) a GT code number of the part that defines the part features in significant detail.

The third ingredient in a generative CAPP system is the capability to apply the process knowledge and planning logic contained in the knowledge base to a given part description. In other words, the CAPP system uses its knowledge base to solve a specific problem—planning the process for a new part. This problem-solving procedure is referred to as the "inference engine" in the terminology of expert systems. By using its knowledge base and inference engine, the CAPP system synthesizes a new process plan from scratch for each new part it is presented.

Benefits of CAPP

Among the benefits derived from computer-automated process planning are the following:

1. *Process rationalization and standardization.* Automated process planning leads to more logical and consistent process plans than when process planning is done completely manually. Standard plans tend to result in lower manufacturing costs and higher product quality.

2. *Increased productivity of process planners.* The systematic approach and the availability of standard process plans in the data files permit more work to be accomplished by the process planners. One system was reported to increase productivity by 600% [6].

3. *Reduced lead time for process planning.* Process planners working with the CAPP system can provide route sheets in a shorter lead time compared to manual preparation.

4. *Improved legibility.* Computer-prepared route sheets are neater and easier to read than manually prepared route sheets.

5. *Incorporation of other application programs.* The CAPP program can be interfaced with other application programs, such as cost estimating, work standards, and others, as indicated in Figure 24.1.

24.2 COMPUTER INTEGRATED PRODUCTION PLANNING SYSTEMS

The principal functions of a production planning and control system were discussed in Chapter 2. In the past, these functions were accomplished by large staffs of clerical personnel. Members of the production planning and control department prepared the schedules, decided what materials and parts needed to be ordered, issued the individual orders to the work centers in the plant, and expedited the orders. For plants with large volumes of parts and complex products, the work involved in these activities was significant.

The types of problems commonly encountered in planning and managing production operations in a plant are the following:

1. *Plant capacity problems.* Production falls behind schedule due to lack of manpower and equipment resources. This results in excessive overtime, delays in meeting delivery schedules, customer complaints, backordering, and so on.

2. *Suboptimal production scheduling.* The wrong jobs are scheduled because of a lack of clear order priorities, inefficient scheduling rules, and the ever-changing status of jobs in the shop. As a consequence, production runs are interrupted by jobs whose priorities have suddenly increased, machine setups are increased, and jobs that are on schedule fall behind.

3. *Long manufacturing lead times.* In an attempt to compensate for problems 1 and 2, production planners allow extra time to produce the order. The shop becomes overloaded, order priorities become confused, and the result is excessively long manufacturing lead times.

4. *Inefficient inventory control.* At the same time that total inventories are too high for raw materials, work-in-progress, and finished products, there are stockouts that occur on individual raw-material items needed for production. High total inventories mean high carrying costs, while raw material stockouts mean delays in meeting production schedules.

5. *Low work center utilization.* This problem results in part from poor scheduling (excessive product changeovers and job interruptions), and from other factors over which plant management has limited control (equipment breakdowns, strikes, reduced demand for products, etc.).

6. *Process planning not followed.* This is the situation in which the regular planned routing is superseded by an ad hoc process sequence. It occurs, for instance, because of bottlenecks at work centers in the planned sequence. The consequences are longer setups, improper tooling, and less efficient processes.

7. *Errors in engineering and manufacturing records.* Bills of materials are not current, route sheets are not up to date with respect to the latest engineering changes, inventory records are inaccurate, and production piece counts are incorrect.

8. *Quality problems.* Quality defects are encountered in manufactured components and assembled products, thus causing delays in the shipping schedule.

These problems give rise to the need for better systems to plan and control production operations. Today, industry has adopted the use of computer systems to perform much of the manual planning and clerical work that was previously accomplished by human beings. In the ideal arrangement, the computerized systems are tied together within the company. Figure 24.3 presents a block diagram illustrating the principal functions and activities that must be performed in a production planning system. The principal functions in a computerized production planning system are:

• *Master production schedule.* The master schedule was defined in Chapter 2 as a listing of the products to be manufactured, when they are to be delivered, and in what quantities. It is developed from customer orders and forecasts of future demand. The master schedule represents the plan of production for the firm, which serves as an input to the material requirements planning function.

• *Material requirements planning.* MRP is a procedure, usually computerized, for determining when to order raw materials and components for assembled products. It can be used to reschedule orders in response to changing production priorities and demand conditions. The term *priority planning* is often used in describing computer-based systems for time-phased planning of raw materials, work-in-progress, and finished products.

• *Capacity planning.* Production capacity was defined in Chapter 2 as the amount of product that a given production facility (e.g., a plant or cell) can produce in a certain time period (e.g., a week or month). Whereas MRP deals with the planning of materials and components needed to produce the products in the master schedule, capacity planning is concerned with the planning of production resources (e.g., labor and equipment) needed to meet the master schedule.

In addition to these production planning functions, there are other functions in the manufacturing cycle that interface with the production planning functions. These include:

• *Engineering and manufacturing data base.* This data base contains the engineering data required to make the components and assemble the products. The engineering data include the product designs, component material specifications, bills of materials,

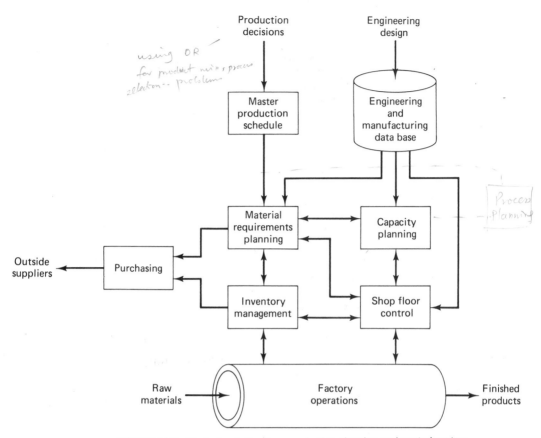

FIGURE 24.3   Typical activities in a production planning and control system.

process plans, and so on. The engineering and manufacturing data base is utilized to perform the planning calculations for the MRP and capacity planning modules.

• *Inventory management.* Inventory management in the manufacturing environment is concerned with keeping the investment in raw materials, work-in-process, finished goods, factory supplies, and spare parts as low as possible without disrupting production operations or jeopardizing customer service.

• *Purchasing.* The Purchasing Department places the orders that are specified by material requirements planning and inventory management. Qualifying vendors and maintaining sources of supply for the company are included within the scope of the purchasing function.

• *Shop floor control.* Shop floor control is concerned with monitoring the progress of orders in the factory and reporting the status of each order to management so that effective control can be exercised. Shop floor control is usually considered to be part of production planning and control.

24.3   MATERIAL REQUIREMENTS PLANNING

Material requirements planning (MRP) is a computational technique that converts the master schedule for end products into a detailed schedule for the raw materials and components used in the end products. The detailed schedule identifies the quantities of each raw material and component item. It also indicates when each item must be ordered and delivered so as to meet the master schedule for final products.

MRP is often thought of as a method of inventory control. While it is an effective tool for minimizing unnecessary inventory investment, MRP is also useful in production scheduling and purchasing of materials.

The concept of MRP is relatively straightforward. What complicates the application of the technique is the sheer magnitude of the data to be processed. The master schedule provides the overall production plan for the final products in terms of month-by-month deliveries. Each of the products may contain hundreds of individual components. These components are produced from raw materials, some of which are common among the components. For example, several components may be made out of the same sheet steel. The components are assembled into simple subassemblies, and these subassemblies are put together into more complex subassemblies, and so on, until the final products are assembled. Each step in the manufacturing and assembly sequence takes time. All of these factors must be incorporated into the MRP calculations. Although each calculation is uncomplicated, the magnitude of the data is so large that the application of MRP is virtually impossible unless carried out on a digital computer.

Fundamental concepts in MRP

Material requirements planning is based on several concepts that are implicit in the preceding description but not explicitly defined. These concepts are:

1.   Independent versus dependent demand
2.   Manufacturing lead times
3.   Common use items

The distinction between independent demand and dependent demand is important in MRP. *Independent demand* means that demand for a product is not directly related to demand for other items. End products and spare parts are examples of items whose demand is independent. Independent demand patterns must usually be forecasted. *Dependent demand* means that demand for the item is related directly to the demand for some other product. The dependency usually derives from the fact that the item is a component of the other product. Not only component parts but also raw materials and subassemblies are examples of items subject to dependent demand.

While demand for the firm's end products must often be forecasted, the raw materials and component parts should not be forecasted. Once the delivery schedule for end products is established, the requirements for components and raw materials can be directly calculated. For example, even though demand for automobiles in a given month can only be forecasted, once the quantity is established we know that five tires will be needed to deliver the car (don't forget the spare).

MRP is the appropriate technique for determining quantities of dependent demand items. These items constitute the inventory of manufacturing: raw materials, work-in-process, component parts, and subassemblies. That is why MRP is such a powerful technique in the planning and control of manufacturing inventories.

The lead time for a job is the time that must be allowed to complete the job from start to finish. There are two types of lead times in MRP: ordering lead times and manufacturing lead times. An *ordering lead time* for an item is the time required from initiation of the purchase requisition to the receipt of the item from the vendor. If the item is a raw material that is stocked by the vendor, the ordering lead time should be relatively short, perhaps a few weeks. If the item is fabricated, the lead time may be substantial, perhaps several months.

Common use items are raw materials and components that are used on more than one product. MRP collects these common use items from different products to effect economies in ordering the raw materials and producing the components.

Inputs to the MRP system

For the MRP program to function properly, it must operate on data contained in several files. These files serve as inputs to the MRP processor. They are:

1. Master production schedule
2. Bill of materials file
3. Inventory record file

Figure 24.4 illustrates the flow of data into the MRP processor and its conversion into useful output reports.

The *master production schedule* is a listing of what end products are to be produced, how many of each product are to be produced, and when they are to be ready for shipment. The general format of the master schedule is shown in Figure 24.5. Manufacturing firms generally work toward monthly delivery schedules; however, in our figure, the master schedule uses weeks as the time periods. The master schedule must be based on an accurate estimate of demand and a realistic assessment of its production capacity. Capacity planning is discussed in Section 24.4.

Product demand that makes up the master schedule can be separated into three categories. The first consists of firm customer orders for specific products. These orders usually include a delivery date that has been promised to the customer by the sales department. The second category is forecasted demand. This is based on statistical techniques applied to previous demand patterns, estimates by the sales staff, and other sources. The forecast may constitute the major portion of the master schedule. The third category is demand for individual component parts. These are repair parts and are stocked in the

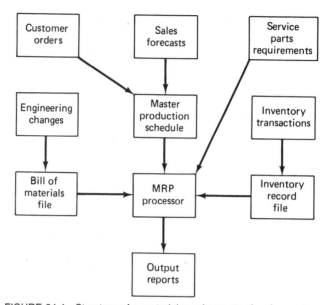

FIGURE 24.4   Structure of a material requirements planning system.

Week number			6	7	8	9	10
Product P1					50		100
Product P2				70	80	25	
etc.							

FIGURE 24.5   Master production schedule for products P1 and P2 showing weekly delivery quantities.

firm's service department. This third category is sometimes excluded from the master schedule since it does not represent demand for end products. In Figure 24.4, it is shown as feeding directly into the MRP processor.

The *bill of materials file* is used to compute the raw material and component requirements for end products listed in the master schedule. It provides information on the product structure by listing the component parts and subassemblies that make up each product.

The structure of an assembled product can be pictured as shown in Figure 24.6. This is a relatively simple product in which a group of individual components make up two subassemblies, which in turn make up the product. The product structure is in the form of a pyramid, with lower levels feeding into the levels above. We can envision one level below that shown in Figure 24.6. This consists of the raw materials used to make the individual components. The items at each successively higher level are called the parents of the items in the level directly below. For example, subassembly S1 is the

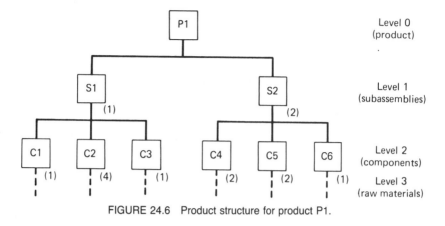

FIGURE 24.6   Product structure for product P1.

parent of components C1, C2, and C3. Product P1 is the parent of subassemblies S1 and S2.

The product structure must also specify how many of each item are included in its parent. This is accomplished in Figure 24.6 by the number in parentheses to the right and below each block. For example, subassembly S1 contains four of component C2 and one each of components C1 and C3.

The *inventory record file* is referred to as the *item master file* in a computerized inventory system. The types of data contained in the inventory record for a given item are shown in Figure 24.7. The file is divided into three segments. The first segment is called the item master data segment and provides the item's identification (part number) and other data as illustrated. The second segment, called the inventory status segment, gives a time-phased record of inventory status. In MRP, it is important to know not only the current level of inventory, but also the future changes that will occur against the inventory. Therefore, the inventory status segment lists the gross requirements for the item, scheduled receipts, on-hand status, and planned order releases. The third file segment provides subsidiary data such as purchase orders, scrap or rejects, and engineering changes.

How MRP works

The material requirements planning processor operates on the data contained in the master schedule, the bill-of-materials file, and the inventory record file. The master schedule specifies a period-by-period list of final products required. The BOM defines what materials and components are needed for each product. The inventory record file contains information on the current and future inventory status of each component. The MRP program computes how many of each component and raw material are needed by "exploding" the end product requirements into successively lower levels in the product structure. Referring to the master schedule in Figure 24.5, 50 units of product P1 are specified in the master schedule for week number 8. Now referring to the product structure in Figure 24.6, 50 units of P1 explode into 50 units of subassembly S1 and 100 units of S2, and the following numbers of units for the components:

ITEM MASTER DATA SEGMENT	Part No.	Description		Lead time		Std. cost		Safety stock	
	Order quantity		Setup		Cycle		Last year's usage		Class
	Scrap allowance		Cutting data		Pointers			Etc.	

INVENTORY STATUS SEGMENT	Allocated		Control balance		Period								Totals
					1	2	3	4	5	6	7	8	
	Gross requirements												
	Scheduled receipts												
	On hand												
	Planned-order releases												

SUBSIDIARY DATA SEGMENT	Order details	
	Pending action	
	Counters	
	Keeping track	

FIGURE 24.7   Record for an inventory item. (Reprinted by permission from Orlicky [7].)

C1: 50 units

C2: 200 units

C3: 50 units

C4: 200 units

C5: 200 units

C6: 100 units

The quantities of raw materials for these components are determined in a similar manner.

There are several factors that complicate the MRP parts and materials explosion. First, the component and subassembly quantities given above are gross requirements. Quantities of some of the components and subassemblies may already be in stock or on order. Hence, the quantities that are in inventory or scheduled for delivery in the near future must be subtracted from gross requirements to determine net requirements for meeting the master schedule.

A second complicating factor in the MRP computations is manifested in the form of lead times: ordering lead times and manufacturing lead times. The MRP processor must determine when to start assembling the subassemblies by offsetting the due dates for these items by their respective manufacturing lead times. Similarly, the component due dates must be offset by their manufacturing lead times. Finally, the raw materials for the components must be offset by their respective ordering lead times. The material requirements planning program performs this lead-time-offset calculation from data contained in the inventory record file (see Figure 24.7).

A third factor that complicates MRP is common use items. Some components and many raw materials are common to several products. The MRP processor must collect these common use items during the parts explosion. The total quantities for each common use item are then combined into a single net requirement for the item.

Finally, a feature of MRP that should be emphasized is that the master production schedule provides time-phased delivery requirements for the end products, and this time phasing must be carried through the calculations of the individual component and raw material requirements.

EXAMPLE 24.1

To illustrate how MRP works, let us consider the requirements planning procedure for one of the components of product P1. The component we will consider is C4. This part happens to be used also on one other product: P2 (see the master schedule of Figure 24.5). However, only one of item C4 is used on each P2 produced. The product structure of P2 is given in Figure 24.8. Component C4 is made out of raw material M4. One unit of M4 is needed to produce 1 unit of C4. The ordering and manufacturing lead times needed to make the MRP computations are as follows:

P1: assembly lead time = 1 week

P2: assembly lead time = 1 week

S2: assembly lead time = 1 week

S3: assembly lead time = 1 week

C4: manufacturing lead time = 2 weeks

M4: ordering lead time = 3 weeks

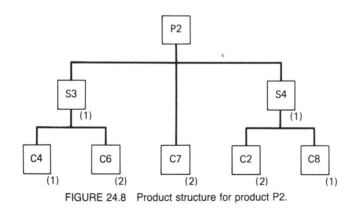

FIGURE 24.8 Product structure for product P2.

Period		1	2	3	4	5	6	7
Item: Raw MATL. M4								
Gross Requirements								
Scheduled Receipts				40				
On Hand	50			90				
Net Requirements								
Planned Order Releases								

FIGURE 24.9   Initial inventory status of material M4 in Example 24.1.

The current inventory and order status of item M4 is shown in Figure 24.9. There are no stocks or orders for any of the other items listed above.

The solution is presented in Figure 24.10. The delivery requirements for products P1 and P2 must be offset by the 1-week assembly lead time to obtain the planned order releases. Since the subassemblies to make the products must be ready, these order release quantities are "exploded" into requirements for subassemblies S2 (for P1) and S3 (for P2). These net requirements are then offset by the 1-week lead time and combined (in week 6) to obtain the gross requirements for part C4. Net requirements are equal to gross requirements for P1, P2, S2, S3, and C4 because of no on-hand inventory and no planned orders. We see the effect of current and planned stocks in the time-phased inventory picture for M4. The on-hand stock of 50 plus the scheduled receipts of 40 are used to meet the gross requirements of 70 units of M4 in week 3. Twenty units remain after meeting these requirements, which can be applied to the gross requirements of 280 units of M4 in week 4. Net requirements in week 4 are therefore $280 - 20 = 260$ units. With an ordering lead time of 3 weeks, the order release for the 260 units must be planned for week 1.

Output reports and benefits of MRP

The MRP program generates a variety of outputs that can be used in planning and managing plant operations. The outputs include:

- Order release notices, which provide the authority to place orders that have been planned by the MRP system
- Report of planned order releases in future periods
- Rescheduling notices, indicating changes in due dates for open orders
- Cancellation notices, indicating that certain open orders have been canceled because of changes in the master production schedule
- Reports on inventory status
- Performance reports of various types, indicating costs, item usage, actual versus planned lead times, etc.

Period		1	2	3	4	5	6	7	8	9	10
Item: PRODUCT P1											
Gross Requirements									50		100
Scheduled Receipts											
On Hand	0										
Net Requirements									50		100
Planned Order Releases								50		100	
Item: PRODUCT P2											
Gross Requirements								70	80	25	
Scheduled Receipts											
On Hand	0										
Net Requirements								70	80	25	
Planned Order Releases							70	80	25		
Item: SUBASSBY S2											
Gross Requirements								100		200	
Scheduled Receipts											
On Hand											
Net Requirements								100		200	
Planned Order Releases							100		200		
Item: SUBASSBY S3											
Gross Requirements								70	80	25	
Scheduled Receipts											
On Hand											
Net Requirements								70	80	25	
Planned Order Releases							70	90	25		
Item: COMPONENT C4											
Gross Requirements								70	280	25	400	
Scheduled Receipts											
On Hand											
Net Requirements								70	280	25	400	
Planned Order Releases					70	280	25	400			
Item: RAW MATL. M4											
Gross Requirements					70	280	25	400				
Scheduled Receipts				40							
On Hand	50	50	50	90	20						
Net Requirements				-20	260	25	400				
Planned Order Release		260	25	400							

FIGURE 24.10   MRP solution to Example 24.1.

Note: All blank cells ≡ 0 qty.

- Exception reports, showing deviations from the schedule, orders that are overdue, scrap, etc.
- Inventory forecasts, indicating projected inventory levels in future periods

There are many benefits claimed for a well-designed material requirements planning system. The benefits reported by users include the following: reduction in inventory, quicker response to changes in demand than is possible with a manual requirements planning system, reduced setup and product changeover costs, better machine utilization, improved capacity to respond to changes in the master schedule, and as an aid in the development of the master schedule.

24.4 CAPACITY PLANNING

The master schedule defines the production plan of the firm in terms of what products, how many, and when. A realistic master schedule must be compatible with the production capabilities and limitations of the plant that will produce the product. Accordingly, the firm must know its production capacity and must plan for changes in the capacity to meet changing production requirements specified in the master schedule. In Chapter 2 we defined production capacity and formulated ways for determining the capacity of a plant or other production system.

Capacity planning is concerned with determining what labor and equipment capacity is required to meet the current master production schedule as well as long-term future production needs of the firm. Capacity planning also serves to identify the limitations of the production resources so that an unrealistic master schedule is not planned.

The relationship of capacity planning to the other planning functions is shown in Figure 24.3. The master schedule is transformed into material and component requirements using MRP. These requirements provide a calculation of the amount of labor hours and other resources required to produce these components. The required resources are then compared to available plant capacity over the planning horizon. If the schedule is not compatible with the plant capacity, adjustments must be made either in the master schedule or in plant capacity. The calculations required in the comparison can be performed on the computer system, and an indication of the required changes in capacity can be provided.

Capacity adjustments can be divided into short-term adjustments and long-term adjustments. Capacity adjustments for the short term include:

- *Employment levels.* Employment in the plant can be increased or decreased in response to changes in capacity requirements.
- *Number of work shifts.* The number of shifts worked per production period can be increased or decreased.
- *Labor hours.* The number of labor hours per shift can be increased or decreased, through the use of overtime or reduced hours.

- *Inventory stockpiling.* This tactic might be used to maintain steady employment levels during slow demand periods.
- *Order backlogs.* Deliveries of the product to the customer could be delayed during busy periods when production resources are insufficient to keep up with demand.
- *Subcontracting.* This involves the letting of jobs to other shops during busy periods, or the taking in of extra work during slack periods.

Capacity planning adjustments for the long term include possible changes in production capacity that generally require long lead times. These adjustments include the following types of decisions:

- *New equipment investments.* This involves investing in more machines or more productive machines to meet increased future production requirements, or investing in new types of machines to match future changes in product design.
- *New plant construction or purchase of existing plants from other companies.*
- *Plant closings.* This involves the closing of plants that will not be needed in the future.

Many of these capacity adjustments are suggested by the capacity equations and models presented in Chapter 2.

REFERENCES

[1] CHANG, T-C., and R. A. WYSK, *An Introduction to Automated Process Planning Systems,* Prentice-Hall, Inc., Englewood Cliffs, N.J., 1985.

[2] FISHER, E. L., "Expert Systems Can Lay Groundwork for Intelligent CIM Decision Making," *Industrial Engineering,* March 1985, pp. 78–83.

[3] GROOVER, M. P., "Computer-Aided Process Planning—An Introduction," *Proceedings,* Conference on Computer-Aided Process Planning, Provo, Utah, October 1984.

[4] GROOVER, M. P., and E. W. ZIMMERS, JR., *CAD/CAM: Computer-Aided Design and Manufacturing,* Prentice-Hall, Inc., Englewood Cliffs, N.J., 1984, Chapters 13, 14.

[5] IBM Corporation, *Communications Oriented Production Information and Control System,* Publication G320-1974.

[6] MCNEELY, R. A., and E. M. MALSTROM, "Computer Generates Process Routings," *Industrial Engineering,* July 1977, pp. 32–35.

[7] ORLICKY, J., *Material Requirements Planning,* McGraw-Hill Book Company, New York, 1975.

[8] PLOSSL, G. W., *Manufacturing Control,* Reston Publishing Co., Inc., Reston, Va., 1973.

[9] WOLFE, P. M., "Computer-Aided Process Planning Is Link between CAD and CAM," *Industrial Engineering,* August 1985, pp. 72–77.

PROBLEMS

24.1. Using the master schedule of Figure 24.5 and the product structures in Figures 24.6 and 24.8, determine the time-phased requirements for component C6. The raw material used in component C6 is M6. Two units of C6 are obtained from every unit of M6. Lead times are as follows:

P1: assembly lead time = 1 week
P2: assembly lead time = 1 week
S2: assembly lead time = 1 week
S3: assembly lead time = 1 week
C6: manufacturing lead time = 2 weeks
M6: ordering lead time = 2 weeks

Assume that the current inventory status for all of the items above is: units on hand = 0, units on order = 0. The format of the solution should be similar to that presented in Example 24.1. *i.e., for C6, M6*

24.2. Solve Problem 24.1 if the current inventory and order status for S3, C6, and M6 is:

— use computer to solve this

S3: inventory on hand = 2, on order = 0
C6: inventory on hand = 5, on order = 10 due for delivery in week 2
M6: inventory on hand = 10, on order = 50 due for delivery in week 2

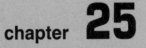

chapter **25**

Shop Floor Control and Automatic Identification Techniques

The various production planning methods discussed in Chapter 24 occur before actual manufacturing. In the present chapter we examine the techniques and technologies by which the progress and status of production is compared to the plans. The term given to this comparison activity in production management is *shop floor control*. Today, shop floor control is often accomplished by means of automated methods such as bar code readers. Descriptions of these technologies are presented in later sections of the chapter.

25.1 SHOP FLOOR CONTROL

Shop floor control is concerned with the release of the production orders to the factory, controlling the progress of the orders through the various work centers, and acquiring current information on the status of the orders. Reducing the definition to the simplest possible terms, shop floor control deals with managing the work-in-process.

We can conceptualize shop floor control in the form of a factory-wide information control system, as shown in Figure 25.1. This diagram relates back to our model of manufacturing introduced in Chapter 1 and discussed in Chapter 2 (see Figures 1.2, 2.2, and 2.4). The input to the shop floor control system is the collection of production plans

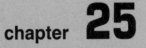

743

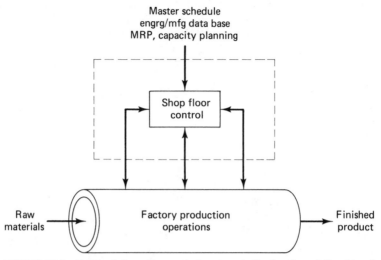

FIGURE 25.1 Factory information control system, indicating the relationship of shop floor control in the system.

(e.g., the results of process planning, MRP, capacity planning, etc.), and the factory production operations are pictured as the process to be controlled. The shop floor control system is indicated by the dashed line in the figure.

A typical shop floor control system consists of three phases. In computer-integrated manufacturing, these phases are augmented by computer. The three phases are:

1. Order release
2. Order scheduling
3. Order progress

The three phases and their connections to other functions in the production management system are pictured in Figure 25.2. In today's implementation of shop floor control, these phases are executed by a combination of computer and human resources. In the computer-automated factory of the future, the role of the computer will dominate.

Order release

The order release phase of shop floor control provides the documentation needed to process a production order through the factory. The collection of documents is sometimes called the *shop packet*. It consists of:

- Route sheet
- Material requisitions to draw the necessary materials from inventory
- Job cards or other means to report direct labor time devoted to the order; also used to indicate progress of the order through the factory

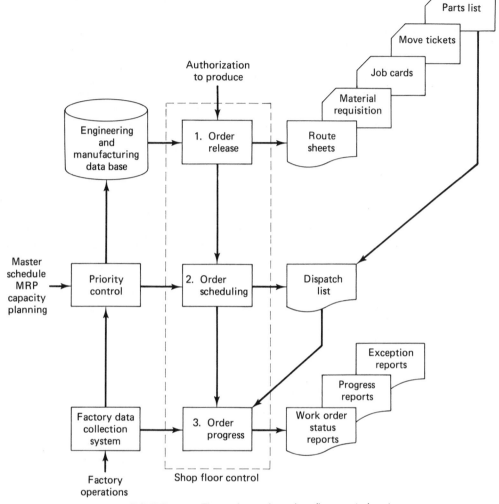

FIGURE 25.2   Three phases in a shop floor control system.

- Move tickets to authorize the material handling personnel to transport parts between work centers in the factory if this type of authorization is required
- Parts list, if required for assembly jobs

In the typical factory of today, characterized by manual labor rather than automated operations, these are the documents that move with the production order and are used to track its progress through the shop. In the factory of the future, more automated methods will be used to monitor the status of production orders, thus rendering these paper documents (or at least some of them) unnecessary. The more modern methods are beginning to be used today, and we explore some of the possibilities in subsequent sections of the chapter.

The order release is driven by two inputs, as indicated in Figure 25.2. The first is the authorization to produce that derives from the master schedule. This authorization proceeds through the various planning functions (MRP and capacity planning) that provide timing and scheduling information. The second input to the order release module is the engineering and manufacturing data base, which provides the product structure and process planning information needed to prepare the various documents that accompany the order through the shop.

Order scheduling

The order scheduling module assigns the production orders to the various work centers in the plant. It follows directly from the order release module. In effect, order scheduling executes the dispatching function in production planning and control. The order scheduling module prepares a dispatch list that indicates which production orders should be accomplished at the various work centers. It also provides information about relative priorities of the different jobs, for example by showing due dates for each job. In current shop floor control practice, the dispatch list guides the shop foreman in making work assignments and allocating resources to different jobs so that the master schedule can best be achieved.

The order scheduling module in shop floor control is intended to solve two problems in production control:

1. The machine loading problem
2. The job sequencing problem

To schedule a given set of production orders or jobs in the factory, the orders must first be assigned to work centers. Allocating the orders to the work centers is referred to as *machine loading*. The term *shop loading* is also used, and this refers to the loading of all machines in the plant. Since the total number of production orders will probably exceed the number of work centers, each work center will have a queue of orders waiting to be processed. A given production machine may have a loading of 10 jobs during a given week. The remaining question is: In what sequence should the 10 jobs be processed?

Answering this question is the problem in job sequencing. *Job sequencing* involves determining the order in which the jobs will be processed through a given work center. To determine this sequence, priorities are established among the jobs in the queue, and the jobs are processed in the order of their relative priorities. *Priority control* is a term used in production planning and control to denote the function that maintains the appropriate priority levels for the various production orders in the shop. As indicated in Figure 25.2, priority control information is an important input in the order scheduling module. Some of the rules used to establish priorities for production orders in the plant include:

- *Earliest due date*. Orders with earlier due dates are given higher priorities.
- *Shortest processing time*. Orders with shorter processing times are given higher priorities.
- *Least slack time*. Orders with the least slack in their schedule are given higher priorities. Slack time is defined as the difference between the time remaining until due date and the process time remaining.
- *Critical ratio*. Orders with the lowest critical ratio are given higher priorities. Critical ratio is defined as the ratio of the time remaining until due date divided by the process time remaining.

The relative priorities of the different orders may change over time. Reasons for these changes include lower- or higher-than-expected demand for certain products, equipment breakdown causing delays in production, cancellation of an order by the customer, defective raw materials, and others. The priority control function reviews the relative priorities of the orders and adjusts the dispatch list accordingly.

When an order is completed at one work center, it enters the queue at the next machine in its process routing. That is, the order becomes part of the machine loading for the next work center, and priority control is utilized to determine the sequence of processing among the jobs at that machine.

Order progress

The order progress module in the shop floor control system monitors the status of the various orders in the plant, work-in-process, and other characteristics that indicate the progress and performance of production. The function of the order progress module is to provide information that is useful in managing the factory based on data collected from the factory.

The information that is presented to production management is often summarized in the form of reports. The reports include:

- *Work order status reports*. These reports indicate the status of the production orders. Typical information listed in the report includes the current work center where each order is located, processing hours remaining before completion of each order, whether the job is on-time or behind schedule, and priority level.
- *Progress reports*. A progress report is used to report performance of the shop during a certain time period (e.g., week or month in the master schedule). It provides information on how many orders were completed during the period, how many orders that should have been completed during the period were not completed, and so on.
- *Exception reports*. An exception report indicates the deviations from the production schedule (e.g., overdue jobs), and similar exception information.

These reports are useful to production management in making decisions about allocation of resources, authorization of overtime hours, and other capacity issues, and in identifying problem areas in the plant that adversely affect achieving the master production schedule.

There are a variety of techniques used to collect data from the factory floor. These techniques range between clerical methods that require workers to fill out paper forms that are later compiled, and fully automated methods that require no human participation. The term *factory data collection system* is sometimes used to identify these techniques.

25.2 FACTORY DATA COLLECTION SYSTEM

The factory data collection (FDC) system consists of the various paper documents, terminals, and automated devices located throughout the plant for collecting data on shop floor operations, plus the means of compiling and processing the data, usually by computer. The factory data collection system serves as an input to the order progress module in shop floor control, as illustrated in Figure 25.2. Using our feedback control system analogy of Figure 25.1, the FDC system is the sensor component of the shop floor control system. Examples of the types of data on factory operations collected by the FDC system include piece counts completed at a certain work center, direct labor time expended on each order, parts that are scrapped, parts requiring rework, and equipment downtime. The data collection system can also include the time clocks used by employees to punch in and out of work.

On-line versus batch systems

The purpose of the factory data collection system is twofold: to supply data to the order progress module in the shop floor control system, and to provide current information to production foremen, plant management, and production control personnel. To accomplish this purpose, the factory data collection system must input data to the plant computer system. This can be done in either an on-line or off-line mode. In an on-line system, the data are entered directly into the plant computer system and are immediately available to the order progress module. The advantage of the on-line data collection system is that the data file representing the status of the shop can be kept current at all times. As changes in order progress are reported, these changes are immediately incorporated into the shop status file. The personnel with a need to know can access this status in real time and be confident that they have the most up-to-date information on which to base any decisions.

In the off-line data collection system, the data are temporarily stored in either a storage device or a stand-alone computer system to be entered and processed subsequently by the plant computer in a batch mode. In this mode of operation, there is a delay in the data processing. Consequently, the plant computer system cannot provide real-time information on shop floor status. This delay, and the requirement for a separate data storage system, are the principal disadvantages of this configuration. The advantage of an off-line collection system is that it is generally easier to install and implement.

Data input techniques

The techniques of factory data collection include manual procedures, computer terminals located in the factory, and other technologies. The following paragraphs discuss the various categories.

The manually oriented techniques of factory data collection are those in which the production workers must fill out paper forms indicating order progress data. The forms are subsequently turned in and compiled, using a combination of clerical and computerized methods. The manual/clerical techniques include [7,10]:

- *Job traveler*. This is a log sheet included in the shop packet that travels with the order through the factory. Workers who spend time on the order are required to record their times on the log sheet together with other data, such as the date, piece counts, defects, and so on. The job traveler becomes the chronological record of the processing of the order. The problem with this method is its inherent incompatibility with the principles of real-time data collection. Since the job traveler moves with the job, it is not readily available for compiling current order progress.
- *Employee time sheets*. In the typical operation of this method, a daily time sheet is prepared for each worker and the worker must fill out the form to indicate the work that was accomplished during the day. Data entered on the form include the order number, operation number on the route sheet, the number of pieces completed during the day, time spent, and so on. Some of these data are taken from information contained in the shop packet for the order. The time sheet is turned in daily, and order progress information is compiled (usually by a clerical staff).
- *Operation tear strips*. With this technique, the shop packet includes a set of preprinted tear strips that can easily be separated from the packet. The preprinted data on each tear strip include order number, route sheet details, and so on. When a worker finishes an operation or at the end of the shift, one of the tear strips is torn off, piece count and time data are recorded by the worker, and the form is turned in to report order progress.
- *Prepunched cards*. This is essentially the same technique as the tear strip method, but prepunched computer cards are included with the shop packet instead of tear strips. The prepunched cards contain the same type of order data, and the workers must write the same kind of production data onto the card. The difference in the use of prepunched cards is that in compiling the daily order progress, mechanized data processing procedures can be used to record some of the data.

There are problems with all of these manually oriented data collection procedures. They all rely on the cooperation and clerical accuracy of factory workers to record data onto a paper document. There are invariably errors in this kind of procedure. Error rates associated with handwritten entry of data average 1/30 [16]. Some of the errors can be detected by the clerical staff that does the compilation of order progress. Examples of detectable errors include wrong dates, incorrect order numbers (the clerical staff knows which orders are in the shop and they can usually determine when an erroneous order number has been entered by a worker), and incorrect operation numbers on the route sheet (if the worker enters a certain operation number but the preceding operation number has not been started, an error has been made). Other errors are more difficult to identify. If a worker enters a piece count of 150 pieces which represents the work completed in one shift when the batch size is 250 parts, this is difficult for the clerical staff to verify. If a different worker on the following day completes the batch and also enters a piece count of 150, it is obvious that one of the workers overstated his/her production; but which one?

Another problem is the delay in submitting the order progress data for compilation. There is a time lapse in each of the methods between when events occur in the shop and when the data representing those events are submitted. The job traveler method is the worst offender in this regard. Here the data might not be compiled until the order has been completed, too late to take any corrective action. This method is of little value in a shop floor control system. The remaining manual methods described above suffer a one-day delay since the shop data are generally submitted at the end of the shift, and a summary compilation is not available until the following day at the earliest.

In addition to the delay in submitting the order data, there is also a delay associated with compiling the data into useful reports. Depending on how the order progress procedures are organized, the compilation may add several days to the reporting cycle.

Because of the problems associated with the manual/clerical procedures, techniques have been developed that use data collection terminals located in the factory. The collection terminals require the workers to input data relative to order progress. The various input techniques include manual entry by simple pushbutton keypads or typewriterlike keyboards. The keyboard entered data are subject to error rates just like the manual/clerical data collection techniques. However, the error rate for keyboard data entry is approximately 1/300 [16], substantially lower than for handwritten entry. Also, error-checking routines can be incorporated into the entry procedures to detect syntax and certain other types of errors.

The data-entry methods also include more automated input technologies, such as magnetic card readers or optical bar code readers. Certain types of data, such as identification of order, product, and even operation sequence number, can be entered with the automated techniques using magnetized or bar-coded cards included with the shop packet. Figure 25.3 illustrates one type of factory data collection terminal that combines keypad entry with bar code technology.

There are various numbers and arrangements of keyboard-based terminals possible in the factory. These include:

• *One centralized terminal.* In this arrangement there is a single terminal located centrally in the plant. This requires all workers to walk from their workstations to the central location when they must enter the data. If the plant is large, this becomes inconvenient. Also, use of the terminal tends to increase at the time of a shift change, and this results in significant lost time for the workers.

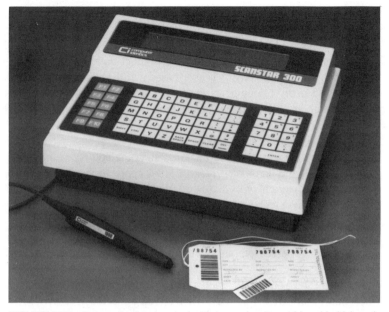

FIGURE 25.3   Data collection terminal with keypad entry and hand-held (wand-type) bar code reader. (Courtesy of Computer Identics Corp.)

• *Satellite terminals.* In this configuration, there are multiple data collection terminals located throughout the plant. The number and locations are designed to strike a balance between minimizing the investment cost in terminals and maximizing the convenience of the workers in the plant.

• *Workstation terminals.* The most convenient arrangement for the workers is to have a data collection terminal at each workstation. This minimizes the time lost in walking to the satellite terminals. However, it seems to be justified only when the number of data transactions is relatively large and when the terminals are also designed for collecting certain data automatically.

The trend in industry is toward more use of automation in factory data collection systems. Although the term *automation* is used, many of the techniques require the participation of human workers. The next three sections discuss the various automated and semiautomated methods of acquiring data from the shop floor.

25.3   AUTOMATIC IDENTIFICATION METHODS

The field of automatic identification is often associated with the material handling industry. In fact, the industry trade association, called the Automatic Identification Manufacturers (AIM), is an affiliate of the Material Handling Institute, Inc. Many of the applications of this technology relate to material handling. We are covering the subject here because it is an emerging technique for tracking materials in shop floor control systems.

Automatic identification is a term that refers to various technologies used in automatic or semiautomatic acquisition of product data for entry into a computer system. These technologies are mostly sensor-based methods that provide a means of reading data that are coded on a document, product, component, container, and so on, without the need for human interpretation of the data. Instead, the computer system interprets and processes the data for some useful application. The applications of automated identification systems are numerous; they include retail sales, warehousing (semiautomated storage and picking), product sortation and tracking, shipping and receiving, and shop floor control.

Some of the automated identification applications require workers to be involved in the data collection procedure, usually to operate the identification equipment in the application. These techniques are therefore semiautomated rather than automated methods. Other applications accomplish the identification procedure with no human participation. The same basic sensor technologies may be used in both cases. For example, certain types of bar code readers are operated by people while other types are operated automatically.

There are some very good reasons for using automatic identification techniques. First and foremost, the accuracy of the data collected is improved, in many cases by a significant margin. To illustrate, the error rate in bar code technology is approximately 10,000 times lower than in manual keyboard data entry. The rate of 1/3,000,000 is used as an error rate for comparison with the handwritten and keyboard entry methods [16]. The error rates of most of the other technologies is not as good as for bar codes, but still better than manual-based methods. A second reason for using automatic identification techniques is to reduce the time required by human workers to make the data entry. The speed of data entry for handwritten documents is approximately 5 to 7 characters per second, and it is 10 to 15 characters per second (at best) for keyboard entry [16]. Automatic identification methods are capable of reading hundreds of characters per second. This comparison is certainly not the whole story in a data collection transaction, but the time savings in using automatic identification techniques can mean substantial labor cost benefits for large plants with many workers.

The technologies available for use in automatic identification systems at the time of this writing include:

- Bar codes
- Radio frequency systems
- Magnetic stripe
- Optical character recognition
- Machine vision

The use of bar codes in factory data collection systems is predominant and growing, and we devote a separate section to this technology. The other techniques are either used in special applications in factory operations, or they are widely applied outside the factory. For completeness, we include brief discussions of them in the paragraphs that follow.

Radio-frequency (RF) systems rely on the use of radio frequency signals similar to those used in wireless television transmission. Although the type of signal is the same, there are differences in the use of RF technology in product identification. One difference is that the communication is in two directions rather than one direction (as in TV). Also, the signal power is substantially lower in factory identification applications (ranging from several milliwatts to 7 watts [9]).

Radio-frequency identification systems consist of the identification tags on the items to be identified, an antenna at some location where data are to be read, and a reader that interprets the data. The identification tag is a transponder, a device that is capable of emitting a signal of its own when it receives a signal from an external source. It is attached to the product, truck, railway car, or other item. The term "tag" is misleading, since the term refers to a small but rugged boxlike container that houses the electronics for data storage and RF communication. The container may be as much as $2.5 \times 2.5 \times 7.5$ in. in size and be capable of withstanding temperatures from -40 to $+400°F$ [9]. The tags are usually read-only devices that contain up to 20 characters of data representing the item identification and other information that is to be communicated. Recent developments in the technology have provided much higher data storage capacity and the ability to change the data in the tag (read/write tags). This opens many opportunities for incorporating much more status and progress information into the automatic identification system.

The antenna is located at an identification station and listens for the RF signal from the identification tag that uniquely indicates the item to which it is attached. The signal is then fed to a reader that decodes and validates the signal prior to transmission of the associated data to the data collection computer system. The hardware required for an RF identification system has tended to be more expensive than for most other data collection technologies. For this reason, RF systems have generally been appropriate for data collection situations in which environmental factors preclude the use of optical techniques such as bar codes. For example, RF systems are suited for identification of products with high unit values in manufacturing processes (such as spray painting) that would obscure any optically coded data. They are also used for identifying railroad cars and in highway trucking applications where the environment and conditions make other methods of identification infeasible.

Magnetic stripes (the term *magnetic strip* is also used) attached to the product or container can also be used for item identification in factory and warehouse applications. These are the same kinds of magnetic stripes that are used to encode identification data onto plastic access cards for use in automatic bank tellers. Their use seems to be declining for shop floor control applications because they are more expensive than bar codes and cannot be scanned remotely. Two advantages they possess is their larger data storage capacity and the ability to alter the data contained in them.

Optical character recognition (OCR) techniques refer to a specially designed alphanumeric character set that is machine readable by an optical sensor device. The substantial benefit offered by OCR technology is that the characters and associated text can be read by human beings as well as machines. The list of disadvantages, at least for factory and warehouse applications, includes the requirement for near-contact scanning, lower scanning rates, and a higher error rate compared to bar code scanning.

Machine vision systems are used principally for automated inspection tasks, as indicated in Chapter 18. The applications also include certain classes of automatic identification problems, and these applications may grow in number as the technology advances. For example, machine vision systems are capable of distinguishing between a limited set of products moving down a conveyor so that the products can be sorted. The recognition task is accomplished without requiring that a special identification code be placed on the product. The recognition by the machine vision system is based on the inherent geometric features of the object.

25.4 BAR CODE TECHNOLOGY

Bar code technology has become the most popular method of automatic identification in retail sales and in factory data collection. The bar code itself consists of a sequence of thick and narrow colored bars separated by thick and narrow spaces separating the bars. The pattern of bars and spaces is coded to represent alphanumeric characters. Bar code readers interpret the code by scanning and decoding the sequence of bars. The reader consists of the scanner and decoder. The scanner emits a beam of light that is swept past the bar code (either manually or automatically) and senses light reflections to distinguish between the bars and spaces. The light reflections are sensed by a photodetector that converts the spaces into an electrical signal and the bars into absence of an electrical signal. The width of the bars and spaces is indicated by the duration of the corresponding signals. The procedure is depicted in Figure 25.4. The decoder analyzes the pulse train to validate and interpret the corresponding data.

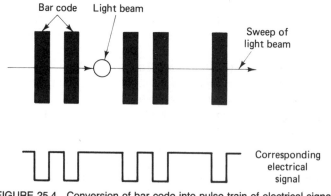

FIGURE 25.4   Conversion of bar code into pulse train of electrical signals.

Certainly, a major reason for the acceptance of bar codes is their widespread use in grocery markets and other retail stores. In 1973, the grocery industry adopted the Universal Product Code (UPC) as its standard for item identification. This is a 10-digit bar code that uses five digits to identify the product and five digits to identify the manufacturer. The U.S. Department of Defense provided another major endorsement in 1982, by adopting a bar code standard (Code 39) that must be applied by vendors on product cartons supplied to the various agencies of DOD.

The bar code symbol

The Universal Product Code is only one of many bar code formats in commercial use today. The bar code standard adopted by the automotive industry, the Department of Defense, the General Services Administration, and many other manufacturing industries is *Code 39,* also known as *AIM USD-2* (for Automatic Identification Manufacturers Uniform Symbol Description—2), although this is actually a subset of Code 39. We describe this format as an example of bar code symbols [2,3,5].

Code 39 uses a uniquely defined series of wide and narrow elements (bars and spaces) to represent 0–9, the 26 alpha characters, and special symbols. The wide elements are equivalent to a binary value of one and the narrow elements are equal to zero. The width of the narrow bars and spaces, called the *X dimension,* provides the basis for a scheme of classifying bar codes into three code densities (this scheme applies to the other bar code standards as well as Code 39):

- *High density:* X dimension is 0.010 in. or less
- *Medium density:* X dimension is between 0.010 and 0.030 in.
- *Low density:* X dimension is 0.030 in. or greater

For bar codes with $X \geq 0.020$ in., the wide elements must be printed with a width of anywhere between $2 \times$ and $3 \times$ (two to three times the X dimension). For bar codes with $X < .020$ in., the wide elements must have a width between $2.2 \times$ and $3 \times$. Whatever the wide-to-narrow ratio, the width must be uniform throughout the code in order for the reader to consistently interpret the bar code. Figure 25.5 presents the character structure for USD-2, and Figure 25.6 illustrates how the character set might be developed in a typical bar code.

In addition to the character set in the bar code, there must also be a so-called "quiet zone" both preceding and following the bar code, in which there is no printing that might confuse the decoder. This quiet zone is shown in Figure 25.6.

The reason for the name Code 39 is that nine elements (bars and spaces) are used in each character and three of the elements are wide elements. The placement of the wide spaces and bars in the code is what uniquely designates the character. Each code begins and ends with either a wide or narrow bar. The code is sometimes referred to as *code three-of-nine.*

Table 1: Character Structure, USD-2

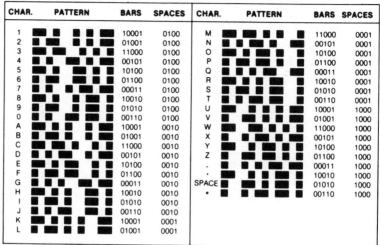

CHAR.	PATTERN	BARS	SPACES	CHAR.	PATTERN	BARS	SPACES
1		10001	0100	M		11000	0001
2		01001	0100	N		00101	0001
3		11000	0100	O		10100	0001
4		00101	0100	P		01100	0001
5		10100	0100	Q		00011	0001
6		01100	0100	R		10010	0001
7		00011	0100	S		01010	0001
8		10010	0100	T		00110	0001
9		01010	0100	U		10001	1000
0		00110	0100	V		01001	1000
A		10001	0010	W		11000	1000
B		01001	0010	X		00101	1000
C		11000	0010	Y		10100	1000
D		00101	0010	Z		01100	1000
E		10100	0010	-		00011	1000
F		01100	0010	.		10010	1000
G		00011	0010	SPACE		01010	1000
H		10010	0010	*		00110	1000
I		01010	0010				
J		00110	0010				
K		10001	0001				
L		01001	0001				

* Denotes a start/stop code which must precede and follow every bar code message. Note that * is used only for the start/stop code.

FIGURE 25.5   Character set in USD-2 bar code, which is a subset of Code 39. (Reprinted from [5] by permission of the Material Handling Institute.)

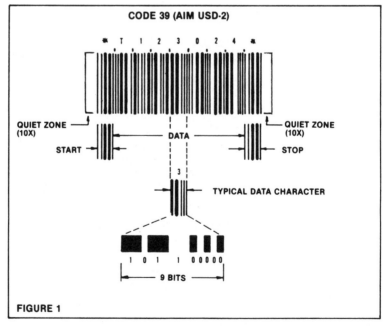

FIGURE 25.6   A typical grouping of characters to form a bar code in Code 39. (Reprinted from [5] by permission of the Material Handling Institute.)

that are performed at the plant level. Payroll, cost accounting, and personnel are examples of these other functions.

The fourth level is the corporate mainframe computer. Data are compiled from the various plants in the corporation at this level. Communication with the individual plant computers can be achieved by means of telephone long lines, satellites, or other wide area communications technologies. The purpose of the corporate computer in the hierarchy is to summarize plant operations and performance for the entire corporation. The CAD/CAM system interface for design engineering is probably at this level although it may be at the plant level depending on corporate philosophy and organization. In addition, the corporate computer must be shared with other departments at the corporate level: sales, marketing, accounting, and so on.

Benefits of the hierarchical structure

The hierarchical computer structure has become the most effective and efficient arrangement for implementing computer systems in manufacturing. At one time in the evolution of computer control of production, it seemed most feasible to use one large mainframe computer to handle all planning, monitoring, and control functions. Indeed, this mode of control became typical of computer control in the process industries. Today, with the proliferation of small computers (e.g., personal computers), the advantage has gone to the hierarchical computer network. The following is a list of the important benefits of the hierarchical approach to CIM:

• *Gradual implementation.* The hierarchical computer system can be installed gradually rather than all at once. Each individual computer project can be justified on its own merits. The company is not required to make an all-or-nothing ("you bet your company") commitment to install a single plantwide computer. The risk is therefore reduced, and the expense can be spread over a number of years, with paybacks realized for each step in the implementation of the hierarchical system.

• *Redundancy.* The hierarchical structure contains redundancy. In the event of a computer breakdown, other computers in the system are programmed to assume the critical tasks of the broken-down computer.

• *Reduced software development problem.* Software development, a very major portion of the total expense in most integrated computer systems, can be managed more easily in the hierarchical configuration. Since the computers are separated in the pyramidal arrangement, programming for each project can be handled separately. Once the project is installed, changes in software are more easily accomplished, with less chance of disrupting the system.

There are significant problems involved in connecting a large number of computers and computer-controlled programmable machines together into the hierarchical structure described here. The following two sections discuss some of these problems.

26.2 LOCAL AREA NETWORKS

The computers in the factory communicate with each other by means of a local area network (LAN). A *local area network* is a nonpublic communications system that permits the various devices connected to the network to communicate with each other over distances from several feet to several miles. The factory devices that can be attached to the network include computers, programmable controllers, CNC machines, robots, data collection devices, bar code readers, vision systems, and so on.

Network topologies

Physically, the communications network does not have the hierarchical configuration described in Section 26.1. Instead, there are three common configurations, or topologies, used in local area networks:

1. Star network
2. Ring network
3. Bus network

The three configurations are illustrated in Figure 26.2. The *star network,* illustrated in part (a) of the figure, consists of a central control station to which each of the individual devices or user stations are connected. For one device to send a message to another device in the network, the message must be routed through the central station. The central station therefore acts as a traffic manager and controls the communications flow between devices. Many telephone systems in office buildings are structured as star configurations.

In the *ring network,* pictured in Figure 26.2(b), the individual stations are connected in a continuous ring. Each station has a neighboring station on either side. For one station to communicate with any other station, the message must be relayed from station to station until it finally arrives at its designated destination station. This is done by assigning a station address to the message. Each station along the ring checks the message to see whether it is the desired recipient. If it is, it loads the message into memory; if it is not, it forwards the message to the next station along the ring.

The *bus network* consists of a single main transmission line to which the individual devices are attached, as shown in Figure 26.2(c). Any device or station can communicate with any other device in the network by sending its message through the bus with the address of the desired recipient. Each station connected to the bus checks the message and loads it if the address is its own.

Among the three topologies, the bus network is the most appropriate for a factory local area network. There are several reasons for this [4]. First, the main transmission line of the bus network can be laid out in a pattern that corresponds closely to the layout of machines in the factory, thus facilitating installation of the communications system. The product flow line layout is the best example of how the network bus line corresponds

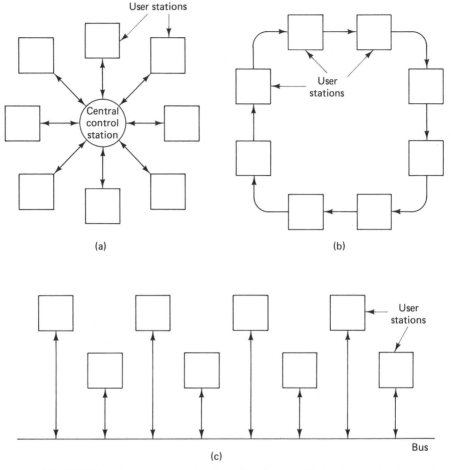

FIGURE 26.2   Three common network configurations used in local area networks:
(a) star; (b) ring; (c) bus.

to the machine arrangement. Second, machines and other devices in the plant are often
being rearranged to match changing production requirements. On a bus network, each
device can be connected to the main transmission bus without major disruptions to the
rest of the network. Third, the bus network is generally easier to maintain and repair
than the star or ring configurations.

Access methods for local area networks

In the star network, the central control station coordinates the flow of communications
from one station to the next. In the ring and bus networks, there must also be a method
for controlling the message transmissions between stations. This is done using schemes

by which the stations can gain access to the network. There are two popular access methods for LANs:

1. Token passing
2. Carrier-sensed multiple access with collision detection

In the *token-passing* method, a special code, called the token, is passed along the network at high speeds from station to station in a predetermined sequence. The sequence can be designed to allow stations with higher priorities to have greater access to the network. In operation, a station can transmit messages only when it possesses the token. If a station has no message to transmit, the token passes to the next station in the sequence. A station wishing to transmit must wait until it is in possession of the token. In this way, access to the network is controlled and coordinated.

The *carrier-sensed multiple access with collision detection* (CSMA/CD) method is also called a *contention-based* method. With this access scheme, any station wanting to transmit on the network first listens to determine if the network is currently being used. If not, it proceeds to send its message immediately. If there is current activity on the network, it waits until the network is free and tries again. In the contention-based access method, there will be occasions when two (or more) stations attempt to transmit along the same transmission line at the same time. This results in a collision that cannot properly be interpreted by any recipient. Each station is capable of detecting the high rate of transmission activity characteristic of a collision, and stops transmitting. The stations each wait a random length of time (different times for different stations) and then try again. The attempts are repeated until a successful transmission is accomplished.

The CSMA/CD access method is appropriate for office networks in which the communications are likely to consist of large blocks of data, but the timing of the transmissions is not critical. For high levels of traffic, the contention-based method is somewhat nondeterministic in terms of knowing how long a given station will have to wait before it is able to send its messages. This is undesirable in manufacturing because the timing of commands to a machine tool may be very important in order to control the process in real time. In the token-passing method, the transmissions between different stations can be coordinated and predicted quite closely under various loadings of the network. Accordingly, the token-passing access scheme is used predominantly in LANs designed for manufacturing environments.

The transmission line

The transmission line is the message- and data-carrying medium that constitutes the physical distribution element of the network. The requirements of the transmission media for factory networks are that they must be capable of a high data transmission capacity, they must be unaffected by electrical noise in the environment, and they must be inexpensive to install, service, and alter.

The data transmission capacity is characterized by a term called *bandwidth*. A large bandwidth means that the medium has a high data-carrying capacity. A related characteristic is whether the transmission is broadband or baseband. *Broadband transmission* means that many independent messages can be transmitted simultaneously over the communications line, each operating at its own frequency. Broadband signals are the standard used for cable television (CATV) transmission. Because of its widespread use in CATV applications, it is considered a mature technology with many technicians trained in its repair and maintenance. In *baseband transmission,* only one signal is carried over the transmission line at a time. Each message requires a certain time to transmit, and no other messages can be carried at the same time. Because of the need for multiple simultaneous data transmission in factory networks, broadband transmission is preferred. On the other hand, many office networks utilize baseband transmission (e.g., those using Ethernet, a commercially available network for offices).

Three types of transmission media are used in local area networks. We will compare the types for use in the factory environment in terms of the foregoing requirements. The three types are:

1. Twisted-pair wire
2. Coaxial cable
3. Fiber optics lines

Twisted-pair wire consists of two (or more) copper wires that are twisted throughout the length of the line. It is an inexpensive transmission medium and is used widely in conventional telephone communications. Its disadvantages are that it is susceptible to electrical noise in the environment and it has a relatively low bandwidth. Because of the electrical noise problem, and the requirement for message integrity in manufacturing control and communications, twisted-pair wire is not a good choice for factory networking.

Coaxial cable consists of one or more strands of wire shielded by a metallic sheath surrounded in turn by insulation. The metal shield reduces the problem of electrical noise. Coaxial cable can have a large bandwidth and is used for either baseband or broadband communications. Broadband coaxial cable is considered to be the most appropriate transmission medium for factory networks, and is currently the type most frequently adopted for these applications. Multiple taps for user stations and other devices are readily installed or removed, as required.

Fiber optics lines consist of several long continuous optical fibers—fibers of glass or other material capable of transmitting light. Its principal attributes are that it possesses a very large bandwidth and it is unaffected by electrical noise in the surroundings. In the operation of a fiber optics transmission line, the electrical pulses representing data at the transmitting station are converted into light pulses, carried through the optical fibers over long distances, and then converted back into electrical signals at the receiving station. At the time of this writing, fiber optics is still a rapidly evolving technology and is relatively costly compared to the alternatives. It is most appropriately used as a high volume data "pipeline" between two points where there is no need for intermediate taps.

Data transmission rate

The transmission rate in communication networks is the rate at which data and messages can be transferred among computers and computer-controlled devices connected to the network. There are two units of measure used to indicate this data transmission rate: baud rate and bit rate.

In digital data communications, characters are generally represented by a series of electrical pulses, as shown in Figure 26.3. Each character has its own individual pattern

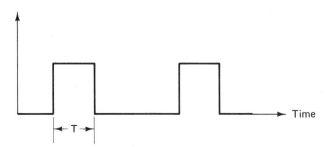

FIGURE 26.3   Series of pulses in digital data communications.

of pulses. These electrical pulses constitute the bits that make up the characters. Each pulse in the series has a certain duration, call it T, and the shortest possible pulse duration that can be handled reliably by the sending and receiving stations and the transmission medium determine the baud rate. That is,

$$\text{Baud rate} = \frac{1}{T} \quad \text{baud}$$

The actual communication of data and information is determined by the bit rate. Although the bit rate is made up of the same basic pulses as the baud rate, there are certain bits in a data transmission that are used up (wasted) because of parity checks, control procedures, initiation and termination of the transmission, and so on. Therefore, the bit rate is generally lower than the baud rate, since these wasted bits are excluded from the count of bits per second. The bit rate and the baud rate are equal only when all of the signal pulses in the data transmission are useful bits.

26.3   MANUFACTURING AUTOMATION PROTOCOL

One of the substantial problems in implementing networks of hierarchical or other con-figuration is that the various computers and computer-based devices in the structure are not always compatible in terms of their ability to communicate with each other. Although they all operate using digital pulses to represent data, the format and interpretation of the pulses differ from one computer-based device to the next. What is required is a set of formalized procedures that can be followed by each device in the computer network whenever data are exchanged between them. Such procedures are referred to as *communications protocols*.

A number of organizations have contributed to the development of a communications protocol called the *Manufacturing Automation Protocol* (MAP). MAP is a set of protocol standards designed for use in a factory local area network such as the hierarchical structure described above. It has become widely adopted in the manufacturing industries due to the efforts of the General Motors Corporation to promote compatibility of computer-based devices in its plants. In the early 1980s, GM became aware of the significant need in their factories for computers and programmable machines from various vendors to be able to exchange data. They developed and adopted MAP and are requiring all of their vendors to satisfy the MAP standard. By this requirement, GM is accelerating the implementation of this communications protocol for all manufacturing networks.

With reference to our previous discussions on communications networks, the Manufacturing Automation Protocol uses a bus network configuration, broadband transmission, a token-passing access scheme, and a data transmission rate of 10 megabits per second. MAP is based on a specification defined by the International Standards Organization (ISO) called the *Open System Interconnection* (OSI) reference model.

The OSI reference model uses seven modules, called *layers,* in its network support software that are based on functionality. Each layer has an assigned function in terms of communicating and exchanging data between peer levels among the various devices in the network. The purpose of each layer can best be explained by first recognizing that there are two classes of functions in a data communication, called *interconnection* and *interworking* [5]. The interconnection functions are concerned with the problems of creating and maintaining a data pipeline that permits two devices to transmit data back and forth in spite of any technological differences between the devices. These problems deal mainly with the physical aspects of data transfer, such as transmission speed, packet size of the transmission, detection of errors in the transmission, and the like.

The interworking functions are concerned with higher-level issues in the data transmission. These issues relate to the data requirements for meaningful dialogue between devices in order to accomplish useful applications. The data requirements tend to be more specific to and dependent on the particular applications. For example, the data requirements for collecting piece counts from a production workstation tend to be quite different from the data requirements for downloading an NC part program to a machine tool. Yet the coding and transmission of the data (the interconnection functions) can be the same.

In the seven-layer structure of the MAP/OSI standards, the first four layers are concerned with the interconnection functions, and the top three layers are concerned with the interworking functions. Descriptions of the seven layers are presented in Table 26.1.

The application layer (the seventh layer) is the highest layer in MAP at the time of this writing. It is possible that this layer may be subdivided into multiple layers as applications of the communications protocol and computer technologies evolve in the future.

TABLE 26.1   Seven Layers of Manufacturing Automation Protocol

1. *Physical layer*. This layer is concerned with the transmission of raw bits across the network lines. It defines the data transmission rate and the type of transmission medium.
2. *Data link layer*. This layer is concerned with the transfer of units of data across the local area network. It deals with the resolution of contentions when two devices are attempting to transmit at the same time, the size of the units of data, detection and correction of errors in data transmission, etc.
3. *Network layer*. The network layer is concerned with the routing of packets of data from source nodes to receiving nodes throughout the network. It stores and relays data travelling between the nodes in the network as part of this function.
4. *Transport layer*. This layer is responsible for the reliable delivery of data from originating device to destination device in the network. It works with layer 3 in order to accomplish this function.
5. *Session layer*. The function of the session layer is to support an orderly dialogue between devices using the network. It deals with network security issues, resynchronizing the data in the event of a transmission failure, and similar problems.
6. *Presentation layer*. This layer is concerned with negotiating syntax and format for the data exchange between the sending and receiving devices. One way of accomplishing this is to require all devices to encode data in a common format.
7. *Application layer*. This layer provides the interface with the user for specific applications requiring the networking capabilities of MAP. These applications deal with problems such as transfer of files between devices, remote job entry, message handling, access of files located at one device from another device, etc.

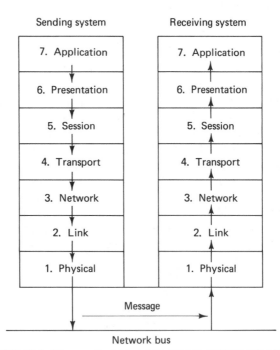

FIGURE 26.4   Diagram illustrating data communications using MAP.

The nature of the communications transmission using MAP is illustrated schematically in Figure 26.4. Messages are formatted according to the seven-layer protocol at the sending station, sent across the transmission line, and then interpreted by the seven-layer protocol at the receiving station. What makes this possible, despite any differences between the internal data processing procedures within each station, is the conformance to the protocol that is mandated when data are transmitted and received.

A related protocol standard that is being adopted for office networks is the *Technical and Office Protocol* (TOP). This standard was developed by Boeing Computer Services. TOP shares layers 3 through 7 with MAP, for the most part. Only layers 1 and 2 (the physical connection layers) differ from MAP, with these layers of the TOP protocol being defined according to the CSMA/CD access method rather than token-passing access scheme defined in the Manufacturing Automation Protocol. Networks based on a combination of MAP and TOP can utilize a "bridge" device to translate signals in both directions between the two protocols.

REFERENCES

[1] ACCAMPO, P. W., "MAP Pilots: Promises and Pitfalls," *CIM Technology*, Spring 1986, pp. 19–23.

[2] CROWDER, R., "The MAP Specification," *Control Engineering*, October 1985, pp. 22–25.

[3] GROOVER, M. P., and E. W. ZIMMERS, JR., *CAD/CAM: Computer-Aided Design and Manufacturing*, Prentice-Hall, Inc., Englewood Cliffs, N.J., 1984, Chapter 17.

[4] MAIRA, A., "Local Area Networks—The Future of the Factory," *Manufacturing Engineering*, March 1986, pp. 77–79.

[5] MOON, D., "Developing Standards Smooth the Integration of Programmable Factory Floor Devices," *Control Engineering*, October 1985, pp. 49–52.

[6] ODREY, N. G., "Integrating the Automated Factory," *Data Processing Management*, Auerbach Publishers, Inc., Pennsauken, N.J., 1985.

[7] "Putting MAP to Work," *American Machinist*, January 1986, pp. 75–79.

[8] REMBOLD, U., K. ARMBRUSTER, and W. ULZMANN, *Interface Technology for Computer-Controlled Manufacturing Processes*, Marcel Dekker, Inc., New York, 1983.

[9] STALLINGS, W., *Local Networks: An Introduction*, Macmillan Publishing Co., Inc., New York, 1984.

[10] STALLINGS, W., *Data and Computer Communications*, Macmillan Publishing Co., Inc., New York, 1985.

[11] TANENBAUM, A. S., *Computer Networks*, Prentice-Hall, Inc., Englewood Cliffs, New Jersey, 1981.

chapter **27**

The Future Automated Factory

Computer integrated manufacturing, CNC machines, robots, flexible manufacturing systems, automated inspection, computer process control—all of the topics we have been discussing throughout this book—are directing the technology of manufacturing toward one goal: the fully automated factory of the future. What will the future automated factory be like, and what will be its impact on society? These are the issues we consider in this chapter. We begin by examining some of the current trends in manufacturing.

27.1 TRENDS IN MANUFACTURING

Certain trends are occurring in manufacturing that will shape the factory of the future. These trends result from management's desire to find new ways to increase productivity and from new opportunities afforded by developing technologies. The trends include:

• *Shorter product life cycles.* Certainly, one of the trends is the competitive pressure on companies to develop and produce new generations of products that are increasingly complex in less time. Automobiles, airplanes, computers, audiovideo equipment, machine tools, and many other products are examples of the trend. This technological "rat race" results in shorter product lives not because the older products wear out but because new offerings make previous items technologically obsolete. The use of CAD/CAM systems makes it possible for companies to accomplish the synthesis, analysis, evaluation, and documentation of the design in much less time than with manual methods.

• *Increased emphasis on quality and reliability.* The Japanese have demonstrated that it is possible to manufacture high-quality products at relatively low cost. American producers, especially in the automobile industry, have responded to consumer pressure for higher quality and the trend has spread to other industries as well. When the consequences of poor product quality are considered (e.g., lower consumer acceptance, reduced sales volume, higher unit costs, more problems in field service, etc.), it makes sense to strive for higher quality in manufactured products.

• *More customized products.* The products available to consumers are becoming more individualized and custom engineered. There are more special options and features to meet the particular needs of the customer. This results in smaller lot sizes. The number of products and components made in small batch sizes (50 or fewer items) is expected to represent the majority of future manufacturing activity in the United States, if that is not already the case.

• *New materials.* New and unconventional materials are being selected by designers of new products. In the automobile industry this trend is exemplified by the use of composite materials for car body panels in place of traditional sheet steel. The advantages of the newer materials include lighter weight and greater shape and styling flexibility. Considering the size of the automobile market each year and the amount of material involved per car, the impact of this material substitution on the U.S. economy will be substantial. The aircraft industry is another growing user of composites. Other materials being used with greater frequency in design applications traditionally satisfied by metals include plastics and ceramics. These nontraditional materials must be shaped by processing techniques that are completely different from those used in metalworking. There are significant challenges confronting the manufacturing industries to deal with these new technologies.

• *Growing use of electronics.* At the time of this writing, the electronics industry is growing at a much faster rate than the traditional mechanical equipment industry. New products of all types (consumer products, business products, and industrial products) are being designed with more and more on-board electronics for data processing, control, and communication with humans. Electronics and microelectronics manufacturing places unusual demands on the workplace for clean environments. Human workers are incompatible with these environmental requirements because they generate contaminants at a high rate. A prevailing viewpoint among electronics manufacturing experts is that human beings must be eliminated from direct participation in the manufacture of microelectronics products. This means automation.

• *Pressure to reduce inventories.* During the late 1970s and during much of the 1980s, interest rates increased to historic levels. Companies realized that there was a very high investment cost associated with keeping inventories. Attempts were made to reduce inventories of all types. In manufacturing the focus was on reducing work-in-process. We have seen in Chapter 3 that the cost of in-process inventory can be significant when the value of the product is high and the manufacturing lead time is long. Some of the following trends are a result of this pressure to reduce inventories.

• *Outsourcing.* Outsourcing is a method used by large companies to subcontract the manufacture of the components of their products to outside firms. Instead of producing these components themselves, they find it more convenient and less expensive to have other companies produce the components. In most cases, the large firms continue to do the final assembly of the product at their own plants where they can maintain better control over product quality. The advantages of outsourcing include reduced labor problems in manufacturing, elimination of equipment that is poorly utilized, avoidance of major investments in new manufacturing facilities, reduction of inventory, and dealing with companies that have become expert at certain manufacturing technologies. The disadvantage of outsourcing is the risk of losing control of the quality and delivery for the components. The alternative to outsourcing for the large firms is to acquire expertise in perhaps a wide variety of processing technologies with the risk that some of these technologies will become outmoded.

• *Just-in-time production.* The concept of just-in-time (JIT) production is simple. It is a means of reducing inventory of raw materials and purchased parts. With JIT, a large company that makes an assembled product will require its suppliers to deliver the components needed for the product within a short time interval before the assembly process. The interval may be one day or less, depending on the reliability of the supplier to make deliveries on schedule. Ideally, the components are delivered immediately before they are needed in assembly (i.e., "just in time"). The benefit to the large company of following a just-in-time policy with its suppliers is that inventories are dramatically reduced. Instead of keeping several days' supply of parts on hand for final assembly, the inventory buffer is reduced to hours. Some observers believe that the burden of maintaining inventories has simply been transferred from the final assembly plant to the suppliers.

• *Point-of-use manufacture.* An approach closely related to JIT but which is applied inside a company is point-of-use manufacture. The approach is used in factories where production of the components and assembly of the final product are both performed on-site. Point-of-use manufacture means that the workstations making the components are located along the assembly line immediately before the assembly operations they serve. In this way the components flow directly into the assembly stations. Instead of a significant time lag between when the parts are made and when they are used, there is almost no time delay. This substantially reduces the amount of work-in-process. The risk suffered by the company is that one of the component production operations will fail and cause the entire assembly line to shut down. To reduce this risk, a small "float" of parts is usually maintained between the workstation that makes the parts and the workstation that assembles them.

• *Greater use of computers in manufacturing.* Computer integrated manufacturing is the term that is used. Over the last decade there has been a growing interest in and implementation of computers to plan, monitor, control, and manage manufacturing operations. There is no sign that this trend will be diminished in the future. Examples include CAD for product design, CAM for manufacturing planning, programmable logic controllers and computers for process control, microprocessors for robots, and personal computers for everyone.

These trends are leading the way toward the computer integrated factory of the future. What will that factory of the future be like?

27.2 THE FUTURE AUTOMATED FACTORY

The concept of the future automated factory is usually applied in the context of discrete-product manufacturing and in connection with products that are made in medium or small batch sizes (down to a lot size of 1). The factory of the future will have to perform the same basic manufacturing functions that were defined in Chapter 2: processing, assembly, material handling and storage, inspection, and control. Our discussion of the future automated factory will address these same issues.

The objective in the automated factory is to achieve a level of untended integrated operation similar to that which currently exists in a computer-controlled production plant which processes chemicals, petroleum, foods, and certain metals. In such a plant, there exists a relatively small crew of perhaps 5 or 10 persons (the number varies according to the size of the plant) who oversee the production operations. These people perform maintenance and repair functions on the equipment, programming of the computer systems, monitoring the computer controlled processes, activities that involve interactions with the outside world (e.g., shipping and receiving), plant security, and general supervision. They do not participate directly in the processing of the product.

In the discrete-product manufacturing industries, complex problems are encountered in achieving the same level of automation because of the difficulties in processing, assembling, handling, and inspecting a diverse mix of products. What makes manufacturing difficult in the multiproduct situation is the huge amount of information that must be processed for each different product made. Each component in the product has its unique geometry specification (i.e., an engineering drawing or a geometric model in a CAD data base), material definition, and processing route sheet. For the product itself, there are parts lists, operating specifications, assembly drawings, and so on. Production schedules must be formulated, materials must be ordered, labor and equipment must be planned, and so it goes. Multiply these data by the number of different products manufactured in the plant, and the amount of information that must be generated and managed in the plant is substantial. It has been estimated that only about one-eighth of the people in the factory are directly concerned with processing the product, while the remaining seven-eighths are handling and processing information [11]. It is the information system in the future factory that will implement the control function in manufacturing.

The information system in the automated factory

Certainly, one of the features that will distinguish the future automated factory is the higher level of information processing and data base management that will be required to operate it. At one time it seemed reasonable that all of the data and information required to operate the plant might be contained in one large central data base. However, the sheer size of the data base and the changing nature of software practices over time is likely to make the single data base impractical. What seems more likely is that there will be a distributed data base system in the plant, and that this arrangement will provide the flexibility necessary to deal with new developments in software and computer technology.

One of the reasons why the factory data base will be so large is that it must be capable of handling not only alphanumeric data (the common medium today in large data bases), but must also be able to store, process, transmit, and display graphical data. The computer systems must be capable of supporting engineering design and analysis functions, and the complex and often time-consuming numerical computations that are associated with these functions, as well as the traditional data processing applications. In other words, the corporate-wide information system must possess data-processing capabilities usually found only in today's CAD/CAM systems. This capability to handle geometric data will provide the opportunity for direct communication of product specifications between the computer systems of the customer firm and its suppliers. Instead of supplying product information in the form of paper documents that require interpretation by human beings, the form of communication will be digital without the need for people to read and analyze every item.

Information systems of the future will probably have the capacity to interpret data in more than the conventional data processing sense. Instead of merely performing repetitive calculations on the data, the system will be able to understand the inherent meaning of the data being manipulated. Large computer systems at the third and fourth levels of the computer hierarchy (described in Chapter 26) will possess attributes of comprehension and intelligence in their processing of information. They will be able to make decisions and initiate actions in the company for the timely execution of procedures that must occur during the manufacturing cycle. As an example, an engineering change related to a given product would be automatically propagated throughout the various data bases that are affected by the change. As another example, the breakdown of a critical machine in the factory would require the rerouting of the parts normally made on that machine to other work centers; the plant computer system would decide how best to manage the problem and work around it. In essence, the information system used to support the automated factory of the future will become a "knowledge base management system" rather than a data base management system.

We have discussed in our book many of the components of the information system that will be used in the future factory. CAD/CAM systems are being used widely in industry today, and the associated computer graphics technology and geometric modeling techniques will become pervasive in the factory information systems of the future. Generative process planning is an example of the intelligence that might be applied by the computer system to automatically develop the sequence of production steps needed to make a product based on the geometry models residing in the engineering data bases. Communication between the different elements of the distributed data base (or knowledge base) in the factory will be made possible by computer networks using the MAP and TOP protocol standards.

Processing and assembly

The processing and assembly functions in manufacturing are the fundamental operations that transform raw materials and add value to them. The scope of our book has been limited to the systems technologies in manufacturing with little attention paid to the processes themselves. Let us consider some of the changes that are likely to occur in processing and assembly technology.

In spite of its disadvantages, machining is likely to remain an important process in manufacturing. Machining operations of the future will likely be carried out at speeds substantially greater than today, perhaps in the range 3000 to 5000 ft/min. (The corresponding conventional speeds today are in the range 200 to 1000 ft/min.) These speed increases will substantially improve productivity in machining operations. Advances in cutting tool materials and machine tool technology will make these increases possible. The use of sintered polycrystalline diamond and other superhard materials and coatings will provide the basis for cutting tools of the future. Machine tools will possess greater rigidity, be equipped with new bearing designs that will permit the very high cutting speeds, and will have more automated features for untended machining. Advances in sensor technology will provide sophisticated tool wear monitoring systems for adaptive control. The high cutting speeds used in machining will generate chips at a high rate, and beneath-the-floor conveyor systems are likely to become prevalent as a means of solving the chip disposal problem.

In addition to machining, the use of *near net shape* processes will grow in importance. Near net shape processes are those which attempt to generate the final shape of the part in a single step (or a limited number of sequential steps). Their objectives and advantages include reduced waste in the form of chips or other scrap material, reduced number of processing operations required to form the part, and reduced manufacturing cost. Examples of near net shape processes include plastic molding, powdered metallurgy, casting and forging. In addition, new processing technologies are being developed to form the newer materials, such as fiberglass and other composites, new plastics, and ceramic materials.

Finally, the growth of microelectronics technology has forced the development of specialized chemical, optical, and physical processing methods to create large-scale integrated (LSI) and very-large-scale integrated (VLSI) circuits on miniature silicon chips. These processes include refined photolithography techniques, chemical etching, chemical vapor deposition, diffusion, ion implantation, and electron beam etching. It is anticipated that some of these processing technologies will find many industrial applications beyond microelectronics.

In the assembly area, some of the biggest productivity improvements are expected to come from a greater awareness of the impact of product design on assembly methodology. By designing parts for ease of automatic assembly, the number of assembly steps and corresponding costs will be reduced. Total product cost can be minimized by achieving an optimum balance between the component costs and assembly costs.

Material handling

The material handling function looms as a significant obstacle that must be overcome if we are to achieve the future automated factory in small- and medium-lot-size manufacturing. Two problem areas will be mentioned here [4]:

- Flexible routings for different parts
- Mechanical interfacing of material handling and production systems

The first of these problems involves the capability of the material handling system to deliver different workparts to different workcells in the plant according to the particular routing of the part. In our conceptual model of the automated factory, the various parts and products will each require its own set of processing operations, and the handling system must be able to provide these flexible routings. This flexibility will be achieved using computer control of the material handling system. Stored in the plant computer will be the process plan for each part, and this information can be converted into the corresponding workcell routing. At the time of this writing the most flexible of the material handling systems is an automated guided vehicle system. Because of its flexibility and capability to be controlled by computer, it is one of the fastest-growing segments of the material handling industry today.

The second problem area is the difficulty in transferring loads (parts) between the material handling systems, production workcells, and storage systems in the plant. We are referring to this problem as the mechanical interface problem [8]. A mechanical interface is required each time a part is transferred from one type of system in the factory to another. The transfer must be accomplished within certain locational requirements. For example, presenting the part to the machine tool must be done with high accuracy to achieve close tolerance requirements in the processing operation. The method of transferring loads between systems in the future automated factory will probably make use of standard-sized pallets. The base of the pallet will be designed using certain standard features and sizes so that it will be compatible with all of the handling, storage, and production systems in the plant. The top surface of each pallet will consist of a fixture designed to accommodate certain part families. Different pallets will have different fixtures to handle the diverse mixture of products made in the factory. We have previously discussed this mechanical interface problem and some of the approaches that can be used to solve it in Chapter 15.

Figure 27.1 presents an artist's sketch of the way the handling and storage systems might be organized to serve production in the future factory. The factory contains several automated storage/retrieval systems, automated guided vehicles, robots, CNC machine tools, and other components that we have discussed in preceding chapters.

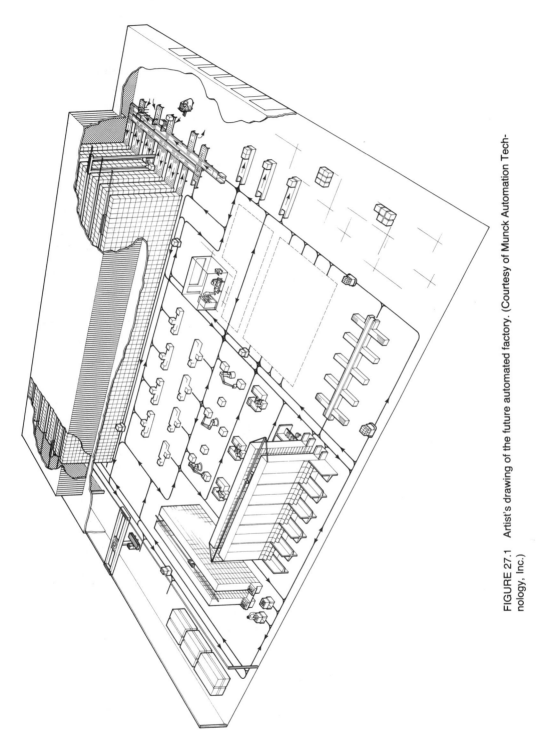

FIGURE 27.1   Artist's drawing of the future automated factory. (Courtesy of Munck Automation Technology, Inc.)

Inspection systems

The inspection function is destined to become more automated in the future as quality continues to remain a high-priority issue. The principles and techniques of automated inspection were presented in Chapter 18. By way of review, current trends in automated inspection suggest that the future factory will be characterized in the quality control area by the following:

- Automated inspection methods will permit the use of 100% inspection of production output rather than the sampling inspection procedures in common use today.
- Inspection procedures will be integrated into the production process to form a closed-loop feedback control system. Processing errors detected in inspection will be corrected on-line so that much closer to 100% good product can be achieved and variations in product specifications from nominal design values will be significantly reduced.
- Noncontact sensors, such as machine vision and other optical techniques, will come into widespread use in automated inspection.
- Computer-controlled inspection technologies that can be adapted to varying product configurations will grow in importance in the future automated factory. These techniques will permit new product specifications to be downloaded from the CAD/CAM data base to the inspection system without the need for special programming of the systems by human operators.

Focused factories

The future automated factory will be an extension of today's flexible manufacturing systems. Many of the problems in workpart handling and storage, machine tool programming, production scecheduling, information processing, cutting tool management, and quality control that are encountered in the design and operation of an FMS are the same problems that must be solved in designing and operating the future factory. One might consider the automated factory to be a very large FMS. However, the problems of operating and controlling the automated manufacturing system become significantly larger as the production capacity of the system increases. There are practical limits that must be imposed on the size of the factory.

The concept of the focused factory, introduced by Skinner [10], is applicable here. The focused factory is one that concentrates its efforts "on a limited, concise, manageable set of products, technologies, volumes and markets." The concept acknowledges that a single factory cannot be successful if it attempts to engage in too many different things. Accordingly, it restricts its mission to certain products and activities, and tries to excel at those things. It practices the principles of group technology. The future automated factory is likely to be a focused factory, limiting its activities to certain families of products which can be produced using a limited set of processing technologies.

In effect, the focused factory uses a modified version of the principle of standardization. It attempts to limit the variety of problems it must deal with, thereby becoming very good at solving the problems that remain. Indeed, there are opportunities for standardization even in the production of small to medium lot sizes of diverse products. These opportunities for standardization include:

- *Design standards.* CAD/CAM systems tend to promote standardization by building it into the design software. Hardware components, fasteners, hole sizes, corner radii, and many other possibilities exist to design products according to standards that reduce problems in manufacturing and assembly.
- *Raw materials.* Products can be selected so that the variety of raw materials is limited to a confined set.
- *Tooling.* Many plants tend to allow the variety of tooling to grow out of hand. It should be possible to limit the numbers of different types of tooling and other supplies that are used.
- *Processes and methods.* The variety of manufacturing processes and methods included in shop practice is limited to a manageable set.

Nonautomated factories of the future

Certainly, not all of the factories of the future will possess the features and the capabilities of the automated factory we are describing in this section. There will probably be a large number of production plants in the future that will still use direct labor to perform their operations. These labor-intensive plants will likely fall into one of the following categories:

- *Foreign factories.* Direct labor will be used to produce goods in underdeveloped countries where labor rates are low and the pressures to automate are not as significant as in the industrialized nations. In these cases, cheap labor competes with automation.
- *Small businesses.* These are typically businesses in which the economic returns are marginal. They are small plants with low capitalization serving commodity markets that are easy to enter. These plants have little alternative but to hire labor at minimum wages and provide no benefits beyond what is required by law.
- *Emerging technologies.* Manual production methods will be utilized in situations where the product is new and the processing technology is not yet mature. Because the technology is still rapidly evolving, it does not lend itself to automation. As the technology matures, it will stabilize, and opportunities for automation will be discovered and implemented.
- *Companies that are going out of business.* These are companies which, due to various circumstances (e.g., poor management, keen competitive environment, economic downturn, mature industry unable to attract new captial), are unwilling or unable to invest in automation. They employ manual labor with old-fashioned methods. These companies are likely to fail.

In all of these categories, the levels of technology will be lower; the skills, training, and education of the employees typically will be less; and the immediate economic prospects will be worse than for those industries served by the automated factory.

27.3 HUMAN WORKERS IN THE FUTURE AUTOMATED FACTORY

What type of work will people do in the future automated factory? It is difficult to foresee at the time of this writing that the automated factory will require no human beings at all in its operations. We are conceptualizing a factory in which there will be no people participating directly in the production and assembly processes. But people will be required to manage and maintain the plant. The kinds of tasks that people will be required to do will include:

- *Equipment maintenance.* As the functions of manufacturing become completely dependent on automatic machines, the reliability and maintenance of those machines grows in importance. In a fully integrated factory, a breakdown of a single critical machine may shut down the entire plant. Highly skilled, highly trained technicians will be needed to maintain and repair the machines.
- *Programming.* The computer systems and programmable machines must be programmed, data must be entered, and so on. Although much of the routine part programming for the production equipment is likely to be done by means of artificial intelligence, there will nevertheless be a need for new computer programs to be written. It is difficult to imagine that the factory information system and data base will remain in a fixed configuration. Just as with today's information systems, there will be a continual demand to update the computer programs and to incorporate new software into the operations of the factory.
- *Engineering project work.* The future automated factory is likely never to be finished. There will be a continual need to upgrade production machines, introduce new processing techniques, try out new cutting tools, and so on. Just as the information systems will need constant updating and improvement, the mechanical systems on the shop floor will also need similar tending. We contemplate that highly educated engineering personnel will find many opportunities in the automated factory of the future.
- *Plant security.* Some of the security functions can be performed by robots and sophisticated sensor systems. There will probably be a need for a limited staff of human security guards to be present to manage the security systems.
- *Factory interface.* The factory will have to interface with the outside world. There will be people at the loading and unloading docks, perhaps a receptionist in the front lobby, and an office staff to support the factory.
- *Plant supervision.* Someone must be in charge of the factory. There will be a limited staff of professional managers and engineers who are responsible for plant operations. We believe there will be an emphasis on the technical skills of managers rather than in today's factory management positions, where the emphasis is more on personnel management skills.

Perhaps when the future automated factory we are describing is achieved, and all of the technological problems associated with that factory have been solved, it will then be realistic to consider a future factory with no people at all. For now, our future factory will require people in order to operate.

27.4 THE SOCIAL IMPACT

There will be a social consequence of the future automated factory, with its reduced number of employees and no direct labor participation in the production processes. The obvious impact is on the unskilled workers who will not be needed to run the production machines and perform the manual labor tasks. But other types of work will also be affected.

It will not happen that all companies in all industries suddenly switch to the automated factory overnight. The building and learning process will take time, with some industries embracing the new CIM and automation technologies more slowly than others. The automated factory will be introduced gradually, and the effects on the work force will be evolutionary rather than revolutionary. Nevertheless, the effects will be noticed.

Impact on labor

The future automated factory means substitution of machines for human workers. The implications for employment in factory operations are clear. As automation is implemented, there will be a shift from direct labor jobs to indirect labor jobs. Direct labor factory work tends to be well defined, manual, and repetitive. Because of these features, the skill level required to perform it is generally low. Indirect labor work in factories is sometimes manual but not as well defined and not as repetitive. Many of the job classifications for indirect labor require skill and training. As we have seen in the preceding section, the need for indirect labor in the future factory will include highly trained technical positions in maintenance, computer programming, engineering (particularly in fields such as electrical and electronics, industrial, manufacturing, and mechanical engineering), and supervision.

As a consequence of the shift from direct to indirect labor in future factories, the ranks of the labor unions are likely to be adversely affected unless the unions can recruit in employment areas where they have traditionally not been successful. Highly skilled professional and semiprofessional workers have tended to be more confident about their employment security, and have identified and associated more with management and professional staffs. Prospects for membership growth in these employment areas pose a difficult challenge for the unions.

Because of the differences in skill requirements, it is not possible that all the workers who currently qualify for direct labor positions in today's conventional factories will qualify for indirect labor positions in the future automated factory. Direct labor jobs in production will be displaced. Some of the unskilled workers can be retrained, but many will not be employable. For the worker who is affected, and for society, there is no denying that job displacement is a negative aspect of automation. However, if companies do not automate their factories of the future, there is likely to be no future for these companies. The negative impact on employment in this case would be far worse.

Retraining and education

One answer to the labor issue is education. As we move toward a more technological society, the importance of technical education seems clear. There are two aspects to the educational solution. The first deals with the education of young people still in school today. It is important that our society trains its young people in sufficient numbers to design, build, and operate the future automated factory and to deal with the other technologies that will be so important to our economic progress and well-being.

The second aspect of the educational solution involves the retraining of the workers that are displaced by new technologies. Some difficult questions arise with regard to retraining: First, who should pay for the retraining? Technical training is costly. Should the company which is introducing automation pay the expense? The labor unions? Or should the federal, state, and local government (which means the taxpayers)?

Another difficult issue involves the obligations of the worker after retraining. If the company provides the retraining, and increases the skill and educational level of the worker, is the worker obligated to remain with the same employer? If there are not enough jobs in the local community, is the worker obligated to move to another geographical area to seek employment? Perhaps the worker has roots in the local area and prefers not to move. The worker may feel that the organization sponsoring the retraining course should also provide employment in the same geographical location.

With the increasing complexity of science and technology, how much retraining is the displaced worker capable of receiving? Given a worker who has been displaced from the local steel mill at age 50 who graduated from a vocational high school more than 30 years ago, imagine how difficult it would be for him to learn computer programming, or the technical concepts and operating principles of a machine vision system, or other sophisticated programmable machine.

Finally, a significant question in the education and retraining issue is: Where does society get the trained teachers and modern laboratory equipment to accomplish the retraining? Many of the new technologies in which training is required are still emerging, and teachers who have been exposed to and educated in these fields are not available. How does society retrain the teachers who are presently in the fading technical fields so that they in turn can retrain the workers to be productive in the emerging technical fields?

We do not have answers to these questions. There do not seem to be any easy answers. For the reader interested in these social issues, we recommend several of the references, especially references [1], [4], [6], and [9].

Social and economic forces

The trend toward the future automated factory seems unavoidable in modern industrialized societies such as the United States, Europe, and Japan. There are several social and economic factors tending to promote the development of such a factory. These include:

- The economic necessity to increase productivity
- The desire to increase machine utilization
- The high cost of in-process inventory
- The desire to reduce manufacturing lead times to respond more quickly to customer demands
- The need to use raw materials and energy as efficiently as possible
- The trend in the labor force to seek employment in the service sector and not in manufacturing
- Federal regulations regarding worker safety

This list includes many of the same factors mentioned in Chapter 1. Hence, we have come full circle. The same factors that constituted the driving force behind the development of transfer lines, automated assembly machines, NC, and other automated production systems of today are also the impetus for further advances, culminating in the computer-automated factory of the future.

REFERENCES

[1] AYRES, R. U., and S. M. MILLER, *Robotics: Applications and Social Implications,* Ballinger Publishing Co., Cambridge, Mass., 1983.

[2] GROOVER, M. P., "Meeting the Challenges of CAD/CAM," *National Productivity Review,* Winter 1982–83, pp. 29–35.

[3] GROOVER, M. P., and J. E. HUGHES, JR., "A Strategy for Job Shop Automation," *Industrial Engineering,* November 1981, pp. 66–76.

[4] GROOVER, M. P., and J. C. WIGINTON, "CIM and the Flexible Automated Factory of the Future," *Industrial Engineering,* January 1986, pp. 74–85.

[5] GROOVER, M. P., and E. W. ZIMMERS, JR., "Automated Factories in the Year 2000," *Industrial Engineering,* November 1980, pp. 34–43.

[6] GROOVER, M. P., J. E. HUGHES, JR., and N. G. ODREY, "Productivity Benefits of Automation Should Offset Work Force Dislocation Problems," *Industrial Engineering,* April 1984, pp. 50–59.

[7] GROOVER, M. P., M. WEISS, R. N. NAGEL, and N. G. ODREY, *Industrial Robotics: Technology, Programming, and Applications,* McGraw-Hill Book Company, New York, 1986, Chapter 18.

[8] JIRANEK, R., "Design Principles for Mechanically Interfacing Production Equipment to Material Handling Systems," Masters thesis, Lehigh University, Bethlehem, Pa., January 1986.

[9] Office of Technology Assessment, "Computerized Manufacturing Automation—Employment, Education, and the Workplace," *OTA Report,* Washington, D.C., April 1984.

[10] SKINNER, W., "The Focused Factory," *Harvard Business Review,* May–June 1974, pp. 113–121.

[11] SKINNER, W., *Manufacturing: The Formidable Competitive Weapon,* John Wiley & Sons, Inc., New York, 1985.

Answers to Selected Problems

CHAPTER 2

2.1 (a) 141 hr, (b) 4.05 pc/hr

2.3 (a) 105 hr, (b) 700 pc/week, (c) 71.43%

2.5 (a) 245 hr, (b) 969.7 pc/month, schedule exceeds capacity by 100 hr, (c) 103.125%, (d) 1531.25 pc, (e) WIP ratio = TIP ratio = 98

2.7 97.6%

2.9 Problem: setup workers are a bottleneck. Solution: hire one more setup worker.

CHAPTER 3

3.1 Manual UAC = $32,441, Automatic UAC = $27,933. Select automatic.

3.3 $1.309/pc

3.5 $33.01/hr

3.7 (a) 96,193 pc/yr, (b) 9619 hr/yr, (c) −$18,477

3.9 Cost/pc = $1.20 + 32,064/Q$

3.11 Manual cost/pc = 0.25, Automated cost/pc = 0.025 + 55,930/Q
3.13 (a) $31.85/pc, (b) h = 102%, (c) $326,400
3.15 (a) $38.40/pc during MLT, (b) $399,360/yr, (c) $266,240/yr

CHAPTER 4

4.1 135 deg drive, 225 deg dwell
4.3 (a) 22 s: 163.6 cycles/hr, 163.6 pc/hr
         21 s: 171.4 cycles/hr, 165.8 pc/hr
         20 s: 180 cycles/hr, 161.6 pc/hr
         19 s: 189.5 cycles/hr, 149.5 pc/hr
         18 s: 200 cycles/hr, 93.6 pc/hr
         (b) 18.55 s: 194 pc/hr

CHAPTER 5

5.1 (a) 0.513 min, (b) 117 pc/hr, (c) 0.649, (d) 0.351
5.3 $0.637/pc
5.5 (a) $F = 0.120$, (b) 90.9 pc/hr, (c) $E = 0.455$
5.7 $D = 0.456$, $E = 0.544$, $R_p = 195.4$ pc/hr
5.9 65,141 pc
5.11 (a) 2.125 min/pc, 28.235 pc/hr, (b) E = 58.8%, D = 41.2%,
         (c) 70.83 hr
5.13 (a) $T_c = 1.35$ min/pc, $F = 0.1456$, $E = 47.5\%$, $R_p = 21.11$ pc/hr, (b)
         Stage 1: $T_c = 1.35$ min/pc, $R_p = 33.58$ pc/hr, $E = 75.5\%$, Stage 2:
         $T_c = 1.00$ min/pc, $R_p = 35.66$ pc/hr, $E = 59.4\%$
5.15 Current line: $C_{pc} = \$1.019$/pc, Proposed line: $C_{pc} = \$0.788$/pc,
         Recommendation: automate station 5
5.17 Current $E_0 = 0.61$, $E_\infty = 0.7576$
5.19 $E = 0.6967$, $R_p = 55.73$ pc/hr
5.21 $E = 0.6854$, $R_p = 54.83$ pc/hr
5.23 Lowest cost buffer capacity $b = 20$ units

CHAPTER 6

6.1 (a) 1.33 units/min, (b) 1.25 min, (c) .75 min/unit
6.3 (a) 0.582 min, (b) 0.5 m/min, (c) 1.72 units/min, (d) 0.291 m/unit
6.5 (a) 6 stations, $d = 0.0789$, (b) One combination that will work is: $T_t = 5.32$
         min, $V_c = 1.128$ ft/min, $s_p = 4.288$ ft/unit.

6.7 (a) 5 stations, (b) 14%

6.9 Station 1: elements 1, 2, 5
Station 2: elements 3, 4
Station 3: elements 8, 7
Station 4: elements 6, 9
Station 5: element 10
(a) 5 stations, (b) 14%

6.11 (b) 20%, (c) Individual workers: UAC = $80,000/yr, Assembly line: UAC = $58,042/yr, Recommend assembly line.

6.13 Station 1: elements 2, 1
Station 2: elements 3, 4, 6
Station 3: element 5
Station 4: element 7
Station 5: element 8

6.15 (a) 5 stations
(b) Station 1: elements 1, 2
Station 2: elements 3, 4
Station 3: elements 5, 6
Station 4: elements 9, 8
Station 5: elements 7, 10
(c) d = 0.1385, (d) 5.2 ft/min, (e) 7.8 ft

CHAPTER 7

7.1 (a) 1.667 min, (b) 40 min,
(c) Proportion on = 0.96, proportion off = 0.04

7.3 R_p = 305.6 asbys/hr, Yield = 0.98705, E = 67.9%

7.5 R_p = 600 asbys/hr, Yield = 0.8861, E = 100%

7.7 R_p = 100.6 asbys/hr, E = 89.43%

7.9 (a) 0.9684, (b) 187.04 asbys/hr, (c) 0.03155, (d) $1.1007/asby

7.11 (a) 0.98, (b) 120 asbys/hr, (c) 97,000 total, 95,060 good, 1940 containing at least one defect

7.13 (a) 260.9 asbys/hr, (b) 0.995, (c) station 4 feed rate = 4 pc/min, (d) 181.9 asbys/hr, 180.9 good asbys/hr

CHAPTER 8

8.1 (a) 0.000667 in, (b) x-axis: 132.5 pulses/s, 53 rev/min, y-axis: 212 pulses/s, 84.8 rev/min

8.3 (a) 0.0004 in, (b) 2500 pulses/s, (c) 60.0 in/min

8.5 (a) 50 step angles, (b) 14 bits

8.7 5.73 in/min, 4.36 min

8.9 3.28 min/cycle

CHAPTER 9

9.1 6111 rev/min, 18.33 in/min

9.3 191 rev/min, 6.11 in/min

CHAPTER 10

10.3 (a) 26.67 min, (b) 8.33 min, (c) 68.8%, (d) 17.33 min

10.5 (a) $200/job, (b) 17.4%, (c) yes

CHAPTER 11

11.7 0.055 in

11.9 8 bits

11.11 (a) 0.0352 in, (b) 0.05882 in, (c) 0.0294 in, (d) 0.0236 in

CHAPTER 13

13.1 67.06 pc/hr

13.3 134.2 pc/hr

13.5 (a) Manual arc-on time = 27.7%, Robot cell arc-on time = 62.9%, (b) Manual R_p = 3.393 units/hr, Robot cell R_p = 9.434 units/hr

CHAPTER 14

14.1 (a) 2180 parts-ft/hr, (b) 0.372, (c) 5860.2 parts-ft/hr

14.3 (a) 2180 parts-ft/hr, (b) 0.4914, (c) 920 ft

14.5 (a) 9000 parts-ft/hr, (b) 200 ft, (c) 18 parts/min

14.7 500 parts-ft/hr, 1.0 part/min

14.9 Two configurations that will work: (1) s_c = 30 ft, n_c = 20, n_p = 1, (2) s_c = 60 ft, n_c = 10, n_p = 2

14.11 (a) R_f = 3.214 parts/min, (b) 25, (c) 7.778 min, (d) Speed rule OK, Capacity constraint OK, Uniformity principle assumed OK

14.13 (a) 3.255 min, $E = 0.335$, 16.6 del/hr, (b) 2 vehicles

14.15 (b) 47.6 ft, (c) 55.35%, (d) 4 vehicles

CHAPTER 15

15.1 $H_s = 26$ ft 10 in, $L_s = 60$ ft

15.3 $V_v = 62.5$ ft/min, $T_{sc} = 3.333$ min, $T_{dc} = 5.28$ min

15.5 $V_v = 23$ ft/min, $V_h = 60$ ft/min

15.7 AGVS: 64.8 loads/hr, AS/RS: 66.8 loads/hr

15.9 196.4 transactions/hr

15.11 (a) One carousel: \$55,615/yr, two carousels: \$98,422.50/yr, (b) One carousel: \$0.62/transaction, two carousels: \$0.39/transaction

CHAPTER 16

16.1 00100

16.3 (a) $3 \rightarrow 1 \rightarrow 4 \rightarrow 2$, (c) in-line

16.5 120 parts/week, A: 40, B: 30, C: 20, D: 20, E: 10, utilization of key machine = 100%, utilization of machines 1 and 2 = 35.95%, utilization of machine 4 = 57.62%

CHAPTER 18

18.1 (a) ± 0.006 in, (b) 0.0124, (c) 0.0241, (d) accuracy = ± 0.0005 in, precision = ± 0.0005 in, standard deviation = 0.0001667 in

18.3 (a) 0.004096 sec, (b) yes, 0.004096 sec $< 1/30$ sec

18.5 (a) 0.0095 sec, (b) 0.00008 sec, (c) yes, resolution more than adequate

18.7 0.0953 in

CHAPTER 19

19.1 $A = 5.0$, $B = 2.0$

19.3 (b) Probably second order, underdamped

19.5 $1/(5s + 2)$

19.7 (a) $-2.68 \pm j2.52$ (oscillatory), (b) 2.52 rad/sec

19.9 (a) $\dfrac{C(A + B)}{1 + CD(A + B)}$

(b) $\dfrac{AB/(1 + A)}{1 + CAB/(1 + A)}$

(c) $\dfrac{B + A}{1 + BC}$

19.13 $\dfrac{3}{s^2 + 9s + 14.9}$

19.15 (b) $\dfrac{15K(s + 8)}{s(s + 8)(s + 6) + 4.5K}$

(c) $\dfrac{15s(s + 8)}{s(s + 8)(s + 6) + 4.5K}$

19.19 (a) $y(s) = \dfrac{-1}{s + 5} + \dfrac{1}{s + 2}$

(b) $y(s) = \dfrac{4}{7s^2} - \dfrac{4}{49s} + \dfrac{4}{49(s + 7)}$

19.23 $y(t) = 1.333 + 1.667 \exp(-3t)$

19.25 (a) 1.0, (b) 13/18, (c) 1/7

19.29 (a) Stable for all K
(b) Unstable for $K > 160$
(c) Marginal stability at $K = 0$
(d) Unstable for $K > 26.25$

19.31 (a) $\dfrac{4K}{(s^2 + 6s + 10)(s + 10)}$

(b) $\dfrac{20K(s + 10)}{(s^2 + 6s + 10)(s + 10) + 4K}$

19.33 $K = 3.285$

19.35 (a) No increase in K, (b) Two ways: (1) increase input x to $x = 8.152$, or (2) add gain block before summing point in Figure 19.28 with gain factor $K = 1.63$

19.37 (a) $K_2 = 3.333$, (b) $K_1 = 2.1$,
(c) $y(t) = 5 - 11.67 \exp(-4t) + 6.67 \exp(-7t)$

CHAPTER 20

20.5 $x_1 = 8.333$, $x_2 = 1.506$, $z = 0.254$

20.7 $x_1 = 17.25$, $x_2 = 11.0$, $z = 441.125$

20.9 (a) $x_1 = 3.885$, $x_2 = 3.387$, $z = \$126.02$,
(b) surplus capacity at operation 1

20.11   (a) $B = 58.38$, (b) $x = 1.3506$, (c) $y = 86.44$

20.13   (a) $y = -42.21 + 51.137x$, (b) $r = 0.99886$, $s_e = 7.51$

20.17   (a) $i25 + j29$, (b) 38.29, (c) $i0.653 + j0.757$

20.19   Gradient = Magnitude = Direction = 0

CHAPTER 22

22.1   4096 levels, 0.01465 V, 0.01465 V, 0.00732 V

22.3   39.84 V

22.5 $V(t) = 36.25 - 3.125t - 0.625t^2$
First order hold: $V = 33.75$ at 4th instant
Second order hold: $V = 32.5$ at 4th instant

Index

A

Absolute positioning, 203
Acceptance sampling, 491
Accuracy and repeatability:
    numerical control, 212–14
    robotics, 310–12
Adaptable programmable assembly system, 352–53
Adaptive control:
    definition, 600–601
    functions of, 601–2
    identification problem, 609, 621
    instantaneous approximation, 610–11
    for machining, 280, 287–94
    practical problems, 621
    regression technique, 611–20
Adhesives for assembly, 139
Addressable points (robotics), 311
AGVS (*see* Automated guided vehicle systems)

ALPACA, 159
Analog-to-digital converters, 678, 680–85
APAS, 352–53
APT, 201, 247, 248–60, 268–78
Assembly:
    assembly processes, 137–39
    automated (*see* Automated assembly)
    function in manufacturing, 20, 23
    future automated factory, 781–82
    mechanical fasteners, 138
    robotics, 352–53
    types of systems, 139
Assembly line:
    automated (*see* Automated assembly)
    flexible manual assembly lines, 162–65
    line balancing, 143–59
    manual, 139–43
    model variations, 142–43
    transfers between stations, 140–41
    ways to improve, 159–61
Asynchronous transfer, 87, 89, 173

Automated assembly:
  analysis of, 180–91
  definition, 139, 170
  design for, 171–72
  in FMS, 467
  parts feeders, 175–78
  types of, 173–75
Automated guided vehicle systems:
  analysis, 393–98
  applications, 386–87
  assembly lines, 164
  blocking system, 390–92
  definition, 363, 383
  guidance, 387–90
  system management, 392
  types of, 383–85
Automated storage/retrieval systems:
  (*see also* Storage systems)
  analysis, 414–17
  components of, 410–12, 413–14
  controls, 412–13
  definition, 407
  in FMS, 472
  types of, 407–9
Automatic identification methods:
  bar codes, 754–60
  definition, 752
  technologies, 752–54
Automation:
  arguments for and against automation, 7–9
  definition, 1
  fixed, 2
  flexible, 3
  numerical control, 199–200
  partial, 115–18
  programmable, 2
  reasons for automating, 6–7, 339
  strategies for, 40–41
  transfer lines, 100–101
  types of, 2
Availability, 37, 39

B

Balance delay, 147–49
Bar code technology, 754–60
Batch model line, 142
Baud rate, 772
Binary sensors, 649

Block diagrams, 536–45
Blocking of workstations, 119, 141
Boolean algebra, 648–49
Bowl feeder, 175–76
Break-even analysis, 56–60
Buffer storage:
  assembly lines, 161
  effectiveness of, 120
  purposes of, 94–95
  partial automation, 118
  storage system for, 423
  transfer lines analysis, 119–28
Business functions, 25

C

CAD (*see* Computer-aided design)
CAD/CAM:
  CAD (*see* Computer-aided design)
  CAM (*see* Computer-aided manufacturing)
  definition, 709, 720–21
  in the future automated factory, 780
  NC part programming, 261–63
  relation to CIM, 5, 720–21
CALB, 158
CAM (*see* Computer-aided manufacturing)
Cam mechanisms for indexing, 93
Capacity, production:
  capacity planning, 26, 730, 740–41
  definition, 33
  mathematical model, 33–35
Capacity planning, 26, 730, 740–41
CAPP (*see* Computer-aided process planning)
Carousel assembly system, 173–74
Carousel storage system:
  analysis, 420–22
  applications, 420
  definition, 417
  construction, 417–18
  control features, 418–19
Cell (*see* Workcell)
Cellular manufacturing, 449
Center column machine, 99–100
CIM (*see* Computer integrated manufacturing)
Classification and coding (*see* Parts
  classification and coding)
CNC (*see* Computer numerical control)
Combinational system, 643
Composite part concept, 447–49

Computer-aided design:
  applications of, 711–16
  definition, 709
  design process, 710–11
  hardware, 716–18
  reasons for, 710
Computer-aided manufacturing:
  definition, 718
  manufacturing control, 26–27, 719–20
  manufacturing planning, 26, 718–19
Computer-aided process planning:
  benefits, 728–29
  definition, 718–19, 724–25
  generative, 728
  retrieval, 725–27
  variant, 725–27
Computer control:
  computer numerical control, 284–87
  coordinate measuring machine, 501–2
  definition, 673
  direct digital control, 692–96
  direct numerical control, 281–84
  flow lines, 96
  FMS, 472–76
  hierarchical, 309, 765–67
  interface to manufacturing process, 674–79
  programming for, 699–705
  robotics, 332
  supervisory control, 696–98
  types of, 691–98
Computer integrated manufacturing:
  definition, 4, 721–23
  relation to CAD/CAM, 720–23
  strategy of automation, 41
Computer numerical control:
  advantages, 287
  control features, 285–87
  definition, 280, 284
  differences with DNC, 284
  relation to NC, 207
Computer process monitoring, 522, 690–91
COMSOAL, 156
Contact inspection, 497
Continuous path, 310
Continuous transfer, 87, 88
Contouring NC, 205–7, 254–60
Control:
  actions, 553–60
  computer (*see* Computer control)

feedback control, 537, 553–60
feedforward, 697–98
function in manufacturing, 20, 23
hierarchical, 309
in FMS, 472–75
instantaneous control, 97, 187
linear systems analysis, 560–65
memory control, 97, 187
optimal control, 592–600
PID control, 554–60, 693, 695
quality control, 27
root locus method, 565–82
robotics, 308–10
sequence control, 95, 333
shop floor control (*see* Shop floor
  control)
Control charts, 491–93
Control resolution, 212, 311
Conveyor:
  analysis, 379–83
  assembly lines, 141–42
  attributes and features, 373
  definition, 362
  transfer lines, 90–91
  types of, 373–78
Coordinate measuring machine:
  benefits, 503–4
  capabilities, 503
  construction, 500–501
  control, 501–2
  definition, 499
  trends, 504
Coordinate system:
  numerical control, 202–3
  robotics, 322
Costs:
  automated assembly system,
    185
  equipment usage, 55–56
  estimating, 718
  fixed, 52
  overhead, 53
  partial automation, 116–17
  transfer line operation, 109
  unit cost of production, 60
  variable, 52
  work-in-process, 62–66
Counters, 656
Cutter offset, 246

Cycle time:
  automated assembly system, 184, 189
  automated flow line, 107–8
  automated storage/retrieval system, 415–17
  carousel storage system, 421–22
  manual assembly line, 145

D

Data acquisition system, 760–61
Delivery, parts, 175–80
Design:
  CAD (*see* Computer-aided design)
  design process, 710–11
  product design, 25–26
Diagnostics, 704–5
Dial index machine:
  automated assembly, 173
  center column machine, 99
  definition, 85
  methods of indexing, 91–93
  rotary indexing machine, 98
  trunnion machine, 99
Differential equations:
  model formulation, 524–33
  Laplace transforms, 546–53
Digital-to-analog converters, 685–88
Direct digital control, 691, 692–96
Direct Numerical Control:
  advantages, 284
  components, 281
  definition, 279, 281
  installation, 294
  types of, 282–83
Dispatching, 27
Distributed numerical control, 295
DNC (*see* Direct Numerical Control)
Downtime:
  assembly system, 185
  transfer line, 109, 122
Drum timer, 654–55

E

Electronics manufacturing, 777, 781
End effectors, 314–15
Error detection and recovery, 702–4
Escapement, 177

F

Factory data collection, 748–51, 760–62
Feed track, 176
Feeders, 176
Feedforward control, 697–98
Fiber optics, 771
Fixed automation, 2
Fixed zero (NC), 203
Flexible assembly systems:
  adaptable programmable assembly system, 352–53
  manual assembly lines, 162–65
Flexible automation, 3
Flexible inspection systems, 504–5
Flexible manufacturing system:
  analysis, 478
  applications, 479–82
  benefits, 482–83
  components of, 463, 466–76
  configurations, 469–71
  control, 472–76
  definition, 463
  GT cell type, 451
  planning of, 465, 476–78
  trends in NC, 295
  types of system, 464
  where to apply, 465
Floating zero, 203
Floor space, cost of, 66
Flow diagram, 367–68
Flow line, automated:
  analysis of, 106–29
  buffer storage, 94–95, 119–28
  computer simulation, 128–29
  configurations, 85
  control functions, 95–97
  definition, 83
  link line, 102
  objectives, 85
  performance of, 108–11
  transfer lines, 86, 101–2
  transfer mechanisms, 89–93
  two stage line, 121–26
  unitized flow line, 104
  work transport methods, 87–89
FMS (*see* Flexible manufacturing system)
Focused factory, 784–85

Ford, Henry, 81
From-to chart, 366–67, 452
Future automated factory:
  definition, 779
  functions of manufacturing, 781–84
  human workers, 786
  impact on labor, 787
  information system, 779–81
  nonautomated factories, 785
  social impact, 787–89

G

Geneva mechanism for indexing, 92–93
Geometric modeling, 712–13
GERTS, 128
GPSS, 128
Gradient search methods, 622–35
Gripper for robots, 314–15
Group technology:
  benefits, 454–56
  definition, 431, 433
  part families, 434–37
  parts classification and coding (*see* Parts
    classification and coding)
  production flow analysis, 437, 445–47
GT (*see* Group technology)

H

Hazard monitoring (*see* Safety monitoring)
Hierarchical control, 309, 765–67
Holding cost (inventory), 64
Hopper, 175
Hopperability, 172

I

Incremental positioning, 203
Information systems, 5, 24–25, 779–81
In-line flow system, 85, 173, 469
Inspection:
  automated, 493–97
  contact and noncontact, 497–98
  coordinate measuring machine, 499–504
  definition, 488
  in FMS, 467
  function in manufacturing, 20, 23
  future automated factory, 784

machine vision, 506–13
measurement errors, 498–99
probes, 505–6
relation to testing, 488–89
sensor technologies, 497–516
strategy of automation, 41
Inspection probes, 505–6
Instantaneous control, 97, 187
Interest:
  definition, 70
  factors, 71–72
  tables of interest factors, 73–80
Interlocks (robotics), 324, 328–29
Intermittent transfer, 87, 88
Interpolation:
  numerical control, 214–15
  robotics, 322–23
Interrupt system, 700–702

J

Joining methods, 138
Just-in-time, 778

K

Key machine concept (GT), 453–54
Kilbridge and Wester method, 152

L

Ladder logic diagrams, 656–61, 666
LAN, 768–72
Laplace transforms, 546–53
Largest candidate rule, 149
Lasers:
  cutting in robotics, 350
  inspection, 513–14
Leadthrough programming (robotics), 320–25
Line, assembly (*see* Assembly line)
Line, flow (*see* Flow line)
Line balancing:
  definition, 143
  methods of solving, 149–59
  terminology, 144–49
Linear programming, 596–600
Linear systems analysis, 560–65
Link line, 102
Local area networks, 768–72

Logic control:
  definition, 643
  logic elements, 644–53
Logic network diagram, 646, 647
Lower bound approach, 112–13, 114

M

Machine cell (*see* Workcell)
Machine control unit, 201, 207, 209, 229
Machine tools:
  machining center, 220–21
  robot tending, 344
  trends in NC, 295
  types of, 219
Machine vision, (*see* Vision, machine)
Machining:
  automation, 97–101
  process variables, 215–19
  unmanned, 295
  untended, 295
Machining center, 220–21, 466
Maintenance, 39
Manufacturing (*see also* Production):
  functions of, 20–24
  information processing, 24–27
  organization of, 24–27
  process model, 22, 590–92
Manufacturing Automation Protocol, 772–75
Manufacturing control, 26–27, 719–20
Manufacturing lead time:
  cost of, 62–66
  definition, 30
  mathematical model of, 30–31
  MRP, 733
Manufacturing planning, 26, 718–19
MAP (*see* Manufacturing Automation
    Protocol)
Material handling:
  AGVS (*see* Automated guided vehicle
    systems)
  analysis techniques, 365–70
  attributes of, 364
  conveyors (*see* Conveyor)
  design of, 371–73
  equipment, 362–64
  FMS, 468–72
  function of, 362

future automated factory, 782
  interfacing with other systems, 425–28
  principles of, 371–73
  relation to manufacturing, 20, 23
  significance of, 361
  strategy of automation, 41
Material requirement planning:
  concepts, 732–33
  definition, 26, 730, 732
  inputs, 733
  operation, 735–38
  reports, 738–40
MCU (*see* Machine control unit)
Memory control, 97, 187
Mixed-model line, 142
Models:
  assembly systems, 141–49, 178–91
  conceptual model of manufacturing, 5, 21
  differential equations, 524–33
  flow lines, 107–28
  manufacturing process model, 22, 590–92
  material handling, 365–70, 379–83, 393–98
  process models, 524–33
  production, 30–39
MRP (*see* Material requirement planning)
Multiplexers, 688–89

N

NC (*see* Numerical control)
Networks (*see* Local area networks)
Noncontact inspection, 497–98, 506–16
Nondestructive testing, 489
Numerical control:
  accuracy and repeatability, 212–14
  applications, 199–200, 215–23
  automated programming, 263–64
  CAD/CAM, 261–63
  CNC (*see* Computer numerical control)
  coordinate system, 202–3
  definition, 199, 200
  DNC (*see* Direct numerical control)
  economics, 223–25
  historical perspective, 201, 220
  interpolation schemes, 214–15
  machine control unit, 201
  positioning system, 208–12
  problems, 280–81

program, 200
part programming (*see* Part programming)
trends, 294–95

O

Occupational Safety and Health Act (OSHA),
    7
Opitz classification scheme, 439–42
Optical encoder, 211–12
Optical inspection methods, 506–16
Optimal control:
    adaptive control, 600–621
    search strategies, 623–35
    steady state, 592–600
Orientor, 176, 178–80
Outsourcing, 778
Overhead costs, 53–55

P

Pallet fixtures, 89
Pallet shuttles, 295
Parsons, John, 201
Part families, 434–37
Part programming for NC:
    APT, 201, 247, 248–60, 268–78
    computer-assisted, 242–48
    definition, 229
    languages, 247–48
    manual data input, 260–61
    manual programming, 239–42
    methods of, 237–64
    tape format and coding, 230–37
Partial automation, 115–18
Parts classification and coding:
    (*see also* Group technology)
    benefits of, 437
    definition, 433–34
    machine cell design, 447–54
    MultiClass, 442–44
    Opitz system, 439–42
    production flow analysis, 437,
        445–47
    types of systems, 438–39
Payback method, 48–49
PID control, 554–60, 693, 695
PLACE (robotics), 330–31

Planning:
    capacity planning, 26
    manufacturing planning, 26, 718–19
    material requirements planning (*see*
        Material requirement planning)
    process planning (*see* Process planning)
    scheduling (*see* Scheduling)
Plant layout:
    definition, 27
    effect on material handling, 370–71
    fixed position, 28
    project layout, 28
    process, 28
    product-flow, 28
    types of, 27–28
Playback robots, 309–10
Point-of-use manufacturing, 778
Point-to-point control, 204, 252–54, 309
Postprocessor, 246–47, 258–59
Power-and-free transfer, 87, 89
Precedence constraints, 143, 146
Precedence diagram, 147
Preplanned control, 691–92
Present worth method, 49–50
Process capability, 490–91
Process control:
    strategy of automation, 41
Process models, 524–33, 608
Process planning:
    computer-aided, 718–19, 724–29
    definition, 26
Processing operations:
    applications in robotics, 346–51
    function in manufacturing, 20, 21–23
    future automated factory, 781
Production:
    batch production, 19
    capacity, 33
    definition, 15
    flow production, 20
    job shop production, 18–19
    mass production, 19–20
    types of, 18
Production economics:
    definition, 47
    evaluation of investment alternatives, 48–52
Production flow analysis, 437, 445–47
Production lines (*see* Flow lines)

Production planning, 729–32
Production rate:
  assembly systems, 184–85
  definition, 32
  flow lines, 108, 113
Programmable automation, 2, 295
Programmable logic controller:
  capabilities, 662, 669
  components, 663–65
  definition, 662
  development of, 662–63
  operation of, 668–69
  programming, 665
  relation to computer control, 673
  in robotics, 332
Programming:
  computer process control, 699–705
  NC (*see* Part programming for NC)
  robot (*see* Robot programming)
Pulse counters, 678, 690
Pulse generators, 679, 690
Punched tape, 230, 280

Q

Quality control:
  definition, 27, 487
  inspection and testing, 488–89
  monitoring in transfer lines, 96
  statistical QC, 489–93

R

Rack and pinion for indexing, 91
Radiation inspection, 516
Ranked positional weights method, 154
Ratchet and pawl for indexing, 91
Rate of return method, 50–51
Regulatory control, 697
Relay, electromechanical, 650
Reliability, 37
Repeatability, 212–14
Resolution:
  analog-to-digital conversion, 682
  numerical control, 212
  robotics, 311
Response surface, 623
Response time, 564

Return-on-investment method, 50
Robot applications:
  assembly, 351–53
  characteristics of, 338–39
  in FMS, 471
  inspection, 353–54
  material handling, 342–46
  processing operations, 346–51
Robot cell (*see* Workcell)
Robot programming:
  computations and logic, 329–30
  definition, 319
  languages, 325–30
  leadthrough, 320–25
  motion, 322–24, 325–27
  off-line, 330–32
  simulation, 330–32
  types of, 319–20
Robotics:
  anatomy, 302–8
  applications (*see* Robot applications)
  control systems, 308–10
  definition, 301
  end effectors, 314
  programming (*see* Robot programming)
  relation to NC, 295
  sensors, 315–16
  speed, 313
  work volume, 308
ROI, 50
Roller conveyor:
  definition, 373
  transfer lines, 90
Root locus method, 565–82
Route sheet, 26 (*see also* Process planning)

S

Safety:
  AGVS, 391
  cost of, 67
  OSHA, 7
  reason for automating, 7
Safety monitoring:
  flow lines, 96
  robotics, 334
Scanning laser beam inspection, 513–14
SCARA robot, 307, 353

Scheduling:
  job sequencing, 746–47
  master schedule, 26, 733
  order scheduling, 746
Search strategies, 623–35
SEE WHY, 128
Selector, 176, 178–80
Sensors:
  binary, 649
  definition, 679
  features, 680
  list of common sensors, 681
  in robotics, 315–16
Sequence control:
  definition, 642–44
  robotics; 333
  transfer lines, 95
Sequencing (control):
  definition, 644
  sequencing elements, 653–56
Shop floor control:
  definition, 27, 731, 743–44
  factory data collection, 748–51, 760–62
  phases of, 744–48
SIMAN, 128
Simulation, 128–29
SLAM II, 128
Social impact of automation, 787–89
Solenoid, 650
Spatial resolution, 311
Spray painting (robotics), 348–50
Stability:
  adaptive control, 621
  control system, 561–62
  robotics, 308–9
Starving of workstations, 119, 141
Statistical quality control, 489–93
Stepping motor, 208
Storage systems:
  AS/RS (see Automated storage/retrieval systems)
  carousel storage (see Carousel storage)
  objectives of, 404–5
  performance measures, 405–6
  types of materials stored, 405
Straight cut NC, 205
Strategies of automation, 40–41

Supervisory control, 691, 696–98
Synchronous transfer, 87, 88, 173

T

Tape control, (see Numerical control, Part programming)
Tape reader, 207–8
Technical office protocol, 775
Timers, 653–56
Timing diagram, 655
TIP ratio, 39
Token passing (networks), 770
Tolerance time, 142
TOP (see Technical office protocol)
Traffic factor, 369
Transducers, 677, 679–80
Transfer functions, 533–36
Transfer line (see also Flow line, automated):
  analysis of, 107–11
  definition, 86, 100–101
  design considerations, 101–4
  link line, 102
  performance of, 108–11
  unitized flow line, 104
Transport work (material handling), 368
Trends in manufacturing, 776–79
Trunnion machine, 99
Truth tables, 645, 652
Two stage production line, 121–26

U

Ultrasonic inspection, 516
Uniform annual cost method, 50
Unit load principle, 371–73
Unmanned machining, 295
Untended machining, 295
Upper bound approach, 111–12, 114
Utilization:
  definition, 36–37
  FMS, 475, 482
  GT machine cell, 454
  interpretation, 39
  storage systems, 406

V

Vibratory bowl feeder, 175–76
Vision, machine:
  applications, 511–12
  definition, 506
  operation, 506–11
  in robotics, 316
Volvo, 162

W

Walking beam transfer mechanism, 90
Waterjet cutting (robotics), 350
Welding:
  assembly process, 138
  robot, 346
WIP (*see* Work-in-process)

WIP ratio, 38
Workcell (*see also* Workcell control):
  GT machine cell design, 447–54
  robotics, 332, 340–41
Workcell control, 317, 332–34, 643–44
Work-in-process:
  cost of, 62–66
  definition, 37
  mathematical model, 37
  measures of, 38–39
  storage of, 422–25
  TIP ratio, 39
  WIP ratio, 38
Work elements, 144
Work standards, 719
Work volume (robotics), 308
World coordinate system (robotics), 322